MW01602031

Founder and Consulting Editor:
Edelgard E. DuBruck

Fifteenth-Century Studies

Volume 25

Edited by
William C. McDonald

Review Editor
Everett U. Crosby

CAMDEN HOUSE

ISSN: 0164–0933
ISBN: 1–57113–077–2

First published 2000
by Camden House

Camden House is an imprint of Boydell & Brewer Inc.
PO Box 41026, Rochester, NY 14604–4126 USA
and of Boydell & Brewer Limited
PO Box 9, Woodbridge, Suffolk IP12 3DF, UK

This publication is printed on acid-free paper.
Printed in the United States of America

Fifteenth-Century Studies appears annually.
Please send orders to Boydell & Brewer at the above addresses.

For editorial correspondence and manuscript submissions, write to:
Prof. Edelgard E. DuBruck,
Modern Languages,
Marygrove College,
Detroit, MI 48221 USA

Articles and book reviews submitted for publication may be edited to conform to *FCS* style. Self-addressed envelopes with return postage must accompany all manuscripts submitted.

Submit books for review to:
Peter Meister
Foreign Languages
University of Alabama
Huntsville, AL 35899 USA

Information on membership in the Fifteenth-Century Society, which entitles the member to a copy of *Fifteenth-Century Studies,* is available from Prof. Edelgard E. DuBruck, Modern Languages, Marygrove College, Detroit, MI 48221 USA

CONTENTS

Essays

Reviews

Theophrastus Bombastus von Hohenheim, Called Paracelsus: Highways and Byways of a Wandeı ing Physician (1493-1541)

Edelgard E. DuBruck

> Medicine should be based upon truth
> and not upon verbal sleight-of-hand.
> — Paracelsus[1]

Introduction

Few men of the early Renaissance had a greater influence, a more controversial reputation, and stronger modern repercussions in science and even literature than Paracelsus. Like Wittenwiler's Bertschi and Grimmelshausen's Simplicius he was born in a tiny village, and like Simplicius and the Lappenhausens (the latter in search of allies) he traveled large distances in pursuit of truth. Doctor of Medicine, of Theology, and *utriusque iuris*, he enjoyed admiration and found implacable hostility. He is still misunderstood today. My article will describe von Hohenheim's life and attempt to highlight his "visionary" contributions to medicine and the medical industry — acknowledged or not, by highways or byways.[2]

The ingenious vagabond with almost superhuman achievements had a tormented career. Born to a Swabian physician (a nobleman) and a commoner mother, he learned practical medicine from his father and began his wanderings at age nine, to Carinthia and Tyrol, where he "studied" metallurgy, chemistry, and alchemy. He enrolled at Vienna and several Italian universities, Paris, Oxford, and Cologne, and then traveled from land to land over all of Europe, learning from bath attendants and magicians, herb-women and Gipsies, monks and peasants, abbots, knights, princes and kings. An excellent surgeon and general physician, he treated wounds, the plague, syphilis, gout, epilepsy, "mountain sickness," and the so-called invisible diseases. Rejecting Avicenna, Hippocrates, Galen and the pathology of the four humors,[3] he introduced inorganic drugs (chemotherapy!), advocated medical ethics, and pioneered modern psychotherapy. He talked about DNA and cloning without, of course, using these terms. His work, *Greater Surgery*, is still used by physicians today.

Altogether, he wrote more than 9,000 pages (29 vols.), including on pharmacology, medicine, mathematics, astronomy, philosophy, theology, social and political science. He lectured and wrote in German. Irascible, a loner without family, restless until the day he died in 1541, Paracelsus managed to turn university faculties against him, academics who might have listened, if his extraordinary message had been clad in more pleasing words. Even his doctoral degrees were questioned. Jolande Jacobi, a modern editor, called him "a true man of the declining fifteenth century, with its deep contradictions."[4] We can merely allude here to the legend "Paracelsus" and to his literary fortune in the following centuries. In English literature, Thomas Nashe, Shakespeare, Ben Jonson, John Donne, Samuel Butler, Robert Browning and Ezra Pound either alluded to him or wrote works about him; in Germany, his doctrine of the four spirits (corresponding to the four elements of water, fire, air, and earth) inspired Jacob Böhme, Herder, Lessing, Goethe and Romanticism, Achim von Arnim, Heine, Fouquet's *Undine* (a water sprite), Gerhart Hauptmann and Rilke.[5] In 1996 alone, ten books on Paracelsus appeared in the USA.

The State of the Medical Art in the Fifteenth Century

To give you an impression of fifteenth-century medicine, let me explain that sickness was experienced by the afflicted and treated by their communities quite differently from today. The Church assumed the care of the sick, of the dying, and the funeral arrangements, and the role of the priest was here at least as important as that of the doctor. The sick (along with healthy people afraid of ailments) went on pilgrimages and prayed to certain saints. People also carried amulets with Bible verses, the monogram of Christ or a cross. A waxen disk called *Agnus Dei* was to help against death in childbed. In domestic nursing, forms of popular medicine prevailed, together with methods learned in herbal and medical treatises (such as that by Ortolff von Bayrland, c.1400, first printed in 1477).[6]

Since the thirteenth and fourteenth centuries European cities started to imitate Italian urban regions which already had better sanitation, and Venice became a model for Nürnberg, for example. The first apothecaries were supported by the city government, and, once thought dishonorable, some former herb vendor/druggists soon acquired burgher status.[7] The Vienna druglist of 1432 contained: pepper, saffron, ginger, cloves, cinnamon rind, nutmeg, caraway, sugar, rice, olive oil, figs, grapes, almonds, soap, wax, plaster, and chocolates. Chemical substances were: sulfur, alum, copper vitriol, theriac, mastic. Here again, Italian prescription practices were imitated.

Medical doctors were employed by the cities, in order to decrease the activities of barbers and shearers. These municipal physicians were not allowed to leave town for longer than twenty-four hours, but some did not have to pay taxes nor to fight in times of war. The ablest physicians were trained in Salerno, Montpellier, or Paris. After a three-year propaedeutic course, five years were spent in specialized areas of study, followed by a year's internship with an experienced practitioner. If the student intended to practice surgery, a year's study of anatomy was compulsory. It goes without saying that the best doctors served above all the upper classes. However, the physicians' oath of Nürnberg (1338-60)[8] specified care of all sick people, whether poor or rich, a modest income, and no manufacture of drugs by a doctor. Physicians were also to supervise the hospitals and the leper colonies. Miraculous healings there often stemmed from the fact that many people with non-leprous eczemas were sent to these colonies, where they recovered eventually. Venereal diseases were occasionally misdiagnosed as leprosy: the examples given by Stephen R. Ell for Denmark were probably valid for other regions as well.[9]

At the beginning of the fourteenth century, surgery was separated from medical practice and was allowed to be performed by barbers, who bled people (at certain times of the astrological calendar), gave enemas, pulled teeth, treated headaches, simple wounds, broken bones and dislocations, skin diseases and ulcers. There was a great deal of uncertainty about diseases, their causes, treatments, and the consequences — which was reflected in the Dances of Death, where the physician figure was usually proud of his professional achievements, but had to admit that he often could not prevent death, including his own.

In conclusion: while great advances were undoubtedly made in the late Middle Ages, it is a fact that for centuries to come medicine and surgery still went hand in hand with magic and astrology. Unfortunately, a good number of unauthorized quacks and herbalists roamed the open country, who have added much to the age-old satire of doctors (especially found in the German carnival plays). They had picked up minimal knowledge in popular treatises or from hearsay, and some had astonishing know-how from practical experience, while others swindled themselves through their itinerant existence.

Paracelsus the Physician

Paracelsus was inspired by a deep love and compassion for his fellow humans. To heal someone came close to priesthood for this very religious man, who considered his profession as God-given. Several times he said to take your time and *talk* to the patients to make them feel better. He despised colleagues who relied on book knowledge and who used their job as a source for making a living or even to gather material goods. Paracelsus got along with no possessions and led a frugal life; wine was the only luxury he allowed for himself. In his treatise on epilepsy he wrote:

> God knows the doctor's heart. He pays no attention to his degrees, to the schools, to pomp, titles, his licence and its seal, but he looks out for the compassionate man and inspires him with the remedy to try.[10]

According to Paracelsus, the qualifications of a good surgeon are:

> A clear conscience,
> Desire to learn and to gather experience,
> A gentle heart and a cheerful spirit,
> Moral manner of life and sobriety in all things,
> Greater regard for his honor than for money,
> Greater interest in being useful to his patient than to himself.
> He must not be married to a bigot.
> ...
> He should not be a runaway monk,
> He should not practise self-abuse,
> He must not have a red beard,
> He must not act without judgment,
> He must not accept belief without understanding,
> He must not scorn the workings of chance,
> He must not boast of knowing anything without experience,
> He must never boast or praise himself,
> He must despise no one.[11]

Furthermore, a physician should receive his experience from nature, whose open-minded servant he remains. In one herb there is more virtue and force than in all the folios read in college. Theory is simply speculative practice which must never be absent from actual from experiments based on eye-sight. It is better to know and understand one remedy, Paracelsus continued, than to rummage through monastery libraries, where of a thousand pages barely one is understood. Study each day without respite, investigate and observe diligently; do not put too much trust in yourself. Travel and explore everything!

The physician should prescribe in accordance with the patient's flesh and blood, with his country's ways and his innate nature, and he must give heed to the region in which the patient lives and be something of a cosmographer and geographer. Medicine rests upon four pillars: philosophy, astronomy, alchemy, and ethics.

Let us now examine his medical works more closely. They are not easy to read, since he jotted down items quite unsystematically, mixing facts with belief and religious considerations, and since he often strayed from his stated topic. According to Jacobi, the Paracelsus editions are flawed, because the original manuscripts contain many errors and distortions, as the handwriting in fifteenth-century German is hard to decipher. Moreover, the author mostly dictated his works, and so rapidly that, as a pupil remarked, "you'd think it was the devil speaking in him." Some parts were written down by students from memory, and others were translated *ex tempore* into Latin (J., xxix). We shall investigate his treatises on epilepsy and on miners' diseases carefully, and also mention the greater divisions of the so-called invisible maladies.

Epilepsy was and is still today frightening by its symptoms. Already Hippocrates, "the father of medicine," had had no patience with the idea that epilepsy was a punishment sent by the gods. He held that "every disease has its own nature and arises from external causes," laying much stress on diet and using few drugs.[12] Paracelsus explained that, in declaring the disease incurable, we declare our ignorance. We don't even know much about a toothache: "You cannot heal toothaches or an eye inflammation, but you compose pompous speeches," he hurled at his colleagues. "Do not waste time with ridiculous cures, urine analyses, oats and barley water, aromas and laxatives — all this will not help an epileptic" (G., 109). Epilepsy is comparable to thunder and lightning, for man's microcosm is related to the macrocosm. (Of course, Paracelsus did not know causes such as electrical rhythms of the central nervous system nor brain activity.) Tempests are caused by the incompatibility of mercury, sulfur, and salt — the same substances as found in the human body, usually in harmony. Other comparisons of the sickness include water spouts and earth quakes.

At the beginning of an attack, Paracelsus continued, the patient's mind is affected. He loses his balance, his normal conduct changes, the harmony is broken. His vision becomes weak, he is perhaps sleepy or melancholy. He breathes heavily and becomes agitated. His stomach and neck swell. Usual remedies, like chasing a cold by its opposite, heat, are useless here. Paracelsus advises grinding mistletoe to a powder; drinking blood of a decapitated man at certain constellations; or grinding down a cranial bone; taking the seeds of a peony and/or nine grains of barley before the crisis, eighteen in the middle, and nine per hour afterwards; or gold leaf or coral dissolved in wine. Camphor and cinders are mild analgesics. The medication must vary for the different ages of humans. He also mentions vitriol (sulfa drugs?). Believing that epilepsy is determined at birth (trauma? constellation? DNA?), he realizes that it can be the consequence of an injury.

Today, epilepsy is treated, according to the type of the disease, with hormones, light sedatives and drugs to prevent major flare-ups. There are more than twenty anti-epileptic drugs, including Dilantin, Phenobarbital, and Milontin; these sometimes produce unwanted side-effects, like rashes. Brain surgery is performed in severe cases. Among young people epilepsy is often cured with aging.[13]

On miners' diseases, Paracelsus writes that such maladies are foremost lung afflictions, but the infection may invade the entire body and even cause stomach ulcers (TB). Underground vapors deposit mercury, salt, and sulfur in the lungs (compared to sediment in wine barrels), a tartar causing coughs and suffocation. Mists cause asthma: today we talk about an allergy, whereas Paracelsus draws the Milky Way into this! Especially damaging are yellow arsenic vapors (orpiment), and such as emanate from crystallized iron pyrites (marcasite). Smelters (founders), money coiners, and alchemists are subject to poisonous gases as well: their mouth and nose are open, as well as those of miners. Each metal has its own gas.

Paracelsus considers the brain as origin for putrefaction (tartar, realgar), also for other symptoms such as migraine, paralysis, lethargy. Only salt minerals do not affect brain, lungs, and stomach, while mercury burns the latter and the liver. Yet mercury is also used in therapeutics, as well as salt and sulfur. Generally, Paracelsus recommends to follow a certain diet and to pay attention to "what is in the air." Realgar (arsenic sulfide) dries out the lungs, alleviates coughing, headaches, constipation, and pain in the spleen. He advises to administer laudanum (opium) as a drug and as a pain-killer, and he recommends to keep miners from breathing mountain emanations. Prescribing an exudate of the ashtree against putrefaction (gangrene), he adds that this drug can also be found in vitriol, nettles, and the lodestone. Anything that causes perspiration is considered valuable, especially hot baths in herbal water with sulfur, like in thermal spas. The recommendation to bathe in bone marrow of humans, wolves or badgers can hardly be taken seriously. Aluminium oxide heals itches, vitriol the loss of hair, and salt cures scabies — all peripheral manifestations of miners' diseases. Tartar deposits on teeth are hard to clean, he wrote, but try toothpaste! Mercury vapor is a laxative, and gas from sublimated arsenic heals the quartan fever, gout, arthritis, and pustules. Herbal ointments alleviate gout, paralysis, and strokes.

It is obvious that Paracelsus does not address disabling mining injuries and deaths resulting from explosions, falls of rock, haulage and others accidents. Rather, the inner damage of the human body is on his mind.

Today, the harmful gases have been defined as methane, hydrogen sulfide, carbon monoxide and dioxide. We are familiar with silicosis (from quartz dust) and black lung (coal dust), and poisoning from lead, arsenic, and mercury. But we also have fairly efficient ventilation equipment, and water spraying minimizes the creation of dust since the early twentieth century. Mine-safety legislation concerns especially coal mining.[14]

Of "invisible diseases" Paracelsus distinguishes four groups and their remedies: 1) maladies of faith, 2) maladies caused by the influence of heaven (stellar constellations) — this book is missing; 3) maladies of the imagination, and 4) maladies by natural forces. Maladies of faith (belief) are mostly superstitions. St. Valentine's Consumption causes terrible convulsions. Although the convulsions were epileptic, it was the saint — seen as a little man with invisible actions — who was blamed. Saint Quirin's disease, where the skin cracks and breaks out (by corrosive salts), as well as varicose veins, were ascribed by the people to this Christian saint.

Holy men or women to whom they prayed for healing a disease were also thought to have caused it. Adoration and priesthood are sometimes based on diabolic falsehoods, Paracelsus continues. St. Anthony's Fire (ergotism) has natural causes as well. As for St. Vitus Dance, this condition is purely imaginary, only resembling epilepsy, and instigated as a form of penitence by persuasion. For syphilis, the so-called French disease, St. Dennis was blamed, when, rather, it was probably caused by succubi, "demons which are begotten through fornication in brothels" (G., 212). Paracelsus cured syphilis with mercury, like his colleagues, which was until recently considered to be the most effective cure. Even the plague was considered God's punishment. Anabaptists and other heretic sects all flourish by the force of imagination.[15] Thus, like medicine, faith can lead to health or to death (G., 213).

In the third book on invisible diseases, Paracelsus treats malformations caused supposedly by the imagination of pregnant women, a determinant which, in the light of reason, cannot be upheld as correct and factual. For him, women are especially subject to the imagination. To demonstrate the latter's power in general, Paracelsus mentions the so-called frog-rain, namely the appearance of little frogs in or after a rain, creatures which seem to have fallen from the sky. He also debunks pregnant women's belief that, if they read about a famous man of wisdom, a warrior or an artist during these nine months, their child would resemble this person. Other circumstances are ascribed to the devil, for example, when the child is paralyzed while its parents were perfectly healthy. (Incidentally, medieval people did not understand impotence and promptly imputed it to the demon.[16]) Unmarried women also imagine or allege incubi and succubi, if they bear children who are really the fruit of debauch. Amorous infatuation (sometimes without a real-life object) is certainly an invisible disease and can lead to death. Under the influence of More's *Utopia*, Paracelsus recommends that governments should keep idle persons well occupied.[17]

In the fourth book, on natural forces, Paracelsus discusses congenital diseases and inherited qualities (that we consider DNA today) and repeats that doctors blame magic, sorcery, the devil, and use superstition for things they do not know. He mentions women rarely, but says here that, no matter what their disposition is, the fruit of their bodies peoples the earth. Finally, while we praise God for our success in healing, we should not forget the art of doctors and pharmacists.

Like alchemists of his time, Paracelsus wrote about an elixir to prolong life and pondered how to produce a human being from sperm in a test tube (cf. Faust's *Homunculus*). Today in fact this has been made possible through artificial insemination, and cloning is indeed the next step, using DNA. Like many Renaissance men of letters, Paracelsus saw man, a microcosm, as comparable to the macrocosm. His emphasis on astrology (which he calls astronomy) and the influence of constellations would not be acceptable to modern physicians — but faith healers, psychics, and even some proponents of alternative medicine do consider stellar configurations among other non-invasive means.[18]

In encyclopedias, Paracelsus is praised for simplifying prescriptions and introducing chemical drugs, for healing syphilis, and, for the first time, having turned attention to miners' diseases. He is credited with keen observation and empirical methods as well as medical ethics. A forerunner of chemical physiology, pathology and therapy (even color therapy!), of hygiene at the workplace, he also pointed to the role of the subconscious in psychiatry. All in all, this wandering physician, who also found time to write works on philosophy, theology, political and social science, often changed highways for byways, and vice versa. The "loneliness of a long-distance runner" hurt him but assured his uniqueness in the history of mankind.

Notes

[1] A quote of Paracelsus's words from Jolande Jacobi's edition, translated into English by Norbert Guterman, of I, 6, 316 in Karl Sudhoff et al., eds. *Sämtliche Werke*, first section, 24 vols. (München: Barth, 1922-33). J. Jacobi, ed. and Norbert Guterman, tr. *Paracelsus. Selected Writings* (Princeton: University Press [Bollingen], 1979, second ed.), 49.

[2] An authentic biography of P.'s life has not yet been written, but there exist a considerable number of fictionalized accounts, of which the most important is Erwin G. Kolbenheyer's *Paracelsus*, 3 vols. (München: Langen/Müller, 1938). Among the many critical works and partial editions we mention Franz Spunda, *Das Weltbild des Paracelsus* (Wien: Andermann, 1941); Alexandre Koyré, *Paracelse* (Paris: Allia, 1997; first ed. Gallimard, 1971); Jean-Pierre Fussler, *Les Idéees éthiques, sociales, et politiques de Paracelse (1493-1541) et leur fondement* (Strasbourg: Université des Sciences Humaines, 1986), and Lucien Braun, ed. and tr., *Évangile d'un médecin errant* (Paris: Arfuyen, 1991). The International Paracelsus Society in Salzburg has, up to 1984, issued at least twenty-three volumes of articles on von Hohenheim. For his works on medicine we have used

Bernard Gorceix's translation into French: *Paracelse. Oeuvres médicales* (Paris: Presses Universitaires de France, 1968).

[3] The notion of the four humors goes back to Empedocles's four elements of the universe: fire, air, earth, and water, accepted by Hippocrates and Galen as the origin of the four humors, hot, cold, dry and moist. The only concession made by Paracelsus is based on his firm belief in four spirits inhabiting the four elements of the universe.

[4] Guterman translation, xli.

[5] On P.'s literary fortune, see Karl-Heinz Weimann, "Paracelsus in der Weltliteratur," *Germanisch-Romanische Monatsschrift*, N.F. 11 (1961), 241-74, and numerous recent articles by other authors on both sides of the Atlantic.

[6] On medieval medicine, see E. DuBruck, *Aspects of Fifteenth-Century Society in the German Carnival Comedies. Speculum Hominis* (Lewiston: Mellen, 1993), 78-92. Also: Ernst Königer, *Aus der Geschichte der Heilkunst von Ärzten, Bädern und Chirurgen* (München: Prestel, 1958); Marjorie Rowling, Life in Medieval Times (New York: Putnam, 1968), 175-95; Harry Kühnel, ed. *Alltag im Spätmittelalter* (Graz: Styria, 1984), 83-91, and Mittelalterliche Heilkunde in Wien (Graz/Köln: Böhlau, 1965); Aryeh Grabois, "Medizin," in Illustrierte Enzyklopaedie des Mittelalters (Königstein: Athenaeum, 1981), 411-12; Joseph Schumacher, *Die seelischen Volkskrankheiten im deutschen Mittelalter* (Berlin: Junker and Dünnhaupt, 1937); Charles Lichtenthaeler, Geschichte der Medizin (Köln: Deutscher Ärzte-Verlag, 1974).

[7] See Werner Danckert, *Unehrliche Leute. Die verfemten Berufe* (Bern: Francke, 1963), 95.

[8] The Hippocratic Oath was adopted in 1747.

[9] "Leprosy and Everyday Life in Fifteenth-Century Denmark," *Fifteenth-Century Studies*, 18 (1991), 83-91. Cf. Also: Saul Nathaniel Brody, *The Disease of the Soul. Leprosy in Medieval Literature* (Ithaca: Cornell University Press, 1974), and Françoise Bériac, *Histoire des lépreux au moyen âge*. Une société d'exclus (Paris: Imago, 1988).

[10] My translation of Gorceix (henceforth: G), 110.

[11] Jacobi (Guterman; henceforth: J), 52-53.

[12] See: *Encyclopedia Britannica*, 23 vols. (Chicago: Benton, 1972), 15: 94B.

[13] *Encyclopedia Americana*, 30 vols (Danbury: Grolier, 1995), 10: 510.

[14] *Ibid.*, 19: 174-75.

[15] See: Fussler, n. 2 above, 44-48. P. rejects the theory of the Anabaptists, but is appalled about their persecution.

[16] See E. DuBruck, "Thomas Aquinas and Medieval Demonology," *Michigan Academician*, 7 (1974), 167-83.

[17] Fussler, 51-56.

[18] Patrick Perry, "Complementary Medicine — Exploring the Alternatives," *The Saturday Evening Post*, 269 (1997), No. 3, 58-62; Jeffrey Kluger, "Mr. Natural. Millions of Americans Swear by the Alternative Medicine of Dr. Andrew Weil," *Time*, 149 (1997), No. 19, 68-75.

Marygrove College

Narrative and Structural Strategies in Early Spanish Sentimental Romance

Louise M. Haywood

In this paper I demonstrate that the three texts usually considered the earliest Spanish sentimental romances share a number of narrative and structural strategies which together offer a new orientation of narrative. Consequently these strategies — the mechanisms of the new orientation — become defining elements in the later development of the genre. They problematicize the nature of fiction and its ability to reflect/refract experience. These texts explore the relation between historically real and fictional characters through the adoption of narrative techniques linked to the *roman à clef*. Specific structural strategies are used to contrast the on-going and unresolved nature of lived experience with the finite form of fiction. Before discussing these strategies I show that Dom Pedro, Con-stable of Portugal, and the anonymous author of *Triste deleytaçión* were familiar with Juan Rodríguez del Padrón's corpus.

Pedro M. Cátedra has argued that the role which Dom Pedro, Constable of Portugal (c. 1429-1466), played in the dissemination of the Spanish sentimental romance is worthy of reconsideration and this view has been supported by both E. Michael Gerli and Regula Rohland de Langbehn. Gerli has argued that, given Dom Pedro's knowledge of Juan Rodríguez del Padrón's literary works, the Constable "might have served as the intellectual focal point for the development of the early sentimental romances during his abortive reign as king of the Catalans" by providing "a crucial eastern literary link in the development of the genre".[1] More recently, Vera Castro Lingl has suggested that Dom Pedro's *Sátira de infelice e felice vida* (1443-53) represents a reworking of Rodríguez del Padrón's *Siervo libre de amor* (c. 1440), particularly in the content of *Sátira*'s glosses and in the romance's structure.[2]

Plot summaries of Rodríguez del Padrón's *Siervo libre de amor* and his *Triunfo de las doñas* in *Sátira's* glosses provide clear evidence that Dom Pedro was familar with Rodríguez del Padrón's work. The author of *Triste deleytaçión* (1458-70) probably knew the same two works; however, *Triste deleytaçión* gives only minimal information about them which need not have been drawn from direct knowledge.[3] The reference to *Siervo*, for example, contains no more information than may be gleaned from Dom Pedro's gloss on Ardanlier whilst references to *Triunfo* merely name the author and state that *Triunfo* praises women:

> segunt que aquel más virtuoso de todos los onbres, Rodrigo del Pedrón, coronándonos de gloria en el triunfo de las senyoras, largamente auía tratado [...] ese cauallero allegado, Rodrigo del Pedrón, quiso por su virtut scubrir, el qu'el restante de los onbres por pura y enbidiosa maliçia nos tenían scondido.[4]

Whilst F. A. d. C. probably knew, possibly indirectly, *Siervo* and *Triunfo*, he was certainly familiar with Rodríguez del Padrón's literary reputation. In the light of this, the aim of this essay is to examine a series of significant narrative and structural strategies and parallels in Rodríguez del Padrón's *Siervo*, Dom Pedro's *Sátira* and *Triste deleytaçión*, possibly by Fra Artal de Claramunt, in order to explore the possibility of the existence of a "direct line of evolution".[5] Regula Rohland de Langbehn has classified these romances as belonging to the first and second of three stages in the development of the genre.[6] The first, strongly allegorical stage, consisting of *Siervo* and *Sátira*, may derive from allegorical *decires* or *coplas* and serves to undermine the moral values of courtly love.[7] The second group consists of *Triste deleytaçión*, and the sentimental romances of Juan de Flores and Diego de San Pedro. These authors make use of the vocabulary of contemporary *cancioneros*, introduce formal debates into the narrative and deal by analogy with the position of the *conversos* immediately prior to the Inquisition. The final stage is made up of the later, mostly sixteenth-century, romances which focus increasingly on the lover's emotional state and manifest a tendency towards the *roman à clef*.

Rodríguez del Padrón's insistence in *Siervo's accessus* that it has a tripartite structure is widely acknowledged but the relation of this allegorical framework to *Siervo's* external structure has been a point of much debate, particularly as the allusion to the "*tres diversos tiempos*" refers to the three stages of loving:

> El siguiente tratado es departido en tres partes principales, según tres diversos tiempos que en sí contiene, figurados por tres caminos y tres árbores consagrados, que se refieren a tres partes del omne, es a saber: al coraçón y al libre alvedrío y al entendimiento, e a tres varios pensamientos de aquellos.
>
> La primera parte prosigue el tiempo que bien amó y fue amado [...] La segunda refiere el tiempo que bien amó y fue desamado [...] La terçera y final trata el tiempo que no amó y fue desamado.[8]

However, it seems at least possible that the "*tres diversos tiempos*" also act as temporal referents and, in fact, this identification is made in Entendimiento's apostrophe to the narrator in a reference to Cerberus, "*¡Ay, amigo, amigo! El passaje a los Campos Ilíasos es peligroso, por el can pavoroso Çervero, de las [tres] cabeças, que son los tres tiempos, presente, passado e por venir*" (168).[9] Of note is the fact that *Sátira*, which offers very close parallels to *Siervo*, makes reference to the "*tres diversos tiempos*" in two places. First in the gloss on Cerberus, "*aquel terrible Can de las tres bocas,*" Dom Pedro notes, "*los poetas [...] quisieron que tuviesse tres bocas o tres cabeças, las quales significan estas tres edades, es a saber, infançia, juventud e senectud*"[10] ; and later the allegorical figure of Prudençia comments:

> Quiero fablar, pues el tiempo lo adebda e lo padesçe, de su inestimable prudençia. E verdaderamente digo que ésta las tres caras de prudençia possee, que son memoria o recordaçión de las passadas cosas, consideraçion de las presentes, providençia para lo porvenir.[11]

In each case, Dom Pedro clearly emphasizes the status of "*los tres tiempos*" as temporal referents and this identification suggests that the three parts of Rodríguez del Padrón's narrative may relate to the past, present and future life of the lover-protagonist: a view which is supported by an analysis of the temporal axes of *Siervo* and *Sátira.* The external structure of *Siervo* comprises the process which leads up to and includes his psychomachic fragmentation (153-74), a vision in the form of the "*Estoria de dos amadores*" (174-202), and an extended lyric sequence followed by a brief section of prose (202-08). *Sátira* consists of a detailed analysis of the lover's current psychomachic fragmentation (3-50), an allegorical vision (actually a court of love representing the judgement of the Lady) (53-150), and finally the lyric plea for mercy followed by a short section of prose (153-75). Each of the romances is narrated largely in the past tense, and moves forward chronologically towards the present position of the narrator.[12] In each the first structural unit takes place in the distant past; the second portrays temporal stasis which analyzes the position of the lover (in *Sátira* through the Virtues' defence of the lady, and in *Siervo* through the Estoria); and the final element focuses on the psychomachic development of the lover up to the present time.

The significance of this in Dom Pedro's text is clarified by his shift into the present tense in the final prose section of *Sátira* to describe the lover still languishing in despair, awaiting the lady's response, at the time of composition:

> E yo, sin ventura, padesçiente, la desnuda e bicordante espada en la my diestra mirava, titubando, con dudoso pensa-

> miento e demudada cara, sy era mejor prestamente morir o asperar la dubdosa respuesta me dar consuelo. La discriçión favoresçe e suplica la espera, la congoxosa voluntad la triste muertereclama, el seso manda esperar la respuesta, el aquexado coraçón, gridando, acusa la postrimería.[13]

In *Siervo* the projection into the future consists of the reintegration of the narrator's faculties which is heralded by the arrival of Syndéresis, construed as Moral Conscience, who "*vino en demanda de mis aventuras*" ("came asking about my adventures"; 208). As Alan Deyermond has observed:

> La narración que acabamos de leer es de hecho su contestación a la pregunta de Syndéresis, y la necesidad de narrarla le cura de la enfermedad de la pasión amorosa. La creación literaria es la tercera parte, y la obra tiene una estructura circular.[14]

Syndéresis' request is answered in the composition of the entire text, "*e yo esso mesmo en recuenta de aquellas*" ("and I [did] just this in retelling them"; 208), with the dual function of a confession and negative *exemplum*, both addressed to Gonçalo de Medina.[15] The self-closure, or circularity, of *Siervo* is made possible by the degree to which the narrator and the author are identified.

E. Michael Gerli has recently suggested that Guillaume de Deguileville's penitential narratives, *Pélerinage de la Vie Humaine* and *de l'Âme* (1330-31 and 1355-58, respectively), are sources for some of *Siervo's* principal motifs, arguing that the *Pélerinages* supply, "[its] central artistic device: an autobiographical narrative of a vision relating a quest to the Other World in which the journey is a metaphor for the spiritual awakening of the narrator [...]".[16]

The two *Pélerinage* narratives circulated together with a third Deguileville text, *Pélerinage de Jésus Christ*, which Gerli does not consider to have been used by Rodríguez del Padrón. Gerli convincingly summarizes the case for the wide recognition of these narratives and their central motifs, including their presence in illuminations without explanatory rubrics. He identifies four of these motifs in *Siervo*: first, the narrator's experience of a nightmare or vision; second, the narrator's journey into "the Deep Valley of Despair"; third, the appearance of a ship at the seashore; and finally, the meeting with Syndéresis. Whilst the occurrence of this set of motifs in both texts adds weight to Gerli's hypothesis, the case that Rodríguez del Padrón's use of them was drawn from direct knowledge is undermined by their wide dissemination.

Gerli goes on to argue that *Siervo* is incomplete and that subsequent motifs from the *Pèlerinage* narratives can be used to reconstruct the missing section of *Siervo*. This would have included an exchange between Syndéresis and the narrator and some kind of reference to the narrator's journey on her ship to, most likely, Jerusalem. He sees the allegorical journey to the New Jerusalem in the *Pélerinage* narratives as figuring Rodríguez del Padrón's historical journey to the Holy City to take the cloth, considering it a "clever conceit" (16) which explains Rodríguez del Padrón's borrowings.

If Gerli's hypothesis that the *Pélerinage* narratives provided source material, either directly or indirectly, for Rodríguez del Padrón's *Siervo* is accepted then how are the limits of Rodríguez del Padrón's borrowings to be calculated? The wide recognition of the motifs of the pilgrimage narratives suggests that there is no need for the motifs to be worked out to their narrative conclusion in *Siervo*. Furthermore, for those familiar with the author's personal history and with Deguileville's narratives, the parallels are significant enough not to need to be spelt out. In fact, for the narrator to undertake a journey to the earthly Jerusalem in this context is to evoke the celestial city and to imply the final judgement of his soul. However if, as I have suggested, Rodríguez del Padrón has composed an unresolved narrative which functions as a negative *exemplum* and confession, then the absence of narrative resolution contributes to the "clever conceit" by suggesting the narrator follows the figural example offered by Deguileville's pilgrim. The exchange between Syndéresis and the narrator which the *Pélerinage* model leads the reader to expect takes the form of the text of *Siervo* itself, and its designated recipient — Gonçalo de Medina — is identified with Syndéresis.[17]

Despite the fact that *Sátira* is constructed upon the same temporal axis as *Siervo*, it does not manifest the same degree of closure, hanging on the anxiety of the lover as he awaits a response from the beloved. Dom Pedro's use of this technique has a twofold impact. Firstly, it creates an open-ended work which appeals beyond its textual limits and seems to beg an extra-narrative lady for mercy. Secondly, the whole text forms a lyrical plea to the lady, with the stasis inherent in the lack of narrative development and the focus on the suffering of the lover in the present calling to mind *cancionero* love poetry. In view of this structural parallel and the similarities listed by Castro Lingl between the two romances, it seems likely that Dom Pedro was imitating Rodríguez del Padrón, and I therefore conclude, with Castro Lingl, that the text of *Siervo* to which Dom Pedro, as a near contemporary, had access was very close to the state of the extant manuscript, that is, in a condition considered by many critics to be incomplete.[18]

A central difference between my approach and that of Castro Lingl is that she argues that *Sátira's* glosses clarify what is unexplained in *Siervo*;

however, of a total of 106 glosses, she counts only around thirty which refer to concepts or figures also present in *Siervo*. It is not my intention to discuss Dom Pedro's glosses here but it should be noted that many occur during the Virtues' defence of the lady and praise "*el femineo linage*" (for example, those on Spuria, Judith, the daughter of Gepte, Porchia, Ceciliana, and the *dueña* of Valida: 66-68, 73-81), whilst several others tell tales of tragic love, including those of Ardanlier and Liesa and Piramus and Thisbe.[19]

In superficial terms it could be argued that *Triste deleytaçión* has a similar structure. After the *accessus*, the *Enamorado* undergoes a fracturing of the faculties of the soul which results in his surrender to love. When his pursuit of the beloved is finally frustrated he experiences a dream vision, described as a *somni*, in which he visits the Other World. At this point the narrative moves into verse which ends with a verse epistle, introduced by the rubric, "*El enamorado, triste de no poder saber nueuas de su senyora, le pide que le scriua, con la presente*" (196), and concludes with a *quintilla* with the double function of explicit to both letter and text:

> Avnque mi querer libré
> con voto y sagramento
> yo jamás no le quité
> de donde primero fue
> con entero complimiento.[20]

Here the pattern of psychomachic fragmentation, vision, and final, open-ended, appeal to the extra-narrative beloved may also be discerned. In addition to this, the *accessus* to *Triste deleytaçión* describes its content and refers to the fact that the action recounted is not complete, which suggests a temporal structure similar to *Siervo* and *Sátira*, "*Es verdat que si la fin d'estos amores en la presente hobra no se muestra, la causa fue no aplicar fiçión, por ser más obligado en tal caso a la verdat que al amigo*" ("It is true that if the end of this love affair is not shown in the present work then the reason was not to make it up [lit. apply fiction, invention], because of being more obliged in that case to the truth than to my friend"; *Triste deleytaçión*, 1). This detail points to the author's awareness of the possible difficulties an audience may experience when presented with a text whose narrative content is left unresolved, such as *Siervo* and *Sátira*.

The existence of an extra-narrative beloved is predicated in the *accessus* of all three texts. *Siervo* and *Sátira* are addressed to a designated recipient — in each case an intimate of the author — who is in possession of information unknown to the public: the identity of the beloved. Juan Rodríguez del Padrón's allusion to a letter which will reveal his lady's identity is well known, "*la grand señora, de cuyo nombre te dirá la su epístola*" ("the great lady whose name you will read in her letter"; 157). However,

Dom Pedro's allusions to the identity of the beloved, and Isabel's possible possession of this knowledge have not been noted. The beloved is described as seeming to be a new St. Catherine in her debating skills, and the propriety of this name over that of the saint for whom the beloved is named is mentioned. This suggests that Isabel, as recipient of *Sátira*, may know the beloved's identity, "*por tan sótiles e agudas determinaçiones pone declaraçión, que más sembla otra sancta Catherina, que por quien es conoscida*" ("for she utters such subtle and pertinent reasonings, that she more resembles another St. Catherine than the saint for whom she is named"; 114). As in *Siervo* and *Sátira*, the *accessus* of *Triste deleytaçión* alludes to the existence of an extra-narrative beloved, "*si aquella senyora de quien soy [...] la presente hobra leiendo, non sólo a ella buelba en la elecçión primera, mas a todas las hotras stimadas senyoras*" ("May the Lady to whom I belong, and not only she but also all the other esteemed ladies, return to their first choice [of lover] through reading the present work"; 1-2).

Parallels are drawn in all three romances between the narrator's personal situation and that of the protagonist of the work. In *Siervo* and *Sátira* the protagonist is identified with the author; whereas in *Triste deleytaçión*, the protagonist's beloved enters a convent thereby denying him her love whilst the narrator hopes that reading *Triste deleytaçión* will cause his own beloved to turn away from any "*nueua fantasía*" towards her "*elecçión primera*" (1). These two parallels suggest the involvement of the author in later sentimental romances and may foreshadow the merging of author and narrator in Flores's *Grimalte* or the active roles played by narrators in other later sentimental fiction, such as that by Diego de San Pedro.[21]

Further to this, *Triste deleytaçión* has clear traits of a *roman à clef*: the author is identified as F. A. d. C.; before moving from the third-person incipit into first-person narrative, the protagonists are identified by initials which refer to their narrative roles:

> Mas ase aquí de considerar una cosa, ca allá donde se allaran aquestas quatro letras ansy fechas cada vna por sy: Sª, Mª, Eº, Aº, se an de comprender la primera por senyora, la segunda por madrastra, la terçera por enamorado, la quarta por amigo,[22]

and later Madrastra and Amigo are identified by their initials (C. J. and M. G.[23]) while in the Other World journey reference is made to realistically named and, in some cases, historically verifiable lovers.[24] The presence of elements typical of a *roman à clef* in *Triste deleytaçión* is particularly notable given that this is a feature which reappears in the stage of the genre classified by Rohland de Langbehn as its third and final stage.

In addition to the strategies shared by the sentimental romances discussed above, Gerli has noticed two points of similarity between *Siervo* and *Triste deleytaçión*: the shift in narratorial perspective and the relevance of the framed story to the narrator's own situation.[25] It is to these points that I should now like to turn.

Although not immediately apparent, the movement from the first person to third person in *Triste deleytaçión,* from the incipit to the main narrative, and in *Siervo* from the frame narrative to the inset romance of the *Estoria de dos amadores* is also exploited in Dom Pedro's *Sátira*. It is found principally in the shifts in tone and narratorial voice between the main narrative of *Sátira* and its supporting glosses. The glosses include extensive sentimental material. They are often relevant to the lover's own situation, occasionally appeal directly to the beloved, and, unlike the main narrative, are presented largely from a third-person narratorial perspective:

> Ninfa Cardiana — Esta es aquella por la qual el mundo conosçe quanto se puede amar, amando secretamente a Eliso, amador suyo [...] E syn fin llorando el su infortunado caso, manifiesta su muy grave dolor. Mirad pues, vos, sola señora de mi, que por vuestra causa yo no sea otro Eliso, e vos por la mia non seays otra Cardiana! (137-38).[26]

Thus all three romances experiment with the juxtaposition of narratorial perspectives.[27]

The structural pattern of fragmentation, vision and unresolved ending is common to all three of the sentimental romances discussed here. It is an important strategy in the exploration of the dynamics of the lover's mind.[28] The authors use these devices to contrast their own unresolved narratives which project into an undefined future with intertextual allusions to resolved narratives. In *Triste deleytaçión* this is evident in the fates of Madrasta and Amigo and the literary and historic lovers encountered in the Other World experience. Explicit literary models are provided by structural elements in *Siervo* through the introduction of Ardanlier and Maçías as exemplary figures in the '*Estoria de dos amadores*' and in *Sátira* through the glosses. The emphasis on the temporal axis of the action found most emphatically in *Siervo* but also in *Sátira* sets the resolved narratives of fictional characters against the unresolved narratives of the protagonists of the sentimental romances discussed here.

This contrast between fictional, or diegetic, and historically real, or extradiegetic, existence is further emphasized by the identification of the author with the narrator. In *Siervo* the roles of author and protagonist are deliberately confused as Rodríguez del Padrón identifies himself as the lover-protagonist in the letter to Gonçalo de Medina which follows the *ac-*

cessus. The author-as-lover's experience is then compared with that of the fictional Ardanlier and that of the legendary Maçías. Finally, *Siervo* ends with the implication that the protagonist retells his unresolved experience as *Siervo* to Syndéresis and as Rodíguez del Parrón to Medina. In *Sátira* the identification of author and protagonist is made explicit in the *accessus* through allusions to an extradiegetic beloved. Dom Pedro then attempts to break the bonds of the fictional construct of a dream vision by appealing to the extra-narrative beloved. In *Triste deleytaçión* the narrator's situation is identified with that of the male protagonist and in the course of the narrative the two are conflated through the use of a shifting narratorial voice.

In fact these three sentimental romances manifest a number of traits — the inclusion of debates, elements of *roman à clef*, treatment of the moral worth of women and the "problem" of the nature of fiction and experience, here through temporal and narrative structure — associated by Rohland de Langbehn with the two later groups in the development of the genre. First, the psychomachic allegory of the soul is a basic narrative element in all three texts which contain a latent debate structure. This is developed to include other types of debate such as the disputation between the College of Virtues, especially Prudençia, and the Lover in *Sátira* and, in *Triste deleytaçión*, the debate between Enamorado and Amigo and the question-and-answer format of the sentimental education offered by Madrina to Senyora.[29] Second, there is a tendency to introduce references to the existence of an extra-narrative beloved which, in *Triste deleytaçión*, becomes more clearly aligned with the *roman à clef*. While the treatment of the figure of the beloved is minimal in *Siervo*, she is described in abstract terms and associated with Saint Catherine in *Sátira* (quoted above) and in *Triste deleytaçión*:

> Cómo el enamorado fue traspostado en su tierra y supo cómo su senyora s'era puesta en religión
> [...]
> me vi sin dilaçión
> traspostado en mi tierra,
> do fallara la strella
> que guía el ser humano
> sotapuesta ad aquélla
> que por su buena querella
> trae la rueda en la mano.[30]

In the earlier text, the beloved's virtues and lack of compassion are described in detail, whilst in the later, Voluntad portrays her qualities allegorically through her dress. Third, both of these texts also include a significant proportion of material on the worth of women: a feature which is particularly marked in the Flores/San Pedro stage of the development of the genre. This is especially important as each author states quite clearly in his *accessus* his intention to defend women, *"este nombre sátira viene de satura, que es loor, e yo a ella primero loando, el femineo linage propuse loar"* ("this name *sátira* comes from *satura*, which is 'praise', and by first praising her I propose to praise women in general"; *Sátira*, 5) and,

> y más, cómo en el razonamiento de las tres senyoras quexosas, la vna llorando manifestaua el grande sujuzgamiento en que las magníficas senyoras por los honbres stauan, mostrándolo ella y confirmándolo la madrina por viuas razones, ser ellas más perfetas y nobles que los onbres.[31]

The presence of material related to the debate about the moral worth of women in two of the earliest romances should be borne in mind by advocates of an analogical reading of sentimental romance which relates the debate to the position of *conversos*.[32] Fourth, *Siervo* and *Sátira* present external tripartite structures consisting of psychomachia, vision and awakening which have strong parallels with the dream-vision convention and internal structures which refer to the past, present and future development of the narrative. This temporal organization may be manifest in *Triste deleytaçión* in the narrator's statement that the action stops before the narrative has reached its conclusion and in the possibility that the final *quintilla* appeals extra-narratively to the narrator's beloved as well as intra-narratively to the *Senyora*.

To conclude, my analysis of the structural and temporal axes of Dom Pedro's *Sátira* and Rodríguez del Padrón's *Siervo* shows that Don Pedro applies *Siervo's* tripartite structure to a similarly unresolved tale of frustrated love thereby strengthening the view that *Sátira* is closely aligned with *Siervo*. Indeed Dom Pedro very likely knew *Siervo* and *Triunfo* well, as Castro Lingl has argued.[33] The parallels I have adduced between *Triste deleytaçión* and the other two sentimental romances under discussion suggest that F. A. d. C. knew Rodríguez del Padrón's *Siervo*, either directly or indirectly, and was influenced by it and/or that he may have known *Sátira*. This last point seems less likely because there are no direct references to *Sátira* in *Triste deleytaçión*.[34] In addition, although there is no evidence that the authors of the later sentimental romances had direct knowledge of the earlier group, continuity in the development of the strategies discussed here can be observed, thereby suggesting that the earlier sentimental romances enjoyed far wider dissemination than has been generally conceded up to this point. In particular, the exploration of the relationship between actual experience and fiction seems to be a new direction in narrative. This concern is taken up by later authors of sentimental fiction and is responsible for producing the active *Autor* figure in *San Pedro*, the intricately crafted metafiction of Flores Grimale and the general tendency toward *roman à clef* in the initial phase of sentimental romance.

Notes

[1] E. Michael Gerli, *Triste deleytaçión: An Anonymous Fifteenth-Century Castilian Romance* (Washington: Georgetown U.P., 1982), "Revaluation," 116.

[2] Vera Castro Lingl, "The Constable of Portugal's *Sátira de infelice e felice vida: A Reworking of Rodríguez del Padrón's Siervo libre de amor,*" *Revista de Estudios Hispánicos* (USA), forthcoming. The present study began as a collaborative project with Dr. Castro Lingl; however, circumstances beyond our control led to the submission for publication of her findings before my own. I should like to express my thanks for her generosity and patience. *Sátira* was originally partially written in Portuguese (1445-49) and then translated into Castilian and completed by Dom Pedro between 1450 and 1453: the Portuguese version is no longer extant.

[3] For dating see Martín de Riquer, "Triste deleytaçión, novela castellana del siglo XV," *Revista de Filología Española* 40 (1956), 54-59. Riquer, "Triste deleytaçión": 61 and Gerli, *Triste deleytaçión,* xviii, argue that Rodríguez del Padrón's *Triunfo* was known to the author of *Triste deleytaçión*.

[4] "As Rodriguez del Padrón, that most virtuous of all men, crowning us with glory in his *Triunfo de las senyoras [Triunfo de las donas/Triumph of Ladies*] has argued at length [...] that aforementioned knight wanted because of his virtue to show what the other men because of their unadulterated [lit. pure] and envious wickedness hid from us." [F. A. d. C.], *Triste deleytaçión*: *novela de F. A. d. C., autor anónimo del siglo XV*, ed. Regula Rohland de Langbehn (Morón: Univ., 1983), 81-82. All quotations from *Triste deleytaçión* are taken from this edition: I have modernized use of accents to facilitate comprehension of the text.

[5] Gerli, "Revaluation," 117.

[6] Regula Rohland de Langbehn "Desarrollo" (see n. 1) and her "Fábula trágica y nivel de estilo elevado en la novela sentimental española de los siglos XV y XVI," in *Literatura hispánica: Reyes Católicos y descubrimiento: Actas del Congreso Internacional sobre Literatura Hispánica en la Época de los Reyes Católicos y el Descubrimiento* (Pastrana, julio 1986), ed. Manuel Criado de Val (Barcelona: PPU for the Diputación de Guadalajara, 1989), 230-36.

[7] Alan Deyermond, "Santillana's Love-Allegories: Structure, Relation, and Message," in *Studies in Honor of Bruce W. Wardropper*, ed. Diane Fox, Harry Sieber and Robert TerHorst, Juan de la Cuesta Monographs Homenajes 6 (Newark, DE: Juan de la Cuesta, 1989), 75-90.

[8] "The following work is divided into three main parts, according to three different times which it contains, represented by three paths and three sacred trees, which refer to the parts of man, namely, Heart, Free Will and Understanding, and to their three different ideas [intentions?]. The first part follows the time of loving well and being loved [...] The second refers to the time of loving well and being

unloved [...] The third and final deals with the time of not loving and being unloved". Juan Rodríguez del Padrón, *Siervo libre de amor, in Obras completas*, ed. César Hernández Alonso, *Biblioteca de la Literatura y el Pensamiento Hispánicos* 48 (Madrid: Editora Nacional, 1982), 153-54. All quotations from *Siervo* are from this edition.

[9] "Alas, friend, friend! The passage to the Elysian Plains is dangerous because of the terrible dog Cerberus with three heads, which are the three times: past, present and future."

[10] "The poets described it as having three mouths or three heads, which signify these three ages, that is Infancy, Youth and Old Age." Condestável Dom Pedro de Portugal, *Sátira de infelice e felice vida, in Obras completas,* ed. Luís Adão da Fonseca (Lisbon: Fundação Calouste Gulbenkian, 1975), 85. All quotations from *Sátira* are from this edition. I modernize use of accents.

[11] 102-03. "I wish to speak, as it is now the appropriate time, of her inestimable prudence. And truly I say that she [the beloved] possesses the three faces of prudence, which are memory or recollection of things past, consideration of [things] present and foresight for the future."

[12] See figure 1 for a schematic representation of the relation of the "*tres diversos tiempos*" to the external structure of the three sentimental romances under discussion.

[13] 174. "And I, unfortunate, suffering, looked at the drawn and double-edged sword in my right hand, with undecided intention and altered expression, wondering whether it was better to die quickly or to hope for the unknown answer to console me. Discretion favours and begs for [me to] wait, grief-stricken Will insists on sad death, Understanding orders [me to] await the reply, aggrieved Heart, wailing, demands the end."

[14] "The narrative we have just read is in fact his reply to Synéresis' question, and his need to tell it cures him of the illness of sexual passion. The act of literary creation is the third part, and the work has a circular structure". Alan Deyermond, "*Estudio preliminar,*" in Diego de San Pedro, *Cárcel de Amor con la continuación de Nicolás Núñez*, ed. Carmen Parrilla and Keith Whinnom, *Biblioteca Clásica* 17 (Barcelona: Crítica, 1995), xv.

[15] Medina's role of confessor/inquisitor has been discussed by Vera Castro Lingl, "Back to the Text: Another Look at Juan Rodríguez del Padrón's *Siervo libre de amor,*" *Romanische Forschungen* 106 (1994), 49-50 and 54, E. Michael Gerli, "*Siervo libre de amor* and the Penitential Tradition," *Journal of Hispanic Philology* 12 (1987-88), 94-96 and Colbert I. Nepaulsingh, *Towards a History of Literary Composition in Medieval Spain*, University of Toronto Romance Series 54 (Toronto: Univ. of Toronto Press, 1986), 168-69.

[16] See E. Michael Gerli, "The Old French Source of Siervo libre de amor: Guillaume de Deguileville's Le Rommant des Trois Pèlerinages," in *Studies on Spanish Sentimental Romance* (1440-1550), *Redefining a Genre*, ed. Joseph J.

Gwara and E. Michael Gerli (London: Tamesis, 1997), 18. I should like to thank Professor Gerli for generously sending me a copy of this article prior to publication.

[17] Gregory Peter Andrachuk identifies Syndéresis as representing the confessor in his, "On the Missing Third Part of *Siervo libre de amor,*" *Hispanic Review* 45 (1977), 177.

[18] Castro Lingl, "Reworking": "it is unlikely that the *Siervo* written by Rodríguez del Padrón differed substantially from the text that we have today." Gregory Peter Andrachuk, "The Function of the Estoria de dos amadores in the *Siervo libre de amor*," *Revista Canadiense de Estudios Hispánicos* 2 (1977-78), 27-29, and Javier Herrero, "The Allegorical Structure of the *Siervo libre de amor*," *Speculum* 55 (1980), 751-64, believe the text to be incomplete; Peter Cocozzella, "The Thematic Unity of Juan Rodríguez del Padrón's *Siervo libre de amor*," *Hispania* (USA) 64 (1981), 188-98, and Colbert I. Nepaulsingh, *A History of Literary Composition:* 166-73, argue that it is complete.

[19] 38-39 and 36-37. On the glosses see Guillermo Serés, "Ficción sentimental y humanismo: la Sátira de don Pedro de Portugal," *Bulletin Hispanique* 93 (1991), 38-58, and Julian Weiss, "Las 'fermosas e peregrinas ystorias': sobre la glosa ornamental cuatrocentista," *Revista de Literatura Medieval* 2 (1990), 103-4.

[20] *Triste deleytaçión*, 197. "Although I freed my desire [love, affections] with vow and sacrament, I never withdrew them from where they first fully dwelt."

[21] On active narrators see Barbara F. Weissberger, "Authors, Characters, and Readers in Grimalte y Gradissa," in *Creation and Re-creation: Experiments in Literary Form in Early Modern Spain; Studies in Honor of Stephen Gilman*, ed. Ronald E. Surtz and Nora Weinwerth, Juan de la Cuesta Monographs Homenajes 2 (Newark, DE: Juan de la Cuesta, 1983), 61-76, and my "Gradissa: A Female Reader in/of a Male Author's Work," *Medium Aevum* 64 (1995), 85-99.

[22] *Triste deleytaçión*, 3. "But something else should be mentioned here, that wherever these four letters are found alone, S^a^, M^a^, E^o^, A^o^, the first should be understood as *Senoyra* [Lady], the second as *Madastra* [Stepmother], the third as *Enamorado* [Lover] and the fourth as *Amigo* [Friend]."

[23] Triste deleytaçión, 109.

[24] Vicenta Blay Manzanera, "El libro llamado *Triste deleytaçión en el marco génerico de la ficción sentimental española: estudio y edición"*, unpubl. thesis, 2 vols. (Univ. de València, 1991), vol. 1, part II, 145-80; Rosa María Gómez-Fargas, "*Triste deleytaçion*, ¿novela clave?," *Revista de Literatura Medieval* 4 (1992), 101-22; Riquer, `*Triste deleytaçión*', 57-60; and E. Michael Gerli ed., *Triste deleytaçión*: xiii and 130.

[25] Gerli, *Triste deleytaçión*, xviii.

[26] "Nymph Cardiana — This is she by whom the world knows how much it is possible to love, loving Elisus, her lover, secretly [...] And endlessly bewailing her unfortunate experience, she shows her very deep grief. Look then, my own Lady,

that I be not another Elisus because of you, nor you another Cardiana because of me!"

[27] For further discussion of point of view see Alan Deyermond, "El punto de vista narrativo en la ficción sentimental del siglo XV," in *Actas del I Congreso de la Asociación Hispánica de Literatura Medieval* (Santiago de Compostela, 2 al 6 de diciembre de 1985), ed. Vicente Beltrán Pepió (Barcelona: PPU, 1988), 45-60; repr. in his *Tradiciones y puntos de vista en la ficción sentimental, Publicaciones Medievalia* 5 (Mexico: UNAM, 1993), 65-88.

[28] See my " 'La escura selva': Allegory in Early Sentimental Romance", forthcoming.

[29] On Madrina's advice see Olga Tudoric Impey, "Un doctrinal para las doncellas enamoradas en la *Triste deleytaçión*," *Boletín de la Real Academia Española 66* (1986), 191-234, and Françoise Vigier, "Le De arte amandi d'André le Chapelain et la *Triste deleytaçión*, roman sentimental anonyme de la seconde moitié du XVe siècle," *Mélanges de la Casa de Velázquez 21* (1985), 167-71.

[30] *Triste deleytaçión,* 195. "How the lover was transported to his land and he found out how his Lady entered holy orders [...] I saw myself without delay transported to my land where I found the star which guides human beings subjected to the one who because of her skilful argument holds the wheel in her hand." I am indebted to Dr Vicenta Blay Manzanera, Universitat de València, who pointed out this parallel in a letter of 4 January 1995.

[31] *Triste deleytaçión,* 3. "And furthermore, how in the discussion between the three querulous ladies, the one weeping showed the great subjection under which splendid ladies were because of men, showing, with the confirmation of the Godmother's lively reasons, that they are more perfect and noble than men."

[32] For differing views on this point see Rohland de Langbehn, her "El problema de los conversos y la novela sentimental," in *The Age of the Catholic Monarchs, 1474-1516: Literary Studies in Memory of Keith Whinnom*, ed. Alan Deyermond and Ian Macpherson, BHS Special Issue (Liverpool: U. P., 1989), 134-43, and my "Female Voices in Spanish Sentimental Romances," *Journal of the Institute of Romance Studies 4* (1996), 17-35.

[33] Castro Lingl, "Reworking": "Dom Pedro most likely had copies of *Siervo* and *Triunfo* in his library, or at least, had them handy when he wrote *Sátira*."

[34] This possibility and its implications are points which Vicenta Blay has proposed to take up in the near future as part of her investigation into the literary relations of Don Carlos of Viana.

University of Saint Andrews

Two Faces of Charisma in Fifteenth-Century Tibet

William A. Magee

D̄zong-ka-b̄a L̄o-sang-drak-b̄a[1] (1359-1417), called Je Rinpoche, was fifteenth-century Tibet's most charismatic religious reformer. This article explores Je Rinpoche's charisma, drawing conclusions primarily from three fifteenth-century hagiographies (*rNam Thar:* literally, "liberation [accounts]"). Tibetan hagiographies generally do not present biographical fact, but instead present their subject's life as a series of events leading to Buddhist nirvana. *rNam Thar* was a popular and well-established genre in fifteenth-century Tibet. Its subjects were initially the great Indian masters of Mahāyāna Buddhism's South Asian past, but increasingly Tibet's own religious heroes were memorialized in *rNam Thar.*

These hagiographies reveal two primary aspects of Je Rinpoche's enduring charismatic appeal: (1) Je Rinpoche had contact with the omniscient sources of Indian Buddhism and (2) Je Rinpoche championed Tibetan cultural superiority over other nations and peoples — primarily those of India and China. These two aspects of his legend show the two faces of charisma in Tibet: religious and political. The religious face looks toward India, the home of Buddhism. The political face observes Tibetan culture as supreme. Thus, three cultures are involved in the charismatic equation. One culture is that of classical Indian Buddhism, the ancient — but long-dead by the fifteenth century — source of Tibetan Buddhism. China often figures as the opposing culture, the culture to be bested. Tibet is always seen as surpreme above these.

Fifteenth-century Tibetan culture was religious in the same way that Islamic culture of the same century was religious: although there were secular activities, there was no secular segment of society. For a culture to be single-mindedly religious in this way, culture itself must be identified with religion. In Tibet, Buddhism was identified with culture. Melvyn Goldstein remarks that:

> Religion in Tibet played a role that went beyond its universal function as an explanation of suffering and a template for salvation. Tibetans saw religion as a symbol of their country's identity and of the superiority of their civilization.[2]

Although Tibetans saw Buddhism as a symbol of their country's identity and the superiority of their civilization, they could not ignore the fact that Buddhism is Indian in origin.[3] Since Tibetan religion is viewed by Tibetans as the basis of the greatness of the Tibetan nationality, we might expect that one role of the charismatic is to neutralize the threat of foreign superiority.

The reform movement inspired by Je Rinpoche and later Ge-luks enjoyed tremendous success in Tibet and established Tibetan orthodoxy well beyond Tibet's borders. Besides Je Rinpoche's influential charisma, a number of political, religious, economic, and social factors contributed to this success. Beginning with the sixteenth century, the Mongol Emperors allied themselves with the Ge-luk faction and lent their political and military strength to enforce religious orthodoxy. Also, maximizing returns in the social sphere, the Ge-luk sect borrowed the reincarnating-lineage system (*yang srid*) from rival sects. They instituted the practice of recognizing deceased eminent lamas in their young reincarnations. This system allows for the transmission of religious charisma and personal wealth within an otherwise childless monastic lineage. The Ge-luk reincarnating-lineage system found and trained the fourteen Dalai Lamas who ruled Tibet for almost three hundred years.

Theories of Charisma

Modern scholarship on charismatic figures and the religious movements they inspire owes much to Max Weber (1864-1920). Weber most often associates economic factors with societal change, but he did not deprecate the affect upon society of charismatic individuals and their influential ideas.[4] Weber respected (and feared) charisma for the transformational power charismatics sometimes hold over society, especially the charisma of prophets and religious reformers. Weber held that charisma is "a certain quality of an individual personality by virtue of which he is considered extraordinary and treated as endowed with supernatural, superhuman, or at least specifically exceptional powers...regarded as of divine origin."[5] Moreover, the charisma of a prophet or religious reformer must be recognized by others in order to be effective. Thus, Weber's theory of charisma suggests this simple model: a remarkable personality that is recognized as such by others.

Of course, there is no consensus as to just what constitutes or causes a charismatic's remarkable personality. Since the 1970s, psychological analyses of charismatic persons have focused on the narcissistic elements of their personalities. Kohout found charismatic personality-types among many of his patients with narcissistic disorder. In particular, his studies drew a parallel between the grandiose self-confidence of his patients and that of charismatic leaders.[6] Kohout felt that charismatic prophets identify with their "grandiose self" as a symbol of omnipotence and the sign that God dwells within them.[7] Len Oakes administered personality tests to charismatic gurus and leaders of religious cults. Oakes's findings describe the behaviors of charismatic personality-types in terms of their self-confidence, energy, revolutionary vision, manipulativeness, aloofness, strength, congruence, and social insight. He also found that charismatics who founded groups possessed the qualities of attached availability, acceptance of others, and a socially classless, unrefined quality.[8]

Although psychologists focus on the psyche and behavior of charismatics, personal qualities alone are not sufficient to explain the immense impact prophets and charismatics have upon society. Weber suggests that charisma is a cooperative and inter-dependent effort between the leader and the followers.[9] In other words, the charisma of a prophet or religious reformer must be recognized by others in order to be effective.

Charisma and the Tibetan Tradition

In order to see how the Ge-luk tradition recognizes Je Rinpoche's charismatic appeal, I consulted three orthodox Ge-luk *rNam Thar* from the late fifteenth-century. The ones consulted herein are authored by two of Je Rinpoche's close disciples. Thus, a careful scholar will not count on them for objective accounts of actual events (a skepticism that should be cultivated with respect to the entire genre of official biography). The other side of the coin is that these biographies *are* reliable as propaganda: we can be sure they display Je Rinpoche's life as charismatically as possible.

Among these are two by Je Rinpoche's disciple, Ke-drup[10] (1385-1438): the *Haven of Faith: The Marvelous Biography of the Great Lama D̄zong-ka-b̄a*[11] and *An Account Expressing a Small Part of the Oceanic Secret Biography of Je Rinpoche.*[12] A third text is by Jam-bel Gya-tso[13] (1356-1428), *Compendium of Good Biographical Statements: Supplement to the Extensive Biography of the Great D̄zong-ka-b̄a.*[14]

These texts and other narratives of the life and legend of Je Rinpoche reveal four biographical themes that explain his charismatic appeal and also illustrate the dual nature of charisma in Tibet:

- Je Rinpoche was prophesied to appear and take miraculous birth;
- Je Rinpoche was divinely sanctioned by an omniscient consciousness;
- Je Rinpoche had direct contact with the sources of Indian Buddhism;
- Je Rinpoche was a champion of Tibetan national superiority.

The legends of many of the world's great religious figures reveal prophesies foretelling the appearance of the great one and detailing the inevitable miraculous events surrounding the birth. Je Rinpoche's legend contains both of these important signifiers of charisma. Ngawang Dhargyey's *A Short Biography of Je Tzong-k'a-pa* discusses the prophetic element of the legend:

> In a previous incarnation, at the time of Buddha Shakyamuni, Tzong-k'a-pa was a young boy. One day he went to see Lord Buddha [at Bodh Gaya] and presented him with a clear crystal rosary. In return the Buddha gave the boy a conch shell. Afterwards the Buddha called his disciple Ananda to Him and prophesied that the boy would be born in Tibet and would found a great monastery between two locations, Dri and Dän. The Buddha gave the young boy the future name of Lo-zang dr'ag-pa. he also said that this person would present a crown to the statue of the Buddha in Lhasa and that the Buddhist teachings would flourish in Tibet.[15]

According to Tibetan dating, the youth presented the Buddha with a crystal rosary in the thirteenth century B.C.E. From that century to the year of Je Rinpoche's birth, twenty-six centuries intervene. During all this time, the individual who is to become Je Rinpoche continually reincarnates while gradually developing his spiritual powers. This long expanse of time between prophesy and birth is a common feature of Buddhist prophesies. As Hopkins remarks, this emphasis on the importance of individual enterprise over long periods of history undermines some scholars' unfounded belief that Buddhists view time as cyclical and individuals' actions as unimportant.[16]

This point is underscored by Je Rinpoche's own reflection upon the effect of his action as described in the prophesy:

> Previously, in Bodh Gaya, I presented Shakyamuni Buddha with prayer beads of white crystal. A partial effect of that has been my generation of the altruistic mind of enlightenment.[17]

Je Rinpoche gives credit for his achievement of the altruistic mind that seeks enlightenment — *bodhicitta* — to his pious offering of a white crystal to the Buddha more than two millenia earlier. This places emphasize on the cause and effect nature of spiritual accomplishments but also places such accomplishments into the proper — i.e., lengthy — time frame. Thus, the prophesy is an indicator of Je Rinpoche's heroic enterprise over a long period of history. The fact that the Buddha purportedly spoke specifically of Tibetan Buddhism in this context adds impact to the political face of Je Rinpoche's charismatic appeal.

Miraculous Events Surrounding Je Rinpoche's Birth

Just as miraculous events surrounded the birth of the Buddha, Jesus of Nazareth, and other charismatic figures, so did extraordinary events portend the birth of Je Rinpoche. Jam-bel Gya-tso relates a number of such dreams and portents in his *Supplement:*

> The birth of the omniscient Je Rinpoche L̄o-sang-drak-b̄a occurred in eastern D̄zong province. His father and mother were faithful and compassionate [Buddhists] who made effort to establish the excellent doctrine [in their lives].
>
> Toward the end of the year of the monkey [nine months before Je Rinpoche's birth], the father had a dream. In his dream a monk who said he was from the Five Mountain Peaks[18] arrived carrying a book. He wore finely stitched monk's robes festooned with many garlands of flowers and had a lower robe that looked to be made of the yellow silk called "Thirty-Three Leafy Branches".
>
> "I wish to stay with you," he said, and so saying he reappeared atop the house inside a temple. Due to this portent, the father offered fervent prayers [to Mañjushrī] and considered the notion that [the child] would be an avatar of Mañjushrī.
>
> Then Je Rinpoche's mother had a dream in which she was in a valley of flowers. She sat in the middle of a thousand women in rows. A boy in white came from the East carrying a vase. A girl in red came from the West carrying a bunch of peacock feathers in her right hand and a large mirror in her left.
>
> They consulted among themselves about the thousand women, the boy asking the girl, "Is this one suitable or unsuitable?" But the girl found some flaw in each of them. Then the boy pointed his finger at Je Rinpoche's mother. "Is she suitable?" he asked. Laughing, the girl said, "She is suitable."
>
> Then they suggested that Je Rinpoche's mother perform an ablution. While she washed, they encouraged her soothingly, saying "You'll be [clean] as a new-born child." Through this she was purified of physical stains and there arose the appearance of clear bliss.
>
> When she awoke from sleep there were many positive signs: her body felt light and her mind was blissful. She won-

dered, "What are these signs? Should I doubt [that my child is an avatar of Mañjushrī]?"

From this day forth, the neighbors and villagers also began having dreams in which many marvels commonly occurred. For instance, many monks appeared within the statue of Atisha [in Lhasa], inviting [the villagers to enter]. The sun, the moon, and the stars all dawned at the same time and flowers rained all day. Incense perfumed the air, the sky loud with the sounds of music. The earth quaked. All of south and central Tibet knew of this.

Then, on the tenth evening of the first month of the year of the bird, Je Rinpoche's mother had another dream. In her dream she experienced an uncountable number of monks and nuns holding victory banners and countless examples of musical instruments, such as the great drums, and so forth. They declared that they were going to host a reception for the arrival of Avalokiteshvara.

[As she recounted her experience:] "At first I saw nothing, though I looked in all directions. Then I saw a golden statue [of Avalokiteshvara], large as a mountain, standing in a vale of clouds. It was surrounded by a retinue of marvelous beings renowned as gods and goddesses, shining like the sun, voicing the sweet sounds of Buddhist doctrine. The golden statue descended, growing smaller and smaller. From a great height, it arrived beside the top of my head. Then it dissolved into my body. I also saw the retinue and the reception committee dissolve into the statue. I dreamed that I prostrated to it and circumambulated it, praying all the while.

"After those on the outside went inside the statue, I felt a great clarity and happiness. Since that dream, even without analysis and investigation, I have venerated [the deity] with my own body. Now, wholesome efforts arise of their own power."

Je Rinpoche's father had another dream. In his dream he saw a flaming golden vajra dissolve into his wife. He thought, "was this thrown down by Vajrapani from Alakāvatī heaven?" He awoke thinking, "Our child will be powerful!"

When the time of the birth came due, Je Rinpoche's mother had a dream. Monks, nuns, and so forth, arrived bearing the five types of offerings. "We wish to visit the temple," they said. "Where is it?"

> Then the white-clad boy who had appeared in an earlier dream appeared again, holding a key of water-crystal. "Here it is," he said. With the key he opened a small golden door in mother's breast and removed the same golden statue [of Avalokiteshvara] that had dissolved into her in an earlier dream.
>
> The red-clad girl who had appeared earlier appeared again. Noticing that the statue was dusty and needed some cleaning, she washed the statue with the water from a vase and wiped it with a bunch of peacock feathers. Then, Je Rinpoche's Mother had the experience of someone singing in a language she thought might be Sanskrit. It appeared to her that the singing was an offering to the statue.
>
> When she awoke from sleep, a great star rose into the sky. That morning, she birthed her child in comfort.[19]

In this narrative of the pre-birth dreams and visions of his father, mother, and community, Je Rinpoche's arrival is heralded by several meaningful dreams displaying auspicious portents, divine visitations, the appearance of adepts, and so forth. It is not surprising that these tales are similar to the birth stories of Jesus, the Buddha, and other religious figures because hagiographic birth legends are designed in part to demonstrate the sacred origins, and thus the profound importance, of the coming infant. In the case of Je Rinpoche, the tales narrated above show him to be an avatar (*sprul sku*) of two Buddhist deities — Avalokiteshvara and Mañjushrī — symbolizing compassion and wisdom respectively.

In this Tibetan Buddhist context, an avatar is a simulacrum mentally emanated through the power of an omniscient Buddha. It is said that all Buddhas emanate humanoid (and non-humanoid) avatar simulacra for the sake of the unenlightened, and that, in fact, these simulacra are a Buddha's primary instrument for compassionate action. Avatars do not have their own mental continua: their minds are dependent on the omniscient minds of their supporting Buddhas.

Je Rinpoche's individuality is not being denigrated by the suggestion that he is an avatar. Rather, the suggestion is that Je Rinpoche was something grander than human: he was the living aspect of two Buddhas. Although it is more usual in Tibet for an individual to be the avatar of just one Buddha, an emanation of both Avalokiteshvara and Mañjushrī in the same individual functions in Tibetan culture as a doubly potent symbol of enlightenment and national superiority.

Not only does Jam-bel Gya-tso's narrative demonstrate the sacred nature and profound importance of Je Rinpoche, it also displays both faces of Je Rinpoche's charisma. There is a face that looks south to India: the link with the Buddha and later Sanskrit writers is preserved in Je Rinpoche's mythical but still powerful connection with the sub-continent. The political face of Je Rinpoche's charisma views Tibet as supreme; to indicate this in dreams, foreign monks and dignitaries travel to the site of his birth, which itself was prophesied to take place in the land of snows. These emissaries pay homage to the infant who will become a champion of Tibetan national superiority.

Je Rinpoche and Mañjushrī

Another important element of Je Rinpoche's biographical narratives is his relationship with Mañjushrī, which displays the two faces of personal charisma in fifteenth-century Tibet: religious and political. The relationship between the deity and the reformer did not begin until Je Rinpoche reached the age of thirty-three. At that time, Je Rinpoche began to settle philosophical issues in consultation with Mañjushrī. At first, he was assisted in these communications by the clairvoyant master, Lama U-ma-b̄a. Later, he was able to attain direct contact with the deity.

Tucci's *Tibetan Painted Scrolls* gives an account of one such meeting from a commentary upon a painting depicting events from the biography of Je Rinpoche:

> Then, while the two, master and disciple [U-ma-b̄a and Je Rinpoche], were meditating in dGa' ba gdong, in the environs of sKyid šod, as he attained the mystical experiences associated with aJam dbyangs [i.e., Mañjushrī], manifestations of a body similar to the one of this (god) occurred; dBu ma pa acting as interpretor, (aJam dbyangs answered) questions, making numberless speeches, in which he revealed the fundamental meaning of the secret instructions.[20]

The clairvoyant Lama U-ma-b̄a and Je Rinpoche continued to have visions of Mañjushrī and other Buddhas and Bodhisattvas. At first, Mañjushrī's role in these virtual meetings followed the traditional Indian model of spiritual preceptor (*dge ba' bshes gnyen*) or guru.

Ke-drup's *Secret Biography of Je Rinpoche* paints a scene of one such meeting that manages to be both supernatural and academic at the same time: each morning, during one of Je Rinpoche's frequent meditational retreats, Mañjushrī would appear and briefly explain one more stanza of a traditional Māhāyana text on Madhyamika School philosophy.[21] On other occasions, the nature of their meetings could be more esoteric: by turns exhortatory, initiatory, or mystical — involving spiritual energy transfer.

Then, in 1394, Je Rinpoche went into meditational retreat with other lamas. It was there that his preliminary period of indirect communication with the deity culminated and he began having direct contact with Mañjushrī. From Ke-drup's *Secret Biography of Je Rinpoche:*

> Then we directly perceived Lord Mañjushrī's body. He was huge and magnificent, surrounded by a retinue of countless Buddhas and Bodhisattvas and the spiritual appearances of the bodies of many paṇḍits: Nāgārjuna, Āryadeva, Buddhapālita, Nāgabodhi, Chandrakīrti, Asaṅga and his brother [Vasubhandu], Dignāga and Dharmakīrti, Guṇaprabha and Shākyaprabhā, Devendrabhuti, Shantirakshita, Kāmalashīla, Abhaya, and so forth. And we directly perceived the spiritual appearances of the bodies of many great adepts: King Indrabhūti, the great brahman Saraha, the great master Lūyipa, Ghantapāda, Kṛṣṇacārya, and so forth.
>
> In consideration of the time when there would be no further spiritual appearances, Lord Mañjushrī spoke as before: "You must accomplish your most difficult aspirations, for there is no liberation in spiritual appearances. Instead, depend on the texts of these [paṇḍits and adepts] to bring about an ocean of benefit for yourself and others."
>
> Then we perceived the terrifying face of Yamantaka [a wrathful aspect of Mañjushrī]. He was huge and magnificent, bearing a full complement of faces and arms. From then on, our practice of the self-generation of Yamantaka took place each day with no interruptions.
>
> Also, in that place as before, we directly perceived the spritual appearance of the body of Lord Mañjushrī. He pressed the hilt of his sword to his own heart and pricked the heart of Je Rinpoche with the tip of his blade. From Lord Mañjushrī's heart, a stream of nectar flowed along the blade into the heart of Je Rinpoche. The nectar was colored white and gold, like the colors of a very oily river. It entered into Je Rinpoche. The nectar in his heart caused a limitless great bliss to fill his entire body, such that he could not speak.[22]

This passage shows a more mystical aspect of Je Rinpoche's relationship with Mañjushrī. In this role, Mañjushrī is less of an educational preceptor and more of an esoteric presence. The transfer of wisdom energy across the swordblade is an interesting detail of Je Rinpoche's relationship with the deity. The energy transfer, with both mystical and initiatory overtones, empowers Je Rinpoche with Lord Mañjushrī's wisdom. This empowerment enables Je Rinpoche to realize the reality nature of things, emptiness — but not immediately. Direct realization of emptiness, the ontological ultimate asserted by the the Middle Way Consequence School (*dbu ma thal 'gyur pa, prāsaṅgika-mādhyamika*) of Buddhist philosophy, brings about a Buddha's omniscient consciousness and accomplishes the purposes of oneself and others. Thus, for Tibetans, the thought of realizing emptiness is inspirational. It is a realization of the truth and not at all the annihilation of reality that is mistakenly seen and deplored by some non-Tibetan scholars.

Although realization of emptiness is inspirational, it is difficult to attain because it involves cutting through the innate ignorance that ignorantly misconceives a self in persons and phenomena. Due to this difficulty, even empowered by Mañjushrī's energy, Je Rinpoche did not complete his realization until his thirty-ninth year. Ke-drup's *Secret Biography of Je Rinpoche* describes the events leading up to this experience:

> While sleeping, Je Rinpoche travelled to the heavenly vale [of Tushita]. There, Mañjushrī propounded to Je Rinpoche a penetrating analysis of the view of the Consequence and Autonomy schools. However, when he awoke to the hermitage at Ra-mo, even though he had been given the teachings, Je Rinpoche was unable to induce the ascertainment that utterly overturns mistaken ideas regarding ultimate points of doctrine.
>
> Remaining in retreat there, Je Rinpoche and his retinue of lamas remained together, offering up numerous prayers. Due to these efforts, one night Je Rinpoche had a significant dream. He dreamed that the master Nāgārjuna and his four spiritual sons [Āryadeva, Bhavaviveka, Buddhapālita, and Chandrakīrti], were debating fine points of doctrine regarding the existence or non-existence of own-being (*rang bzhin, svabhava*). Je Rinpoche recognized Buddhapālita amongst the group of debaters by the pandit's blue skin and large body. Buddhapālita approached Je Rinpoche with a text in his hand. He blessed him [with the text]. This was a sign [that Je Rinpoche would experience full realization].
>
> Later, [when Je Rinpoche awoke] that day, he re-read *Buddhapālita's Commentary on (Nāgārjuna's) Treatise on the Middle*. Without effort, Je Rinpoche generated certain ascertainment unlike any he had experienced before regarding the fine points of the Consequence school view and the limits of the object of negation [the absence of which constitutes emptiness] and he dispelled without remainder all mistaken grasping after signs [of inherent existence] and all

> superimpositions which reach conclusions other than the meaning of thusness [i.e., emptiness].[23]

Ke-drup's description of Je Rinpoche's ascertainment of the view of emptiness depicts a gradual process of struggle and attainment. The process of realization is presented as a spiritual drama involving many lifetimes and many attainments. Je Rinpoche is presented as having set into motion currents of causality across many centuries, ranging from the time of the Buddha, through the era of Indian Mahayana Buddhist civilization (second to thirteenth centuries) to the present day of fifteenth-century Tibet. In the story presented here by Ke-drup, Buddhapālita appears in a dream of the past to bestow upon Je Rinpoche what appears to be a textual empowerment (*lung*).[24] Je Rinpoche awakens from India's past into Tibet's present. Assisted by Buddhapālita's textual empowerment, his own scholarship enables Je Rinpoche to penetrate the meaning of the text and ascertain the view.

It is important for Je Rinpoche and his followers to be able to claim this type of connection with Indian sources of omniscience and scholarship because Je Rinpoche is claimed to have restored authentic Indian Buddhist doctrine in Tibet. Tenuous as this contact within a "significant dream" is, no actual contact with Indian Buddhism was possible in the fifteenth century. Tibet's physical connection with India had been severed in the fourteenth century due to Muslim deprecations of Buddhist institutions in Northern India. No fifteenth-century Tibetan could claim the charisma of actual contact with Indian paṇḍits, but Je Rinpoche's dream serves as one credential enabling his followers to claim for him this type of charisma.

Je Rinpoche as Cultural Champion

Not only was Je Rinpoche one of Tibet's greatest scholars, but his millions of followers within the Ge-luk tradition portray him as a champion of Tibetan cultural superiority. A champion of Tibetan cultural superiority is most often one who creates a religious or political tradition that unifies and strengthens the Tibetan nation. Many champions of Tibetan cultural superiority fit this description besides Je Rinpoche: Marpa, Sakya Pandita, Jang-chup Gyaltsen, the Fifth Dalai Lama, and Döl-b̄o-b̄a S̄hay-rap-gyel-tsen (before his discreditation in the texts of Je Rinpoche). Like these others, Je Rinpoche did not became a champion of Tibetan cultural superiority solely due to his scholarship. Events following his death were also necessary to shape his legend as a cultural champion.

During his life, Je Rinpoche created a novel synthesis of Buddhist doctrine and practice in the *Great Exposition* and other texts, and initiated millenarian-style reforms among his followers.[25] The tradition that Je Rinpoche's reforms were in rebellion against was the Empty of Other (*gshan stong*) movement of Döl-b̄o-b̄a S̄hay-rap-gyel-tsen[26] (1292-1361), the founder of the Jo-nang sect. In many respects, Döl-b̄o-b̄a's charisma resembles that of Je Rinpoche, but their philosophical positions were very different. For instance, the two scholars differ regarding which sutras of the Buddha are definitive and which require interpretation. Perhaps their most dramatic difference is that Döl-b̄o-b̄a asserted the existence of an omniscient Buddha nature within each individual, empty of all other (i.e., all conventional) phenomena, whereas Je Rinpoche did not. Due to Döl-b̄o-b̄a's assertion that a Buddha is immanent in each individual, his Jo-nang sect was able to hold out the promise of sudden enlightenment and became very popular in fourteenth-century Tibet.[27]

Despite their popularity, Je Rinpoche found these and other Jo-nang doctrines so heterodox as to be non-Buddhist. In his *Great Exposition* he states:

> Such assertions are outside the sphere of all the scriptures of the Greater and Lesser Vehicles because (1) those [Jo-nangs] assert that it is necessary to overcome the conception of self that is the root binding persons in cyclic existence and (2) the bases that are apprehended by this [conception] as self are these [phenomena] realized as not existent by nature. Hence, without overcoming that, they assert that the conception of self is overcome through realizing some other phenomenon unrelated with that [conception of self] as true.[28]

Je Rinpoche makes the point that the Jo-nangs themselves assert that individuals must overcome the conception of inherent existence to free themselves from cyclic existence. Although they assert this, they attempt to reverse the conception of inherent existence not through realizing the lack of inherent existence, as Je Rinpoche would have it, but instead through realizing some other, unrelated phenomenon — the Buddha nature. Je Rinpoche presents a telling analogy to illustrate this point:

> Regarding this [Jo-nang view], it is no different than if [some person] conceives there is a snake to the east and becomes distressed, and if [someone else] thinking the distress cannot be overcome by thinking there is no snake to the east instead says, "Think on the fact that to the west there is a tree. Through this, you will get rid of your conception of a snake in the room and will overcome your distress."[29]

In this analogy the snake in the east is inherent existence, the mistaken apprehension of which is seen by Buddhists as the root cause of all suffering. For Je Rinpoche, putting forth the Other Emptiness of Döl-b̄o-b̄a's system is akin to speaking of a tree in the west to dispell the conception of the snake in the east — it is completely beside the point. This analogy helps Je Rinpoche clarify his primary point: the positive, independent nature spoken of by Döl-b̄o-b̄a does not address the main issue of Buddhist soteriology, which is abandoning the conception of inherent existence that underlies all afflictions.

Je Rinpoche saw Döl-b̄o-b̄a's views as wildly incorrect and thus dangerous for the practitioner, but Je Rinpoche himself did not attempt to establish orthodoxy over other Tibetan sects. Rather, he spent his life in meditational retreats, scholarly pursuits, and other activities befitting a Buddhist monk. After his death, his followers in the Ge-luk sect extended the author's sphere of influence across much of Asia. Je Rinpoche's politicized descendents forged military connections and forcibly converted Jonang monasteries in the seventeenth and eighteenth centuries. Despite these partisan aggressions, the Ge-luk reform movement continued as the dominant religious movement in Central Asia until the twentieth century, inspiring millions of followers across a vast territory from Peking to St. Petersburg and from Katmandu to Ulan Batar. Today, for the displaced persons of the Tibetan diaspora, the significance of Je Rinpoche's charismatic appeal is as an important source of religious inspiration and Tibetan national pride.

Conclusion

The narratives recounted here from Je Rinpoche's biographies are certainly not reliable accounts of historical fact, but they do reveal that his charisma has two faces. The religious face looks toward India, the home of Buddhism: alone among fifteenth-century Tibetans, Je Rinpoche had contact with the omniscient sources of Indian Buddhism. This contact helped him to reform the philosophical view of emptiness and to dispell doctrinal and monastic corruptions. The political face observes Tibetan culture as supreme: Je Rinpoche championed Tibetan cultural superiority over India and China. Je Rinpoche's descendents in the later Ge-luk sect established Buddhist orthodoxy across a vast portion of Asia.

It is interesting to note that many aspects of Je Rinpoche's charismatic appeal also surround Tenzin Gyatso[30] (born 1936), the fourteenth and current Dalai Lama of Tibet. The fourteenth Dalai Lama is the first of the Dalai Lamas to become an international figure, and much has been written about his humble warmth, his intelligence, his scholarship, his impeccable ethics; and so forth. Tibetans everywhere (with some partisan abstainers) worship him as a perfect being and a fountainhead of hope and truth. His personal charisma is recognized the world over, but Tibetans — and others within the Tibetan cultural region — experience Tenzin Gyatso's charisma in an intensified manner.[31]

Without attempting to draw large conclusions about Tibetan charisma in general, I will point out that Je Rinpoche and Tenzin Gyatso share many of the same cultural signifiers of charisma. Prophesies and auspicious events occurred at both their births, and the oracles and mysterious events surrounding the choosing of new Dalai Lamas are analogous to the prophesy and miraculous events at Je Rinpoche's birth. Moreover, just as Je Rinpoche had contact with Indian omniscience, so Tenzin Gyatso is divinely sanctioned by an omniscient consciousness. He is said to be an emanation of Avalokiteshvara, as is Je Rinpoche. Also, Tenzin Gyatso symbolically reestablished contact with India through *geographically* moving his seat from Tibet to India. Finally, Tenzin Gyatso is like Je Rinpoche in that they are both champions of Tibetan national superiority. Je Rinpoche's tradition championed Tibetan culture as religiously superior throughout Central Asia. Tenzin Gyatso, Nobel laureate, champions Tibetan culture as morally superior to Communist Chinese oppression by personal example throughout the world.

Thus, the charismatic constellate is similar for Je Rinpoche and Tenzin Gyatso, and their charismatic appeal has two faces: religious and political. The public image of Je Rinpoche as a charismatic five hundred years ago depended on prophesies and miraculous events, divine sanction, direct contact with the sources of Indian Buddhism, and being a champion of Tibetan national superiority. These same signifiers are present today in the life and legend of the fourteenth Dalai Lama, a source of religious inspiration and a living symbol of Tibetan national identity.

Notes

[1] *tsong kha pa blo bzang grags pa*. For Tibetan romanization I employ the standard Wylie transcription scheme with some capitalization. See Turrell V. Wylie, "A Standard System of Tibetan Transcription." *Harvard Journal of Asiatic Studies*, Vol. 22, 1959, 261-267.

[2] Melvyn C. Goldstein, "The Revival of Monastic Life in Drepung Monastery." In *Buddhism in Contemporary Tibet*, edited by Melvyn Goldstein and Matthew T. Capstein (Berkeley: University of California Press, 1998), 15.

[3] Chinese Buddism is also Indian in origin, and it is worth asking if Tibetan and Chinese Buddhist cultures were sometimes vulnerable to feelings of cultural inferiority because their religion was a product of India.

[4] Jones and Anservitz, "Saint-Simon and Saint-Simonism: A Weberian View." *American Journal of Sociology* (1975; vol. 80 no. 5), 1098.

[5] Max Weber, *Economy and Society,* ed. Guenther Roth and Claus Wittich (Berkeley: University of California Press, 1968), 241.

[6] G. Little, "Leaders and Followers: A Psycho-social Prospectus", *Melbourne Journal of Politics* (1980; 12), 15.

[7] Len Oakes, *Prophetic Charisma: The Psychology of Revolutionary Religious Personalities* (Syracuse: Syracuse University Press, 1997), 31. Oakes quotes Heinz Kohut, "Forms and Transformations of Narcissism", *Journal of the American Psychoanalytic Association* (1966; 14), 250.

[8] Oakes, 12-18.

[9] Max Weber, *Economy and Society,* 241-242.

[10] mkhas sgrub dge legs dpal bzang po.

[11] rje btsun bla ma tsong kha pa chen po'i ngo mtsar rmad du byung ba'i rnam par thar pa dad pa'i 'jug ngogs. From The Collected Works of Rje Tson-kha-pa Blo-bzan-grags-pa, vol. 1 (Delhi: Ngawang Gelek Demo, 1979), 1-143.

[12] rje rin po che'i gsang ba'i rnam thar rgya mtso lta bu las cha shas nyung ngu zhig yongs su brjod pa'i gtam rin po che'i snye ma. From The Collected Works of Rje Tson-kha-pa Blo-bzan-grags-pa, vol. 1 (Delhi: Ngawang Gelek Demo, 1979), 167-201.

[13] 'jam dpal rgya mtso.

[14] rje btsun tsong kha pa'i rnam thar chen mo'i zur 'debs rnam thar legs bshad kun 'dus. From The Collected Works of Rje Tson-kha-pa Blo-bzan-grags-pa, vol. 1 (Delhi: Ngawang Gelek Demo, 1979), 144-166.

[15] Geshe Ngawang Dhargyey, *A Short Biography of Je Tzong-k'a-pa* (Dharamsala, Library of Tibetan Works and Archives, 1975), 7.

[16] See Jeffrey Hopkins on Nagarjuna's life story, in *Buddhist Advice for Living and Liberation* (Ithaca: Snow Lion Publications, 1998), 9-21.

[17] Supplement to the Extensive Biography, 164.5

[18] The Five Mountain Peaks of China are said to be an abode of Mañjushrī.

[19] *Supplement,* 145.2-149.1.

[20] Tucci, Tibetan Painted Scrolls, 343.

[21] Candrakīrti's Commentary on the "Introduction to (Nāgārjuna's) 'Treatise on the Middle"; dbu ma la 'jug pa'i rang 'grel, madhaymakāvatārabhāshya. Peking 5263, Vol. 98. See the Secret Biography, 57.3-4.

[22] *Secret Biography*, 179.2-180.2.

[23] Secret Biography, 184.5-185.6

[24] Tibetan lamas traditionally receive a textual empowerment before beginning their study of a text.

[25] The term "millenarian" originally was used to indicate a complex of Christian beliefs surrounding the second coming of Christ, but recent scholarship employs the term "millenarian" more widely to describe religious phenomena unrelated to the Christian millennium. For modern scholars, signs of millenarianism include a religion's promise of a future transformation and rebellion against a given tradition, as well as the founder having visionary experiences, divine warrant, and a program for action to set right that which has gone wrong. Je Rinpoche's reform movement was millenarian in all these respects except that his program for action was meditative rather than political. It was up to his followers in the sixteenth century to forge a political movement with Mongolian military backing.

[26] dol po pa shes rab rgyal mtshan.

[27] See Cyrus Stearns, "The Buddha from Dol po and his Fourth Council of the Buddhist Doctrine" (University of Washington, Ph.D. dissertation, 1996).

[28] Great Exposition, 869.1-3.

[29] Great Exposition, 869.3-6.

[30] bstan 'dzin rgya mtsho.

[31] It is common for pilgrims to walk hundreds of miles in order to circumambulate the Dalai Lama's residence.

University of North Carolina at Greensboro

The Spiritual and Civic Meaning of Pollaiuolo's Berlin Annunciation

Kornelia Imesch

Pollaiuolo's Berlin *Annunciation*, situated in a villa outside and above Florence, has, compared with the traditional paintings of the *Incarnation* of the Florentine Quattrocento, two peculiarities: the one-point perspective construction of the pictorial space has a vanishing point located to the left of the center. It differs therefore from the usual scheme with its so-called "corridor motive," which enhances the sacred middle through a centralised vanishing point. Furthermore the window in the left background opens onto a view of an actual landscape: the city of Florence.

Starting with such observations, my interpretation will rely upon contemporary Florentine writings about Mariology, the Florentine city-state with its holy visage, and the special relationship between the city and the cult of the *Annunciation*, i.e., the *Annunziata*, which Pollaiuolo's painting visualizes. It documents the analogy, made by historiographers of this time, between the *Incarnation* of Christ in the *Annunciation* to Mary and the *Incarnation* of the Florentine *Civitas*. Through the transfer of this *Incarnation* model to the *Civitas*, the civic body becomes a mariological body that had given birth to the Messiah and from which one could derive a claim to salvation and government with Messianic connotations. Pollaiuolo's *Annunciation* can therefore be considered as a metaphor of a paradisiacal historic era: it represents the *summa beatitudo* of the anti-republican, oligarchic Florence of the Medici times. And in the sacrally connoted theme of dignity, given by the so-called view from above on the town, the patron of Pollaiuolo's painting asserts a claim on domination and power in the Florentine city-state and, at the same time, a guiding influence on the local cult of the *Annunziata*.

Piero Pollaiuolo's magnificent painting on wood showing the *Annunciation to Mary*, now kept at the Gemäldegalerie in Berlin,[1] is thought to have been painted circa 1470 and was probably intended for the private chapel of a villa to the north or north-west of Florence (Fig. 1).[2] On account of the view from the windows in the left and right-hand background of the painting, this country-house is generally identified as either the Villa *Careggi* of the Medicis or Benedetto Salutati's Villa *Petraia*. The Villa *Careggi* is situated to the north of Florence, the Villa *Petraia* to the north-west.[3]

The painting reproduces the central salvific moment of Christ's becoming man on 25 March.[4] The action takes place in the foreground of a divided room of a villa which is located on a hill.[5] The room itself is sparsely, but very elegantly furnished. Two twin windows situated respectively in the left and right background of these princely chambers grant the beholder a wide view of a distant landscape that includes a town on the left (Fig. 2), and villas and farmyards on the right (Fig. 3). As seen from the left window, the view of the lowland plain with its farmyards merges into distant hills and mountains; it includes a group of riders and servants who approach the villa on a winding path and evoke a passage from Leon Battista Alberti's *Treatise on Architecture* (1452/1485), in which the author, talking about the elevated position of a country-house that he recommended, tells us:

> It will receive the arriving guest with its most magnificently furnished rooms. He will be noted as he approaches and will see the city [...], have the spreading plain, the peaks of the mountains, magnificent gardens, fish ponds and joyful hunting under his eyes.[6]

Mary and the Archangel, facing each other in silent dialogue, are arranged close to the front edge of the picture, so close as to be seemingly touchable (cf. Fig. 1). Both are of above-normal stature in relation to the room. The importance of the two figures is further underscored by the fact that they are viewed from below, which contrasts with the room and the high horizon of the landscape with its Dutch inspiration, both viewed from a higher perspective.[7] Pollaiuolo does not portray the Holy Spirit in the form of a dove.

Gabriel, on his knees, turns to the future Mother of God, a lily in his left hand and his right raised in the gesture of a blessing. The celestial greetings of the Archangel, *Ave Maria Gratia Plena* (Lk 1,28) are embroidered with pearls on the sleeves of his tunic. The Queen of Heaven is shown as a meditative type, with prayer book on her lap and her hands crossed in front of her bosom. She keeps her head and eyelids lowered in modesty. She neither looks at the angel, nor does she try — by throwing a so-called Albertian look from within the picture — to enter into dialogue with the beholder.[8] The bedstead in the right background shows that the room is to be seen as the representation of Mary's lap as a celestial bridal chamber. As suggested by Psalm 19,6, Christ, as the sun, entered this chamber by becoming man. Pollaiuolo's painting alludes to this with the solar ornamentation above the bed. ("In them he has set a tent for the sun, which comes forth like a bridegroom leaving his chamber")[9] (Fig. 4).

Both the structure of the action and the iconographic motives show that Pollaiuolo's painting owes a great deal to the traditional formula of Florentine representations of the *Annunciation* dating to the fifteenth century. Even the renunciation of the dove as the embodiment of divine creative power cannot be regarded as an unusual feature.[10] Donatello did not use it in the *Cavalcanti Annunciation* in *Santa Croce*, Florence, and it is likewise missing in various *Annunciations* painted by Fra Angelico. The dogmatic content is thus pushed into the background to stress the pious character of the representations.[11]

But there are two aspects that distinguish Pollaiuolo's painting from other Florentine *Annunciations*: the room shown in the picture has an excentrically situated vanishing point in the left part of the picture and thus deviates from the traditional formula with the so-called "corridor motive" that served to visualize the sacral centre (Fig. 5). The window in the left background does not grant a view of an ideal city, a cloister district or the *Hortus conclusus*, the gardens of Paradise, as is the case, for example, in the *Annunciations* of Fra Angelico (Fig. 6), Botticelli or Filippo Lippi (Fig. 7), but rather draws the eyes onto a real landscape, onto Florence and its surroundings.

The view of the entire city and not just a part of the inner area, as in Ridolfo Ghirlandaio's fresco in the *Palazzo Vecchio*, reproducing Florence's church of *SS. Annunziata* (Fig. 8), is quite unusual for the narratively conceived fifteenth-century Florentine *Annunciations* (Fig. 9).[12] Equally unusual is the view of the city from the north or the north-west. As pointed out by Sonja Brink, views of Florence dating to the fifteenth and sixteenth centuries normally show the city as seen from the south or south-west, as is the case in the so-called *Chain Plan* (ca. 1482, Fig. 10)[13] or in Jacopo del Sellaio's painting of *Saint John the Baptist* (ca. 1485, Fig. 11). In Pollaiuolo's painting one can readily recognize the most important religious and political buildings of the city state, namely the *Palazzo Vecchio*, the *Baptistery*, the *Bell Tower*, and the cupola of *Santa Maria del Fiore*.[14]

The dignity formula of the so-called view from above[15] lets our eyes range over the native town of the artist and the person who ordered the picture. The view from the left window thus enabled the commissioner, as it does the modern beholder, to "totam licet estimare Florentiam" — these being the words that Angelo Poliziano, somewhat euphorically and possibly alluding to Martial, used in a letter to Marsilio Ficino in which he described the view of Florence from Cosimo de Medici's villa in Fiesole.[16] The "where and when" (Edgerton) analyzed by Archbishop Antoninus (1389-1459) in Florence in the fifteenth century and discussed by Samuel Edgerton in connection with another *Annunciation* is thus very clearly specified and made tangible in Pollaiolo's painting. The place of Christ's *Incarnation* is the Florence area or the city itself circa 1470. The light flooding in from the left, i.e., from the east-north-east, and the rather short shadows suggest that the event that promised the rising of the sun of Christ over the earth must be taking place in the latter part of the morning.[17]

Does this early Florentine view represent a merely decorative, naturalistic motif, a reference to the fidelity to reality that had been sought since the late Middle Ages? Research has not yet concerned itself with this problem.[18] It seems to me that a purely decorative interpretation of this motif is contradicted both by the setting of the view in the picture and by the part that the Mother of God in general, and the *Annunciation to Mary* in particular, played in the self-concept of the city-state of Florence in the fifteenth century.

Florence, Mary and Paradise

Let us first consider the way the view is set in the picture (cf. Figs. 1, 2, 9). In fact, only the extreme left of Pollaiuolo's painting is constructed in an exact linear perspective. Here the orthogonal lines of the picture converge onto a common vanishing point above the view of Florence.[19] The vanishing point, the seemingly infinite point of convergence of the picture orthogonals, is situated in the south or south-east, in the direction of salvation, of resurrection and Paradise.[20] Put in other words: the vanishing point draws its origin from the city in the background of the picture and, from the point of view of the composition, is bound to the city, to the left-hand twin window as symbol of Christ in the centre, and to the Archangel in the foreground.[21] According to a fifteenth-century exegetist of the *Annunciation*, the previously mentioned Florentine Archbishop Antoninus, Gabriel is also the harbinger of light and the Holy Spirit;[22] he is the annunciator of the divine wisdom and power of creation,[23] which draws its origin from Paradise or, in Pollaiuolo's picture, as also in Filippino Lippi's representatively staged *Annunciation* (Fig. 12), from the city on the banks of the Arno.[24] The city's coat of arms is graced by the lily, the same lily that the Archangel of the *Annunciation* holds in his hand and which is a symbol of both Mary and Christ.[25]

The thematics of Paradise also have a close bearing on the symbolics of Mary, protagonist of the picture. As Mother and Bride of Christ, *Sponsa Christi*, Mary is the archetype of the *Ecclesia* (Fig. 13),[26] the very church of which the dome can be seen in the background as the symbol of Florence. The Church, in her turn, was understood as the faithful image of the heavenly Jerusalem and of Paradise.[27]

According to Archbishop Antoninus, in fact, Mary is therefore also the door to Paradise;[28] just like Christ, she stands for the window through which the light of divine mercy passes to illuminate the darkness of this sinful world.[29] Filippo Lippi, for example, gave direct and concrete form to this thought in his *Madonna in front of the window*, now on view at the *Uffizi* in Florence (Fig. 14).

But the Mother of God is also a sanctified and purified place.[30] In her the earth profaned by Eve's misdemeanour becomes re-sacralized. She is therefore understood as *terra vera*, *terra beata* and *terra promessa*, she is the place of everlasting spring, the *hortus conclusus* in which the flower of Christ is budding. Mary embodies the Paradise that was given back to Christian humanity by God's decision to redeem humankind.[31] The concept of Paradise is recalled also by the reproduction of the Archangel, by the details of the motives and by the picture structure. Gabriel has wings made of peacock feathers, an iconographic reference to the fact that the divine messenger has come from eternal Paradise (cf. Fig. 1). The twin window on the left allows the eyes to settle on a peacock standing on the parapet of a loggia (cf. Fig. 2.). In its positive connotation the peacock is a symbol of immortality and everlasting life. In representations of the Mother of God this bird alludes to the expectation of eternal life in Paradise.[32] In Pollaiuolo's picture, moreover, the peacock on the loggia parapet and the tip of Mary's right foot are joined by one of the orthogonals of the left-hand side of the painting, which — just like all the other orthogonals of this side of the picture — strives towards the vanishing point that, as was already mentioned, is situated in the paradisiac south or south-east above Florence.

Since the mother of God is a sanctified place, she is considered not only as the symbol of the *Ecclesia*, but also, as Antoninus of Florence once again tells us, as embodiment of the *Civitas*, the city.[33] In Italy during the fourteenth century, and therefore also in Florence, the aforesaid significance of the Church was transferred to the city as a whole, thus conferring sacral connotations upon the city and not just upon its walls, which had always been considered sacred. The city, at least in its positive symbolics, has ever since been likewise understood as a symbolic image of celestial Jerusalem and Paradise.[34] Around 1465, for example, this interpretation of Florence was given expression in a painting by Domenico di Michelino, where the city on the Arno stands for Dante's *Paradise* (Fig. 15).[35]

Mary is also identical with the palace of a city in general and the hall or room, since Christ, by virtue of his *Incarnation*, took up his residence there.[36] In fifteenth-century theory of architecture and the state, the palace was deemed a simile of the villa and the villa, in its turn, as Paradise (as Leon Battista Alberti tells us).[37] For the palace or the villa were understood, again according to Alberti, as a *Città piccola* or *Civitas piccola*.[38] Since Mary is the *terra beata* and the new place of salvation, indeed, the embodiment of Paradise, she is not only identical with the *Civitas* or the palace in their interpretation as Paradise, but also identical with the villa in which Pollaiuolo's Annunciation is taking place. As *città piccola*, i.e., as state body, the villa appears in fifteenth and sixteenth century Italy as an elite-type enlargement of the body of the city or the state.[39] In Pollaiuolo's painting it appears as the *Florentia piccola* and thus as the simile of the Paradise that is reproduced in the left background of the picture and embodied by Mary. The paradisiac city on the Arno and the villa of the *An-*

nunciation in its symbolic significance as *Florentia piccola* or Mary, are joined by a winding path that seems inserted in the landscape in the manner of a monumental M (cf. Fig. 2).[40] City and villa are thus joined not only by this path and the perspective view described at the beginning, but also by the initial of the name of the one who is the bearer of the Christian logos and the new *Ark* of salvation.[41] Mary is also the road to salvation, the *Old* and the *New Testament* come together in her, as also divine and human nature, for it was she who bore the body of the Lord within her.

The Annunciation, the Marian-Paradisiac "Body" and the "Holy Face" of Florence

Though John the Baptist was the Patron Saint of Florence,[42] both the city and the state had considered themselves as eminently Marian ever since the thirteenth century.[43] For Mary, the finest flower as Dante would have it,[44] stands for the flower *Florentia*, whose coat of arms, as we know, bears the Marian symbol of the virtuous lily. Ever since the late thirteenth century, the city's most important cult images had therefore been representations of Mary,[45] namely Mary of the *Annunciation* in *SS. Annunziata* (Fig. 16), the *Madonna* of *Or San Michele*, and the *Madonna* of *Impruneta*. The two Florentine *Madonnas* had "begun to unfold" their miraculous activities, or lets say were venerated for them, since 1280, respectively 1292,[46] at a time of important changes in the socio-political life and the physical structure of the city: in 1282 the institution of the priors was created, to be followed in 1293 by the so-called *ordinamenti di giustizia*, which can be described as the city's basic constitution or government statutes.[47] Work on the third wall had started in 1284,[48] and towards the end of the nineties, the building of the government palace (*Palazzo Vecchio*) and the cathedral as we know it today — the symbol of the commune[49] — was begun. Following the completion of Brunelleschi's cupola, it was consecrated in 1436, specifically on the anniversary of the *Annunciation to Mary*. Both the new name and the day of the consecration were to make it clear, as a resolution of the city council dated 29 March 1412 would have it, that "[...] the benign, humble and gracious *Incarnation* of the Son of God announced by the angel on the 25th day of March was the flower and beginning of our redemption."[50] The name of the cathedral was also understood as an allusion to the name of the city and the prosperity of the community: "The title [...] of this wonderful basilica is Santa Maria del Fiore, thus called to allude to the name of *Fiorentia*, or to the florid state in which the Republic found itself when it resolved to build this magnificent Temple [...]".[51]

Since Florence was understood by its historiographers also as a simile of Rome, as the most beautiful and famous successor of the eternal city,[52] it is not at all surprising that the city on the Arno, just like Rome with *Veronica*, should possess a holy visage. And in the case of Florence this sacral visage was the face of the Mother of God, of the Mary of the *Annunciation* (cf. Fig. 16), which brings us back to the subject of Pollaiuolo's painting. Out of the Mary of the *Annunciation*, the pure lily, there had come the flower of Christ, the most beautiful and well proportioned of bodies,[53] who was chosen by Savonarola at the end of the fifteenth century and again in 1528 by the followers of the Dominican, as the King of the city on the Arno.[54] But Mary, the pure lily, had also given birth to the flower *Florentia*, the most flourishing and beautiful of states, because, as one of the city counsellors put it in 1431: "Deus est Respublica".[55]

The transfer of the *Incarnation* model to the *Civitas* and the transformation of the civic body into a mariological body that had given birth to the Messiah and from which one could derive a claim to salvation and government with Messianic connotations occurred at the same time in which the above mentioned Marian images of the city had begun their miraculous activities (1280 and 1292) and coincided also with the aforementioned socio-political and architectural changes.

The *Incarnation* of Christ began to play an important part in the self-concept of the city and state of Florence in the thirteenth century.[56] Even in the fifteenth century, it was still customary to announce important political decisions on the *Feast of the Annunciation* and thus to associate them directly with the *Incarnation* of Christ.[57] This was also the case in other cities, among them Ascoli, where the attainment of the city's autonomy was linked with this salvific event, as Carlo Crivelli's painting of the *Annunciation* for *SS. Annunziata* bears splendid witness (Fig. 17).[58] For the formation of the *Civitas*, just like God's becoming man on the occasion of the Annunciation to Mary, was seen as an act of revelation and as the reconstitution of the divine order of salvation after the fall from Paradise. The fundamental concepts of the *Civitas* were order, law and justice, and so Hrabanus Maurus believed that the city had to realize and implement the divine order. This turned the *Civitas* or the city into the previously mentioned reflection of the celestial Jerusalem, into the *spaeculum* of the *Civitas Dei*. Both the incarnation of Christ and the formation of the *Civitas* were therefore situated in a cosmic context of salvation and understood as *summa beatitudo*.[59]

In Florence or in Venice, therefore, the year did not begin on the first day of January, but rather on March 25, the anniversary of the Annunciation to Mary. This day was celebrated as a fertility feast; it stood for the Marian-paradisiac image of everlasting spring.[60] Ever since St. Augustine, this day had been dedicated to the cosmic expectation and fulfillment of salvation and, among other events, also as the day of Christ's death on the cross.[61] This same day, it was believed, had witnessed Adam's creation by

God, Adam and Eve's expulsion from Paradise, the slaying of Abel and the beheading of John the Baptist, patron saint of the city of Florence, to give but a few examples of the events that were traditionally associated with this day of expectation.[62]

But the so-called *Incarnation* of the Florentine *Civitas*, unlike its Venetian counterpart, was not underscored by a legendary city foundation date of March 25, though on the basis of an etymological interpretation of the city's name that was still widely held in the fifteenth century it was nevertheless very closely connected with God's becoming man. In fact, Antoninus of Florence and such popular preachers as Roberto Caracciolo translated the Hebrew word Nazareth with the Latin *flos*, which means flower,[63] or *Florentia*, a notion which was backed by Jacobus de Voragine's *Legenda Aurea* (ca. 1300), a work well known in fifteenth century, which states: "Nazareth is spoken the flower; Saint Bernard writes that the flower wanted to be born of the flower, in the flower, in the time of the flowers."[64] As far as the Archbishop and Roberto Caracciolo were concerned, Nazareth thus became Florence.[65]

Ever since 1250, the Florentine Republic had possessed a church dedicated to the Annunciation to Mary, the SS. Annunziata, which had been founded on the day of the *Incarnation of Christ*.[66] Right from the beginning, this church had formed part of the area of influence of the Guelphs, the papal party.[67] The church became the symbol of Catholic orthodoxy and the monument of the anti-imperial and anti-Ghibelline popular movement that had adopted its constitution in the year of the foundation of the church, when the city had declared its independence from the empire, from Frederick II.[68] The church became the city's central place of cult, understandable since the church was the principal centre of the Florentine custom of life-size and highly realistic votive wax figures.[69] Male members of the upper social classes sought to have themselves preserved for posterity here, often "[...] with *lucchi* or cassocks worn in the cìvilian manner [...]."[70] Florentine burghers were placed on one side of the nave, foreign dignitaries on the other.[71] In 1401, the privilege that permitted Florentine burghers to donate a wax image to SS. Annunziata while still alive was limited to "Uomini di Repubblica" and members of the topmost social layers, in accordance with the ancient *Jus imaginum*:[72] "Non poteva [...] metter Voto alla Nunziata in figura, chi non er' Vomo di Repubblica, abile a' tre maggiori [...]."[73] Florentine women were thus excluded by decree from donating their life-size votive figures, not surprising, considering the juridical and social position of women in Florentine society.[74]

The law just mentioned reflects the appropriation of the Annunziata cult and its Messianic claim to government and power by the elitist, neoaristocratic regime that had come into being during the transition from the fourteenth to the fifteenth century.[75] SS. Annunziata and its wax statues became a masculine image city within the city, and even the elitist centre of the world, since the church, as we saw, accepted also the votive statues of foreign dignitaries.[76]

This votive custom achieved its peak in the fifteenth century and reflects the attempted *Imitatio Christi* or the sacralizing trends of the Florentine nobility.[77] For just like Christ, the Florentine "Eletti", namely the male members of the upper social classes, through their waxen images, a symbol of the Incarnation of Christ,[78] took up residence in the city's Church of the *Annunciation* and thus in Mary or in the Marian "body" of the Florentine city state.

Ever since the thirteenth century, this church, the SS. Annunziata, had also been the site of the adoration of the fresco with the *Annunciation* that had given Florence its holy visage. This fresco was said to have been completed in a miraculous manner in 1252 and to have commenced its own miraculous activities in 1280. According to these legends, in fact, the face of the Mother of God had been painted by an angel or a *spirito celeste.*[79]

This face, and with it also the "city face" of the flower *Florentia*, was therefore due as Francesco Bocchi held in the sixteenth century not to any human artistic gift, but rather to the direct action and intervention of *divino sapere*, divine wisdom.[80] The fresco of the Church of the *Annunciation*, together with the *Madonna* of Or San Michele and the *Madonna* of Impruneta, formed part of the most important Florentine images of Mary.[81] In the fourteenth century and after, it grew into the frequently copied cult image of the city[82] and was associated with miraculous activities that could be activated on behalf of both individuals and the city as a whole.[83] The fresco of the *Annunciation* with its holy face thus became the identification image of the Florentine republic. It therefore assumed an altogether central position in the sacral topography, in the city's political geography. On arrival, foreign visitors were first taken to this image of grace in SS. Annunziata, where, as we have just seen, the Florentine nobility was also assembled in effigy. It was only after their visit to the church that they were received at the seat of government or at the palace of the Medicis.[84]

This cult of the *Annunciation* image became particularly important in the fifteenth century.[85] Following their return from exile in 1434, the Medicis adopted not only the cult of the three *Magi*,[86] but on the accession of Cosimo de' Medici also took possession of the cult of the Annunciation, altogether central for the Florentine *Civitas*. Foreshadowing, as it were, Bocchi's much later saying (1592) to the effect that "[...] tutte le arti sono alla Politica soggette"[87] or that painting and "sacra Politica" had the same goals,[88] the Medicis closely bound the fresco and its church to their family.[89] The claim to the image and the church became expression of their messianically connotated claim to power, their right to rule the republic. For, as the previously mentioned city counsellor would have it: "qui gubernat Respublicam gubernat Deum."[90] The Medicis' appropriation of the fresco sustained their appropriation of the state.

Who Commissioned Pollaiuolo's Picture: Lorenzo de' Medici or Benedetto Salutati?

Against this background we may now attempt a review of the old problem of where Pollaiuolo's picture was originally hung and therefore who actually commissioned the work. Was it to be seen in the Villa Careggi, which at the time the picture is presumed to have been painted, belonged to Lorenzo de' Medici, or in Villa Petraia, which had been acquired by Benedetto Salutati in 1468?

As mentioned at the beginning, researchers have not agreed on this matter. Since at the moment no records that provide certain information about the original destination of the picture and the person who commissioned it, are at our disposal, the answer to both questions remains doubtful, but can at least be hypothetically re-discussed in the light of the historical context set out in this article.

Both the Villa Careggi and the Villa Petraia had chapels at the time the painting was painted. Both of these country houses also offer fine views of the city of Florence and its immediate environment.[91] Let us therefore begin by considering the view. As I already mentioned, it leaves a certain margin of doubt as regards the direction, and does not therefore constitute a sound basis for settling the question of the location of the villa.[92] Moreover, the arguments in favour of the view from either villa are about as broad as those against it are long.[93]

It may therefore be fruitful to consider the personalities of the two presumed erstwhile owners. We know that both of them commissioned work from the Pollaiuolo brothers. In 1469, for example, Salutati commissioned Antonio to produce a decorative helmet for Lorenzo de' Medici's famous *giostra*, while Piero was asked to make him a banner for the same occasion.[94] Both brothers executed paintings and sculptures at the behest of the Medicis as well.[95]

As compared with Lorenzo de' Medici, we have relatively little information about Benedetto Salutati. He was a nephew of the famous Coluccio Salutati and worked as a banker and wool merchant. In 1472 he held the honorary office of a prior and was therefore a member of the Florentine government. Just like Lorenzo de' Medici, he is said to have had a penchant for magnificence on the occasion of festivities and to have assumed a very costly style of life. He had only one child, a daughter named Lisbetta, whom he gave in marriage to Antonio di Filippo Tornabuoni.[96] Salutati's participation in the *giostra* in honour of Lorenzo de' Medici, his priorship and his marriage alliance with the Tornabuoni — the family of Lorenzo de' Medici's mother, lead one to conclude that Salutati was either a member of the Medici party or, at least, a sympathizer and supporter of the governing clan. Against the background of the Florentine Annunziata cult, Pollaiuolo's painting could thus be interpreted as a public profession of his membership of the governing party and as a reference to the Guelph-dominated priorship which held Salutati in 1472.[97] Pollaiuolo's *Annunciation* in "casa di villa" (cf. Fig. 1) would thus be a pendant, an analogon as it were, of the other *Annunciation* "in città" that to this very day graces the Chapel of the Prior (cf. Fig.8) in Palazzo Vecchio in Florence.

But the arguments maintaining Lorenzo de' Medici as the person who commissioned the painting, seem to me to be more convincing. Among these the fact that the Medicis controlled the Annunziata cult in the fifteenth century — a control thas was exercized very actively during Lorenzo's reign,[98] the view of Florence — rather unusual for Florentine *Annunciations*, and the view from above onto the *Civitas* — a dignity motif with sacral connotations since the days of antiquity and thus constituting a claim to dominion over this selfsame *Civitas*, is the most forceful. Read in this way, Pollaiuolo's work would be a Medicean fifteenth-century version of the ruler portrait in front of a view of Florence that became customary in the sixteenth century, of which a fine example is constituted by Vasari's 1534 painting of Duke Alessandro de' Medici (Fig. 18).

According to this interpretation, then, Pollaiuolo's *Annunciation* must have hung in the famous Villa Careggi, associated with certain historical traditions. All the fifteenth-century Medicis were wont to withdraw to this villa. It contained selected works of art and an important library, and the city's most important artists, philologists and philosophers were frequent visitors. Careggi was said to have been the seat of the so-called Platonic Academy and it was here that Cosimo Pater Patriae (1464), Piero the Gouty (1469) and Lorenzo the Magnificent (1492) met their deaths. Following the Medicis' fall from power, the villa was sacked and set on fire by supporters of the republican party.[99]

Lorenzo de' Medici, this "glorious man" and "wise head",[100] became unofficial regent of Florence in 1469. According to Guicciardini, he had established his power as early as 1470[101] and a year later, in 1471, was appointed as *Sindaco* of the city.[102] People expected him to usher in the hoped-for *Golden Age*, the beginning, as it were, of an everlasting spring.[103] And the ruler reflected this hope in his motto "Le Temps revient".[104]

May we therefore interpret Pollaiuolo's painting as the Incarnation metaphor of a paradisiac Golden Age that the rise to power of Lorenzo the

Magnificent seemed to promise, almost to reveal, as the picture's half-open curtain seems to suggest? Whatever the answer, as we now know, the *summa beatitudo* of this Medicean Incarnation was to come to a sudden end, as revealed in Botticelli's so-called *Mystical Crucifixion* of 1497, in which the republican coat of arms appears. The scene is likewise set in front of the gates of Florence (Fig. 19), though here the city is seen from the opposite direction. As Lightbown's interpretation would have it, following the death of Lorenzo de' Medici (1492) and the banishment of his son Piero (1494), the *Bella Donna*, as the city on the Arno was often referred to, became under Savonarola the penitent Magdalene whom we see in Botticelli's painting at the foot of the cross.[105] In Botticelli's painting, indeed, the place of Pollaiuolo's *divina incarnazione in casa di villa* is taken over not only by divine judgement, but also by the promise of new salvation through Christ's death on the cross on March 25 on the republican Golgotha in front of the gates of Florence.

(I am indebted to Herbert Garrett, Rome, for the English version of this article.)

List of Figures and Sources

Fig. 1: Pollaiuolo, *Annunciation*, in Hildebrand/Magnani 1989 (see n. 7 below): no page numbers; Fig. 2: Pollaiuolo, *Annunciation*, detail, in Hildebrand/Magnani 1989 (see n. 7 below): no page numbers; Fig. 3: Pollaiuolo, *Annunciation*, detail, in Brink 1990 (see n. 1 below): plate 4; Fig. 4: Pollaiuolo, *Annunciation*, detail, in Brink 1990 (see n. 1 below): plate 1, excerpt; Fig. 5: Lorenzo di Credi, *Annunciation*, 1480-85, Uffizi, Florence, in Didi-Huberman 1991 (see n. 25 below): plate 59; Fig. 6: Fra Angelico, *Annunciation*, 1430-32, Prado, Madrid, in Didi-Huberman 1991 (see n. 25 below): plate 82; Fig. 7: Filippo Lippi, *Annunciation*, San Lorenzo, Florence, in Gloria Fossi, *Filippo Lippi* (Florence: Scala, 1989): plate 20; Fig. 8: Ridolfo del Ghirlandaio, *Annunciation*, Florence, Palazzo Vecchio, Chapel of the Priors, in *Firenze nella pittura* 1994 (see n. 14 below): plate 99; Fig. 9: Pollaiuolo, *Annunciation*, detail, in Hildebrand/ Magnani 1989 (see n. 7 below): no page numbers; Fig. 10: Lucantonio degli Uberti, *Chain Plan*, Berlin, Kupferstichkabinett, in Brink 1990 (see n. 1 below): plate 6; Fig. 11: Jacopo del Sellaio, *Saint John the Baptist*, Washington, National Gallery of Art, Samuel H. Kress Collection, in *Firenze nella pittura* 1994 (see n. 14 below): plate 56; Fig. 12: Filippino Lippi, *Annunciation*, Museo di Capodimonte, Naples, in *Firenze nella pittura* 1994 (see n. 14 below): plate 60; Fig. 13: *Mary as Ecclesia*, Exultet Roll of Monte Cassino, 11th cent., London, in Gertrud Schiller, *Ikonographie der christlichen Kunst, 4,1. Die Kirche* (Gütersloh: Gerd Mohn, 1976): plate 209; Fig. 14: Filippo Lippi, *Madonna in front of the window*,

Uffizi, Florence, in Gloria Fossi, *Filippo Lippi* (Florence: Scala, 1989): plate 44; Fig. 15: Domenico di Michelino, *Dante and Florence*, Florence, Santa Maria del Fiore, in *Firenze nella pittura* 1994 (see n. 14 below): plate 49; Fig. 16: Fresco of the *Annunciation* in SS. Annunziata, Florence, in Didi-Huberman 1991 (see n. 25 below): plate 46; Fig. 17: Carlo Crivelli, *Annunciation*, National Gallery, London, in Pietro Zampetti, *Carlo Crivelli* (Florence: Nardini, 1986): plate 74; Fig. 18: Giorgio Vasari, *Portrait of Alessandro de' Medici*, Florence, Depositi della Soprintendenza, in *Firenze nella pittura* 1994 (see n. 14 below): plate 70; Fig. 19: Sandro Botticelli, *Mystical Crucifixion*, Cambridge Mass., The Harvard Art Museums, Fogg Art Museum, in Lightbown 1989 (see n. 105 below): plate 100.

Fig. 1: Pollaiuolo, *Annunciation*, in Hildebrand/Magnani 1989 (see n. 7 below): no page numbers.

Fig. 2: Pollaiuolo, *Annunciation*, detail, in Hildebrand/Magnani 1989 (see n. 7 below): no page numbers.

Fig. 3: Pollaiuolo, *Annunciation*, detail, in Brink 1990 (see n. 1 below): plate 4.

Fig. 4: Pollaiuolo, *Annunciation*, detail, in Brink 1990 (see n. 1 below): plate 1, excerpt.

Fig. 5: Lorenzo di Credi, *Annunciation*, 1480-85, Uffizi, Florence, in Didi-Huberman 1991 (see n. 25 below): plate 59.

Fig. 6: Fra Angelico, *Annunciation*, 1430-32, Prado, Madrid, in Didi-Huberman 1991 (see n. 25 below): plate 82.

Fig. 7: Filippo Lippi, *Annunciation*, San Lorenzo, Florence, in Gloria Fossi, *Filippo Lippi* (Florence: Scala, 1989): plate 20.

Fig. 8: Ridolfo del Ghirlandaio, *Annunciation*, Florence, Palazzo Vecchio, in *Firenze nella pittura* 1994 (see n. 14 below): plate 99.

Fig. 9: Pollaiuolo, *Annunciation*, detail, in Hildebrand/ Magnani 1989 (see n. 7 below): no page numbers.

Fig. 10: Lucantonio degli Uberti, *Chain Plan*, Berlin, Kupferstichkabinett, in Brink 1990 (see n. 1 below): plate 6.

Fig. 11: Jacopo del Sellaio, *Saint John the Baptist*, Samuel H. Kress Collection, in *Firenze nella pittura* 1994 (see n. 14 below): plate 56.

Fig. 12: Filippino Lippi, Annunciation, Museo di Capodimonte, Naples, in *Firenze nella pittura* 1994 (see n. 14 below): plate 60.

Fig. 13: *Mary as Ecclesia*, Exultet Roll of Monte Cassino, 11th century

Fig. 14: Filippo Lippi, *Madonna in front of the window*, *Uffizi*, Florence, in Gloria Fossi, *Filippo Lippi* (Florence: Scala, 1989): plate 44.

Fig. 15: Domenico di Michelino, *Dante and Florence*, Florence, *Santa Maria del Fiore*, in *Firenze nella pittura* 1994 (see n. 14 below): plate 49.

Fig. 16: Fresco of the *Annunciation* in *SS. Annunziata*, Florence, in Didi-Huberman 1991 (see n. 25 below): plate 46.

Fig. 17: Carlo Crivelli, *Annunciation*, National Gallery, London, in Pietro Zampetti, *Carlo Crivelli* (Florence: Nardini, 1986): plate 74.

Fig. 18: Giorgio Vasari, *Portrait of Alessandro de' Medici*, Florence (see n. 14 below).

Fig. 19: Sandro Botticelli, *Mystical Crucifixion* (see n. 105 below): plate 100.

Notes

[1] Pollaiuolo research has so far paid little attention to this picture. A detailed description has as yet been given only by Sonja Brink, "Die Berliner *Verkündigung* und der *David* von Pollaiuolo", in *Jahrbuch der Berliner Museen* 32 (1990), 153-171. On the dating, style and state of research of the *Annunciation*, cf. Maud Cruttwell, *Antonio Pollaiuolo* (London: Duckworth and Co., 1907), 97-99; Leopold D. Ettlinger, *Antonio and Piero Pollaiuolo. Complete Edition with a Critical Catalogue* (Oxford: Phaidon, 1978), 30, 138; Eric Marshall Frank, "Pollaiuolo Studies" (Diss. University of New York, 1988, Ann Arbor, 1989), 37; Nicoletta Pons, *I Pollaiolo* (Florence: Cantini, 1994), 17, 98-99. The painting arrived at the Berliner Museum in 1821 as part of the collection of an English merchant. It is painted on a poplar board, preserved in a good original condition and measures 152.5cm x 176.9cm. It is neither signed nor dated. Originally thought to have been painted by Alesso Baldovinetti, it has been considered as a work of either the Pollaiuolo brothers, Antonio (ca. 1430-1498) and Piero (1443-96), or of the latter only since the end of the 19th century. Since Cruttwell (1907), research has justified the attribution to the Pollaiuolo brothers or to Piero alone, and the dating circa 1470 by the stylistic affinities between the Mary of this *Annunciation* and Piero del Pollaiuolo's *Virtues* of the *Arte della Mercanzia* (1469).

[2] As read from the buildings represented in it, the orientation of the view in the left-hand background of Pollaiuolo's picture cannot be determined beyond doubt. It seems to reproduce the city as seen either from the north or the north-west, and in the following analysis of the picture I have assumed this to be the case. Consequently, the location of the villa in which the picture must originally have hung cannot be exactly determined. Brink, for example, has gone on record in favour of a view of the city from the north (Brink 1990 [see n. 1 above], 162), while Pons prefers a view from the north-west (Pons 1994 [see n. 1 above]).

[3] Cruttwell was the first to suggest Villa *Careggi* (Cruttwell 1907 [see n. 1 above], 97), while Villa *Petraia* was recently proposed by Brink (Brink 1990 [see n. 1 above], 161-163). Both these were recently called into question by Pons, though without any supporting arguments (Pons 1994 [see n. 1 above], 17). On the location of the villa and the question of who commissioned the painting, see further on.

[4] Concerning the dating and the importance of the event in the history of salvation, cf. *Die Legenda aurea des Jacobus de Voragine.*, ed. and trans. by Richard Benz (Heidelberg: Lambert Schneider, 1984[10]), 255, 490.

[5] On the description about to be given, cf. Brink 1990 (see n. 1 above).

[6] Leon Battista Alberti, *Zehn Bücher über die Baukunst*, ed. and trans. by Max Theuer (Darmstadt: Wissenschaftliche Buchgesellschaft, 1991), Book V, chap. 17: 272.

[7] On the non-uniform perspective of the painting, the combination of upward and downward view and the different horizon lines, cf. Josephine Hildebrand and Sabina Magnani, *Die Darstellung des Raumes in der Renaissance. Überlegungen und Untersuchungen zur Perspektive ausgehend von dem Gemälde "Die Verkündigung" von Pollaiuolo* (Berlin: Staatliche Museen Preussischer Kulturbesitz, 1989), 19-20. The high landscape horizon is characteristic of the works of the Pollaiuolo brothers (Ettlinger 1978 [see n. 1 above], 50).

[8] But Brink points out, very rightly, that Mary turns her body towards the beholder (Brink 1990 [see n. 1 above], 156).

[9] Brink 1990 (see n. 1 above), 158. On the metaphor of the bridal chamber in relation to the *Annunciation*, cf. Maria Elisabeth Gössmann, *Die Verkündigung an Maria im dogmatischen Verständnis des Mittelalters* (Munich: Hueber, 1957), 56.

[10] The dove of the Holy Spirit is already missing in most of the illustrations of the Annunciation in Dante's *Divine Comedy*. Cf. Peter Brieger, Millard Meiss and Charles S. Singleton, *Illuminated Manuscripts of the Divine Comedy*, vol. 2 (Princeton N.J.: Princeton University Press, 1969), 356, pl. a; 359, pl. a; 360, pl. a; 361, pl. a. I am indebted to Ulrich Pfisterer, Rome, for having drawn my attention to this aspect of the *Divine Comedy*.

[11] This is also demonstrated by the aforementioned *Annunciations* in Dante's *Divine Comedy*. The dove is generally missing in representations that, like the cases mentioned in note 10, served as examples of modesty.

[12] A further fifteenth-century *Annunciation* with a view of Florence in the background has been preserved in Filippino Lippi's work, now in the Capodimonte Museum in Naples, where it is seen between John the Baptist and Saint Andrew (Fig. 12). But this picture, which must have come into being in the late seventies or early eighties, is not narrative and is conceived as a representative image. On this picture, see further on; regarding its dating, more particularly, cf. Luciano Berti and Umberto Baldini, *Filippino Lippi* (Florence: Il Fiorino, 1991), 182.

[13] Brink 1990 (see n. 1 above), 161, 162. As this author is not the only one to stress, we are concerned here with one of the earliest views of Florence to be found anywhere. It was painted more than ten years before the famous *Chain Plan* (Fig. 10) of circa 1482. On the *Chain Plan*, cf. Giovanni Fanelli, "Topografia e forma urbana nelle vedute di Firenze," in *Firenze e la sua immagine. Cinque secoli di vedutismo*, ed. by Marco Chiarini and Alessandro Marabottini (Venice: Marsilio, 1994), 13-17, 13 as well as 69, Cat. No. 7.

[14] Concerning the individual buildings in the context of views of Florence, cf. Silvia Blasio, "La rappresentazione simbolica: i monumenti illustri nella pittura e nelle

scenografie teatrali," in *Firenze nella pittura e nel disegno dal Trecento al Settecento*, ed., Mina Gregori and Silvia Blasio (Florence: Silvana, 1994), 9-50.

[15] As explained by Hans Blumenberg in his analysis of Petrarch's ascent of Mont Ventoux, this was reserved for God until the late Middle Ages: Hans Blumenberg, *Die Legitimität der Neuzeit* (Frankfurt: Suhrkamp, 1966), 336-338.

[16] Cf. Martial about the villa of a cousin: "totam licet aestimare Romam" cited from Paul Holberton, *Palladio's Villas. Life in the Renaissance Countryside* (London: Murray, 1990), 114.

[17] Samuel Y. Edgerton, Jr., "Mensurare temporalia facit Geometria spiritualis: Some Fifteenth-Century Italian Notions about When and Where the Annunciation Happened," in *Studies in Late Medieval and Renaissance Painting in Honor of Millard Meiss*, vol. 1 (New York: New York University Press, 1977), 115-130, with a detailed specification of the passages in Antoninus of Florence. The exegesis and interpretation of the *Annunciation* always stated either sunrise and morning (Antoninus of Florence) or mid-day (Roberto Caracciolo) as the time of the *Incarnation* of Christ. On the exegesis of the Florentine Archbishop, cf. Edgerton 1977 (see above); for that of Roberto Caracciolo, cf. Michael Baxandall, *Die Wirklichkeit der Bilder. Malerei und Erfahrung im Italien des 15. Jahrhunderts* (Frankfurt: Suhrkamp, 1988[2]), 69.

[18] Only Brink (Brink 1990 [see n. 1 above], 159-161) goes into the details of the view of Florence, which forms the starting point of a discussion of who could have commissioned the picture (Ibid.: 161-163). The author's argumentation does not affect my own. On views of Florence in general, see Giuseppe Boffito and Attilio Mori, *Piante e Vedute di Firenze. Studio storico topografico cartografico* (Florence: Giuntina, 1926); *Firenze e la sua immagine* 1994 (see n. 13 above); *Firenze nella pittura* 1994 (see n. 14 above). For the views due to Pollaiuolo, cf. Marco Chiarini, "Firenze e la sua immagine," in *Firenze e la sua immagine* 1994 (see n. 13 above), 3-11, 3; Silvia Blasio, "Il Mito di Firenze nelle vedute d' insieme. La città ideale dei Cristiani e degli Umanisti, l'immagine del potere mediceo," in *Firenze nella pittura* 1994 (see n. 14 above), 51-84, 58. The author describes the view of Florence summarily as a symbolic image of the celestial city.

[19] Concerning the perspective construction, cf. Hildebrand/Magnani 1989 (see n. 7 above). A fifteenth-century *Annunciation* with a similar construction, i.e. a vanishing point in the left-hand part of the picture, is constituted by Carlo Crivelli's painting for the Church of *SS. Annunziata* in Ascoli (cf. Fig. 17).

[20] On the significance of the cardinal points, the south as the cardinal point of grace and mercy and the east as the one of Paradise, cf. Edgerton 1977 (see n. 17 above), 120, 121, 122.

[21] On the concept of the vanishing point as starting point in connection with Masaccio's *Trinity* in Florence, cf. Alexander Perrig, "Masaccios *Trinità* und der Sinn der Zentralperspektive," in *Marburger Jahrbuch für Kunstwissenschaft* 21 (1986), 11-43.

[22] Edgerton 1977 (see n. 17 above).

[23] On the interpretation of the name of Gabriel as *fortitudo Dei* by Jeremy, cf. Gössmann 1957 (see n. 9 above), 12. About the Archangel as annunciator of the divine power of creation, see also Jutta Ströter-Bender, *Die Mutter Gottes. Das Marienbild in der christlichen Kunst. Symbolik und Spiritualität* (Cologne: DuMont, 1992), 69.

[24] On Lippi's representative-image *Annunciation*, see n. 12 above.

[25] About the lily as a symbol of Christ, cf. Georges Didi-Huberman, *Beato Angelico. Figure del dissimile* (Milan: Leonardo, 1991), 173.

[26] About Mary as the type of the *Ecclesia*, cf. Wolfgang Beinert, "Die mariologischen Dogmen und ihre Entfaltung, 4.2. Maria als Typus der Kirche," in *Handbuch der Marienkunde*, ed. by Wolfgang Beinert and Heinrich Petri (Ratisbon: Pustet, 1984), 297-301.

[27] Wolfgang Braunfels, *Die Verkündigung* (Düsseldorf: Schwann, 1949), XVII.

[28] On the analogy between Mary and door or window in general or in Antoninus of Florence in particular, cf. Edgerton 1977 (see n. 17 above), 121; Anselm Salzer, *Die Sinnbilder und Beiworte Mariens in der deutschen Literatur und lateinischen Hymnenpoesie des Mittelalters. Mit Berücksichtigung der patristischen Literatur. Eine literar-historische Studie* (Darmstadt: Wissenschaftliche Buchgesellschaft, 1967), 525-526.

[29] According to Augustine, cf. Salzer 1967 (see n. 28 above), 526.

[30] About the sanctification of the Mother of God and the concept of *Maria locus*, cf. Gössmann 1957 (see n. 9 above), 52, 244 et passim; Georges Didi-Huberman, "Le lieu virtuel: l' Annonciation au-delà de son espace," in *Symboles de la Renaissance*, vol. 3, *Arts et langage* (Paris: Presses de l' Ecole Normale Supérieure, 1990), 65-93, 80-86; Didi-Huberman 1991 (see n. 25 above), 195 et passim.

[31] On these interpretations of the Mother of God, cf. Gössmann 1957 (see n. 9 above), 89, 179; Braunfels 1949 (see n. 27 above), XVII; Didi-Huberman 1991 (see n. 25 above), 171.

[32] On the symbolics of the peacock, cf. *Lexikon christlicher Kunst. Themen, Gestalten, Symbole*, ed. by Jutta Seibert (Freiburg Basel Vienna: Herder, 1982), 252.

[33] About this interpretation of Mary in the composition of hymns and sequences and in Antoninus of Florence, cf. Edgerton 1977 (see n. 17 above), 120, note 20; Gössmann 1957 (see n. 9 above), 110, 123.

[34] Hermann Bauer, *Kunst und Utopie. Studien über das Kunst und Staatsdenken in der Renaissance* (Berlin: de Gruyter, 1965), 5; Wolfgang Braunfels, *Mittelalterliche Stadtbaukunst in der Toskana* (Berlin: Gebrüder Mann, 1979), 22-23. About the concept of the city as a pool of evil and sin (Petrarch, Boccaccio), on the other hand, cf. Bernhard Rupprecht, "Villa. Zur Geschichte eines Ideals," in *Probleme der Kunstwissenschaft. Second volume. Wandlungen des Paradiesis-*

chen und Utopischen. Studien zum Bild eines Ideals (Berlin: de Gruyter, 1966), 210-250, 211-217.

[35] Concerning this picture, cf. *Firenze e la sua immagine* 1994 (see n. 13 above), 64, 66, Cat. No. 4.

[36] On this interpretation of Mary, cf. Salzer 1967 (see n. 28 above), 37. — According to Adam of St. Viktor, whose writings were received in fifteenth-century Florence, the Mother of God is "[...] Mens, castellum, aula, templum, Thalamus et civitas." (Adam of St. Victor, cited from Gössmann 1957 [see n. 9 above], 110) The reception of Adam of St. Viktor is demonstrated by Fra Angelico's great fresco of the *Annunciation* in the cloister of *San Marco* in Florence, which as its main title bears a sequence from his writings. Cf. Gössmann 1957 (see n. 9 above), 273.

[37] Leon Battista Alberti, "I Libri della Famiglia," in Leon Battista Alberti, *Opere volgari*, ed. by Cecil Grayson, vol. 1 (Bari: Laterza, 1960), 3-341.

[38] Cf. Leon Battista Alberti, *L' Architettura*, ed. and trans. by Giovanni Orlandi and Paolo Portoghesi (Milan: Il Polifilo, 1989), Book I, chap. 9: 36; Book V, chap. 2: 179; Book V, chap. 14: 210. Alberti equates the city house or palace with the country villa (Ibid., Book V, chap. 17). Concerning this concept of central importance for Alberti's architecture, cf. Hanno-Walter Kruft, *Geschichte der Architekturtheorie. Von der Antike bis zur Gegenwart* (Munich: Beck, 1991), 48.

[39] Regarding the villa as an enlargement of the sacral body of the state or city in sixteenth-century Venice, cf. Kornelia Imesch Oehry, "Serenissima und *Villa*. Skizze zu einer Rhetorik der architektonischen Form in Palladios venezianischen Villen der Terraferma," in *Georges-Bloch-Jahrbuch des Kunstgeschichtlichen Seminars der Universität Zürich* 2 (1995), 75-85.

[40] I am indebted to Prof. Liana De Girolami Cheney, University of Massachusetts Lowell, for drawing my attention to this feature.

[41] About Mary as the type of the *Ecclesia* and therefore also as the type of the *Ark*, cf. Beinert 1984 (see n. 26 above).

[42] Bocchi calls him "protettore, et avvocato de' Fiorentini." Francesco Bocchi, *Le Bellezze della citta di Fiorenza [...]* (Florence, 1591), 11.

[43] As Peyer states, at the end of the Middle Ages, about 1300, John the Baptist had lost his prominent role as Patron Saint of Florence. Cf. Hans Konrad Peyer, *Stadt und Stadtpatron im mittelalterlichen Italien* (Zürich: Europa, 1955), 51, 55.

[44] On this interpretation of Mary in Dante, cf. Gössmann 1957 (see n. 9 above), 261.

[45] On the circumstance that the city's most important images were pictures of Mary, cf. Richard C. Trexler, "L' esperienza religiosa fiorentina: l' immagine sacra," in David Herlihy und Richard C. Trexler, *L' Impruneta, una pieve, un santuario un comune rurale* (Florence, 1988), 47-81, 51.

[46] The miraculous activities of the fresco of the *Annunciation* in *SS. Annunziata* commenced in 1280 (Marcello Fantoni, "Il culto dell' Annunziata e la sacralità del potere mediceo," in *Archivio storico italiano* 147 [1989], 771-793, 772), those of the *Madonna* of *Or San Michele* in 1292. The cult of the *Madonna* of Impruneta can be traced from the middle of the fourteenth century to the end of the sixteenth. Impruneta's *Madonna* was one of those images that unfolded their miracles elsewhere rather than in situ, and that was why it was taken to Florence (Trexler 1988 [see n. 45], 51).

[47] On the creation of the priorship, cf. Giovanni Villani, *Istorie fiorentine fino all' anno 1348*. Vol. 3, book 7, chap. LXXVIII (Milan: Società Tipografica de' Classici Italiani, 1802), 142-143. On the institution and nature of the *ordinamenti di giustizia*, cf. Karl Mittermaier, *Die Politik der Renaissance in Italien* (Darmstadt: Wissenschaftliche Buchgesellschaft, 1995), 106-113.

[48] Nicolai Rubinstein, "Vasari' s Painting of The Foundation of Florence in the Palazzo Vecchio," in *Essays in the History of Architecture presented to Rudolf Wittkower*, vol. 1 (London: Phaidon, 1967), 64-73, 66.

[49] On this interpretation of the cathedral, cf. Peyer 1955 (see n. 43 above); Thomas Szabo, "Die Visualisierung städtischer Ordnung in den Kommunen Italiens," in *Anzeiger des Germanischen Nationalmuseums und Berichte aus dem Forschungsinstitut für Realienkunde* (1993), 55-68. For the importance of the cathedral in relation to the Italian city, cf. also Braunfels 1979 (see n. 34 above), 145-147, 245-246.

[50] Cited from Eugenio Casalini, "La Santissima Annunziata nella storia e nella civiltà fiorentina," in *Tesori d' arte dell' Annunziata di Firenze* (Florence: Alinari, 1987), 75-95, 78.

[51] *Guida di Firenze e d' altre città principali della Toscana*, ed. Gaspero Ricci, vol. 1 (Florence: Ricci, 1820), 16.

[52] About the concept of Florence as similar to and successor of Rome, which can be found in Dante, Villani and other Florentine historiographers, cf. Nicolai Rubinstein, "The Beginnings of Political Thought in Florence," in *Journal of the Warburg and Courtauld Institutes* 5 (1942), 198-227; Braunfels 1979 (see n. 34 above), 131-134; David Friedman, *Florentine New Towns. Urban Design in the Late Middle Ages* (Cambridge, Mass. and London: MIT, 1988), 200. The Florentine claim as a second Rome was underscored also by Roman indulgences granted between the fourteenth and the sixteenth centuries. On these indulgences, cf. Richard C. Trexler, *Public Life in Renaissance Florence* (New York and London: Academic Press, 1980), 6.

[53] See, for example, Sacchetti on Christ: "fu il piu' bello e 'l meglio proporzionato corpo, che mai fosse, e non ebbe gli occhi travolti nè spaventati." (Sacchetti, cited from Andrew Ladis, "The Legend of Giotto' s Wit and the Arena Chapel", in *Art Bulletin* 68 (1986), 581-596, 582, note 4. Cataneo, a sixteenth-century

architecture theoretician, expressed himself in similar terms. Cf. Kruft 1991 (see n. 38 above), 88.

[54] Peyer 1955 (see n. 43 above), 55-57; Volker Reinhardt, *Florenz zur Zeit der Renaissance. Die Kunst der Macht und die Botschaft der Bilder* (Freiburg and Würzburg: Ploetz, 1990), 233, 235.

[55] Cited from Trexler, though in connection with a different argument. Trexler 1980 (see n. 52 above), 45: "Deus est Respublica, et qui gubernat Rempublicam gubernat Deum. Item Deus est iustitia, et qui facit iustitiam, facit Deum."

[56] Cf. note 43 above.

[57] On important events, decisions and privileges that were announced or taken in Florence on the Feast of the Annunciation, cf. Luca Landucci, *Ein florentinisches Tagebuch 1450-1516. Nebst einer anonymen Fortsetzung 1516-1542*, ed. and trans. by Marie Herzfeld (new edition Düsseldorf and Cologne: Diederichs, 1978), 30, 52, 63.

[58] Just like Pollaiuolo's *Annunciation*, the painting by Crivelli, which dates to 1486 and is today kept in London's National Gallery, has a vanishing point in the left-hand part of the picture. The work owes its existence to an important political event. Pope Sixtus IV had granted administrative independence to the city of Ascoli in 1482, an event to which the picture refers with the diction "libertas ecclesiastica". The grant was announced to the people on March 25 and this day has been celebrated ever since in Ascoli as the anniversary of the city's autonomy and as the Feast of the *Annunciation to Mary*. On Crivelli's painting, cf. Anna Bovero, *L' opera completa del Crivelli* (Classici dell' Arte, 80) (Milan: Rizzoli, 1975), 96.

[59] On the concept of the *civitas*, cf. Wolfgang Braunfels, "Italienische Stadtbaukunst im Mittelalter und der Begriff der Civitas", in *Beiträge zur Kunst des Mittelalters. Vorträge der Ersten Deutschen Kunsthistorikertagung auf Schloss Brühl 1948* (Berlin: Gebr. Mann, 1950), 39-45, 40, 43; Wolfgang Braunfels 1979 (see n. 34 above), 18-20. On the significance and interpretation of the *Incarnation* of Christ, cf. *Legenda Aurea* 1984 (see n. 4 above), 249. For the understanding of the Annunciation as *summa beatitudo*, cf. Gössmann 1957 (see n. 9 above), 152.

[60] On the commencement of the Florentine year on March 25, cf. Rubinstein 1967 (see n. 48 above), 71; Volker Breidecker, *Florenz, oder "Die Rede, die zum Auge spricht". Kunst, Fest und Macht im Ambiente der Stadt* (Munich: Fink, 1992[2]), 204. About March 25 as a feast of fertility, cf. Louis Réau, *Iconographie de l' art chrétien*, vol. II/2 (Paris: Presses universitaires de France, 1957), 175. On the interrelations between Mary, Paradise, Garden and the idea of everlasting spring, cf. Didi-Huberman 1990 (see n. 30 above), 68; Didi-Huberman 1991 (see n. 25 above), 171.

[61] Gössmann 1957 (see n. 9 above), 25.

[62] Thus the *Legenda Aurea*, which also lists the following as having taken place on March 25: Melchisedek's sacrifice, Peter's release from his chains, God's granting grace to the good thief on the cross, Abel's death, Abraham's sacrifice of Isaac, the fall from Paradise, etc. Cf. *Legenda Aurea* 1984 (see n. 4 above), 255.

[63] On the interpretation of Nazareth as *flos*, which Antoninus of Florence took from the so-called *Mariale*, cf. Gössmann 1957 (see n. 9 above), 225; Didi-Huberman 1991 (see n. 25 above), 122, 170. It is well known that in the days of Antoninus the *Mariale* was attributed to Albertus Magnus. The library of *San Marco* in Florence, of which Antoninus was prior, contained a copy of the *Mariale* (Didi-Huberman 1991 [see n. 25 above], 250-251, note 34).

[64] *Legenda Aurea* 1984 (see n. 4 above), 250.

[65] On this interpretation in Antoninus of Florence, cf. Edgerton 1977 (see n. 17 above), 129, note 48; Didi-Huberman 1991 (see n. 25 above), 254, note 141. For the corresponding interpretation of Roberto Caracciolo, an observant Franciscan, cf. Baxandall 1988 (see n. 17 above), 69. Another tradition, formulated by Giovanni Villani in the fourteenth century, traced the name of the city of Florence back to Florianus. Villani held in 1300 that the name of the city was derived from "Floria", since Florianus, a flourishing knight and warrior, had died in Florence and thus became the founder of the city, which had always been surrounded by flowers and lilies in full bloom. Cf. Giovanni Villani: "Wie die Stadt Florenz errichtet wurde (1300), " in *Florenz. Lesarten einer Stadt*, ed. by Andreas Beyer (Frankfurt: Insel, 1983), 15-17, 17.

[66] Various Florentine *Annunciations* of the late fifteenth and the sixteenth century reproduce the square and the church of *SS. Annunziata* as the site of the sacred event. They include, over and above the previously mentioned freso by Ridolfo Ghirlandaio (cf. Fig. 8), the *Annunciations* by Monte di Giovanni, Santi di Tito and Jacopo da Empoli. On these paintings in the context of a different argumentation, cf. Silvia Blasio, "L' innovazione realistica: dai disegni 'dal naturale' alle vedute fiorentine di Gaspar Van Wittel," in: *Firenze nella pittura* 1994 (see n. 14 above), 85-154, 86, 91.

[67] On the Servite convent as a bulwark of the Guelphs, cf. Zygmunt Wazbinski, "L' Annunciazione della Vergine nella chiesa della SS. Annunziata a Firenze: Un contributo al moderno culto dei quadri," in *Renaissance Studies in Honor of Craig Hugh Smyth*, vol. 2 (Florence: Giunti Barbèra, 1985), 533-549, 538. On the conflict between Guelphs and Ghibellines, cf. the summary given in Mittermaier 1995 (see n. 47 above), 76-81.

[68] Casalini 1987 (see n. 50 above), 76, 77.

[69] On the votive figures of the Church of the Annunciation, cf. Susann Waldmann, Die lebensgrosse Wachsfigur. Eine Studie zur Funktion und Bedeutung der keroplastischen Porträtfigur vom Spätmittelalter bis zum 18. Jahrhundert (Munich: tuduv, 1990), 20-43.

[70] Ferdinano Leopoldo Del Migliore, *Firenze città nobilissima*, Florence 1684 (Repr. Bologna: Forni, 1968), 286. The waxen figure of Lorenzo de' Medici donated to the church after the Pazzi plot, for example, was dressed in this manner. In this connection, see Giorgio Vasari, "Vita del Verrocchio," in *Le Vite de' piu' eccellenti pittori scultori ed architettori, con nuove annotazioni e commenti di Gaetano Milanesi*, vol. 3 (Florence: Sansoni, 1878), 374.

[71] Del Migliore 1684 (see n. 70 above), 286-287.

[72] On the resolution of the council, cf. Aby Warburg, "Bildniskunst und florentinisches Bürgertum," in Aby M. Warburg, *Ausgewählte Schriften und Würdigungen*, ed. by Dieter Wuttke (Baden-Baden: Koerner, 1979), Appendix, 89. For the *Jus imaginum*, cf. Julius von Schlosser, *Tote Blicke. Geschichte der Porträtbildnerei in Wachs. Ein Versuch*, ed. by Thomas Medicus (Berlin: Acta humaniora, 1993), 19.

[73] Del Migliore 1684 (see n. 70 above), 285.

[74] This exclusion did not apply to non-Florentine women. On the votive figures of foreigners, see also note 76. Florentine women, among them the two "First Ladies", Contessina de' Bardi Medici and Lucrezia Tornabuoni Medici, nevertheless donated smaller *ex voti* made of silver. In this connection, see *Tesori d' arte dell' Annunziata* 1987 (see n. 48 above), 97. On the donation of Lucrezia Tornabuoni for the altar of the *Annunciation*, cf. Francesco Bocchi, *Opera sopra L' Imagine miracolosa della Santissima Nunziata di Fiorenza; Dove si narra, come di quella è grande la maestà* (Florence, 1592), 31.

[75] On the formation of the elitist, neoaristocratic regime in Florence, whose history Macchiavelli was later to turn into world history, cf. Trexler 1980 (see n. 52 above), XIX; Sharon T. Strocchia, *Death and Ritual in Renaissance Florence* (Baltimore and London: The Johns Hopkins University Press, 1992), 105. On the notion and trend of oligarchy in the Italian city states of the Renaissance, cf. Lauro Martines, *Power and Imagination. City-States in Renaissance Italy* (New York: Vintage Books, 1980), 130-161.

[76] For the waxen figures of foreign dignitaries, cf. Del Migliore 1684 (see n. 70 above), 286-287.

[77] On the sacralization trend in the Florentine city-state in a different context of argumentation, cf. Marvin B. Becker, *Florence in Transition*, vol. 1: *The Decline of the Commune* (Baltimore: Johns Hopkins Press, 1967); vol. 2: *Studies in the Rise of the Territorial State* (Baltimore: Johns Hopkins Press, 1968). The above mentioned sacralization trend of the fifteenth-century Florentine patriciate, particularly marked among the entourage of the Medici, can also be understood by virtue of the custom of reproducing events of the history of salvation in familiar environments and with contemporary burghers either as protagonists of the events or as simple bystanders, as is the case, for example, in Ghirlandaio's fresco cycles of the Sassetti and Tornabuoni chapel in SS. Trinità and in Santa Maria Novella in Florence. What is expressed here is not just the presentation of the history of

salvation or even its profanation, but the sacralization of the Medicean-stamp civic culture of Florence's grande bourgeoisie. Girolamo Savonarola (1452-1498) probably had picture cycles of this type in mind when, in his sermons of the nineties of the fifteenth century, he severely criticized the custom of locating the events of the history of salvation in Florentine environments and reproducing the likenesses of prominent citizens in them, deeming this custom to be blasphemous.

[78] Regarding wax as symbol of the Incarnation of Christ, cf. Waldmann 1990 (see n. 69 above), 11.

[79] Casalini 1987 (see n. 50 above), 78.

[80] Bocchi 1591 (see n. 42 above), 217-218. As Bocchi put it in his tractate of 1592 the face of the Mother of God was "[...] non da terrena mano, ma da divino sapere miracolosamente con maestà ineffabile effigiato" (Bocchi 1592 [see n. 74 above], 10). He expressed himself in the same sense in *ibid*: 19, 25-26 et passim. On the origin of the fresco, cf. Wazbinski 1985 (see n. 67 above), 534; Fantoni 1989 (see n. 46 above), 772.

[81] Trexler 1988 (see n. 45), 51.

[82] In this connection cf. Fantoni 1989 (see n. 46 above); Wazbinski 1985 (see n. 67 above). Since the second half of the fourteenth century copies could be found not only in churches in Florence, among them Ognissanti and San Marco, but also outside the city, Prato being a case in point (Wazbinski 1985 [see n. 67 above], 535; Casalini 1987 [see n. 50 above], 79).

[83] On the miraculous activities of the *Annunziata*, cf. Del Migliore 1684 (see n. 70 above), 288. Even foreigners relied on the miraculous force of this fresco. Landucci, for example, reports that the Swiss confederates, before the battle against Charles the Bold, recommended themselves to the protection of the Florentine *Annunziata* by entering battle under an Annunciation banner. In token of gratitude for their victory, they later donated the banner to the Florentine church. Cf. Landucci 1978 (see n. 57 above), 29.

[84] More in Trexler 1980 (see n. 52 above), 9. On the state references cited against SS. Annunziata, cf. Del Migliore 1684 (see n. 70 above), 292.

[85] Trexler 1980 (see n. 52 above), 7. Under the Medici dukes it was developed into a dynastic or state cult. Cf. Fantoni 1989 (see n. 46 above), 774-793; Wazbinski 1985 (see n. 67 above), 536.

[86] On the cult of the *Magi* in Florence and its appropriation by the Medici, cf. Rab Hatfield, "The Compagnia de' Magi," in *Journal of the Warburg and Courtauld Institutes* 33 (1970), 107-161. On the cultural politics of the Medici and the political situation, cf. Alison Brown, *The Medici in Florence. The Exercise and Language of Power* (Florence: Leo S. Olschki and Perth or University of Australia Press, 1992); Paula C. Clarke, *The Soderini and the Medici. Power and Patronage in Fifteenth-Century Florence* (Oxford: Clarendon Press, 1991).

[87] Bocchi 1592 (see n. 74 above), 1. Bocchi also derives the control of the images in public and private life by the potentate from this subordination of the "arti" to "politica" (Ibid.: 1-2).

[88] Bocchi 1592 (see n. 74 above), 55, 61.

[89] This claim was also underscored in architecture. Cosimo de' Medici commissioned Michelozzo to undertake a comprehensive restructuring of the church and monastery of the Servites in 1444, and some years later his son Piero donated a precious marble tabernacle for the miraculous fresco. On Piero's gift, cf. Bocchi 1592 (see n. 74 above), 30; Wolfgang Liebenwein, "Die 'Privatisierung' des Wunders. Piero de' Medici in SS. Annunziata und San Miniato," in *Piero de' Medici "il Gottoso" (1416-1469). Kunst im Dienste der Mediceer*, ed. by Andreas Beyer and Bruce Boucher (Berlin, 1993), 251-290. The reconstruction of the church was an integrated component of the urban restructuring of the northern part of the city by Cosimo de' Medici. In this connection, see Kunibert Bering, *Baupropaganda und Bildprogrammatik der Frührenaissance in Florenz—Rom—Pienza* (Frankfurt: Peter Lang, 1984), 11-42.

[90] Cf. note 55 above.

[91] On Villa Careggi, cf. the review of the state of research in Carlo Cresti and Massimo Listri, *Civiltà delle ville toscane* (Udine, 1992), 100; Margherita Azzi Visentini, *La villa in Italia. Quattrocento e Cinquecento* (Milan: Electa, 1995), 49-53. The view of Florence from this villa is today hindered by the growth of trees behind the building, partly very tall and dense, and by modern construction on the intervening land. On Villa Petraia, which passed into the hands of the Medicis in the sixteenth century, cf. Cresti/Listri, ibid., 1992: 196.

[92] See note 2 above.

[93] Brink mentions quite rightly that what speaks in favour of Villa Petraia is its somewhat higher situation and the better view it commands of Florence with the surrounding plain and Prato (Brink 1990 [see n. 1 above], 162); but she does not take into account the fact that from Villa Petraia one can see a large part of the cathedral's facade, which does not seem to agree with Pollaiuolo's view. This aspect therefore speaks in favour of Villa Careggi, which in the fifteenth century most probably already had a loggia extension of the type shown at the back of Pollaiuolo's painting.

[94] Brink 1990 (see n. 1 above), 162; Pons 1994 (see n. 1 above), 12.

[95] Cf. Ettlinger 1978 (see n. 1 above); Pons 1994 (see n. 1 above); F. W. Kent and Patricia Simons, "Renaissance Patronage: An Introductory Essay," in *Patronage, Art, and Society in Renaissance Italy*, ed. by F. W. Kent and Patricia Simons (Oxford, 1987), 1-21, 20.

[96] Giacomo De Nicola, "Opere perdute del Pollaiuolo," in *Rassegna d' Arte* 18 (1918), 210-214, 212-214; Brink 1990 (see n. 1 above), 161-163 and note 46.

[97] As already mentioned, the dating of Pollaiuolo's *Annunciation* circa 1470 is based solely on considerations of style, cf. note 1.

[98] Lorenzo de' Medici had the General of the Servites banned from Florentine territory, because he had arranged for the miraculous painting of the *Annunciation* to be copied for Emperor Frederick III. We learn this from a 1471 letter from Cardinal Francesco della Rovere to Lorenzo de' Medici in which he asks that the General be pardoned. In this connection, cf. Casalini 1987 (see n. 50 above), 79. According to this author, the use of copies of the painting in SS. Annunziata was forbidden or limited in the second half of the fifteenth and the first half of the sixteenth century (Casalini 1987 [see n. 50 above], 80).

[99] On Villa Careggi, see the literature in note 91 above and Gerda Bödefeld and Berthold Hinz, *Die Villen der Toscana und ihre Gärten* (Cologne: DuMont, 1991), 173. The villa was plundered and set on fire by Florentine republicans after 1494 and again 1529. The wax images of the Medici popes Leo X and Clemens VII in SS. Annunziata in Florence were likewise destroyed on the latter occasion. In this connection see Herzfeld, in Landucci 1978 (see n. 57 above), 323, note 1. The foundation of the Platonic Academy by Cosimo de' Medici has recently been called into doubt. Cf. James Hankins, "Cosimo de' Medici and the *Platonic Academy*," in *Journal of the Warburg and Courtauld Institutes* 53 (1990), 144-162.

[100] Epithets used after the ruler's death and reported by Landucci 1978 (see n. 57 above), 96. On the myth of Lorenzo de' Medici and the culture and politics under his reign, cf. *Lorenzo dopo Lorenzo. La fortuna storica di Lorenzo il magnifico*, ed. by Paola Pirolo (Florence: Silvana, 1992); *All' ombra dell' Lauro. Documenti librari della cultura in età laurenziana*, ed. by Anna Lenzuni (Florence: Silvana, 1992); *Consorterie politiche e mutamenti istituzionali in età laurenziana*, ed. by Maria Augusta Morelli Timpanaro (Florence: Silvana, 1992).

[101] "In questo tempo e anno 1470, Lorenzo de' Medici comincio' in Firenze a pigliare piede [...]" (Francesco Guicciardini, quoted by Hatfield 1970 [see n. 86 above], 143, note 168).

[102] Cf. Ammirato as regards the year 1471: "[...] onde per pubblico decreto fu creato sindaco del comune Lorenzo de' Medici [...]" (*Istorie fiorentine di Scipione Ammirato*, ed. by Luciano Scarabelli, vol. 5 [Turin: Pomba and Comp., 1853], 381).

[103] On the idea of the Golden Age in Florence in the fifteenth century, cf. Ernst H. Gombrich, "Die Renaissance und das Goldene Zeitalter," in Ernst H. Gombrich, *Die Kunst der Renaissance I. Norm und Form* (Stuttgart: Klett-Cotta, 1985), 44-50, 183-184.

[104] This motto appears on the freeze on the facade of Lorenzo de' Medici's Villa Poggio a Caiano (1485/95). As is well known, this entrance in the form of an antique temple porch, represents the first modern use of a motif of the sacral architecture of antiquity in a civil building. On the freeze and the temple front, cf. Bödefeld/Hinz 1991 (see n. 99 above), 48-49, 212.

[105] Ronald Lightbown, *Sandro Botticelli* (Milan: Fabbri, 1989), 246. At this point it should be noted that during the Medici rule the themes of the passion of Christ were pushed into the background on the occasion of processions, so-called "living pictures" and religious plays, occasions when preference was given to triumphant Christian contents. Cf. for example, Ammirato as regards the year 1471: Ammirato 1853 (see n. 99 above), 382 and Matteo Palmieri as regards 1454. In this connection, cf. Herzfeld, in Landucci 1978 (see n. 57 above), 39, note 1.

University of Zürich

From Twelfth-Century Cortezia *to Fifteenth-Century* Courtoisie*: Evolution of a Concept or Continuation of a Tradition?*

Deborah H. Nelson

The meanings of *corteisie* and *cortezia* with their corresponding adjectives *corteis* and *cortes* fall into four categories in medieval French and Occitan:

1. pertaining to a court, as in *littérature courtoise;*
2. pertaining to a high social class, or the nobility;
3. a particular code of behavior that prescribes social relationships between individuals, both men and women;
4. an abstract term associated with *fin'amors* variously defined as a collection of qualities or as a quality in and of itself that an individual must possess in order to love in this special way and which he can no longer possess when his love ceases.[1]

Often, the reader is obliged to infer from the text in question which one or more of the meanings the author intends. And unquestionably, the writers play on the ambiguity inherent in the closely related but separate meanings of the terms while not always being in agreement with each other on the meanings. To explore the overlapping concepts described by these terms, it is useful to examine a series of texts that range from the twelfth to the fifteenth century in order to attempt to discern their specific meaning or meanings and to demonstrate the breadth and depth of possible interpretations.

The complexity of these words becomes apparent early in Occitan literature with Marcabru, who wrote in the first third of the twelfth century a *pastorela* "L'autrier jost'una sebissa"[2] in which he uses the adjectives *cortes* and *corteza* with a double meaning to play on the disparity between appearance and reality. A knight riding through the countryside sees a shepherdess, whom he describes clearly in the first strophe as "*mestissa*" ("of lowly birth," v. 2) and as dressed "*cum filla de vilana*" ("as the daughter of a peasant woman," v. 4). To emphasize further her social status, he refers to her as "*la vilana*" in every strophe but the last. However, her witty and articulate resistance to his advances causes the knight to suggest that she is the daughter of a "*cavaliers*" by a "*corteza vilana*" (vv. 30-32). The combination of these two words, an oxymoron if the sense pertains only to class distinction, adds another dimension to the word *corteza*. Breaking out of the boundaries of social class implied by the use of "*mestissa*" and "*vilana*," *corteza* now takes on the meaning of personal qualities that remain undefined here but are associated with the noble class. The shepherdess holds firmly to her peasant background and asserts that good sense dictates that members of the two social classes should seek amorous adventures among their own kind: "*Cerca fols sa follatura,/Cortes cortez aventura,/E il vilans ab la vilana*" ("A fool seeks his folly while a noble seeks courtly adventure, and the peasant man [seeks] the company of a peasant woman." vv. 79-81).[3] Marcabru uses the word *cortes* to denote class and, at the same time, to indicate behavior appropriate to that class. Thus, the knight can be "*cortes*" by class but "*vilan*" by behavior as the shepherdess can be "*vilana*" by class but "*corteza*" by other qualities that are implied, not specified. Marcabru's deliberate juxtaposition of these terms indicates that the two meanings of *cortes* and *corteza* were well-established early in the troubadour tradition.[4]

While *cortes* in the *pastorela* probably refers simply to class and behavior, other songs by Marcabru indicate that for him an intimate connection exists between *cortezia* and love. In "*Cortesamen vuoill comenssar*" ("In a Courtly Manner I Wish to Begin." Song XV) he states firmly and clearly that: "*Mesura es de gen parlar,/E cortezia es d'amar*" ("*Mezura* consists of speaking politely and *cortezia* consists of loving." vv. 19-20). Elsewhere, he notes that "*Aicel cui fin'amors causitz/Viu letz, cortes e sapiens*" ("That man whom pure love singles out lives happy, courtly and wise." XL, 8-9). Cercamon further clarifies and delineates the interdependence between *cortezia* and *amors* when he writes: "*Greu er cortes/hom qui d'amor se desesper*" ("Hardly will that man be courtly who gives up all hope of love." Song I, 57-58).

Cortezia is only one of a complex, interrelated group of positive qualities that do not in themselves produce *fin'amors* but without which *fin'amors* cannot exist. Taken together, these qualities, which include *cortezia*, *mezura*, *jovens*, *jois*, *donars*, *pretz e valors*, produce the ennobling aspect that contributes to making *fin'amors* a unique concept. They are emphasized differently by the different poets, who do not agree on which ones engender the others, and which ones are absolutely vital for the existence of love.[5] Arnaut Daniel, for example, identifies *cortezia* as the source of all the virtues that came to be associated with *fin'amors*, when he says: "I have been in many courts, but here with her I found a great deal more to praise: moderation and intelligence and other good qualities, beauty, youth, excellent deeds and pleasant diversions. Courtliness (*Cortezia*) nobly taught and instructed her, so far from herself has she banished all obnoxious deeds that I do not think that anything more of good can be said of her."[6] Bernard de Ventadour reflects the same mind-set when he states: "*Tota corteza fazenda:/solatz, chanz e jocs e ris,/mou ben d'amor, so m'es vis*" ("Every courtly deed: bliss, song and diversion and laughter indeed arise from love, so it seems to me").[7] This tie between love and *cortezia* is so firm that when love ceases to exist, these good qualities disappear or turn into their negative counterparts, as is stated in a *tenson* between Bernard de Ventadour and Peire d'Auvérgne: "Hardly will that man be of worth or courtly who cannot persevere in love."[8]

As with the other qualities associated with love by the *troubadours*, the words *cortes* and *cortezia* are either not defined or defined narrowly and differently by each *troubadour* depending on the content and form of his song. An understanding of the connotation that came to be associated with this concept can be attained only by a systematic examination of a large number of songs as was undertaken by Denomy and, a little later, by Moshé Lazar.[9] Denomy summarizes that "...*cortezia* is concerned primarily with the moral side of behavior, with liberality, moderation, fidelity, rather than with the social aspects of life...The *troubadours* were concerned...with moral worth and moral perfection; their stress and accent is on the ethical aspect of behavior...."[10] They are not concerned "with the social niceties of social intercourse, [there is] nothing of the *politesse recherchée* of the chivalric ideal."[11]

Denomy's explanation of *cortezia* is certainly valid. Since, however, the presence of *cortezia* in an individual is demonstrated by his outward behavior, it is not difficult to ascertain why the denotation of the word was so easily reduced to a much simpler meaning. Given the interrelatedness of the different meanings of *cortes* and *cortezia*, it is evident that, for example, when the troubadours used "*cortes*" and "*cortezia*" to denote social class or a certain type of behavior as in Marcabru's *pastorela*, these terms did not totally lose the abstract connotation that existed from their association with *fin'amors*. This fact makes it quite impossible and undesirable to isolate completely one meaning from the others, since these multiple meanings provide mutual enrichment to the texts.

The meanings of "*corteis*" and "*corteisie*" developed simultaneously in northern France, with the earliest record of "*corteis*" employed in the *Chanson de Roland* to describe Olivier's moderation and wisdom, qualities which differentiate him from the impetuous Roland.[12] The noun *corteisie* does not appear until the third quarter of the twelfth century in the *Roman de Troie* (v. 5546) when Troilus is described as follows: "*Bien fu sis frere de proece,/De courtoisie et de largesse*" (He was full of prowess, courtesy, and generosity).[13] At about the same time, Marie de France characterizes her patron as "*Ki flurs est de chevalerie, /D'enseignement, de curteisie*" (He is the flower of chivalry, instruction, and courtesy).[14] These three uses of the terms are examples of the first three meanings mentioned above (i.e., pertaining to the court; of noble class; and a code of behavior). Whether the tradition of lyric love poetry moved north from Occitania into France or whether it developed on its own in the north, the content of the songs and the concept of love differ radically. The *trouvères* virtually never analyse the quality of love and do not speak about the many abstract qualities required of the lover. They do not imitate the *troubadours'* obsessive and complex expression of the subtleties inherent in the different kinds of love and lovers. Instead, the *trouvères* paint with a broad brush the joys and sorrows experienced by lovers to create an agreeable picture of interplay between the sexes, but a picture that lacks the intensity of the ambiance evoked by the *troubadours*. Therefore, the fourth and very abstract meaning of *cortezia* associated with *fin'amors*, while probably not unknown among the *trouvères*, was not part of the conventions that make up the content of the northern lyric. Another factor that contributes to the difference in expression lies in the fact that, while there existed a large number of lyric songs in Old French, the dominant genre in the north, in fact, was the *roman* whereas in the south it was unquestionably lyric poetry. Given the different requirements of these genres and the divergent literary traditions that dominate in the *langue d'oil*, it is not surprising that the evolution of the meanings of words would be different from the *langue d'oc* (Frappier, 14).

Northern writers, exemplified by Chrétien de Troyes in the third quarter of the twelfth century, tend to highlight the concrete rather than the abstract aspects of love and echo Ovid more consistently than the southern poets when they describe the symptoms of love as a physical illness instead of emphasizing the worthiness or lack of worthiness of the lover. When Fénice and Cligès fall in love, their first symptoms seem to be those of a strange new malady. Fénice describes how she feels to her nurse:

> *Tessala mestre, car me dites,*
> *Cist max don n'est il ipocrites,*
> *Qui dolz me sanble, et se m'angoisse?*
> *Je ne sai comant jel conoisse,*
> *Se c'est anfermetez ou non.*
> *Mestre, car m'an dites le non,*
> *Et la meniere, et la nature.* (vv. 3045-3051)[15]
>
> ("Thessala, my nurse, tell me, isn't this illness two-sided, which seems pleasant and oppresses me at the same time: I don't know how to tell whether it is an illness. Nurse, tell me what it is called and what it is like.")

Cligès's love is described as a wound: "*Por ce sa plaie li reoncle,/Et plus li grieve et plus li dialt,/Qu'il n'ose dire ce qu'il vialt*" ("His wound gets worse and causes him much suffering because he does not dare express his desire." vv. 3866-3867).

Chrétien and his successors spend many verses in the dissection of the psychology of their characters who are in love. Beginning with the *roman classique*, the first of the *romans courtois*, the northern writers link the lover with the warrior, a connection not found in Occitan poetry (Frappier, 15). This link alters radically the image of the lover and the issues with which he must wrestle in his internal dialogues. In Chrétien's romances, we regularly see the protagonist in anguish over his conflicting obligations, the love of a woman versus the need to demonstrate his prowess at arms, a conflict not experienced by Occitan lovers. Another romance writer, Jean Renart, states straightforwardly that his *Roman de la rose ou de Guillaume de Dole* will tell a "*conte d'armes et d'amors Et chante d'ambedeus ensamble*" (a tale about arms and love and it sings of both together).[16] This combination is more acceptable to the culture of the land of the *langue d'oil* than is the inherent adulterous quality of *fin'amors* with which northern writers feel uncomfortable, and which rarely survives in the north, with the notable exceptions of Chrétien's *Lancelot* and the *Tristan* legend. Chrétien manages to emphasize Lancelot's obligations to maintain his reputation for prowess while recounting, as he was instructed by his patroness, the knight's passion for the queen. In the *Tristan*, the love element is also an overwhelming obsession, explained in Thomas's text by the *philtre*, and retains, of course, its adulterous quality finally resulting in death, the fate often mentioned but virtually never experienced by both the French and Occitan poets (Frappier, 16-17). It is noteworthy that Bernard de Ventadour also identified elements familiar to the Occitan tradition in Tristan's love: "*Plus trac pena d'amor/de Tristan l'amador/que.n sofri manhta dolor/per Izeut la blonda*" ("I endure more suffering from love than the lover Tristan who suffered much pain because of the blond Isolde." Lazar, ed., Song 4, 45-48).

In one of two extant love songs by Chrétien de Troyes, he speaks directly of the difference in the quality of love as an obsession and as a choice:

> Je n'ai jamais bu du breuvage dont Tristan fut empoisonné, mais ce qui me fait aimer mieux que lui, c'est tendresse profonde du coeur et volonté droite. Je dois consentir à cet amour de mon plein gré, car jamais il ne me prit de force, sauf dans la mesure où je me suis fié à mes yeux qui m'ont guidé vers le chemin dont je ne sortirai jamais et que toujours j'ai voulu suivre.[17]

This statement applies not only to Tristan's love for Iseut but also to the entire obsessive and uncontrolled passion about which the troubadours sing. Because the concept of *fin'amors* did not translate into the culture or into the language of France, the abstract concept of *cortezia* so closely linked to it disappeared. As a result, the most important use of the word in the north came to be as it applied to the code that embodied the exterior signs of the lovers' behavior as summarized by Henri Dupin:

> il est nécessaire qu'ils ne manquent pas à l'obligation du salut, du congé, du baiser, de l'accueil et de l'hospitalité, qu'ils soient loyaux et fidèles, bons et portés à la pitié, doux, libéraux et larges, joyeux, épris de bonne renommée, mesurés, et qu'ils aiment, et que dans leur amour ils appliquent ces vertues courtoises.[18]

Thus, love in northern France is still associated with the concept of *courtoisie,* but *courtoisie* has become simply another external obligation rather than inextricably linked in nature to a particular kind of love. An excellent example of Dupin's definition is Bartlett Jere Whiting's study in the French and English texts of the portrayal of Gawain, whose outstanding quality is consistently identified as *courtoisie.*[19] Whiting lists twenty-six nouns and adjectives that are often combined with *courtois* and *courtoisie* in the depiction of Gawain and other knights, words which reinforce their nobility of character, such terms as *bel, vaillaint, sage, enseigné, bonté, beauté,* etc. (221). These are all characteristics linked with *fin'amors* in the Occitan tradition, but here the field of meaning has been expanded beyond love to include the entire character. Only Kay is consistently described as not "*courtois*," but this depiction is never related to his behavior in love situations but in his general lack of finesse in his relations with those around him at court (222).

Le Roman de la Rose[20] offers extensive confirmation of the importance of *courtoisie* for the development of love and also for the definition of the term as a code of behavior. *Courtoisie*, whose son is *Bel Accueil* (vv. 2776-2777), was "*sage et raisonnable*" (v. 1234) not "*orgueilleuse, folle, niaise, or mélancolique*" and never quarreled with anyone (vv. 1227-1240). The God of Love recommends that the knight imitate the behavior of Gawain known for his *courtoisie* and avoid that of Kay, who was "*cruel, méchant, sarcastique, médisant*" (vv. 2077-2086). Here as elsewhere, it appears easier to define courteous behavior by a list of prohibitions.

Moving now into the fifteenth century to examine the fate of *courtoisie*, it is appropriate to examine texts by Charles d'Orléans, Christine de Pizan, Alain Chartier, and François Villon, the first three of whom are normally associated with the courtly tradition (i.e., they wrote for an audience composed of members of the royal court) and the fourth who broke ranks with convention and usually composed in a style that contrasts sharply with that of the others.

In her *Cent ballades d'amant et de dame*, Christine de Pizan recalls not only the French courtly lyric of the twelfth and thirteenth centuries but also the Occitan lyric of the same period. Christine recounts in a series of one hundred ballads an adulterous love affair with the innovation of giving the married lady an equal voice. This work is courtly in that its characters are noble, in that it was written for a noble audience, and in the gentility of the behavior of both protagonists. The word *courtoisie* appears only one time in this work, in Ballad XXXI, in which the lady describes the behavior that she expects from her suitor: she requests his discretion to protect her honor, truthfulness, loyalty, and willingness to help others. She says then: "*prens desplaisir/En orgueil, et soyes renté/De courtoisie et en langaige/Doulz, salue amiablement,/Soyes aux dames serviteur,/Se tu veulx faire mon plaisir.*"[21] Once again, *courtoisie* appears among other qualities prescribed for good behavior of a nobleman who wishes to please a lady. Conspicuously absent though are the Occitan concerns for the quality of love and those characteristics that must combine to create *fin'amors*. The *Cent ballades d'amant et de dame* recounts an elegant dance of seduction that ends very badly for the lady. The links to the *fin'amors* tradition are evident in the extra-marital quality of the relationship, the presence of *mesdisans*, the necessity for discretion to protect the lady's reputation, and the shadowy presence of the husband referred to as *le jaloux*. Absent and forgotten, however, is the analysis of the love itself.

Alain Chartier's *La Belle Dame sans merci* resembles Christine's *Cent Ballades de dame et d'amant* in that he uses the dialogue to present a discourse on love. However, Chartier introduces a narrator who initially sets a sorrowful tone by relating his own misfortunes in love. At an evening party, he distances himself from the merrymaking to contemplate his own unhappiness. Hidden behind an arbor, he overhears a man designated as "*L'Amant*" speaking to a lady "*La Dame*", in an attempt to persuade her to graciously accept his amorous attentions. Though cloaked in the traditional vague language, the lover's intentions are obvious to the lady, the narrator, and the reader. *L'Amant* invokes *courtoisie* as support for his cause: "*Elas! ma dame, il vault trop mieulz/Pour courtoisie et bonté faire/D'un dolent faire deux joyeux*" ("Alas, my lady! To act courteously and to do good, it is best to make one sorrowful person into two joyous ones.").[22] Later, the lover makes much the same argument by stating that "*...sembleroit en vous perie/Courtoisie qui vous semont/Qu'amours soit par amour merie*" ("It would seem that Courtesy, which would exhort you to repay love with love, has perished within you." vv. 406-408). The lady's response to the lover's comments is confident and self-possessed: "*Courtoisie est si alïee/D'Onneur, qui l'aime et la tient chiere,/Qu'el ne vuelt estre a riens lïee/Ne pour devoir ne pour prïere*" ("Courtesy is so tightly linked to honor, which loves it and holds it dear, that it does not want to be tied to anything else because of duty or demand." vv. 409-412). *Courtoisie* in all of these instances denotes polite and proper behavior but nothing more. Alain Chartier's lovers' dialogue lasts only a short period of time during one evening and not the several months of Christine's *Cent Ballades d'amant et de dame.* Chartier's lady is extremely concerned about her honor but exhibits much more strength and firmness of character than Christine's. When Chartier's lover suggests that only the lady can cure his suffering that could lead to his death, the lady responds by telling him that "*Mieulx en vault un dolent que deux*" ("It is better that one person suffer, not two." v. 272). She is not swayed by the lover's promises to protect her honor nor by any argument that he can make.

Charles d'Orléans who also wrote for a courtly audience, has been referred to as the last *trouvère* and is universally characterized with both praise and criticism as an exponent of *courtoisie*. The word itself, he uses rarely and conventionally: In *La Retenue d'Amours,* Jeunesse advises the young lover, "*Soies courtois et en faiz et en dis*" (v. 130).[23] Otherwise, the word is used in the expressions "*de courtoisie" and "par courtoisie*," simply "*formules de politesse.*"[24] His poetry is elegant, restrained in the expression of both joy and sorrow, typified by a vocabulary that elicits rather than dictates a response from the reader. The courtliness of Charles's poetry is defined by its audience, its elevated tone, its intellectualized imagery, its delicate and limited number of themes, and the quality of its subjectiveness, personal but without the intimate and graphic details found in Villon. The reader is made gently aware of Charles's state of mind, usually marked by sadness if not depression which he names "*Merencolie*."

Just as Charles d'Orléans looks back in time and creates one last expression of courtly conventions, François Villon looks forward, rejecting almost entirely the poetic conventions that had been in vogue for three hundred years. The term "courtly" is virtually never applied to his poetry. His poems are full of graphic images of life and death: prostitutes, taverns, imprisonment, rotting bodies, eyes plucked out of cadavers by birds. The assumptions that he makes concerning the context of his poems indicate that he normally wrote for his peers,[25] those who lived on the edge of poverty, immorality and lawlessness. However, at least two of his poems, written for the court of Charles d'Orléans, are more elevated in tone: "*Je meurs de soif auprès de la fontaine*" for a contest at Blois and the "*Epitre à Marie d'Orléans*" on the occasion of the birth of Charles's daughter. "*Je meurs de soif*" consists of contrasts that recall Guillaume IX's "*Farai un vers de dreyt nien*" in which the poet describes his world, which love has turned upside down and inside out (Song IV). Villon, however, simply lists contradictions that serve to reflect the complexity of his world without giving a specific cause, but with a reference at the end to financial problems. The poem written for Charles's daughter is a conventional *poème de circonstance,* with a religious tone that appears to be an unsubtle effort to earn money through flattery. Both these poems are courtly in the sense of their audience and elevated tone but in no way associated with love.

In a rondel in *Le Testament* that cries out against the ravages of death, Villon demonstrates that he is capable of writing in a style very similar to that of Charles d'Orléans: "*Mort, j'appelle de ta rigueur/Qui m'as ma maistresse ravie....*"[26] However, his temperament combined with the new spirit of his time to give most of his poetry an entirely different quality. A simple comparison of the number of words found in each poet's vocabulary provides the beginning of an understanding for the basis of the vast difference in tone: Charles uses 1,790 words in his ballades as compared with Villon's 2,950 in all his poetry.[27]

Is fifteenth-century *courtoisie*, then, the evolution of a concept or the continuation of a tradition? The answer seems to be "neither of the above." Three of the four meanings of the words *corteisie* and *cortezia* (*corteis* and *cortes*) developed separately and similarly in the two languages. Thus, in the fifteenth century *courtoisie* and *courtois* retained the meanings of "pertaining to a court," "pertaining to a high social class, or the nobility," and "a particular code of behavior that prescribes social relationships between individuals, both men and women." However, *courtoisie* in Old French virtually never had the abstract, complex meaning that it possessed in Occitan with its link to the qualities necessary for the existence of *fin'amors,* even though it often appears in similar lists of characteristics expected to make up the behavior of members of the nobility and is often specified in northern French texts as a necessity in a lover. The narrow meaning of *cortezia* merged quietly and naturally, almost without notice, with the broader meaning of "a refined code of behavior" at the same time as *fin'amors* became *amour courtois.* Moshé Lazar calls the abstract denotation of *courtoisie* a moral meaning as contrasted with the other social meanings.[28] Even in a work such as Christine de Pisan's *Cent Ballades d'amant et de dame* where the text recalls the dialectic of love of the twelfth-century Occitan lyric, the so-called moral meaning has been totally displaced by the social one.

Notes

[1] Moshé Lazar, "Les Eléments constitutifs de la "Cortezia" dans la lyrique des troubadours," *Studi mediolatini volgari*, vi-vii (1959), 73.

[2] Jean-Maire-Lucien Dejeanne, ed. *Poésies complètes du troubadour Marcabru* (New York: Johnson Reprint Corp. 1971), xxx.

[3] This translation and those that follow are mine unless otherwise indicated. In his *De arte honeste amandi* (translated as *The Art of Courtly Love,* John Jay Parry, ed. [New York: Norton, 1941]), Andreas Capellanus includes a chapter entitled "The Love of Peasants" in which he suggests that if one falls in love with one of them, he should "puff them up with lots of praise" and then "take what you seek" and "embrace them by force" (p. 150). Written between 1184-86, i.e., some fifty years after Marcabru's career, this text reflects the tone of the *pastourelles* of both northern and southern France.

[4] Cercamon, a contemporary of Marcabru, also contrasts *cortes* with *vilans,* again with reference to undefined personal qualities: "*Per lieys serai o fals o fils,/.../ O totz vilas o totz cortes*" (Because of her, I will be either false or faithful, completely base or completely courtly). Alfred Jeanroy, *Les Poésies de Cercamon* (Paris: Champion, 1922), Song I, 51-53.

[5] Alexander J. Denomy, "Courtly Love and Courtliness," *Speculum* 28 (1953), 48.

[6] Ben ai estat a maintas bonas cortz/Mas sai ab lieis trob pro mais que lauzor; /Mesura e sen et autres bos mestiers,/Beutat, joven, bos faitz e bels demors./Gen l'enseignet Cortezia e la duois;/Tant a de si totz faitz desplazens rotz/De lieis ne cre rens de ben sia a dire." Réné Lavaud, ed., *Les Poésies d'Arnaut Daniel* (Geneva: Slatkine Reprints, 1973), XV, 15-21. Cited by Alexander J. Denomy, 60.

[7] vv. 8-9. Carl Appel, ed. *Bernart von Ventadorn: Seine Lieder* (Halle a. d S: M. Niemeyer, 1915), 345. The song "*Mandat m'es que no m recreja*" is attributed to BdV in MS. V and to Pons de la Gardia in MS. E.

[8] "Bernartz, greu er pros ni cortes/que ab amor no.s sap tener." Moshé Lazar, ed., *Chansons d'amour* (Paris: Klincksieck, 1966), Song 28, 15-16.

[9] "Les Eléments constitutifs de la "Cortezia" dans la lyrique des troubadours," *Studi mediolatini volgari*, vi-vii (1959), 67-96.

[10] Denomy 62.

[11] Denomy 62. See also Jean Frappier, *Amour courtois et table ronde* (Geneva: Droz, 1973), 7, for a discussion of the meaning of *cortezia* among the troubadours.

[12] William Calin ed. (New York: Appleton-Century-Crofts), 1968. vv. 576, 3755.

[13] Léopold Constans, ed. I (Paris: Firmin-Didot, 1904), v. 5546. Cf. also vv. 3180, 5353. As cited by Denomy, 47.

[14] Alfred Ewert and Ronald Carlyl Johnston, eds. *The Fables of Marie de France* (Oxford: Blackwell, 1942), Prol. v. 32.

[15] Alexandre Micha, ed. *Cligès*. Paris: Champion, 1982).

[16] Rita Lejeune, ed. (Paris: Droz, 1936) and Félix Lecoy, ed. (Paris: Champion, 1962), vv. 24-25.

[17] Onques del bevraje ne bui/don Tristans fu anpoisonez,/mes plus me fet amer que lui/fins cuers et bone volantez./bien an doit estre miens li grez,/qu'ains de rien

esforciez n'an fui,/fors de tant, que mes iauz an crui,/par cui sui an la voie antrez,/don ja n'istrai, n'ains n'i recrui. Karl Bartsch, ed. *Chrestomathie de l'ancien français, viiie-xve siècles* (New York: Hafner, 1958).

[18] *La Courtoisie au moyen âge* (d'après les textes du xiie et du xiiie siècle) (Paris: Picard, 1931), 127.

[19] "Gawain: His Reputation, His Courtesy and His Appearance in Chaucer's *Squire's Tale*," *Mediaeval Studies* 9 (1947), 189-234.

[20] Guillaume de Lorris, *Le Roman de la Rose*. Tome I. (Paris: Champion, 1971).

[21] Jacqueline Cerquiglini, ed. (Paris: Union Générale d'Editions, 1982), vv. 11-20.

[22] J. C. Laidlaw, ed. *The Poetical Works of Alain Chartier* (Cambridge: Cambridge University Press, 1974), 341, vv. 273-275.

[23] Pierre Champion, ed., *Charles d'Orléans, Poésies.* (Paris: Champion, 1982), 5.

[24] Daniel Poirion, Le Lexique de Charles d'Orléans dans les Ballades (Geneva: Droz, 1967), 60. Claudio Galderisi, Le Lexique de Charles d'Orléans dans les rondeaux (Geneva: Droz, 1993), 170.

[25] David A. Fein, *François Villon and His Reader* (Detroit: Wayne State University Press, 1989), 19.

[26] John Fox, *The Lyric Poetry of Charles d'Orléans.* (Oxford: Clarendon Press, 1969), 100-101.

[27] Baudelaire used 4,000 words in the *Fleurs du Mal*. Daniel Poirion, *Le Lexique de Charles d'Orléans dans les ballades*. (Geneva: Droz, 1967), 31.

[28] "Les Eléments," 70.

Rice University

Fortune's Double Face: Gender and the Transformations of Christine de Pizan, Augustine, and Perpetua

Lori J. Walters

In *La Mutacion de Fortune* (*Fortune's Transformation*, 1403) Christine de Pizan gives an allegorized version of her personal history as introduction to a universal history spanning the Creation to her own modern-day France. If there is a Christine-narrator who presents human history as a function of the workings of Fortune, her narrator also recounts the none-the-less capricious operations of this same deity on a Christine-protagonist. In the latter's story nothing is more arbitrary than the determination of the child's gender: whereas Christine was born a girl, she resembled her father in everything except her gender. This is how she expresses the troubling circumstances of her birth: "I fully resembled my father in all things, only excepting my gender: in manner, body, face, we so resembled each other that you would have thought that we had them in common."[1] More surprising to modern readers, however, than Christine's birth, which gave her an ambiguously gendered identity, is her transformation into a man by Fortune, the central event of her mini-autobiography. As she tells us herself in *L'Avision Christine* (*Christine's Vision*, 1405), her metamorphosis symbolized the profound changes that she had to make in order to assume financial responsibility for herself and her family after her husband's death,[2] changes that led her to become the author of the present book.

Christine's account of the change from woman to man in *Fortune's Transformation* does not, however, represent the last word on the gender of her authorial self. At the beginning of *La Cité des Dames* (*The City of Ladies*, 1404-05), a work in which Christine-narrator refutes the misogynistic tradition by providing countermodels of admirable women in history and legend, she rejects speaking as a masculinized persona. While at first she may lament having been born a woman, Christine, drawing on her book learning and her lived experience as a woman,[3] comes to accept and even rejoice in her status. Thus Christine constructs a differently gendered authorial self — masculine in *Fortune's Transformation*, feminine in *The City of Ladies* — as a function of the aims of each work. In this article I will argue that two well-known metamorphoses experienced by saints underlie her ambiguous or "double faced" gender identity. Christine transforms her earlier male and female models of saintliness into the more secular, humanist ideals,[4] those of the chaste and hardworking widow (*Fortune's Transformation*)[5] and the devoted scholar (*The City of Ladies*). Medieval French readers, all Catholics who regularly attended mass, would, I think, be especially sensitive to what we now call the intertextual resonances of Christine's gender change that I will consider in this study.

Critics have found the modern terminology of intertextuality particularly appropriate for describing how medieval writers and readers approached a work. Defined by Gérard Genette as "la présence effective d'un texte dans un autre,"[6] intertextuality takes into account the "already textualized" context of literary creation, a notion that is especially germane to medieval practice. With its emphasis on the establishment of *auctoritas* within a received tradition, medieval *inventio* prescribed a process of writing and interpretation in which a text was defined largely by the expectations established by prior ones. Much of what a medieval text "means" comes from the way it transforms elements in earlier works. Michel Riffaterre's definition of the intertext as "l'ensemble des textes que l'on peut rapprocher de celui que l'on a sous les yeux"[7] suggests how each new text provides a commentary on a vast ensemble of earlier ones.[8] In a textual environment dominated by adaptation and rewriting, medieval writers would signal their debt to predecessors by citing the name of an author or by echoing phrases, images, situations from their works (the majority of texts in the medieval period were anonymous).

I wish to examine the possibility that two important subtexts of Christine's gender change are Augustine's well-known account of his conversion to Christianity and a gender change undergone by Perpetua, a popular third-century Carthaginian martyr. Although Christine does not make direct mention of the respective metamorphoses of these two figures in *Fortune's Transformation*, she refers to Augustine extensively in her earliest prose text, the *Epitre Othéa* of 1400 (Christine begins her career composing lyric poetry around 1394, four years after her husband's death.[9]). Augustine would remain one of the major authority figures in Christine's subsequent works, as they increasingly assume a religious cast. Perpetua is also closely associated with Augustine, who discusses her martyrdom in three of his sermons and one of his religious treatises.[10]

Christine herself pointedly connects her self-portrait in *Fortune's Transformation* to saintly paradigms when, following the account of her birth, she tells us that her name is the same as that of the most perfect man who ever lived, plus the letters "I N E"; in other words, it corresponds to the name "Christ" with the addition of the female diminutive.[11] When Christine refers to her name as a variant of Christ's, she virtually instructs her reader to see it as an allusion not only to Christ, but to his saints as diminutive Christs as well. Christine's nameplay implies that her gender identity is as mutable as the form of her name; correspondingly, her models of transformation are justly male and female. Unlike Augustine's metamorphic experience, Perpetua's includes a gender change from woman to man that likens it even more closely to Christine's. Perpetua's transformation therefore may be seen as a kind of female recasting of male conversion narratives like those of Saint Paul and Augustine.

There are other references in *Fortune's Transformation* that give the impression that, in imitating Christ, Christine is styling herself on the model of a female saint. Christine's "transmutacion" account (v. 1161, Solente) is preceded by her rewriting of three Ovidian metamorphoses — Ulysses's men changed into animals by Circe, Tiresias transformed into a woman and back again, and Iphis transformed into a man — whose immediate source in each and every case is the *Ovide moralisé*, cited by Christine (vv. 13913-17, Solente). Christine thus calls upon her reader to interpret her transformation as if it figured in the latter work,[12] which routinely interprets classical myths as if they were saints' lives.[13] The anonymous commentator of the *Ovide moralisé* claims that the best reading of Iphis's metamorphosis, as opposed to the negative readings of Iphis as a woman of perverted sexuality or the sinful soul,[14] is the Incarnation (IX, vv. 3158-61). So that we do not fail to grasp the analogy between Ovidian fable and Christian truth, Christine calls "miracles" the three Ovidian metamorphoses that introduce her own gender change (vv. 1037, 1153,1159, Solente). According to the logic of the readings offered by the *Ovide moralisé*, Iphis's transformation from woman to man can be read as a prefiguration of the gender change of Christine and of a female saint like Perpetua.

At the beginning of *Fortune's Transformation* Christine-narrator proposes to tell her readers how the goddess Fortune conspired to change Christine's gender from feminine to masculine when she was twenty-five years old. After Christine-protagonist has spent ten blissful years at Hyménée's court as the wife of an exceptionally good man, Fortune, envious of the young woman's happiness, calls her back into her service. During the sea voyage which Christine and her family undertake in order to rejoin Fortune, her husband perishes in a storm. Fortune arrives to comfort her in her despair and help her avoid shipwreck. Here is how Fortune transforms Christine into a man so that she can pilot the ship:

> Wearied by long crying, I remained, on one particular occasion, completely overcome; as if unconscious, I fell asleep early one evening. Then my mistress came to me, she who gives joy to many, and she touched me all over my body; she palpated and took in her hands each bodily part, I remember it well; then she departed and I remained, and since our ship was following the waves of the sea, it struck me with force against a rock. I awakened and things were such that, immediately and with certainty, I felt myself completely transformed. I felt my limbs to be stronger than before, and the

> great pain and lamentation, which had earlier dominated me, I felt to be somewhat lessened. Then I touched myself all over my body, like one completely bewildered. Fortune had thus not hated me, she who had transformed me, for she had instantly changed the great fear and doubt in which I had been completely lost. Then I felt myself much lighter than usual and I felt that my flesh was changed and strengthened, and my voice much lowered, and my body harder and faster. However, the ring that Hymen had given me had fallen from my finger, which troubled me, as well it should have, for I loved it dearly.
>
> Then I stood up easily; I no longer remained in the lethargy of tears which had been increasing my grief, *I found my heart strong and bold*, which surprised me, but I felt that *I had become a true man*; and I was amazed at this strange adventure.[15] (1.12, 106; my emphasis)

After the unexpected death of her husband, Christine-protagonist undergoes a symbolic gender change in order to be able to assume the masculine role of provider not only for herself, but for the other remaining members of her household, which included two children, her mother, and a niece. Christine turned her misfortune to her advantage by becoming a writer, an extraordinary decision since she appears to have been the first woman in France to support herself from this activity.[16]

Christine's gender change shares many characteristics with Augustine's conversion to Christianity. Augustine describes his conversion in Book VIII of the *Confessions*,[17] composed between 397 and 401. It, like *Fortune's Transformation*, is a first-person narrative connected to a universal history.[18] Augustine, who had been in a state of despair marked by profound weeping because of his inability to come to a decision on the matter, finds the strengh to undergo conversion by reading a passage from an Epistle (Rom. 13: 13-14)[19] where Saint Paul preaches the virtues of a new way of life in Christ.[20] Paul, we recall, was the erstwhile persecutor of the Christians who had himself experienced a spectacular change of heart on the road to Damascus, a change reflected in the substitution of his old name "Saul" for "Paul." After reading Paul's words, Augustine says:

> I neither wished nor needed to read further. At once, with the last words of this sentence, it was as if a light of relief from all anxiety flooded into my heart. All the shadows of doubt were dispelled.[21]

After Augustine's conversion in 386, he became the fervent apologist of the Christian faith who in *De civitate Dei*, composed between 413 and 427, wrote the definitive defense of Christianity against its critics. Christine's metamorphosis is similar to Augustine's in that a great feeling of consolation follows a moment of deep despair. It differs from his because her despair arises from another source, the death of her husband. Both transformations involve a renouncement of the erotic: Augustine chooses celibacy, a solution that Christine adopts after the death of her beloved husband.[22] In each case the transformation of the self eventually leads to a dedication to the contemplative life[23] and a new vocation as writer, Augustine, as religious writer with a humanist bent,[24] Christine, as Christian humanist.[25]

Through her metamorphosis into a man, Christine attempts to appropriate some of Augustine's prestige as a male authority figure in his *Confessions* for her own *Fortune's Transformation*. Although, as Peter Brown remarks, Augustine could have modeled his autobiography on stories already circulating such as Perpetua's very moving and popular narrative,[26] he instead patterned his tale on conversion narratives written by men. Brian Stock shows how the part of the *Confessions* dealing with conversion in fact consists of three interrelated stories:

> Simplicianus, the successor of Ambrose as bishop in Milan in 397, tells Augustine of the conversion of Marius Victorianus, which took place in 355. Ponticianus, a Christian official of the imperial court, tells Augustine and Alypius of the conversion of two state agents, which occurred sometime after 381. Finally, Augustine describes his and Alypius' conversions in the garden of their house in Milan in August 386.[27]

That each and every storyteller and convert is male suggests that Augustine constructed his conversion narrative as a quintessentially masculine one. By becoming a man, we may suppose that Christine is harking to Augustine's position that for a woman to be a man's equal, she needs a man's body. In the *Confessions* Augustine claims about woman that "in mental power she has an equal capacity of rationale intelligence, but by the sex of her body she is submissive to the masculine sex" (xxxii [47], 302). The meaning of Augustine's statement is captured by Christine's contention that although by her intelligence and virtue she was a man's equal, she was limited by having a woman's body. Through her metaphorical "*mutacion*" into a man, Christine circumvented many of the negative values associated with being female that existed in Augustine's time and in her own.

While Christine borrows for her narrative the authority of the male conversion narrative, she reorients her transformation in a feminine direction through her echoes of Perpetua's gender change. Perpetua describes events leading up to her execution in the first-person section of the *Passio Sanctarum Perpetuae et Felicitatis*. A testimonial believed to have been written in Perpetua's own hand, this is one of the first examples of female "autobiography." The two-part *Passio* (a male eyewitness account of several martyrs' deaths, including Perpetua's, frames her prison diary) was a key text in forming the norms of the female saint's life. Thomas J. Heffernan calls the *Passio* "the primal document in the conventions which were to shape female sacred biography for a millennium."[28] Although largely forgotten today, Perpetua's story would have been well known in outline form by devout Parisians.[29] It played as focal a role in determining the paradigms of female saintliness as Augustine's *Confessions* later did in establishing those of male saintliness.[30]

Vibia Perpetua, a recent convert to Christianity, was martyred for her beliefs on March 7, A.D. 203. The high points of her diary are her four dream visions. It is her fourth and final one that is recalled in *Fortune's Transformation*. Here is an excerpt from her moving account of that dream:

> And I saw the immense, astonished crowd. And as I knew I had been condemned to the wild beasts, I was amazed they did not send them out at me. Out against me came an Egyptian, foul of aspect, with his seconds: he was to fight with me. And some handsome young men came up beside me: my own seconds and supporters. And I was stripped naked, and *became a man*. And my supporters began to rub me with oil, as they do for a wrestling match [...] (my emphasis).[31]

When Christine asserts, "I felt that I had become a true man," an affirmation that is reinforced by her statement, "I found my heart strong and bold," she seems to echo Perpetua's words at the moment of her own transformation. Although "becoming male" became a staple of the female saint's life, this convention originated in Perpetua's second-century story; indeed, she appears to be the only female saint to have ever experienced an actual bodily transformation.[32] Christine follows Perpetua's lead in describing a physical gender change in a dream vision that is part of a larger first-person "autobiographical" narrative.[33]

Christine imitated the words pronounced by the future martyr at the moment of her transformation into a man in order to appropriate for her own first-person text the strengths of Perpetua's. Christine resembles Perpetua in viewing her dream as a prediction of her eventual triumph over her misfortunes. Here is how Perpetua interprets her forthcoming trials in the arena:

> And I awoke. And I knew I should have to fight not against wild beasts but against the Fiend; but I knew the victory would be mine.[34]

Although Christine will be spared the fate of martyrdom, she does contemplate committing suicide after her husband's death. She decides against this expedient solution because of her responsibilities to her family members.[35] Her triumph over adverse circumstances ultimately lies in becoming a writer. May we say that in her singular position as France's first professional woman of letters she resembles Perpetua, who was able to better a man in unarmed combat, an accomplishment denied to most women?

By echoing Perpetua's words, Christine also tries to duplicate the effect of Perpetua's story on her own audience. The most unusual aspect of Perpetua's document is that it communicates a sense of her uniqueness as a human being. It is the author's own words that we seem to hear as she recounts her reactions to frightful experiences. Medieval and modern audiences alike fell under the spell cast by her story. Augustine's warning that local Christians who read her prison diary on her feast day were in danger of confusing it with sacred scripture[36] is a measure of the strength of Perpetua's hold on fifth-century North African popular imagination. Moderns cannot help but be struck by what Canadian historian Brent Shaw calls "the overpowering singularity of her achievement."[37] Commenting on the quality of her language, Shaw claims that Perpetua expresses herself "with such a power and simplicity of rhetoric that the very words she wrote contained an irrefutable self-empowerment."[38] Perpetua's first-person account conveys an arresting sense of female dignity that contrasts markedly with the indignities to which the female body is subject in the redactor's framing narrative, indignities whose violent and pornographic qualities were aggressively exploited by the Roman authorities in their campaign of terror against the spread of Christianity.[39] What Christine wants to appropriate for *Fortune's Transformation* and *The City of Ladies,* both universal histories guaranteed by the author's personal history, is the dignity and power of Perpetua's voice speaking about herself in the first-person.[40]

Besides Christine's description of a physical gender reversal and her establishment of her gender change within the context of a female *imitatio Christi*, there is yet another reason for seeing Perpetua's first-person account of her gender shift as a model for Christine's. Michael Riffaterre informs us that what he terms "ungrammaticalities," elements that do not quite fit the new context, often reveal the traces of an intertext.[41] Fortune's massage is one such "ungrammaticality." Fortune's loving stroking of each of Christine's limbs could be a recasting of the massage given Perpetua by her male supporters, a detail absent from all versions of the earlier Ovidian models of gender changes (the stories of Tiresias and Iphis that precede her "*mutacion*"). After Christine contemplates suicide when the ship's pilot has drowned, Fortune revives her for the battle that she will have to fight in life in the same way that Perpetua's male supporters prepared her for combat. The direct action of female figures on other female figures will be repeated in *The City of Ladies*, when, for instance, the three Ladies, Reason, Rectitude, and Justice appear to Christine-protagonist in a vision and authorize her to construct her city. One woman's influence on another expresses the essential structure of the female genealogy that Christine seeks to establish by writing her work.

Following her gender change in *Fortune's Transformation*, Christine adopts a new female literary persona in *The City of Ladies,* where the author, no longer the man of the prior work, offers a direct response to the disparaging depiction of women in literature written by men. In order to establish the legitimacy of her new text, a collection of portraits of female figures whose achievement and moral excellence is worthy of imitation by present and future women, Christine now has to clear away centuries of defamation of women's character by male writers. Overwhelmed by the extent of the antifeminism she finds in books composed by even the most respected male authorities, Christine despairingly asks God why she was not born a man[42] and begins to question what she thinks she knows about herself and other women. The preceding unflattering literary representation of women contradicts her understanding of her own behavior, which she characterizes as that of a "natural woman." Christine's concept of the "natural woman" blurs the distinction between anatomy and gender because the concept takes into account experience[43] and learning, elements that today we ascribe to environment as opposed to heredity. *Fortune's Transformation* and *The City of Ladies* provide a challenge to the idea that bodily characteristics determine gender. Judith Butler's contention that the enactment of gender through performance can attain an authority approaching that of biological characteristics[44] recalls Christine's take on gender in these two works.[45]

After having heard the lengthy exposition on the merits and capabilities of women throughout the ages given by Reason, Rectitude, and Justice, Christine discards her desire to have been born a man. Christine-protagonist's lesson from Reason is that she should not reject what she knows from her own experience,[46] whatever recognized male authorities may say. Reason dismisses Christine's desire to have been born male with a scoffing parable of a man who was tricked into thinking he was a woman:

> You resemble the fool in the prank who was dressed in woman's clothes while he slept; because those who were making fun of him repeatedly told him he was a woman, he

> believed their false testimony more readily than the certainty of his own identity.[47]

Renate Blumenfeld-Kosinski explains the outcome of the above scene:

> At that moment, of course, Lady Reason begins to instill pride in Christine, pride in her female body and her female intellect. While before she had been an "unnatural" albeit effective woman, she now no longer needs her male disguise since she will be in the company of the most excellent and successful women of her own creation.[48]

Christine's "natural woman" of *The City of Ladies* nevertheless retains elements from her "unnatural" time spent as a man. Even though at the beginning of the work Christine's bodily form has been restored to a woman's, several aspects of her self-portrait correspond to traditionally male paradigms. First is her self-representation as scholar seated in her library, which is based on the customary representation of male authority figures. Second is the courage she exhibits in refuting generations of male antifeminism, which corresponds in the moral realm to male valor on the battlefield. The "woman with the heart of a man" that characterizes Christine-protagonist's transformed state in *Fortune's Transformation* remains the ideal of both the pagan women and Christian saints who populate Christine's city[49] as well as of Christine herself in her role as crusader against antifeminism in *The City of Ladies*. Whether Semiramis in *The City of Ladies*[50] or Joan of Arc in the last work composed by Christine, the *Ditié de Jehanne d'Arc* (*The Poem of Joan of Arc*; 1429),[51] the heroic woman would remain a constant in Christine's writings.[52]

Reminiscences of the transmutations of Augustine and Perpetua appear in several instances in *The City of Ladies* as well as in *Fortune's Transformation*. Christine evokes memories of Augustine's conversion in refusing a gender change for her protagonist in a work written in the first-person replete with allusions to Augustine and in representing herself as a figure of authority and heroism in traditionally male molds. In *The City of Ladies* Christine refers to Augustine as "the glorious Doctor of the Church," and has him standing "at the fore of the Holy Church which he completely brightens and illuminates" (1.10.4, 28). She shows him correcting the error of Aristotle, even though the Greek philosopher is, according to all, the "prince of philosophers"(I.2.2, 7). By means of the title of her work, *The City of Ladies* (*La Cité des Dames* in Middle French) she capitalizes on the prestige of the defense of Christianity that Augustine made in *The City of God*, a text well known in fifteenth-century France in both the original Latin and in the vernacular French version of Raoul de Presles (1371-75), known under the title *La Cité de Dieu*. This was a translation that had been commanded by Charles V, the same king who had invited Christine's father to join the royal court as his own physician and advisor. In other words Christine's *City of Ladies* is in many ways a continuation of Augustine's work that would assure a select spot for virtuous women in his City of God.

Can we not see a reassertion of the Perpetua subtext alongside Augustine's? After her time spent as a man in *Fortune's Transformation*, Christine chooses to take back her female face in *The City of Ladies*. While assuring a place of choice for women in the ideal of perfection imagined by Augustine, Christine's *City of Ladies* reorients *The City of God* in terms of gender. In one of her earliest works, *L'Epistre au Dieu d'Amours* (*The God of Love's Letter*, 1399) Christine had commented that if more women were writers, women would not be misrepresented in literary works. Perpetua's testimony to the ultimate meaning of her forthcoming martyrdom is more pertinent to Christine's project of disseminating notions of women's heroism and nobility throughout the ages than Augustine's typically male conversion narrative. Perpetua, who had dared to write about her own experience and affirm her dignity as a woman despite the humiliating treatment to which she was to be subject in the arena, was consequently a fitting model for Christine both as woman autobiographer and as a protagonist responding heroically in particularly difficult circumstances.[53] Besides the similarities already discussed, Christine resembles Perpetua in her role as self-sacrificing mother. Perpetua nursed her infant son throughout many of her harrowing days in prison, and Christine became a writer in order to support family members.

In *The City of Ladies*, a work that makes the implicit claim that women were the hidden but ubiquitous founders of civilization, Christine's self-representation as a heroic woman and as a first-person author thus posits Perpetua as a significant precursor of her self-transforming persona alongside Augustine. Christine's reference to Augustine's mother Monica's role in her son's conversion (I.10.4), which is based on his own account in the *Confessions,* makes the reader sensitive to the presence of heretofore concealed female models for male success stories. Brown's comment that Perpetua's story was a readily available prototype for Augustine's autobiography could even lead us to suspect that Perpetua's transformation served as a blueprint for Augustine's, a fact that he attempted to obscure by his representation of his conversion in an exclusively male context. If in transmitting Perpetua's story in his sermons and writings, Augustine made it more acceptable in terms of the gender expectations of the fourth-century Church, in which women were examples of human frailty rather than of strength, he nonetheless distorted its message.[54] We cannot ignore the possibility that

Augustine was motivated by personal insecurities concerning Perpetua's popularity.[55] When in *The City of Ladies* Christine teaches us to look for female ancestors where males had established exclusively male ones,[56] could she not be hinting that Augustine's transformation and first-person narrative need to be complemented by female ones like Perpetua's?

In giving metaphorical representation to the misfortunes that had befallen her — such as her birth as a woman and the death of her husband that forced her to assume a male role — Christine takes on an ambiguously gendered persona that has models in male and female saints' lives, most particularly in those of Augustine and Perpetua. Memories of the well-known stories of Augustine's conversion and Perpetua's gender change would have enriched the readers' appreciation of Christine's transformation from woman to man in *Fortune's Transformation* and her reappearance as a woman at the beginning of *The City of Ladies*. In constructing her self-portrait as a Christian humanist, a writer who, like the author of the *Ovide moralisé*, read Christian meaning into pagan myths, Christine builds upon Augustine's humanist preservation of classical values in the new context of Christian culture. She also shares his vision of the place of temporal history in a higher providential scheme. Echoes of Perpetua's first-person narration of her heroic resistance to the forces of evil help accredit Christine's new vocation as writer in secular and specifically feminine terms. Christine's allusions to Augustine and Perpetua contribute to a self-portrait that would retain a double perspective throughout her career. She would continue to write with the authority of a male Christian humanist while making humanism more responsive to issues affecting women.

Notes

[1]What Christine desired above all was to acquire the great learning and informed judgment of her father, Tommaso di Benvenuto da Pizzano, who had served as physician and advisor to Charles V of France. Referring to the constraints imposed on women's education in fifteenth-century France, she describes herself as being reduced to gathering crumbs from her father's table. Despite the limitations of her society, Christine did manage to educate herself, a process she recounts, again in an allegorical mode, in the *Chemin de long estude* (*The Path of Long Study*, 1402-03), a text that Christine interrupted to begin work on *Fortune's Transformation*. See: *The Book of Fortune's Transformation*, tr. Kevin Brownlee, *The Selected Writings of Christine de Pizan* (New York: Norton, 1997), 1.6, 94. Brownlee translates from the standard edition of Suzanne Solente, ed., *Le Livre de la mutacion de Fortune de Christine de Pisan*, 4 vols. (Paris: Picard, 1959-66). To facilitate comparisons between texts written in Middle French and Latin, I have used English translations, which in each and every case are based upon the standard editions and are excellently rendered. When I refer to lines in

the original which are not present in the translation I am using, I include the editor's name in parentheses.

[2]"Now I had to go to work (which, being indulgently raised on rich meats, I had not learned to do) and pilot the ship remaining without master or captain on the stormy sea, that is, the desolate household misplaced and in a foreign land," *Christine's Vision*, tr. and intro. Glenda K. McLeod, (New York: Garland, 1993), III, 6, 112.

[3]The instability of Christine's gender identity is suggested by two of the examples of Ovidian metamorphoses that introduce her own transformation. Whereas the change of Iphis from woman to man reproduces most closely Christine's own gender change in *Fortune's Transformation*, Tiresias's changes from man to woman and back again to his original form is a foreshadowing of the fluidity of Christine's gender position as she moves from *Fortune's Transformation* to *The City of Ladies*.

[4]For a discussion of Christine's humanism, see E.J. Richards, "Christine, the Conventions of Courtly Diction, and Italian Humanism," in *Reinterpreting Christine de Pizan,* ed. E.J. Richards, Joan Williamson, Nadia Margolis, Christine Reno (Athens: University of Georgia Press, 1992), 250-71; Nadia Margolis, "The Cry of the Chameleon: Evolving Voices in the Epistles of Christine de Pizan," *Disputatio* 1 (1996), 37-70 and Lori J. Walters, "Chivalry and the (En)Gendered Poetic Self: Petrarchan Models in the *Cent Balades*," *The City of Scholars: New Approaches to Christine de Pizan*, ed. Margarete Zimmermann and Dina De Rentiis (Berlin: Walter de Gruyter, 1994), 44-66.

[5]See Kevin Brownlee, "Widowhood, Sexuality, and Gender in Christine de Pizan," *Romanic Review* (1995), 339-53, and Liliane Dulac, "Un mythe didactique chez Christine de Pizan: Sémiramis ou la veuve héroïque," *Mélanges Charles Camproux*, 2 vols. (Montpellier, Centre d'Etudes occitanes de l'Université Paul Valéry, 1978), 1; 315-40, for Christine's self-representation as a widow.

[6]Gérard Genette, Palimpsestes: La littérature au second degré (Paris: Seuil, 1982).

[7]Michel Riffaterre, "L'intertexte inconnu," *Littérature* 41 (1981), 5-6.

[8]In preparing this paragraph, I have used the entry on intertextuality prepred by Hans-George Ruprecht for the *Dictionnaire international des termes littéraires*, pre-published in *Texte* 2 (1983), 13-22.

[9]Charity Cannon Willard, *Christine de Pizan: Her Life and Works* (New York: Persea, 1984), 43.

[10]4.18.26 of *De natura et origine animae*, a work that Christine could have known since it was present in the Sorbonne library in the early fifteenth century.

[11]For a study of Christ's "maternal" characteristics, see Carolyn Walker Bynum, *Jesus as Mother: Studies in the Spirituality of the High Middle Ages* (Berkeley: University Press of California, 1982).

[12]*Ovide moralisé en vers*, ed. Cornelis de Boer, 5 vols. (Wiesbaden: Martin Sandig, 1915-38).

[13]In Book I Dané is interpreted as the Virgin Mary (vv. 3065-260); Io, who turned to prostitution after having been seduced by Jupiter, is compared to Saint Mary the Egyptian (vv. 4013-30).

[14]Renate Blumenfeld-Kosinski, "Christine de Pizan and Classical Mythology: Some Examples from the *Mutacion de Fortune*," *The City of Scholars: New Approaches to Christine de Pizan*, ed. Margarete Zimmermann and Dina De Rentiis (New York: Walter de Gruyter, 1994), 9.

[15]Fortune's Transformation, 106.

[16]We do not know much about the historical identity of the late twelfth-century writer, Marie de France, but it seems probable that she was either a noblewoman or an abbess (or a noblewoman who later became an abbess), who did not live from her writings. For an overview of the research on this question, see the Introduction of Glyn S. Burgess and Keith Busby, *The Lais of Marie de France* (London: Penguin Books, 1986), 17-19.

[17]See the *Secretum* (composed between 1346-53) for Petrarch's description of Augustine's conversion as his transformation into "another man."

[18]In *The City of God* Augustine continues the history of Creation as recounted in Scripture that is the subject of the final books of the *Confessions*.

[19]*The Confessions of Saint Augustine*, tr. Henry Chadwick (Oxford: Oxford University Press, 1991), xii (29), 152.

[20]On p. 144 of her notes to Book III of *Christine's Vision*, Glenda McLeod points out the parallels between Paul's blinding by God's light on the road to Damascus (Acts 22: 6-13) and the brilliant light accompanying Philosophy's apparition to Christine ("For as soon as it did, such a brilliant light struck me in the face and eyes that I believed myself forever blinded; from fear and because of the wondrous event, I fell on the threshold of light, faint and repentant for having risen so high. As I was lying on the ground, a woman's voice came from the high enclosure, sounding neither horrifying nor terrible but sweet, beautiful, and very gracious" III, i, 106). Given the general concerns of this study, it is noteworthy that in the analogy with the Biblical passage, Christine replaces God the Father with Lady Philosophy!

[21]*The Confessions*, xii (29), 153.

[22]The wedding ring that drops from Christine's finger has a meaning in a Christian context. It signifies that a saint must renounce familial ties in order to realize her sacred vocation and thus be "wed" to Christ. Although a ring does not figure in Perpetua's account, what the ring signifies is conveyed when she repudiates her father's demands to renounce her identity as a Christian and separates herself from her infant. It is also conveyed by the absence of her husband from the narrative, a fact about which Perpetua does not comment. The conventions of the

female saint's life had undergone considerable elaboration between the time of Perpetua's martyrdom and Christine's reworking of a large corpus of female saints' lives in the fifteenth century. Consequently, although renunciation of familial ties is a prominent motif in Perpetua's story that was focal in forming the conventions of female hagiography, this motif did not receive symbolic form in the wedding ring in that particular narrative.

[23]Robert J. O'Connell, *Images of Conversion in St. Augustine's 'Confessions'* (N.Y.: Fordham University Press, 1996), 251.

[24]On Augustine's humanist role in preserving the culture of the ancients by transposing it into the new Christian order, see Henri-Irénée Marrou, *Saint Augustin et la fin de la culture antique* (Paris: Boccard, 1938).

[25]Renate Blumenfeld-Kosinski, *Reading Myth: Classical Mythology and Its Interpretations in Medieval French Literature* (Stanford: Stanford University Press, 1997) makes a perceptive comment on the development of Christine's humanism: "I would suggest that the *Chemin* can be read as a dramatization of the role classical learning should play in medieval culture" (196).

[26]Peter Brown, *Augustine of Hippo* (Berkeley: University of California Press, 1967), 159.

[27]Brian Stock, Augustine the Reader: Meditation, Self-Knowledge, and the Ethics of Interpretation (Cambridge, MA: Harvard University Press, 1996), 90.

[28]Thomas J. Heffernan, *Sacred Biography: Saints and Their Biographers in the Middle Ages* (Oxford: Oxford University Press, 1988), 186.

[29]I thank Janet Martin for this insight. See my "Metamorphoses of the Self: Christine de Pizan, and Perpetua," *Sur le chemin de longue étude: Actes du colloque d'Orléans, juillet 1995, Etudes chrétiennes*, 3 [Paris: Champion, 1998], 159-81. Since the names of Perpetua and Felicity had figured in the Roman canon as early as the fourth century, Christine would have been reminded of her story each time she went to mass. Given that in the early fifteenth century it was still general practice to read and discuss Latin saints' lives in a variety of church settings (Heffernan, *Sacred Biography*, 214), Christine may have heard a reader of Perpetua's story in addition to or in place of having access to a copy of a manuscript of the *Passio*. Latin saints' lives were read aloud from a lectionary or sung on occasion in a liturgical or semi-liturgical setting, commonly in the Liturgy of the Hours or in the refectory or chapter, sometimes even in the mass itself (Evelyn Birge Vitz, "From the Oral to the Written in Medieval and Renaissance Saints' Lives," *Images of Sainthood in Medieval Europe*, ed. Renate Blumenfeld-Kosinski and Timea Szell [Ithaca and London: Cornell University Press], 97-115 at p. 99).

[30]Elizabeth Alvida Petroff, *Medieval Women's Visionary Literature* (Oxford: Oxford University Press, 1986), 15, 27.

[31]Peter Dronke, *Women Writers of the Middle Ages: A Critical Study of Texts from Perpetua (†203) to Marguerite Porete (†1310)* (Cambridge: Cambridge

University Press, 1984), 4. Dronke bases his translation on the standard edition of Cornelius Joannes Maria Joseph Van Beek, 2 vols. (Nijmegen: Dekker and Van de Vegt, 1936). Besides Dronke's short but informative discussion, other important studies of Perpetua's story include Brent Shaw, "The Passion of Perpetua," *Past and Present* (139), 3-45, and the recent book by Joyce E. Salisbury, *Perpetua's Passion: The Death and Memory of a Young Woman* (New York: Routledge, 1997). See Van Beek's introduction to vol. 1 for information on the manuscript diffusion of the *Passio*. There are nine surviving manuscripts of the Latin work dating from the twelfth century or earlier. In particular, the provenance of the tenth-century MS Paris, Bibliothèque Nationale de France, lat. 17626 has been localized to the monastery of Saint Cornelius in Compiègne, a town just north of Paris. After the *Passio* had circulated for a time on its own, writers began to rework the story. A shortened version of Perpetua's life was readily available in the *Acta minora*, a collection of saints' lives that enjoyed a wide diffusion in France during Christine's lifetime.

[32]Margaret R. Miles, *Carnal Knowing: Female Nakedness and Religious Meaning in the Christian West* (Boston: Beacon Press, 1989), 53-63. See Salisbury, *Perpetua's Passion*, 108-09, for hypotheses concerning Perpetua's sense of her own transformation.

[33]In *Langue, texte, enigme* (Paris: Seuil, 1975), Paul Zumthor, citing the case of Christine de Pizan among others, contends that whereas the "I" first represented a fluid and changeable entity capable of being adopted by many subjects, it tended to be identified with the person of the author in the fifteenth century (167). In his *History of Autobiography in Antiquity*, 2 vols. (Cambridge, MA: Harvard University Press, 1951), Georg Misch points to the existence of much earlier models; in particular he stresses the importance of the *Confessions* for the conception of first-person writing in the Middle Ages.

[34]Dronke, *Women Writers*, 4. On comparisons between Perpetua's first-person account and the third-person narrative of the male hagiographer who recounts her actual death in the arena, see my "Metamorphoses of the Self," 166.

[35]"I would have thrown myself into the sea [...] but I was held back by my household," *Fortune's Transformation*, 1.12, 105.

[36]Heffernan, *Sacred Biography*, 193.

[37]Shaw, "Perpetua's Passion," 45.

[38]Shaw, "Perpetua's Passion," 33.

[39]Shaw, "Perpetua's Passion," 4-6.

[40]See Helen Solterer, *The Master and Minerva: Disputing Women in French Medieval Culture* (Berkeley: University of California Press, 1995), 151-75, on Christine's writing, which Solterer characterizes as combining "Minervan wisdom and Roman eloquence," 175.

[41]Riffaterre, "L'intertexte inconnu," 5.

[42]*The Book of the City of Ladies*, tr. Earl Jeffrey Richards (N.Y.: Persea Books, 1982), I.1.2, 5.

[43]See Mary Anne C. Case, "Christine de Pizan and the Authority of Experience," *Christine de Pizan and the Categories of Difference*, ed. Marilynn Desmond (Minneapolis: University of Minnesota Press, 1998), 71-88. Case, a law professor at the University of Virginia, discusses Christine's views in light of modern legal terminology: "[...] Christine presages the 'sameness' feminism of the legal academy by arguing on behalf of the exceptional woman who succeeds in traditionally male fields of endeavor and by insisting that differences between the sexes, apart from those directly connected to reproductive physiology, are the product of education and custom, not of nature [...] Finally, in her use of narrative and personal experience to give voice to oppressed women, Christine may be one of the earliest proponents of what has come to be called outsider jurisprudence. Christine realized that what critical race theorist Mari Matsuda has called an 'outsider' perspective is just as importantly an 'insider' perspective--a characteristic of subordinated groups is that they are spoken about, described, and defined by 'outside experts' from the dominant group; the 'inside story' from a member of the group discussed can thus be a powerful corrective to the authority of these experts...(71).

[44]Judith Butler, *Gender Trouble; Feminism and the Subversion of Identity* (New York: Routledge, 1990), 136. For Butler, all gender is performative; it is constructed by means of discourse and bodily signs.

[45]Another illustration of the notion of gender as performance is found in the story of Iphis. The Roman goddess of marriage Vesta gives Iphis a man's body so that she can consummate her union with a woman: "Vesta, who undid her woman's body and made her a son" (*Fortune's Transformation*, 1.11.,104). Like Christine-protagonist, Iphis receives the male body that corresponds to her performance as a man. In light of Christine's declaration that metaphorical language can be truthful ("And it is not a lie or a fable to speak according to metaphor which does not exclude truth," *Fortune's Transformation*, 1.11, 102), the gender change of Christine-protagonist and Iphis imply that performance can supercede innate characteristics in the determination of gender.

[46]In basing her attack on antifeminism on what she knows personally about women's moral character, Christine was ascribing to Aristotle's view that experience was a reliable means of gaining knowledge. For a more extended discussion of Christine's borrowings from Aristotle's concept of experience, see Lori J. Walters, "Boethius and the Triple Ending of the *Cent Balades*," *French Studies*, 50 (April 1996), 1-9.

[47]The City of Ladies, I.2.2, 6.

[48]Renate Blumenfeld-Kosinski, "Christine de Pizan and the Misogynistic Tradition," *The Selected Writings*, 311; rpt. *Romanic Review* 81 (1990).

[49]See Barbara Newman, *From Virile Woman to Woman Christ* (Philadelphia: University of Pennsylvania Press, 1995) on the importance of the notion of the "strong woman" in medieval religious and literary thought.

[50]See Dulac, "Un mythe didactique."

[51]Christine asks if the warrior Joan is not something "beyond nature" in stanza 35; see *The Selected Writings*, 258.

[52]In the *Avision*, Christine-narrator represents her transformation into a man as time spent as a captain of a ship lost in a storm without a master (III, 6), and in *Le Trésor de la Cité des Dames* she tells widows that they should be prepared to take on the heart of a man (III, 4).

[53]Although Perpetua is not mentioned *per se*, memories of Perpetua are certainly not absent from *The City of Ladies*, a work that abounds in examples of female heroism. The third and final section is devoted entirely to female saints' lives. We can perhaps explain the lack of a portrait of Perpetua in *City* III by noting that her life does not figure in the *Miroir historial*, Jean de Vignay's vernacular adaptation of Vincent de Beauvais's *Speculum historial*, Christine's source for all the saints' lives in that section. Perpetua, however, *is* closely related to several saints — Christine, Felicity, and Blandina — whose portraits Christine does include. Although many parallels exist between Saints Perpetua and Christine, for example, Saint Christine better suits the author's purpose in that work, since her name has an obvious onomastic link with Christ's and it designates her as Christine's patron saint. See Walters, "Metamorphoses of the Self," 178.

[54]Salisbury, *Perpetua's Passion*, 178: "Sometimes Perpetua's words were refracted through a lens of gender that caused male writers like Augustine to add to the text meanings that had nothing to do with the intelligent, passionate young Roman matron." Shaw, "The Passion," 45: "From the very start [the story] was buried under an avalanche of male interpretations, rereadings, and distortions." Miles, *Carnal Knowing*, 62: "The *Martyrdom of Saints Perpetua and Felicitas* is an unusually vivid example of the appropriation of a woman's writing as support for theological and ecclesiastical concerns that her text does not acknowledge as her own." For a discussion of Augustine's distortion of the meaning of Perpetua's gender change in his *De natura*, see Walters, "Metamorphoses of the Self," 175-76.

[55]Augustine's statement concerning Perpetua's popularity, discussed above, suggests that he attempted to contain or limit her authority because it posed a threat to his own. See Walters, "Metamorphoses of the Self," 174-76, and Salisbury, *Perpetua's Passion*, 171-79. In this regard it is interesting to note that in the *Confessions* Augustine never mentions his sister named Perpetua who entered the religious life.

[56]For ways that Christine establishes her relation to her patron saint Christine, see Kevin Brownlee, "Martyrdom and the Female Voice: Saint Christine in the *Cité*

des Dames," *Images of Sainthood in Medieval Europe*, ed. Renate Blumenfeld-Kosinski and Timea Szell (Ithaca: Cornell University Press, 1991), 115-35.

Florida State University

The York/Towneley Harrowing of Hell?

Michelle M. Butler

It is commonly recognized that several plays (with slight variations) appear in both the York and Towneley cycles. As Peter Meredith says, it has been known "since Lucy Toulmin Smith's edition of the *York Plays* in 1885" that "five of the Towneley pageants are closely related to the parallel pageants in York."[1] Meredith also notes that later studies of these parallel pageants have recognized that the plays are not as identical as Smith suggests. However, while scholars have long acknowledged generally that parallel plays in York and Towneley contain variations, the York and Towneley plays of the *Harrowing of Hell* have consistently been treated as if they are essentially the same.[2] While the York and Towneley *Harrowing of Hell* plays are textually similar, an analysis of the differences between them, particularly the use of battle-imagery and role of the character David, shows that these plays are distinct. The Towneley *Harrowing of Hell* seeks to representationally reconcile Christ's forcible overcoming of hell with the other aspects of his nature, which creates dramatic conflict that is not present in the York play.[3] The plays are thus quite different and should be dealt with separately. Furthermore, this finding that the York and Towneley *Harrowing of Hell* plays are distinct suggests that scholars of medieval drama should feel confident in approaching our texts with attention to the particular wording and phrasing, a methodology frequently employed by scholars of later drama but avoided by medieval drama scholars because of the problematic nature of the surviving manuscripts.

Both the York and Towneley *Harrowing of Hell* plays are considerably more interested in the battle-like elements of the harrowing than either N-town or Chester.[4] In N-town, the assault on the gates of hell takes only 15 lines. Christ calls (25-32), and the devils capitulate immediately (33-40). In Chester, one devil offers Christ some resistance (157-160), but most of the fifty-one lines of the assault consist of Satan declaring himself beaten. In Towneley and York, the assault lasts much longer, and the devils are defiant. In Towneley, Belzabub calls for the gates to be shut and watches set (125-126); Belial performs the same duty in York (139-140). In both plays David has two speeches which emphasize the battle-like aspects of the harrowing. In both Towneley and York, Satan orders that the devils should get their weapons and be ready to strike Christ down (T: 185-8; Y: 177-80), and is answered that he should try to do so himself (T: 225-228; Y: 205-208). Finally, in both plays Satan resolves to deal with the problem personally, and calls for his armor (T: 231-2; Y: 211-12).

While both the York and Towneley *Harrowing of Hell* plays evince more interest in the battle aspects of the harrowing than do either N-town or Chester, Towneley emphasizes this motif more than does York. In Towneley, Christ declares that he will go to hell to "chalange that is myne" (9-10). The *Middle English Dictionary* defines this use of "chalange" as: "To lay claim to (sth.); claim as one's due, right, privilege, or property; heritage, lordship, etc.; of right, have to right to claim."[5] Christ is claiming the souls in Limbo as his own. Moreover, the word "chalange" is used elsewhere in Middle English to mean "demand."[6] In York, Christ says he simply needs to go "unbynde" the souls (8). No claim seems required. The souls have already been bought, and all that remains is for Christ to "unbynde" them.

The treatment of Satan in the Towneley *Harrowing of Hell* also serves to draw attention to the idea of the harrowing as a battle. Satan's appearance is delayed in Towneley. His original absence heightens the perception that when he finally does come to deal with the problem personally, there will be battle between him and Christ. Satan shouts orders, but isn't actually present until after the gates of hell break. While David Bevington suggests that Satan joins the other devils at line 147, later lines indicate otherwise.[7] At line 149, Satan says, "And me, if I com nar,/Thy brain bot I brist owte!" Satan cannot yet be present if he is threatening that he will join the other devils only in order to beat Belzabub's brains out. A more logical point for his arrival is line 231-2, when he orders, "Loke in haste my gere be grayd/Myself shall to that gadling go." In contrast, in the York play, Satan is present from the beginning of the assault. It is he who answers Christ's first call for the gates of hell to open. Towneley gives this duty to Rybald. Cawley and Stevens agree that Satan's appearance is delayed in Towneley, but that he is present in York from the beginning of the assault: "Satan, in the Towneley version, makes his first appearance only after all the other devils have been unable to contain Christ; in York, he is the first to respond to Christ's challenge at the gates (37/125)."[8] Satan's delayed appearance in Towneley creates tension, and when he finally does come, after having called for his armor, we expect that Satan will try to fight Christ.

The warlike elements of the harrowing are likewise emphasized in Towneley in its treatment of the binding of Satan in hell. In York, Christ calls for Michael, who binds Satan:

> Mighill myne aungell, make þe boune,
> And feste yone fende, þat he noght flitte.
> And, Deuyll, I comaunde þe go doune,
> Into thy selle where þou schalte sitte. (339-42)

The Towneley Christ handles the situation without angelic assistance: "Devill, I commaunde the[e] to go downe / Into thy sete where thou shall sit!" (367-8).

Towneley stresses the warlike aspects of the harrowing by heightening the confrontation between Christ and Satan, and showing Christ amply powerful enough to handle the situation. Michael is not there. Christ alone harrows hell and binds Satan.

The Towneley *Harrowing of Hell* emphasizes the warlike aspects of the harrowing as well by having the devils describe their situation as "besieged." Belzabub calls to Satan, "Thou must com help to spar;/We ar beseged abowte" (151-2) and Satan replies, "Besegyd aboute! Whi, who durst be so bold/For drede to make on vs afray? (153-4)." 'Besieged' is a term which clearly has warlike connotations. These lines have no parallel in York.

The assault on the gates receives more attention in Towneley than in York, which also draws attention to the concept of the harrowing as battle. In York, Christ twice orders that the gates be opened (121-124; 181-184). In Towneley, Christ calls three times. His third demand is striking:

> Ye princes of hell, open youre yate
> And let my folk furth gone!
> A prince of peasse shall enter therat,
> Wheder ye will or none. (197-200)

Christ's speech clearly characterizes the harrowing as battle-like; he is coming into hell whether the devils want him to or not. Furthermore, this speech would call considerable attention to itself when performed. The Towneley Christ's two previous demands for hell to open up are in Latin. This speech is in English. The York Christ's two demands are a mixture of Latin and English. This third demand, for which no parallel exists in York, emphasizes the battle-like elements of the harrowing, which is enhanced by the striking shift in language.

Nor is there a parallel in York for thc lines which follow Christ's third demand in the Towneley play, in which Rybald and Belzabub declare their defiance and their faith in hell's defenses. Christ declares that he is coming in. Rybald replies, "What art thou that spekys so?" (201). Christ answers, "A king of blis that hight Jhesus" (202). Rybald responses, "Yee, hens fast I red thou go, / And mell the not with us!" (203-4), and Belzabub says, "Oure yates I trow will last, / Thay ar so strong, I weyn; / Bot if oure barres brast, / For they shall not twyn (205-8)." Rybald and Belzabub's expressing their confidence in hell's gates, and Rybald's "advice" to Christ not to fight with them, emphasize the warlike aspects of the harrowing. In York, the devils, at the last moment before the gates burst, do not express continued confidence in hell's strength.

The Towneley *Harrowing of Hell* emphasizes the warlike elements of the harrowing considerably more than do any of the other Corpus Christi cycles' *Harrowing of Hell* plays, including York, to which the Towneley version is generally considered to be virtually identical. This emphasis on the motif of battle in the harrowing concentrates attention on Christ's forcible overcoming of hell, and raises the question of whether Christ misuses his power, which becomes the dramatic conflict of the play. The dramatic conflict in Towneley is thus summed up neatly in Christ's lines:

> Ye princes of hell, open youre yate
> And let my folk furth gone!
> A prince of peasse shall enter therat,
> Wheder ye will or none. (197-200)

The York *Harrowing of Hell* does not contain these lines; they have been added in the rewriting of York into Towneley, and underscore the Towneley *Harrowing of Hell's* concern with Christ's forcible entry into hell.

In considering this question of Christ's use of his power to remove the souls from Limbo, the Towneley *Harrowing of Hell* associates the character David with the warlike elements of the harrowing, establishes David as a symbol for Christ's power in battle, and uses David to reconcile the dramatic conflict. David is associated with the battle imagery in three ways. First, the placement of David within the action of the play suggests that David is to be associated with Christ's warlike power. The Towneley *Harrowing of Hell* breaks logically into five sections. The first is Christ's opening speech in which he declares his intention to go to hell and "chalange that is myne." This first scene runs from lines 1 to 24. The second section (25-88) consists of souls in Limbo relating their prophecies which foretold the light that they now see, and the souls anticipate their coming redemption from hell. A third section begins with the appearance of Rybald (89) and lasts until after the gates fall and Satan himself comes up to take on Christ (232). The debate between Satan and Christ is the fourth 'scene,' lines 233 to 372, ending with the binding of Satan. In the fifth and last section, Christ greets the souls in Limbo and they express their joy to see him (373-415). The battle imagery is concentrated in section 3. Not all of the battle imagery occurs between lines 89-232--Jesus declares his intent to "chalange" in his opening speech (10), and the devil is bound at the end of his debate with Jesus (370)--but the bulk of the warlike language occurs within this middle section. This is not surprising since the major action of the third scene is the actual assault on and breaking of the gates of hell. What is interesting, though, is that the character David also has his major action in the third section. Two of his three speeches occur within this section. It is not odd to find Christ and the devils associated with the battle aspects of the harrowing. However, David is not a necessary or obvious participant in this fight, although David's history does make him an ideal candidate to be a spokesman for warlike power. David himself is warlike: the boy-slayer of Goliath, and king of Israel, whose throne the Christ was said to be coming to reestablish. David acting as a symbol for Christ's warlike power is a more much natural connection than someone like Isaiah or John the Baptist, who are also waiting in Limbo. David's presence, then, in the section of the play in which is concentrated most of the heightened battle imagery, is of interest. Moreover, his speeches occur during the heat of the assault, and follow closely upon calls from Christ for the gates to open. That the bulk of David's activity occurs here suggests that he is to be closely associated with the action of this section, the assault, and thus the battle-aspects of the harrowing.

David is also linked to the motif of battle in the harrowing because his speeches are war-like, declaring how fierce and mighty Christ is. David says that Christ is "king and conqueroure" (134), and "full fers in fight" (139). David tells the devils that Christ is coming to "breke / Youre barres and bandys by name, / And of your warkys take wreke" (193-5). David's words emphasize Christ's warlike power, and David's commentary on it links him with Christ's might.

Third, David is associated with the battle imagery and Christ's warlike power by his isolation from the other patriarchs. In the second section of the Towneley Harrowing of Hell, six souls in Limbo — Adam, Eve, Isaiah, Simeon, John the Baptist, and Moses — discuss the hope of salvation which the light gives them. We should notice that David does not speak with them. He must be on stage: he is in Limbo, just as the other souls are. However, they speak, and he does not. This silence is certainly not for lack of something to say. Psalms 24 and 107 are generally taken as referring to hell. Since David was considered to be the author of all the psalms, he could have been given one of those psalms to declare as his prophecy of the harrowing. Yet he is silent, and that silence draws attention to him.

Moreover, we should note that there are *seven* souls in Limbo. At the beginning of the Towneley *Harrowing of Hell,* the perfect number of patriarchs is disrupted. David does not speak with the other patriarchs. In section three, when David does speak, the others are silent. The play does not initially encourage us to group David with the other patriarchs. David instead becomes associated with the battlelike aspects of the harrowing in section three, in which he does participate.

David's association with the heightened battle imagery in the Towneley *Harrowing of Hell* serves to resolve its dramatic conflict. David is used to show the reconciliation of Christ's warlike nature with his other aspects. He becomes a symbol for Christ's power, exerted in forcibly removing the souls from Limbo. When, at the end of the play, David expresses his gratitude to Christ with the other patriarchs, he has been reintegrated into their number. Thus, symbolically, Christ's power is reconciled with the rest of his nature, as David, serving as representation of that power, is reconciled into the group.

Having established that the Towneley *Harrowing of Hell* contains dramatic conflict, it remains to show why this argument does not also hold for the York play. As shown above, the York *Harrowing of Hell* contains less battle imagery than Towneley, and thus does not use an emphasis on such imagery to set up dramatic conflict around the question of Christ's power. There are other reasons as well why the dramatic conflict is not present in York.

First, Christ's opening speech in York suppresses any dramatic conflict. In both Towneley and York, Christ declares his intention to foray into hell. He says he will send a light before him, so that the souls in Limbo know he is coming, and that his body will remain in its grave until he is finished. At this point, the Towneley Christ's speech ends. However, in York, he continues:

> My fadir ordand on þis wise
> Aftir his will þat I schulde wende,
> For to fulfille þe prophicyes,
> And als I spake my solace to spende.
> My frendis þat in me faith affies,
> Nowe fro ther fois I schall þame fende,
> And on the thirde day ryght vprise,
> And so tille heuen I schall assende.
> Sithen schall I come agayne
> To deme bothe goode and ill,
> Tille endles joie or peyne
> Thus is my fadris will. (25-36)

The audience would of course already be familiar with what was going to happen, but with Christ explicitly reminding everyone how the story ends — the harrowing and the cosmic story both — dramatic conflict is difficult to maintain. Moreover, the harrowing clearly becomes in York merely a step in God's overall plan for mankind, a point which is not brought up in Towneley. Davidson's suggestion that the *Harrowing* represents only a mock battle seems apt.[9]

Secondly, the York *Harrowing of Hell* does not contain the dramatic conflict found in the Towneley play because David's speeches function quite differently in York. The texts are similar, but the contexts are very different.

In Towneley, David volunteers his first speech. Christ calls *Attollite portas* for the first time. Belzabub orders Rybald to "Go spar the yates" (125) and tells Rybald that if Christ again orders for hell to open up, he (Rybald) should strike him (Christ) soundly and make him continue on his way. David's speech is a response to this impertinent command of Belzabub:

> Nay, with hym may ye not fyght,
> For he is kyng and conqueroure,
> And of so mekill myght
> And styf in euery stoure.
> Of hym commys all this light
> That shynys is this bowre.
> He is full fers in fight,
> Worthi to wyn honoure. (133-40)

In the Towneley *Harrowing of Hell,* David interjects himself to assert Christ's fierceness and the futility of fighting with him. However, in the York play, David speaks in response to a question. Satan asks:

> What page is þere þat makes prees,
> And callis hym king of vs in fere? (125-6)

And David replies:

> I lered leuand, withouten lees,
> He is kyng of vertues clere.
> A lorde mekill of myght,
> And stronge in ilke a stoure,
> In batailes ferse to fight,
> And worthy to wynne honnoure. (127-32)

In York, David's answer bears witness to Christ's power, but the impetus of the speech is to answer the question. 'Who is he?' Satan asks. "He is a kyng of vertues clere," David replies. In Towneley, the very similar words of the speech are given a stronger opening statement ("Nay, with hym may ye not fyght" [133]) and become not an answer of who Christ is, but a rather defiant proclamation by David of Christ's might.

Likewise, the text of David's second speech is nearly identical in both plays. In both Towneley and York, David responds to the same question. In Towneley, Rybald asks, "Outt, harrow! What harlot is he / That sayes his kingdam shal be cryde?" (189-90). In York, Satan says, "Owte, harrowe! What harlot is hee / ∂at sais his kyngdome schall be cryed? (185-86). We could hardly ask for a closer parallel between the two plays. David's answer is also the same in both. In Towneley, he says:

> That may thou in sawter se,
> For of this prince thus ere I saide:
> I saide that he shuld breke
> Youre barres and bandys by name,
> And of youre warkys take wreke;
> Now shall thou se the same. (191-96)

And in York:

> That may þou in my Sawter see
> For þat poynte I prophicied.
> I saide þat he schuld breke
> Youre barres and bandis by name,
> And on youre werkis take wreke,
> Nowe schalle ye see þe same. (187-92)

The only textual difference between the Towneley and York versions of David's second speech is one line. Towneley changes the position of the second line to "For of this prince thus ere I saide" (192). However, the position of these two speeches in their plays is not identical.

As shown above, the Towneley *Harrowing of Hell* emphasizes the warlike elements of the harrowing more than does the York play. Many of these differences occur around Christ's assault on the gates of hell. The assault lasts significantly longer in Towneley than in York. In Towneley, between David's first speech and his second, the devils characterize their situation as "besieged." As discussed above, these lines have no parallel in York. In York, immediately after David's second speech, Christ calls for the final time and the gates fall. In Towneley, more diabolic defiance follows David's second speech, as well as another instance of Christ demanding for the gates to open.

This extra emphasis in Towneley on the assault on the gates of hell makes the assault a moment of higher tension in Towneley than in York. David's second speech, while textually similar to its analog in York, functions within the context of this moment of higher tension. In York, David's second speech does not participate in a such a heightened moment of tension around the gates' final breech. In York, David's second speech occurs just before the gates fall and functions mostly to clue the audience that the break is imminent. In Towneley, David's speech helps to extend and extenuate the tension of the assault, and thus the dramatic conflict of the play.

Finally, the York *Harrowing of Hell* does not achieve dramatic conflict as does the Towneley play because the reintegration of David with the other patriarchs is not emphasized. In York, the reference to David comes in the middle of a speech by John the Baptist (line 369 of speech 361-372). In Towneley, the same speech is split between John the Baptist and Moses. Moses' begins with the reference to David, emphasizing it much more than does its position in York (John: 389-96; Moses: 397-400).

David's final speech follows, expressing his gratitude to Christ as do the speeches of other freed souls. As with his second speech, his third speech is textually very similar to that in York. In Towneley David says:

> As I saide ere, yit say I so:
> *"Ne derelinquas, domine,*
> *Animam meam in inferno"*
> "Leyfe never my saull, Lord, after the[e],
> In depe hell wheder dampned shall go;
> Suffre thou never thy saintys to see
> The sorow of thaym that won in wo,
> Ay full of filth, and may not fle. (401-8)

In York, David says:

> Als I haue saide, yitt saie I soo,
> *Ne derelinquas, domine,*
> *Animam meam in inferno,*
> Leffe noght my saule, lorde, aftir þe,
> In depe helle where dampned schall goo,
> Ne suffre neuere saules fro þe be,
> The sorowe of þame þat wonnes in woo
> Ay full of filthe, þat may repleye. (373-380)

Again we see that David could have spoken with the other patriarchs at the beginning; he has a prophecy he could have recited. While the final words that David speaks are nearly the same in both plays, they do not function in the same way. In York, David's final speech is simply another soul's expression of gratitude. In Towneley, the same words, being spoken when and by whom they are, symbolize that Christ's warlike power is indeed reconciled. David, once isolated from the other souls, has been reintegrated with them. Symbolically, Christ's power is reconciled with the rest of his nature, as David, serving as representation of that power, is reconciled into the group. The context of David's speeches in Towneley's *Harrowing of Hell* evokes a very different meaning than the parallel speeches in York.

Thus the Towneley *Harrowing of Hell* contains dramatic conflict, whereas the York play does not. The Towneley *Harrowing of Hell* has dramatic conflict pertaining to whether Christ's forcible overcoming of hell is a misuse of his power; it is concerned with the seeming paradox of a "prince of peasse" who "shall enter therat, / Wheder ye will or none" (197-200). The play uses David, as a representative of Christ's warlike power, to symbolize the reconciliation of this power with the rest of Christ's nature. With dramatic conflict present in Towneley, and absent from York, a crucial difference exists between the two texts. We must therefore call into question critical stances which treat the Towneley and York *Harrowing of Hell* plays as equivalent texts. The Towneley and York plays of the *Harrowing of Hell* make meaning very differently, and should be treated as separate texts.

Moreover, the significant differences in meaning created by these seemingly small differences between the Towneley and York *Harrowing of Hell* plays suggest that medieval drama scholars will find it fruitful to apply similar methodologies elsewhere. Because of the problematic nature of surviving medieval dramatic manuscripts, we are frequently hesitant to examine closely the phrasing and wording of medieval drama. However, this study of the Towneley and York *Harrowing of Hell* plays indicates that such careful consideration is warranted. Scholars of later drama do not hold back from examining the text of *King Lear* or *Dr. Faustus* as carefully chosen and deliberately crafted simply because of the well-known textual difficulties with these works. Scholars of medieval drama should feel confident that the authors of medieval drama were as conscientious about their work as their successors, and give their work the detailed consideration that it deserves.

Notes

1. Peter Meredith, "The Towneley Cycle," in *The Cambridge Guide to Medieval English Theatre*, ed. Richard Beadle (Cambridge: Cambridge University Press, 1994), 145.

2. For example: V. A. Kolve states, "the Towneley play is borrowed, with only minor changes, from York" (*The Play Called Corpus Christi*, [Stanford: Stanford University Press, 1966], 196). Clifford Davidson, as is implied by the title of his article, treats the two as interchangeable: "From *Tristitia* to *Gaudium:* Iconography and the York-Towneley *Harrowing of Hell*," *American Benedictine Review* 28 (1977), 260-75. Richard Beadle, in his notes on the *Harrowing of Hell* in his edition of the *York Plays* says that "[a]nother copy of this play exists in the Towneley manuscript, and its readings (*T* in the Textual Notes) occasionally assist with difficulties in the York text. The two copies are substantially the same" (*The York Plays*, [London: Edward Arnold, 1982], 452). Harry S. Anderson and Leanore Lieblein ask, "How is it that essentially the same basic text could serve at both York and Wakefield where, it seems, the plays were staged quite differently?" ("Staging Symbolic Action in the Medieval Cycle Drama: The York/Towneley *Harrowing of Hell*," *Fifteenth-Century Studies* 13 [1988], 211). Martin Stevens

and A.C. Cawley say, "While the Towneley editor added or replaced some 100 lines of the extant play, the remaining lines, approximately three quarters of the play, have the same or very similar phrasing as the York version" (*The Towneley Plays,* 2 vols. [Oxford: EETS, 1994], 591). Chester G. Curtiss recognizes that the Towneley text has significant differences from the York text, but seems to suggest that these revisions spice up "dull scenes" and downplay the didacticism; Towneley is York modified, not its own play ("The York and Towneley Plays of *The Harrowing of Hell,*" *Studies in Philology* 30 [1933], 24-33). Mendal G. Frampton likewise acknowledges that variations exist but not that Towneley is therefore necessarily a separate play ("The Towneley *Harrowing of Hell,*" *PMLA* 56 [1941], 105-119). Finally, Peter Meredith's "The Iconography of Hell in the English Cycles: A Practical Perspective" refers to the "York-Towneley" Harrowing of Hell episode as it they were one play (in *The Iconography of Hell,* ed. Clifford Davidson and Thomas H. Seiler. [Kalamazoo: Medieval Institute Publications, 1992], 158-86).

3. There is scholarly disagreement as to whether the "York/Towneley" *Harrowing of Hell* contains dramatic conflict. In his article "From *Tristitia* to *Gaudium:* Iconography and the York-Towneley *Harrowing of Hell,*" Clifford Davidson asserts that there is no real dramatic conflict in the *Harrowing of Hell* plays of York and Wakefield. Davidson says, "The battle indeed has already taken place, and thus here there is no real 'contest between light and darkness.' All that remains in the harrowing episode is a mock battle and ceremonious rescue of souls" (263). Christ has already undergone the real battle, the Crucifixion, and thus "when Christ, having won the victory on the cross, arrives at the gates of hell, no great struggle is forthcoming" (265-266). On the other hand, Martin Stevens and A. C. Cawley, in their notes to the new EETS edition of the Towneley plays, claim that both the York and Towneley plays of the *Harrowing of Hell* "add dramatic suspense to the harrowing by adopting the 'Abuse of Power' theory in developing the plot" (592). The confusion here probably arises from the propensity to conflate these two plays.

4. Quotations from the York, Towneley, Chester, and N-town Cycles are from the following editions, and are cited in parentheses in the text according to the following abbreviations. When line numbers are sufficient, no abbreviation is given in the text:

T: Martin Stevens and A. C. Cawley, *The Towneley Plays.* 2 vols. (Oxford: EETS, 1994).

Y: Richard Beadle, *The York Plays* (London: Edward Arnold, 1982).

C: R.M. Lumiansky and David Mills, *The Chester Mystery Cycle,* 2 vols. (Oxford: EETS, 1974).

N: Stephen Spector, *The N-Town Play,* 2 vols. (Oxford: EETS, 1991).

5. *Middle English Dictionary.* (Ann Arbor: University of Michigan Press, 1952), Volume C. 146.

6. Middle English Dictionary, Volume C. 146

[7] Editorial stage direction. David Bevington, *Medieval Drama* (Boston: Houghton Mifflin, 1975), 599.

[8] Martin Stevens and A. C. Cawley, *The Towneley Plays*, 592.

[9] Clifford Davidson, "From *Tristitia* to *Gaudium*: Iconography and the York-Towneley *Harrowing of Hell*," 263.

Duquesne University

When the World was Half a Thousand Years Younger: Color and Concept in Johan Huizinga's Autumn of the Middle Ages

David Pickus

One of the twentieth century's best-known historical works, Johan Huizinga's *The Autumn of the Middle Ages* begins with an opening line that could start the pages of a novel: "when the world was half a thousand years younger all events had sharper outlines than now."[1] Huizinga first composed his *Herfsttij der Middeleeuwen* in 1919. Yet despite the attention it has received, and the praise it has garnered, there is something elusive about the book's message. What does it mean for events of the fifteenth century to have sharper outlines than those of the twentieth century? The very idea of "outlines" itself is enigmatic. Considered from this standpoint, there is something unusual about the fact that this opaque work is one of *the* books through which non-specialists (undergraduates particularly) are introduced to the era. Moreover, there are even two different versions available to the English speaking reader, *The Waning of the Middle Ages* (1924) and a new translation, *The Autumn of the Middle Ages* (1996). But despite or because of Huizinga's popularity, it is in no sense easy to determine what he meant to tell us about the world of half a millennium before.

The following essay will attempt an assessment of *The Autumn of the Middle Ages* by exploring some of the achievements and ambiguities of that classic. I will not try to pass judgment on the accuracy and validity of Huizinga's use of sources. Nor will I try to decide if the book is or is not appropriate for beginning students. Most of these points have been covered by Paul L. Ward who, in a trenchant essay, drew attention to some of the inconsistencies in Huizinga's overall scheme, and found more value in it as an "impressionistic background study,"[2] than a basic historical statement. Yet the question of what impressions Huizinga cultivated remains, and my goal is to consider Huizinga as a twentieth-century thinker who approached the fifteenth century within the context of a specific, but complex, intellectual milieu.

I begin with the idea that there is a connection between the way Huizinga told his story and the meaning he derived from it. The thesis I shall argue is that Huizinga's work has not grown obsolete — and is not likely to despite both new research and its own difficulties — because its author succeeded in forging a link between the cultural moods of the twentieth century and that of five hundred years before. The nature of this link is complex and is best explicated by showing what Huizinga did when he depicted the forms or "colors" of culture. In particular, I want to show that Huizinga used his study of the late Middle Ages to unite disparate but powerful sensibilities, ones that continue to shape the attitudes of the twentieth century. These are romanticism and modernism. Implicit in Huizinga's argument is a plaintive sense of loss at the wholeness of a culture vanished. This melancholy is the converse to his celebration of the medieval world's devotion to its ideals, and thus his lament at this culture's eventual "failure" is reminiscent of a certain kind of romanticism. At the same time, it is important to bear in mind that Huizinga never expressed this romantic mood unambiguously, nor did he parade it as a message. In fact, he avoided any kind of propagandistic (or didactic) subordination of history to a predetermined ideological end. Instead, Huizinga went very far in eschewing any narrative that creates a single story with a single moral. This, I think, is due to the fact that his "modernist" technique works by juxtaposing powerful images in order to create a montage of moments of historical illumination. Of course, the terms "romantic" and "modernist" are indeed amorphous enough to admit of several definitions, and little is gained by simply attaching labels.[3] Our task, rather, is to understand the specific ways these concepts apply to Huizinga. This application, I argue, helps explain the overall appeal of *The Autumn of the Middle Ages,* as well warning us of some of the dangers of this appeal.

Given the aim of reflecting on the book as whole, I will not try to decide whether Huizinga was right or wrong to write as he did. Undoubtedly, specialists in Franco-Burgundian culture have in Huizinga rich opportunities to debate interpretations of texts and methods. But over and above individual controversies is the larger question of what an imaginative and influential twentieth-century scholar might have sought in examining the close of the Middle Ages. However, this is no easy task, and the best place to begin explicating is to look at some of the reasons why the text is so difficult.

In 1996 the University of Chicago Press brought out what it called "the definitive new translation of Huizinga's masterpiece."[4] The reason a new edition was in order went deeper than the fact that some seventy years had passed since F. Hopman first translated the book from Dutch into English. As co-translator Rodney Payton pointed out in the preface to the new edition, the Hopman edition was a work of "adaptation, consolidation and condensation."[5] Although the preface to the 1924 work has Huizinga's explicit endorsement, Payton and collaborator Ulrich Mammitzsch suggest that Huizinga only gave this consent because he was under pressure from publishers to bring out a popular edition of his work.[6] This is why he agreed to a version that was shorter by approximately a third, having eliminated many quotations and authorial reflections.

Taking their cue from the opinion of the Dutch-born historian Karl Joachim Weintraub, who called the 1924 *Waning of the Middle Ages* a "very inferior, crippled version of the original,"[7] Payton and Mammitzsch set out to present the work in its totality. Their choice of the more literal title, *The Autumn of the Middle Ages,* testifies to their commitment to capture the precise meaning of Huizinga's words. Whether or not they fully succeeded in this difficult task has sparked some debate. For instance, in a highly critical review in *Speculum*, Walter Simon took issue with a number of their choices and concluded that "readers who are familiar with Huizinga's inimitable Dutch are bound to feel a sense of loss."[8] Yet whatever verdict is ultimately reached, the fact that Payton and Mammitzsch endeavored to make all of Huizinga's text accessible to English speaking readers provides an important historical service. Their translation makes it clear that the *Autumn of the Middle Ages* has a broader and different ambition than a typical historical study. Huizinga's book does not take up a circumscribed set of historical questions, but instead aims to make us see the world in a different way. In particular, Huizinga wants us to see two things. First, he wants us to notice the energy which late medieval men and women expended in the attempt to beautify their lives. Second, he wants us to reflect on what it means for this search for beauty to be a cultivation of what he calls an "artful life of play."[9] This cultivation is a participation in dramatic and expressive activity. Its seldom articulated goal is to make an otherwise hostile and unattractive world colored in more inviting shades.

The interpretive difficulties of *The Autumn of the Middle Ages* truly begin once we try to grasp this broader point. For even if there were a complete consensus on the translation, it is difficult to imagine a complete consensus on Huizinga's meaning. It is evident, even to a reader without Dutch, that the book is written in a highly poetic style. It invites diverging responses from individual readers. On top of this is the fact that Huizinga nowhere provides a master explanation as to how he wants his book to be understood. It is true that in the preface to the German edition he said that he chose to study the culture of France and the Netherlands in the fourteenth and fifteenth centuries because in it we can see the end of medieval times, rather than the start of the Renaissance or the modern age.[10] However, his argument does not provide an explicit and straightforward account of why this particular time and place should be seen in this way, nor does he always keep our attention focused on the idea of the era's end. Instead, Huizinga simply presents his findings, organizing chapters around themes like "The Heroic Dream" or "The Vision of Death." These particular themes, flowing past the reader, are what occupy center stage. Furthermore, Huizinga steadfastly refuses to suggest that the mentalities he examines were fully determined and thus neatly "explained" by some prior historical reality, especially class. This undeniably enriches Huizinga's definition of the purpose of culture, yet it also complicates an understanding of his positions. Hence, given the looseness of his structure, it seems fair to conclude that Huizinga is simply not pursuing an explicit argument about the periodization of eras or the relationship between economics and culture. Instead, his historical argument has an artistic plan. What makes him begin his chapters at one point and end them at another is an aesthetic intuition about the proper way the story of the medieval "autumn time" should be told. This intuition is that in describing an "end" one call dwell on particulars as they display themselves and as they seek their ideal goals. Hence, the framework of the waning Middle Ages is introduced to enable Huizinga to focus on significant details for their own sake.

From this perspective of treating a narrative as an end in itself, it appears that Huizinga anticipates what has come to be called a "post-modern" view of historiography in that he suggests that history is a "construct" created by the historian.[11] However, it is important to bear in mind that Huizinga himself, in his essay on the tasks of cultural history, polemicized against any blurring of the distinction between history and literature. In fact, in his own way, he is almost the antipode of the post-modern, since he remained committed to writing history *wie es eigentlich gewesen*. Where he truly differs from his more traditional colleagues is in thinking that this historic actuality lies not in patterns beyond cultural forms, but in the "colors" or expressive moments of culture itself. Thus the logic that takes Huizinga from one page to the next is the necessity of explaining what it means for cultural forms — art, religion, learning, sport, battle, entertainment, etc. — to have characters of their own which cannot be reduced to something other than a pageant of expressive activity.

It is to display these characters that Huizinga asks us to believe a proposition that, if stated in another context, would be open to question. He asserts that half a millennium ago:

> ...all events had sharper outline than now. The distance between sadness and joy, between good and bad fortune, seemed to be much greater than for us; every experience had that degree of directness and absoluteness that joy and sadness still have in the mind of a child. Every event, every deed was defined in given and expressive forms and was in accord with the solemnity of tight, invariable life style.[12]

Consequently, to grasp this world fully, we need an aesthetic sense of empathy:

> We have to transpose ourselves into this impressionability of mind, into this sensitivity to tears and spiritual repentance, into this susceptibility, before we can judge how colorful and intensive life was then.[13]

The poetry of this language makes one reluctant to criticize it. Nevertheless, its propositions are still open to objection. First, it is not only the culture of the fifteenth century that was characterized by such extreme contrasts. Brief consideration of, for instance, classical Athens or tenth-century Japan shows that the notion of the "passionate intensity" of life is equally applicable to a wide variety of cultural milieux. Moreover, the very idea of a world of "sharper outlines" is only true in some respects. For instance, Huizinga may indeed be correct in remarking that, in those times, "sickness contrasted more strongly with health,"[14] but that does not mean that our own age is devoid of moments where the same fundamental difference between contrasting states becomes as poignant — and as desperate — as it ever was.

However, to take these objections as refutations is surely to miss the point. Huizinga is not reporting facts as much as he is alerting us to his program of lifting the veil on those moments where the "colors" of a vanished culture reveal themselves. It is by signaling out these intense, passionate and *contrasting* moments that Huizinga is able to communicate his distinct historical message. Hence, it is in this task of selecting revealing moments that Huizinga is at his strongest, for in the words of Carlo Antoni, "he is a master at correlating episodes, phrases and documents to the end of creating an affective atmosphere in which both individuals and masses are immersed."[15] But this "immersion" only serves to reveal the nature of individuals and masses more clearly. Here, we must turn to the text itself. It is impossible to select the most revealing moments in The *Autumn of the Middle Ages*, as every reader will choose their own. However, it is necessary to provide a specific explanation of how Huizinga presents his detail. These specifics are the best means of explicating Huizinga's overall message, since they show us how he succeeds in capturing the imagination.

Take a few example of moments where our sensual imagination can grasp Huizinga's world. For instance, there is the sound of trumpets and trombones wafting through the night on the eve of the battle of Agincourt. The opposed armies are relying on music to muster their courage and it is reported that the French feel "subdued" because they do not have as many musicians as their foes.[16] Alternately, there is a story of Philip the Good (a man of extravagant festivities and numerous bastards, of political calculation, of tremendous pride and rage"[17]) refusing, out of religious ardor, to rise from prayer, even though his army had just conducted a surprise attack on Luxembourg. When his entourage, riddled with anxiety and impatience at the continuing battle, wanted him to say his Our Fathers another time, "*Si Dieu m'a donné victorie, il la me gardera*,"[18] was the response they received, and one can see the looks on their faces. Indeed, we can "see" throughout, since these are moments whose significance can be grasped without reducing them to an abstract formula. In doing so, Huizinga reminds us of the powerful role of anecdotes in modern historical understanding. Despite, or perhaps because of, the endless flow of historical information, vivid anecdotes do more than embellish comprehension. If presented with the kind of care and finesse which characterizes Huizinga at his best, they become vehicles of understanding itself.

Furthermore, Huizinga's capacity for evoking strong and compelling images is not confined to descriptions of stirring scenes. It can be found in the expression of cultural ideals in learned and everyday life. For instance, the message of the *danse macabre* is well known to students of the Middle Ages, but Huizinga's quotations make even the familiar seem gripping, such as when quotes Death to the Laborer, "Laborer, who in care and toil/Have lived all your time,/You must die, that is certain,/No drawing back, no struggling./Death should make you happy because it frees you from great sorrow."[19] However, it is not only the preoccupation with death that captures Huizinga's eye. In describing the *Roman de la Rose* he not only explains why its opponents could denounce it as a kind of "sensuous mysticism," but why it defenders could be enraptured with this very sensuality.[20] Thus Jean de Gerson, in attacking the *Rose*, had to confront an adversary who said outrageous things:

> He dared to claim that Solomon's high song had been composed to praise Pharaoh's daughter. Those who denounced the book of the *Rose* had bent their knee before Baal since Nature did not intend that one man would be enough for a woman and the genius of nature is God. Verily, he even dares to misuse Luke 2: 23 to prove with the help of the gospel itself that formerly the female sexual organ, the Rose of the novel, had been sacred. And, fully confident in all of these blasphemies, he calls on the defenders of this work, on a number of witnesses, and threatens that Gerson himself will fall victim to an irrational love as had happened to other theologians before him.[21]

Finally, Huizinga has no compunction about reminding us of how easy it was in common culture, as well as learned culture, for the lines between sacred and profane to blur. In describing the carrying of the shrine of St. Liéin to the fair at Houthen, he recounts the lament at the spectacle's degeneration, "they carry it (the shrine) screaming and howling, singing and dancing, mocking everything in sight, and they are all drunk. Moreover, they are armed and indulge themselves in whatever they wish. Everything is at their mercy, given the excuse of their holy burden."[22] In all of these cases, Huizinga makes it clear that the intermingling of personal and religious ideas is too complex to ever be separated by analysis. Individuality is not abolished by explanation. We must visualize these forms against the backdrop of the harshness which serves as their screen.

This goal of avoiding reductive oversimplification clarifies Huizinga's concern with "color." However, this concern explains more of what he does not wish to do than what he wishes to accomplish. The question still remains of what all his particular images add up to; what, if anything, is "behind" them. Antoni's suggestion that *The Autumn of the Middle Ages* "is not a history of ideas, nor even of interests, but of sentiment and feeling"[23] is somewhat misleading in that Huizinga himself did not draw an explicit distinction between idea and sentiment. Rather, in theorizing about cultural history, he laid stress on the activity, not the result, which is clearly defined by means of visualization:

> The cultural historian has abandoned the design of deducing generally valid rules for the knowledge of society from phenomena. He not only sketches the contours of the forms he designs, but colors them by means of intuition and illuminates them with visionary suggestion. Quite apart from any conscious program, the great cultural historians have always been historical morphologists: seekers after the forms of life, thought, custom, art. The more clearly they define those forms the better they succeed.[24]

As a way of summarizing this philosophy, Karl Weintraub noted that Huizinga's "epistemological master-word was *verbeelden*, to take account of the datum of the past by forming an image of it."[25] Simultaneously, Weintraub stressed that this process did more than perceive particulars, "the specific subject of investigation must ever be seen in relation to the whole of cultures."[26] In this respect, we can draw the conclusion that there is nothing behind the images Huizinga presents in the same sense that there is nothing behind the colors of a painting. The meaning lies in the images, but the im ages color the canvas as a whole.

But if the *Autumn of the Middle Ages* is indeed such a "canvas" what do its colors depict? This is the point where it is profitable to return to the notions of modernism and romanticism. It is not only Huizinga's method — with its collage of presented images — that can be called modernist. He takes delight in signaling out moments of vibrant illumination, ones serving as epiphanies of cultural meaning. Yet it is not only modern humanity that seeks such moments. His message is that fifteenth-century culture also cultivated their version of ideal moments. This is the link between twentieth century modernism and Huizinga's Franco-Burgundian culture, and it is worth asking if both epochs were traumatized in ways that required them to develop a culture that seeks out and celebrates moments which must be made ideal. Perhaps, then, the "sharper" contrasts of the world of five hundred years before were only sharper because the pageant is over?

This affinity between late medieval and modern times is further strengthened if we realize that, in Huizinga, seeking celebratory moments is not always finding. Over and again he reminds us how deeply late medieval men and women only *wanted*, but did not fully succeed in beautifying their lives with the richness of their culture. This is where romanticism helps us understand Huizinga. He does more than simply portray this desire to enrich life with its color, he endorses its impetus and laments when the quest fails or falls short. More than his theoretical statements, the time he spends describing the incapacity of medieval culture to beautify life testifies to what he finds most sad in its "autumn" or "waning." This degeneration takes many forms. It comes when religious language loses its concrete and immediate vitality; when chivalric gestures clearly no longer correspond to the realities of politics, and when artists and poets surrender genuine content to the service of stereotyped moods. In saying this, Huizinga is not sentimental. He does not try to make us feel nostalgia for the fifteenth century. However, in a way that deserves to be called romantic, he inculcates a bit of reflective melancholy at a passionate intensity that is no longer there. The distinction between nostalgia and melancholy, therefore, is that nostalgia wishes for bygone days, while this sort of melancholy dwells on its own sense of deprivation. This is a more complex and problematic mood, and a common one in modern culture as well.

Stepping back, and considering all these points together, we can ask where *The Autumn of the Middle Ages* leaves us. Two considerations can serve as final reflections. First, behind the notion that Huizinga shows an affinity of moods between the fifteenth and twentieth centuries is the idea that gestures mean something more than themselves. Huizinga's fifteenth century, therefore, is a mirror for us because, though it expressed its color in different ways and with a different content, both eras consider the cultivation and celebration of peak moments as a necessary good. Moreover, both know they cannot always achieve them, and they also have moments where each recognizes that this search for beautiful sensation degrades more than it ennobles. Hence, the great advantage of Huizinga's work is that by awakening the reader's own love of color (which is nothing less than our implicit acknowledgment of our participation in a culture of peak moments), he enables us to empathize with the passionate intensity of the fifteenth century. This perhaps is the underlying reason why the book remains a "classic." Huizinga speaks to a sensibility that remains important to us.

At the same time, it is clear that the concepts of "color" and intensity" could use more specific elaboration. More investigation is needed as to why Huizinga chose the cultural categories that he did, and how these categories mesh with contemporary research on the late medieval period.[27] Economic and political issues that he treated glancingly cry out for more attention. Furthermore, it should be regretted that Huizinga did not confide more of his agenda to the reader. A writer this idiosyncratic and "impressionistic" helps rather than distracts the reader by explaining how he understands himself in relation to his project. Why, ultimately, did the passionate intensity come to an end? Why did Huizinga himself feel the need to recall it? Indeed (though I do not intend it as a reductive explanation) it is at least worth voicing the suspicion that just as Huizinga's characters created their ideal worlds to fend off all-too-real ones, so too did Huizinga himself use the writing of history to live out an ideal that contrasted against an increasingly empty modernity.

This leads to a final point. Without dwelling upon the pessimism of it, Huizinga always let his reader know that the world of beauty could only cover over, but never replace a world of desperation and pain. As well as being an era of beauty, his "autumn" is a time of ceaseless and destructive wars, as well as all the attendant maladies a suffering world holds. From this perspective, it seems proper to conclude that Huizinga himself was dedicated to the cultivation of moods. Indeed, precisely because they were their own end, these moods served both as an escape from and a pointer to the brutality of his own time. In this context, it is worth remembering that Huizinga wrote his book in the wake of the First World War, and that he himself died, after being brutalized by the Nazis in the Second. As the Keats ode reminds us, colors of autumn may be glorious, but their very fullness, in the end, directs our thoughts toward winter. Huizinga's *Autumn of the Middle Ages* both describes the beauty of this autumnal mood, and calls up some of its sadness as well.

Notes

[1] Johan Huizinga, *The Autumn of the Middle Ages*, trans. Rodney Payton and Ulrich Mammitzsch (Chicago: University of Chicago Press, 1996).

[2] "Huizinga and the Middle Ages" in *Teachers of History: Essays in Honor of Laurence Bradford Packard*, ed. H. Stuart Hughes (Ithaca: Cornell University Press, 1954), 168.

[3] For a clear overview of styles of modernism in relation to contrast and montage see Eugene Lunn, *Marxism and Modernism* (Berkeley: University of California Press, 1982). For a helpful account of the varieties of romanticisms see Arthur O.

Lovejoy's "On the Discrimination of Romanticisms" in *Essays in the History of Ideas* (Baltimore: The Johns Hopkins University Press, 1948).

[4] Dust-jacket note.

[5] *Autumn*, x.

[6] Autumn, xi.

[7] In *Visions of Culture* (Chicago: University of Chicago Press, 1966), 212.

[8] Speculum: A Journal of Medieval Studies, April 1997, vol. 72, no. 2, 489.

[9] *Autumn*, 39.

[10] *Autumn*, xxi.

[11] The Dutch philosopher F. R. Ankersmidt has given Huizinga credit for anticipating the postmodern view of historiography. See his *History and Tropology: The Rise and Fall of Metaphor* (Berkeley: University of California Press, 1994), 209.

[12] *Autumn*, 1.

[13] *Autumn*, 7.

[14] *Autumn*, 1.

[15] *From History to Sociology*, trans. Hayden V. White (Detroit: Wayne State Press, 1959), 187.

[16] *Autumn*, 114.

[17] *Autumn*, 207.

[18] *Autumn*, 207.

[19] *Autumn*, 171.

[20] *Autumn*, 139.

[21] *Autumn*, 139.

[22] *Autumn*, 184.

[23] From History to Sociology, 187.

[24] "The Task of Cultural History" in *Men and Ideas: History, The Middle Ages, The Renaissance* (New York: Meridian Books, 1959), 59.

[25] Visions of Culture, 229.

[26] Ibid., 231.

[27] Huizinga has attracted more attention from Dutch scholars, and hopefully some of this work will be made available in English.

Arizona State University

"Arestyus is Noucht bot Gude Vertewe": The Perplexing **Moralitas** *to Henryson's* **Orpheus and Erudices**

John Marlin

Relations between affect and intellect are often uneasy in the act of reading poetry. This tension is inherent in the very act of exegesis, which reorders aesthetic constructs into analytic categories, often by bringing a poem into a relationship with a complex of ideas external to it. Sometimes, however, this tension is also inherent within a literary work itself. As Wesley Trimpi has argued, a poem, when seeking an affective response, will often be at odds with its attempt to engage the intellect if one aim is pursued at the expense of the other, a problem he calls "the ancient dilemma of representation and knowledge."[1] A decorous discursive relationship between affect and reason in a poem requires that these aims be properly balanced.

It is just this balance that is at stake in Robert Henryson's *Tale of Orpheus and Erudices his Queene*.[2] It is a two-part composition, the first part composed of a mostly rhyme-royale adaptation of the story of Orpheus in the Underworld, and the second part offering a 218-line allegorical *moralitas* explicating that story in decasyllabic couplets — thus, an ostensibly self-interpreting work. Henryson stands near the end of a long line of medieval writers who adapted and allegorized Orpheus,[3] and the Middle-Scots Chaucerian is a credit to the tradition. Like other medieval classicists, Henryson conflates and adapts the Orpheus stories of Ovid, Boethius, and Virgil into a composite account; unlike many of his predecessors, he sensitively amplifies the humanity and pathos of Orpheus's plight. In these regards, the first part of Henryson's poem is rivaled perhaps only by *Sir Orfeo*, earning it considerable appreciation from scholars of Henryson and the medieval Orpheus tradition.

Less charitable reviews have been the lot of the *moralitas*. It ostensibly follows Nicholas Trivet's (c.1265-1334)[4] commentary on Boethius's version of the Orpheus story, found in Book III of *De Consolatione Philosophiae*.[5] Trivet, an English Dominican, wrote a number of theological and historical treatises, as well as a number of commentaries on patristic and classical works. His commentary on Boethius, surviving in 38 manuscripts, was one of the most widely disseminated treatments of *De Consolatione* in the late Middle Ages;[6] it would have been known not only to Henryson, but to any of his readers schooled in the liberal arts. Trivet's allegorization follows closely the spirit, and even the letter of the long medieval tradition of Orpheus commentary; indeed, it has been called "almost plagiarized" from Guillaume of Conche's twelfth-century commentary on Boethius.[7] To the extent Trivet varies from Guillaume, it is to lay a coat of Aristotelian varnish over Guillaume's Platonism, the sort of revision that might be expected near the end of the age of scholasticism. Trivet also incorporates some minor concepts that seem to be derived from the works of the Second and Third Vatican mythographers and Bernardus Silvestris.[8] Guillaume's commentary, in turn, elaborates and extensively revises earlier commentaries by Notker of Labeo (11th c.) and Remigius of Auxerre (10th c.).

At the core of all of these allegorizations is the moral Boethius himself draws from the Orpheus story in *De Consolatione Philosophiae*: "This fable applies to all of you who seek to raise your minds to sovereign day. For whoever is conquered and turns his eyes to the pit of hell, looking into the inferno, loses all of the excellence he has gained."[9] Boethius uses the Orpheus story to illustrate and amplify the *Consolatio*'s thesis, that man's happiness depends on his rational faculties ruling him, not his appetite for the temporal gifts of a blind, unjust Fortune. Hence, Guillaume and Trivet allegorize the story as the progress of a bifurcated soul: Orpheus represents some form of the intellect, and Eurydice some form of the appetites ("natural concupiscence" in Guillaume; the "affections of man" in Trivet). In this scheme, when the intellect masters the appetites or affections, the soul is rightly ordered and can ascend to genuine beatitude. But when love of concupiscence overpowers the intellect, as represented by Orpheus's look back, the disordered soul becomes re-enslaved to *temporalia* and forfeits its bliss.

Following this line, Henryson's allegory figures Orpheus as the "part intellectiue" of the soul (428) and Erudice as "oure affection / Be fantasy oft movit vp and doun" (431-2). Erudice's death is caused by the affection's flight from virtue and toward worldliness. Orpheus's ascent through the planets, Henryson's original contribution to the tale, signifies contrition for misdirected appetites (446), and his descent into the underworld signifies the intellect's attempt to recover sovereignty over the affections. The poet's musical performances in the underworld represent "quhen reson and perfyte sapience / Playis apon the harp of eloquens, / And persuadis our fleschly appetyte / To leif the thoct of wardly delyte" (507-510). The reunion of Orpheus and Erudice marks "Quhen oure desire wyth reson makis pes" (617); Orpheus's fatal backward glance, is, predictably, a return to worldliness and sin (624-6).

Typical of the *moralitas* detractors is Douglas Gray, who writes that it "does its best to drag [the poem] down into the mass of poems which are simply typical of their age."[10] While this judgment stems from a general perception that the *moralitas* deflates the tale's tragic power, a good part of what disturbs readers is a perplexing contradiction between the poem and the *moralitas* with respect to the character Aristaeus. In classical antiquity, Aristaeus appears only in Virgil's version of the myth,[11] and is responsible for Eurydice's death. Medieval adapters regularly brought him into their conflations of the story's several versions; in his, Henryson casts him as a "bustuos" herdsman:

> And whan he saw this lady solitar,
> Barfute, with shankis quhytar than the snawe,
> Prikkit with lust, he thocht withoutin mar
> Hir till oppres — and till hir can he drawe. (98-102)

Fleeing him, she steps on a venomous serpent, is bitten, dies, and is carried to the Underworld. In allegorizing this passage, the *moralitas* states, surprisingly: "Arestyus, this hird that couth persewe / Erudices, is noucht bot gude vertewe" (435-6).

Unlikely as it seems to have a ravisher "prikkit with lust" signifying virtue (and Henryson and his sources clearly refer here to morality and not potency), the poet seems to be merely following Trivet's and Guillaume's commentaries, both of which figure Aristaeus the same way; hence, Nicholas: "aristeus qui interpretatur virtus" (Aristaeus, who is interpreted as virtue), and Guillaume: "Aristeus ponitur virtute: *ares* enim est virtus" (Aristeus is set down for virtue, for "ares" [a contraction for the Greek "aretes," moral excellence] is virtue).[12] But such tension between tale and allegory is not evident in their versions, as their Aristaeus is merely a name, a flat or abstract type; indeed, he doesn't even appear as a character in the version of the tale they are allegorizing, but is brought into their commentaries through long-standing tradition.[13] In adapting his sources, Henryson depicts the herdsman as an individual with personality, mannerisms and real desires, even to the idiosyncrasy of a foot fetish. He likewise deviates from his classical source material: Virgil's Aristaeus is not explicitly "bustuos"; any lecherous intent on his part is at best understated.[14] Further, the *moralitas*'s "Arestyus... / is noucht bot gude vertewe" expresses a certainty about the herdsman's signification — almost the certainty of a bluff — not so evident in Trivet's "Aristaeus qui interpretatur virtus." It is as if Henryson purposely adapted his sources at this point to drive the tale and its *moralitas* in opposite directions.

This dissonance between tale and allegory has generated some critical consternation. Friedman observes somewhat modestly that "relations between the story and the *moralitas* are uneasy, with the *moralitas* sometimes contradicting the fable itself."[15] Louis puts it more bluntly: "Henryson apparently forgot his moral when he was writing the actual poem."[16] MacQueen creatively attempts to reconcile the discrepancy by considering Aristaeus' role as a beast-keeper[17] (line 98) allegorically equivalent to moral virtue's role in keeping control over the carnal passions — the beastly part of man.[18] The text frustrates this reading, however, as the "bustuos" herdsman (Henryson used this same word to describe the natural inclination of the bear in his *Morale Fabilles*) is as much one of the herd as he is over it: he desires "to oppres" Eurydice, rather than bring her into the flock.[19] Despite this problem with Aristaeus, readers see the *moralitas* as the key to the tale's meaning, at least to a degree. MacQueen's reading of the poem is thoroughly grounded in the *moralitas*; McDiarmid believes that "Henryson expects the clerkly reader to recognize the moral meaning in the tragedy that will follow, to reconsider the story once he has read the concluding *moralitas* and still feel it as a tale of human beings, and not merely abstractions."[20] Dorena Wright attempts a mean between accepting and rejecting the allegory, speculating that "either Henryson has wavered uneasily between an allegorical and a non-allegorical method, or (as I prefer to believe) he intended the *moralitas* to provide an optional and added level of meaning, not the obligatory key to the entire poem."[21]

Regardless of their stance on the *moralitas's* role in explicating the myth, the critics almost universally declare it a poetic failure, a great letdown after the sensitive and expressive pair of stanzas that end the tale. Barron writes, "there is a paucity of invention in its application to the narrative, a lack of zest in the plodding couplets which make it difficult to accept as the poet's primary interest" in the poem.[22] The dissonance between the two parts of the work render it "a defective expression of what the poet has to say," according to McDiarmid.[23]

These arguments over the function and poetic worth of the *moralitas* hinge on two critical assumptions, both arising from its explicit claims. The first is that the *moralitas* is supposed to be a harmonious decoding of the tale: after all, it is rather long, translates characters into allegorical figures, and states that the tale's "doctryne and gude instruction" are "hid vnder the cloke of poesie" (418, 420).[24] The second assumption is that the *moralitas* is, as it claims to be, a careful rendering of Nicholas's commentary. Even McDiarmid, who observes some discrepancies between the *moralitas* and its sources, believes Henryson "would not have wished to differ from [the commentary's] analysis or been conscious of the differences of meaning that he does introduce."[25]

Reasonable as these assumptions seem at first glance, they deserve a second, and not merely because adopting them dooms the poem aesthetically. Henryson was a Chaucerian poet who was probably a schoolmaster, practicing lawyer, and well-traveled humanist;[26] most likely he understood all too well the discrepancies introduced into a text through translation. Hence, a more satisfying understanding of the poem might stem from suspending these assumptions and examining whether the tale and its *moralitas* might be reconciled through irony. Such a reading must begin with not a little critical circumspection and justification; due to the privilege irony receives in New Criticism and more recent theoretical schools, questionable ironic considerations of medieval poets and especially of Chaucer have proliferated in recent years. In his biography of Chaucer, Derek Pearsall aptly remarks that readings based on an ironic narrator often "substitute for the enigmatic and elusive intentions of the author the only too obvious intentions of the critic. The cult of the [Chaucerian fallible] persona has thus become a technique for systematically ironizing the text and appropriating it to the service of particular kinds of programmatic interpretation."[27] How then, might we ascertain the presence of irony in this poem without merely asserting it at those points where the literal text inconveniences our theoretical preconceptions?

A useful if conservative approach would be to consider what irony meant to medieval writers and readers. Rhetorical theorists and encyclopedists of the period generally defined irony as a verbal structure that says one thing but "means" its opposite (or at least means something else), and that opposition is signaled verbally or vocally. Representative of this definition is Isidore of Seville's *Etymologies*, which states, "Ironia est sententia per pronunciationem contrarium habens intellectum" (Irony is a statement having, through the manner in which it is uttered, a contrary meaning).[28] Hence, it is a deliberate act on the part of the author; it "presupposes conscious intention (of a character in the work or the poet) and cannot arise fortuitously."[29] This sense of intentionality differentiates irony in medieval exegesis from the discovery of unconscious verbal or conceptual contradictions that characterizes many contemporary psychoanalytic and poststructuralist treatments of poetry. The role of authorial intention in explicating poetry is, to say the least, a problematic issue amongst modern critics — to many it is anathema — but to medieval readers uncovering the writer's intended meaning was a normal part of literary interpretation. Hugh of St. Victor, for instance, argued in his *Didascalion* that readers should try to determine "quod potissimum scriptor senserit" (what, above all, the author meant) as well as the "voluntas scriptoris" (the inclination of the author).[30] Hence, in developing an ironic reading of the text we might first look for signs of "conscious artistry with which the poet imposes his view of things on the material handed down to him,"[31] through adaptation or re-rendering. Further, we must consider whether the poem's most likely original audiences would have recognized the presence of a set of ironic signifiers, that is, Isidore's *per pronunciationem*, as irony presupposes an audience of initiates that can see the intended reversal of the literal sense.[32] We might also inquire into whether irony is a characteristic or common practice in the larger body of the poet's works, or the tradition within which he normally writes, although these alone cannot confirm that any particular work is to be taken ironically. Finally, we should ascertain whether the proposed ironic reading plays back into the poem's announced thematic concerns.

Conscious artistry seems to be at work in the numerous points of tension between the main parts of the poem. As noted earlier, both the character of Aristaeus in the tale and his symbolic value in the *moralitas* have been meaningfully altered from the form in which they appear in the original sources in such a way as to intensify their incompatibility. Aristaeus represents but one of many conflicts between the tale and the *moralitas* that have been heightened through such adaptation. From the outset, differences in style and manner drive the poem's parts against each other. By developing Orpheus's psychology and subjectivity beyond what one finds in the classical renditions of the story, Henryson's tale achieves a heightened emotional intensity, most notably in Orpheus's *planctus* (135-183) and in his despair at seeing Eurydice's beauty corrupted in hell (352-356). This amplified *pathos* marks all the more strongly the vocal shift at the beginning of the *moralitas*, signaled by the prosodic shift from rhyme royale to couplets, as well as by the direct address, "Lo, worthy folk" (415): this change in *pronunciatio* invites the audience to adopt a new mode of reading, to leave the world of realized, sympathetic characters and enter the world of analytic commentary. Further, the *moralitas* reduces the tale's more rounded human characters to one-dimensional personifications of intellectual qualities, such that the experience of moving from Orpheus's tragic discovery to the moral's propositional discourse is quite jarring. It is a shift from affect to reason — the integration of which is the theme of the *moralitas*.

These vocal and methodological tensions between commentary and tale echo through their substantive dissonances. A slight rupture occurs early in the *moralitas*, where it identifies Calliope as eloquence (426). That this is a traditional interpretation there is no doubt;[33] but it is noteworthy that the tale associates Calliope purely with music (43-5, 68-70) while assigning eloquence to Mercury (213), the classical god of rhetoric. In other words, the poem recognizes music and rhetoric as distinct arts with their own methods. While this is a slight distinction — after all, in medieval allegory the same quality can be indicated by different figures[34] — it does suggest that the poem and the *moralitas* might be working out of different interpretive schemata. Yet the most important substantive discrepancies are those which occur in the *moralitas*'s allegory of plot. Although Orpheus's descent from Phoebus and Calliope (61-3) mark him as an apt figure of the intellect, his thorough characterization as a courtly lover undercuts that figuration.[35] His "accord" (84) with Eurydice is not an image of reason controlling the desires, but of "myrth, blythnes, gret plesans, and gret play," (88). His long complaint at Eurydice's passing shows "His hart was sa apon his lusty quene" (149), and when he petitions the planets for her return, he confesses to Venus that "I am your avin trewe knycht" (206). When Orpheus recognizes Eurydice in the deepest part of Tartarus, he bemoans the loss of "thy rude as rose with chekis quhite, / Thy cristall eyne with blenkis amorouse, / Thi lippis red to kis diliciouse" (354-6). Returning from the Underworld the couple are "talkand of play and sport" (385), underscoring Orpheus's consistent motivation to recover the "warldlie ioye" (89) they once had. Throughout, the hero wants to indulge, not redeem, his desires: he, not Eurydice, seems a proper figure of the affections. The conventions of courtly romance that Henryson imports into the traditional story strain those of the moral and theological allegory customarily attached to it, and this juxtaposition of traditions creates an instance of the "generic instability" Fyler finds characteristic of both Chaucerian and Ovidian irony, that is, the practice of extablishing one set of generic expectations, only to undermine them by shifting genre.[36]

Orpheus's cupidity wedges tale and moral apart at other points. The *moralitas* equates the hero's long and moving lament on his queen's death with when "parfyte reson wepis wondir sare, / Seand oure appetite thusgate mys-fare" (445-6), ostensibly an expression of contrition for misplaced desire. But in the actual complaint Orpheus regrets only the loss of "plesance and play" (154); he repeatedly cries, "Quhar art thou gane, my luf Erudices?" (143). Here again the gap between tale and allegory widens from the poet's adaptations of his sources. While Orpheus's lament in the woods is stock in both classical and medieval versions of the story, it is rarely developed in the courtly and unambiguously cupidinous terms Henryson deploys. And while Nicholas's commentary mentions the intellect weeping for the affect, he figures it not as a sign of contrition; rather, he holds the intellect culpable: "et ideo [intellectus] non debet flectere aspectum ad [a]effectum" (ll. 76-7). Indeed, Henryson's tale reflects Nicholas's commentary better than his *moralitas*, which follows a logic of its own. A similar disjunction occurs in the *moralitas*'s rendering of the journey to the spheres, which ostensibly symbolizes repentance and a turn to spirituality: Orpheus "passis vp to the hevvn belyue, / Shawand till us the lif contemplatyve" (447-448). Yet in the tale, no such repentance occurs. Orpheus's only motive for visiting the heavens is his desire to recover Eurydice: his pleas to Jupiter, Apollo and Venus all make this plain. Orpheus here may be a figure of praying amiss, but not of "the lif contemplatyve."

This exegetical discord continues in the *moralitas*'s account of Orpheus's five concerts in hell (the classical sources depict only one, another case of Henryson's crafting his material, gaining emphasis through repetition). The *moralitas* figures the cessation of punishments in Hades following Orpheus's songs as a reordering of the soul — that reason, combined with eloquence, are quieting the desires:

> Bot quhen oure mynd is myngit with sapience,
> And plais apon the harp of eloquence;

> Thàt is to say, makis persuasioun
> To draw oure will and oure affection
> In ewiry elde, fra sin and foule delyte,
> This dog our saule has no power to byte. (469-74)

But again, this is not what happens in the poem. Orpheus plays the music of the spheres, which he discovers as if by accident in his trip to heaven (218-246), not to quell his desires, but in response to either fear of the tormentors or pity for the tormented — perhaps the same misplaced pity for which Virgil chastises Dante in the Inferno.[37] In essence, his eloquence helps him gratify his desire, rather than subordinate it. Moreover, the moral effects of his music are dubious. While Cerberus and the furies doze off to Orpheus's lullaby, Ixioun "out of the quhele can crepe / And stall away" (272-3) presumably to continue his "hardy and curageouse" lechery. Similarly, Tantalus steals a sip from the river (286-8), and Tithyus, while still bound, gains lasting relief from the ravenous grip (300-2). If the tormented represent wrong desires, Orpheus's music actually quiets the guards that hold those desires in check — exactly opposite to the *moralitas*'s interpretation.[38] Henryson cannot plead that he is merely following his *auctoritees*. In Ovid and Boethius, as well as Nicholas's commentary, when Orpheus plays his harp the furies weep instead of sleep, Ixioun's wheel merely stops for a short spell, Tantalus is so moved by the song that he ignores the waters he could drink, and the eagle tearing at Tityus's bowels pauses a moment instead of flying away.[39] Nicholas's commentary emphasizes the furies' role as avengers of sin ("ultrices," ll. 182-3), and notes that the sapience and eloquence figured by Orpheus's music quiet the desires rather than give them opportunities for release. Once again Henryson's adaptations have created a tension which would not have existed otherwise.

The final discord between tale and moral comes when the *moralitas* announces its thesis: "Than Orpheus has wone Erudices / Quhen oure desire wyth reson makis pes, / And sekis vp to contemplacion" (616-618). Where, exactly, in the tale Orpheus achieves this moment of psychic reintegration is hard to find. Even standing before Pluto, Orpheus mourns Eurydice's loss of beauty, indicating his concern for material rather than spiritual good. And after being reunited, "thai went, talkand of play and sport" (383), hardly an image of the reason seeking "vp to contemplacion," as the *moralitas* figures it to be (618). As with the case of Aristaeus, the character of events throughout the fiction seems at odds with their allegorical figuration. That so many of the discrepancies stem from the way sources have been adapted argues that the cumulative dissonance between tale and moral is designed; and, given the wide dissemination of Nicholas's commentary, not to mention the general popularity of the Orpheus legend in medieval schooling, Henryson's most literate readers would likely have been sensitive to these adaptations.

Given the number of moments at which tale and moral seem in conflict, it seems surprising that anyone accepts the *moralitas*'s claim that it interprets the tale. But several parts of the *moralitas*, especially in the beginning, are in concord with the poem. For example, Orpheus, given his parentage, seems a good figure of the soul's intellective faculty. Eurydice, in demanding marriage of Orpheus and in her penchant to wander in the meadows, seems an apt figure of human affect. The marriage arrangement, in which Eurydice tells Orpheus "In this province ye sall be king and lord" (83), clearly figures the proper relationship between reason and desire. However, the farther into the *moralitas* one reads, the more the discrepancies compound, creating a wider gap between fiction and interpretation. It is as if the *moralitas* begins on solid premises but then takes on a life of its own, independent of the tale, driven less by the language and context of the poem than by its own conceptual framework. This is not to say that the *moralitas* is intellectually bankrupt. It contains moments of fine insight: the notion of reason making peace with desire is appealing in terms of medieval psychology and spirituality, and the figuring of Orpheus's harp as reason and eloquence quieting the desires is a lovely rendering of the medieval idea of the proper role of rhetoric. Arguably, it reaches the same moral conclusion as the tale it supposedly interprets — that is, that ungoverned affections will take you straight to hell. But when the *moralitas* arrives at such moments, it is by its own methods and pursuing its own purposes, inspired by the tale, but not explicating it.

We perhaps should not be surprised to see such a gap between fiction and allegory in a work by Henryson. His later and more famous work, the *Morale Fables* is full of surprising moralities that deploy unpredictable allegorical values that make the reader dependent upon the commentator. And as in *Orpheus*, throughout the *Fables* the morals routinely upset the expectations set up in the tales. This pattern of reversal works by gaining our emotions for the tales' sometimes mean-spirited, sometimes good-natured characters and evoking a visceral judgement on their black-comedic outcomes, but then examining them in the light of what is often rather stern moral reasoning.[40] The tension between tale and moral evident throughout the fables suggests that the morals do not dictate our understanding of the tale; rather, they temper it. The fables engage our affections; the morals cause us to examine them, just as they cause us to reconsider our moral judgment.[41] The reader is invited to negotiate apparently valid claims to truth from different sources — from affect and intellect.[42]

Does a comparable negotiation occur in Orpheus? An approach to that problem may be found in the poem's Chaucerisms. We could virtually ignore the *Testament of Cresseid* and the Tale of *Chauntecleir* and infer Chaucer's influence on Henryson from *Orpheus and Erudices* alone. Written mostly in rhyme-royale, the stanza form of *Troilus* and several of the *Canterbury Tales*, the poem resonates with Chaucerisms. As Friedman notes, Orpheus's petitions to Jupiter, Apollo and Venus are reminiscent of Palamon and Arcites's prayers in the *Knight's Tale*, and Orpheus's moving complaint (134-183) has echoes of the complaint of the Black Knight in The *Book of the Duchess*.[43] Many of the poem's Chaucerisms are more direct. The poem's naming of Proserpine as the Queen of Faery comes from the *Merchant's Tale* (IV (E) 2236f)[44] (and Proserpine seems to get the last word in Henryson's hell, just as she does in January's garden). Henryson's figuring of Watling Street as the Milky Way (188) derives from the *House of Fame* (935-44); that work may be the source for Orpheus's flight to the spheres, as well.

Henryson borrows not only from Chaucer's material, but also from his manner. Narrating Orpheus is an apologetic persona such as we find in Chaucer's dream poems and a few of the *Canterbury Tales*. After reciting the long list of musical terms, the narrator confesses, "Of sik musik to wryte I do bot dote, / Thar-for at this mater a stra I lay, / For in my lif I coud newir syng a note" (240-3). Naturally, he goes on at a later point to speak of how Orpheus "playit mony suete proporcion / With base tonys in ypodorica, / With gemilling in ypolerica" (played many sweet chords, with bass tones in the Hypodorian mode, with harmony in the Hypolocrian[45] mode) (368-70), somewhat like the Knight and other pilgrims who say they will speak no more on a subject and then tarry on it — albeit to a purpose. Further, Henryson's work is rife with Chaucerian digression. The prolix catalogs of the muses, musical terms, and notables in hell all draw us out of the plot's essential action, and these moments of somewhat tedious erudition and arcana smack just a bit of the pedantic eagle in the *House of Fame*. Finally, bookishness, a Chaucerian concern for *auctoritee*, pervades the poem. The narrator carefully identifies and enthusiastically endorses his sources, and reminds us at points that his commentary comes from the library: "I sall the tell sum part, as I haue red" (490). And as we have seen above, we can trust Henryson to follow faithfully his announced sources about as much as we can Chaucer.

This accumulation of Chaucerisms suggests that we might search for one more: a fallible narrator, fallible because he is naive, self-deceived or self-interested. Positing such a narrator may answer a question many have asked, which is, why does Henryson include the *moralitas* at all? There is lesson enough in Orpheus's reversal and his discovery of the simple but profound truth that the weakness of human love (the look back) undermines its power (to raise the dead); those who want more of a moral might examine the poem's political trappings for lessons on princely conduct. MacQueen's notion that a medieval reader would typically see such a commentary at the end of a poem is not persuasive. Whether or not morals might be found at the end of texts is a matter of genre. Middle-English and Middle-Scots vernacular adaptations of classical mythology did not universally or even characteristically include allegorical commentary: none appear appended to the text of *Sir Orfeo* or the works of Gower, James I and Dunbar.

A fifteenth-century Scottish reader might come across a glossed classical text — like the *De Consolatione* containing Nicholas's commentary — or hear a lector expound upon an ancient myth. In any case, the commentary would be by someone other than the poet, and it seems that this is exactly what Henryson has mimicked in the *moralitas* to *Orpheus and Erudices*; this would have been more evident to an audience hearing an oral performance of the poem than it may be for readers. The shift in *pronunciatio* signaled by the change in meter and verse form is accompanied by a shift in address: the third-person narration that dominates the tale gives way to a direct address to the reader — "Lo, worthy folk" (415) — suggesting a fictive rhetorical situation wherein a lecturer addresses several auditors. Throughout the *moralitas* the speaker identifies with his audience: he refers to "our affection" (431), "oure myndis" (436), "our myndis ee" (453), "the feruent lufe / We suld have" (449-50), "oure appetit" (445), and "oure desyre" (455). The *moralitas* becomes personal and communal, with a tone more of speaking than of writing (another deviation from Nicholas's commentary, which remains impersonal and expository entirely in the third person, with the pronoun *nos* occurring only once near the end). Hence, we might examine the speaker of the *moralitas* as a character as individuated and idiosyncratic as Orpheus or Aristaeus, a character whose interests and weaknesses influence our reading of the poem.

This speaker is pedantic and bookish, and, while not quite the ostensible bore of the House of Fame's eagle, he is verbose and confident in his sources. Like Chauntecleir, he exudes confidence for the "olde bookes" that buttress his argument, which is "Rycht full of frute and seriositee" (424). Significantly, his presentation is marked by moments where he loses logical and rhetorical control of his material, perhaps suggesting personal enthusiasms. For instance, with respect to the crimes of Tantalus he translates two clauses of Nicholas ("Tantalus avarum significat…quia non sustinet in necessitatibus suis ea [diuicias] expendere, quia delectatus uisu peccunie non uult aceruum diminuere" [214-219])[46] into a fourteen line invective on miserliness (531-544); one almost hears the annoyance of the scrivener or barrister who hasn't been paid. He likewise treats Tityus's desire to divine the future, which Nicholas (222-236) handles with dry, scholastic etymologies, with a lengthy (571-599) outburst against divination, witchcraft, and sorcery. Caught up in this diatribe, he omits from his exegesis of Tityus the formula with which he ends that of each of the other monsters — how Orpheus's harp of reason and eloquence stills the inordinate or misplaced desire figured by each creature. As silence is often significant in Chaucer, it is also so in Henryson: could this absence mark the narrator's personal disquiet of mind? The subject of his invective is divination, and he is striving to divine intellective meaning from a poetic text, something which is hardly among "sic maner of thingis / Quhilk vpoun trew and certaine causis hingis" (590-1), self-proclaimed as the proper object of divination. Perhaps he senses at this moment that his own presentation judges itself, and he loses his thread.

With his moralizing, faith in intellection and love of study, full of "doctryne and gude instruction" (417), this narrator stands in marked contrast to the characters of the tale, who are explicitly driven by affection and appetite, the commentator's figurations notwithstanding. As a man who trusts to things discernible "be calculatioun" (595), and unwitting of the divide between his own theory and its practice, he fulfills his own picture of Orpheus: a widowed reason (627), an intellect out of touch with its affections. It is revealing that he recognizes affect "Is alway prompt and redy to fall doun" (628), but not intellect. His scheme of the relationship between reason and emotion finds no space even for his own righteous indignation or his own enthusiasm for study and commentary. Indeed, the only affection finding a place in his allegory is contrition — an emotion consequent to moral reasoning and, hence, a validation of his own theory.

There may be other and better ways to psychologize the lapses in logical and narrative control within the *moralitas*, its progressive deviation from the text on which it comments, and its manner of creating expectations only to frustrate them. What matters is that these rhetorical features are present and therefore can be psychologized, that the *moralitas* is colored by the concerns of a subjective narrator; moreover, that coloring falls squarely into the most common medieval *topoi* of irony: feigned praise.[47] The *moralitas* seems to be endorsing Trivet's commentary, but actually presents an instance of the "vatic pretense" that Fyler finds in many of Chaucer's and Ovid's narrators,[48] that is, a narrator who, like the *House of Fame's* persona, promises the profound and the remarkable, but then systematically deflates those promises and undercuts his own authority. So read, the *moralitas* becomes an artful demonstration of how commentary, through the obsessions and personal concerns of its author, takes on a life of its own independent of its literary object. As such, it is also a demonstration, almost a self-satire, of the digressive style, interpretive excesses and personal enthusiasms, all mixed with moments of wisdom, that mark medieval commentary, especially when it emanates from a mind in which reason and desire are at odds. As happens in the *Canterbury Tales*, the tale sets a standard that judges the teller.

By postulating a fallible narrator we might also understand how the poem's two divisions work together as a literary unit. The *moralitas*'s announced theme is the right relationship between affect and reason, and its ideal is a harmony between the two — the balance about which Trimpi writes. Achieving that balance is the problem Henryson's work explores. The tale, with its narrative structure driven by discoveries and reversals, its poetic diction and decoration, and its affect-seeking hero himself "be fantasy oft movit vp and doun" (432) engages our affect and seeks an emotional catharsis. The *moralitas*, with its ratiocinative narrator insisting to the point of self-validation on the primacy of the intellect, depicts a widowed reason, an intellect out of touch with, or at least operating independent of, its affections. As in the morals to the *Fabilles*, the commentator insists on his own interpretive authority while drawing our intellect in a direction our affect might resist. Because he pursues a purely intellective aim (Trimpi's "knowledge") at the expense of and ignoring its related affect ("representation"), he soon diverges from the tale and follows his own path to a self-contradictory destination. But following the affective route is no more satisfactory: the tale's Orpheus seeks the object of his affections through heaven and hell and finds in the end that those affections themselves betray him. Hence, in terms of medieval psychology, the will is left to shift anxiously between affective and cognitive impulses, recognizing the potential danger in pursuing either to its ultimate consequences.

The potential for harmonious cooperation between affect and intellect remains problematic. There are points where the tale and *moralitas* find concord, but these are at best ephemeral, similar to what Robert Frost called "a momentary stay against confusion." In the end, the poem is a representation of its stated theme — that is, the inherent tension between the soul's faculties, whose integration can last no longer than Orpheus's and Eurydice's reunion. Perhaps here Henryson reflects the anxieties of his own age, a period of intellectual turmoil, wherein long-standing scientific, political, and religious certainties were in question, and wherein faith in an overarching intellectual order that dissolved all contradictions had long been on the wane.[49] While Henryson may not have been genius enough to devise new poetic forms to express these tensions, he fully recognized and exploited the potential of the Chaucerian tradition. And in grasping the spirit of Chaucer, Henryson has also grasped something of the spirit of that other great ironist, Ovid, whose *Metamorphoses* inspired the medieval Orpheus tradition. Indeed, Henryson's artfully problematic *moralitas* to *Orpheus and Erudices* exposes the dubious wisdom of persistent medieval attempts to fix a stable meaning on a work whose theme is *omnia mutant*.

Notes

1. *Muses of One Mind* (Princeton: Princeton University Press, 1983).

2. All quotations from Henryson are from Denton Fox, ed., *The Poems of Robert Henryson* (Oxford: Oxford University Press, 1981).

3. For a review of the medieval Orpheus tradition, see John B. Friedman, *Orpheus in the Middle Ages* (Cambridge: Harvard University Press, 1970).

4. For more on Trivet's career, see Beryl Smalley, *English Friars and Antiquity in the Early Fourteenth Century* (Oxford: Basil Blackwell, 1960), 58-65.

5. B.L. Addit. MS 19585, ff. 61b-63b, and B.N. MS lat. 18424. Line numbers in this essay refer to the extract of Nicholas's commentary appearing in Fox, 384-391.

6. Friedman, *Orpheus,* 110.

7. Fox, *Poems,* cvi.

8. Trivet's emphasis on Orpheus's eloquence may stem from the Vatican mythographers, who noted the civilizing effect of music. Bernardus used Orpheus's geneology to establish his allegorical value, as do Trivet and Henryson. Friedman, 110, 112. Henryson elaborates this genealogy even further; see lines 1-70 of the poem.

9. Boethius, *The Consolation of Philosophy*, trans. Richard Green (Indianapolis: Bobbs-Merrill, 1962), 74.

10. *Robert Henryson* (Leiden: E.J. Brill, 1979), 240.

11. *Georgicon* IV, 436f.

12. Fox, *Poems,* 385, l.47; Friedman, *Orpheus,* 108.

13. Aristaeus enters allegorizations of Orpheus as early as the sixth century, in the *Mythologiae* of Fulgentius. Subsequently, he appeared as a matter of course in commentaries on Ovid and Boethius, even when not a character in the primary text: Fox, 415; Friedman, 89. For instance, see the marginal gloss to X.10 in *The 'Vulgate' Commentary on Ovid's Metamorphoses*, ed. Frank T. Coulson (Toronto: Pontifical Institute of Medieval Studies, 1991), 119.

14. Virgil describes the incident as follows:

illa quidem, dum te fugeret per flumina praeceps,
immanem ante pedes hydrum moritura puella
seruantem ripas alta non uidit in herba. (457-9)

(This one, indeed, when she fled from you headlong through the river, the fated girl did not see before her feet an observer on the bank, a monstrous serpent in the tall grass.) R.A.B. Mynors, ed., *P. Vergili Maronis Opera* (Oxford: Oxford University Press, 1969), 97. All translations are my own unless otherwise attributed.

15. Friedman, *Orpheus,* 203.

16. Kenneth R.R.G. Louis, "Robert Henryson's Orpheus and Eurydice and the Orpheus Traditions of the Middle Ages," *Speculum* 41 (1966), 654.

17. In the *Georgics*, Aristaeus is a beekeeper. In early medieval commentary, he became a herdsman, so the change in occupation is not Henryson's original contribution. See Friedman, 108f.

18. John MacQueen, *Robert Henryson: A Study of the Major Narrative Poems* (Oxford: Clarendon Press, 1967), 34-5.

19. Friedman writes, "there is little evidence to support [MacQueen's reading] in either the Orpheus tradition or in Henryson's poem, *Orpheus,* (239 n69). Matthew McDiarmid simply states, "I do not understand MacQueen": *Robert Henryson* (Edinburgh: Scottish Academic Press, 1981), 61 n13.

20. McDiarmid, *Robert Henryson,* 55. Gray, *Robert Henryson,* 237, is somewhat less committal; while he sees sufficient points of contact between the tale and the *moralitas* to make the latter something of a guide to the former, he feels the two are in conflict enough that "It would be wrong...to force the allegorical reading of the *moralitas* on to every detail of the story."

21. Dorena A. Wright, "Henryson's Orpheus and Eurydice and the Tradition of the Muses," in *Medium Aevum*, 40 (1971), 46-7.

22. William Raymond Johnston Barron, *Robert Henryson: Selected Poems* (Manchester: Fyfield, 1981), 12. Louis, 646, concurs: "He makes his characters and their tragedy so attractive that the *moralitas*, by comparison, becomes dull and ineffectual. His primary interest is clearly not in the *moralitas* at all."

23. McDiarmid, *Robert Henryson,* 59-60.

24. The *moralitas*'s remark that Nicholas "Applyis it [the tale] to gud moralite" might suggest that the *moralitas* is not deployed as an allegorical decoding of the poem, but rather as one moral application of the poem among many potential modes of understanding it. However, "apply" in Middle Scots also meant "to apply by interpretation" (Douglas used it in this sense); hence, the term still carries the sense of exegesis, and probably does in this context. See *A Dictionary of the Older Scottish Tongue*, ed. William A. Craigle (Chicago: University of Chicago Press, 1937), I. 96.

25. McDiarmid, *Robert Henryson,* 43. Fox, *Poems,* clx, echoes this sentiment: "although [Henryson] departs from [Trivet] in some particulars, he does not make any essential changes in Trivet's allegory."

26. See Barron, 9-10; Smith, xxii-xxv; McDiarmid, *Robert Henryson,* 1-23.

27. Derek Pearsall, *The Life of Geoffrey Chaucer* (Oxford: Basil Blackwell, 1992), 86. Cf. Jonathan Culler: "Irony, the cynic might say, is the ultimate form of recuperation and naturalization, whereby we ensure that the text says only what

we want to hear." *Structuralist Poetics* (Ithaca, New York: Cornell University Press, 1975), 156.

28. *Etymologiarum*, ed. William Lindsay (Oxford: Clarendon Press, 1911), I:73. Likewise, Augustine, *On Christian Doctrine*: "Now irony indicates by inflection what it wishes to be understood, as when we say to a man who is doing evil, 'You are doing well'"; trans. D.W. Robertson (Indianapolis: Bobbs-Merrill, 1958), 103. For an introduction to the treatment of irony in the medieval encylopediae and rhetorical treatises, see the first chapter of Simon Gaunt, *Troubadors and Irony* (Cambridge: Cambridge University Press, 1989).

29. Dennis H. Green, *Irony in the Medieval Romance* (Cambridge: Cambridge University Press, 1979), 6.

30. Vi.xi *Patrologia Latina*, 176, 808. Likewise, John of Salisbury complains that teachers of philosophy rendered interpretations "contra mens auctoris" (contrary to the mind of the author); *Metalogicon, ii.xvii, PL* 199, 874. In a paper on "Interpretation and Scholastic Method," (Conference on Representation and Interpretation, Canisius College, Buffalo, NY, April 20, 1995), Prof. Jorge Garcia argued that twelfth-century interpreters of Aristotle and other authors routinely claimed that they were attempting to recover the "intellegens auctoris" and even the "intentio auctoris."

31. Green, *Irony,* 6.

32. Green, *Irony,* 3.

33. See Friedman, *Orpheus,* 112.

34. This type of covalence is suggested by Bernardus Silvestris in his *Commentary on the First Six Books of the Aeneid*, ed. E.G. Schreiber and T.E. Maresca (Lincoln and London: Univ. Nebraska Press, 1979), 11.

35. Gray finds the root of Orpheus's characterization in the romance tradition, as does Louis.

36. John Fyler, *Chaucer and Ovid* (New Haven: Yale University Press, 1979), 3, 4-8, 13, 20.

37. There are other allusions to Inferno in the tale, which suggests that Henryson may have had this meaning in mind. For example, the "ferefull strete" that "For slidderiness scant" (305, 307), and the "mony pape and cardinal," "bischopis" and "Abbottis" in hell (338-42) are Dantesque.

38. Incidentally, these features of the text call into question MacQueen's allegorization, in which the figures in hell represent "various dangers which beset the intellectual power in its quest for the appetites.... Orpheus overcomes all these obstructions, only to succumb finally when he is on the very brink of complete success."

39. See Ovid, *Metamorphoseon* X, 40-48, and Boethius, *De Consolatione Philosophiae*, L. III m. 12.

[40] For a more thorough development of this thesis, see Harold. E. Toliver, "Robert Henryson: From *Moralitas* to Irony," in *English Studies* 46 (1965), 300-9.

[41] Toliver finds a similar distance between poem and narratorial commentary at work in Henryson's *Testament of Cresseid*, as does Sydney Harth, "Henryson Reinterpreted," in *Essays in Criticism* 11 (1961), 471-80. It seems the poet's consistent practice.

[42] Although Henryson's poems are not definitively dated, most likely the *Fabillis* came later than *Orpheus*. I am suggesting, then, that Henryson adopted this method of ironic distancing earlier in this career than has previously been indicated.

[43] Friedman, 199-200. The complaint might also find roots in Lydgate's *Complaint of the Black Knight* or in any number of secular lyrics circulating at the time. Fleeing to the woods and sobbing "farewell" were common tropes in fourteenth- and fifteenth-century lyrics about lost love.

[44] In Sir Orfeo the queen and king of faery take Eurydice away, but they are not explicitly identified as Proserpine and Pluto. Friedman notes that "There are, to my knowledge, no other references to Proserpine as queen of the Fairies except by Chaucer" (198).

[45] Conjectural translation; Fox notes that there is no evidence of this musical mode being known in Henryson's; it might be a "nonce formation" that might not "make musical sense" (411-12); presumably a knowing audience would see a parody on hyperspecialized musical terminology.

[46] "Tantalus symbolizes the avaricious man, who cannot bear to spend those riches for his own necessities, as he, delighted by the sight, does not wish to diminish his heap of money."

[47] See Gaunt, 9, and Green, 139-40; feigned praise is the most common example of irony used in medieval rhetorics; see the example from Augustine, n28 above.

[48] Fyler, 22, 43.

[49] Hence, Gray, 30: "It is certainly not surprising that in a period when past certainties were being undermined we should find in literature a liking for enigmas, contradictions, and ironies."

College of St. Elizabeth

Giorgio Vasari's Judith and Holofernes: *Athena or Aphrodite?*[1]

Liana De Girolami Cheney

> ...God has sent me to do things with thee
> at which the whole world will be astonished.
> —Judith 11:16

The story of Judith and Holofernes has been a popular theme for artists for many centuries, the sixteenth-century in particular. The story is taken from the Book of Judith in the Apocrypha:[2] Nebuchadnezzar, who reigned over the Assyrians in Ninevah, sent his general, Holofernes, against the Jews who had refused to help him in his war against King Arphaxad of the Medes. Holofernes laid siege to Bethulia which blocked his route to Jerusalem and cut off its water supply. Its despairing inhabitants were persuaded by their chief priest, Ozia, to surrender. Judith, a beautiful and deeply religious widow, came to Bethulia to assist her people and presented them with a bold plan.

Abandoning her widow's sackcloth, she bathed and anointed herself with rich perfume. She arranged her hair elaborately, tied it with ribbons and dressed in all her finery, and went with her maid, Abra, to the enemy camp. The Jews of Bethulia had broken the laws of their God and were about to lose His protection, she told Holofernes. But she was his ally, and if he allowed her to pray in private outside the camp every night she would help him to victory over her people. The Assyrian general, struck with her beauty and her courage, agreed.

For three days and three nights, Judith ate alone the fruits and grains brought from her home, and prayed. The next day, Holofernes invited her to have dinner with him. Trembling with passion, he ordered a feast for her where he consumed vast quantities of food and drank a great deal of more wine than he had ever drunk before.

After the banquet he lay sprawled on his bed, dead drunk. Taking advantage of this moment, alone in the tent with Holofernes, Judith quickly and cautiously reached for his sword. Drawing close to the bed, she gripped him by the hair, prayed for strength, struck his neck twice with all her might, and severed his head, then wrapped it in the canopy of the couch. She hurried from the tent and gave the head to Abra, who put it in her food bag. The two women went out of the camp to pray, as they did every night, then hastened to walk through the enemy lines back to Bethulia. There Judith stood on the city walls and showed the prized head of Holofernes to the Assyrians, who had already found his headless body. They fled in terror as the Israelites attacked them. Judith sang a hymn of thanksgiving.

The Book of Judith became very popular among Jewish intellectual circles, as demonstrated by the elaboration of the midrashic literature from the Greek original writings. The tale's importance can also be reinforced and understood through the association with midrashic literature and the struggle of the Hasnomeans against the Greeks and with the festival of Hanukkah by the Maccabees.[3]

Since biblical times and antiquity, a heroic parallelism was noted between Judas of Maccabeus, who had freed his Jewish people from the Greeks, and Judith, from the Assyrians. She was also affiliated with the Jewish heroes who had freed their people, such as Samson, Jason, and David.[4] Her virtues of humility and heroism connected her with the founders of the Jewish nation, such as Moses and Aaron, and her name became identified with Israel.[5] Her faithful trusting in the Divine Providence and her willingness to be guided by God in order to save her people connects her with Abraham, whose faith and trust in God's demand for the sacrifice of his son, Isaac, made him a symbol of obedience to the Jewish people. Both figures become parental role models and mentors for their people — Abraham as father and Judith as mother.

In the visual arts, the story of Judith interested artists for many reasons and they interpreted it in a variety of ways. Through the centuries, the theme of Judith and Holoferness changed in terms of artistic representations, involving many different texts and voices, from the narrative or epic depiction to the single image. In the epic depiction the entire story from beginning to end is illustrated on one page, as seen in biblical texts of the Middle Ages, such as the Bible of Charles the Bald of 870 where the scenes of *Judith Departing Bethulia*, *Judith Before Holofernes*, and *Judith Slaying Holofernes* were all depicted sequentially on one page.[6] During the Renaissance this format changed to a selection from or fragment of the story: the decapitation (Donatello's *Judith and Holofernes*, 1456, in the Palazzo Vecchio, Florence) [Fig. 1]; placing the severed head in a sack or basket (Andrea Mantegna's drawing of *Judith and Her Slave* of 1491, Uffizi, Florence [Fig. 2]; Coreggio's *Judith* of 1512, Musée des Beaux-Arts, Strasbourg; Rosso's drawing of *Judith and Holofernes*, 1525, Los Angeles County Museum of Art [Fig. 3]; Parmigianino's etching of *Judith*, 1526, Rosenwald Collection, Washington, D.C.; and Paolo Veronese, *Judith*, 1570, Kunsthistorisches Museum, Vienna); standing on the severed head (Giorgione, *Judith*, 1504, Hermitage, Leningrad [Fig. 4];[7] presenting the head to the viewer (Titian's *Judith* of 1516, Doria Pamphili Collection, Rome,[8] Lavinia Fontana's *Judith and Holofernes*, 1595, Museo Davia Bargellini, Bologna [Fig. 5], and Hendrick Goltzius's engraving after Bartholomaeus Spranger,

Judith, 1585 [B. III. 83.272]; or fondling the severed head (Lorenzo Sabatini's *Judith*, 1565, Carimonte Banca, Bologna [Fig. 6]).

The numerous visual interpretations can also be seen associated with the symbolic reference alluded to the imagery of Judith. From the Middle Ages to the end of the sixteenth-century, the story of Judith or the portrayal of Judith and Holofernes alluded to diametric concepts of virtue over vice: *virgo–virago*; *humilitas–superbia; fortitudo–acedia; pudicita–libido* or *intellectus–luxuria;*[9] woman's beauty triumphant over a man's physical weakness; woman's mental strength over man's physical power; and civic pride and patriotism over subjugation and domination. Throughout the Middle Ages, the portrayal of the spiritual combat between good and evil or the conflict between the virtues and vices was best illustrated in Prudentius's *Pyschomachia*, since he was able to draw and compile in his manuscript the already established tradition of the allegorical interpretation of the Bible. Biblical commentaries and literary texts could best represent the human's spiritual conflict through abstract imagery such as personifications of virtues or vices —Judith as virtue and Holofernes as vice.

Since the Book of Judith was included in the canonical books of the Old Testament, Christian typology of Judith becomes a prefiguration of Virgin Mary, as St. Bonaventure commented on the virtuous similarity between Mary and Judith for their fight against the Devil.[10] In part this association can be found with the meaning of the name Bethulia or *betulah*, which in Hebrew means not only *virgin* but also an innocent and pure young woman.[11] In addition, the Hebrew word *betulah* was understood as *bêt éloah,* which meant the house of the Lord, that is the Temple in the Old Testament or the city of Jerusalem, a prototype in the New Testament for the Christian church. Judith not only represents Mary in that she is symbolically pure, but also prefigures her in the Bible; as Mary foreshadows the Church and the New Testament, Judith prefigures the synagogue and the Old Testament. Since the time of the Middle Ages, Judith as a symbol of virtue was considered a precedent for Mary, because she had defeated the villain, Holofernes, just as Mary had conquered the Devil, as illustrated in *Speculum humane salvationis* [Fig. 7].[12] Judith in the Old Testament and Mary in the New Testament become the antetype of the victorious Church (*ecclesia*). This is best illustrated in *The Story of Judith and Lucifer's Fall* in the Pamplona Bible of 1200 Harburg, where the two stories are paralleled.[13] The Devil falls at the exact moment that Judith offers the decapitated head of Holofernes to the Israelites of Bethulia.

Moreover, all virtues were considered to be derived from the Church and all vices from the Devil alluding to the conquest of virtue and vice, as Mary had conquered Satan with her chastity and humility. Judith had triumphed over Holofernes in the same manner. His desire to conquer Bethulia, for personal gain of land and money, contrasts with Judith's charity. Although she stayed humble and chaste during her widowhood, she sacrifices her chastity to save her people. Mary parallels Judith's *humilitas* by accepting the incarnation and the sacrifice of her Son for the sake of Christianity.

Other allusions to Judith's virtue such as purity or humility can be seen referred to in the *Speculum virginum* from the twelfth century, where the figure of Judith is identified in the inscription *Humilitas* (Humility and Chastity) for her willingness to give up her household to save her people as she prayed for divine guidance.[14] In contrast, Holofernes symbolizes *Superbia* (Pride and Avarice) for his wishes to conquer the Bethulia land and its richness.

During the Middle Ages the importance of divine guidance during Judith's murderous action was constantly stressed in the biblical writings referring back to the Book of Judith. Of course, divine intervention can also be seen in other Hebrew stories, such as God's intervention during Abraham's sacrifice of Isaac and God's assistance in David's killing Goliath. Of course, all of them allude to God's guidance and protection for His chosen people. Thus, Judith became a personification of a multitude of virtues, such as chastity, obedience, prudence, and fortitude, whose attribute, the sword, symbolized her adroitness.

In the Renaissance it became popular to depict the story of Judith in a symbolic act rather than in epic narrative, selecting the aesthetic moment of suspension or "pregnant momement"[15] of the story when Judith, holding the sword high in the air (a symbolic gesture of victory), is about to strike Holofernes, as seen in Donatello's *Judith and Holofernes* of 1456 (Palazzo Vecchio, Florence [Fig. 1]).[16] Ingeniously, Donatello departs from the artistic tradition not only by creating the aesthetic "pregnant moment" but also by narrating the epic story as a prolegomenon to the execution in a series of reliefs at the base of the sculpture. The most important influences for Donatello's imagery were the Bible, Prudentius's *Psychomachia*, the Medici family as patrons, and the cultural history of Florence. Donatello adheres to the medieval symbolism of pyschomachia — virtue (Judith) triumphing over vice (Holofernes) — as well as to the classical Renaissance tradition of Christianizing pagan myths (such as personifying the gods of antiquity: Minerva as Wisdom or *Humilitas* in Judith, and the Centaur as Ignorance or *Superbia* in Holofernes, as seen in Botticelli's *Minerva and The Centaur* of 1480, Uffizi). Using ancient statues and reliefs from the Medici collection for his monument, Donatello was promoting the artistic attitude of the Florentine and Medici love for antiquity.[17]

Under the patronage of the Medici, Donatello raises to another level of symbolism the civic action and patriotism of Judith — she freed Bethulia as the Medici protected Florence. The Medici family presented a strong voice in the creation of Judith and Holofernes. Many of its motifs can be traced back to difficulties in the history of the family — their exile and their losses. The Medici struggle and survival paralleled the Florentines' endurance and victory in battles and wars. The general idea of virtue against vice or the strong of mind defeating the weak of heart became a metaphor for Florence's good government and civic patriotism.[18] This metaphor embraced other biblical images, such as David. For the Florentine, Judith, like David, came to personify heroism, freedom, and the city of Florence.

Donatello introduces the perception of Judith as temptress who uses her feminine wiles to kill a man. He minimizes divine intervention and stresses the humanist and civic aspects of Judith's victory. The theme of a woman victorious over a man or killing a man, even an enemy, was disconcerting to the Hebrew people[19] as well as the Florentines. Paradoxically, although Judith heroically saved her people and their town, her heroism was not completely virtuous because she had killed Holofernes through betrayal and seduction. However, virtuous and courageous Judith, like Mary, had trod on evil: Judith's foot pressed on Holofernes's head, Mary's on the serpent. Both had triumphed over vice.

Inspired by the medieval tradition, fifteenth and sixteenth century attributes focused on Judith's brutal action as symbols of justice and victory, as seen in Botticelli's diptych paintings of *Judith and Holofernes* of 1470-72 in the Uffizi; Andrea Mantegna's paintings and engravings of *Judith with the Head of Holofernes* of 1491, in the National Gallery of Art, Washington, D. C., Dublin and Uffizi [Fig. 2]; Michelangelo's *Judith and Holofernes*, 1509-11, a pendentive on the Sistine Chapel Ceiling, Vatican; Paolo Veronese, *Judith and Holofernes* of 1570 in the Musée des Beaux-Arts, Caen; and Lavinia Fontana's *Judith and Holofernes*, 1595, in the Oratorio del Ritiro di San Pellegrino, Bologna.

Michelangelo's pendentive on the Sistine Chapel Ceiling is coupled with the theme of *David and Goliath*. The moment selected by the artist is the flight from the camp after the decapitation. Judith, her back to the viewer, covers the severed head held on a platter by Abra, turning her face toward the open tent where Holofernes's body lies. By omitting the sword and its violent action, Michelangelo accentuates the completion of Judith's deed, and her fear, rather than her heroic action [Fig. 8].

By contrast, Giorgio Vasari's *Judith and Holofernes*, 1554, now in the Saint Louis Art Museum [Fig. 9], conceived of Judith as an universal hero, or *heros-theos*, a term embodying all the characteristics and manifestations of *arete* and *virtù* associated with the pagan warrior and the Christian knight.[20] This association, combined with the legendary story of Judith from the Apocrypha,[21] created a new image of Judith in sixteenth-century art.

According to Vasari's account books, he designed three versions of the story of Judith and Holofernes. The first version, now lost, was a small painting (one braccia or approximately twenty-five square inches) commissioned by Francesco Lioni, a Florentine merchant residing in Venice, and completed in 1541 when Vasari was visiting his friend Pietro Aretino, a satirist and virtuoso poet. Vasari describes this painting as "a Judith who cuts off the head of Holofernes while an old woman holds the severed head."[22]

The Saint Louis version was painted for Antonio Bracci of Florence in 1554.[23] In his *Ricordanze,* Vasari writes: "I remember that at the end of the year I finished one of those painted panels which shows a Judith who is cutting off the head of Holofernes, with life-size figures, which was given to Antonio Bracci. I requested a payment of twelve *scudi*."[24]

Only two drawings have survived of Vasari's third version of the Judith theme: one is in the Habich Kassel Collection in Germany, the other in the Farnesina Collection in Rome [Fig. 10]. Because of its simplified composition, with fewer soldiers, women, and children represented in the lower half of the work, the Kassel drawing of 1561 is perhaps an earlier version of the Roman drawing.[25] The Roman pen-and-ink drawing with washes is recorded in a letter from Vincenzo Borghini in Poppiano to Vasari in Florence in 1564, in which he describes it as "a sketch depicting Judith showing the head of Holofernes to her people."[26]

From Vasari's description of the Judith paintings and drawings, it is clear that the first, or Lioni version, was a conventional Quattrocento and Cinquecento depiction of the Judith story, showing Judith with her maid, Abra, as she places Holofernes's head in a sack or basket. Botticelli's painting of about 1470-72, in the Uffizi, is representative of the Quattrocento conception of Judith,[27] as is Mantegna's painting of 1491, in the National Gallery of Art, Washington, D.C., and his Uffizi and Dublin drawings of 1491,[28] and Michelangelo's Sistine Chapel Ceiling drawing and fresco of 1509-11.[29] Other, similar treatments of the story include Parmigianino's etching of 1526 in the Rosenwald Collection, Philadelphia,[30] Lorenzo Sabatini's painting of 1565, Carimonte Banca, Bologna,[31] and Lavinia Fontana's painting of 1595 in the Museo Davia Bargellini, Bologna.[32] In these examples, as in Vasari's depiction, the image of Judith as a heroic and victorious woman is softened by her graceful physical beauty and fine clothes. This new aesthetic quality — *pulchritudo* (beauty) — added to the imagery of Judith an implication of forgiveness, as physical beauty attested to spiritual beauty or innocence of the heart. In this manner, Judith's violent act was somehow excused as a necessary moral deed.[33] The moral tradition to hide a didactic meaning within a story and to explain human behavior was part of the antique culture and appropriated in Renaissance

Neoplatonic philosophy.[34] By endowing mythological or historical characters with edifying meaning — Minerva as Prudence, Venus as Beauty — passions or comportments could be explained and understood.

In some Cinquecento representations of Judith and Holofernes — such as Hans Sebald Beham's engravings of 1532, in the Rosenwald Collection [Fig. 11][35] and Rosso Fiorentino's red chalk drawing of 1540 at the Los Angeles County Museum of Art [Fig. 3][36] — the image of Judith as a hero is even more disguised, if not completely negated, because she and her maid are portrayed naked. Judith's beautiful nude body and her feminine sexuality negate her heroic *virtù*. In these last Cinquecento examples, it is not Judith's *virtù* but her voluptuousness that has turned a moral act into a homicidal act, and her sexuality leads the viewer to this interpretation.

The Cinquecento artists's desire to alter the meaning of Judith's story is also evident in Vasari's later versions, which were composed under the direction of Borghini's *invenzione*. In the first version, the Roman drawing ("a sketch depicting Judith showing the head of Holofernes to her people"),[37] Vasari represents a new image of Judith. This time she is not a voluptuous beauty but a victorious conqueror who presents the head of Holofernes to her Bethulian people and to his Assyrian soldiers. Perhaps Vasari's *invenzione* was meant to relate more closely to the familiar heroic or victorious representations of public heroes like David in his triumph over Goliath or even Perseus with the head of the Medusa.[38]

Vasari has created a *publicly praised* Judith — someone whose significant acts are no longer confined to the private world of the home, the tent, or the bedroom. Vasari consciously embeds his Judith into a composition dependent on Raphael's tapestry cartoon depicting *Saint Paul Preaching to the Multitudes* of about 1515-20, now in the Victoria and Albert Museum, London. Vasari's Judith is not the Venus Pudica transformed into a vicious executioner by Albrecht Altdorfer, neither is she infected with a death-dealing sensuality as seen in Bartholomeus Spranger's *Judith* (both engravings of about 1520-30 in the Rosenwald Collection [Fig. 12]).

In the Cinquecento, depictions of Judith and Holofernes varied. Many emphasized female sexuality illustrated through the expressiveness of sheer beauty, both unclothed and clothed, as well as by the female virago and *pudica victrix* role.[39] In addition to the examples already cited, other variations include Barthel Beham's engraving of 1526 in the Rosenwald Collection, which shows a clothed, pregnant Judith holding the cut-off head — a most unusual depiction of the chaste Judith [Fig. 13]. Hans Sebald Beham's engraving of 1547, also in the Rosenwald Collection [Fig. 14], represents a nude Judith seated at a window, contemplating the severed head of Holofernes. The Latin caption above her head states: "The Lord has taken away the head of Holofernes by the hand of Judith"[40] as if her very voluptiousness and beauty were the primary means of her heroic act. Perhaps the most astonishing representation of Judith is Barthel Beham's engraving of 1525 [Fig. 15], also in the Rosenwald Collection, showing a nude, sensuous, angry Judith seated on the naked body of Holofernes holding a sword and his severed head.[41] In these later examples, Judith's sexuality becomes as alluring as her violence is repulsive. Her virago figure as a Mannerist conceit combines the sensuality of the female body with the assumed heroic *virtù* of the male figure.[42]

In these representations we also notice a clear connection between the association of the female sexuality with the depiction of her body or clothing. In the Renaissance, according to Anne Hollander, "the compartmentalized conception of feminine nudity came from perceiving women's bodies in relation to a visually compelling style of dress,"[43] or the powerful suggestion of removed clothing, which gives the nude image its erotic force as well as its power. This sexual paradox of dressed or undressed female body representations in sixteenth-century paintings arose with the classical and mythological response to female beauty and action, as invested in Athena (Minerva) who wore military armor over a flowing *himatia* veiling her feminine body and representing a heroic male body. By contrast, Aphrodite (Venus) can be seen undressed or nude, alluding to female revealment and the power of seduction through sight, while Athena's power of seduction is through action. These representations of Judith clearly combined the classical mythological tradition with Renaissance religious interpretations of a heroine.

Consistent with Cinquecento artists' desire to find new ways of interpreting old themes, Vasari presents an inventive conception of Judith in the Saint Louis painting [Fig. 9]. Vasari's figure appears as a Mannerist *concetto* (conceit) which combines the sensuality of the beautiful female body (Aphrodite-Venus) with the assumed heroic *virtú* implied by women endowed with the male trait of heroism (Athena-Minerva). Furthermore, Vasari's *concetto* is based on his adroitness fusing classical mythology with Judeo-Christian iconography as promoted in Renaissance Neoplatonic philosophy.[44] This intellectual ability is manifested in the visual representations of Vasari's paintings, as in *Judith and Holofernes*. His image of Judith is unlike most of the faithful, conservative, and passive virago representations of the Quatrocento or Cinquecento, for he portrays Judith as a beautiful, strong woman in an active male role. The ambiguity of male/female imagery in Vasari's Judith is unsurpassed in his century.

Vasari choses to depict the most dramatic moment in the story of Judith — when the young widow from Bethulia, beautifully dressed, enters the tent of the drunk Holofernes. She seizes him by the hair with her right hand, wielding a sword in her left to strike and sever his head. Furthermore, Judith, as a paradigm of a hero, is paradoxically portrayed by Vasari as Aphrodite-Venus with feminine qualities such as beauty and sensuality — aesthetic elements highly admired by *Maniera* painters — and as an Athena-Minerva figure as well, empowered with manly attributes. Her attire evokes both eroticism and prudishness. A decorated and musculated cuirass of classical armor articulating the parts of upper body, like the late armors worn by military men, evokes sexual allure. In contrast, Judith's long skirt and triple girdle of chastity with an elaborate metal belt denote her modesty.[45] The arrangement of her braided hair, with a scarf intertwined through its tresses, creates a helmet shape as well as a veiled beret, again alluding to a defined Vasarian depiction of Judith in an ambivalent sexual role, through her attire as well as her action.[46]

In this new, complex interpretation, Vasari transforms Judith's female sexuality, endowing it with the potency of a male hero, and she manifests a desexualized valor that transcends gender. Vasari's figure combines the images of Athena-Minerva and possibly even Hercules, incorporating their symbolic associations with the virtues of courage, fortitude, and wisdom. Vasari's Judith as Athena, in her valiant purposefulness devoid of what Elena Ciletti called "feminine wiles,"[47] stands for the *Maniera* concept of *virtù* — under the guidance of Fortune, the imitation and assimilation of ancient moral actions and good deeds for humankind and God.[48]

Vasari's conception of Judith as a universal hero, or *heros-theos,* is unprecedented in the art of the Cinquecento and derives much from his familiarity with Roman sarcophagi, such as the Antonine Battle Sarcophagus of the second-century A.D. in Villa Doria Pamphili, Rome [Fig. 16] and the Amazonomachy Sarcophagus of 180-190 A.D. in the Palazzo dei Conservatori, Rome [Fig. 17].[49] The depiction of a heroic Judith has its roots in part in Vasari's knowledge of the legendary Amazons, and from his familiarity with such works as the Medicean sarcophagus depicting an Amazonomachy of 180-190 A.D.[50] *Amazon* is, of course, a Greek word for the powerful woman with one breast from Cappadocia (which, perhaps significantly, was also the birthplace of Holofernes). According to the legend, Amazons amputated their breasts to facilitate physical mobility as well as self-protection during battle.[51] The ancient Amazon and the biblical Judith embody female beauty and heroism. Judith's heroism is an example of a Christian Amazon or *virago*. In "Virgo et Virago," Margaret King defines *virago* as referring to a "female military hero who achieves equivalence, or indeed eminence, in the world by becoming not a greater woman, but, as it were, a man (*vir*)."[52] Judith's physical and spiritual beauty represents both a threat and a lure for Holofernes because, like the Amazons, she has chosen to defy, even deny, her own sexuality (widowhood). Furthermore, she has risked a permanent blemish (loss of her chastity) in order to dispatch the enemy of her people.[53] Dismemberment is a form of both disintegration and reintegration in the action of Judith, where the mutilation or decapitation occurs as a moral sacrifice in defense of Bethulia, as well as her spiritual sacrifice to offer her sexual services to Holofernes in order to save her people (Judith, then, becomes a prefiguration of Christ).

The bond between the ancient Amazon and the biblical Judith is deeper than imagined. Like the Amazon, Judith yields to physical dismemberment for heroic reasons.[54] Both are symbols of fortitude and human strength, and both are triumphant liberators; Judith is especially valiant because she is a widow acting alone. Both surface out of a mythical tradition in order to explain sources of conflict and tension in the social order and human condition of their respective patriarchal society — Athens and Bethulia.

According to William Blake Tyrrell, the Greek mythical system for categorizing male and female roles depends on three mythmaking motivations as well as sexual conflicts: one focuses on the male, as a symbol for culture, superiority and normality; the second, on the opposite, the female, which denotes whatever is not valued by men — nature, inferiority, chaos, and abnormality; and the third, the feminine, combines a mediation between male/female and culture/nature.[55] Obviously for the mythical tradition, the feminine fuses positive aspects of female nature with physical and mental strength that are similar to male culture and valued by men, such as courage, astuteness, and heroism. However, the negative aspects of the female nature — of course, similar to men but not viewed as such in the mythical culture — such as her seduction and self-gratifying sexuality were feared by men because of her potential to destroy them.

Vasari sought to visualize these iconographical implications by searching for antique representations of male/female heroes as well as Quattrocento or Cinquecento interpretations or sources for a seductive Herculean Judith. He found in Antonio Pollaiuolo's *Hercules and the Hydra* of about 1460-75, now at the Uffizi, an image that he greatly admired for its vitality: "truly a marvelous thing, particularly the serpent, the coloring of which is so vividly done, and so appropriately, that it is impossible that anything could be more lively."[56] Hercules served as a pagan guardian of Florence, just as David has served as a Christian guardian.

Another Hercules known to Vasari is Caraglio's 1525 engraving after Rosso's drawing of *Hercules Fighting Cacus,* in the Bibliothèque Nationale, Paris [Fig. 18]. The biographer of the *Lives* admired this work because "the print revealed an energetic response to the Roman and pagan artistic milieu."[57] Vasari's knowledge of classical literature and his immersion in Florentine and Roman humanism provided him with a subtle understanding of the myth of Hercules, whose very name meant force.[58] In Euripides's *Alcesti*, Heracles's force is described as mute and within himself.[59] Euripides further comments on how Heracles achieves this force by speaking to his vigorous arm.[60] The power of Hercules is concentrated in the arm of the hero.

In the Saint Louis painting, Vasari has invested the force of Hercules in his Judith as she looks toward her left hand which pulls Holofernes's hair, while in her right hand she courageously holds the deadly weapon. The beautifully exposed nude arm of Vasari's *Judith* can be compared to the revealed nude leg in Giorgione's *Judith* of 1504, in the Hermitage, Leningrad, in both cases alluding to the old notion of strength [Figs. 9 and 4].[61]

While looking at her arm, Judith gazes at the image on the medallion on her cuirass in which stands the figure of Athena, holding her lance and shield. The wise war goddess protected heroes like Hercules by helping him to outwit his enemies. By depicting Athena-Minerva on Judith's cuirass, Vasari implies that wisdom and power will assist the woman in her heroic act.[62] A classical source for Vasari's image of Minerva is found in the Roman copy of a Greek statue of Athena now in the Museo Archeologico, Florence [Fig. 19], which was even known to Botticelli, who drew it in 1480.[63] Other possible Renaissance sources include coins, gems, and Tarot cards depicting *Philosophia* or Athena (for example, Mantegna's Tarot card of *Athena* or *Philosophia*, 1490, in the British Museum, London), and drawings (such as Mantegna's *Judith and Her Slave*, 1491, now at the Uffizi, which Vasari owned [Fig. 2]).[64]

Traditionally, Vasari's depiction of Judith seen from the back has been associated with Michelangelo's *Libyan Sibyl* of 1509-11, on the Sistine Chapel Ceiling, both artists appropriating the imagery from the Torso Belvedere.[65] However, the most obvious source of inspiration for the entire composition of the Saint Louis painting was Rosso's *Moses Defending the Daughters of Jethro,* about 1523-24, at the Uffizi [Fig. 20]. It is not by accident that Vasari assimilated Rosso's Herculean Moses for the representation of Judith. From his early career onward, Vasari sought Rosso's advice and assistance, so once again in the Saint Louis Judith, Vasari relies on his teacher's art to create a new and powerful image.

Vasari's familiarity with traditional Renaissance representations of Judith, associating her with Florentine civic humanism, with moral implications of Neoplatonism, as well as with the medieval psychomachy and classical mythmaking assisted him in creating a Judith who expresses the very meaning of the word "Jewess." The heroine symbolizes Israel's faith and spirit. For Vasari, Judith was a strong and resourceful individual as well as womanly, beautiful, and sensual.

In the Saint Louis painting, Vasari intended also to make an emblematic analogy between Judith and Moses, both of whom had the task of freeing their people, and both of whom struggled to abide by the law of God.

These two Old Testament figures believed in God's commitment to the Jewish people and in their own ability to obtain victory and freedom for God's chosen people.

Moreover, Vasari composed an image of Judith that combines two conceits: when the Vasari *Judith* is viewed in the role of Athena, Hercules, and Moses, she personifies fortitude, courage, wisdom, and freedom. In this instance, Vasari allows Judith to adopt a male model of moral and physical strength. However, Vasari's Judith does not discard Aphrodite or associations with idealized female beauty or with the chastity of the virgin-widow and even with charity — the gift of the widow who wills to sacrifice her body and her honor for the sake of her people. As a result, the Vasarian Judith personifies a Mannerist psychomachia in a heroine-goddess: Athena-Aphrodite.[66] A finely tuned paradox — the quintessential Mannerist conceit.[67] Thus, Vasari's various depictions of Judith and his reliance on ancient and contemporary sources to work out this evolving image created a new iconography in representing the story of Judith in Cinquecento art.

Figure 1. Donatello, *Judith and Holofernes*, 1456. Bronze sculpture. Florence, Palazzo Vecchio.

Figure 2. Andrea Mantegna, *Judith and Her Slave*, 1491.
Drawing. Florence, Uffizi.

Figure 4. Giorgione, *Judith*, 1504.
Oil painting. Leningrad, Hermitage.

Figure 3. Rosso, *Judith and Holofernes*, 1525.
Drawing. Los Angeles, Los Angeles County Museum of Art.

Figure 5. Lavinia Fontana, *Judith and Holofernes*, 1595-1600.
Oil painting. Bologna, Museo Davia Bargellini.

Figure 6. Lorenzo Sabatini, *Judith*, 1565.
Oil painting. Bologna, Carimonte Banca.

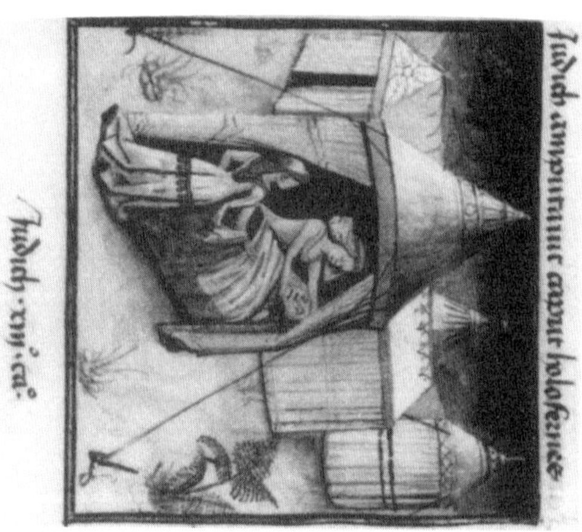

Figure 7. Mary Conquers the Devil and Judith Decapitates Holofernes in *Le Miroir de l'humaine Salvation*.

Figure 8. Michelangelo, *Judith and Holofernes*, 1509-11.

Figure 9. Giorgio Vasari, *Judith and Holofernes*, 1554.
Oil painting. Saint Louis Art Museum.

Figure 10. Giorgio Vasari, *Judith and Holofernes*, 1561. Drawing. Kassel, Habich/Kassel Staatliche Kunstsammlungen.

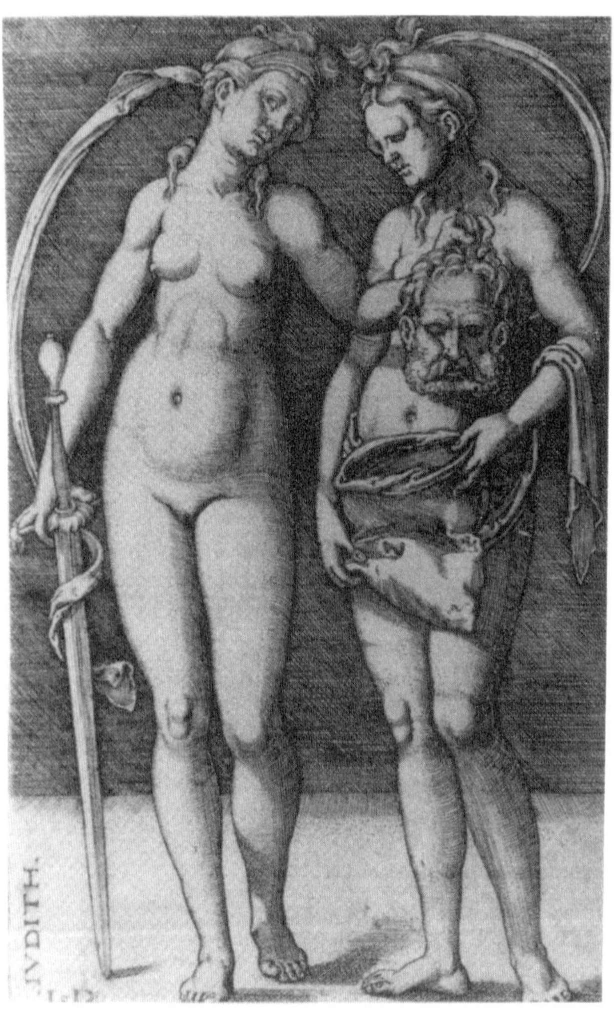

Figure 11. Hans Sebald Beham, *Judith and Holofernes*, 1547.
Rosenwald Collection.

Figure 12. Albrecht Altdorfer, *Judith with the Head of Holofernes*, 1520-30. Rosenwald Collection.

Figure 13. Barthel Beham, *Judith with the Head of Holofernes*, 1526. Rosenwald Collection.

Figure 14. Hans Sebald Beham, *Judith Sitting in a Window,* 154. Engraving. Washington, D.C., National Gallery of Art, Rosenwald Collection.

Figure 15. Barthel Beham, *Judith Seated on the Body of Holofernes*, 1525.

Figure 16. Antonine Battle Sarcophagus, second-century A.D.
Rome, Villa Doria Pamphili.

Figure 17. Amazonomachy Sarcophagus, 180.
Rome, Palazzo dei Conservatori.

Figure 18. Caraglio, *Hercules Fighting Cacus*, 1525. Engraving after Rosso's drawing, Eb 6b Réserve. Paris, Bibliothèque Nationale.

Figure 19. *Athena-Minerva*. Roman copy of a Greek statue. Florence, Museo Archeologico.

Figure 20. Rosso Fiorentino, *Moses Defending the Daughters of Jethro*, 1523-24. Oil painting. Florence, Uffizi.

Notes

[1] This study greatly benefited from the numerous comments and observations of Profs. Jane Aiken, Virginia Technology University, Yael Even, University of Missouri at Saint Louis, and William C. McDonald, University of Virginia. A research grant from the University of Massachusetts Lowell made my study possible.

[2] I have relied on the Oxford Bible and its commentaries in considering the theme. This book was originally written in Hebrew, but only the fourth-century Greek versions have survived. In the Christian Church it was known to Clement of Rome, and this version was also consulted in the Renaissance. It is not the aim of this presentation to discuss historical, philosophical, theological, or archeological controversies related to the book of Judith. See M. Jack Suggs, Katharine Doob Sakenfeld, and James R. Mueller, eds., *The Oxford Study Bible: Revised English Bible with the Apocrypha* (London/New York: Oxford University Press, 1992), 1071-86. See also Bruce Metzer, ed. *The Oxford Annotated Apocrypha* (New York: Oxford University Press, 1977) and J. C. J. Metford, *Dictionary of Christian Lore and Legend* (London: Thames & Hudson, 1983), 151-52.

[3] Gabrielle Sed-Rajna, *The Hebrew Bible* (New York: Rizzoli, 1987), 148.

[4] Mira Friedman, "The Metamorphoses of Judith," in *Jewish Art* 5 (1986), 231, for an informative study on the early representations of the story of Judith.

[5] Friedman, 225.

[6] See also the Catalan Bibles of Rhoda Ripoll and Arsenal Bible (ms 11639 and ms 2626 in the British Museum, London) and the Jerusalem Bible (from the Rothschild Miscellany, MS. 180, Jerusalem, Israel Museum of 1470-80 in Ferrara).

[7] Serena Romano, "Giuditta e il Fondaco dei Tedeschi," in *Giorgione la cultura veneta tra '400 e '500: Mito, Allegoria, Analisis iconologica* (Rome: De Luca, 1981), 103-25, for an excellent iconographic study on the story of Judith, particularly as it relates to the Venetian depictions of Judith in Giorgione, Titian, and Catena, and relation to the Venetian Judith as a symbol of Justice.

[8] Paul Jonnides, "Titian's *Judith* and its Context: The Iconography of Decapitation," presents an interesting discussion of the concept of the trencher, or plate, as a symbol of offering and trophy, and as the correlation between the image and iconography of Judith with Salome.

[9] Jennifer O'Reilly, *Studies in thc Iconography of the Virtues and Vices* (London: Garland Publishing, Inc. 1988), 10. This excellent study on Prudentius's *Pyschomachia* explains the medieval cultural framework and imagery of good and evil. Throughout the Middle Ages, the enormous popularity of Prudentius's work rested in its illustrations as a well in its inspiration.

[10] F. L. Cross, *The Oxford Dictionary of the Christian Church* (Oxford: Oxford University Press, 1983), 186.

[11] Friedman, "The Metamorphoses of Judith," 225.

[12] See the miniature of *Mary Conquers the Devil and Judith Decapitates Holofernes* in *Le Miroir de l'humaine Salvation*, Chapter XXX, MS. 40, fol. 30 verso, Newberry Library, Chicago, and another version in MS. Fr. 139, Musée Condé, Chantilly. See also Figs. 9 and 11 of Judith as Humilitas in Herrade de Landsberg, *Speculum Virginum* sec. 12, Zwettl MS. 180, fol. 45 (MS. 44 Arundel fol. 34, British Museum Library, London) and Judith and Mary in *Speculum Humanae Salvationis*, sec. 14 (no location cited), in Serena Romano, "Giuditta di Leningrado," in *Giorgione la cultura veneta tra '400 e '500: Mito, Allegoria, Analisis iconologica* (Rome: De Luca 1981), 103-104.

[13] Collection L.E.K. Fürst von Oettingen Wallersterin. MS. I. 2, lat. 4, 15, fol. 168r. See illustration Fig. 11 in Friedman, "The Metamorphoses of Judith," 233.

[14] Adolf Katzenellenbogen, *Allegories of the Virtues and Vices in Medieval Art* (New York: W. W. Norton & Company, 1964), 57, and R. Tuve, "Notes on the Virtues and Vices," *Journal of the Warburg Institute* (1964), 44-72. See *Speculum virginum*, twelfth-century manuscript (MS. Arundel 44, fol. 34v, British Museum Library, London), for an illustration of the scene.

[15] Marvin Levich, ed. *Aesthetics and the Philosophy of Criticism* (New York: Random House, 1963), 31, for a discussion of the theory of painting in Gotthold Ephraim Lessing's *Laocoön*. In a painting, the "pregnant moment" is experienced by perceiving in a single instance the coexisting visual elements of the composition, thus easily apprehending what preceded and what follows.

[16] H. W. Janson, *The Sculpture of Donatello* (Princeton: Princeton University Press, 1957), 198-296. Other Florentine Renaissance sculptors also represented Judith, such as Ghiberti's Judith of 1450 in the left-hand area of the East Doors of the Baptistery and Antonio Pollaioulo's *Judith*, 1455, in the Detroit Institute of Arts. What is unusual about Pollaioulo's bronze statue is that the figure of Holofernes is omitted and Judith stands holding a sword in her raised arm. See Samuel Sachs II and Edmund P. Pillsbury, eds., *Italian Renaissance Sculpture in the Time of Donatello* (Detroit: Detroit Institute of Arts, 1985), 99-201.

[17] Other visual sources for classical reference may have been sarcophagi reliefs depicting bacchanals, such as the *Frenzied Maenad*, stucco relief, first century A. D. in the Basilica Sotterranea di Porta Maggiore. See Friedman, "The Metamorphoses of Judith," p. 246, nn. 78 and 79, Fig. 30.

[18] Christine Sperling, "Donatello's Bronze *David* and the Demands of the Medici Politics," *The Burlington Magazine* 134 (April 1992). For variations on these ideas see Yael Even, "The Loggia dei Lanzi," *Woman's Art Journal* (Spring/Summer 1991), 10-14; Yael Even, "Mantegna's Uffizi Judith: The Masculination of the Female Hero," *Konsthistorisk Tidsskrift* 61 (December 1992), 1-13; Mary Garrad, *Artemisa Gentileschi* (Princeton: Princeton University Press, 1989), 285-297; and

James Vanderkam, ed., *No One Spoke Ill of Her: Essays on Judith* (Atlanta, GA: Scholars Press, 1992).

[19] Suggs, et al., *The Oxford Bible*, Book of Judith 13:16, 1083: "The Lord has struck him down by a woman's hand." To be struck down by a woman was the ultimate disgrace for a warrior.

[20] I am using Pindar's meaning of hero and god or hero-god. See Pindar, *Third Neman*, 22, cited in Yves Bonnefoy, ed., *Greek and Egyptian Mythology* (Chicago: University of Chicago Press, 1992), 180.

[21] See n. 2.

[22] "Apresso si mando a detto Francesco Lioni un quadro di un bracchio per ogni verso. Drentovi una mezza figura, che era una Judit, che aveva tagliato la testa a Oloferne; e drentovi una vecchia, che teneva la testa del morto tagliata." Karl Frey, "Le Ricordanze di Giorgio Vasari," in *Der Literarische Nachlass Giorgio Vasari*, 3 vols. (Munich, 1930), 2, App., 858.

[23] Giorgio Vasari's *Judith and Holofernes* (oil on panel, cm 108 x 80 or 42 1/2 x 31 1/2 in.), was acquired by the Saint Louis Art Museum in 1982 (inv. 12.1982). The museum purchased it through Colnaghi in London, which obtained it from a private collector in England. Antonio Bracci was a Florentine for whom Vasari had previously painted two portraits (locations unknown), and later in 1557 a *Cupid and Psyche* in the Gemäldegalerie Staatliche Museen, Berlin. He is listed among Vasari's correspondents, and when the artist and his family moved from Arezzo to Florence early in 1555, Vasari probably delivered the *Judith and Holofernes* to him. See D. Colnaghi, *Italian Paintings: 1550-1780* (London: P. and D. Colnaghi and Co. Ltd, 1976), entry 1. See Nora W. Desloge and Laura Lewis Mieyer, "Italian Paintings and Sculpture," *Saint Louis Art Museum Bulletin* (Winter 1988), 43-45.

[24] "Riccordo, come al fine dell anno (1554) fini un di que quadri bozati; che vera dentro una Judit, che tagliava la testa a Oloferne, grande quanto il naturale, che si dono a messer Antonio Bracchi. Mando a donar argenti per 12 scudi." Frey, "Ricordanze," App., 871, and Alessandro del Vita, *Il Libro delle Ricordanze di Giorgio Vasari* (Rome, 1938), Carta 21, 73.

[25] See Vincenzo Borghini's letters to Giorgio Vasari of August 14 and 17, 1564, quoted in Frey, "Ricordanze," 100-102 and 105-6. In the first letter Borghini suggests and describes the biblical subject to Vasari: "In questa fara l'historia di Giudit che e semplice e piana; et queste historie bisogna che favellino senza lingua et esprimino quel fatto che segui il meglio et piú naturalmente che si puo." See also Alessandro Cecchi, "Vasari, Naldini e la 'Giuditta'," *Paragone* 28 (1977), 100-107, Figs. 61-64. The Farnesina drawing is located in the Istituto Nazionale per la Grafica, inv. FC12419, Rome.

[26] Frey, "Le Ricordanze." See Borghini to Vasari, August 3, 1564, 89-90: "Vi ricordo quel poco di schizzo di Judit, che mostra la testa d'Oloferne al popolo." According to Borghini, Vasari executed this drawing to assist his fellow artist

Battista Naldini in doing a painting on the same subject commissioned by the prior of Arezzo.

[27] See Elena Ciletti, "Patriarchal Ideology in the Renaissance Iconography of Judith," in *Refiguring Woman: Perspectives on Gender and the Italian Renaissance*, eds. Marilyn Migiel and Juliana Schiesari (Ithaca: Cornell University Press, 1991), 35-70.

[28] See Yael Even, "Mantegna's Uffizi *Judith*," 8-20. In his drawing collection, Vasari owned a drawing of Mantegna, *Judith and Her Slave* of 1491 (now at the Uffizi); however, it is unclear whether the Uffizi drawing is the same one. See Licia Ragghianti Collobi, *Il Libro de' Disegni del Vasari* (Florence: Vallecchi, 1974), 84, Fig. 232, for a discussion of the drawing attribution. In his *Il Libro de' Disegni*, Vasari comments on Mantegna's *Judith and Her Slave*: "Nel nostro libro e in un mezzo foglio reale un disegno di mano d'Andrea finito di chiaroscuro, nel quale è una Judit che mette nella tasca d'una schiava mora la testa di Oloferne, fatto d'un chiaroscuro non piú usato, avendo egli lasciato il foglio bianco, che serve per il lume della biacca tanto nettamente, che visi veggono i capegli sfilati e le altre sottigliezze." See also Jane Martineau, ed., *Andrea Mantegna* (Milan: Olivetti/Electa, 1992), 435-44.

[29] I belive that the drawing of *Judith and Holofernes* of 1509-11 (FD1036, in the Collección de Dibujos Italianos, Museo del Prado, Madrid), is probably a study by Michelangelo for the fresco painting. See Mira Friedman, "The Metamorphoses of Judith," 225-46.

[30] H. Diane Russell with Bernadine Barnes, *Eve/Ave: Woman in the Renaissance and Baroque Prints* (Washington, D.C.: National Gallery of Art, 1990), 63.

[31] M. Scolaro, *Carimonte. La raccolta d'arte* (Bolonga: Carimonte Banca, Spa, 1993), 24. Sabatini depicts a brutal and erotic scene where Holofernes's dismembered body can be viewed through the canopy of the tent while Judith triumphantly gazes at the viewer. With her right hand, she holds the sword erect as a banner, while caressing the soft beard of the severed head with her left. The objects of victory — helmet, cut-off head, sword — are placed on a table in the tent as trophies and still-life decorations of success. The apprehension of the barbaric and voyeuristic depiction of the scene parallels contemporary Surrealist paintings.

[32] Maria Teresa Cantaro, *Lavinia Fontana bolognese: "pittora singolare" 1552-1614* (Milan: Jandi Sapi Editori, 1989), 197, and Vera Fortunati, *Lavinia Fontana: 1552-1614* (Milan: Electa, 1994), 204-05.

[33] Edgar Wind, *Pagan Mysteries in the Renaissance* (New York: W. W. Norton & Company, 1958), 73, for a discussion of the Neoplatonic definition of Love (*Pulchritudo-Amor-Voluptas* or *Castitas-Pulchritudo-Amor*), "Love is Passion aroused by Beauty" or "Beauty is Love combined with Chastity."

[34] Jean Seznec, *The Survival of the Pagan Gods* (Princeton: Princeton University Press, 1972), 86.

[35] Russell with Barnes, *Eve/Ave*, 64-66.

[36] Eugene Carroll, *Rosso Fiorentino: Drawings, Prints, and Decorative Arts* (Washington, D. C.: National Gallery of Art, 1988), 364.

[37] Frey, "Le Ricordanze." See Borghini to Vasari, August 3, 1564, 89-90: "Vi ricordo quel poco di schizzo di Judit, che mostra la testa d'Oloferne al popolo."

[38] See Yael Even, "The Loggia dei Lanzi: A Showcase of Female Subjugation," *Woman's Art Journal* 12 (Spring/Summer 1991), 10-14.

[39] The purpose of this paper is not to survey or focus on the Renaissance models of virago and *pudica victrix* images as seen in heroines such as Artemisia, Diana, Lucretia, Agatha, Mary Magdalen, or the Virgin Mary ... or female warriors of the Western lore. Future study needs to be done on this subject. See Margaret L. King, "Virgo et Virago," *Women of the Renaissance* (Chicago: University of Chicago Press, 1991).

[40] Quoted in Russell with Barnes, *Eve/Ave*, 68.

[41] See Russell with Barnes, 67.

[42] I am using the term conceit, or *concetto*, in the Panofskian manner. See Erwin Panofsky, *Idea: A Concept in Art Theory* (Columbia: University of South Carolina Press, 1968).

[43] Anne Hollander, *Seeing Through Clothes* (Berkeley, CA: University of California Press, 1993), 215. See also the following chapters on "Nudity," 83-156, and on "Undress," 157-236, and Jonathan Sawday, *The Body Emblazoned: Dissecting and the Human Body in Renaissance Culture* (London: Routledge, 1995), 16-22, for a discussion on the unity of the body and soul and the revelation of the struggle for the body to house the desire of the soul.

[44] Liana De Girolami Cheney, *Botticelli's Neoplatontic Images* (Potomac Park, MD: Scripta Humanistica, 1993), 27-33.

[45] Hollander, *Seeing Through Clothes*, 214-16, 266 and 472, and Nora W. Desloge, "Italian Paintings and Sculpture," 44.

[46] For a discussion of the symbolism of hair in biblical times see Veda Cobb-Stevens, "Speech, Gesture and Women's Hair in the Gospel of Luke and First Corinthians," in *The Symbolism of Vanitas in the Arts, Literature, and Music*, ed. Liana De Girolami Cheney (New York/London: The Edwin Mellen Press, 1989), 315-51, and "Locks, Tresses, and Manes in Pre-Raphaelite and Victorian Paintings," in *Pre-Raphaelitism and Medievalism in the Arts* (New York/London: The Edwin Mellen Press, 1992), 159-93.

[47] Ciletti, "Patriarchal Ideology," 52.

[48] See Mario Bonfantini, ed. *Opere di Niccolò Machiavelli* (Milan: Riccardo Riccardi, 1963), 497-508: "Non ci può essere utile imitazione degli esempi antichi senza adeguata preparazione morale; e ancora, la *virtù* di un uomo siffatto non potrà farsi valere senza la opportuna occasione, che ` e dalla *fortuna*."

[49] See Phyllis Pray Bober and Ruth Rubinstein, *Renaissance Artists and Antique Sculpture* (New York: Oxford University Press, 1986), 186, no. 153, and 175-80, nos. 139-141.

[50] William Blake Tyrrell, *Amazons: A Study in Athenian Mythmaking* (Baltimore, MD: The Johns Hopkins University Press, 1984), xv. See Bober and Rubinstein, 177, no. 140.

[51] No ancient images represent the Amazons without a breast. Why? Is it because of a sense of decorum, the horror of a woman without a breast, or is it because of the Greek aesthetic concept of the idealized? See Liana De Girolami Cheney, "The Cult of Saint Agatha," *Woman's Art Journal* 17 (Spring/Summer, 1996), 3-10, and Mareily Yalom, *A History of the Breast* (New York: Alfred A. Knopf, 1997).

[52] Margaret L. King, "Virgo et Virago," *Women of the Renaissance* (Chicago: University of Chicago Press, 1991), 192.

[53] Giual Sissa, *Greek Virginity*, trans. Arthur Goldhammer (Cambridge: Harvard University Press, 1990), 87-104. Sexuality and virginity were compatible in ancient times only if sexual activity remained secret. In our case, Judith talks to her people and asks them not to interfere but to trust her actions.

[54] Caroline Walker Bynum, *The Resurrection of the Body in Western Christianity, 200-1336* (New York: Columbia University, 1995) for a discussion on this topic.

[55] Tyrrell, *Amazons: A Study in Athenian Mythmaking*, xv. This scholar eloquently explains Greek mythmaking through sexual polarization.

[56] Gaetano Milanesi, *Le opere di Giorgio Vasari: con nuove annotazioni e commenti*, 9 vols. (Florence 1878-85), 3, 294 (to be noted in this text as *Vasari-Milanesi*). When reversing Pollaiuolo's image it is obvious that Vasari assimilated the Herculean act, which must have fascinated him because he also used it in other later paintings, such as the warrior figure in the fresco of the Sala Regia, Rome. See Philipp Fehl, "Vasari's Extirpation of the Huguenots," *Gazette des Beaux-Arts* 84 (1974), 257-83. Furthermore, in his *Libro de' Disegni*, Vasari collected several drawings on this theme by artists such as Bartolomeo Ammannati, Baccio Bandinelli, and Domenico Beccafumi. See Collobi, *Il Libro de' Disegni*, 282, 235, and 231, respectively, for illustrations of these images. In addition, Vasari provided drawings for Cristofano Gherardi for his painting on the Hercules theme in the Palazzo Vecchio (see Paola Barocchi, *Complementi al Vasari Pittore* [Florence: Leo S. Olschki Editore, 1964], 269-79.)

[57] Vasari-Milanesi, 1878, 5:424; and Carroll, *Rosso Fiorentino*, 75-86.

[58] Bonnefoy, ed., Greek and Egyptian Mythology, 181.

[59] Richard Lattimore, trans., "*Alcesti*," *Euripides* I, ed. David Grene and Richard Lattimore (Chicago: University of Chicago Press, 1955), 52.

[60] Lattimore, "*Alcesti*," 40-41.

[61] Hollander, Seeing Through Clothes, 216.

[62] In previous paintings, to symbolize strength and audacity, Vasari decorated personifications of Fortitude and Courage with military cuirasses like the one seen on Judith. See Liana De Girolami Cheney, "Vasari and Naples: The Monteoliveto Order," *Papers in Art History by Pennsylvania University Press* 5 (1994), 48-126.

[63] Botticelli's drawing of *Minerva* is located at the Uffizi, inv. 201E.

[64] See nn. 10 and 25. Furthermore, the association of Judith with Athena is emphasized by the fact that they both act as wise women, whose skillful and persuasive powers orchestrate freedom for their people. For example, Athena assists the Greeks in conquering the Trojans by suggesting the offer of a gift — the horse; similarly, Judith helps the Israelites overcome the Assyrians by offering her body. Because of their moral and deliberate actions Athena and Judith personify wisdom or illustrate the emblem of *Philosophia*. It is interesting to note that Vasari's image anticipates Cesare Ripa's emblem on *Philosophia*. See Cesare Ripa, *Iconologia* (Padua, 1618), 126.

[65] Liana De Girolami Cheney, "Giorgio Vasari and Antiquity," paper delivered at the International Society for the Classical Tradition, Boston University, March 8-10, 1995. In this presentation (and forthcoming article), I discuss the impact of the Torso Belvedere in Vasari's work, in particular by the personification of the arts that frame the artists's portraits in the *Vite* of 1568. Of note: the Torso Belvedere came from the antique collection of Vasari. See Francis Haskell and Nicholas Penny, *Taste and the Antique* (London: Yale University Press, 1981), 312.

[66] Sissa, *Greek Virginity*, 73-86, and Edgar Wind, *Pagan Mysteries in the Renaissance* (New York: Oxford University Press, 1980), 75, 200, and 203 for the concept of *venus-virgo*.

[67] Obviously Vasari's ambiguous *desexualization* of Judith manifests the Italian *Maniera* style as well as his assimilation of the Quattrocento and Cinquecento conventions of Donatello, Botticelli, Mantegna, Michelangelo, Parmigianino, Rosso, Titian, and later Lavinia Fontana, Veronese, and so on. Furthermore, Vasari's new psychomachia in Judith, in which the virile and violent act dominates the scene, anticipates the representations of Judith in Phillippe Galle's engraving of 1610 (after Maerten van Hemmskerck) for the book *The Fatal Power of Women*, 1610. See also the representation on this topic by Caravaggio, Artemisia Gentileschi, Fedele Galizia, and Elizabetta Sirani during the Baroque period.

University of Massachusetts at Lowell

La Dramaturgie des Jeux Allemands de Carnaval

Jean Marc Pastré

Ininterrompue à Nuremberg au cours des XV° et XVI° siècles, les *Jeux de Carnaval*, les *Fastnachtspiele*, oscillent entre la forme brève et dense d'une action continue et la répartition de la matière en scènes et actes à la manière de la dramaturgie classique des comédies ou drames de Hans Sachs et de Jacob Ayrer. Mais ces deux derniers grands auteurs du XVI° siècle connaissaient encore bien la première manière, si bien que leurs *Jeux* présentent à chaque fois une solution bien particulière du traitement dramaturgique de la matière scénique. Chaque cas mérite donc à la fois l'attention et une analyse détaillée, seule cette dernière permettant de dégager la manière dont s'y prit à chaque fois l'auteur. Pour bien montrer en quoi la dramaturgie des *Jeux* du XV° siècle perdure pour partie au siècle suivant, nous avons choisi pour exemple la pièce 47 de Jacob Ayrer, *Ein fassnachspiel, der uberwunden eifferer.*[1] A l'instar de Hans Sachs, qui s'était inspiré pour ses *Jeux* de bon nombre des nouvelles de Boccace,[2] Ayrer y adaptait pour la scène la huitième nouvelle de la septième journée du célèbre *Décaméron*.[3]

Boccace y conte l'histoire d'un vieux marchand, Arriguccio Berlinghieri, qui, devenu jaloux et méchant, renonce à ses tournées pour mieux surveiller sa jeune femme, Sismonda, tombée follement amoureuse d'un jeune homme qui la courtise depuis longtemps, Roberto. Pour duper le mari, la belle invente le stratagème d'une ficelle qui, attachée à son orteil, lui permettra de savoir que l'amant est au jardin. Ayant découvert la supercherie, l'époux sort armé de la maison et poursuit l'amant. Alarmée par le vacarme, la belle envoie sa servante dans son lit. Le marchand confie l'affaire aux frères et à la mère de l'épouse. Tous accourent chez le marchand et trouvent, à la stupeur du mari, Sismonda en train de coudre calmement, le visage sans trace des coups qu'il a cru lui donner. La belle n'aura pas de mal à convaincre les siens que son époux va chaque nuit trouver les filles à la taverne et qu'il aura, pris une fois encore de boisson, transféré sur sa femme quelque aventure qu'il aura connue avec l'une de ces filles. On pardonne au marchand pour l'ivresse qui l'a égaré, mais il aura garde de ne pas recommencer et laissera désormais les coudées franches à Sismonda.

L'histoire était bien connue en Allemagne comme en France. Le fabliau *Des tresces*, du début du XIII° siècle, la contait déjà, mais sans le stratagème de la ficelle.[4] Vers la moitié du XIII° siècle, Hugues de Mâcon donnait dans ses *Gesta militum* la première version qui alliait à la fois la substitution de la belle au lit et le motif de la ficelle.[5] L'Allemagne connaît l'alliance des deux motifs dès le XIV° siècle avec *Der verkêrte Wirt* de Herrand von Wildonie, version dans laquelle on substitue en outre au galant surpris un âne,[6] puis, au XV° siècle, avec *Der Pfaffe mit der Schnur*, fabliau proche de Boccace et qui finit par une scène comique d'exorcisme pour guérir le mari de sa jalousie maladive.[7] Jörg Zobel reprend enfin à la même époque le fabliau français des *Tresces* dans *Das untergeschobene Kalb*.[8]

Ayrer s'inspira sans aucun doute de la nouvelle de Boccace, bien qu'il fasse attacher la ficelle au doigt de la belle, et non pas à son orteil. Comme chez Boccace, le mari, appelé sobrement par Ayrer *maritus*, a acquis la noblesse par le mariage (2794, 17); incapable d'assurer un métier lucratif (2793, 30), le mari du *Jeu* a de plus épousé sa femme pour sa fortune (2793, 31-34), qu'il dissipe, comme le déplorent le frère de l'épousée et son ami, *amicus*. De même qu'Arriguccio a cessé son commerce pour mieux surveiller sa jeune femme, le mari du *Jeu*, délaissant ses activités de messager, revient à la maison pour tenter de surprendre l'amant dont il sait l'existence (2794, 2-3). Chez Boccace, le frère et l'ami ne cherchent pas à séparer les époux, mais veulent amender le comportement du mari. Ayrer reprend la même idée (2795, 17-19), tout en la transférant aussi sur la servante, dont il amplifie le rôle ici comme ailleurs: la soubrette voit bien la mésentente du couple, mais ne veut pas l'accroître en prenant parti pour l'un ou pour l'autre (2799, 13-14), bien qu'elle penche plutôt, morale oblige, pour son maître (2799, 8-10).

Pour ce *Jeu* comme pour tant d'autres de Sachs et d'Ayrer, la répartition de la matière obéit au principe de sa distribution en "scènes," démarquées par l'entrée et la sortie des personnages. Ce sont donc les "scènes vides" qui permettent de découper l'action en tranches successives.[9] Or l'analyse minutieuse des mouvements des personnages permet de dégager des ensembles cohérents qui distribuent harmonieusement la matière scénique.

Le premier ensemble de trois scènes bien démarquées sert d'exposition. La jeune femme, *Uxor*, déplore d'abord dans un bref monologue le peu d'empressement de son mari. A son amant qui arrive justement, elle explique le stratagème de la ficelle qui lui permettra de la rejoindre la nuit pendant que le mari dormira. L'amant quitte la scène; la belle annonce qu'elle va faire passer la ficelle par la fenêtre (2793, 19). Voilà donc présentés dans cette première scène la femme et son amant. Arrive alors le mari qui, dans un monologue entrecoupé de grognements (2794, 14), déplore son sort, tout en reconnaissant qu'il a épousé sa femme pour son argent, car il est incapable d'exercer un vrai métier. Il part faire une course (2794, 18). A cette deuxième scène succède l'arrivée du frère de la belle et de son ami, *frater* et *amicus*, lesquels déplorent le sort de la belle et déclarent être venus pour observer un peu ce qui se passe dans le ménage (2795, 27). Voilà donc présentés successivement, outre la belle et son amant, le mari et les proches de la belle. On voit que, dans ces trois scènes d'exposition et de présentation des personnages du *Jeu*, Ayrer prépare la fin du drame en introduisant les proches de l'épouse dès les premières scènes, à l'inverse de Boccace, qui ne les fait apparaître qu'au moment du dénouement.

Après la mise en place des personnages et après l'exposé de l'intrigue, un second groupe de trois scènes présente l'exécution même de l'action, la réalisation du plan ourdi par la femme et l'amant. L'épouse accroche d'abord la ficelle à la croisée (2796, 10); *Amator* arrive sur ces entrefaites dès la nuit tombée et tire sur la ficelle; la femme le fait entrer (2796, 22). Ainsi vidée de ses acteurs, cette première scène permet l'arrivée du mari, qui annonce qu'il rentre surveiller sa femme (2797, 3). Cette courte scène est suivie d'un habile chassé-croisé au cours duquel la femme fait subrepticement sortir son amant (2797, 18), occupe la scène après son départ et voit arriver le mari. Elle lui prend le peu d'argent qu'il a gagné, se plaint de son inefficacité et le renvoie à ses courses (2799, 2).

A la triple exposition a donc suivi un groupe de trois scènes dans lesquelles la femme mène le jeu, mais voit son plan contrecarré par l'arrivée inopinée du mari. Après cet ensemble de six scènes, l'action connaît un nouveau départ. Ayrer fait en effet entrer sur scène pour la première fois la soubrette. Elle fait le point de la situation dans un bref monologue, évoque les va-et-vient d'hommes dans la maison, mais se gardera de prendre position pour ne pas envenimer les choses (2799, 2-16). Les deux scènes qui suivent cette nouvelle exposition constituent la reprise inversée de la première scène du dernier groupe précédent. Le mari entre, voit la ficelle, comprend le stratagème et part se préparer à accueillir l'intrus (2800, 3). Arrive alors l'amant, qui tire la ficelle, ce qui déclenche la sortie de l'époux en armure, lequel poursuit l'intrus (2801, 8). Tous deux sortent donc précipitamment. Dans le groupe précédent de trois scènes, c'est la femme qui tirait parti de la ficelle et accueillait l'amant, à l'inverse de ces trois scènes où le mari ravit pour la première fois l'initiative à sa femme. Les trois scènes précédentes montraient le stratagème en action; ces trois scènes montrent comment le mari le déjoue.

A ce premier dénouement succède alors la mise en place d'un nouveau subterfuge, qui prendra la forme de la substitution de l'épouse par la servante, rebondissement qui correspondait au deuxième mouvement de la nouvelle de Boccace. Dans ce nouvel ensemble de trois scènes encore, la femme demande à sa servante d'aller se mettre au lit à sa place; elle en tirera une riche récompense (2802, 4). Toutes deux disparaissent. Entre alors le mari, qui fait le point de la situation dans un très bref monologue: il a chassé l'intrus et va battre sa femme dans sa chambre (2802, 18). Reste donc une troisième et dernière scène, très longue (2802, 19 — 2808, 20), qui apporte à ce groupe de scènes tout autant qu'à l'ensemble du jeu un nouveau dénouement et une conclusion: le nouveau subterfuge confond le mari dont la vengeance est déjouée.

Dans cette dernière scène, qui a l'ampleur du premier mouvement de six scènes et qui constitue une sorte d'acte final, l'action se répartit très habilement en cinq moments. Tout comme la Sismonda de Boccace se cachait dans un coin pour observer le déroulement de la substitution mise en place, la femme du *Jeu* revient en scène avec un travail de couture et se met dans un coin. Ayrer recourt alors à un procédé qu'il avait appris des troupes anglaises de passage à Nuremberg et fait chanter le personnage. Ce chant permet à l'auteur de faire en neuf strophes le point de la situation et surtout d'annoncer point pour point l'action qui suit, si ramassée qu'un résumé préalable pouvait sembler nécessaire à l'auteur pour une meilleure compréhension de la scène. Hans Sachs connaissait d'ailleurs bien cette manière très pédagogique de préparer le public aux détours d'une action parfois touffue. Dans sa chanson, la femme reprend d'abord les motifs du début du *Jeu*, son insatisfaction, la dilapidation de sa fortune et sa décision de prendre un amant (str. 1 et 2). Puis elle évoque l'action la plus immédiate, les coups que le mari va donner à la servante (str. 3). Elle annonce enfin la suite du déroulement du *Jeu*: sa famille sera bien étonnée de la voir coudre si sereinement lorsque le mari la conduira jusqu'à sa parentèle (str. 4), car la ruse féminine est grande (str. 5); si grande que le mari, qui pensait se venger d'elle, recevra en fait les coups qu'il destinait à son épouse (str. 6); une petite femme vient ainsi à bout d'un grand mari (str. 7). Entendant ce dernier mari descendre l'escalier, elle interrompt son chant et annonce qu'elle restera assise dans son coin (str. 8 et 9).

La scène n'est donc pas vide, ou plutôt elle l'est à demi, puisque la femme reste visible et assiste à ce qui va se passer. Dans le deuxième "moment" du déroulement de l'action, le mari saisit la servante par son bonnet de nuit, la roue de coups et annonce qu'il va chercher la famille de sa femme (2804, 2). Reste donc en scène la soubrette, qui se plaint à sa maîtresse, toujours assise tout à côté, laquelle l'envoie se faire soigner par *Amicus* (2804, 14). A ce troisième moment, moment charnière en ce que la servante prépare le témoignage d'*Amicus*, qui va réapparaître dans le moment suivant, à cette troisième étape succèdent, en un crescendo propre à tout *finale*, le frère de l'épouse et le mari, suivis de l'ami. Confondu par le bon état physique de sa femme et par le témoignage de l'ami, l'époux est à son tour battu par le clan de la belle par deux fois. Le mari promet de ne plus dire un mot quoi qu'il arrive. Tous quittent la scène (2808, 6), sauf l'épouse qui, dans un bref monologue à la manière de l'*Ausschreier* des

Jeux, conclut le tout et souligne combien les hommes doivent prendre soin de leur femme et combien aussi la roue de Fortune tourne en peu de temps, précipitant bientôt ceux qui se croyaient au faîte de leur pouvoir (2808, 20). On notera qu'Ayrer a inventé cette scène de coups donnés au mari, absente de la nouvelle de Boccace, mais que, curieusement, Steinhöwel mentionnait dans le résumé qu'il faisait de sa traduction. Il est vrai que bien des *Jeux* du XV° siècle ponctuaient de coups le déroulement de leur action, surtout à titre de démarcation de scènes.[10] Ayrer reprend donc là une tradition bien établie de la dramaturgie des *Jeux* de Nuremberg.

Cette grande scène de la dimension d'un acte est en fait construite avec la rigueur d'un acte. Bien que la scène n'y soit jamais vide, il est aisé d'y déceler de petites "scènes", cinq moments de l'action. A la scène 1, qui sert d'exposition, répond la scène finale qui conclut le *Jeu*, l'une et l'autre mettant en scène pour seul personnage la femme. A la scène 2, celle des coups que le mari donne à la servante, répond la scène 4, dans laquelle le mari reçoit à son tour tout autant de coups. La scène 3 sert de charnière à cet ensemble: la soubrette à la fois reprend la scène 2 — elle a été battue — et annonce la scène 4. *Amicus* pourra témoigner de la confusion grossière du mari sans doute pris d'ébriété.

L'ensemble du *Jeu* répartit d'ailleurs tout aussi harmonieusement la matière scénique: aux deux groupes de trois scènes qui constituent le premier mouvement du *Jeu*, avec une triple exposition et le début de l'action, répond un ensemble de deux groupes de trois scènes, un second mouvement narratif qui comprend la reprise, mais dans l'échec, de l'action qui avait réussi tout avant, puis un second subterfuge destiné à déjouer la vengeance du mari. La femme d'abord mène le *Jeu*, puis l'époux, qui toutefois perd la main et tombe victime de son propre plan.

Ce type de prouesse technique ne doit pas nous étonner. Ayrer prouve dans bien d'autres Jeux qu'il excelle en la matière, à preuve le *Jeu* 2 de l'édition Keller, le *Fassnachtspil von Antreuxo*, qui répartit l'action en deux ensembles de trois scènes, précédés et suivis d'une exposition et d'une conclusion.

Et cette manière n'était pas nouvelle, puisque Sachs savait en faire autant déjà, à preuve le *Jeu* 23 de l'édition Götze, *Der jung Kauffeman Nicola mit seiner Sophia*, tiré de la dixième nouvelle de la huitième journée des *Cent nouvelles*, *Jeu* dans lequel la matière se répartit avec une parfaite régularité dans deux ensembles égaux de cinq scènes chacun, les parties des deux ensembles se répondant scène pour scène avec une parfaite symétrie.[11]

Hormis la dernière scène, le *Jeu* d'Ayrer a donc pour démarcatif les scènes vides à l'instar de tant de *Jeux* de Sachs. La scène finale, si longue, relève d'un autre principe, celui d'un continuum narratif, d'une suite de moments qu'aucune scène vide ne sépare. Sachs connaissait aussi cette manière: il l'emploie dans *Das Weib im Brunnen*, jeu tiré de la quatrième nouvelle de la septième journée du *Décaméron*. Fondé sur le parallélisme inversé de deux mouvements, le jeu ne présente toutefois aucune interruption scénique. C'était là reprendre la tradition des *Jeux de Carnaval* du XV° siècle, dans lesquels les personnages se succèdent sur l'avant-scène, puis passent en arrière-scène sans qu'on ait jamais de scène vide.[12] On voit qu'Ayrer n'hésite pas à allier dans un même jeu les deux manières, tant il est vrai qu'il n'existait pas de forme dramaturgique fixe, rigide et figée des *Jeux* de cette époque.

Moins stricte que la forme arrêtée de la comédie, que Sachs et Ayrer connaissaient aussi, le *Jeu* garde ainsi beaucoup de cette liberté de mise en scène qui faisait la force et la diversité des *Jeux* du siècle précédent. Notre Jeu en garde les traces. Comme pour eux, le personnage qui conclut la pièce s'adresse au public, "vous avez vu dans ce Jeu ...", "*In diesem Spiel habt jhr gesehen*" (2808, 8). Ayrer y apporte toutefois sa marque personnelle. Il précise ainsi dans uns indication technique que le *Maritus* peut, si l'on veut, prendre la forme du clown anglais qui avait marqué si fort Ayrer, Jahn Posset, "*Maritus ob man will, in gestalt eines Englendischen Jahnns*" (2793, 20-21). En outre, l'épouse, au dernier vers de la dernière strophe de sa chanson lors de la grande scène finale, s'adresse au public et lui enjoint de se taire, car le mari et la soubrette arrivent, "*O schweigt! sie kommen warlich schon*" (2803, 32). Or Ayrer est un habitué de cette manière. Dans le jeu d'Antreuxo, déjà cité, *Amicus*, le valet d'une belle, accompagne le jeune homme, qu'elle dupe, jusqu'aux latrines, lui éclaire la fosse d'une torche, l'éteint après la chute du jeune homme dans le trou, puis rit et fait signe au public de se taire (2346, 19). Eva, la soubrette, observe la scène, cachée derrière le rideau; elle rit aussi et fait signe à *Amicus* de ne rien répondre à Antreuxo, *Amicus* faisant à son tour signe au public de n'en rien faire non plus (2347, 26-27). Actrice, mais aussi spectatrice de la scène, la soubrette observe donc la scène en connivence avec le public dont elle partage le regard: c'est un peu déjà le théâtre dans le théâtre, les acteurs partageant avec le public le rôle de spectateur. La soubrette de notre *Jeu* ne fait pas autrement.

Ayrer est en effet un homme de théâtre. Il n'est pour s'en convaincre que de voir la manière dont il recourt aux indications scéniques. Il est très probable que les premiers *Jeux* du XV° siècle ne présentaient pas ces notations, le texte suffisant à sa mise en scène, les termes mêmes des dialogues ou monologues suffisant à déterminer les positions et les mouvements des personnages. La pièce 24 de l'édition Keller, *Ein hubsch vasnachtspil*, de Rosenplüt, en fournit un bon exemple.[13] Les auteurs des *Jeux* du XVI° siècle connaissaient encore cette manière, à preuve le *Consistory Rumpoldi* de Vigil Raber.[14] Tout à l'inverse, Sachs, dans ses

Jeux, libérait le texte de ce genre de notations en introduisant de nombreuses et précises indications scéniques, lesquelles ne faisaient pas double emploi avec le contenu du texte. La pièce 84 de l'édition Goetze, *Die jung witfrau Francisca*, et la pièce 16, *Der schwanger Bawer*, en fournissent de bons exemples. Or, rares sont chez Ayrer les cas où le texte se suffit à lui-même et où l'auteur n'éprouve pas le besoin d'ajouter une indication scénique. Notre *Jeu* n'en compte même qu'un. Le mari, qui vient de découvrir la ficelle, annonce qu'il part pour se préparer à la riposte et faire semblant de dormir "*Ich wil gehn wie ich gsagt hab, than*" (2800, 3). De fait, Ayrer n'ajoute au texte aucune indication scénique.

Notre jeu contient au contraire plus de trente passages dans lesquels le texte se suffirait à lui-même, mais Ayrer, metteur en scène prudent, préfère souligner le trait et répéter par l'indication scénique ce que le texte contient déjà. Bien souvent, il s'agit de l'entrée en scène ou de la sortie des personnages, annoncées pourtant par le texte, telle l'arrivée d'*Amator*, "*Amator geht ein*" (2792, 7), annoncée pourtant par l'épouse, "*Schau! dort kommt der Hertzlichste mein*" (2792, 5), telle celle de *Maritus* (2793, 21: 2793, 22; 2797, 32: 2797, 27) ou telle celle d'*Amator* (2800, 4: 2800, 5). Ce peut être aussi le départ d'un personnage, celui d'*Amator*, "*Er gibt jr die Hand und geht ab*" (2793, 9), annoncé pourtant par lui-même par avant, "*Itzt scheid ich von euch mit wissn ab*" (2793, 6), celui de la femme (2793, 20: 2793, 14; 2794, 19: 2794, 16: 2796, 11: 2796, 8). Le texte parfois enchâsse l'indication scénique, par exemple lorsque *Amator* annonce son départ, "*Dissmal muss es geschieden sein*" (2797, 15), précisé par l'épouse, qui lui dit de partir, "*Mein Hertzeslieb, dein Strassen fahr!*" (2797, 6), le tout entourant l'indication scénique, "*geht ab*" (2797, 16). Mais les notations reprennent toutes sortes d'éléments du récit. La femme dit aussi à l'amant de pousser la porte qu'elle a laissée ouverte, "*Ach Hertzlieb, stoss an der Thür an!/Ich hab euch auffgezogen schon*" (2796, 19-20), ce qui aurait dû rendre superflue la notation de 2796, 23, "*Er geht hinein.*" Ou bien elle demande à son mari rentré de courses ce qu'il a d'argent dans la poche, "*Sag! wie bist du im Beutl staffirt ?*" (2798, 6), ce que reprend la notation qui vient aussitôt, "*Sie greifft jhn in die Taschen, nimmt das Gelt rauss*" (2798, 7). On voit qu'Ayrer tient à diriger lui-même les acteurs plutôt que de leur laisser l'initiative de mettre leurs gestes en conformité avec leurs dires. Lorsque le mari trouve la ficelle, "*Ja, find ich da dieses Wahrzeichn*" (2799, 19), Ayrer préfère ainsi préciser dès avant une mimique que pourtant la situation exigeait de l'acteur, "*Maritus geht ein und sihet als balt umb nach der Schnur*" (2799, 17-18). Il en va de même un peu plus loin, lorsque l'amant, qui vient de tirer sur la ficelle, sent la résistance souhaitée, signe que la dame est prête, "*Die Schnur hat sie mir zucket wider*" (2800, 13), ce qu'une notation annonçait déjà, "*die Schnur wird wider gezuckt*" (2800,

11). Ou bien la femme déclare être restée assise à coudre, pour gagner un peu d'argent, "*Sonder da gesessen, hab geneht*" (2805, 1), ce qu'Ayrer précisait quelque vingt vers avant, "*Die Frau sitzt dort und neht*" (2804, 15). Et c'est bien le jeu des acteurs que le dramaturge-metteur en scène tient à souligner, comme dans le passage où le mari battu tombe à genoux, suppliant qu'on l'épargne, "*O lieben Herrn, ich bitt umb Gnad*" (2807, 2) et "*Ich bitt umb Gottes willn umb Gnad*" (2807, 14), attitude de l'acteur imposée par deux indications scéniques, "*Maritus felt zu fuss*" (2807, 1 et 13).

A la manière de Sachs, Ayrer se contente dans un bon tiers des cas — dans quelque 15 passages — de guider le jeu des acteurs par la seule indication scénique. Il s'agit le plus souvent de l'entrée des personnages après une scène vide, ce qui correspond à une nécessité dramaturgique, comme l'entrée en scène de la soubrette (2799, 2), du mari (2799, 17) ou de la femme et de la soubrette (2801, 9). Il peut s'agir aussi d'une sortie des personnages que le texte ne laisse pas prévoir, manière d'alléger d'autant ce dernier. C'est le cas de la sortie de scène du frère et de l'ami (2795, 26), du mari (2797, 4), de la soubrette (2799, 17) ou de l'amant (2801, 5). Metteur en scène aussi, Ayrer recourt souvent à ces notations pour imposer aux acteurs un jeu de mimique ou l'emploi d'accessoires. La femme doit ainsi monter faire passer la ficelle par une fenêtre, "*Uxor geht oben auff die zinnen, hengt ein lange schnur oben rab*" (2795, 28-29); lorsque l'amant tire à la ficelle, elle doit apparaître à la fenêtre en bonnet de nuit, vêtue d'une pelisse, "*Uxor geht herfür, sicht oben rauss in einer Schlaffhauben und Nachtbeltz*" (2796, 16-17). Au moment de surprendre l'amant qui vient de tirer la ficelle, le mari doit tirer l'épée du fourreau, "*Maritus geht besser rauss, hat ein Harnisch uber sich geworffen*" (2801, 29-30); il poursuit bientôt l'amant en fuite, quittant la scène avec un grand cri et frappant le pavé de son épée, "*Maritus laufft mit eim grossen geschrey rauss, schlägt ins Pflaster*" (2801, 5-6). Pour ne rien laisser au hasard de l'interprétation, Ayrer arrête donc tous les détails du geste et de la tenue des acteurs.

En bon dramaturge, Ayrer fournit en outre dans le texte toutes sortes de détails qui précisent et limitent au mieux la durée de l'action comme les lieux de son déroulement. Chez Boccace, les amants se voient depuis longtemps et doivent trouver un stratagème pour duper un mari devenu excessivement méfiant. A bien lire Ayrer, les amants du Jeu en sont encore à organiser leur premier rendez-vous nocturne (2792, 8-16). L'action, ainsi ramassée, commence de jour; l'amant salue l'épouse par un "bonjour" significatif, "*Ach Hertzlich, einen guten tag*" (2792, 8). La femme attend de l'amant qu'il revienne plus tard, de nuit, "*Wenn ji zu nachts kommt für mein hauss*" (2792, 22). Le mari arrive sur ces entrefaites, assez tôt toutefois pour repartir peu après pour une autre course (2794, 15-18): nous sommes donc en fin d'après-midi. Suivent alors deux rendez-vous nocturnes, Ayrer redoublant le motif de la visite nocturne qu'il trouvait chez Boccace. Le premier rendez-vous, interrompu, se situe dans le premier mouvement de six scènes. L'amant est venu en l'absence du mari; il doit quitter la maison lorsque ce dernier rentre nuitamment après une longue course, "*Die gantz Nacht bin ich heut gloffn*" (2796, 24). Les amants sortent en fait d'un bon souper, "*Das essn und trincken war als gut*", dit *Amator* (2797, 10), mais le retour du mari écourte le reste, ce que l'amant déplore, "*So hett wir sonst auch unsern Muth/Nach alles unsers Hertzen lust*" (2797, 11-12). Mais la femme le console: il n'a qu'à revenir cette même nuit, plus tard, "*Heint zu Nacht wider kommen thut!*" (2797, 6). Il revient en effet bientôt, mais se fait surprendre: le second rendez-vous appartient au second mouvement de six scènes et se solde par un complet échec. Le mari frappe alors de coups sa servante et annonce qu'il fera venir la parentèle de sa femme au matin, "*Dass man dich morgen kennen sol/Und wil es deinen Freunden klagn*" (2803, 36-37). Cette dernière pourra alléguer à la parentèle accourue qu'elle a passé toute la nuit assise à coudre, "*Die Nacht hab ich kein Schlaff gethan/Und bin auch kommen in kein Beht*" (2805, 34-35). Tout s'est donc passé entre la fin d'un après-midi et le petit matın qui suit la nuit des deux rendez-vous.

L'unité de temps chère à la dramaturgie classique est donc bien respectée. Boccace d'ailleurs y conduisait naturellement dans cette nouvelle. Il en va de même pour l'espace, limité chez Boccace à la maison d'Arriguccio. Ayrer n'eut donc pas grand peine à respecter l'unité de lieu. Il n'en précise pas moins les détails, afin, ici aussi, de tracer les lignes majeures de la mise en scène. L'exposition de l'action des trois premières scènes se passe manifestement devant la demeure de la belle. Elle dit ainsi vouloir y rentrer pour accrocher la ficelle (2793, 14-15). Le mari prend la place de l'épouse, rentrant de courses pour repartir aussitôt (2793, 21-22). Le frère et l'ami de la belle reviennent, disent-ils, observer la vie du couple (2795, 19); ils sont donc dans les parages, sans doute aussi devant la demeure. Le deuxième groupe de scènes se passe dans le même décor. L'amant arrive devant la porte de la maison et tire sur la ficelle (2796, 11617); la femme apparaît alors à la fenêtre: le public la voit donc de l'extérieur, devant la façade de la demeure, lieu du drame jusqu'à présent. Le mari arrive, la femme congédie l'amant, retrouve le mari, toujours devant la maison, car le mari déplore de ne pas la trouver couchée (2798, 2). Lors du second mouvement, le mari revient devant la maison et, ayant découvert la ficelle, annonce qu'il va monter se coucher après avoir attaché la ficelle à son propre doigt (2800, 3). L'amant s'approche, tire sur la ficelle (2800, 4), le mari sort et poursuit l'amant (2800, 21 et 29). Nous sommes donc toujours devant la maison. La femme demande alors à la servante de monter en vitesse dans sa chambre, "*Geh eylend hinaufl!*" (2801, 19); elle annonce ensuite qu'elle va partir s'asseoir dans un coin, "*Denn will ich mich hinsetzen dort*" (2801, 23). Tout indique ainsi que les deux personnages se trouvent toujours en bas devant la demeure. Elles laissent la place au mari revenu, lequel déclare avoir chassé l'intrus et s'apprête à monter battre l'infidèle, "*Ich will gehn still zu jhr nauff schleichn*" (2802, 18). La scène n'a toujours pas changé de lieu. Est-elle ensuite transférée à l'intérieur de la maison ? Ayrer n'en dit rien. Une seule chose est claire: le public ne voit rien se dérouler dans la chambre. La femme est en effet descendue, elle s'assied dans un coin (2802, 29-20). La soubrette est couchée à sa place, au-dessus, dans sa chambre, "*Mein Magd ligt droben in seim Bett*" (2803, 1), mais le mari la fait descendre pour la battre en bas. La femme entend en effet son mari descendre les escaliers, "*Mein Mann tumpelt dir Stiegen rab*" (2803, 27), traînant avec lui la servante en tenue nocturne; il est, répétera plus tard la femme à sa parentèle, sorti de sa chambre avec elle, "*Das aber hab ich wol vernommen,/Dass er ist auss der Kammer kommen*" (2805, 4-5). Une fois battue, la soubrette va jusqu'à sa maîtresse (2804, 2-3), bien que sans quitter la scène. Surgissent alors le frère et l'ami, qui s'adressent à la femme toujours assise dans son coin en train de coudre (2804, 14). Tout peut donc se passer à l'extérieur, en bas de la même demeure, ce qui simplifie d'autant la mise en scène, et, par là, la compréhension de l'action, le même lieu réel du théâtre, la scène, se prêtant sans grand luxe de décor à l'évolution d'un *Jeu* qui fait entrer et ressortir d'une même maison les personnages pour les réunir enfin devant ou en bas dans cette même demeure, les mouvements de passage d'une étape à l'autre relevant du récit indirect et non de l'action vue par le public.

En ne formalisant pas plus le décor, en lui laissant une certaine souplesse d'interprétation, Ayrer garantissait à la pièce la sobriété de fonctionnement qui fit toujours la force des *Jeux de Carnaval*. Bâtie avec rigueur, simple dans sa forme, à la fois très élaborée, mais de structures très forte, le *Jeu du Jaloux* témoigne, à l'instar des *Jeux* de Sachs, d'une dramaturgie particulièrement efficace, sans cesse renouvelée et qui requiert de ce fait à chaque fois l'analyse la plus minutieuse. Comme Sachs, Ayrer était en effet un excellent dramaturge.

Notes

[1] Jacob Ayrer, *Dramen*, éd. Adalbert von Keller (Stuttgart: Litterarischer Verein, 1865), 76-80.

[2] Voir notre article, “L’Italie et l’Allemagne, Boccace et Hans Sachs: de la nouvelle au Jeu de Carnaval”, in “Die kulturellen Beziehungen zwischen Italien und den anderen Ländern Europas im Mittelalter,” *Wodan* 28 (1993), 135-145.

[3] Boccace, *Décaméron,* traduction de Jean Bourciez (Paris: Garnier, 1952).

[4] *Recueil général et complet des fabliaux des XIII° et XIV° siècles*, éds. Anatole de Montaiglon et Gaston Raynaud (Paris: Librairie des Bibliophiles, 1880), vol. IV, 94: 67-81. Jean Rychner, *Contribution à l’étude des fabliaux*, tome II, *Textes*, X (Neuchâtel-Genève: Droz, 1960), 136-148. Philippe Ménard, *Fabliaux français du Moyen âge* (Genève: Droz, 1979), tome 1, VII: 95-108.

[5] *Die Gesta militum des Hugo von Mâcon. Ein bisher unbekanntes Werk der Erzählliteratur des Hochmittelalters*, Teil I: *Einleitung und Text*, éd. Ewald Könsgen (Leiden: Brill, 1990), Mittellateinische Studien und Texte, XVIII, 1. Voir notre article “Une nouvelle version des *Tresces* et du *Chainse* ou l’utilisation des fabliaux dans les *Gesta militum* de Hugues de Mâcon”, in *Reinhardus* 7 (Amsterdam: Benjamin, 1994), 103-112.

[6] Herrand von Wildonie, *Der verkerte wirt*, éd. Friedrich Heinrich von der Hagen, *Gesamtabenteuer* (Stuttgart/Tübingen: Litterarischer Verein, 1850), vol. 2, XLIII: 332-347.

[7] *Der Pfaffe mit der Schnur A*, éd. Heinrich Niewöhner, *Neues Gesamtabenteuer* (Berlin: Weidmann, 1937), 140-151.

[8] Jörg Zobel, Das untergeschobene Kalb, éd. Hanns Fischer, Die deutsche Märendichtung des 15. Jahrhunderts (Munich: Beck, 1966), 378-383.

[9] Voir notre article “Fastnachtspiel et récit bref: l’interférence de deux genres littéraires en Allemagne aux XV° et XVI° siècles”, in *Récit bref au Moyen Age*, *Wodan* 2 (1989), 141-150.

[10] Voir notre article “De la fonction des coups dans les Jeux allemands de Carnaval,” in *Les “realia” dans la littérature de fiction du Moyen Age*, *Wodan* 25 (1993), 109-118.

[11] Jean Marc Pastré, “L’Italie et l’Allemagne”, op. cit. Hans Sachs, *Sämtliche Fastnachtspiele*, éd. Edmund Goetze, 1-20 (Halle: Niemeyer, 1881), 23.

[12] Jean Marc Pastré, “Fastnachtspiel et récit bref.”

[13] *Fastnachtspiele aus dem 15. Jahrhundert*, éd. Adalbert von Keller, vols. 1-3 (Darmstadt: Wissenschaftliche Buchgesellschaft, 1965-66).

[14] *Fastnachtspiele des 15. und 16. Jahrhunderts*, éd. Dieter Wuttke (Stuttgart: Reclam, 1973), 91-130.

Université de Rouen

Cain in the Mysteries: The Iconography of Violence

Clifford Davidson

I

In one of the choir windows of York Minster is a panel of sixteenth-century painted glass showing the fallen Adam and Eve being expelled from the Garden of Eden and followed by the Seven Deadly Sins. The glass is not part of the original glazing of York Minster or even English (it is from Rouen),[1] but it illustrates how the Fall was regarded as the entry point for transgressive behavior in the history of humankind. In the epistle of Clement of Rome, written in c.100 A.D., the Fall is defined as the source of emulation, envy, and strife as well as sedition, persecution, disorder, and war.[2] Adam and Eve had themselves not fallen into such sins directly, but the act of eating the forbidden fruit started the slide toward crime and eventually toward murder. Hence while the origins of the lapsarian condition were understood to be found in the Fall — the succumbing of Eve and Adam to the suggestions of the serpent in the garden — the first person to be fully suffused with evil was Cain, who functions as the initial human villain in the religious drama of the Middle Ages.[3] As such, he is the figure out of primordial time who establishes a spiritual progeny that will join him in eternal damnation — a kinship that will continue to exist upon this earth until the last day of history. Cain was thus regarded as central to the presentation of the problem of violence and evil in history; his act of fratricide was for St. Augustine the "archetype of crime,"[4] and for the dramatists of the late medieval vernacular plays of England it was the pattern of all subsequent violence, including the strife that would lead to the torture and death of the Redeemer.[5]

The present paper will attempt to examine the late medieval understanding of the first murder in its full visual dimension as it provided the ground against which violence would be presented on the civic religious stage in England.[6] In so doing I will be implicitly asserting the validity of studying the dominant urban culture — that is, the conventional views held by citizens, their wives, parish clergy, and others. This is not to say that the popular response to all biblical characters was uniform or that there was not an element even of indifference toward their stories from some quarters — or that the comic elements were not perceived from quite different perspectives by different members of the audience.[7] But with regard to acts of violence, and to their potential for repetition through acts of revenge, the complexity of public reaction nevertheless does not erase the people's generalized concern or the earlier legal response, which in Germanic countries was to substitute the concept of public justice for the idea that murder was a private matter between the families affected. In place of the Anglo-Saxon practice of *Wergild*, the *Laws of Henry I* had recognized murder as an offense against the crown. The acceptance of public responsibility for bringing the murderer to justice may, at least theoretically, be seen as an attempt to limit transgressive behavior in a time when there was intense concern about social instability. Violence was often a real presence, especially as it existed outside the walls of the city (in 1520 Coventry, for example, closed its gates between 8 in the evening and 5 in the morning "for the preseruacion of good rulee etc."[8]) but not infrequently internally. The York *Ordo Paginarum*, an official civic document, found it necessary to decree "þat no man go armed in þis Citee with swerdes ne with carill axes ne none othir defences in distourbaunce of þe kynges pees & þe play or hynderyng of þe processioun of Corpore christi" except for "knyghtes and sqwyers of wirship þat awe haue swerdes borne eftir thame."[9] Even in the Christian era when salvation was held to be available to all, Cain's act of murder was being replicated in the society — and would continue to be replicated as long as the world would continue to stand. To understand this threat to good order was to give it a historical basis in imagining the first act of murder, which was hence an obligatory episode in the dramatic presentation of the history of the world.

The story of Cain and Abel, which highlighted both the failure of Cain to sacrifice satisfactorily and his homicide, cannot have been visualized in the vernacular drama — or, for that matter, in art — merely as a response to some perceived external threat to the sacrifice of the Mass. For example, some Lollards objected strenuously to the sacramental theology of the Church, denied the element of sacrifice in the Eucharist, and refused to attend Mass or take communion. While such attitudes may plausibly have been in the mind of the dramatist who created the Towneley Cain, the story of the murder of Abel had a much broader application,[10] and it was dramatized not only in Continental drama[11] but also in a much earlier play, possibly written in England, of the early history of the world. In no sense could the latter play bear any relationship whatever to the beliefs of Wyclif or the Lollards.

A useful perspective may nevertheless be gained from glancing back at this earlier play, the twelfth-century Anglo-Norman *Ordo Representationis Adae*,[12] which was written long before the earliest of the great civic drama cycles. In one sense the *Ordo*'s Cain may be seen primarily as an illustration of the consequences of the Fall for human behavior, but it has some extremely interesting features. Unusually, in this play both Cain and his brother Abel are tillers of the soil, an occupation that is reminiscent of the task to which Adam had typically been set following his expulsion from Eden. As Adam's task earlier in this play had been complicated by the devil's act of planting thistles and thorns on his land, so now Cain will himself be a physical sign of human decadence. His victimizing of his brother Abel will cause him to be in turn a victim of devils, who beat him and thrust him into hell where he will be the first permanent resident.[13] Cain's immediate demise is a surprise, since this symbolic conclusion follows a rapid dramatization of the main events up to that point of the biblical story, which emphasizes the sacrifice, Cain's envy, his murder of his brother, and the curse of God, here identified as Figura. While, as Lynette Muir points out, the tithing and sacrifice have their rationale as "love of God, and an attempt to repair the sin of the First Parents,"[14] these become the source in the play of Cain's wrath when his own sacrifice is rejected. Cain absorbs in full measure the *cupiditas* that had been the motive for the Fall of his parents initially.[15] Herein, then, lies the very origin of violence among human beings — violence which will resound through history until the Last Day.

In the later vernacular drama of England, the story of Cain is even more clearly the presentation of an archetype of violence in history. Cain serves as a point of reference throughout each of the play cycles and collections, even though all are composite works by several hands and lacking the artistic unity which a single author might introduce. Cain represents the reprobate who is at once a transgressor and a sufferer from despair because of his expectation of damnation. Thus he provides a model of alienation and violence for the subsequent villains that are presented in the course of the plays, which survey human history as it was understood from the traditional accounts in the Bible and other sources. Four of these dramatizations of Cain's story are written in Middle English, while two are in Cornish.

II

The ultimate source of the story of Cain, the narrative in Genesis 4, is to be sure a passage of considerable ambiguity, though biblical scholars agree that it is part of the earliest layer of writing attributed to one known in higher criticism as the Yahwist (J), as distinguished from the later priestly redactors.[16] In one sense the narrative is straightforward in its description of events following the sexual coupling of Adam and Eve: the birth of their sons Cain and Abel, their different occupations, their offerings, Cain's envy and murder of his brother, and God's curse of the murderer. As a story about the first human beings to be born into earthly life it has a terrifying message of violence, and at its end Cain has become both a wanderer and an exile and a founder of cities.

But what is the reason for God's rejection of Cain's sacrifice? The conventional explanation is that Abel as a shepherd represented the preferred pastoral way of life, as opposed to Cain's choice of tilling the soil, for an author who romanticized a nomadic Israelite past.[17] The Hebrew God prefers the younger son, the shepherd, rather than the farmer. Why? Was it, as the gloss in the Geneva Bible (1560) insisted, merely that Cain was a "hypocrite and offred onely for an outwarde shew without sinceritie of heart"? If so, how was it that the very first man to have been born rather than created should also have been a hypocrite who only outwardly would go through the motions of piety demanded by a still present Creator? The Genesis text itself is silent in this regard. It says only in effect that God did not like Cain's offering while Abel's offering was acceptable to him.[18] As Harold Bloom comments, "J offers us no motive for Yahweh's choice, and is equally laconic as to the provocation for Cain's gratuitous, sudden murder of Abel."[19] The author, J, tantalizes and leaves room for multiple interpretations. Was it that Cain's sacrifice was fruit of the ground that God had cursed? If so, we may regard this curse as reversed at the Flood, and certainly in the rogation rites of fifteenth- and sixteenth-century England the blessing of the fields established a very different view of the ground and its fruits.[20]

Another interpretation, which contradicts the Genesis account,[21] even suggests that Cain's father was not Adam but the devil. The idea that Satan, under the guise of the serpent, was the first seducer of a woman was known in the Christian West.[22] Some lesser known Jewish writers and Manichaean heretics included Cain's demonic paternity as an explanation for his thoroughly bad behavior.[23] More important was the authority of 1 John 3:12: "Not as Cain, who was of the wicked one, and killed his brother...because his own works were wicked: and his brother's just." The *Cursor Mundi* appears to affirm this view: "And caym was þe feindes fode,/ was neuer wers of moder born."[24] The Wakefield Master's Cain, on account of his perverse and even demonic behavior throughout the Towneley play, seems not very far removed from this Cain, though so far as I know there is no proof that the author drew upon the notion that he was physically sired by the devil. This Cain, however, swears by the devil even as he attempts to light the fire under his sacrifice: "Now bren in the dwillys name" (2.280). The York play's Cain, similarly willful, likewise invokes the devil in response to Abel's urging: "Ya, daunce in þe devil way,.../ For I wille wyrke euen as I will" (VII.52–53). Being on the side of the devil does not, of course, prove diabolical paternity except in a symbolic sense. Yet there is merit in Peter Travis's observation that the Chester Cain bears comparison with the Lucifer of the Fall of the Angels, for he too appears to be "a 'congeon,' a subtle deceiver whose evil desires, although slowly revealed, are in retrospect seen to have been operative in his first words"; further, "like Lucifer, Cain shows no signs of guilt...."[25] The *Cursor Mundi* says that

Cain sacrificed out of an "iuel will," and for this reason "vr louerd loked noght þar-till."[26]

The nature of Cain's sacrifice, which many interpreters described as defective in quality or quantity, is also important. The biblical text does not specify either defect, of course, only that God did not like the sacrifice. But commonly it was believed that Cain picked out for sacrifice the inferior fruits of the earth and saved the best for himself. So Cain in the Chester play will offer the worst of his harvest ("For cleane corne, by my faye,/ of mee gettst thou nought" [II.543–44]), and the Wakefield Master's Cain also offers his poorest sheaves, mixed with "Thystyls and brerys," which when it burns "stank like the dwill in hell" (Towneley 2.204, 285). The Cain of the N-town specifically offers only his worst; he will, he says, "tythe þe werst," for which he searches through his fields (3.96–100). When to Abel's horror he brings forth his "werst," he announces: "Here I tythe þis vnthende sheff" (101). The Chester Cain grasps at straw instead of sheaves of wheat; "Hit weare pittye, by my panne," he says, "those fayre eares for to brenne" (II.537–38). And in the Cornish *Ordinalia* Cain insists that it is folly to consign to the fire that "which a man can live on" (*Origo Mundi* 474–75), while in the *Creacion of the World* he adulterates his sacrifice not only with brambles and thorns but also with cow dung (Cornish: *glose*) to burn for his sacrifice (1086–90). This depiction of Cain's sacrifice is consistent with the criticism developed in St. Ambrose's *Of Cain and Abel*,[27] a work that would prove to be most influential in subsequent centuries. In the *Stanzaic Life of Christ*, for example, Cain offers "fuylet corn," which therefore burned without "light" — that is, without open flame.[28]

Hence Cain offered not the "first fruits" of his labor but inferior produce instead, nor indeed did he give willingly.[29] Cain's hostility to God, his malice toward his brother, and his blasphemous unwillingness to sacrifice anything of value are evident in all the English and Cornish plays, and these attitudes may be translated into delaying actions that, while enhancing the dramatic interest, subvert the very purpose of sacrifice, which is, as René Girard has suggested, designed "to restore harmony to the community, to reinforce the social fabric."[30] Such perversity also offends against the demand enunciated by Ambrose for speed in making one's sacrifice. As John E. Bernbrock notes, the Towneley Abel "reiterates this need for haste four times," while Cain very obviously demonstrates his indifference and reluctance.[31] The N-town Cain announces that he is "loth" to go to sacrifice and would rather "gon hom, well for to dyne" (3.49, 52). In the Cornish *Ordinalia*, on the other hand, Cain's haste is a sign of his impatience with the whole process of sacrifice, for he rushes off before receiving his father's blessing and then seems to resent both the time involved in making the sacrifice and the loss of good grain.

Other writers, perhaps following Josephus, were convinced that Cain, as the establisher of weights, measures, and limits, offended by offering only a limited sacrifice — and hence not out of his whole heart.[32] The *Ordinalia* shows him holding back a portion of his tithe. The Wakefield Master, who represented the sacrifice as defective in both quality and quantity, makes much of the way in which Cain counts out sheaves and uses his arithmetic to exclude God. Such ingratitude, one might expect, would thoroughly offend the Creator of all things.[33] The play especially provides corroboration of the view of Cain as a false tither. This interpretation of his character should not be surprising in the light of Ambrose's derivation of his name, Cain, from "getting [*acquisitio*], because he got everything for himself."[34]

Less ambiguous is Cain's reaction to his rejection, for it is explicitly established that he was both resentful and envious.[35] His envy of his brother leads directly to his fratricide, his lifting of his hand against his kin. It was this murder that defined Cain in the religious drama of the Middle Ages, and it was through this act that he was believed to have established himself as a model of self-destructive infidelity and violence. Among his numerous spiritual progeny will be the biblical Judas and the mythological Grendel, who is specifically identified as "Cāines cynne" in the Anglo-Saxon epic, *Beowulf*.[36] When he appeared in the visual arts, his failed sacrifice and, even more often, his murder of his brother were depicted. These scenes are included in the *Bohun Psalter* (Bodleian Library MS. Auct. D.4.4, fol. 40) of c.1370–80 along with the infancy of Cain and Abel, one of whom is at his mother's breast, and the imposition of the mark of Cain. A fifth scene depicts the death of Cain from an arrow shot by Lamech from his bow.[37]

None of the scenes in the *Bohun Psalter* possesses the detail and elaboration that are displayed in the fourteenth-century *Holkham Bible Picture Book* (British Library MS. 47,680), which has been associated with a London workshop. There is no reason to believe, as W. O. Hassall has suggested, that there was a connection between these illuminations and the religious drama,[38] but the manner in which the biblical account was expanded cannot fail to be seen as a foreshadowing of the Cain and Abel episode in the Towneley *Mactacio Abel*, though the opening of the pictorial narrative is closer to the ordering in the N-town collection and the Cornish plays with Adam's admonition to his sons to sacrifice their first fruits.[39] On the lower half of the illumination on fol. 5r in the *Holkham Bible Picture Book* Adam lectures his sons, who stand by in postures that signify their attitudes toward him and his suggestions. Cain, standing beside sheaves of grain and grasping a two-pronged pitchfork, has his back to his father but turns his head toward him. His jaw juts out, and the expression on his face is meant to convey hostility.[40] In contrast, Abel, who is positioned among his sheep, holds his shepherd's staff in his left hand and extends his right upward with his palm turned toward his father in what is clearly intended to be a gesture of acceptance. The contrast between the two brothers is continued above in the upper portion of the miniature which shows their sacrifices. Here Cain, his face turned so his eyes glare with even greater hostility at his father, is pitching another bundle onto the fire, which, unlike Abel's clean burning sacrifice with its smoke going upward toward heaven, emits a smudge that does not rise but instead goes downward and joins the smoke emitted by a hell mouth positioned below it. This example may be compared with an early fourteenth-century wall painting in the church of All Saints at East Hanningfield, Essex, in which the smoke from the sheaves of grain of Cain's sacrifice likewise descends into the mouth of hell.[41] Emerson notes that the description of the smoke from Cain's fire as going downward was a common addition to the story that appeared first in the prose *Lyff of Adam and Eue*: "Crist vnderfong wel fayre þe tiþe of Abel: for þe smoke wente euene vpward, as hit brende; and þe smoke of Caym wente dounwart, for he tiþede falsliche."[42] Often elsewhere, too, smoke and flames ascend from Abel's offering but drift downward from Cain's offering. So it is, for example, in the fifteenth-century blockbook *Speculum Humanae Salvationis* printed in the Low Countries but widely distributed and in painted glass of c.1480 at St. Neot, Cornwall.[43] The smoke and flame also come down upon Cain in a carving in the Chapter House at Salisbury.[44] In the Towneley play Cain's sacrifice does not burn cleanly but, as noted above, produces a cloud of evil-smelling smoke that almost chokes him.[45] A further aspect of the hell mouth near Cain's sacrifice in the *Holkham Bible Picture Book* illumination is that it is located exactly in the same position as the mouth of hell in conventional depictions of the Last Judgement — that is, at the left of those in the scene and below.[46] The typological connection between the first Adam and his good and bad sons on his right and left in this scene, and the second Adam, Christ, with the good and bad thieves also on his right and left, should be obvious,[47] but the scene also therefore looks forward to the separation of the good and the evil human beings at Doomsday.

On fol. 5v of the *Holkham Bible Picture Book*, Cain, having led Abel to a different place, grasps him by the shoulder with his left hand and delivers the fatal blow to his head with his right. The instrument that he uses for this irrational act of violence is the jawbone of an ass, which had become the conventional murder weapon in England from Anglo-Saxon times and also appeared in some Continental examples in the visual arts.[48] In the Caedmonian *Genesis* (Bodleian Library MS. Junius 11) the instrument had been a club (p. 49),[49] but the jawbone would appear perhaps for the first time in an eleventh-century manuscript of Aelfric's translation of the Pentateuch (British Library, Cotton MS. Claudius B.iv, fol. 8).[50] Meyer Schapiro's explanation of the adoption of the jawbone as the result of an association between the Anglo-Saxon *cinbān* and *Cāin bana* has been convincingly refuted by George Henderson, who argues that the jawbone as weapon was adapted from book illustration showing Samson's slaying of one thousand Philistines in Judges 15:15.[51] The Towneley and N-town plays and the Cornish *Creacion of the World* call for this instrument. As the rubrics in the Cornish play indicate, Cain has a "*chawbone readye*" as he threatens Abel with a beating, whereupon he hits him with it and he dies (s.d. at ll. 1099, 1115).[52] In the N-town play, Cain says, "With þis chavyl bon I xal sle þe" (3.149), and he of course does as he has promised to do: "With þis strok I þe kylle" (152).[53] In the blockbook version of the *Speculum Humanae Salvationis* Cain holds Abel by the throat as he lies on the ground; his right arm is raised with his hand grasping the jawbone in preparation for striking another blow at his brother.[54] In the *Holkham Bible Picture Book* Cain will now try to cover over his brother's body, and in the *Cursor Mundi* his attempt to hide the corpse fails — it will not stay buried.[55] Exhibiting an unfeeling nature, the Cain of the Cornish *Creacion of the World* will simply "*Cast Abell into a dyche*" (s.d. at 1136). In the Towneley play Cain quakes with fear and tries to hide,[56] while in the York play he is challenged by an angel who pronounces God's curse on him.[57] The most terrifying detail is his despair, for he believes that his "synne it passis al mercie" (York VII.119).

But in the other plays and in the *Holkham Bible Picture Book* Cain will now be challenged directly by God rather than an angel. Again in the manuscript illumination Cain has his back turned to the speaker with only his face turned in the direction of God. His face is even more filled with hostility than before, if that is possible. Cain, a diminutive human with his right hand still clutching the jawbone, is standing before the large figure of God who accuses him of crime. In the Cornish *Creacion of the World* he looks down when the Father speaks to him, but he does not repent. In this play as in the *Ordinalia* the disembodied voice of Abel's blood cries out.[58] The scene is actually a key to the entire narrative, for here it becomes clear that, as Ricardo Quinones has argued, Cain's anger against his brother has in fact been "a displaced anger that is really directed against God.... The quarrel of envy is ultimately a quarrel with God — its arena, or façade, is a hatred of those whom God favors."[59] Violence, then, is seen as a theological problem and as the ultimate form of rebellion against both the Creator and things-as-they-are. Violent acts serve to separate persons from the community — "I haue no frende," Cain says in the N-town play (3.177) — and precipitate them into an abyss of alienation. In the Towneley play Cain will go forth "And to the dwill be thrall,/ Warld withoutten end" (2.468). Here the phrase "Warld withoutten end" is a direct translation of concluding words of the *Gloria Patri*. Violence without repentance and forgiveness reverses the song of praise to the Trinity and insures an ultimate place in a "stall" in hell "With Sathanas the feynd" (377, 470). For the time being, however, he will be marked by God so that the one who slays him will in turn be "punishid sevenfold" (375).

The *Holkham Bible Picture Book* does not illustrate the imposition of a mark upon Cain by God, but in the *Bohun Psalter* this is shown as God with his finger making a sign on Cain's forehead. There is some confusion about what the mark of Cain meant, whether a physical mark on his body or a shaking or trembling of his head, as indicated in the *Historia Scholastica* of Peter Comestor.[60] In the *Holkham Bible Picture Book* Cain's mark is visible as a pair of horns on his forehead (fols. 6v–7r).[61] In the Cornish *Creacion of the World* the mark is placed on his forehead, and it is the Greek letter Omega (s.d. at 1180) — a sign of closure, of the closing of the book of history at the Last Day. In the Great East Window at York Minster the topmost tracery panel shows God with the Book of Creation open before him with the words "Ego sum alpha & *omega*,"[62] the beginning and ending letters of the Greek alphabet representing the beginning and end of the world. Yet this mark will protect Cain from the immediate death that he deserves,[63] at least until he is mistaken for a beast and killed by his descendant Lamech — a popular episode shown, for example, in the *Holkham Bible Picture Book* (fols. 6v–7r), in a window at St. Neot, Cornwall,[64] and on a nave roof boss at Norwich Cathedral.[65] The death of Cain appears as an extended segment in the *Creacion of the World* (1429–1725). The Cain of this play is at this time deformed and "overgrown with hair" (1664–65) — a wild man of medieval and Renaissance tradition but also a demonic figure destined for hell.[66] The mark on his forehead here is appropriately identified as a horn (l. 1616; Cornish: *corne ow thale*),[67] which of course has associations with demons since they also very often have horns in depictions in the visual arts. At the end of the scene in the Cornish play two devils come forth to carry the "outcast Cain" (Cornish: *Cayne adla*) to the place of torment "*with great noyes*" (1712–13, s.d. at 1720). In the Lamech episode inserted into the Noah play in the N-town collection, Cain is mistaken for a "best" under a "grett busche" by the boy who is assisting the blind Lamech (4.166). As in the Cornish *Creacion*, the ending is violent. Lamech, attacking the boy, beats and kills him, then in his despair goes into hiding as an outlaw — a repetition of Cain's attempt to hide following his fratricidal act against Abel.

Prior to the crucial events of Cain's story — i.e., the sacrifice and murder — in the Chester cycle he is shown with a plough, a symbol which defines his role as a farmer (s.d. at II.516), and this is an implement which the Wakefield Master also introduced in association with Cain in the Towneley

Mactacio Abel. The plough in the latter play is more than a simple wheeled plough that Cain can push onto the stage. It must be an actual wheeled farm implement that is pulled by a team, which has consistently been interpreted as including several draught animals. (A. C. Cawley specified four horses and four oxen.[68]) A recent study, however, has reduced the number to a more reasonable two, a horse and a mare named Don and Molly.[69] The different names that Cain calls out may thus be attributed to a combination of rural practice in driving teams of animals and his verbal aggressiveness, which also is displayed in the language he uses to address his servant and his brother. Hostility in language extends to physical aggression, as when Cain initially beats his boy Pikeharness (2.50). Gestures, such as his invitation to Abel to kiss his posterior (61), are a preliminary to his refusal to enter into the sacrifice with a right spirit — and to his fratricide thereafter.

The plough, an implement used in Plough Monday ceremonies in rural England,[70] also appears in the *Holkham Bible Picture Book* on fol. 6ʳ, between the page illustrating the sacrifice and the murder of Abel and the two pages (fols. 6ᵛ–7ʳ) which contain the story of Cain's death. While in Plough Day ceremonies this farm implement is associated with beneficence, Cain's plough here and in the Towneley and Chester plays is hardly symbolic of goodness. The illumination in the *Holkham Bible Picture Book* shows a mixed team of two oxen and one ass pulling the plough, which is guided by Cain, who wears a hood that covers the mark on his forehead. He is looking down as he ploughs, and the expression on his face is apparently to be interpreted as displaying anger and malice.[71] The oxen seem to show signs of stress, and a boy wearing a hat stands with a whip over them. A third man is sowing, while below are shown the wicked children of Cain. The illustrator has chosen to present a picture of alienation and hostility in an agricultural setting rather than of Cain as the founder of cities. At his death in the subsequent illuminations Cain will become himself a victim of violence. The *Holkham Bible Picture Book*, like the vernacular plays of medieval England, has attributed to him the deadly sins of Covetousness, Sloth (for not being quick about attending to sacrifice), Envy, and Wrath. To these may be added Pride, which is central to his behavior and stands in direct contrast to Abel's humility.

Cain is ultimately an exemplar of the antisocial principle. In the Towneley play Cain orders Pikeharness to take the plough away from the acting area; then his farewell to the audience is followed by a statement of his intention to find a place to hide, perhaps for the forty days mentioned previously in the text (2.342) since that would be the time allotted under the English law for sanctuary granted to outlaws.[72] Quite clearly the pardon which the Towneley Cain attempted to proclaim for himself could not have been taken seriously even if it had not been undermined by the sarcasm of

Pikeharness. Cain's felonious act of violence against his brother is not a pardonable offense, and would have merited execution immediately upon apprehension in late fifteenth-century England.[73]

While it may be difficult to reconcile the accounts of the outlaw Cain in the late medieval vernacular plays with the biblical writer's claim that he established cities, there is nevertheless a connection with St. Augustine's view of him as the founder of the earthly city, Babylon, as enunciated in his *City of God*.[74] For the earthly city is ruled by supreme selfishness, a culture antithetical to salvation. Persons who participate in this culture and do not repent will have no hope of salvation, and symbolically it represents the dominance of those who share with Cain a kinship of despair. It is a culture of "getting," of possession, and hence of violence. In contrast, those who are of the City of God have, like Abel, a different spiritual orientation, for they are motivated by a different love — not of self but "by the love of God, even to the contempt of the self."[75] St. Ambrose commented that Abel, unlike his brother, "did not...refer everything to himself. Devotedly and piously, he attributed everything to God, ascribing to his Creator everything that he had received from Him."[76] Thus the followers of Abel, of the City of God however imperfectly realized, are the "true wanderers and wayfarers" of this world — pilgrims in an alien land whose great wish is to reach the heavenly city that can be entered only by means of the sacraments and a "good death."

III

As Alexandra F. Johnston remarks, the Wakefield Master's Cain "sets the pattern for all the evil figures who will follow him in this sequence of plays."[77] But this view of Cain's legacy is hardly limited to the Towneley cycle alone. In historical terms, Cain was regarded as a prototype of both those Jews who rejected Christ — and thus subjected him to violence even unto death on the cross — and all those who lived after Christ but rejected grace. In contrast are those who have served the principle of goodness and who have taken on the role of peacemakers rather than promoters of dissension. These are the two nations, the Church and the Synagogue, described as "two classes of people" by St. Ambrose.[78] The Jews who rejected Jesus are represented in the visual arts of the Middle Ages by a common symbolism, as in an example of painted glass at in the York Minster Chapter House vestibule;[79] in contrast to the crowned figure of the Church, which holds a cross and a model of a church building, is the figure of the Synagogue, with her banner staff breaking, her eyes blindfolded, and her crown falling from her head — that is, with her authority crumbling and her intellectual and spiritual vision limited. So those who question, arrest, torture, and execute Jesus in the vernacular plays in Middle English and the Cornish *Ordinalia* are of this class of people. Significantly, their acts are, like Cain's, directed out of envy at their brother Christ — the one who has, in Anselm's terms, become incarnate in order to be our brother.[80] The identification of Abel as a type of Christ at the Betrayal that began his Passion ordeal is made clear in the blockbook *Speculum Humanae Salvationis,* not only in the arrangement of the woodcuts but in the texts below each of them: "Cristus dolose traditus"; "Caym dolose interfecit fratrem suum Abel."[81] Abel's name, according to St. Augustine, signified "grief" ("luctus"),[82] while Christ of course will be revealed as the "Man of Sorrows."

The Middle English text of the *Speculum Humanae Salvationis* outlines a direct kinship between those who tortured and executed Christ and "the enevyous Kaym" who "slewe his innocent brothere þat neuer trespast til him." The scene that is invoked is the Betrayal:

> With glosing wordes tillid forth his brothere this fals Cayme,
> And having forth at the large with wikkid strokes he slewe hym:
> So Judas with faire wordes Oure Lord Crist he salutyd,
> And til his enemys to slee vndere that hym presentid.
> Abel his wombes brothere be Kaym to deth done was,
> And Crist, thaire fadere and brothere, slewe the Jewes and Judas.[83]

Among the enemies of Christ, Judas is the one who is of course most like Cain, and in the Towneley *Suspencio Iude* he describes himself as of "That cursyd clott of Camys kyn" (32.17).[84] In the *Conspiracy* in the same play collection, Pilate names those who are intent on violence against Christ as "kamys kyn" (20.663). And in the Harrowing in the York cycle, Anima Christi, speaking to Satan, links "cursed Cayme þat slewe Abell" with other suicides, including Judas, "And alle of þare assente,/ Als tyrantis euerilkone/ Þat me and myne turmente" (XXXVII.306–12). These lines are retained with only minor changes in Harrowing as it was adapted from the York text in the Towneley collection.

The brutality of the torturers in the vernacular plays of the Passion has long been recognized. In the Towneley Resurrection play Christ is said to have been wounded 5,400 times, with wounds covering his entire body from the top of his head to the soles of his feet (26.292). Representations in the visual arts showing his wounded body were ubiquitous and were often, as in the illuminations illustrating the Passion in the *Holkham Bible Picture Book* (fols. 29v, 30v, 31v–33r) and in the example of East Anglian painted glass showing Our Lady of Pity at Long Melford, Suffolk, extremely detailed in the depiction of the effects of the scourging and crucifixion.[85] The wounded body was commonly set forth as a devotional image, which might be on the cross (every church had a rood with Jesus, Mary, and, usually, St. John) or in some other form such as alabaster carvings showing Christ with his torturers, many of whom had darkened faces to represent their anger.[86] One of the signs of the Passion on the roof bosses of Winchester Cathedral shows a torturer spitting in contempt[87] — a gesture that is present also in the *Holkham Bible Picture Book*, which presents the faces of the soldiers and torturers as grotesque and distorted in representation of their hostility and anger. Here, as in the case of the murder of Abel, violence and killing are directly associated with sacrifice, in this case the atonement of the innocent Christ for the sins of all. While the malevolence is here directed against the one who is to surrender his life out of unlimited love for humankind, the spiritual progeny of Cain as often turn their violence against others of their own kind. The sons of Cain are liable in their wickedness to involve both Christ and his followers as well as members of their own wicked people in all manner of rapine and murder.[88]

Doomsday will be a time when such earthly violence and dissension are put down forever. In spite of spectacular representations of the end of history according to the book of Revelation in manuscript tradition and in such examples of public art as the East Window of York Minster,[89] the usual depiction of the Last Judgment followed the account in Matthew 25.[90] This iconography was ubiquitous and very often appeared above the chancel arch of parish churches, as in the case of the famous restored wall paintings in the church of St. Thomas of Canterbury in Salisbury[91] or the church of the Holy Trinity in Coventry, the latter depiction now totally obscured by grime and in need of restoration.[92] The York play, for which a remarkable inventory of 1433 corroborates the iconography suggested by the play text,[93] culminates in a scene of good and bad souls being consigned to heaven and hell. This play, like the final play in the other Middle English cycles and collections, dramatizes the recitation of the Seven Corporal Acts of Mercy as a test by which the souls are judged.[94] The wicked know in advance that they are destined "to dwelle with feendes blake" in hell (York XLVII.143) even before they are separated from the good by the archangel Michael and the Judge descends to perform the ritual that seals their fate. Jesus shows his "woundes wide" as a sign of the violence that was wrought upon him and mentions the specific acts that were committed against him (245ff).[95] These violent acts were suffered, he says, for love of humankind; he was the human sacrifice for all men and women if they would only reciprocate his love. But for the sacrifice to have been effected, of course, it was necessary for the act to be committed by those who, like Cain, were hostile to God and to the welfare of their fellow men.

Those who have performed the Corporal Acts of Mercy have comforted and aided the homeless, the hungry and thirsty, the sick, prisoners, and those lacking clothing — deeds depicted in a famous window in the church of All Saints, North Street, York.[96] Such acts are precisely opposed to the selfishness and egoism of Cain and his followers, who are specifically designated as the "cursid caytiffis of Kaymes kynne" that will for their selfishness and lack of concern for others be consigned to dwell in sorrow and "dole" through eternity (XLVII.317–20). This designation of the wicked at the Last Day appears in precisely the same terms as the "cursid catyfs of Kames kyn" in the Towneley *Iudicium* (30.648) in a section of the text of that play which is borrowed from York. For those, whether high or low in either the secular or ecclesiastical hierarchy, who have refused grace there will be no mercy. In the N-town play, the devils specifically contrast the Corporal Acts of Mercy with the Deadly Sins, beginning with Pride, which is identified by a mark on the forehead, and Covetousness: "On covetyse was all thy thought" (42.100). Reference to Wrath, Envy, Sloth, Gluttony, and Lechery follows. Augustine's Babylon, the city founded by Cain, will be handed over to the torture house of hell, where violence and indeed all manner of malevolence will prevail without ending in the isolation of that infernal kingdom.

IV

There is no doubt that in the main the citizens of cities and towns such as York, Coventry, and Chester took very seriously their obligation to perform the Corporal Acts of Mercy, support their parish churches and chantry chapels, and live amicably. While they may have violated such ideals on occasion, as when the Cordwainers were "mysbehauyng in bering of þer torches" and fighting with the Weavers in the Corpus Christi procession at York over the matter of their specific position in the Corpus Christi procession[97] — and hence over their standing in the social order within the city — their determination in these matters is well documented in civic records, generosity in building programs, and wills. Violence, especially against guild brethren and kinsmen, was strongly condemned, perhaps no more strongly than during the Wars of the Roses when violent and disorderly acts in the larger society were being committed in the course of the struggle among the aristocracy. In such an era of shifting loyalties and sporadic fighting, their belief in the historical origin and pattern of violence allowed people to categorize acts of transgression and therefore to come to terms with the evil represented by them. Herein must lie an important social role of the Cain and Abel plays, for they reinforced a collective memory that connected the present to the past — indeed, to the earliest instance of violence.

It will further be useful to note as a kind of postscript to this article that the story of Cain and Abel remained of very great significance in this regard through the early modern period. Shakespeare, whose parentage and roots were in the social order represented by craftsmen, merchants, and yeomen, would make much of social prohibitions against violence, especially as these involved family, kinsmen, and residual feudal obligation. Macbeth's murder of his kinsman and king is one example, but more explicit is Claudius's homicide in which he killed his brother and thereafter specifically identified himself as one who has replicated Cain's crime. His "offence" has "the primal eldest curse upon't,/ A brother's murder" (*Hamlet* 3.2.36–37).[98]

Notes

[1] Peter Gibson, "The Stained and Painted Glass of York," in *The Noble City of York*, ed. Alberic Stacpoole (York: Cerialis Press, 1972), 143, pl. 39.

[2] Epistle of Clement of Rome to the Corinthians 3; in *The Apostolic Fathers*, 2 vols. (London: Griffith, Farran, Okeden, and Walsh, n.d.), 1:161.

[3] Rosemary Woolf aptly comments on the significance of the emphasis in medieval drama on Cain rather than on Abel, who is not treated in depth; she sees this emphasis as demonstrating the "dramatists' interest in showing a continuation of the Fall" (*The English Mystery Plays* [Berkeley and Los Angeles: University of California Press, 1972], 124). Citations in the present article are to the following editions: *The York Plays*, ed. Richard Beadle (London: Edward Arnold, 1982); *The Towneley Plays*, ed. Martin Stevens, 2 vols., EETS, s.s. 13–14 (Oxford: Oxford University Press, 1995); *The Chester Mystery Cycle*, ed. R. M. Lumiansky and David Mills, 2 vols., EETS, s.s. 3, 9 (London: Oxford University Press, 1974–86); *The N-Town Play*, ed. Stephen Spector, 2 vols., EETS, s.s. 11–12 (Oxford: Oxford University Press, 1991); *The Ancient Cornish Drama*, ed. and trans. Edwin Norris, 2 vols. (Oxford: Oxford University Press, 1859); *The Creacion of the World*, ed. and trans. Paula Neuss (New York: Garland, 1983). Quotations are identified in parentheses in my text by line numbers, preceded, in the case of the Middle English plays, by the number of the pageant.

[4] St. Augustine, *The City of God* XV.5; trans. Marcus Dods et al. (New York: Random House, 1950), 482.

[5] Cf. T. W. Craik, "Violence in the English Miracle Plays," in *Medieval Drama*, ed. Neville Denny, Stratford-upon-Avon Studies 16 (London: Edward Arnold, 1973), 173–95, esp. 187–92. For the observation that domestic dissention and violence could be included, see David C. Fowler, *The Bible in Middle English Literature* (Seattle: University of Washington Press, 1984), 260.

[6] The methodology adopted in this paper is intended to examine the larger cultural context in which the iconography of the plays may be located. I have elsewhere studied the use of local iconography to illuminate the visual aspects of the plays both in instances where a direct connection between drama and art exists and where local art provides insight indirectly into the design of the plays' spectacle.

[7] See especially the excellent analysis of Hans-Jürgen Diller, *The Middle English Mystery Play* (Cambridge: Cambridge University Press, 1992), 224–31.

[8] *The Coventry Leet Book*, ed. Mary Dormer Harris, EETS, o.s. 134–35, 138, 146 (London: Kegan Paul, Trench, Trübner, 1907–13), 3:669.

[9] Alexandra F. Johnston and Margaret Rogerson, *Records of Early English Drama: York*, 2 vols. (Toronto: University of Toronto Press, 1979), 1:24.

[10] In this respect my argument is similar to Ann Eljenholm Nichols's assertion with regard to the Croxton *Play of the Sacrament* — that is, that finding a cause of its anti-sacramentalism in Lollardy is reductive, and instead attention needs to be turned to look to the broader aspect of Eucharistic piety in East Anglia or, in the case of the Towneley play, the West Riding of Yorkshire; see "The Croxton *Play of the Sacrament*: A Re-Reading," *Comparative Drama* 22 (1988), 117–37.

[11] See Lynette R. Muir, *The Biblical Drama of Medieval Europe* (Cambridge: Cambridge University Press, 1995), 70–71, 207–08.

[12] See for convenience the text and translation of this play in *Medieval Drama*, ed. David Bevington (Boston: Houghton Mifflin, 1975), esp. 103, 105–13.

[13] Abel will, of course, be among those delivered from hell at the Harrowing. In the Cornish *Ordinalia*, Abel is likewise taken off to hell, but Lucifer is quite mistaken in insisting that he will be a permanent resident "Notwithstanding all thy true tithe" (555–57).

[14] Lynette R. Muir, *Liturgy and Drama in the Anglo-Norman Adam* (Oxford: Basil Blackwell, 1973), 87, citing Hugh of St. Victor (*PL* 176:344).

[15] See Muir, *Liturgy and Drama*, 85.

[16] See E. A. Speiser, trans., *Genesis*, Anchor Bible (Garden City, N.Y.: Doubleday, 1981), xxvi–xxviii.

[17] See Northrop Frye, *The Great Code: The Bible and Literature* (New York: Harcourt, Brace, Jovanovich, 1982), 142–43. But something more complex is going on here; cf. René Girard, *Violence and the Sacred*, trans. Patrick Gregory (Baltimore: Johns Hopkins University Press, 1977), 4.

[18] See also Hebrews 11:4: "By faith Abel offered to God a sacrifice exceeding that of Cain, by which he obtained a testimony that he was just, God giving testimony to his gifts; and by it he being dead yet speaketh." Biblical citations in my paper are to the Douay-Rheims edition, which is chosen because it the most faithful to the Vulgate.

[19] *The Book of J*, trans. David Rosenberg, Introd. and Commentary by Harold Bloom (New York: Grove Weidenfeld, 1990), 188.

[20] See Eamon Duffy, The Stripping of the Altars: Traditional Religion in England, 1400–1580 (New Haven: Yale Univ. Press, 1992), 136–37.

[21] See Genesis 4:1: "And Adam knew Eve his wife: who conceived and brought forth Cain, saying: I have gotten a man through God."

[22] Robert E. Kelly, *The Bible in the Early Middle Ages* (Westminster, Maryland: Newman Press, 1959), 36, and, thereafter, by Richard Axton, *European Drama of the Early Middle Ages* (London: Hutchinson, 1959), 125.

[23] Oliver F. Emerson, "Legends of Cain, Especially in Old and Middle English," *PMLA* 21 (1906), 835–37.

[24] *Cursor Mundi*, ed. Richard Morris, 6 vols., EETS, o.s. 57, 62, 66, 68, 99, 101 (London: Kegan Paul, Trench, Trübner, 1874–93), 1:69 (ll. 1056–57).

[25] Peter Travis, *Dramatic Design in the Chester Cycle* (Chicago: University of Chicago Press, 1982), 93. This observation applies to the Cain of the other cycles and collections as well.

[26] *Cursor Mundi*, ed. Morris, 1:70 (ll. 1065–66).

[27] See Emerson, "Legends of Cain," 849; John E. Bernbrock, "Notes on the Towneley Cycle *Slaying of Abel*," *Journal of English and Germanic Philology* 62 (1963), 320; and St. Ambrose, *Of Cain and Abel* 1.10.40; *Hexameron, Paradise, and Cain and Abel*, trans. John J. Savage (New York: Fathers of the Church, 1961), 396; Latin text in *PL*, 14:315–59.

[28] *A Stanzaic Life of Christ*, ed. Frances A. Foster, EETS, o.s. 166 (London: Oxford University Press, 1926), 79 (ll. 2339–40). In the Lucerne Passion, Cain has a sheaf of wheat that had "im wasser gelegen" and hence was wet (M. Blakemore Evans, *The Passion Play of Lucerne* [New York: Modern Language Association, 1943], 194).

[29] See Ambrose, *Of Cain and Abel* 1.7.25-28; trans. Savage, 383-86.

[30] Girard, *Violence and the Sacred*, 8. For corroboration of aspects of Girard's view of the purpose of sacrifice in terms of the sacrifice of the Mass in the Middle Ages, see John Bossy, "The Mass as a Social Institution, 1200–1700," *Past and Present* 100 (Aug. 1983), 29–61, and Susan Brigden, "Religion and Social Obligation in Early and Modern Sixteenth-Century London," *Past and Present* 103 (May 1984), 67–112. Girard's discussion is not, of course, to be regarded as the final word on the subject of sacrifice.

[31] See Bernbrock, "Notes on the Towneley *Slaying of Abel*," 318; Towneley 2.74, 106, 132, 144.

[32] See Josephus, *Jewish Antiquities*, ed. and trans. H. St. J. Thackeray, 6 vols., Loeb Classical Library (Cambridge: Harvard University Press, 1930–65), 1:28–29 (1.2.2 [61]).

[33] This does not mean that comedy is not an important element in the contribution of the Wakefield Master to the Towneley collection; see my "Jest and Earnest: Comedy in the Work of the Wakefield Master," *Annuale Mediaevale* 22 (1982), 65–83. Other important aspects of the Wakefield Master's work are discussed in J. W. Robinson, *Studies in Fifteenth-Century Stagecraft*, Early Drama, Art, and Music, Monograph Ser. 14 (Kalamazoo: Medieval Institute Publications, 1991), though this book does not focus on the *Mactacio Abel*.

[34] Ambrose, *Of Cain and Abel* 1.1.3; trans. Savage, 360. Ambrose apparently received this derivation of the name from Jewish writers. See Josephus, *Jewish Antiquities*, 1:24–25 (1.2.1 [52]), and Philo, *On the Birth of Abel and the Sacrifices Offered by Him and by His Brother Cain*, in *Philo*, Loeb Classical Library, 10 vols. (Cambridge: Harvard University Press, 1929), 2:94–97 (1:1). Cain's avarice was to be stressed by Peter Comestor (*Historia Scholastica*, Liber Genesis, 26) and others.

[35] It is perhaps to be emphasized also that Cain is usually depicted as "out of charity" with his brother Abel throughout his sacrificing; for the importance of being in charity with one's neighbors prior to Mass, see Brigden, "Religion and Social Obligation," 67–84. Brigden quotes (p. 73) a poem in British Library Harl. MS. 2252, fol. 160[v], which insists that whoso "þat charyte forsakythe dothe not well/ but may be comparyd to the devyll of hell."

[36] For Judas, see below, and for Grendel see *Beowulf*, ed. F. Klaeber, 3rd ed. (Boston: Heath, 1950), 5 (l. 107), and David Williams, *Cain and Beowulf: A Study in Secular Allegory* (Toronto: University of Toronto Press, 1982), passim.

[37] Ruth Mellinkoff, *The Mark of Cain* (Berkeley and Los Angeles: University of California Press, 1981), fig. 1; the manuscript is briefly described by Otto Pächt and J. J. G. Alexander, *Illuminated Manuscripts in the Bodleian Library, Oxford*, 3: *British, Irish, and Icelandic Schools* (Oxford: Clarendon Press, 1973), No. 665. For Continental iconography, see Louis Réau, *Iconographie de l'art chrétien*, 3 vols. (Paris: Presses Universitaires de France, 1955–59), 1, Pt. 2:94–97.

[38] W. O. Hassall, *The Holkham Bible Picture Book* (London: Dropmore Press, 1954), 34–36. While useful for its preservation of much iconography of biblical narrative as it was commonly understood, this work, on account of its provenance and date (c.1320–30), needs to be used with considerable care as a document corroborating stage picture in drama that is dated a hundred or two hundred years later and from different regions in England.

[39] Hassall, *Holkham Bible Picture Book*, 66, notes the source of Adam's admonition as the *Historia Scholastica*, Liber Genesis 26 (*PL* 198:1077). At Lucerne, Abel's sacrifice was a wooden effigy of a lamb, filled with shavings so that it would burn brightly (Evans, *The Passion Play of Lucerne*, 194). However, there was apparently a live lamb for which the effigy was exchanged in the course of the scene; see also Peter Meredith and John E. Tailby, *The Staging of Religious Drama in Europe in the Later Middle Ages, Texts and Documents in English translation* Early Drama, Art, and Music, Monograph Ser. 4 (Kalamazoo: Medieval Institute Publications, 1983), 118.

[40] Cain's hostile facial expressions are also noted in the prose *Lyff of Adam and Eue*, in *Sammlung altenglischer Legenden*, ed. Carl Horstmann (Heilbronn: Henninger, 1878), 224.

[41] E. W. Tristram, *English Wall Painting in the Fourteenth Century*, ed. Eileen Tristram (London: Routledge and Kegan Paul, 1955), 177.

[42] Emerson, "Legends of Cain," 848; *Lyff of Adam and Eue*, in Horstmann, *Sammlung altenglischer Legenden*, 224. The fire for the sacrifice fails to be ignited in the N-town and Chester plays and the Cornish *Ordinalia*. In the *Creacion of the World* Cain apparently breaks off before completing his sacrifice, though he has promised that his bad produce will make "a huge bush of smoke" (1091). The York play is defective and lacks the folios that contained the sacrifice.

[43] Adrian Wilson and Joyce Lancaster Wilson, *A Medieval Mirror: Speculum Humanae Salvationis* (Berkeley and Los Angeles: University of California Press, 1984), 177; G. McN. Rushforth, "The Windows of the Church of St. Neot, Cornwall," *Exeter Diocesan Architectural and Archaeological Society* 15 (1937), 156, pl. 39.

[44] William Burges, "The Iconography of the Chapter-House, Salisbury," *The Ecclesiologist* 20 (1859), 149; Selby Whittingham, *Salisbury Chapter House* (1974; reprint Salisbury: Dean and Chapter of Salisbury Cathedral, 1986), fig. 13; M. D. Anderson, *Drama and Imagery* (Cambridge: Cambridge University Press, 1963), 144, 212. Anderson also reports another example of smoke from Cain's offering descending downward on the Fitzroy tomb at Framlingham, Suffolk (144).

[45] In contrast, the smoke from Abel's sacrifice is described as "sweet" in the *Creacion of the World* (1100).

[46] Further it should be noted that hell was conventionally associated with unpleasant odors; thus a closer association may exist between this one aspect of the iconography of the *Holkham Bible Picture Book* illumination and the Towneley play than previously suspected. For the odor of hell, see Thomas Seiler, "Filth and Stench as Aspects of the Iconography of Hell," in *The Iconography of Hell*, ed. Clifford Davidson and Thomas H. Seiler, Early Drama, Art, and Music, Monograph Ser. 17 (Kalamazoo: Medieval Institute Publications, 1992), 132–40.

[47] With regard to this typology see also Gertrud Schiller, *Iconography of Christian Art*, trans. Janet Seligman, 2 vols. (Greenwich, Conn.: New York Graphic Soc., 1968), 2:124.

[48] See Meyer Schapiro, "Cain's Jaw-Bone That Did the First Murder," in *Late Antique, Early Christian and Mediaeval Art: Selected Papers* (New York: George Braziller, 1979), 255. Schapiro was apparently not aware of Scandinavian examples: see Knud Banning, *A Catalogue of Wall-Paintings in Medieval Denmark, 1100–1600: Scania, Halland, Blekinge*, 4 vols. (Copenhagen: Akademisk Forlag, 1976), 1:42–44, figs. 45, 48, 50.

[49] Thomas Ohlgren, *Anglo-Saxon Textual Illustration* (Kalamazoo: Medieval Institute Publications, 1992), 550.

[50] George Henderson, "Cain's Jaw-Bone," *Journal of the Warburg and Courtauld Institutes* 24 (1961), pl. 16b.

[51] Ibid., 111–12. For another suggestion, see A. A. Barb, "Cain's Murder-Weapon and Samson's Jawbone of an Ass," *Journal of the Warburg and Courtauld Institutes* 35 (1972), 386–89.

[52] The term *challa*, meaning jawbone, is used in the *Origo Mundi*, but is transferred to Abel's anatomy. Norris translates: "That thou mayest never thrive,/ Take this on the jaw-bone" (539–40). Immediately thereafter the rubric commands Cain to hit his brother on the head: "*Tunc percuciet eum in capite et morietur....*"

[53] See the discussion in Cherrell Guilfoyle, "The Staging of the First Murder in the Mystery Plays in England," *Comparative Drama* 25 (1991), 42–51. The York play probably also utilized the jawbone of an ass, according to Guilfoyle; this instrument is named in works with associations with the York play (ibid., 42). For discussion of the iconography of a panel in the East Window of York Minster in relation to the missing section of the York play, see Clifford Davidson, *From Creation to Doom* (New York: AMS Press, 1984), 15. The figure of Abel in this panel was made up in the restoration of 1953, but there is no doubt about either his head or Cain with his jawbone lifted high to bring it down on his brother's head. See also Clifford Davidson and David E. O'Connor, *York Art*, Early Drama, Art, and Music, Reference Ser. 1 (Kalamazoo: Medieval Institute Publications, 1978), 25, fig. 6; Thomas French, *York Minster: The Great East Window*, Corpus Vitrearum Medii Aevi, Summary Catalogue 2 (Oxford: Oxford University Press, 1995), 52. Muir also notes the use of the jawbone as the murder instrument at Valenciennes (twenty-day play) (*The Biblical Drama*, 208).

[54] Wilson and Wilson, *A Medieval Mirror*, 177.

[55] *Cursor Mundi*, ed. Morris, 1:70 (ll. 1075–80).

[56] Subsequently the Towneley Cain will want to hide Abel's corpse "For som man myght com at vngayn," so he calls for Pikeharness to help bury him (2.380–87). For dramatic treatment elsewhere, see Muir, *The Biblical Drama*, 71, 208.

[57] Eleanor Prosser suggests a reason for the substitution of the angel for God: "Clearly because our author confuses dramatic 'action' with violence and wants Cain to strike back physically at the curse-giver. Since he certainly could not strike God, God thus becomes an angel..." (*Drama and Religion in the English Mystery Plays* [Stanford: Stanford University Press, 1961], 75).

[58] Compare the painted glass at St. Neot, Cornwall, which includes the text "En sanguis fratris tui" ("Behold thy brother's blood"); see Rushforth, "The Windows of the Church of St. Neot," 157. In an early wall painting on the south wall of the parish church at West Kingsdown, Kent, a small figure representing Abel's blood is crying out for vengeance (Hassall, *Holkham Bible Picture Book*, 68, and, for verification, I am grateful to James Gibson and also the churchwarden, Neale J. Muller). For the use of a small child to represent Abel's blood crying out for vengeance at Mons, see Meredith and Tailby, *The Staging of Religious Drama*, 96–97.

[59] Ricardo Quinones, The Changes of Cain: Violence and the Lost Brother in Cain and Abel Literature (Princeton: Princeton University Press, 1991), 16.

[60] *PL* 198:1078, as cited by Mellinkoff, *The Mark of Cain*, 49, 118–19. According to the prose *Lyff of Adam and Eue*, "Crist" placed "a marke vp on him: þat he waggede alwey forþ his heued" (Horstmann, *Sammlung altenglischer Legenden*, 224). For a Continental play that follows this tradition, see Muir, *The Biblical Drama*, 71. A literal translation of the original Hebrew text designates Cain as a "totterer and wanderer" (Speiser, *Genesis*, 31).

[61] For further examples of horns as the mark of Cain, see Mellinkoff, *The Mark of Cain*, figs. 7–8 (capital at Vézelay), 15 (Pamplona Bible), 19–20 (Cambridge, St. John's College MS. K.26).

[62] Davidson and O'Connor, *York Art*, fig. 2; French, *York Minster: The Great East Window*, 17.

[63] For discussion of the mark of Cain in terms of a protective sign (*sphragis*), see Jean Daniélou, *The Bible and the Liturgy* (Notre Dame, Indiana: University of Notre Dame Press, 1956), 60–61.

[64] Rushforth, "The Windows of the Church of St. Neot," 157, pl. XXXIX.

[65] C. J. P. Cave, *Roof Bosses in Medieval Churches* (Cambridge: Cambridge University Press, 1948), fig. 148; the boss is noted by Anderson, *Drama and Imagery*, 89, 145.

[66] See, for example, the wild man and woman in Walter de Milemete, *De Nobilitatibus, Sapientiis, et Prudentiis Regum* (Oxford, Christ Church MS. 92, fol. 64[v]), reproduced in Clifford Davidson, *Illustrations of the Stage and Acting in England to 1580*, Early Drama, Art, and Music, Monograph Ser. 16 (Kalamazoo: Medieval Institute Publications, 1991), fig. 120. For discussion of the Lamech episode in the medieval English drama, see Edmund Reiss, "The Story of Lamech and Its Place in Medieval Drama," *Journal of Medieval and Renaissance Studies* 2 (1972), 35–48.

[67] See R. Morton Nance, *A New Cornish English Dictionary* (St. Ives: Federation of Old Cornwall Societies, 1938), s.v. 'corn.'

[68] A. C. Cawley, ed., *The Wakefield Pageants in the Towneley Cycle* (Manchester: Manchester University Press, 1958), 91, 186–87.

[69] Margaret Rogerson, "The Medieval Plough Team on Stage: Wordplay and Reality in the Towneley *Mactacio Abel*," *Comparative Drama* 28 (1994), 182–200.

[70] See A. R. Wright, *British Calendar Customs*, ed. T. E. Lones, 3 vols. (London: Folk-Lore Soc., 1938), 2:101–03; John Brand, *Observations on Popular Antiquities* (London: Chatto and Windus, 1913), 273–75. A ceremonial plow is still retained, for example, at Selby Abbey in Yorkshire.

[71] See Hassall, Holkham Bible Picture Book, 68–69.

[72] See Bennett A. Brockman, "The Law of Man and the Peace of God: Judicial Process as Satiric Theme in the Wakefield *Mactacio Abel*," *Speculum* 49 (1974), 704.

[73] *Ibid.*, 704-07.

[74] Augustine's discussion of Cain and Abel appears in *The City of God,* XV.

[75] Ibid., XIV.28; trans. Dods et al., 477. See also the comments by Alexandra F. Johnston, "Evil in the Towneley Cycle," in *Evil on the Medieval Stage*, ed. Meg Twycross (Lancaster: Medieval English Theatre, 1992), 97–99.

[76] Ambrose, *Of Cain and Abel* I.i.3; trans. Savage, 360.

[77] Johnston, "Evil in the Towneley Cycle," 100. See also my article "The Unity of the Wakefield 'Mactacio Abel'," *Traditio* 23 (1967), 497–99.

[78] Ambrose, *Of Cain and Abel* I.ii.5; trans. Savage, 361–62.

[79] Davidson and O'Connor, *York Art*, 183. Another York example of the Synagogue, in a painted ceiling in the Chapter House, was removed in 1798; see Joseph Halfpenny, *Gothic Ornaments in the Cathedral Church of York* (York, 1795), pl. 95.

[80] See Anselm, *Cur Deus Homo.*, esp. II.viii–xiii. Anselm emphasizes the point that Christ's death could have saved his murderers, for their sin was done out of ignorance: "no man could ever, knowingly at least, slay the Lord; and therefore those who did it out of ignorance did not rush into that transcendental crime with which none others can be compared" (St. Anselm, *Basic Writings*, trans. S. N. Deane [LaSalle, Illinois: Open Court, 1962], II.xv 264).

[81] Wilson and Wilson, *A Medieval Mirror*, 176–77.

[82] *The City of God* XV.18; trans. Dods et al., 504; *De Civitate Dei*, ed. Emmanuel Hoffmann, 2 vols. (1900; reprint New York: Johnson Reprint, 1962). The etymology is incorrect; Hebrew scholars are instead more likely to see Abel's name as meaning "puff, vanity," though this too may be fanciful. See Speiser, *Genesis*, 30.

[83] *The Mirour of Mans Saluacioune*, ed. Avril Henry (Philadelphia: University of Pennsylvania Press, 1987), 113 (ll. 2087–88, 2095–2100). This text preserves the traditional notion that Cain and Abel were twins. Cain in all accounts is the elder of the two.

[84] For physical resemblances between Cain and Judas, see Ruth Mellinkoff, *Outcasts: Signs of Otherness in Northern European Art of the Late Middle Ages*, 2 vols. (Berkeley and Los Angeles: University of California Press, 1993), 1:134.

[85] Christopher Woodforde, *The Norwich School of Glass-Painting in the Fifteenth Century* (London: Oxford University Press, 1950), pl. XXVII.

[86] See Francis Cheetham, *English Medieval Alabasters* (Oxford: Phaidon, Christie's, 1984), nos. 159, 163–64, 166, 168, 170. In alabasters of the Betrayal on which some paint remains the faces of all except Jesus and Peter were either black or dark brown; see ibid., nos. 151, 156–57. Executioners and torturers in alabasters showing the martyrdom of saints were similarly presented with darkened faces; see, for example, ibid., nos. 15, 25–26. Cain also has a dark face — and

Negroid features — in Cambridge, St. John's College MS. K.26, fol. 6v; see Mellinkoff, *Outcasts*, 1:134, and vol. 2, pl. VI.50

[87] Cave, Roof Bosses in Medieval Churches, fig. 245.

[88] See Josephus, *Jewish Antiquities*, 1:30–31 (1.2.2 [66]).

[89] See *The Apocalypse in the Middle Ages*, ed. Richard K. Emmerson and Bernard McGinn (Ithaca: Cornell University Press, 1992), esp. 105–289; French, *York Minster: The Great East Window*, 72–136, pls. 6–17.

[90] See especially Pamela Sheingorn and David Bevington, "'Alle This Was Token Domysday to Drede': Visual Signs of Last Judgment in the Corpus Christi Cycles and in Late Gothic Art," in *Homo, Memento Finis: The Iconography of Just Judgment in Medieval Art and Drama*, Early Drama, Art, and Music, Monograph Ser. 6 (Kalamazoo: Medieval Institute Publications, 1985), 121–45.

[91] This wall painting has been frequently reproduced; see, for example, ibid., fig. 14.

[92] Clifford Davidson and Jennifer Alexander, *The Early Art of Coventry, Stratford-upon-Avon, Warwick and Lesser Sites in Warwickshire*, Early Drama, Art, and Music, Reference Ser. 4 (Kalamazoo: Medieval Institute Publications, 1985), 37; George Scharf, Jr., "Observations on a Picture in Gloucester Cathedral and Some Other Representations of the Last Judgment," *Archaeologia* 36 (1855), pl. XXXVI, fig. 1; Jennifer Alexander, "Coventry Holy Trinity Doom," *EDAM Newsletter* 11 (1988), 37.

[93] Alexandra F. Johnston and Margaret Rogerson, *Records of Early English Drama: York* (Toronto: University of Toronto Press, 1979), 1:55–56.

[94] The Cornish *Ordinalia* does not conclude with a Doomsday play.

[95] In the Chester Last Judgement, a rubric indicates that Christ's wound in his side actually appears to be bleeding (XXIV.428 s.d.)

[96] The York play omits visiting prisoners here; this is added in reference to the evil souls (XLVII.355) and in the Towneley play: "In hard prison when I was sted/ On my penance ye had pyté" (Towneley 30.620–21). For the Corporal Acts window, see Eric A. Gee, "The Painted Glass of All Saints' Church, North Street, York," *Archaeologia* 102 (1969), 162–64, pls. XXV–XXVII; Davidson and O'Connor, *York Art*, 116–17. A seventh Corporal Act, not pictured in the All Saints glass, is the Burial of the Dead. This Act derives from Tobit 1:17–18 rather than from the account in Matthew 25:35–36; it does not appear in the York Doomsday play, but is mentioned in the N-town play (42.85). Further examples of the Corporal Acts in painted glass are noted in Woodforde, *The Norwich School of Glass-Painting*, 193–96, pl. XLII; Richard Marks, *The Stained Glass of the Collegiate Church of the Holy Trinity, Tattershall (Lincs.)* (New York: Garland, 1984), 204–08, pl. 28. For examples of the Corporal Acts of Mercy in wall paintings, see Tristram, *English Wall Painting of the Fourteenth Century*, 99–101; A. Caiger-Smith, *English Medieval Mural Paintings* (Oxford: Clarendon Press, 1963), 53–55, pls. XVIII, XIXb.

[97] Johnston and Rogerson, *REED: York*, 1:158–59. The fine for the Cordwainers' offense was a hefty £10.

[98] The citation is to William Shakespeare, *The Complete Works*, gen. ed. Stanley Wells and Gary Taylor (Oxford: Clarendon Press, 1988). For a recent study which treats the first murder as a paradigm for subsequent violence in Shakespeare's time, see Naomi Conn Liebler, "Shakespeare's Medieval Husbandry: Cain and Abel, Richard II, and Brudermord," *Mediaevalia* 18 (1995 [for 1992]), 451–73.

Western Michigan University

The Crucified Heart of René D'Anjou in Text and Image

Shira Schwam-Baird

As Paul Klee movingly said, art does not render the visible but renders visible: "Art has the power of thought, and what makes something a work of art rather than a mere thing is that it gives embodiment in a sensuous idiom to a thought, the grasping of which is like understanding a proposition."[1]

René d'Anjou's *Mortifiement de Vaine Plaisance* (1455) tells the story of an allegorical Soul who, troubled by her wayward heart, sends it to be purified of its vain striving for worldly pleasure through a beneficent act of crucifixion. The image of the heart nailed to the cross in the miniatures is a powerful one (fig. 1), which, on one level, simply illustrates the climax of the narrative. But on another level, the image "renders visible" moral precepts whose mere exposition in language could never affect the reader the way visual representation shapes the spiritual experience of the spectator. Deep experience was the goal of late-medieval pious practice, and this paper will situate the *Mortifiement* and René himself in the tradition of lay piety and devotional literature. It will then proceed to discuss which thoughts and propositions are to be grasped through the image of the crucified heart and which of the reader/spectator's needs may be fulfilled by the creation of this particular image.

Text and Author

After the opening dedication to René's personal confessor, the work describes the Soul (*l'Ame*)[2] seated in her dilapidated hut and complaining of the flighty heart that drags her into the mire of *vaine plaisance*. As she mourns, she is approached by two women, Fear of God (*Crainte de Dieu*) and Contrition (fig. 2). A long dialogue ensues in which the two women, exhorting the Soul to give up all attachment to vain, worldly pleasure, demonstrate to her the shortness of life, the vanity of pride, wealth and power, the vileness of concupiscence, and the need to love God and his creatures through Him. Like good medieval preachers, they embellish their sermon with three lengthy *exempla* or parables, which illustrate with meticulous allegory the need to embrace the virtues they expound.[3]

Convinced by their discourse, the Soul entrusts her heart to Fear of God and Contrition. They bear the guilty one up a mountain to an enclosed garden where it is purified in an ultimate act of *imitatio Christi* by three virtues, Faith (*Foy*), Hope (*Esperance*), and Love (*Amour*), and a fourth figure, Divine Grace (*Grace Divine*). When Fear of God and Contrition return the heart, still nailed to the cross, to the Soul, the latter is moved to offer prayers of praise and thanksgiving to God for the purification of her heart (fig. 4). The text ends with an appeal to the archbishop to accept René's little work and to pray for his soul and for forgiveness of his sins.

The *Mortifiement de Vaine Plaisance* was composed in 1455, the year following the widowed René's marriage to Jeanne de Laval, a woman twenty-five years his junior. It might seem odd that René wrote such a somber work so soon after his remarriage, but the death of his first wife, Isabelle, had occurred only a year prior to what was primarily a political marriage to Jeanne in 1454. In addition, many events in René's life, including serious political setbacks, could have caused him to ponder the vanity of life and question the value of earthly aspirations. He was the sometime prisoner of the Duke of Burgundy from 1431 to 1436, and suffered repeated defeats in trying to realize the Angevin claim in Italy. Moreover, he fell out of royal favor when Louis XI succeeded Charles VII (René's brother-in-law), and lost all but one of the many duchies and counties he had at one time ruled.[4] His own creation, Contrition, reminds him that

> true and perfect happiness is truly not in leading a life of show, nor in being victorious in arms, nor in finding oneself in high command, nor in having royal preeminence, nor in having many followers or retinues of people, nor in infinite riches, nor in fertile lands, nor in possessing pleasant manors and sumptuous palaces, nor in governing strong castles and powerful cities.[5] (211-12)

René's was a life of contrasts. Military campaigns, elaborate tournaments, literary production (particularly his better-known *Livre du Cuer d'Amours espris* of 1455) and the amassing of a significant library shared time and resources with numerous acts of piety such as gifts and commissions for churches and monasteries.[6] But the gruesome *Roi mort* figures (crowned skeletal shapes) decorating two of his personal books of hours and his tomb attest particularly to René's spiritual preoccupations.[7] Very much a prince of the fifteenth century, René embodied that exuberant mixture of sacred and profane passions that characterized his period.[8] Thus the composition of the *Mortifiement* likely arose from René's participation in a culture of piety and lay devotion that had been steeped in mysticism.

Sources and Influences

Mystical writings differ from the more strictly devotional works of the later Middle Ages. Mysticism concerns itself with transcendental experiences in which the soul senses an "immediate awareness" and "direct intimate consciousness of the divine Presence."[9] The way of the mystic is the way of contemplation (the medieval word for mysticism), that is, the renunciation of earthly comfort and pleasure that prepares the body and mind for the soul's domination of its experiences. The institutionalized asceticism and discipline of monastic life fostered such experiences, yet many outside the cloister were mystics, and, more importantly for our purposes, elements of mysticism filtered into non-mystical lay devotion.

René's *Mortifiement*, not in itself a mystical work, exhibits thematic links to such texts. For example, Hugh of St. Victor, the twelfth-century mystic, writes in the prologue to *The Moral Ark of Noah* that his brethren have asked him to explain the "unstableness and disquiet of the human heart." They desire instruction on how to remove this evil, for otherwise the soul is not prepared for mystical contemplation. The inclination to earthly desires is due to the Fall, Hugh explains, and the subsequent forgetting of the sweetness of the divine:

> So man's heart which had been kept secure by divine love, and one by loving One, afterward began to flow here and there through earthly desires. For the mind which knows not to love his true good is never stable and never rests. Hence restlessness, and ceaseless labor, and disquiet, until the man turns and adheres to Him. The sick heart wavers and quivers; the cause of its disease is love of the world; the remedy, the love of God.[10]

Though we have no evidence of René's having read Hugh's tract himself,[11] his *Mortifiement* demonstrates his absorption of similar sentiments, as seen in the Soul's opening complaint. She cannot attain the divine, which is her true desire, she despairs, because of the "desir abusé" (deceived desire) of her heart. "Ainsi samblablement et souventes foiz apres luy si me tire ce dolent cuer, et tresbucher me fait en la fange et ordure de sa vaine plaisance" (Thus does this painful heart often drag me after it and make me stumble in the mire and ordure of its vain pleasure) (61-62, 197). She further complains that her heart is "volaige" (flighty or unstable) (99, 121). Indeed, "love of God," the remedy Hugh promotes, appears as one of the allegorical characters that carries out the crucifixion of the Soul's heart in the *Mortifiement*.

From the fourteenth century on, lay thought and lay piety began to occupy an important place in religious thought that had previously been occupied exclusively by philosophy and academic theology,[12] and produced devotional works that influenced René's text more directly than did mystical writings. In his use of *exempla*, for instance, and in the forceful didacticism of the work, René draws heavily on the sermon tradition of the late

Middle Ages.[13] That tradition was supported by sermon books, religious handbooks, and collections of *exempla* that formed a sort of common font ("une espèce de trésor commun") for all to draw upon.[14] Gerald Robert Owst's exhaustive studies of preaching and the pulpit in medieval England demonstrate the relative abundance of material available in the vernacular (devotional tracts, manuals of moral and spiritual instruction, and commentaries on Scripture) that was obviously intended for lay as well as pastoral reading.[15]

An influential aspect of contemporary religious thought was the relentless contemplation of death, the *ars moriendi*, elaborated and pictorialized in the various *danses macabres* of the period. Death, the great equalizer, leads away both king and peasant, young and old, beautiful and ugly, rich and poor. As mentioned above, René, a man of his times, commissioned *Roi mort* figures for his tomb and personal books of hours to instruct himself and others on the vanity of earthly power and the fact of personal mortality. How fitting then that his devotional work likewise lectures the reader, through the voices of Fear of God and Contrition, on the inevitability of death and the need for God's grace. Such are the lessons that convince the Soul to deliver up her heart to her instructresses for appropriate "treatment."

The focus on the heart may well have been aroused by the developing cult of the Sacred Heart of Jesus. The official cult dates from the seventeenth century, but prior to formal recognition by the church, its way was prepared by ritual veneration of Jesus's wounds, an active devotion already in early Christianity. In the Middle Ages, the objects that caused Christ's many wounds, that is, the instruments of the Passion, were known as the *arma Christi*, for they belonged to the victor, Christ, through whose sufferings salvation was won.[16] The advent of the crucifix as a replacement for the simple cross focused attention on the wounds of the crucifixion as opposed to the wounds of the flagellation or the crown of thorns, and fostered the veneration of those wounds.[17] From the eleventh and twelfth centuries, special attention was paid to the side wound that leads to the heart. Texts from the thirteenth and fourteenth centuries recounting the various visions of the unofficial cult are summarized in the *Dictionnaire de Théologie Catholique*:

> Favors granted to the privileged are: permission to place one's lips on the side wound in order to draw from it the love and riches of the Heart; penetration into the Heart in order to rest there as in an oasis, or to walk there as in a beautiful garden; plunging into the Heart as in a furnace of love and purity; to be set ablaze by a spark from the Heart; sometimes

> to exchange one's own heart for that of Jesus and to live by means of the divine Heart;...etc.[18]

René's text would add to the list: to place one's own heart on the cross in imitation of the Savior's Passion and of the sufferings of the Sacred Heart.

From the thirteenth century on, the Franciscans maintained a celebration of the side wound on the very day that later became the calendar day to celebrate the feast of the Sacred Heart.[19] By the end of the fifteenth century, the iconography of the *arma Christi* was well-known, including a heraldic display in which the detached hands and feet of Jesus, showing the marks of their wounds, are disposed around a pierced heart — Jesus' heart — which was supposed penetrated by the same lance that Longinus thrust into Christ's side.[20] It is reasonable to assume that the increasingly common images of the Sacred Heart, which arose from this devotion, influenced René's adaptation of Christ's Passion to the passion of the heart in the *Mortifiement*, as well as the illustrations of the crucifixion scene in all the extant manuscripts.

Thus René's work is very much the product of these several modes in religious thought and literary production. Its didactic tone draws on the tradition of the late-medieval sermon with its instructional *exempla* and exhortations to piety, and its yearning for the purity that leads to grace derives from the obsession with death. But what stands out in grisly calm, like the visions of mystics who yearned to embrace the sacred wounds and enter the Sacred Heart, is the culminating purgation of *vaine plaisance* by crucifixion, the focal point of this study.

The Crucified Heart

Eight illustrated manuscripts of the *Mortifiement* survive.[21] In virtually all of them the same eight narrative scenes are depicted, a relative rarity in miniature cycles. The one notable difference is the omission of the central crucifixion scene in the Paris manuscript.[22] But consistency is the more striking characteristic, and the reasons for this stability in the miniature cycle are not difficult to surmise. René himself probably devised the original pictorial cycle, working closely with the artist illuminator of his personal copy and/or of the presentation copy for the archbishop.[23] However, the consistency in the miniature programs can be linked no less to the imperatives in the text itself, whose internal structures demand a certain succession of visual images, than to René's original design. The program is as follows: 1) the lamenting Soul clasps her heart to her bosom; 2) the Soul is approached by Fear of God and Contrition; 3) the parable of the cart driver; 4) the parable of the old woman taking her wheat to the mill; 5) the parable of the valiant man-at-arms; 6) the Soul entrusts her heart to Fear of God and Contrition;

7) the crucifixion; and 8) the Soul receives her purified heart from Fear of God and Contrition.[24]

Some of the miniature cycles are more faithful than others in depicting the details of the text. Though the paintings are done in the "naturalistic" style of late-medieval manuscript painting, that is, with receding landscapes and atmospheric perspective, the "naturally" shaped characters that inhabit them are strictly allegorical in nature. Each represents a moral quality (such as Contrition) or a spiritual essence (such as Divine Grace), and the Soul, as a kind of Everysoul representing the divine spark in the human, is the sign for the spiritual subject. Her heart is an allegorized synecdoche, the expansion of a part for a whole; here, the sign for the affective attribute. Unlike the other personified abstractions, the heart never speaks, and in the illustrations, it is the only allegorical character not given human form. Rather, it retains the schematic shape of a heart as it is clasped by the prostrate Soul or nailed to the cross of its own passion.

The climactic scene of the *Mortifiement* is a moment of high allegory, in which every character and object is significant. The text is excruciatingly explicit in its description of the lovely walled garden, the summer weather, the clothes worn by the virtues, the instruments they employ, and the allegorical significance of each item. The first lady virtue, Faith, wears a white ecclesiastical cape whose borders are embroidered with scenes of Christ's life and Passion. Her steel nail, driven into the lower portion of the heart, represents duration, and her hammer, perfect knowledge. The blue mantle of Hope, the second virtue, is decorated with gold anchors signifying firmness (the anchors) in celestial actions (the blue ground). She drives the silver nail of valor into the heart's left side with the hammer of charitable compassion. Love, the third virtue, wears a crimson mantle embroidered with white doves representing works of the Holy Spirit. She wields the hammer of complete obedience to drive a golden nail signifying perfect sovereign charity into the right side of the heart. Last is Divine Grace, an empress in an imperial tunic, wielding a lance whose head is inscribed with "Knowledge of Eternal Glory," and whose worm-eaten shaft bears the inscription "Concern for Worthless Earthly Goods" (162-67)(fig. 5).[25]

Despite differences in the extent of detail, all the manuscript miniatures render this scene as a compression of events, in which the four ladies bend to their tasks simultaneously rather than in succession. They group around the heart and cross in frozen animation, like a tableau in a mystery play. Indeed the *Mortifiement* contains only the bare bones of a narrative with the bulk of the text comprised of lengthy discourses, so that, once illustrated, these static scenes resemble nothing so much as the tableaux of mystery plays.

The resemblance is probably not accidental. René was a great aficionado of mystery plays and spent considerable sums mounting them. Court accounts attest to spectacles at Angers in 1454 and 1456, at Saumur in 1462, and at Aix-en-Provence in 1474, and they must have been lavish, for details in the accounts indicate that spectators came to Saumur from Berry, Normandy, Touraine and even Paris.[26] Mysteries drew their inspiration from treatises on the Passion that heightened the less melodramatic gospel accounts with gruesome detail. In one text

> [t]he welts and bloody wounds of [Christ's] body are made septic by the admixture of spit from those who mock him, and are inflamed by the soil rubbed into them; burning egg-shells are applied to his face; he is stretched beneath big and heavy tables, squashed by the double pressure of the cross and the tormentors who assail him. All the while the affectionate nature of the beholder's relationship is insisted upon.[27]

Focus on the torments endured by Christ, on the empathetic reliving of the events was an integral part of lay devotion. In sermons, for example, preachers would dwell on the dramatic, morbid and poignant details of the Passion, urging listeners to see what they described.[28] Exaggeration and embroidery were generic, as sermon and treatise supported and inspired each other. One text in particular, *Meditations on the Life of Christ*, by a thirteenth-century Franciscan monk, supplied numerous details to flesh out the stories of Christ's life. Enjoying a relatively wide distribution, it not only inspired writers of mystery plays, but had as well a profound influence on contemporary art, providing the source for images such as Mary's fainting at the foot of the Cross, and her supplication of Longinus.[29] Indeed, this morbid fascination with the tortured body of Christ causes Grünewald's crucifixion from the *Isenheim Altarpiece* (1512-1515) to come immediately to mind, and connects the various fifteenth-century paintings of Christ surrounded by grotesque tormentors, such as Bosch's *Christ Carrying the Cross,* to the embellished gospel accounts, of which they are probably the offspring.[30] Although both paintings postdate the *Mortifiement*, they are masterpieces of a tradition already developed in René's time.

René set his story of spiritual purging in a garden, an earthly paradise, comparable to the Garden of Eden in its beauty and the bounty of its fruit, and perhaps even surpassing it in that none of its fruit, we are told, is forbidden. The *locus amoenus* has a long history in the visionary landscape of allegory: usually remote, often walled off, paradisal in its beauty, it can serve, as it does in the *Mortifiement*, as "the scene of…the solution of a problem."[31] Though the Soul accepts the arguments presented by her two instructresses, she can hope for salvation only through an act, the purging of *vaine plaisance* from her heart, and that solution is carried out in a space that reverberates with references to Antiquity, Genesis, and the *Romance of the Rose*.

It is a protected location, perfect for the bloodletting, which in real terms was common medieval medical practice.[32] René insists on its benefits as the silent figures drive their nails, one by one, into the flighty heart and through to the wood of the cross. Faith's nail brings forth three drops of blood, one of excessive indulgence, one of fleshly corruption, and one of covetous deceptions, all dark and stinking. Hope's nail brings forth the black drop of impatience, and that of negligence. From Love's nail come the drops of envy and presumption. But when the silent Divine Grace pierces the heart with her lance, the blood of vain pleasure bursts forth in a stream:

> Desquelles goutes de mauvaiz sang qui pour les cloux hors du cuer issirent ne me pouoye assez merveillez, pensant comment il avoit tant et si longuement peu endurer ne porter telles apostumes et ordures ne si detestables sans estre mort comme porte avoit, jusques a lors que le clouerent les tresbenoistes dames....
>
> (I could not marvel enough that these drops of bad blood issued from the heart, thinking how it had been able to endure and carry so many and such detestable abcesses and filth without being dead, since it had borne them until the time when the blessed ladies nailed it...) (176, 267).

The *locus amoenus* extends the medical metaphor. Only by removing the heart from the scene of its sin into a pure domain, that is, from an *infected* to a *sanitary* location, can the operation be successfully completed.

It is a powerful and compelling narrative moment. When read in an unillustrated manuscript (and such do exist of the *Mortifiement de Vaine Plaisance*), such description sparks the mind to create its own images. All reading of narrative inspires mental images. But what is rendered visible, as Klee put it, beyond the simple illustration of the narrative, when miniatures accompany such a text?

Images have a special function in the lay piety of the period under consideration, although the use of images was not unambiguously desirable in Christian aspirations to spirituality. Though various saints regularly reported seeing visions, the true mystic was theoretically supposed to avoid the mental images accompanying prayer and devotion. St. Bernard admitted that the praying individual would tend to imagine scenes from Christ's life, death and resurrection, and that such images could be beneficial. But this was a concession on his part, justifiable only because

> the invisible God had assumed carnal shape in order to make it possible for those "who cannot love otherwise than carnally" to fix their affection on Him, and hence gradually ascend to spiritual love. But, he says, "you have not reached very far unless you can, by the purity of the mind, raise yourself above the phantasms of corporeal likenesses rushing in from every direction."[33]

Along with the moral purification necessary to prepare one's soul for contemplation, Hugh of St. Victor likewise stressed the need for the soul "to recede from sensible reality and from the realm of images that distract its inner vision."[34]

The ideal of imageless spiritual experience was apparently not universal, and, as Sixten Ringbom demonstrates, later mystics (Saint Teresa of Avila and Julian of Norwich) recorded and even classified their visions.[35] Thus, as mysticism influenced the spread of private meditative devotion in the latter part of the Middle Ages, leading to the proliferation of personal books of hours and other religious texts, it also led to an increasing demand for devotional images or *Andachtsbilder*.[36] As Ringbom points out, the distinction between mental image (rejected by St. Bernard and embraced by St. Teresa) and visual image (as art image) became blurred. The "formative power of art for the apparitions" seen by inspired visionaries was recognized, and everybody wanted to own his own images. Small diptychs and triptychs were regularly commissioned for use in private devotions, a fact testified to by a miniature of Philip the Good at his prie-dieu with a devotional image before him.[37] A fascinating case of an image in this tradition is a miniature in Mary of Burgundy's personal book of hours (c. 1480). Mary is seated at her devotions in front of an open casement, which, in turn, frames a church interior. There the Virgin and Child sit enthroned before an altar where (a second) Mary kneels before them in devotion.[38] Is the praying Mary of the outer frame inspired by the image in the book of hours open before her to enjoy a vision of the Virgin adored by Mary herself? If so, what of the actual observer of this miniature, who was originally Mary, since the volume that contains this image within an image is known as the *Book of Hours of Mary of Burgundy*? It is a neat example of *mise en abyme*, especially since the image in the book that the Mary of the outer frame is looking at may be the same one we are looking at (and that the historical Mary used to look at). What is devotional image and what is vision? Can they even be separated in this instance?

A parallel phenomenon was the indulgenced image which won remission for the one who pronounced specified prayers in front of it — a far remove from Bernard's ideal of imageless devotion. Though he condemned such abuses, including the preference for the beauty of an image to the neglect of its spiritual significance, Jean Gerson himself accepted the role of the pictorial image as a spur to proper contemplation of the life and Passion of Christ: "And we ought thus to learn to transcend with our minds from these visible things to the invisible, from the corporeal to the spiritual. For this is the purpose of the image."[39]

In fact, there always was a role and a purpose for religious art in Christianity, formally recognized from the time of Gregory the Great, who scolded the bishop of Marseille for having removed the images from his churches. "Images are to be employed in churches, so that those who are illiterate might at least read by seeing on the walls what they cannot read in books." This sentiment was echoed in Gregory of Nyssa's famous statement that pictures were the books of the illiterate, and further justified by Bonaventure who added two further reasons; namely, "so that people who are not excited to devotion when they hear of Christ's deeds might at least be excited when they see them in figures and pictures, as if present to our bodily eyes; and...so that by seeing them we might remember the benefits wrought for us by the virtuous deeds of the saints." As Freedberg explains in *The Power of Images*, Bonaventure thus expresses the

> conviction that images are more effective than words in rousing our emotions and in reinforcing our memory. [They allow us] to understand the full import of Christ's sufferings and deeds... We come closer to him and more easily model our lives on his and those of his saints when we suffer with them... We attain compassion when we concentrate on images of Christ and his saints and of their sufferings. This is the view that underlies the whole tradition of empathic meditation.[40]

And Bonaventure was seconded by his contemporary, Thomas Aquinas, who believed images were good for "awakening feelings of piety."[41]

If vivid embroidered descriptions of the Passion in works such as *Meditations on the Life of Christ* were intended to elicit empathetic responses, how much stronger they would be, Bonaventure is saying, if provoked visually. And so they were, in numerous images of the bleeding Man of Sorrows, of Christ surrounded by grotesque tormentors on the way to Calvary, and of Crucifixions that culminate perhaps in the magnificently gruesome *Isenheim Altarpiece*. Such images inspired the empathy needed for the kind of imitation of Christ that Thomas à Kempis urged on his readers in the *Imitatio Christi* (c. 1425).[42]

Like other practitioners of the *Devotio moderna*, which urges constant meditation on Christ's life and Passion, and imitation of his example to foster progress along the road to God, Thomas calls upon his readers to take up the cross like their Lord, for it represents the purest life, one of renunciation of worldly desires:[43]

> There is no salvation for our souls, no hope of life everlasting, but in the cross. Take up your cross, then, and follow Jesus; and you will go into life that has no end. He has gone ahead of you, bearing his own cross; on that cross he has died for you, that you may bear your own cross and on that cross yearn to die. If you have died together with him, together with him you will have life; if you have shared his suffering you will also share his glory.[44]

By "dying" with him, one would have life, not death, so that dying and coming to life is an act of purgation, of cleansing. Like the crucifixion of the heart on the cross in the *Mortifiement*, the suffering is salutary. It is worth quoting Thomas at some length here, for he gives the best insight into the unusual image that René has provided:

> You see, the cross is at the root of everything; everything is based upon our dying there. There is no other road to life, to true inward peace, but the road of the cross, of dying daily to self.... [Y]ou will always find you have some suffering to bear, whether you like it or not; you will always find the cross. Either you will be in bodily pain or your soul will be inwardly in distress.[45]

And:

> Make no mistake about it; the life you are to lead must be one of death-in-life. The more a man dies to himself, the more he begins to live to God. No one is fit to grasp heavenly things unless he resigns himself to bearing affliction for Christ's sake. There is nothing more acceptable to God, nothing so conducive to your *soul's health* in this world, than willingly to suffer for Christ's sake. If you had the choice, you ought to choose rather to suffer affliction for Christ's sake than to be refreshed by much comfort; that would make you resemble Christ more nearly, make you follow more closely

> the pattern of all the Saints. Our merit, you see, our progress in virtue, doesn't consist of enjoying much heavenly sweetness and consolation; no, it lies in bearing heavy affliction and trouble.[46]

The medical metaphor is reminiscent of René's use of the medical procedure of bleeding as a model for the "operation" carried out on the heart, and the emphasis on the suffering all must undergo as part of living would ring true for the prince who saw so many of his worldly aspirations dashed during his lifetime:

> Give me the sweet balm of your spirit instead of all the delights of the world; empty my heart of fleshly love and fill it instead with the love of your name.[47]

And:

> Ah, when will it come, that blissful and longed-for hour, when the joy of your presence shall brim to overflowing the depths of my desire, and you be my all in all? Until you grant me that, my joy cannot be full. Still does the man I was — I grieve to say it — stir to life within me; he is not completely *nailed to the cross*, not finally and utterly dead. Still do his lusts make violent war against the spirit, making my heart the battle-ground of civil war, so that the kingdom of my soul may not be at peace.[48]

Like the Soul's flighty heart, Thomas's heart is still pulled to the joys of earthly pleasures, which Thomas takes as a sign that he himself is not yet completely "nailed to the cross." In René's imagination, the heart as object becomes the sign for the human creature who must be purged of moral infection so that the "kingdom of his soul" may be at peace.

Images were supplemental aids to the spiritual exercise of *imitatio Christi* urged by Thomas and effected by René in his devotional tract, and this has to be seen as one of the factors in the illustration of the *Mortifiement de Vaine Plaisance*. Art was something to be used and experienced, not simply admired. As James Marrow points out, art "structures experience and interpretation."[49] Crucifixion images of the Virgin with a sword piercing her heart, or the influential "Descent from the Cross" by Roger van der Weyden, which portrays Mary swooning in her sorrow, were meant to evoke the idea of compassion in their viewers.[50] And the generation of pious responses led, in extreme form, to incidents of stigmatization and groups like the Flagellants.[51] According to Marrow, even the new illusionistic space developing in the fourteenth and fifteenth centuries implicates the beholder in new ways.[52] The viewer is no longer set at a distance, in another dimension as it were, as if a line were drawn between the fiction or history depicted within the frame and our reality without. Rather, we the viewers are implicated in the image; we simply cannot be seen because we are on our side of the frontal picture plane. Could we but move forward and cross that line, it is suggested, we would be in the picture, as is Mary of Burgundy, both in the frontal plane of her chamber and in the inner plane of her vision of the church interior graced with the Madonna's presence.

A less dizzying *mise en abyme* but one that draws in the viewer is found in the Brussels manuscript of the *Mortifiement* (fig. 6). The crucifixion miniature depicts René (recognizable from his numerous portraits), neatly framed in the doorway to the garden, gazing on the marvelous scene before him. It is as if the picture were framed by the garden wall and he, as observer, had managed just to penetrate that frame, while we, the other observers, remain one step removed outside the plane of the picture frame.[53]

The heart, as a separate detached entity, is the center and focus of the *Mortifiement*. Like the Sacred Heart of Jesus, it has become an object of attention in its own right. (In fact, Bainval's article in the *Dictionnaire de Théologie Catholique* points out that in the development of the cult of the Sacred Heart of Jesus, theologians had to stress the union of the heart with the divine body.[54] Therefore, the folk tendency to make a totem of the Sacred Heart as object and venerate it apart from the total notion of the Savior must have been a particularly strong one.) Most interesting, moreover, is the fact that, despite all sources and influences that might have inspired René to place his heart on the cross, the passion of a mortal heart in the *Mortifiement de Vaine Plaisance* is René's original construct, apparently unprecedented in both Latin and vernacular literature.[55]

René repeated the gesture of extracting the heart as the locus of affect when he allowed the god Love to send his heart (transformed into a young armed knight) on a quest to win the lady Sweet Grace in the *Livre du Cuer d'Amours espris*. The quest failed when the Heart (Cuer) lost his lady to the clutches of Denial and Refusal, the enemies of Love, and he was left to finish his days in prayer. The heart of the *Mortifiement* is never fully allegorized like the Cuer of the *Livre du Cuer*. Yet it constitutes the dramatic focus of the narrative, is never offstage (for the parables are in fact only narrative asides in Fear of God's discourse), and the climax of the text, the crucifixion scene, centers on the heart as the locus of penance. Yet the heart itself never speaks. In the opening dedication René states: "...me suis mis a faire cy apres ung traictié entre l'ame devote et le cuer plain de toute vanite" (I have started to write hereafter a treatise between the devoted Soul and the heart full of every vanity) (56, 195). Expectations are raised of a debate between two opposing abstractions, expectations that are never fulfilled, for there is no discussion between the Soul and her heart. She is often said to be addressing her heart — "et disant en ce point a son cuer ..." (and speaking thus to her heart ... [62, 198]); "Mais gaires ne tarda apres les motz que l'Ame au cuer eust dit ..." (But scarcely had the Soul said these words to the heart ... [64, 199]) — but the heart never answers. It never transcends passive object status, which is confirmed by the illustrations. Throughout the miniature cycles of all the extant illustrated manuscripts of the *Mortifiement de Vaine Plaisance* the heart is an object, painted in the universally recognized schema. In this fashion it seems barely allegorized. Its role of willful creature hungering after vain worldly pleasures is determined only as addressee, as defined by the Soul's plaint. Yet, when the heart is placed on the cross to be purged, it bleeds, suffers, is humbled and transformed. It is, in fact, and this despite its passive mode, the only "character" in this little drama to undergo any transformation. The Soul is the heart's mouthpiece, detailing its shortcomings and sins, but she herself is morally static. Without a transformation in her heart, she is unable to change her own moral fate. The moral vitality of the heart is suggested in the miniatures by the drops, or rivulets, of blood issuing forth from the wounds inflicted by nail and lance.

Thus does the heart concentrate the moral lesson of René's allegory. One's heart finds expression through other means — the mouth, the eyes ("windows of the soul"), one's deeds — but it is in the heart that *moral* action takes place. Only if purged of its evil, here defined as desire for earthly vanities, will the soul attain grace. The somber tableau of crucifixion that constitutes this important advance in moral progress inspires desire for the very process it visualizes on parchment. It renders visible, in Klee's phrase, the grand human enterprise of spiritual ascension.

APPENDIX

Illustrated Manuscripts of *Le Mortifiement de Vaine Plaisance*

New York, Pierpont Morgan Library, Ms. 705
Brussels, Bibliothèque Royale Albert Ier, Ms. 10308
Cambridge, Fitzwilliam Museum, Ms. 165
Paris, Bibliothèque Nationale, Ms. fr. 19039
Berlin, Kupferstichkabinett, Ms. 566 (shelf number 78C5)
Chantilly, Musée Condé, Ms. 1477
Geneva, Bibliothèque Martin Bodmer, Cod. Bodmer 144
Metz, Médiathèque Municipale, Ms. 1486

Figure 1. Crucifixion.
New York, Pierpont Morgan Library.

Figure 2. The Soul approached by Fear of God and Contrition.
New York, Pierpont Morgan Library.

Figure 3. Poor woman taking her wheat to the mill.
New York, Pierpont Morgan Library.

Figure 4. Fear of God and Contrition return crucified heart to the Soul. New York, Pierpont Morgan Library.

Figure 5. Crucifixion.

Figure 6. Crucifixion.

Notes

[1] Arthur C. Danto, "Description and Phenomenology of Perception," in *Visual Theory: Painting and Interpretation*, eds. Norman Bryson, Michael Ann Holly, and Keith Moxey (New York: Harper Collins, 1991), 211, 212.

[2] In the original, her name is always preceded by a definite article, i.e., "l'Ame," thus "the Soul." (The Middle French orthography omits the modern circumflex accent over the letter *A*.)

[3] The second parable demonstrates particularly well the extreme detail in late-medieval allegory (fig. 3). A poor woman, who has worked all year plowing, cultivating, harvesting and threshing her wheat, finds that she has to cross a dilapidated bridge over a treacherous river to bring her sack of grain to the mill to be ground into flour. Fear of death by starvation if she does not get her precious sack to the mill struggles with fear of losing her year's labor and possibly drowning if she steps onto the rotten planks of the bridge. Attracted by her lamentations, a wise stranger stops to advise her that she must use the senses God has given her to guide herself across the bridge. By carefully testing each plank with one foot before deciding where to step, she should be able to cross safely. Following the stranger's advice, she picks her careful way across the bridge to the mill, and is rewarded with flour and abundance from her wheat. The explanation follows: the woman represents a person's endeavor; the sack of wheat, merit; the bridge, conscience; the wooden planks, a person's thoughts; the poor woman's foot, a person's decisions; the river, the wrath of God; and the mill, the glory of Paradise. Thus must each endeavor to test his thoughts, restraining decision, until one may be sure that the thoughts are good and solid. For the bridge (conscience) groans, if the thoughts are evil, and it is preferable to take one's time and be sure of one's decisions, for, otherwise, Fear explains, one's merit and good deeds are for naught and one falls into God's wrath, which is hell everlasting. Eriko Amino, "*Le Mortifiement de Vaine Plaisance* of René d'Anjou: Text, Translation and Commentary" (Diss. Columbia University, 1981), 125-35 (text) and 237-43 (translation). All further references to the text and its translation will be by page number only.

[4] For accounts of René's life, see Noël Coulet, Alice Planche and Françoise Robin, *Le Roi René: Le Prince, le mécène, l'écrivain, le mythe* (Aix-en-Provence: EDISUD, 1982); Albert Lecoy de la Marche, *Le Roi René: Sa vie, son administration, ses travaux artistiques et littéraires*, vol. 2 (Paris, 1875; rpt. Geneva: Slatkine Reprints, 1969); Frédéric Lyna, *Le Mortifiement de Vaine Plaisance: Etude du texte et des manuscrits à peintures* (Brussels: Ch. Weckesser, 1927); Daniel Poirion, "Le Miroir Magique" in *Le Coeur d'Amour épris*, eds. Marie-Thérèse Gousset, Daniel Poirion and Franz Unterkircher (Paris: Philippe Lebaud Editeur, 1981); Comte de Quatrebarbes, *Oeuvres complètes du roi René*, vol. 1 (Angers: Cosnier and Lachèse, 1845-46). The earlier authors in this

selection take the more sentimental view of René's attachments to his two wives, whereas the modern authors understand the various monuments that René raised to his first wife as at least partly conventional, and the legend of René's having fallen in love with his second wife after seeing her portrait as just that, a legend.

[5] "... la vraie et parfaite bieneurte n'est pas vraiement a mener vie pompeuse, ne estre victorieux en armes, ne a soy trouver en haulte dominacion ne avoir preminences royaulx, ne en multitude de suites et acompaignemens de gens, ne d'avoir richesses infinies, ne en assiete de fertil pays, ne en posseder plaisans manoirs et sumptueux palais, ne seigneurier fors chasteaux et puissantes cites."(85) I have amended Amino's diplomatic edition of the text (adding punctuation, differentiating between *u* and *v*, *i* and *j*, etc.) and changed her translation where I found it necessary to do so.

[6] The great *Virgin in the Burning Bush* altarpiece by Nicolas Froment [1476] is probably the best known. See James Snyder, *Northern Renaissance Art: Painting, Sculpture, the Graphic Arts from 1350 to 1575* (New York: Harry N. Abrams, 1985), 121, fig. 157.

[7] See reproductions in Coulet et al., 66 and 120.

[8] Johan Huizinga, *The Waning of the Middle Ages* (New York: Doubleday, 1954). Such is the basic theme of Huizinga's book, but see especially Chapter Thirteen, "Types of Religious Life," and page 181 for a reference to René.

[9] Ray C. Petry, ed., *Late Medieval Mysticism* (Philadelphia: Westminster Press, 1957), 18.

[10] Petry, *Mysticism*, 92-93.

[11] None of Hugh's works is listed in the inventory of René's library in Lecoy de la Marche, 182-91.

[12] Heiko Oberman, "Fourteenth-Century Religious Thought: A Premature Profile," *Speculum* 53 (1978), 92-93.

[13] Amino, "*Mortifiement*," 22-23.

[14] Albert Lecoy de la Marche, *La Chaire française au moyen age* (1886; repr. Geneva: Slatkine Reprints, 1974), 270. See also Jean-Thiebaut Welter, *L'Exemplum dans la littérature religieuse et didactique du moyen âge* (1827; repr. Geneva: Slatkine Reprints, 1973).

[15] Gerald Robert Owst, Preaching in Medieval England: An Introduction to Sermon Manuscripts of the Period c. 1350-1450 (1926; repr. New York: Russell and Russell, 1965), 279. See also Literature and the Pulpit in Medieval England (1933; repr. New York: Barnes and Noble,1961).

[16] Henk van Os, *The Art of Devotion in the Late Middle Ages in Europe: 1300-1500*, trans. Michael Hoyle (Princeton: Princeton University Press, 1994), 114.

[17] Dom Louis Gougaud, *Dévotions et pratiques ascétiques du moyen âge*, Collection Pax 21 (Paris: Desclée de Brouwer, 1925), 79.

[18] J. Bainval, "Dévotion au Coeur Sacré du Jésus," *Dictionnaire de Théologie Catholique* (Paris, 1908), 311-12. The original text reads:

> Les faveurs faites aux privilégiés sont: d'être admis à coller ses lèvres sur la plaie du côté pour y puiser l'amour et les richesses du Coeur; de pénétrer dans ce Coeur pour s'y reposer comme dans une oasis, ou pour s'y promener comme dans un beau jardin; de s'y plonger comme dans une fournaise d'amour et de pureté; d'être embrasé d'une étincelle partie du Coeur; parfois d'échanger son coeur avec celui de Jésus et de ne vivre en quelque sorte que par le Coeur divin; ... etc.

[19] Gougaud, *Dévotions*, 94.

[20] Gougaud, *Dévotions*, 89. An excellent reproduction of the heraldically displayed *arma Christi* may be seen in van Os, *Art of Devotion*, 117 (colorplate 36). The wounded heart, though not nailed to the cross, is placed centrally in much the same fashion that the Soul's heart is placed in fig. 6.

[21] See the appendix for the list of manuscripts.

[22] The second, less notable, is an additional miniature of the discussion between the Soul, Fear of God and Contrition that precedes the parables in the Cambridge manuscript. Some of the manuscripts include an author portrait (the Brussels and Paris manuscripts), or presentation miniature (the New York and Chantilly manuscripts), while the others have neither.

[23] Durrieu tried to divine the process in which books of René's own works were produced in his court:

> On commençait par faire une première copie sur papier, une sorte de minute originale; dans cette minute on introduisait le modèle rapidement esquissé, la 'pourtraiture,' suivant l'expression du temps, des illustrations qui devaient accompagner le texte. On avait ainsi un premier état, qui se prêtait à être transcrit ultérieurement sous forme de volume posément calligraphié sur parchemin, avec de brillantes enluminures et les 'pourtraitures' transformées en miniatures peintes en toutes couleurs.

Paul, comte du Durrieu, "La Bibliothèque du roi René," in *Procès-verbaux et mémoires du Congrès international des bibliothécaires et des bibliophiles*, eds. P. Mazerolle and Ch. Mortet (Paris: 1925), 445. Also quoted in Frédéric Lyna, *Le Mortifiement de Vaine Plaisance: Etude du texte et des manuscrits à peintures* (Brussels: Ch. Weckesser, 1927), lxxii. Durrieu arrived at his conclusions by studying, in particular, the extant manuscripts of René's *Livre des tournois*, especially the paper manuscript (Paris, Bibliothèque Nationale, Ms. fr. 2695), which may be the original.

[24] This cycle is preceded in two of the manuscripts (Brussels MS 10308 and Paris, B.N. MS fr. 19039) by author portrait miniatures (depicting René at his writing), and in three others (New York, Morgan Ms. 705 and Chantilly Ms. 1477) by dedication miniatures (showing presentation of the manuscript as a gift to some figure).

[25] "This grouping of four agents of purification may be traceable to four sister virtues who appear in numerous commentaries, sermons, and mystery plays:" Owst, *Literature and Pulpit*, 90-91. See also Isa Ragusa and Rosalie Green, eds., *Meditations on the Life of Christ* (Princeton: Princeton University Press, 1961), 6-9.

[26] Jacques Levron, *Le Bon Roi René* (Paris: Arthaud, 1972), 143-44.

[27] David Freedberg, *The Power of Images: Studies in the History and Theory of Response* (Chicago: University of Chicago Press, 1989), 171.

[28] Owst, Literature and Pulpit, 507-10.

[29] Emile Mâle, *L'Art religieux de la fin du moyen âge en France* (Paris: Armand Colin, 1969), 28-34.

[30] See Snyder, *Northern Renaissance*, on Grünewald, 349 (colorplate 53), on Bosch, 208 (fig. 199).

[31] Paul Piehler, *The Visionary Landscape: A Study in Medieval Allegory* (London: Edward Arnold, 1971), 77-78.

[32] See Charles H. Talbot, *Medicine in Medieval England* (London: Oldbourne, 1967), 130-31.

[33] Sixten Ringbom, "Devotional Images and Imaginative Devotions," *Gazette des Beaux-Arts* 73 (1969), 163. Ringbom is quoting from Bernard's sermons on the Song of Songs (*Cantica* XX,8).

[34] Petry, *Mysticism*, 82.

[35] Ringbom, "Devotional Images," 163-64.

[36] See Eugène Honée, "Image and Imagination in the Medieval Culture of Prayer: A Historical Perspective" in van Os, *Art of Devotion*, 157-172 for an excellent account of the development of private meditative devotion and the images that stirred piety and accompanied prayer.

[37] Ringbom, "Devotional Images," 164, and Honée, "Image and Imagination," 160-161.

[38] Snyder, *Northern Renaissance*, 194 (colorplate 34).

[39] Cited in Ringbom, "Devotional Images," 165.

[40] All cited in Freedberg, *Power of Images*, 163-64.

[41] Cited in Honée, "Image and Imagination," 159.

[42] I am grateful to Eriko Amino, who, in her unpublished dissertation, pointed out the many parallels between the text of the *Mortifiement* and Thomas à Kempis.

[43] The "Modern Devotion" was a movement of lay piety that emphasized the virtue of simplicity in thought and life while rejecting "formalism of belief in

dogma and in ecclesiastical ceremonies," and, most of all, sought "the fulfillment of the human striving for perfection in divine grace and in the example of Christ:" Regnerus Richardus Post, *The Modern Devotion: Confrontation with Reformation and Humanism* (Leiden: E.J. Brill, 1968), 9 and 679.

[44] Thomas à Kempis, *The Imitation of Christ*, trans. Ronald Knox and Michael Oakley (New York: Sheed and Ward, 1959), 78-79.

[45] Thomas à Kempis, *Imitation*, 79.

[46] Thomas à Kempis, *Imitation*, 82. Emphasis added.

[47] Thomas à Kempis, *Imitation*, 124.

[48] Thomas à Kempis, *Imitation*, 135.

[49] James H. Marrow, "Symbol and Meaning in Northern European Art of the Late Middle Ages and the Early Renaissance," *Simiolus* 16 (1986), 152. Marrow claims to have borrowed the formulation from Joseph Koerner.

[50] Marrow, "Symbol and Meaning," 153-54.

[51] Marrow, "Symbol and Meaning," 154. See also André Vauchez, *Religion et société dans l'occident médiéval* (Turin: Bottega d'Erasmo, 1980), 327.

[52] Marrow, "Symbol and Meaning," 158.

[53] René's position within the door frame is a variation on ubiquitous portraits of donors who usually gaze at a devotional image from a side panel or from the edge of a single panel, and are sometimes flanked by an interceding patron saint. Among all the illustrated manuscripts of the *Mortifiement*, this is the only one where René is inserted into the crucifixion miniature.

[54] Bainval, "Dévotion," 283.

[55] Amino, "*Mortifiement*," 41.

University of North Florida

Method in Her Malice: A Reconsideration of Lynet in Malory's Tale of Sir Gareth

Miriam Rheingold Fuller

Lynet, in the *Tale of Sir Gareth*, is one of the most powerful, original, and misunderstood of Malory's women. She is the hero's mentor and guide, instrumental in helping him achieve his quest, but her unkind behavior towards Gareth has caused critics to malign her unjustly, describing her as a "fiery termagant,"[1] a "dismal damsel,"[2] and even accusing her of trying to thwart Gareth in a manner akin to that of Morgan le Fey.[3] Even those who praise her in other matters consider her abuse of Gareth capricious and gratuitous.[4] However, Lynet's treatment of Gareth is appropriate and serves many functions particular to Malory's narrative, and an analysis of the method behind her ostensible mistreatment of Gareth reveals that Lynet is Gareth's most effective teacher and one of his greatest friends.

Although Malory does not give much evidence for motivation, the fact that Lynet's treatment of Gareth, whether positive or negative, helps him to become a better knight, strongly suggests that she means to help Gareth all along. Her scorn makes him more effective in battle, and is a form of reverse — or perverse — encouragement. When Gareth fights with the Green Knight, Lynet exhorts the latter to win, and disparages Gareth: "...why for shame stonde ye so longe fyghtynge with that kychyn knave? Alas! hit is shame that evir ye were made knyght to se suche a lad to macche you, as the wede growyth over the corne."[5] Gareth is "a lytyll ashamed... of hir langage," gives the Green Knight a hard blow, and soon defeats him (306: 5-10). Gareth himself is aware of the tonic effect of Lynet's scorn, for he tells her that it made him angry and his anger made him fight better:

> ... for the more ye seyde the more ye angred me, and my wretthe I wrekid uppon them that I had ado withall. [And therefore all] the mysseying that ye mysseyde me in my batayle furthered me much and caused me to thynke to shewe and preve myselffe at the ende what I was... (313: 1-6)

Gareth is grateful for Lynet's scorn, assuring her that "ye dud nothyng but as ye sholde do, for all youre evyll wordys pleased me" (313: 15-17). Gareth, it appears, appreciates the method behind Lynet's malice.

Lynet uses positive encouragement, but with a similar effect as that of her scorn, at the Castle Perelous, before the climactic battle of Gareth and Ironsydes. She tells Gareth about Ironsydes's fighting style and evil customs in order to prepare him better for his fight, and warns him to remain brave, despite the ghastly sight of the forty dead knights, in order to prevail: "Fayre sir ... abate nat youre chere for all this syght, for ye muste corrage yourself, other ellys ye bene all shente" (320: 4-6). For her most successful encouragement, Lynet uses her sister, Lyones. After Gareth has sounded the horn, challenging Ironsydes to battle, Lynet tells him to "be glad and lyght, for ... at yondir wyndow is my lady, my sistir dame Lyones"(321: 22-23). Lynet's showing Gareth Lyones puts the final seal on his courage, for upon seeing her, he declares that "she besemyth afarre the fayryst lady that ever I lokyd uppon, and truly... I aske no better quarell than now for to do batayle, for truly she shall be my lady and for hir woll I fyght" (321:26-29). Lynet again invokes Lyones in a fashion similar to her former encouragement of Gareth's opponents when Ironsydes momentarily overcomes Gareth: "A, sir Bewmaynes! Where is thy corrayge becom? Alas! my lady my sister beholdyth the, and she shrekys and wepys so that hit makyth myne herte hevy" (324: 12-14). Her words cause Gareth to recover and double his assault, and shortly afterwards, Ironsydes yields.

Lynet's two modes of behavior strongly resemble each other, further evidence that she does intend to help Gareth through her mistreatment. During the first part of their journey Lynet tests Gareth's courage and spurs him on to fight by denigrating his prowess and scornfully urging him to flee. Her exhortations make him even more determined to fight, as she no doubt intends: "What sey[st th] ou?' seyde the damesell, 'woll ye macche yondir two knyghtis other ellys turne agayne?' 'Nay,' seyde sir Bewmaynes, 'I woll nat turne ayen, and they were six mo!" (301: 33-35) Lynet continues to test Gareth after she stops rebuking him. But now she does so by acting concerned for him, rather than by casting aspersions on his courage. She tests him in this way when he is about to fight Sir Persaunt:

> "I pray the save thyself and thou may, for ... thou have had grete travayle...and all perelous passage[s] we are paste sauff all only this passage, and here I drede me sore last ye shall cacche som hurte. Therefore I wolde ye were hens, that ye were nat brused nothir hurte with this stronge knyght. But I lat you wete this sir Persaunte of Inde is nothyng of myght nor strength unto the knyght that lyeth at the seege aboute my lady" (312: 12-21).

Lynet is as clever with kind words as she is with "foule" ones. Although she appears to be dissuading Gareth, she is testing his courage by implying that he will be badly hurt and seeing if he will still take up the challenge. She also hints that not fighting Sir Persaunt would be detrimental. By telling him that Sir Persaunt's strength is nothing to that of Ironsydes, she implies that if Gareth does not prevail against the former knight, he will certainly not prevail against the latter. Gareth takes the hints and fights Sir Persaunt, just as he has fought his previous opponents, spurred on by the perverse encouragement of Lynet.

Gareth also passes her next, final test of his chivalry, when she warns him not to challenge Sir Ironsydes until noon, since his strength waxes to that of seven men in the morning (320-21: 36-3). Again, Lynet is testing Gareth under the guise of concern for his safety, a ruse similar to Lady Bercilak's tempting Gawain with the green belt in *Sir Gawain and the Green Knight*. Gareth shows his awareness of this temptation when he tells Lynet that he will "wynne worshyp worshypfully othir dye knyghtly" (321: 6-8). Her concern is as challenging as was her scorn, for it is often easier to be fooled by apparent helpfulness as it is by disparagement. Lynet's positive testing and encouragement of Gareth is similar in method and effect to her earlier mistreatment of him, signaling that this mistreatment is deliberate, that it springs from necessity rather than malice, and that it is intended for Gareth's benefit.

Lynet's strategy recalls Chrétien's *Perceval*, where Blancheflor encourages the hero to fight Engygeron by pretending to dissuade him. Chrétien is explicit about Blancheflor's deception and the motivation behind it:

> "Car vostre cors ne vostre aaiges
> N'est tex, ce saichiez de seür,
> Que vos a chevalier si dur
> Ne a si fort ne a si grant
> Con cil est qui la forz atant,
> Vos poïssiez contretenir
> [N']estor ne bataille fornir.
> -- Ce verroiz vos, fait il, encui,
> Que je m'iré conbatre a lui,
> Je no lairai por nul chasti."
> Tel plait li a cele basti
> Qu'ele lo blasme, et si lo viaut,
> mais sovant avient que l'en siaut
> Escondire sa volanté,
> Quant an voit bien entalanté
> Home de fair son talant,
> Por ce que mielz li entalant.
> Ansin fist ele come saige,
> Qu'ele li a mis blasme molt fort.[6]

> ("For neither your body nor your age are such, be sure of this, that you could oppose or do battle against a knight as hard, as strong and as big as he who awaits you out there. — You will see it, said he, today, for I will go fight him, I will

> not tarry for any warning." She concocted such a plea for him, she spoke against what she really wanted him to do. But often it happens that one opposes what one wants when one sees a man well inclined to do one's will, in order to make him still better inclined. Thus she acted wisely, by encouraging him to do what she very strongly opposes.)

Thus, Lynet is following a time-honored ploy with which a contemporary audience would be familiar, if not through Chrétien's text then through more recent versions, a ploy meant to make a man more effective in battle.

Much of Lynet's purpose in making Gareth a better knight is to prepare him adequately for his battle with Ironsydes. Textual evidence suggests that Gareth must successfully complete certain "perilous passages," that is, the fights with the varicolored knights, in order to achieve his final adventure. Lynet refers to these "passages" throughout their journey. Before they encounter each of the knights, she warns Gareth that he will soon meet a knight who will defeat him (302: 23-24; 304: 30-36; 308: 17-21), giving the impression that each encounter is a stage in a contest.[7] Significantly, Lyoness's castle is called the Castell Perelus (331: 20), so it is appropriate that Gareth must complete the perilous passages in order to succeed at the perilous castle. Gareth's dwarf, too, in his conversations with Lyoness and Ironsydes, implies that Gareth's having achieved the perilous passages implies good odds for his ultimate victory.[8] It is evident from the importance placed on these passages that Gareth's having achieved them presages his triumph over Ironsydes, or at least renders such triumph possible. It is also significant that the forty knights who failed to save Lyoness probably did not attempt the passages, since the varicolored knights are undefeated prior to fighting Gareth. The scornful attempts of Lynet to discourage him from fighting with the knights are intended precisely to spur him on. Thus Lynet gives Gareth favorable odds, or at least even money, against Ironsydes.

The long duration and intensity of Lynet's abuse build up Gareth's endurance in adverse situations, a quality necessary to his victory. He learns to fight well under duress, defeating his foes even when Lynet taunts him and encourages them. These experiences, though unpleasant, prove invaluable when Gareth fights Ironsydes, with whom the fight lasts all day. Lynet knows about the solar strength that Ironsydes possesses and realizes that Gareth will have to fight a long time, the first part of which under a distinct physical disadvantage. Her stream of "foule wordys" and negative cheerleading, while they do not duplicate the circumstances of his bout, nevertheless well prepare him for it.

There is not only encouragement but education in Lynet's mistreatment. Joseph Ruff notes that she trains Gareth in courtesy,[9] and Larry Benson observes that Gareth learns noble manners, notably chivalric self-control, from Lynet.[10] She constantly alerts Gareth to upcoming dangers, and many of her taunts are warnings or instructions in disguise. She tells him of the dangers awaiting him in the Pace Perelous well before they reach it, under pretext of disparaging him: "Caste away thy shylde and thy spere and fle away… or thou shalt sey ryght sone 'Alas!' For and thou were as wyght as sir Launcelot, sir Tristrams or the good knyght sir Lamerok, thou shalt not passe a pace here…" (308:16-20). Lynet's early warning, though scornful, gives Gareth sufficient time to prepare himself for combat with the Red Knight. She in fact warns him beforehand about all of his opponents except the first, behavior that resembles in content, if not in form, Enide's warnings to Erec,[11] and ensures that Gareth is prepared for the various combats awaiting him.

Lynet's mistreatment of Gareth constitutes a test of his courtesy. Edmund Reiss notes that with Lynet Gareth "experiences a real test of … his *gentillesse*."[12] Lynet is also testing Gareth's lineage, which like his courtesy, is a particular concern of this tale and its relation to Malory's cycle. Stephen Knight suggests that in *Gareth*, Malory addresses the question of how new knights fit into society, arguing that Gareth at first exemplifies "the *arriviste* whose strength is a threat that must somehow be absorbed, acculturated into the aristocratic society," and that Lynet voices this threat.[13] Dhira Mahoney argues that: "Gareth's acceptance of the role of menial requires that he demonstrate his worth specifically with the context of class, that inclusion in the body result from a precise definition of his right to belong."[14] She points out that many of Lynet's taunts, such as: "What art thou but a luske, and a turner of brochis, and a ladyll-washer?" (300: 13-14) are class-based, and notes that the apparent dismay of Lynet at a "kychyn knave" triumphing over a knight stems from the fact that such a triumph offends chivalry.[15]

What Mahoney and Knight do not point out, however, is that Lynet attempts to solve the dilemma of Gareth's lineage at the same time that she raises it. The above-quoted taunt is not merely a rhetorical question designed to humiliate Gareth: it is a challenge to him to prove to her that he *is* something more than a ladle-washer. He cannot simply tell her who he really is, for that would defeat the purpose of his masquerade, which is to prove himself by his conduct alone. Lynet solves this problem by disparaging Gareth in front of other knights in order to discover his lineage. She tells the Black Knight, that Gareth "is but a kychyn knave that was fedde in kyng Arthurs kychyn for almys" (303: 14-15). The Black Knight in turn rebukes Gareth: "hit besemed never a kychyn knave to ryde with such a lady" (304: 9). Gareth responds by hotly asserting that: "I am a jantyllman borne, and of more hyghe lynage than thou, and that woll I preve on thy body!" (304: 10-12). Lynet deliberately makes the Black Knight provoke Gareth into admitting his high rank, which he would not otherwise reveal in her hearing.

Lynet mistreats Gareth in front of his defeated opponents, manipulating them into asserting his lineage and prowess. When she refuses to eat with him at the Green Knight's castle, the Green Knight sits with Gareth himself and chastises Lynet, emphasizing Gareth's nobility and prowess:

> ...for I warne you he is *a full noble man*, and I knowe no knyght that is able to macche hym. Therefore ye do grete wronge so to rebuke hym, for he shall do you ryght goode servyse. For whatsomever he makyth hymself he shall preve at the ende that *he is com of full noble blood and of kynges lynage* (307: 17-23) (emphases mine).

When the Green and Red Knights put their own men at Gareth's disposal, Lynet gains further assurances of his worth, and it is possible that she helped bring about these gestures of fealty. The knights may have been so impressed by the courtesy of Gareth under fire that they wished to reward him.

Lynet's behavior satisfies Gareth's own need to prove himself. As Benson points out, Gareth differs from the typical Fair Unknown hero, since he knows his name and lineage; his quest is "to prove himself worthy of that name."[16] Like Ipomedon, who deliberately provokes — and delights in — others' scorn by the ridiculous disguises he assumes, Gareth deliberately provokes Kay's scorn by asking for food and Lynet's disdain by asking to undertake her adventure looking like a kitchen boy. Critics have noted that he acts in such a way to prove himself,[17] and Beverly Kennedy suggests that Gareth does not want to be knighted merely because he is Arthur's nephew,[18] but no one has discussed *why* Gareth is the only one of his brothers to reject such nepotism. His moral superiority to his brothers is in part an explanation, but the main reason probably stems from his being the youngest of four brothers by many years.[19] If the splendid turnout with which Morgawse equips him on his journey to Arthur's court and the consternation she shows at his degradation and disappearance (339: 6-10) are any evidence, Gareth has probably been spoiled much more than have his brothers. No doubt chafing under too much privilege, he wishes to prove that he can stand on his own.

Lynet, who probably suspects early on what Gareth is doing, satisfies his need for "roughing it" with a vengeance. Indeed, she perversely obliges Gareth by giving him more opportunities to prove himself than he probably wanted. Seen in this light, Gareth's suffering is humorous, as it becomes clear that he gets more testing than he bargained for. Lynet's reaction to

Gareth's disguise could stem from the contrast between their situations. Gareth, by adopting the Fair Unknown persona, is dramatizing himself. Like the Earl of Warwick with his sumptuous tournaments and intricate disguises, the idealistic Gareth attempts to locate himself within the context of chivalric, and particularly Arthurian, romance. He can afford to do this, as he has no responsibilities and plenty of security. Lynet, however, has no time for courtly idealism. She has a vital task to accomplish, and although her situation is replete with romance conventions, she is too aware of its harsh realities to appreciate its scope for chivalric fantasy. By treating Gareth as she does she expresses her impatience with the fictionalized view of knighthood, which treats the dilemma facing her and her sister as a vehicle for proving male prowess, rather than as a social crisis. Lynet does Gareth more of a service than he realizes, for by making him aware of knighthood's unpleasant realities, she transforms his idealism into social responsibility, helping him to develop it in practical, beneficial directions, and making him more conscientious.

Lynet's needs and those of her sister make her conduct appropriate and necessary. Lynet must test Gareth because of her justified doubt of his class and courtesy, which he himself causes with his disguise. His fight with Kay discourages her faith in his chivalry. Gareth's reaction to Kay, when the latter challenges him, is unmannerly: "Yee, I know you well for an unjantyll knyght of the courte, and therefore beware of me!" (298: 14-15). Gareth's choleric response is understandable to the audience, who knows of his long trial under the caustic Kay. Lynet, however, does not know about it, and is probably bewildered at Gareth's words, which to her would indicate discourtesy. It is also possible that the manner in which Gareth fights Kay makes Lynet doubt his chivalry. When he unhorses Kay, he takes Kay's horse and gear, and rides away without either stopping to help Kay arise, as Launcelot does when he and Gareth unhorse each other, or proffering to fight Kay on foot, as Gareth does Launcelot (298: 20-24, 27-32). Malory also notes that Gareth fights "more lyker a gyaunte than a knyght" in his bout with Launcelot (299: 1-2). This bout takes place immediately after Gareth's fight with Kay, so Gareth probably fights like a giant there too, since he wishes for revenge. While his strength may impress Lynet, his discourteous manner of combat would not strike her as appropriate to the man whom she wishes would rescue — and possibly wed — her sister.

Lynet's treatment of Gareth, then, ensures that her sister will be rescued by a courteous knight. Malory makes clear that if the vanquisher of Sir Ironsydes is not courteous, then the victory will be an empty exchange of one bad knight for another. Both Lynet and Lyoness stress that Ironsydes's discourtesy and murderousness cancel out his prowess, nobility, and wealth. Lyoness calls him: "a full noble knyght, but he is nother of curtesy, bounté, nother jantylnesse; for he attendyth unto nothyng but to murther, and that is the cause I can nat prayse hym nother love him" (318: 23-26). Lynet describes him similarly: "... in hym is no curtesy, but all goeth to deth other shamfull mourther. And that is pyté ... for he is a full lykly man and a noble knyght of proues, and a lord of great londis and of grete possesions." (320: 15-19) The sisters' speeches encapsulate the code of *gentillesse* expressed in earlier romances that informs Malory's own code of knightly conduct. It is vital, then, that Lynet ascertain Gareth is morally capable of achieving this adventure. Her testing him parallels the trials undergone by the knights on the Quest of the Sangkreall. There too, moral character rather than prowess determines a knight's success, as the examples of Gawain and Launcelot illustrate.

Lynet is conscious and deliberate in her treatment of Gareth, which consists of testing and training him. Each element of it has a specific goal, be it determining his lineage or preparing him for his final adventure, and the beginning and ending of her mistreatment are triggered by specific actions or words on his part that indicate to Lynet the need to test him and the cessation of that need. Lynet does not start to taunt Gareth until after she sees him defeat Kay; indeed, she ignores him.[20] When she sees him defeat Kay, however, she realizes that he might have merit, so she decides that it is worthwhile to test him. Damsels in other Fair Unknown romances abuse the hero before they see him fight, because they think he has no ability, and cease their abuse once he proves his prowess. Eleyne, in *Lybeaus Desconus*, "chydes" the hero until he defeats his first opponent.[21] Lynet changes her behavior, however, when Gareth tells her, after enduring many days of her abuse, that "I had lever do fyve batayles than so to be rebuked" (312: 8-9). His speech is the seal on his mild behavior, showing that words wound him more than combat, thus proving to Lynet that he is courteous and of good birth, and so she stops rebuking him. Her apologetic speech: "I mervayle what thou art and of what kyn thou arte com... ever curteysly ye have suffyrde me, and that com never but of jantyll bloode" (321: 10-11, 32-34) reveals her and Malory's belief that *gentillesse* is irrevocably joined to noble lineage. Her abuse, then, is useful and does not spring from anger or caprice.

Indeed, Lynet suffers as much or more than Gareth from her mistreatment of him, for she risks her own name in order to help her sister, since, in being so abusive to Gareth, she herself is discourteous. She sacrifices her reputation particularly when she and Gareth are with others. Whenever she rebukes him in front of other knights she herself is rebuked. They leave her to dine by herself, and the Green and Red Knights set guards over Gareth while he sleeps to protect him against her possible "treson," "shame," or "vylony" (307: 31-33, 310: 16-20). It must be as frustrating for Lynet to be treated as a villainess when what she is really doing is aiding her lady — and in the long run, Gareth — as it is for Gareth to be treated as a kitchen knave when he is really a king's son. That both voluntarily undertake these masquerades does not mitigate the discomfort of either.

In fact Lynet, like Gareth, is a type of Fair Unknown, who is mistreated at Arthur's court, and by this mistreatment reveals the inadequacies of the court. Like Gareth, she will not tell Arthur her name, nor that of her sister. She tells Arthur only that her sister "is a lady off grete worshyp and of grete londys," and the name of the knight besieging her (296: 27-30). This causes Arthur and his knights to dismiss the importance and urgency of her request, even though Gawain vouches for Ironsydes's reputation, just as Gareth's request for food causes the court to question his lineage. Arthur will not grant Lynet a knight because she will not reveal her sister's name or estate:

> "Fayre damesell," seyde [the] kynge, "there bene knyghtes here that wolde do hir power for to rescowe your lady, but bycause ye woll not telle hir name nother where she dwellyth, therfore none of knyghtes that here be nowe shall go with you be my wylle." (296-7: 36-3)

Arthur's refusal to grant Lynet a knight reveals serious inadequacies in the Round Table. The Pentecost oath specifies that the Round Table knights must "allwayes to do ladyes, damesels, and jantilwomen and wydowes [socour:] strengthe hem in hir ryghtes..." (120: 20-22). Arthur should grant Lynet a knight because of his oath to protect ladies, not because of her lady's status. In refusing to aid her, Arthur breaks his own oath. He and his knights fail this test of their chivalry and courtesy. It is fitting, therefore, that Gareth be the one to undertake Lynet's adventure and pass her test.

Further, it must be humiliating for Lynet, to whom courtesy is so important, to be considered discourteous. That she values the courtesy of others is evident from her testing of Gareth and her criticism of the discourteous Ironsydes; that she values her own courtesy is evident from her self-castigation in front of Gareth and others. She tells Gareth, after she stops rebuking him, that "so fowle and so shamfully dud never woman revyle a knyght as I have done you, and ever curteysly ye have suffyrde me" (312: 31-33), and the fervent exclamation with which she prefaces her apology reveals her distress at how she has treated him: "Alas!... fayre Bewmaynes, forgyff me all that I have myssesyde or done ayenste you" (313: 13-14). This regret for her discourtesy colors her speech when she praises Gareth to her siblings:

> ... he is curtyese and mylde, and the most sufferynge man that ever I mette withall. For I dare sey there was never jantyllwoman revyled man in so foule a maner a[s] I have rebuked hym. And at all tymes he gaff me goodly and meke answers agayne. (330: 5-9)

It is significant that Lynet feels remorse for her treatment of Gareth, even though it is ultimately for the good, while she expresses no compunction for preventing Gareth from sleeping with Lyones, an action that, like her mistreatment, is necessary but frustrating to Gareth. The difference between Lynet's reactions to her various actions is that the latter involves no discourtesy while the former does. It is apparent, then, that in her mistreatment of Gareth, necessary as it is to her sister's security and Gareth's triumph, Lynet makes a sacrifice similar to that which Brengien makes for Iseult on the latter's wedding night.

Lynet's thwarting the lovers' pre-nuptial tryst is, like her earlier mistreatment of Gareth, done for his welfare — and that of Lyones. Lynet tells Gareth — when he protests at having his tryst so rudely interrupted — that "all that I have done shall be to your worshyp and to us all" (336: 2-3). The "worshyp" that Lynet brings about involves the couple's chastity, and, by extension, the social standing of Lyones. Her brother has already approved the marriage, but Morgawse and Arthur have not. If Lyones consummates the marriage privately, she would be guaranteeing it according to canon law — and probably according to some ecclesiastical authorities as well[22] — but she would be indicating that she feels she is not high-ranking enough for Gareth, and that she fears that Arthur and Morgawse would not permit a public marriage.[23] Such an action would reflect negatively not only upon the honor of Lyones, but upon that of her family. Lynet, then, is indeed acting for "us all" when she thwarts the lovers. Her concern for her sister and family resembles that of Lunete for the Dame de Landuc in Chrétien's *Yvain*, and recalls Lunete's reminder to the lady that her excessive grief — which is a type of *demesure* similar to Lyones's "hoote lustis" — is not becoming to such a noble lady.[24]

Lynet's interventions keep Gareth on the proper moral track. Reiss argues that Lynet's actions on Gareth's behalf make her "a kind of conscience based on Christian and chivalric ideals."[25] Wilfred Guerin maintains that Lynet "acts with a sense of righteousness" when she prevents the lovers from their "hoote lustis" and that her "efforts are well-directed" since the lovers' goal is marriage and not illicit love, and since Malory stresses the happiness of married love in the tale as opposed to the ultimately disastrous loves that occur later in the cycle.[26] Benson notes that Lynet is acting as a teacher, and that the overhasty Gareth learns patience from her timely interventions.[27] Lynet's unwelcome but necessary chaperonage is similar to

Eleyne's rescuing Lybeaus from his luxurious interlude with the Dame d'Amore in *Lybeaus Desconus* in order to get him back on his quest (1417). Thus, the interventions of Lynet enable Gareth and his tale to proceed appropriately in both a moral and narrative context.

Lynet, as Malory's authorial agent, must maintain proper sexual conduct between the lovers in order to uphold Malory's strict standards of morality for this tale. These standards come from a contemporary preference for married love and concurrent aversion to illicit love, a preference apparent in works like the early fifteenth-century romance *Sir Degrevant*, whose heroine refuses to consummate her love with the hero until their marriage.[28] Kennedy notes that by the fifteenth century, attitudes towards marriage and *fin'amor* "had changed considerably, in literature if not in real life. In both French and English romances marriage was now viewed as the ideal consummation of the love between a knight and his lady."[29] Benson attributes this change to the increasing role of romances as manuals of correct behavior:

> ... the one rule of courtly love that was not promulgated in the late Middle Ages was... that love is impossible between a man and wife. That was a harmlessly amusing idea so long as chivalric love was mainly a matter of literature... When chivalric romances became a guide to conduct, the condonation of adultery was no longer acceptable. This may be why English romances, which are all from this later period, seem so moral when compared to their French antecedents. Though fifteenth-century nobles were eager to be known as model lovers equal to Tristram or Launcelot, they obviously did not want to be known as adulterers.[30]

Since Arthurian material was regarded as quasi-historical, Malory, as Benson notes, "had to find a means of mediating between his convictions and his inherited plot.... When he is free to invent, as in *Gareth*, marriage is clearly preferred to love *para-mours*; this was usually the case in fifteenth-century fiction."[31] Lynet shares Malory's "convictions" when she tells Gareth that she has acted for his worship. She clearly regards pre-marital chastity as a matter not only of morality, but of honor, and she upholds Malory's agenda by maintaining the lovers' "worshyp."

As the foiled-consummation scenes show, Malory trusts Lynet more than any other character to keep the narrative progressing correctly. Lyones, who assumes Lynet's role as Gareth's mentor,[32] cannot control his behavior, and thus is unable to maintain an appropriate narrative process. She begins properly, insisting that Gareth prove himself further in order to win her: "thou shalt nat have holy my love unto the tyme that thou be called one of the numbir of the worthy knyghtes. And therefore go and labour in worshyp this twelve-monthe, and than ye shall hyre new tydyngis" (327: 7-11); and sweetly but firmly overriding his protests: "go on your way and loke that ye be of good comforte, for all shall be for your worshyp and for the best; and, pardé, a twelve-monthe woll sone be done" (327: 22-25). However, she does not make Gareth uphold her command, and she grants him her love soon after he comes to her brother's castle. She also gives in to Gareth's sexual desire. While her actions are understandable, given her love for Gareth, she is in danger of eroding the hard-won discipline Gareth acquired under Lynet's stern tutelage, as well as diminishing his reputation by her conspiracy in his luxurious *recreantise*. This stance directly opposes her earlier one of enabling Gareth to achieve status as one of "the worthy knyghtes." Lynet must reassume her duties as his mentor, and it is no accident that her assertion she is acting for his worship echoes the earlier assurance of Lyones that their long separation would be for his worship.

Gawain too fails in his duty to Gareth. He is trying to find Gareth and bring him back to Arthur's court, but winds up fighting him instead. Lynet is the one who recognizes Gareth and gets Gawain to stop fighting him: "Sir Gawayne! leve thy fyghtynge with thy brothir, sir Gareth" (357: 8-9). She also reminds Gawain that Arthur ought to be informed of Gareth's whereabouts: "Now what woll ye do?... Mesemyth hit were beste that kynge Arthure had wetynge of you bothe..." (357: 32-34). Again, Lynet succeeds where others fail. In parallel passages in *Yvain* and *Ipomadon*, the two knights discover each other without the damsel's help. By making Lynet crucial to Gawain's discovery of Gareth, Malory underscores her narrative authority and her importance to the smooth progression of his plot.

Indeed, Lynet guarantees Gareth's continued success throughout the tale, and always acts for his honor and his ultimate happiness. Her being rewarded with marriage to his brother Gaheris indicates that both Gareth and Malory wish to honor her. Far from being his nemesis, then, Lynet is Gareth's most loyal ally, and rather than being classed with the antagonistic Morgan le Fey, she ought to share the spotlight with Nynyve and similar ladies as one of the Round Table's greatest benefactresses.

Notes

[1] Victor Angelescu, "The Relationship of Gareth and Gawain in Malory's 'Morte Darthur," *Notes and Queries 8* (1961), 8.

[2] Donald L. Hoffman, "Malory's 'Cinderella Knights' and the Notion of Adventure," *Philological Quarterly* 67 (1988), 146. Interestingly, although Hoffman

refers to Lynet in uncomplimentary terms, he credits her "rebukes" with forming Gareth's character.

[3] Wendy Tibbetts Greene describes both Launcelot and Gareth as winning their quests "despite the machinations of enchantresses," a summary that shows a misunderstanding of Lynet's role in Gareth's adventure: "Malory's Uses of the Enchanted: A Study in Narrative Technique:" (Ph.D. diss., Indiana University, 1982), 76.

[4] Edmund Reiss, *Sir Thomas Malory* (New York: Twayne Publishers, Inc., 1966), 105. Reiss considers Lynet "too rash, too outspoken, and too full of *demesure*," in her treatment of Gareth (105), and Hoffman claims that she "scorns his knighthood undeservedly" ("Malory's 'Cinderella Knights," 149).

[5] *The Works of Sir Thomas Malory*, ed. Eugene Vinaver. 3 vols., 2nd ed. (Oxford: Clarendon Press, 1967), 305-6: 37-2. All quotations are from this edition.

[6] Chrétien de Troies, *Le Conte du Graal ou Le Roman de Perceval*, ed. and trans. Charles Méla (Paris: Librairie Générale Française, 1990), 2076-95. All quotations are from this edition.

[7] Dhira Mahoney, "Malory's *Tale of Gareth* and the Comedy of Class," in *The Arthurian Yearbook*, ed. Keith Busby (New York: Garland Publishing, 1991), 171. Mahoney notes that "The color-differentiation of the knights that Gareth defeats as he works his way through the perilous passages itself conveys a sense of hierarchy and gradation."

[8] The dwarf tells Lyoness how Gareth defeated the varicolored knights, and she is so impressed that she sends him food, wine, and a costly gold cup (318: 9-16). When the dwarf informs Ironsydes that Gareth "hathe passed all the perelouse passages," Ironsydes assumes that the mysterious knight must be either Lancelot, Tristrams, Lamerok, or Gawain (319: 7-15).

[9] "She gives him instruction in conduct appropriate to a knight, although her remarks tend to be comments on what he has done badly. Even so she directs attention to his knightly prowess.... She is the one who observes his conduct and shapes his behavior in his first adventures..." Joseph R. Ruff, "Malory's *Gareth* and Fifteenth-Century Chivalry," in *Chivalric Literature: Essays on Relations between Literature and Life in the Later Middle Ages*, eds. Larry D. Benson and John Leyerle (Toronto: University of Toronto Press, 1980), 109.

[10] Larry D. Benson, *Malory's Morte Darthur* (Cambridge: Harvard University Press, 1976), 103.

[11] Roger Sherman Loomis, *Arthurian Tradition and Chrétien de Troyes* (New York: Columbia University Press, 1949): 128-29.

[12] Reiss, *Sir Thomas Malory*: 104-5.

[13] Stephen Knight, *Arthurian Literature and Society* (New York: St. Martin's Press, 1983), 119-20.

[14] Mahoney, "Malory's *Tale of Gareth* and the Comedy of Class," 167.

[15] "Malory's *Tale of Gareth* and the Comedy of Class," 169.

[16] Benson, Malory's Morte Darthur,102.

[17] Benson, *Malory's Morte Darthur*, 97, 102; Beverly Kennedy, *Knighthood in the Morte Darthur*, 2nd ed. (Cambridge: D. S. Brewer, 1992), 132.

[18] Kennedy, Knighthood in the Morte Darthur, 132.

[19] When Morgawse comes to Arthur's court in search of Gareth, Malory notes that her other sons have not seen her for twelve years (339: 1-4). Gareth was most likely the only child left with his mother for a long time.

[20] Lynet directs her anger and frustration at Arthur at being denied a proven knight for her adventure: "Fy on the... shall I have none but one that is your kychyn knave?" and rides off without a backwards glance or word for Gareth (297: 21-23).

[21] *Lybeaus Desconus*, ed. M. Mills (London: Oxford University Press, 1969), 256-76, 445-50. All quotations are from this edition.

[22] Kennedy, Knighthood in the Morte Darthur, 142.

[23] Kennedy, Knighthood in the Morte Darthur, 143.

[24] As it says:

> A si haute dame ne monte,
> Que duel si longuemant maintaingue.
> De vostre enor vos ressovaingne
> Et de vostre grant jantillesce!"
>
> ("It is not seemly for so noble a lady to maintain her grief for so long. Recall your honor and your very gentle birth!")

Chrétien de Troyes, *Yvain*, ed. Wendelin Foerster (Manchester: Manchester University Press, first printed 1942; reprinted 1984), 1670-73. All quotes are from this edition.

[25] Reiss, Sir Thomas Malory, 108.

[26] With their (Gareth and Lyones's) marriage and with those of two of Gareth's brothers, Malory brings full stress upon the happiness of all concerned. As with the married love of Pelleas and Nineve, Gareth's is an index to the noblest elements of the chivalric ideal — and an effective contrast to the loves that will later wither the flower of chivalry. Wilfred L. Guerin, "The Tale of Gareth' Chivalric Flowering," in *Malory's Originality: A Critical Study of Le Morte Darthur*, ed. R.M. Lumiansky (Baltimore: The Johns Hopkins Press, 1964), 110-11.

[27] Benson, Malory's Morte Darthur, 106.

[28] L. F. Casson, ed., *The Romance of Sir Degrevant* (London: Oxford University Press, 1949), 1523-36. All quotes are from this edition.

[29] Kennedy, Knighthood in the Morte Darthur, 90.

[30] Benson, Malory's Morte Darthur, 159.

[31] Benson, Malory's Morte Darthur, 160-61.

[32] Ruff, "Malory's *Gareth* and Fifteenth-Century Chivalry," 109.

Central Missouri State University

Rituelle Symbolik, Theatralität und die 'Ambivalenzen des geistlichen Spiels': Das mittelenglische Spiel 'Secunda pastorum'[*]

Jörn Bockmann / Judith Klinger

1 Ritual und Theater?

Die literaturwissenschaftliche Auseinandersetzung mit dem geistlichen Spiel des späten Mittelalters ist überwiegend von oppositionellen Kategorien geprägt: Untersucht wird die irritierende Koexistenz von Sakralem und Profanem bzw. christlichen und außerchristlichen Elementen (auf der Ebene des Inhalts), Ernst und Komik (auf der Ebene der Rezeptionsästhetik), Unterhaltung und Andacht (auf der Ebene der Pragmatik). Den Rahmen dieser Diskussion bildet die Frage nach dem Übergang vom christlichen Ritual zum neuzeitlichen Theater, das sich als Literatur- und Inszenierungsform gegenüber der Vermittlung verbindlicher Glaubensinhalte verselbständigt hat. Aus diesem Grunde haben Spiele, die im Umfeld dieser Grenze zwischen 'Ritual' und 'Theater' angesiedelt werden, erhöhte Aufmerksamkeit gefunden: Ein besonders intensiv diskutiertes Beispiel ist das mittelenglische 'Zweite Hirtenspiel' des sogenannten Meisters von Wakefield, die *Secunda pagina pastorum*.[1] Und dies nicht ohne Grund: Der Text zeichnet sich durch eine auffällige Verschränkung alltagsweltlicher mit religiösen Bezügen, komisch-burlesker Elemente mit sakraler Feierlichkeit aus, wie bereits ein Blick auf den Handlungsverlauf zeigt.

Das Spiel wird auf freiem Feld eröffnet (Szene 1, V. 1-295). Die drei Hirten Coll, Gib und Daw klagen über das schlechte Wetter, zu hohe Steuern und die häuslichen Lasten als Ehemänner und Familienväter (V. 1-189). Zu ihnen gesellt sich Mak, der bereits als notorischer Schafsdieb bekannt ist (V. 224f.). Auch Mak beklagt seine häusliche Not, da ihn die ausgesprochene Fruchtbarkeit seiner Frau Gyll, die pro Jahr mindestens ein Kind zur Welt bringt, zu Hunger und Krankheit verurteilt (V. 190-252). Nachdem sich die Hirten bereits zur Ruhe gelegt haben, spricht Mak zur Sicherheit noch einen Schlafzauber, um ihnen daraufhin ein besonders fettes Schaf zu stehlen (V. 253-295).

In seiner Hütte angekommen, wird Mak von seiner Frau mit Vorwürfen empfangen (Szene 2, V. 296-349), da Gyll befürchtet, die Hirten könnten den Verlust des Schafes bemerken und ihn verdächtigen. Auf ihren Vorschlag hin beschließt das Paar, das gestohlene Schaf in einer Wiege zu verbergen, während Gyll selbst sich ins Kindbett legen soll, um die Geburt eines Kindes vorzutäuschen (V. 332ff.).

Mak kehrt zu den Hirten zurück (Szene 3, V. 350-403), die soeben erwacht sind und ihn vermissen; der Schafsdieb erklärt, er müsse sofort zu seiner Frau eilen, da er von der Geburt eines weiteren Kindes geträumt habe. Mak und Gyll können so ihre Pläne ausführen (Szene 4, V. 404-448), bevor die Hirten, wie vom betrügerischen Ehepaar erwartet, den Verlust bemerken und tatsächlich Mak und dessen Frau verdächtigen (Szene 5, V. 449-475).

In Maks Hütte wird den Hirten die verabredete Geschichte über den neugeborenen Sohn aufgetischt, werden deren Verdächtigungen zurückgewiesen, bis der Schwindel letztlich doch auffliegt und Mak bestraft wird (Szene 6, V. 476-628). Gyll schwört so z.B., daß sie, falls die Hirten betrogen worden seien, das Kind in der Wiege essen wolle (V. 534ff.); Mak vermag sogar die Taufpaten aufzuzählen (V. 561ff.). Als die Hirten aber das vorgebliche Kind beschenken wollen, stellen sie eine lange Schnauze, Hörner und vier Beine an ihm fest, bis einer der Hirten das Schaf schließlich an einer Ohrmarke erkennt (V. 575-615). Gyll versucht sich herauszureden, indem sie behauptet, das Kind sei von Elfen entführt und verwandelt worden (V. 616ff.). Die Ausreden nützen jedoch nichts: Mak wird zur Strafe in einer Decke geprellt (V. 620ff.).

Nach diesem ‘Spottmysterium’ setzt unvermittelt die Inszenierung des Weihnachtsgeschehens ein: Die selben drei Hirten befinden sich wieder auf freiem Feld, wo ihnen ein Engel des Herrn erscheint und die Geburt des Erlösers verkündet. Lobpreisend und singend machen sich die Hirten auf den Weg (Szene 7, V. 629-709). Das Spiel schließt mit der traditionellen Nativität-Szenerie, der Anbetung des Kindes durch die Hirten im Stall zu Bethlehem (Szene 8, V. 710-754).

Die auffällige Kombination des profanen mit dem sakralen Geschehen im Spiel hat in der Literaturwissenschaft zu Charakterisierungen geführt, die Maynard Mack folgendermaßen zuspitzt: “a long farcical tail wagging a small sacred dog.”[2] In dieser Beschreibung klingt neben der Opposition des Komisch-Burlesken und des sakralen Ernstes auch die Vorstellung einer allmählichen Verselbständigung des Theaters gegenüber dem Ritual an, den das quantitative Übergewicht der ‘profanen’ Handlung anzukündigen scheint.[3] Es ist schließlich ein Gemeinplatz der Literaturgeschichtsschreibung geworden, das weltliche Theater des Mittelalters aus einer allmählichen Loslösung von der Liturgie, den liturgischen Feiern und den geistlichen Spielen herzuleiten, wobei die rituellen Elemente mit den sakralen abnehmen.[4]

Tatsächlich wirkt die Kombination der burlesken Geschichte vom gestohlenen Schaf mit einem Zentralereignis der christlichen Heilsgeschichte auf den modernen Rezipienten irritierend: Es stellt sich aber die Frage, wie mit dieser Irritation über die *coincidentia oppositorum* im Spiel interpretatorisch umzugehen ist. Festzustellen ist nämlich auch, daß sich offenbar weder die Autoren noch die zeitgenössischen Rezipienten — von Einzelfällen theologischer Kritik abgesehen — an dieser dramatischen Einheit der Gegensätze gestört haben.[5] Ein solcher Befund muß nachdenklich stimmen, scheint er doch die Kategorien selbst in Frage zu stellen: Entweder ist ihr Zusammenhang anders zu denken als im Modus wechselseitiger Ausschließlichkeit, oder es sind die oben genannten Kategorien ungeeignet, dem historisch anderen Rezeptionsmodus gerecht zu werden. Die Irritation, die die überlieferten Texte beim modernen Rezipienten in der Regel auslösen, könnte zum Anlaß genommen werden, Kategorien wie 'Ernst' und 'Komik' in ihrer Historizität zu reflektieren. Es hat den Anschein, als verdanke sich die Vorstellung grundsätzlicher Unvereinbarkeit christlicher Vorstellungsinhalte mit komischen Präsentationsformen einem spezifisch neuzeitlichen, nämlich nach-reformatorischen Religionsverständnis, das der Interpretation spätmittelalterlicher Spiele nicht ohne weiteres zugrunde gelegt werden darf.

Die Forschung zur *Secunda pastorum* berücksichtigt nun durchaus die Möglichkeiten einer Kombination von 'Komik' und 'Ernst', indem etwa von einer Funktionalisierung des Komischen für den lehrhaften Zweck ausgegangen wird. Da schon der erste und umfangreichere Teil ('Mak-Spiel') vielfältige (Bild-)Bezüge zum Heilsgeschehen aufweist, können Schafdiebstahl und 'Spottmysterium' (die Betrachtung des Schafs in der Wiege durch die Hirten) nach typologischem Muster als Präfiguration der Nativität aufgefaßt werden. Ein Großteil der Forschung zur *Secunda pastorum* beschreibt, in der Formulierung Theo Stemmlers, das Mak-Spiel als "eine vollständige Anti-Szene zur Geburt und Anbetung Christi"[6]. Komische Verkehrungen und profane Elemente sind dieser Lektüre zufolge vollständig in die religiöse Sinnkonstellation eingebunden, die sie im Negativ-Entwurf noch erkennen lassen, und damit dem Glaubensinhalt untergeordnet, zu dem sie hinführen: Das Lächerliche wird dem Erhabenen dienstbar gemacht. Die Zuordnung von Bild und Gegenbild führt dazu, die *mock-nativity* als sekundäre Ableitung zu verstehen, die das Sakrale nicht stört, seine Entfaltung vielmehr noch zu steigern erlaubt. Umgekehrt ist es ebenso denkbar, den ersten Teil als Parodie des Heilsgeschehens zu lesen, das im zweiten Teil zwar noch vorgeführt, durch die komische Verzerrung jedoch beschädigt wird, womit der sakrale Ernst letztlich dekonstruiert würde.[7]

Solche Überlegungen zum Wechselbezug zwischen dem Profanen und dem Sakralen, dem Komischen und dem Ernsten führen indes abermals zu einer dualistischen Perspektive, die das Spiel entweder als geistliche Verkündigung oder als weltliche Parodie klassifiziert. Ob dieser Dualismus des einander Ausschließenden auch die Perspektive des Spiels selber darstellt, ist aber erst zu prüfen: Zu deutlich ist auf der einen Seite die Abweichung von Inhalten und Handlungsformen des christlichen Glaubens und seiner Verkündigung, zu deutlich auf der anderen Seite die Abhängigkeit der Spiele von einem klerikalen Umfeld, als daß sich auf Dauer mit diesen Fragestellungen eine Beschreibung der Struktur und Funktion von Spielen wie der *Secunda pastorum* erreichen ließe. Die Gegenüberstellung von Parodie vs. Verkündigung führt zum Problem der 'Evolution' des neuzeitlichen Theaters zurück,[8] da ihr die Vorstellung einer allmählichen Entwicklung des Dramas aus rituellen über pararituelle Formen hin zur theatralischen Eigenständigkeit zugrundeliegt. Um einen neuen Blick auf die *Secunda pastorum* zu ermöglichen, scheint es daher sinnvoll, diese Voraussetzung selbst zu befragen.

Neuere Forschungen stellen zunehmend die Konzeption einer linearen Entwicklungsgeschichte des modernen Theaters von der christlichen Liturgie über die Zwischenstufe des geistlichen Spiels in Frage. In diesem Sinne hat Hans-Ulrich Gumbrecht dafür plädiert, die 'Schwelle' zwischen vortheatralischen Formen und mittelalterlichem Theater als Komplex verschiedener Komponenten zu differenzieren,[9] etwa die Ausgestaltung des Theaterraums, die zur Trennung zwischen Darstellern und Zuschauern führt, den Einsatz eines Vorhangs oder die zunehmende Rollenindividualisierung durch Kostüm, Masken und Gesten,[10] aber auch Indizien für die Durchsetzung einer aus der Alltagsrealität abgehobenen Theaterwirklichkeit im Spiel-Text. Diese Komponenten können im einzelnen Spiel teilweise oder sämtlich mit je unterschiedlicher Gewichtung auftreten. Interessant für unsere Fragestellung ist an Gumbrechts Vorschlägen der Versuch, die verschiedensten Kriterien nicht mit einem systematischen, geschlossenen Konzept von 'Ritual' oder 'Theater' zu verrechnen, sondern mit Hilfe des so gewonnenen Instrumentariums den Blick auf die Kombinationsmöglichkeiten solcher Merkmale in spätmittelalterlichen Theaterformen zu richten.

In der Konsequenz führt dieser Vorschlag von einer Beschreibung gegeneinander abgeschlossener Systeme — Ritual und Theater — und dem Übergang vom einen zum anderen weg: In Hinblick auf jeweils spezifische Formen, Wissen zu vermitteln und Erfahrung zu strukturieren (die Gumbrecht 'Erfahrungsdispositive' nennt[11]), können 'Ritual' und 'Theater' Eckdaten auf einer Skala bezeichnen, im Sinne idealtypisch gedachter Inszenierungsformen, die dann zur Beschreibung eines Spielraums von Variationen und Kombinationen tauglich sind. Während im Rahmen der Frage nach einem generellen "schwer faßbaren Wandel im kollektiven Erfahrungsstil" Texte,[12] Regie-Anweisungen oder Aufführungsformen als 'Symptome' eines solchen Wandels begriffen werden, ist es umgekehrt auch denkbar, den einzelnen Text als Erfahrungsdispositiv zu analysieren. Die oben skizzierten Dualismen sind so zugunsten einer interpretatorischen Verfahrensweise aufgehoben, die sich einerseits — auf inhaltlicher Ebene — mit den im Text vorfindlichen Wissenssphären und ihrer Kombination befaßt, andererseits — hinsichtlich der Strukturierung von Rezeption — die jeweiligen Strategien der Wissensvermittlung in einem Koordinatensystem theater- bzw. ritualspezifischer Formen verortet.

Die Frage nach rituellen Handlungs- und theatralischen Inszenierungsformen im geistlichen Spiel, die in dieser Sichtweise auch nebeneinanderstehen und sich wechselseitig überlagern oder beeinflussen können, basiert auf einem Literaturbegriff, der wesentlich von dem Konzept der 'Aufführung' geprägt ist. Als Aufführung stellt der mittelalterliche Text eine Interaktionsform dar, ein Gemeinschaftshandeln von körperlich miteinander kommunizierenden Trägern dieser Gemeinschaft, bei dem Wissen strukturiert und vermittelt wird.[13] Eine Beschäftigung mit geistlichen Spielen unter dieser Perspektive führt zu einer "Verschiebung des Interessenschwerpunktes vom Sinn der Texte hin zu Texten als Indizien für Aufführungs- und Interaktionsformen, die ihrerseits als Dispositive für historisch spezifische Modalitäten des Erfahrens gedeutet werden können."[14] Erst eine solche Forschungsperspektive scheint uns dazu geeignet, die oben genannten Dualismen zu suspendieren: Statt eine Entscheidung hinsichtlich einander ausschließender Kategorien wie Parodie *oder* Verkündigung, Ritual *oder* Theater vorzunehmen, wollen wir versuchen, ausschnitthaft die spezifische Komplexion von Komponenten zu beschreiben, die die 'Modalität des Erfahrens' in der *Secunda pastorum* bestimmen.

Dieser Ansatz kann nicht nur für die Rekonstruktion der tatsächlichen Aufführung eines Spiels, über deren konkrete Form nur sehr begrenzt Aussagen möglich sind, fruchtbar gemacht werden.[15] Gumbrechts Vorschlag, die "Formen des mittelalterlichen Theaters als Erfahrungsdispositive [zu] verstehen,"[16] kann auf den überlieferten, schriftlichen Text insofern übertragen werden, als dieser selbst ein bestimmtes Wissen voraussetzt, aktualisiert oder vermittelt, indem er auf bestimmte Wissenssphären bezugnimmt, diese miteinander kombiniert und schließlich durch seine Strategien der Vermittlung auf eine spezifische Weise Erfahrung strukturiert. Insofern wird im hier diskutierten Modell der Text als Teil des Erfahrungsdispositivs 'mittelalterliches Theater' begriffen: Er liefert durch Inhalte und Handlungen, Akteure und situative Konstellationen Indizien einer spezifischen Erfahrungsweise. Der damit angezeigte Inszenierungs- und Erfahrungstyp kann durch die individuelle Aufführung, im Zusammenspiel von historisch-konkreter Inszenierung und Rezeptionssituation, verengt oder erweitert, verstärkt oder konterkariert werden. Wir beschränken uns in diesem Zusammenhang auf die im Text selbst angelegten Rezeptions*möglichkeiten*, also die Text-Funktion des impliziten Rezipienten.

Im Fall der *Secunda pastorum* ist nun konkret zu beobachten, daß das Spiel eingangs die ökonomisch-materielle Alltagswelt der Hirten entfaltet, während an seinem Ende die Verkündigung christlicher Glaubensinhalte steht. Diese inhaltlich voneinander getrennten Sphären sind durch die burleske Handlung um den Schafsdiebstahl miteinander verbunden. Wenn hier nach Wissenssphären und ihrer Kombination sowie den Modi der Wissensvermittlung gefragt werden soll, so ist zunächst die Strukturbeschreibung zu modifizieren. Zwar hebt sich das gesamte Mak-Spiel von der Nativität durch Ortswechsel und den partiellen Austausch des Personals (an die Stelle Maks und Gylls treten der Engel, Maria und das Kind) deutlich ab, doch sind auch innerhalb des ersten Teils zwei voneinander unterscheidbare Handlungsabschnitte auszumachen[17]: Auf den handlungsarmen, ersten Abschnitt, in dem sich die drei Hirten über ihre Lage austauschen und diverse Mißstände beklagen, folgt der aktionsreiche Schafsdiebstahl mit mehrfachem Ortswechsel. Es ist die nun folgende, eigentliche Mak-Handlung (ab V. 190), in der es zu einer Überblendung des Alltäglich-Materiellen mit dem Sakral-Transzendenten kommt. Während der erste Abschnitt ökonomische und familiäre Probleme mit Tendenz zur Verhaltensdidaxe ausbreitet (s.u., 2.2 und 3.), im Rahmen der Nativität dagegen Heilswahrheiten verkündet werden, kennzeichnet die Mak-Handlung keine derart gerichtete und unmittelbare Wissensvermittlung. Stattdessen fällt in diesem vermittelnden (Haupt-)Teil eine Häufung von Anspielungen auf den christlich-heilsgeschichtlichen Horizont auf, die jedoch nicht in eindeutig artikulierte Lehre münden. Zentral ist vielmehr die bildlich hergestellte Analogie zwischen den beiden 'Familiengruppen' — Mak, Gyll und das gestohlene Schaf in der Wiege einerseits, Maria und das Kind andererseits — sowie der scheinbaren und der tatsächlichen Verehrung eines ganz besonderen Kindes. Dem in der Forschung entsprechend intensiv diskutierten Motiv des Schafs[18] kommt dabei die Rolle eines Symbols zu, das die verschiedenen Erfahrungssphären miteinander verbindet.

Angesichts dieses Befundes kann die Frage nach den Charakteristika der *Secunda pastorum* als Wissensdispositiv präzisiert werden. Die Struktur des Spiels legt es nahe, am Knotenpunkt der Vermittlung zweier gegeneinander abgegrenzter Sphären, die zu Anfang und Ende jeweils klar konturiert sind, anzusetzen und zuerst nach der Spezifik der symbolgestützten Wissensvermittlung in der Mak-Handlung zu fragen. Im Anschluß daran kann der Blick auf die Verknüpfungsstrategien und die Gesamtstruktur des Spiels erweitert werden. Es stellt sich also zuletzt die Frage, welchen besonderen Erfahrungsmodus des Alltäglichen und des Heiligen die *Secunda pastorum* eröffnet.

2 Die Symbolik der Secunda pastorum

Das Ungleichgewicht der 'profanen' und der 'sakralen' Handlung in der *Secunda pastorum* wird von der Forschung immer wieder vermerkt, wobei stets auf den unterschiedlichen Umfang sowie den Kontrast des Komischen und Burlesken im ersten Teil mit dem religiösen Ernst der abschließenden Szene verwiesen wird. Gleichwohl hat das Hauptaugenmerk literaturwissenschaftlicher Analysen sich stets darauf gerichtet, einen inneren Zusammenhalt aus der Stringenz heilsgeschichtlicher bzw. typologischer Referenzen abzuleiten.[19] In der Tat steht der mittlere Handlungsabschnitt — das 'Spott-Mysterium' der Gottesgeburt — im Schnittpunkt einer Vielzahl heilsgeschichtlicher Bezüge, die im Bild des gestohlenen Schafs in der Wiege kulminieren. Diese Bezüge sind in der Forschung entschlüsselt und ausführlich diskutiert worden. Angesichts ihrer Fülle muß dann aber ein weiteres Ungleichgewicht auffallen: Die Mak-Handlung erweist sich in ihrer Bildlichkeit als äußerst komplex und mehrdeutig, während die abschließende Anbetung das Heilsereignis mit eindeutigem Verkündigungsgehalt in Szene setzt. Zu beobachten ist also in der Mak-Episode eine deutlich *höhere Komplexität der symbolischen Vermittlung von Bedeutung bzw. Wissen*, da christliche Vorstellungsinhalte zunehmend im Kontext des Alltäglich-Materiellen aktualisiert werden.

Diese bildhafte Bezugnahme auf die Sphäre des Sakralen läßt für den mittleren Abschnitt des Spiels, das 'Spott-Mysterium', einen ritualspezifischen Modus der Wissensvermittlung vermuten, zumal man in Ritualen — der prominenten Definition Durkheims gemäß — nichts anderes sehen kann als Handlungen, die dem Menschen die Annäherungen an das Heilige (bzw. die sakralen Dinge) ermöglichen.[20] Im Rahmen der oben formulierten, grundsätzlichen Frage nach der Bedeutung rituellen Handelns für mittelalterliche Theater-Formen[21] ist zunächst die spezifische Form der Wissensvermittlung und der Strukturierung von Erfahrung im Ritual zu klären. Angesichts der Prominenz eines mehrfach überdeterminierten Symbols in der *Secunda pastorum* wird ferner nach der Funktionsweise von Symbolen im Ritual zu fragen sein. Die theoretischen Überlegungen verstehen sich dabei (im oben beschriebenen Sinne) als Merkmalsraster, das einer heuristischen Beschreibung dienen soll.

Wir orientieren uns im folgenden an einem soziologischen bzw. sozialanthropologischen Ritualbegriff. Rituale sind in Anlehnung an Hans-Georg Soeffner zu verstehen als eine "Verknüpfung von Symbolen und symbolischen Gesten in gleichbleibenden vorstrukturierten Handlungsketten."[22] Ein Ritual ist Gemeinschaftshandeln, in dem eine bestimmte Ordnung, welche die Mitglieder einer Gemeinschaft miteinander verbindet, zum Ausdruck kommt und konstituiert wird. Rituale sind somit sowohl

Repräsentanten als auch Träger einer bestimmten sozialen Ordnung. Reformuliert man dieses Ritualverständis kommunikationstheoretisch, indem man Rituale als eine Kommunikationsform unter anderen auffaßt, dann ergibt sich folgendes Bild — mit charakteristischen Unterschieden und Gemeinsamkeiten gegenüber sprachlicher Kommunikation[23]:

• Rituale haben per Definition eine feste Form, die eingehalten werden muß, damit das Ritual auch wirklich Ritual ist.

• Als Handlungsform ist ein Ritual auf Wiederholbarkeit angelegt, als Ausdrucksmittel gehört es zu den herausgehobenen Typen der Interaktion und ist nur in begrenztem Rahmen zu spezifischen Kommunikationszwecken einsetzbar.

• Rituale markieren in ihrer Herausgehobenheit aus den anderen Formen der Interaktion einen Übergang, der sich häufig in den Oppositionen von Alltag vs. Fest manifestiert und die Teilnehmenden in einen anderen als den vorher eingenommenen sozialen Status führt.

• Im Gegensatz zur sprachlichen Kommunikation erscheinen den Teilnehmern eines Rituals die Beziehungen zwischen dem rituellen Ausdruck und dem ausgedrückten Inhalt keineswegs willkürlich, sondern vielmehr 'natürlich'.

• Wie die Arbeiten von Mary Douglas zeigen, kommt im Ritual die einer Gesellschaft zugrundeliegende Ordnung zum Ausdruck, die — symbolisch vermittelt — als die natürliche und richtige bestätigt wird.

Von zentraler Bedeutung für die spezifische Form der Erfahrung im Ritual ist die 'Symbolik', sei es in Form symbolischer Handlungen oder symbolischer Objekte. Die Konzentration auf die 'rituelle Symbolik' der *Secunda pastorum* wird zunächst durch den Umstand nahegelegt, daß Symbolik und bildhaft-konkrete Vermittlungsformen für die mittelalterliche religiöse Praxis zentral sind. Wesentliches Merkmal vorneuzeitlicher Formen des Wissens und der Wissensvermittlung ist der geringe Stellenwert schriftsprachlicher Medien gegenüber der Dominanz direkter Interaktion, die durch verbale Vermittlung in der *face to face*-Situation und den Einsatz von im weitesten Sinne bildlichen Medien gekennzeichnet ist. Außerhalb des gelehrten theologischen Diskurses vollzieht sich (auch) die christlich-religiöse Praxis weitestgehend in vorgegebenen Handlungsmustern; Glaubensinhalte werden überwiegend durch 'Bilder' weitergegeben, die diesen Handlungsmustern angepaßt sind.[24] Im Fall des geistlichen Spiels liegt es darüber hinaus nahe, die Vermittlung von Wissen und den im Spiel konstituierten Erfahrungsmodus in ritualisierten Handlungen und Symbolen zu sehen, wie sie auch in den liturgischen Formen eine Rolle spielen.[25]

"Symbol" ist natürlich ein notorisch vager und mehrdeutiger Ausdruck. In der Bestimmung dieses Begriffs legen wir wiederum ein sozialanthropologisches Verständnis zugrunde.[26]

• Wie Rituale sind auch Symbole Teil der Ordnung, die mit ihnen zum Ausdruck kommt. Als kulturspezifische Zeichen sind sie von den Sinnsystemen einer je bestimmten Gesellschaft abhängig.

• Dennoch kann ein "Symbol" im Zusammenhang mit dem Ritualhandeln keineswegs als Zeichen im Sinne der klassischen Formel 'ein Ding steht für ein anderes' verstanden werden. Ein Symbol erscheint dem, der es als Teil seiner Kultur benutzt oder versteht, wie das Ritual als 'natürliches Zeichen.'[27]

• Ein Symbol steht nicht in einer bloßen Signifikationsrelation zum Symbolisierten, sondern eher in einer Teilhaberelation zu diesem, die bis zu völliger Identität reichen kann.

• Das Symbolisierte ist im Symbol gegenwärtig und erhält seine Legitimation erst durch dieses.

• Das Symbol ist überdeterminiert und von einer grundsätzlichen Bedeutungspolarität geprägt; d.h., es kann einen Gegenstand genauso wie sein Gegenteil bedeuten.[28]

Im folgenden ist nun zunächst die Symbolik in der Mak-Handlung der *Secunda pastorum* zu beschreiben: einerseits hinsichtlich der (durch explizite oder implizite Referenzen) aktualisierten Vorstellungsgehalte, andererseits hinsichtlich der Strategien einer Verknüpfung profaner und sakraler Inhalte. Die Komplexität der symbolischen Wissensvermittlung wird im Anschluß der eindeutigen Inszenierungsform des Sakralen und dem Verkündigungsgestus in der Nativität des Spiels gegenüberzustellen sein (2.1). Auf dieser Grundlage ist dann nach der spezifischen Form der Vermittlung zweier im wesentlichen statischen Wissenssphären durch die Mak-Handlung zu fragen (2.2). Zuletzt sollte es damit möglich werden, Antworten auf die eingangs gestellte Frage nach Erfahrungs und Inszenierungstyp zu skizzieren (3).

2.1 Sakrale Symbolik und Bedeutungsverdichtung

Folgt man denjenigen Forschungspositionen, die dem 'Spott-Mysterium' eine außerordentlich hohe religiöse Anspielungsdichte zusprechen, so drängt sich erneut die Frage nach dem impliziten Rezipienten auf: Angesichts der Fülle der möglichen Assoziationen kann der Eindruck entstehen, daß sich ein derartiger Bedeutungsreichtum nur dem theologisch gebildeten Publikum erschließt. Demgegenüber gilt es zu betonen, daß die Vermittlung von Burleske und Gottesgeburt in der *mock-nativity* einer 'Bilderlogik' folgt: Nicht nur werden hier komplexe Glaubensinhalte bildlich-konkret eingespielt, diese Einspielungen selbst sind auch auf dem Horizont populärer ikonographischer Traditionen beschreibbar. Obschon einzelne Referenzen strittig bleiben müssen, operiert die Symbolik der *Secunda pastorum* mit der Verknüpfung bildlicher Vorstellungen, die auch dem Laienpublikum zugänglich und bekannt sind. Religiöse Bildlichkeit wird hier im weiteren Sinne gefaßt: Bezeichnet sind damit einerseits konkret sinnliche Eindrücke, die durch 'Inszenierungen' im Gottesdienst, die sinnstiftende Raumordnung der Kirchen-Architektur, aber auch durch Fresken, Plastiken etc. vermittelt werden; andererseits die sprach-bildliche Veranschaulichung abstrakter und theoretischer Glaubensinhalte durch Metaphern, Allegorien, Personifizierungen etc.[29]

2.1(a) Explizite religiöse Referenzen und Anspielungen

Direkte Anspielungen auf christliche Vorstellungsinhalte finden sich in verschiedenen Reden der Protagonisten. Diese Verweise auf 'zukünftige Ereignisse' (z.B. durch Anrufung Christi, obschon das Spiel zur Geburt des Gottessohns erst hinführt) können indes nur behelfsweise als 'Anachronismen' bezeichnet werden, da nicht historische Chronologie, sondern vielmehr die Universalpräsenz des Heils das Zeitgefüge nicht nur dieses Spiels, sondern des gesamten Zyklus prägt.[30]

Die hineinzitierten Themen gruppieren sich vorrangig um die heilsgeschichtlichen Zentralereignisse der Passion und Auferstehung Christi. So erwacht einer der Hirten mit dem Ausruf *Resurrex a mortruus!* aus dem Schlaf, den Maks Zauber hervorgerufen oder zumindest vertieft hat (V. 350),[31] um den Diebstahl des Schafs zu bewerkstelligen. Mit dem generellen Hinweis auf die Auferstehung ließe sich hier wohl die konkrete Grab-Szenerie assoziieren, in der die Grabwächter einem ebenso ohnmächtigen Schlaf hingegeben sind.[32] Mak leitet seine Verzauberung der Hirten mit den Worten *Manus tuas commendo, / Poncio Pilato* (V. 266f.) ein: Christi Worte am Kreuz (Lk 23, 46) stehen hier neben der Anrufung Pilatus', die sich vermutlich magischen Praktiken verdankt.[33]

Verschiedentlich begegnen ferner Bezugnahmen auf den Teufel in seiner Eigenschaft als Verführer und Betrüger, der deutlich mit der Person Maks in Verbindung gebracht wird (V. 210, 217, 229).[34] Mak stellt sich gegenüber den Hirten zunächst als adliger Herr vor, indem er einen südenglischen Akzent imitiert. Der vorgebliche 'Heilige' (*saynt*: V. 209) wird jedoch entlarvt, die versuchte Täuschung mit dem Teufel assoziiert. Eine Anspielung auf den Teufel enthält auch Daws Traum von Mak als Wolf unter den Schafen (V. 368, 371): Neben der verbreiteten Figuration des Wolfs als Teufel ist hier mit Mt 7, 15 auch an die 'falschen Propheten, die in Schafskleidern gehen, inwendig aber reißende Wölfe sind', zu denken. Zumal das biblische Gleichnis vom guten Hirten (Joh 10, 1-16) insgesamt den weiteren Bild-Horizont abgeben dürfte, erscheint Mak in der Rolle des Bösen, der sich der Schafe — also der Gläubigen — zu bemächtigen sucht.[35]

2.1(b) Kontrastive und typologische Bezüge in der Doppelstruktur

Durch die Doppelungsstruktur des Spiels ergeben sich sowohl kontrastierende als auch 'typologische' Bezüge, die Mak, aber auch Gyll und das vorgebliche Kind als Vorläufer Christi bzw. Präfiguration der eigentlichen Nativität zu sehen erlauben. Wichtig — auch für die heilsgeschichtlichen Referenzen (s.u.) — ist allererst die Konfiguration von Mak und dem Lamm, das bildhaft auf das Agnus Dei vorausweist. Im Anschluß an das Johannes-Evangelium (Joh 1, 36 *Ecce, agnus Dei*) wird Johannes dem Täufer ikonographisch das Lamm als Attribut zugeordnet,[36] so daß über die Assoziation mit dem (Opfer-)Lamm Mak in struktureller Analogie zu Johannes als Vorläufer Christi aufgefaßt werden kann.[37] Strukturell ergibt sich eine Zuordnung von Präfiguration und Erfüllung ferner zwischen Mak und dem Engel der Verkündigung: Maks Behauptung, er habe in einem (prophetischen) Traum von der Geburt seines Sohnes erfahren, korrespondiert in der Aktionsfolge Schlafen / Erwachen / Verkündigung mit dem Erscheinen des Engels in der letzten Szene des Spiels.[38]

Entscheidend für das Darstellungsmuster der Präfiguration ist im weiteren die Konstellation der Familie und der Hirten, die als Gesamtbild auf die Geburt Christi vorausdeutet. Vater, Mutter, ein auf wundersame Weise in die Welt gesetztes Kind sowie die Hirten, die dieses Kind beschenken wollen (V. 571ff.), geben ein der Nativität vollkommen analoges Gruppenbild ab.[39] Im Detail wird diese Parallele etwa dadurch verstärkt, daß beide 'Kinder' mit dem für Christus topischen Bild des Morgensterns — *lytyll day-starne* (V. 577, 727) — belegt werden.[40] Die Andeutung einer wunderbaren Geburt bzw. übernatürlicher Vorkommnisse in ihrem Zusammenhang[41] legt dann auch eine Parallelisierung von Gyll und Maria nahe, wobei Gyll typologisch als Eva erscheinen kann.[42] Die beunruhigende Fruchtbarkeit von Maks Frau steht ferner in Opposition zur jungfräulichen Geburt als einem einmaligen Ereignis; Mak selbst schließlich wird die Rolle des Vaters eines höchst besonderen Kindes zugewiesen.[43]

Die Simultanität von typologischer und antithetischer Verweise läßt bereits ahnen, mit welcher Komplexität die Bildlichkeit des Spiels operiert: Das 'Spottmysterium' geht im Entwurf eines 'sekundär abgeleiteten' bloßen Antitypus schon deswegen nicht auf, weil eben nicht alle Bezüge den Typus Nativität schlicht negieren.[44] Typologie und Kontrast überlagern einander vielmehr.

2.1(c) Sakrale Parodie in der Theologie des Bösen

Linda Marshall hat unter dem Stichwort der 'sakralen Parodie' eine Lektüre der *Secunda pastorum* vorgeschlagen, die parodistische Züge nicht als profanen Zusatz, sondern vielmehr als integralen Bestandteil der Figuration des Bösen im 'Spottmysterium' begreift: Die Inszenierung der *mock-*

nativity nehme auf die Antichrist-Legende Bezug, und für diese wiederum sei die Parodie zentral.[45] Auf dem biblischen Hintergrund der Johannes-Apokalypse und ihrer Gegenüberstellung des 'wahren' und des 'falschen' Lamms[46] entfalte die Legende nämlich die Zeugung des Antichrist als Parodie der Inkarnation.[47] Dieser parodistische Zug ist Konsequenz einer nach mittelalterlicher Auffassung elementaren Substanzlosigkeit des Bösen, das sich allein in Negation und Verkehrung des Heiligen artikulieren kann. Das Böse parodiert mithin das Heilige und erscheint als dessen verzerrte Imitation.

Die dieser Deutung zugrundegelegte Typologie bezieht Inkarnation und Parusie des Gottessohns aufeinander, wodurch Maks vorgebliches Kind als Figuration des Antichrist erscheint. Gyll kann damit zugleich als Parodie der Mutter Gottes wie auch als Anspielung auf die Hure Babylon in der Apokalypse gelesen werden. In Marshalls Lektüre evozieren also insgesamt nicht spezifische Inhalte, sondern die Struktur der imitierenden Verdoppelung im Spiel den Sinnhorizont der Apokalypse. Dieser Aspekt ist schon deswegen zu betonen, weil in der *Secunda pastorum* endzeitliche Begleiterscheinungen sowie eine Anbetung des 'falschen Lamms' fehlen. Insofern ist aber auch kaum von einer Antitypik im strengen Sinne zu sprechen, da sich der Antagonismus Christus — Antichrist hier zugunsten der parodistischen Struktur verschiebt, also nicht direkte Verkehrung, sondern Verzerrung — die Imitation und Übertragung in ein fremdes Milieu — im Vordergrund steht. Deutlich erkennbar ist das auch an der Parodie der unbefleckten Empfängnis, da Gyll die Geburt des 'Kindes' nurmehr vortäuscht, nicht aber einen vom Teufel gezeugten Sohn zur Welt bringt.

Die hier nachgezeichnete Simultanität von Präfiguration, Kontrastierung und Parodie im ersten Teil der *Secunda pastorum* läßt einen souveränen Umgang mit den theologischen Verknüpfungsverfahren erkennen, für die die Gegenbildlichkeit der beiden zentralen Szenen nur eine unter mehreren Darstellungsformen ist. Das Bild des Schafs in der Wiege erweist sich dann hinsichtlich seiner heilsgeschichtlichen und sakramentalen Konnotationen, die wir abschließend der Nativität-Szene gegenüberstellen, als komplexe symbolische Verdichtung der bereits angesprochenen Glaubensinhalte.

2.1(d) ikonographische Verdichtung der Heilsgeschichte

Die in der Forschung ausführlich entfalteten ikonographischen Bezüge des Spott-Mysteriums führen wir hier nur stichwortartig auf: Dominant ist das Bild des Agnus Dei, womit einerseits auf die Passion (das von den Propheten angekündigte Opferlamm), andererseits auf die Parusie (das Lamm der Offenbarung) vorausgewiesen wird. Es bedarf hier nicht einmal der Bezugnahme auf die Antichrist-Legende, da das apokalyptische Lamm Gottes eine äußerst starke ikonographische Tradition hat.[48] Das Mysterium des Heiligen Kindes, das zugleich das Opferlamm ist, wird hier in die Entdekkung des Schafs anstelle eines Kindes verkehrt, zugleich aber in seiner weltumspannenden Bedeutung aufgerufen.[49]

Im Umfeld der *mock-nativity* begegnet ferner der sakramentale Bezug der Eucharistie; Gylls doppeldeutiger Eid (V. 535ff.) sowie ihre Erklärung, das 'Kind' habe sich verwandelt (V. 616ff.), weisen prägnant darauf hin:[50] Der Schwur, dieses 'Kind' aufessen zu wollen, wenn sich das gestohlene Schaf im Hause finde, und die imaginäre Transformation des Kindes zum Lamm konnotieren die Transsubstantiation: die Verwandlung der Hostie in den geopferten Leib Christi. Diese bildliche Verdichtung der Bezüge, die zentrale Glaubensinhalte anschaubar macht, erscheint — wie oben beschrieben — in Form von Präfiguration, Verkehrung und verzerrender Imitation. Ein Vergleich dieser Darstellung mit der Nativität im zweiten Teil des Spiels kann ihre Komplexität abschließend noch schärfer konturieren.

In der Szene des Spiels, die die Verkündigung des Engels schildert (V. 629ff.), begegnen abermals explizit biblische Referenzen, als sich die Hirten über alttestamentarische Messias-Prophezeiungen verständigen und dabei David und Jesaja nennen (V. 675, 680ff.). Auf die bevorstehende Erlösung durch den Gottessohn weist der Engel — unter Anspielung auf die Typologie Adam / Christus — voraus (V. 639 f.). In der folgenden Nativitäts-Szene steht das Heilsereignis indes ganz für sich selbst: Mit zusätzlicher Bedeutung aufgeladen werden hier allein die Gaben der drei Hirten, der Ball, der Vogel und die Kirschen, indem sie bildlich beispielsweise auf die Weltherrschaft, die spirituelle Reinheit oder die künftige Passion Christi hinweisen.[51] Eine Spannung oder Mehrdeutigkeit ist dieser Symbolik der Gaben indes nicht abzulesen, sie ordnet sich dem Verkündigungszusammenhang vollständig unter. Die Nativität bietet eine homogene und in sich vollkommen abgeschlossene Inszenierung der Rolle des Gottessohns im Heilsgeschehen. Das Bild des Kindes in der Krippe wird hier durch Prophezeiungen und zeichenhafte Attribute gerahmt, die zweifelsohne die heilsgeschichtliche Bedeutung des Moments illustrieren, ohne indes an die ikonographische Verdichtung zentraler christlicher Glaubensinhalte und heilsgeschichtlicher Ereignisse, wie sie im Bild vom Schaf in der Wiege zu erkennen waren, heranzureichen.

Die Symbolik der *mock-nativity* zeichnet sich also durch Überdeterminierung und Ambivalenz aus, die durch ein Spiel der Konnotationen und durch Überlagerung auch des einander Ausschließenden — z.B.: das 'echte' und das 'falsche' Lamm Gottes — erreicht wird. Zu fragen ist im folgenden, ob die dichte Symbolik des Spott-Mysteriums die Wahrnehmung auch der abschließenden Szene mitstrukturiert, hätte dies doch Konsequenzen für den inneren Zusammenhang zwischen Mak-Spiel und der abschließenden Nativität.

2.2 Profanes und Sakrales oder Die Amalgamierung von Wissenssphären

Resümierend läßt sich feststellen, daß die textuellen Verfahren des 'Zweiten Hirtenspiels' im Wakefield-Zyklus in ihrer Komplexität so eigenständig sind, daß sie sich nicht auf die Formeln der gegenbildlichen Verkehrung oder der Antitypik bringen lassen: Das zum Schluß des Spiels dargestellte Weihnachtsgeschehen würde als exakte gegenbildliche Verkehrung eine andere Geschichte hervorbringen als die in der Mak-Episode dargestellte. Diese steht mit ihren Handlungselementen, dem Personal und vor allem mit der zentralen Symbolik des Schafs in der Wiege nicht nur in gegenbildlichem Kontrast, sondern zugleich immer auch in substanzieller Analogie zur eigentlichen Nativität. Es ist keineswegs unwichtig zu betonen, daß die meisten Elemente der Mak-Episode in Bezug auf das Weihnachtsgeschehen Kontrast und Ähnlichkeit zugleich anzeigen, wobei die Ähnlichkeit über eine rein strukturelle Analogie hinausgeht, die trivialerweise immer dann entsteht, wenn Bild und Gegenbild aufeinander bezogen sind. Die Bezüge, die die Mak-Handlung zum Heilsgeschehen aufweist, sind vielmehr polyvalent, indem sie unterschiedlichste Oppositionen und Steigerungslinien miteinander verbinden. Das läßt sich beispielsweise deutlich an der Gegenüberstellung Gyll/Maria zeigen: Eine beängstigende, ökonomische Not produzierende Fruchtbarkeit kontrastiert hier mit der Geburt des Erlösers, das Wunder der Jungfrauengeburt mit der Fälschung einer nurmehr vorgetäuschten Geburt eines Kindes, das dann — ebenso unrichtig — für verzaubert erklärt wird. Zugleich kann die profane Geburt die Geburt des Gottessohns, kann Gyll als 'Eva' Maria präfigurieren.[52] Die oppositionellen Kategorien — Bedrohung/Erlösung, falscher Zauber/Wunder, irdische Leiblichkeit/übernatürliche Jungfrauengeburt — sind aber nicht bloß in einen typologischen Verweiszusammenhang eingebunden, sie entfalten sich auch auf dem Hintergrund unterschiedlicher Erfahrungssphären: der alltäglich-materiellen und der sakral-spirituellen. Die Verschmelzung verschiedener Bereiche des Wissens und Erlebens, wie sie im 'Spott-Mysterium' durch die Hereinnahme christlicher Denkfiguren und Figurationen gegeben ist, hebt die Mak-Handlung gegen den einleitenden Teil des Spiels (V. 1-189) und die Nativität ab.

Für alle hier diskutierten Verweiszusammenhänge ist festzustellen, daß religiöse Konnotationen untrennbar mit der alltäglichen Lebenssphäre der Hirten verbunden sind. So deutlich etwa die Figur des Mak den Satan konnotiert, so prägnant sind zugleich ihre einem ganz anderen Milieu entlehnten Züge. Mak reiht sich in die Gruppe der über allgemeine Mißstände lamentierenden Hirten ein; sein mißtönender Gesang, seine Probleme mit der Ehefrau, selbst seine magischen Künste ordnen ihn dieser Protagonistengruppe eher zu, als daß sie ihn aus ihr herausheben. Die Verwendung magischer Zauberoder Segensformeln in verballhorntem Latein, ob sie nun *Iudas carnas dominus* (V. 351) oder *Manus tuas commendo* (V. 266) lauten, begegnet sowohl bei Mak als auch den Hirten. Vorgeführt wird damit die alltägliche Umgangspraxis mit einer von diesen Akteuren ganz anders begriffenen Sprache des Heiligen und des gelehrten Wissens, die keineswegs diabolisch erscheint oder als verwerflich ausgestellt wird. Entsprechend ist Gyll eben nicht eine eindeutige Figuration der Eva oder der Hure Babylon, sondern eine klug kalkulierende und selbstbewußte Frau, die den Betrug an den Hirten weitgehend dominiert, wodurch sich Maks Rolle als 'Satan' um ein weiteres reduziert. Die Rede über die Last der Haushaltsführung und den Fluch des Kinderreichtums führt über die Inszenierung der Vaterschaft am Schaf zuletzt zur Heiligen Familie und der jungfräulichen Empfängnis. Die mit dem gehörnten Lamm in der Wiege gegebene Antichrist-Vorstellung tritt in diesem Milieu des Alltäglichen und Konkret-Materiellen in Erscheinung.[53]

Anhand der Begutachtung des vorgeblichen Kindes läßt sich diese kontinuierliche und keineswegs nur in eine Richtung verlaufende Metamorphose vom Alltäglichen zum Heiligen genauer als Strategie der Kombination und Verdichtung von Bildern beschreiben. Das Kind, das zugleich das Lamm Gottes ist, verwandelt sich: In der Eucharistie-Referenz des Spiels wird dieses Mysterium als konkrete Transformation angespielt, die zugleich auf die profane Geschichte vom Wechselbalg zutrifft. Ein ganz konkretes Kind soll sich unter Einwirkung übernatürlicher Mächte in ein Mischwesen verwandelt haben. Doch diese Geschichte, die Gyll den Hirten auftischt, ist selbstverständlich erlogen. Mitten im derart potenzierten Betrug wird aber die Heilswahrheit, das Wunder, noch anschaubar, da das Heilige Kind selbstverständlich auch das Opferlamm ist, dessen Leib die Gläubigen verspeisen. Mit dem hier angesprochenen Thema einer wunderbaren Verwandlung gibt sich im Text zugleich die Symbolproduktion als Prozeß steter Transformation des einen in das andere sowie der wechselseitigen Anreicherung zu erkennen. Angesichts dieses Befundes müssen eindeutige Bestimmungen wie etwa die einer weltlichen Parodie geistlicher Inhalte oder auch die Einbettung des Heiligen in einen alltäglichen Zusammenhang — als didaktische Strategie — zu kurz greifen. Greifbar werden stattdessen ein komplexes Spiel mit Bedeutungen sowie die Prozesse der Aufladung und Anlagerung von Bildern und Motiven, in deren Zentrum eben das Symbol — das Schaf in der Wiege — steht.[54]

Dabei zeigt sich nicht nur, daß magische, folkloristische oder konkret-alltägliche Gegenstände dem Mysterium integrierbar sind: Das Mysterium der Gottesgeburt und seine heilsgeschichtlichen Implikationen werden vielmehr in der transformationellen Struktur um eben diese Gegenstände bereichert, auf eine Weise, die mit 'Parodie', 'Verkehrung', 'Travestie' etc. nicht angemessen bezeichnet werden kann. Auf die Kombination von Bedeutungen in der Symbolik der *mock-nativity* scheint zuzutreffen, was Victor Turner über die Funktionsweise des Rituals schreibt: Es vollzieht sich darin die Aktualisierung kultureller Bedeutung, indem symbolische Zusammenhänge in ihre Bestandteile zerlegt und neu zusammengesetzt werden.[55] Die *Secunda pastorum* gibt sich in ihrem mittleren Handlungsteil als Vollzug einer solchen Neukombination zu erkennen, in der kollektiv erfahrbar die Vermittlung zweier Erlebnisbereiche durchgeführt wird.

Bereits auf den ersten Blick ist erkennbar, daß die im Spiel thematisierten Inhalte einerseits unterschiedlichen Wissenssphären — der ökonomisch-materiellen und der religiösen — angehören, andererseits durch Motivanalogien miteinander in Verbindung gebracht werden. Die Vermittlung des häuslich-familiären mit dem sakralen Erfahrungsbereich eröffnet in der Interpretation Anschlußmöglichkeiten an Entwicklungen des Spätmittelalters, die beispielsweise aus kunsthistorischer Sicht als 'Domestikation' des Heiligen beschrieben worden sind.[56] Dieser Prozeß läßt sich einerseits als Form der Aufwertung des familiären Privatraums als gesellschaftlichem Nukleus, andererseits im sozialhistorischen Rahmen der Reformation als 'Privatisierung' des Religiösen beschreiben. Die *Secunda pastorum* zeichnet sich indes weniger durch spezifische Inhalte denn durch die Komplexität der Form aus, ist also als *Inszenierung einer Vermittlung der Wissenssphären* besonders interessant.

3 Der Inszenierungs — und Erfahrungstyp des Spiels

Kommen wir auf die einleitend angesprochenen Fragen und methodischen Kategorien zurück, dann bleibt für die *Secunda pastorum* als ganze zu klären: (a) wie sich das Spiel in Hinblick auf die 'Aufführungsperspektive' in das Spektrum ritueller und theatralischer Inszenierungsformen einordnen läßt; (b) auf welche Weise es in seiner Verlaufsstruktur Wissen vermittelt (Inszenierungstyp); (c) wie dabei Erfahrung für einen potentiellen (zeitgenössischen) Rezipienten strukturiert wird (Erfahrungstyp).[57] Mit Hilfe eines jeweils neu ansetzenden, kurzen Durchgangs durch die drei Teile des Spiels (Hirteneinleitung, Mak-Episode, Nativität) wollen wir versuchen, diese Fragen zu beantworten.

3.1 Ritualität und Theatralität

Natürlich handelt es sich bei der *Secunda pastorum* weder um Ritual noch um Theater (im neuzeitlichen Sinn), auch wenn das Spiel Momente der Theatralität und der Ritualität besitzt. 'Theatralität' beruht auf einer Trennung von Darstellern und Zuschauern, einer Distanzierung der internen Sprechsituation von der textexternen Rezeptionssituation, wie sie für die Entstehung von Fiktionalität notwendig ist, während Ritualität durch die Partizipation aller Beteiligten an der Aufführung gekennzeichnet ist.[58] Das spätmittelalterliche Fronleichnamsspiel besitzt nun bereits eine spezifische Art von Theatralität, die nicht nur in der vermuteten Aufführungsform auf einer Bühne außerhalb des unmittelbar kirchlichen Rahmens, sondern darüber hinaus in seiner Entfaltung einer eigenständigen Spielrealität begründet liegt. Die Figuren der *Secunda pastorum* sind, wie besonders deutlich die einleitenden Abschnitte der miteinander interagierenden Hirten zeigen, in gewisser Weise individualisiert; Alters und Hierarchieunterschiede sind so z.B. genauso wie persönliche Eigenschaften der Figuren in die Darstellung mit eingeflossen.[59] Die Mak-Episode ist sodann keineswegs eine alltägliche, sondern eine 'unerhörte Begebenheit', ein Schwankstoff, der nicht zuletzt zum Vergnügen der Zuschauer in Szene gesetzt wird und sich so von der Vergegenwärtigung des bereits Bekannten, wie es die Gattung Fronleichnamsspiel mit ihren überwiegend biblischen Stoffen anzeigt, unterscheidet. Darüber hinaus hat das Stück mit dem Theater gemein, daß es über eine Form individualisierter Exemplarik dennoch Allgemeingültiges zur Anschauung zu bringen vermag: wie sich Schäfer gegen einen Betrüger und Schafsdieb zur Wehr setzen, woran man einen Betrüger erkennt oder wie sich eine zänkische Ehefrau verhält.

Ein weiteres Mittel, diese Eigenständigkeit der dargestellten Welt zu erzeugen, besteht in der Strategie, die anfängliche und abschließende Szenenfolge jeweils gegen die Erwartung des Rezipienten zu gestalten. So legt die Szenerie 'Hirten auf dem Feld' zu Anfang sicher die Erwartung der biblischen Hirten nahe, denen die Geburt des Erlösers verkündet wird; stattdessen trifft man auf normale Schäfer, denen eines ihrer Tiere gestohlen wird. Die erwartete Weihnachtsgeschichte wird hingegen am Ende des Stücks in Szene gesetzt; in dem Moment, in dem auch dieser Stoff nach dem Abschluß der Mak-Handlung wieder unerwartet zu wirken vermag. Die Abgrenzung des aufgeführten Geschehens von der Aufführungssituation, wie sie Merkmal des Theaters ist, zeichnet daher Anfang und Schluß des Spiels aus, während sie sich in der Mak-Episode bereits aus der Außergewöhnlichkeit der geschilderten Ereignisse ergibt. Diese sind von der Alltagswelt der Hirten und Zuschauer etwa ebenso weit entfernt wie von der Sinnsphäre der Religion, insofern sie eben weder der einen noch der anderen Sphäre zuzuordnen sind, sondern als deren Amalgamierung inszeniert werden. Theatralität betrifft daher nicht bestimmte Szenen; auch wenn man verlockt sein könnte festzustellen, daß sie die Mak-Episode in besonders starkem Maße prägt, während die einleitende Szene und die Nativität weniger theatralisch sind, insofern sie eine deutliche Rollentrennung zwischen Darstellern und Zuschauern vermissen lassen.[60]

Die Ritualität des Stücks läßt sich ebenfalls hauptsächlich an der Mak-Episode festmachen, die mit ihrem zentralen Symbol — dem Schaf in der Wiege, das ein Kind sein soll — alle Merkmale der rituellen Symbolik zeigt, ohne dadurch selber Ritual zu sein.[61] Ritualität und Theatralität treffen sich darüber hinaus in der "analytische(n) Zerlegung der Kultur in Faktoren" und einer "freie(n) oder 'spielerischen' Neukombination dieser Faktoren zu jedem nur möglichen Muster, wie verrückt dies auch sein mag".[62] So können auch dem geistlichen Spiel des Spätmittelalters die Merkmale jenes 'Schwellenzustandes' (Liminalität) zugeschrieben werden, der sich primär auf eine bestimmte Phase in einem Übergangsritus bezieht, der aber ebenso andere herausgehobene und 'spielerische' Interaktionsformen kennzeichnet.[63] Diese dienen — neben der entlastenden Funktion des spielerischen Umgangs mit sonst ungefragt Gültigem — auch der Selbstvergewisserung, Identitätsbildung und Reflexion einer Gesellschaft über ihre eigenen Kategorien.

3.2 Inszenierungstyp

Aufschluß über die Funktion der einzelnen Teile sowie des gesamten Spiels läßt sich durch eine Betrachtung der jeweils inszenierten Kommunikationssituationen gewinnen, welche diese unterschiedlichen Modi bestimmen. Während die Mak-Episode die beschriebene Amalgamierung des Sakralen und des Profanen über die Symbolik und das Spiel der Konnotationen betreibt, sind für den ersten und den dritten Abschnitt des Spiels einsinnigere Formen der Wissensvermittlung bezeichnend. Der erste Teil des Spiels (Szene 1, V. 1-295) zeigt die Hirten in lebhafter, geradezu 'realistisch' anmutender Interaktion[64] untereinander: Bereits an der Unterhaltung der beiden Hirten Coll und Gib über ihren Gefährten Daw ebenso wie an Daws Schwierigkeiten, sich in seiner offensichtlich untergeordneten Stellung der Gemeinschaft einzufügen, ist zu erkennen, daß hier alltagspraktische, soziale Probleme im Dialog der Akteure thematisiert und über konfligierende Standpunkte ausgehandelt werden. Eine mehr oder minder direkte Kommunikation zwischen Akteuren und Publikum stellt sich darüber hinaus durch die Reden der Hirten her, denen handlungsleitende Züge eigen sind. Am deutlichsten wird dies, wenn sich Coll an die jungen Männer im Publikum wendet und ihnen aufgrund seiner Erfahrungen als Ehemann von der Ehe abrät (V. 91ff.). Mit den Fragen nach häuslicher Ökonomie und familiärem Zusammenleben ist dieser einleitende Abschnitt des Spiels offensichtlich darauf ausgerichtet, ein inhaltliches Einverständnis zwischen Akteuren und Publikum zu erzielen, damit aber die stilisierte Kommunikationsform gerade zum Verschwinden zu bringen und eine Identifizierung der aufgeführten Situation mit derjenigen der Aufführung zu erreichen. Mit der Thematisierung ökonomischer und sozialer Konflikte wird ein 'Rezeptwissen' über verschiedene Elemente der 'Welt in Reichweite' vermittelt, das für Protagonisten wie Publikum gleichermaßen zustimmungsfähig ist.[65] Diese auf integrativen Momenten basierende Interaktionsstruktur nimmt in der Mak-Episode einen anderen Charakter und eine andere Komplexität an. Der Unterschied zeigt sich schon im Vergleich der Klagereden der Hirten mit jenen des Schafsdiebes. Während Coll und Gib über das Wetter, die finanziellen Bedrückungen durch den Adel und die Sorgen als Ehemänner a parte und damit z.T. auch explizit zum Publikum sprechen, sind Maks redsam mitgeteilte Bekümmernisse über den Kindersegen seiner Frau, erst recht aber seine Beteuerung, krank zu sein und daher trotz Armut und Not keinen Hunger zu haben (V. 226ff.), strategische Reden in Hinblick auf den beabsichtigten Schafsdiebstahl — und für das Publikum auch als solche erkennbar. Obschon die Ebene des Besprochenen also kohärent bleibt, ist das Gesagte nunmehr funktionalisiert für den geplanten Betrug, der sich dem Publikum nicht über die Bekundungen der Akteure, sondern nur noch über die interne Situation — die dargestellte Handlung — erschließt. Deren Deutung wird indes dem Rezipienten selber abverlangt; mit dieser komplexeren Form die Wissensvermittlung ändert sich dann aber auch die Status vermittelten Wissens.

In den Expositionsszenen gestaltet die *Secunda pastorum* einen Bereich pragmatischen Wissens, für den die Nähe der Lebenswelt von Publikum und Protagonisten konstitutiv ist. Diese Konstellation ändert sich in der Mak-Episode radikal, wenn die Handlung, die fortan nicht mehr aus dem internen Rahmen der Protagonistenebene ausbricht, damit nicht nur zu einer eigenen 'Spielrealität' wird, für die eine textinterne Deutungsinstanz fehlt, sondern zudem durch 'Lug und Trug' bestimmt ist. Die Betrugsabsicht der handelnden Instanzen blockiert dann aber die Möglichkeit, ihre Reden in Form handlungsleitenden Rezeptwissens zu rezipieren.

Handeln und Sprechen der Protagonisten sind in der Mak-Episode überwiegend strategischer Natur und angesichts der nicht mehr ausgleichbaren Interessen beider Protagonistengruppen antagonistischer Art. Verstellungen, gegenseitiges Mißtrauen sowie versuchte, gelungene oder gescheiterte Übervorteilungen oder Rachemanöver bestimmen die Kommunikation: angefangen von Maks Verkleidung als Ritter (V. 201ff.) über die verschiedenen Täuschungsversuche des wirtschaftlich bedürftigen Ehepaares bis hin zu Maks Bestrafung durch die Hirten. Es kommt so zu einer permantenten Infragestellung der Richtigkeit des Gesagten, die eine Vermittlung eindeutigen und 'positiven' Wissens durchkreuzt. An seine Stelle tritt im Mittelteil die Hypertrophie sowohl der vermittelten Elemente des kulturellen Wissens als auch der Modi ihrer Vermittlung, deren Uneindeutigkeit, Ambivalenz und Vielschichtigkeit bereits deutlich zu sehen waren (s.o., 2.). Wissen — gleich welcher Sphäre — wird hier nurmehr über die Brechungen seiner Inszenierung (seiner Verdichtungen in einer komplexen Symbolik und nahezu grotesken Handlungslogik) präsent gehalten, aber nicht mehr an festen Maßstäben und gleichbleibenden Adressaten ausgerichtet.

Mit dieser im Mittelteil vorherrschenden Kommunikationssituation und ihrem entsprechend 'mehrstimmigen' Inszenierungstyp bricht erst die abschließende Szene im bethlehemitischen Stall. Von einer Figureninteraktion im eigentlichen Sinne kann hier nicht mehr die Rede sein, da in der Nativität die Sender-Empfänger-Struktur auf ein Mindestmaß reduziert ist. An die Stelle echter, d.h. zumindest potentiell in alle Richtungen verlaufender Sprech und Handlungsakte, treten nun einerseits die an das Erlöser-Kind gerichteten Huldigungen der Hirten in Gestalt stark formalisierter Ansprachen und Gabenüberreichungen (V. 764ff.), andererseits die formelhaften Worte und Segnungen Marias (V. 737-745).[66] Die Kommunikationssituation hat sich freilich nicht ohne Grund gewandelt: Zumal die Aussagen der Gottesmutter über die Geburt des Erlösers eine überzeitlich gültige, transzendente Wahrheit artikulieren, müssen sie nicht mehr an bestimmte Personen — weder in der Protagonistenwelt noch in der des Publikums — gerichtet sein. Mit diesem Verkündigungsgestus ist die vorangegangene 'Mehrdeutigkeit' der Vermittlungsweisen aufgegeben, an ihre Stelle tritt eine unhinterfragbare Eindeutigkeit des vermittelten Wissens, wodurch ferner der Inszenierungstyp der einleitenden Hirtenszenen mit jenem der Schlußszene vergleichbar und verknüpfbar wird. In beiden Abschnitten haben die vermittelten Inhalte den Status positiven, 'fraglosen' und damit anscheinend auch nicht beweisbedürftigen Wissens. Mit der Mak-Episode wird dann aber eine jenseits jeder Beweiskraft liegende Szenenfolge zwischengeschaltet, in der einerseits — durch die Akte der Täuschung und Verstellung — explizit vermitteltes Wissen infragegestellt wird, andererseits die symbolische Verdichtung und Vermischung der Wissenssphären an die Stelle direkter Mitteilung tritt. Die Verlaufsstruktur des Stücks bedarf nun allerdings einer funktionalen Deutung: Eine Interpretation des Stücks als Erfahrungstyp und 'Wissensdispositiv', die letztlich auf seinen historischen Sinn verweist, muß vom Verhältnis zwischen (interner) Struktur und (externer) Funktion ausgehen. Welche Funktion kommt gerade dieser Struktur zu, wie ist sie mit dem Texttyp des 'Fronleichnamsspiels' in Verbindung zu setzen?

3.3 Erfahrungstyp

Die interne Struktur des Spiels ist von einer deutlichen Dreiteilung gekennzeichnet, wobei den drei Teilen der Handlung[67] je bestimmte Personen-konstellation, ein spezifischer Modus der Wissensvermittlung sowie bestimmte Sinnsphären korrespondieren.

Der erste Teil spielt in der Lebenswelt der Hirten, die von einer relativ eindeutigen Wissensvermittlung geprägt ist, wobei die herrschende Sinnsphäre die des Alltags dieser Hirten ist. Der dritte, abschließende Teil wartet zwar immer noch mit diesem Personal auf, durch den Handlungskontext sind die Hirten nun aber mit jenen der Bibel gleichzusetzen. Die Wissensvermittlung ist monologisch; das Heilsgeschehen wird nurmehr verkündet und in szenische Darstellung umgesetzt; die allein gültige Sinnsphäre ist die der christlichen Religion und Religiosität. Dazwischen steht die Mak-Episode, die in der Verlaufsstruktur des Stücks die eine Sinnsphäre in die andere verwandelt bzw. zwischen ihnen vermittelt. Die Hirten sind sowohl die alltagsweltlichen Bewohner einer englischen Stadt als auch die biblischen Zeugen, denen die Geburt des Erlösers verkündet wird. Maks Hütte ist ihnen nur Station auf der Durchreise. Die angespielten Sinnspären sind hauptsächlich die der Alltagswelt und die der Religion, die sich hier im Anspielungsstil des Stücks in gegenseitiger Verkehrung und Analogisierung untrennbar vermischen. Es kommen jedoch auch weitere Sinnsphären, wie die der Magie und des Volksglaubens, hinzu. Der Modus der Wissensvermittlung ist im wesentlichen dialogisch und intertextuell. Welches Wissen eigentlich Gültigkeit besitzt, darüber gibt es in diesem Teil keine festen Maßstäbe mehr. In allen drei genannten Hinsichten (Sinnsphären, Personal, Wissensvermittlung) nimmt die Mak-Episode also eine vermittelnde Stellung ein, womit nun die interne Struktur des Stücks beschrieben, aber noch nicht erklärt ist. Es bleibt also die Frage, wie sich diese geschilderte Verlaufsstruktur des Spiels im Gattungskontext verorten läßt.

Auch in Hinblick auf die (externe) Funktion, d.h. unter Rezeptionsperspektive, läßt sich — wie im Fall der Mak-Episode innerhalb des Spiels — der Terminus der 'Vermittlung' gewinnbringend verwenden. Im geistlichen Spiel insgesamt wurden verschiedene Sinn — und Handlungssphären einander vermittelt — die der Religion und des Alltags, der Volkssprache und des Lateinischen, des Klerus und der Laien.[68] Diese gattungstypische Vermittlungsfunktion kommt den Fronleichnamsspielen in besonderem Maße zu, da sie nicht auf ein bestimmtes biblisches Thema festgelegt waren und so die Sphärenvermischung besonders begünstigten. Die externe Funktion der Vermittlung von Handlungs — und Sinnsphären sowie entsprechenden Wissenselementen in einem neuen Modus der Präsentation ist der *Secunda pastorum* also mit den anderen Spielen der Gattung gemeinsam, auch wenn dieses Spiel keineswegs als repräsentativ gelten kann.[69]

Das Besondere des Spiels besteht darin, daß es die Funktion, die ihm als 'Aufführung' zweifelsohne zukommt, in seine interne Struktur hinein-nimmt. Die *Secunda pastorum* übersetzt also die externe Vermittlungsfunktion in ihre interne Struktur, macht die externe Funktion, für ein zeitgenössisches Publikum vermittelndes Erfahrungsdispositiv zu sein, zu ihrer internen Verlaufsstruktur. Die Vermittlung von Sinn — und Wissenssphären wird in der *Secunda pastorum* nicht nur implizit geleistet, wie dies bei allen Fronleichnamsspielen der Fall ist, sondern ist dem Spiel-Text selber eingeschrieben. Damit ist das Spiel selbst so etwas wie ein 'Realsymbol' eben jener Übergänge und Sphärenvermischungen, die zu bewältigen seinen gattungstypischen, historischen Sinn ausmacht. Und nur der Umstand, daß dieses Spiel genau jene Vermittlung in Szene setzt, die es leisten möchte, bleibt eine Ausnahme, deren Faszinationskraft die Forschung weiterhin beschäftigen wird.

Literaturverzeichnis

(1) Hilfsmittel

HWdA: *Handwörterbuch des deutschen Aberglaubens*. 10 Bde. Hrsg. v. Hanns Bächtold-Stäubli, Berlin / New York 1987.

LCI: *Lexikon der christlichen Ikonographie*. 8 Bde. Hrsg. v. Engelbert Kirschbaum (Bde. 1-4) und Wolfgang Braunfels (Bde. 5-8). Rom u.a. 1968ff.

LMA: *Lexikon des Mittelalters*. München/Zürich 1980ff.

TRE: *Theologische Realenzyklopädie*. Hrsg. v. Gerhard Krause und Gerhard Müller. Berlin 1977ff.

(2) Ausgaben

Cawley 1958: Arthur C. Cawley, *The Wakefield Pageants in the Towneley Cycle* (Manchester: Old and Middle English Texts, 1958).

Cawley 1958a: Arthur C. Cawley, *Everyman and Medieval Miracle Plays*. (London/New York: Everyman's Library 381, Poetry & Drama, 21958).

Cawley/Stevens 1976: *The Towneley Cycle. A Facsimile of Huntington MS HM 1*. With an Introduction by A.C. Cawley and Martin Stevens. (Leeds: Leeds Texts and Monographs. Medieval Drama Facsimiles II, 1976).

(3) Forschungsliteratur

Blanch 1972: Robert J. Blanch, "The Symbolic Gifts of the Shepherds in the 'Secunda pastorum'," *Tennessee Studies in Literature* 17 (1972), 25-36.

Braungart 1992: Wolfgang Braungart, "Ritual und Literatur. Literaturtheoretische Überlegungen im Blick auf Stefan George," *Sprache und Literatur in Wissenschaft und Unterricht* 69 (1992), 2-31.

Braungart 1996: Wolfgang Braungart, *Ritual und Literatur* (Tübingen: Konzepte der Sprach und Literaturwissenschaft 53, 1996), 255-312.

Brinkmann 1966: Hennig Brinkmann, "Zum Ursprung des liturgischen Spiels," in *Studien zur Geschichte der dt. Sprache u. Literatur*. Bd. 2: Literatur (Düsseldorf, 1966; Nachdruck Genf, 1974).

Cawley et al. 1983: Arthur C. Cawley et al. (Hgg.), *The Revels History of Drama in English*. Bd. I. Medieval Drama (London/New York, 1983).

Cawley 1983: Arthur C. Cawley, "The Staging of Medieval Drama," Cawley et al. 1983: 1-66.

Chambers 1903: E.K. Chambers: *The Medieval Stage*. 2 Bde. (Oxford, 1903).

Cutts 1970: John P. Cutts, "The Shepherds' Gifts in The Second Shepherds' Play and Boschs 'Adoration of the Magi'," *Comparative Drama* 4 (1970), 120-124.

Diller 1970: Hans-Jürgen Diller, "The Wakefield Master. Secunda pastorum," *Das englische Drama vom Mittelalter bis zur Gegenwart*, hrsg. v. D. Mehl. Bd. 1. (Düsseldorf, 1970), 21-38.

Douglas 1993: Mary Douglas, *Ritual, Tabu und Körpersymbolik. Sozialanthropologische Studien in Industriegesellschaft und Stammeskultur* (Frankfurt/Main: Fischer Wissenschaft, 1993).

Durkheim 1994: Emile Durkheim, *Die elementaren Formen des religiösen Lebens* (Frankfurt/Main, [1912] 1994).

Eco 1985: Umberto Eco, *Semiotik und Philosophie der Sprache* (München: Supplemente 4, 1985).

Foucault 1977: Michel Foucault, *Der Wille zum Wissen. Sexualität und Wahrheit I* (Frankfurt/Main, 1977).

Gumbrecht 1992: Hans Ulrich Gumbrecht, "Für eine Erfindung des mittelalterlichen Theaters aus der Perspektive der frühen Neuzeit," *Festschrift Walter Haug und Burghart Wachinger*. Bd. II (Tübingen, 1992), 827-848.

Hardison 1965: O.B. Hardison Jr., *Christian Rite and Christian Drama in the Middle Ages. Essays in the Origin and Early History of Modern Drama* (Baltimore, 1965).

Harris 1992: John Wesley Harris, *Medieval Theatre in Content. An Introduction* (London/New York, 1992).

Helterman 1981: Jeffrey Heltermann, *Symbolic Action in the Plays of the Wakefield Master* (Athens/Georgia: South Atlantic Modern Language Association Award Study, 1981).

Jakobson 1988: Roman Jakobson, "Mittelalterliches Spottmysterium. Der alte tschechische 'Salbenkrämer'," *Semiotik. Ausgewählte Texte 1919-1982* (Frankfurt/Main, 1988), 335-364.

Jetter 1986: Werner Jetter, *Symbol und Ritual. Anthropologische Elemente im Gottesdienst*, *Göttingen* 2 (1986).

Jungmann 1982: Robert E. Jungmann, "Mak and the Seven Names of God," *Lore and Language* 3 (1982), 31-41.

Kuhn 1980: Hugo Kuhn, "Versuch über das 15. Jahrhundert in der deutschen Literatur," *Entwürfe zu einer Literatursystematik des Spätmittelalters* (Tübingen, 1980), 77-101.

Mack 1978: Maynard Mack, Jr., "The Second Shepherds' Play: A Reconsideration," PMLA 93 (1978), 78-85.

Marshall 1972: Linda E. Marshall, "'Sacral Parody' in the Secunda pastorum," *Speculum* 47 (1972), 720-736.

Meredith 1994: Peter Meredith, "The Towneley Cycle," *The Cambridge Companion to Medieval English Theatre*, hrsg. v. Richard Beadle (Cambridge, 1994), 134-162.

Mills/McDonald 1983: David Mills/Peter F. McDonald, "The Drama of Religious Ceremonial," Cawley et al. 1983: 67-210.

Morgan 1964: M.M. Morgan, "'High Frau': Paradox and Double-Plot in the English Shepherds' Play," *Speculum* 39 (1964), 676-689.

Müller 1996: Jan-Dirk Müller (Hrsg.), *Aufführung und Schrift in Mittelalter und früher Neuzeit* (Stuttgart, 1996).

Oelkers/Wegenast 1991: Jürgen Oelkers/Klaus Wegenast (Hgg.), *Das Symbol — Brücke des Verstehens* (Stuttgart u.a., 1991).

Preuss 1906: Hans Preuß, *Die Vorstellungen vom Antichrist im späten Mittelalter, bei Luther und in der konfessionellen Polemik* (Leipzig, 1906).

Ross 1972: Lawrence J. Ross, "Symbol and Structure in the Secunda pastorum," *Medieval English Drama*, hrsg. v. Jerome Taylor and Alan Nelson (Chicago, 1972), 177-211.

Rossiter 1950: A.P. Rossiter, *English Drama from Early Times to the Elizabetheans* (London, 1950).

Salaquanda 1978: Jörg Salaquanda, "Artikel 'Antichrist'," TRE III (1978), 20-50.

Schütz/Luckmann 1994, 1/2: Alfred Schütz and Thomas Luckmann, *Strukturen der Lebenswelt*. 2 Bde. (Bd. 1: Frankfurt/Main: stw 284, 1994; Bd. 2: Frankfurt/Main: stw 428, 1984).

Soeffner 1989: Hans-Georg Soeffner, "Emblematische und symbolische Formen der Orientierung," *Auslegung des Alltags - Der Alltag der Auslegung. Zur wissenssoziologischen Konzeption einer sozialwissenschaftlichen Hermeneutik* (Frankfurt/Main: stw 785, 1989), 158-184.

Soeffner 1991: Hans-Georg Soeffner, "Zur Soziologie des Symbols und des Rituals," Wegenast/Oelkers 1991: 63-81.

Soeffner 1992: Hans-Georg Soeffner, "Rituale des Antiritualismus - Materialien für Außeralltägliches," *Die Ordnung der Rituale. Die Auslegung des Alltags 2* (Frankfurt/Main: stw 993, 1992), 102-131.

Speirs 1951/52: John Speirs, "The Mystery Cycle: Some Towneley Plays," *Scrutiny* 18 (1951/52), 86-117; 246-65.

Stearns 1989: Mary Stearns, "Gyll as Mary and as Eve: Order and Disorder in Secunda pastorum," *Fifteenth-Century Studies* 15 (1989), 295-304.

Stemmler 1970: Theo Stemmler, *Liturgische Feiern und geistliche Spiele. Studien zu Erscheinungsformen des Dramatischen im Mittelalter* (Tübingen: Buchreihe der Anglia 15, 1970).

Turner 1968: Victor Turner, "Artikel 'Myth and Symbol'," *International Encyclopedia of the Social Sciences* Bd. 10 (1968), 576-582.

Turner 1989: Victor Turner, *Das Ritual. Struktur und Anti-Struktur* (Frankfurt/New York, 1989).

Turner 1989a: Victor Turner, *Vom Ritual zum Theater. Der Ernst des menschlichen Spiels* (Frankfurt/Main, 1989).

Warning 1974: Rainer Warning, *Funktion und Struktur. Die Ambivalenzen des geistlichen Spiels* (München: Theorie und Geschichte der Literatur und der schönen Künste 35, 1974).

Warning 1983: Rainer Warning, "Der inszenierte Diskurs. Bemerkungen zur pragmatischen Relation der Fiktion," *Funktionen des Fiktiven*, hrsg. v. Dieter Henrich and Wolfgang Iser (*München*: *Poetik und Hermeneutik* 10, 1983), 183-206.

Watt 1940: Homer A. Watt, "The Dramatic Unity of the 'Secunda pastorum'," *Essays and Studies in Honor of Carleton Brown* (New York, 1940), 158-166.

Weimann 1967: Robert Weimann, "Realismus und Simultankonvention im Misteriendrama: Mimesis, Parodie und Utopie in den Towneley-Hirtenszenen," *Shakespeare Jahrbuch* 103 (1967), 108-135.

Wenzel 1995: Horst Wenzel, *Hören und Sehen, Schrift und Bild: Kultur und Gedächtnis im Mittelalter* (München, 1995).

Young 1933: Karl Young, *The Drama of the Medieval Church*. Bd. II (Oxford, 1933).

Notes

* Der Aufsatz geht auf einen Vortrag zurück, den wir beim internationalen Symposion der 'Fifteenth Century Studies', das vom 2. bis 7. Juli 1995 in Kaprun (Österreich) stattfand, gehalten haben. Für Anregungen und Kritik danken wir Corinna Dörrich und Christoph Petersen (München).

1 Entstanden in der ersten Hälfte des 15. Jahrhundert, gehört das Spiel zu den mittelenglischen Fronleichnamsspielen, deren Aufführung von den Handwerkszünften oder religiösen Gilden organisiert wurde. Der einzige Überlieferungsträger datiert aus dem letzten Drittel des 15. Jahrhunderts; es handelt sich um das nach einem früheren Besitzer so benannte Towneley-Manuskript (heute in San Marino, Californien; Huntington Library Ms. HM 1). Von den 32 überlieferten Spielen dieser vermutlich als 'Register' für städtische Autoritäten angefertigten Sammelhandschrift (vgl. Cawley, 1958, xiif.) gehören insgesamt sechs Spiele zur Wakefield-Gruppe (in der Betitelung des Herausgebers), *Mactacio Abel* (fol. 3^r-7^r), *Processus Noe cum filiis* (fol. 7^v-12^v), *Prima pastorum* (fol. 32^v: Incipit Pagina pastorum; fol. 38^r: Explicit Vna pagina Pastorum), *Secunda pastorum* (fol. 38^r: Incipit Alia eorundem; fol. 46^v: Explicit pagina Pastorum), *Magnus Herodes* (fol. 55^r-60^r) und *Coliphizacio* (fol. 73^v-78^v). Mit Ausnahme der *Mactacio Abel* sind die genannten Spiele in einer außerhalb des Towneley-Zyklus nicht auffindbaren neunzeiligen Strophenform abgefaßt (Wakefield-Strophe), die im Verbund mit anderen sprachlichen Eigenschaften Hauptanhaltspunkt für die Autorschaft eines Verfassers, des 'Wakefield-Masters', ist. Aufführungsort und Zielpublikum der Spiele sind aufgrund lokaler Anspielungen auf die Stadt Wakefield und ihre Region begrenzbar. Zu Autor, Entstehung und historischem Umfeld vgl. Cawley, 1958, Introduction, xi-xxxiii sowie Cawley, 1983, 50-66. Zur Hs., ihrer Datierung und der Überlieferung der Spiele vgl. Cawley et al., 1983, xxxii und 295f. (Übersicht zum Inhalt des Towneley-Ms.) sowie die Einleitung in der Faksimile-Ausgabe von Cawley/Stevens, 1976, vii-xix. Wir zitieren nach der Verszählung in der maßgeblichen kritischen Ausgabe von Cawley, 1958. Bei der nachfolgenden Inhaltsangabe geben wir — der Übersichtlichkeit halber — zusätzlich die Szeneneinteilung der gut zugänglichen Ausgabe in der 'Everyman's Library' (Cawley, 1958a, 79-108) an. Die Szeneneinteilung hier folgt dem Schauplatzwechsel im Stück.

2 Mack, 1978, 78.

[3] Beide Teile stehen in einem Verhältnis von 6:1 zueinander; das 'Mak-Spiel' reicht von V. 1-628, die Nativität von V. 629-754. Allerdings läßt sich auch der 'profane' Teil weiter untergliedern: s.u.

[4] Vgl. Chambers, 1903; Young, 1933: Dabei herrscht trotz des 'evolutionären' Beschreibungsmodells die Tendenz vor, Ritual und Theater als kategorial unterschiedene Systeme gegeneinander abzugrenzen.

[5] Zur zeitgenössischen Kritik der Spiele vgl. etwa den '*Tretise of Miraclis pleyinge*' (um 1400); hierzu Mills/McDonald, 1983, 83-91.

[6] Stemmler, 1970, 298. Von einer Unterordnung der komischen Elemente in Hinblick auf eine religiöse Didaxe gehen beinahe alle Forschungsbeiträge aus (vgl. etwa Watt, 1940, Speirs, 1951/52, Mack, 1978), selbst wenn sie dem Spiel eine Umkehrung christlicher Rituale im Sinne von 'Verkehrungsriten' (hierzu Turner, 1989, 161-170) zugestehen. Cawley, 1958, Introduction, xxivf., vergleicht das Spiel so z.B. mit dem 'Narrenfest' ("Feast of Fools"), welches ja ein im Weihnachtsfestkreis vom niederen Klerus ausgeführtes Fest der Stausumkehrung und der 'Verkehrung' der Liturgie darstellt. Cawley vergleicht die Nativitäts-Parodie in der *Secunda pastorum* mit den "burlesque ceremonies" im Narrenfest und gesteht zu: "the spirit of nonsense has infected the Wakefield playwright, who wrote his pageant for Corpus Christi day, just as it did the subdeacons who played the fool on the feast of the Circumcision" (ebd.). Zwischen Narrenfest und Hirtenspiel will er aber dennoch einen wichtigen Unterschied gewahrt wissen: "in the Feast of Fools an irreverent comic use was made of sacred ritual, while in the *Secunda pastorum* the comedy is subservient to the sacred theme it so closely parallels" (ebd.) Diese Formulierung entspricht der *Opinio communis* der Forschung bis heute.

[7] Eine in diese Richtung zuspitzende Lektüre der *Secunda pastorum* ist unseres Wissens bislang nicht vorgeschlagen worden. Exemplarisch für verschiedentlich geäußerte Zweifel an der Homogenität des sakralen Ernstes ist die Interpretation Rossiter, 1950 anzuführen, die von einer ironischen, unauflösbaren Ambivalenz des Spiels spricht (bes. 53ff., 72).

[8] Kritik an der einsinnigen Linearität der Entwicklungsgeschichte und den impliziten Biologismen schon bei Hardison, 1965.

[9] Gumbrecht, 1992, bes. 830, 847.

[10] Gumbrecht, 1992, 833ff.

[11] Gumbrecht, 1992 benutzt den Begriff für die medien — und gattungsspezifische Form der Erfahrungs- und Wissensvermittlung. Auch wenn sich bei ihm keine Definition des Begriffs findet, ist dieser offenkundig in Anlehnung an den Sprachgebrauch Foucaults verwendet (vgl. Foucault 1977, 95ff.).

[12] Gumbrecht, 1992, 831.

[13] Paradigmatisch sind hier die Arbeiten von Zumthor geworden. Vgl. zu diesem Literaturbegriff auch Gumbrecht, 1992, sowie Müller, 1996.

[14] Gumbrecht, 1992, 829.

[15] Cawley, 1958, xxvif. stellt so z.B. in der Einleitung seiner kritischen Ausgabe die bipolare Raumorganisation in den Spielen der Wakefield-Gruppe fest, wie sie den überlieferten Dramentexten selber zu entnehmen ist. Zu den Aufführungsbelegen und der mutmaßlichen Bühnenform vgl. Cawley, 1983, 50-66. Grundsätzlich zur Aufführung der Misterienspiele vgl. Harris, 1992.

[16] Gumbrecht, 1992, 830.

[17] Unsere Interpretation wird im folgenden zeigen, daß es sinnvoll ist, von drei gegeneinander abgegrenzten Teilen des Spiels (Szene 1: Hirtenbegegnung; Szene 2-6: Mak-Episode; Szene 7-8: Nativität) zu sprechen; s.u. 3.

[18] Vgl. dazu ausführlich unten, Abschnitt 2.1.

[19] Vgl. z.B. Mack, 1978.

[20] Durkheim, 1994, 61ff.

[21] Vgl. Gumbrecht, 1992, 847f.

[22] Soeffner, 1989, 178.

[23] Wir orientieren uns an Soeffner, 1989, 1992 und 1991 sowie an Douglas, 1993. Zusammenfassend zum Thema 'Literatur und Ritual' vgl. Braungart, 1992 sowie Braungart, 1996. Die Tatsache, daß das Ritual in jüngerer Zeit zunehmend das Interesse von Literaturwissenschaftlern findet, ist wohl nicht so sehr auf die Entdeckung eines neuen 'Stoffbereiches' bzw. eines plötzlich modischen Gegenstandes *in* der Literatur zurückzuführen, sondern eher auf die Entdeckung eines Funktions-Aspektes von Literatur: ihrem Aufführungscharakter und ihrer 'Ritualität'. Vgl. zu dieser Umorientierung der Forschung "vom sozialgeschichtlichen und funktionsgeschichtlichen Forschungsparadigma" zu "anthropologischen Fragestellungen" Braungart, 1992, 8 (Anm.) sowie Braungart, 1996 (mit umfänglicher Bibliographie, 255-312). Im Fall des mittelalterlichen Dramas wurde der ritualähnliche oder pararituelle Charakter der Spiele schon seit Beginn ihrer Erforschung diskutiert (Chambers, Young), wenn auch hauptsächlich unter der Fragestellung der Abhängigkeit von christlichen und außerchristlichen Ritualen. Eine leider kaum rezipierte Ausnahme stellt Warning, 1974 dar, der in den Spielen ein Ritual vollzogen sieht (das 'Sündenbock-Ritual'), für das die christliche Liturgie in dieser Form keinen Platz ließ.

[24] 'Bild' im weiten Sinn soll den Begriffsumfang von *pictura* und *imago* genauso abdecken wie Fälle sprachlicher Bilder und bildhafter (visueller oder visualisierter) Vorgänge und Handlungen. 'Bildlichkeit' kann daher im Sinne von Modellhaftigkeit, Imaginierbarkeit, Piktorialität oder schlichter (intendierter) Ikonizität verstanden werden; sie meint aber ebenso Vor-Bildlichkeit und Exemplarik. Die mittelalterliche Kultur bediente sich häufig nicht-diskursiver Unterweisungsformen, deren Hauptkennzeichen ihre Bezogenheit auf die 'Sinne' war. Vgl. grundsätzlich hierzu Wenzel, 1995. Zum hier angezielten, weiten Verständnis von 'Bild' vgl. auch unten 2.1 und Anm. 30.

[25] Zur Rolle von Ritual und Symbol in der Liturgie vgl. als neuere, ritualtheoretisch interessante Beiträge: Jetter, 1986 sowie Oelkers/Wegenast, 1991.

[26] Im Fall des Symbols konkurrieren zeichentheoretische, ästhetische und weitere Disziplinen um das Definitionsrecht; sie heben die Rolle der internen Struktur, der Rezeption und Pragmatik oder spezifischer inhaltlicher Aspekte hervor. Faßt man Rituale als Form des symbolischen Handelns auf (wie es naheliegend und Forschungskonsens ist), dann gehört eine Definition des Symbolbegriffs als integraler Bestandteil zu jeder Ritualtheorie. Vgl. hierzu Durkheim, 1994, 284ff., Douglas, 1993, 1-10, passim; Soeffner, 1989, 161-163; Soeffner, 1991, 69-75 sowie Turner, 1968. Zum wissenssoziologischen Symbolverständnis vgl. Schütz/Luck-Mann, 1994/2, 195-200.

[27] Soeffner, 1992, 105f. verweist auf Helmuth Plessners Begriff der "natürlichen Künstlichkeit", welche sich durch den institutionalisierten Gebrauch von Zeichen konstituiere. Douglas' Untersuchungen sind in der englischen Ausgabe mit 'Natural Symbols. Explorations in Cosmology' (Erstausgabe, 1970) betitelt, womit ebenfalls die Naturalisierung kulturspezifischer Konzepte, wie sie jede Kultur selber vornimmt, hervorgehoben wird.

[28] Zur grundsätzlichen Ambivalenz und Überdeterminiertheit von Symbolen vgl. Soeffner, 1989, 163f. sowie Turner, 1989, 55f.

[29] Das sprachliche Bild wird im Zusammenhang einer weit aufgefaßten Bildlichkeit als dominante Denk- und Vermittlungsform mittelalterlicher Kultur aufgefaßt. Vgl. hierzu Wenzel, 1995, bes. 292-337, 414-478.

[30] Vgl. Speirs, 1951/1952, 90; vgl. auch Jakobson, 1988, 353, der für dieses Phänomen den Begriff der "Panchronie" bereithält.

[31] Nach Cawley, 1958, 109 (Apparat zur Stelle) aus „resurrexit a mortuis" des Credo gebildet.

[32] Neben der populären ikonographischen Tradition der schlafenden Wächter am leeren Grab (vgl. LCI 1, 203ff.; LCI 2, 55ff.) steht die dramatische Ausformulierung der entsprechenden Bibelstelle in den Osterspielen. Zu denken ist ferner an die Korrespondenz des hier zugrundegelegten Weihnachtstropus (*Quem quaeritis in praesepe...*) mit dem Ostertropus (*Quem quaeritis in sepulcro...*); vgl. Jakobson, 1988, 338, 340. Gesichert ist allerdings nur, daß sich das Osterspiel aus dem Ostertropus entwickelt hat, während letzterer das Vorbild für den Weihnachtstropus abgegeben hat (vgl. Young, 1933, 4f. sowie Brinkmann, 1974, 6), aus dem wiederum die Weihnachtsspiele (Hirtenspiele, Nativitäten, Josephsspiele) hervorgehen.

[33] In der Vulgata findet sich keine vergleichbare Formulierung bei der Überstellung Christi an Pilatus, und die Anrufung Gottes vom Kreuz aus — *in manus tuas commendo spiritum meum* — begegnet ausschließlich an der zitierten Stelle des Lukas-Evangeliums. Die Anrufung Pilatus' wird daher in Verbindung mit der volkstümlichen Tradition, die Pilatus als Herrn des Wetters auffaßt, zu sehen sein (vgl. HWdA 7, Sp. 25ff.).

[34] Die zitierte Redensart *Seldom lyys the dewyll dede by the gate* (V. 229) überträgt Cawley (Stellenkommentar in Cawley, 1958a, 89) als: *appearances may be deceptive*. Zur Assoziations Maks mit dem Teufel vgl. Helterman, 1981, 104ff.

[35] Vgl. Helterman, 1981, 110f. Zur Ikonographie des Wolfs als Teufel, die aus Joh 20, 1-16 hervorgeht, vgl. LCI 4, 538. Der Gute Hirte wird ikonographisch sowohl mit der Auferstehung als auch mit der Taufe Jesu in Verbindung gebracht (vgl. LCI 2, 291f.). Beide Momente spielen auch für den heilsgeschichtlichen Referenzrahmen eine Rolle (s.u., ad b/c).

[36] Vgl. LCI 7, 167f.

[37] Vgl. LCI 7, 174.

[38] Vgl. Mack, 1978, S81f., der hier auch spekuliert, Mak und der Engel seien möglicherweise durch denselben 'Schauspieler' verkörpert worden. Die Vorbereitung der Hirten auf Maks 'Kind' durch dessen Reden korrespondiert ferner mit ihrem Wissen um die Prophezeiungen, die Christi Geburt ankündigen (vgl. Watt, 1940, 162).

[39] Die Inszenierung kann dies betonen, indem beispielsweise Wiege oder Darsteller der Mutter (Gyll bzw. Maria) sowie Bühnenort identisch sind (vgl. Helterman, 1981, 111f.).

[40] Vgl. Speirs, 1951/1952, 110.

[41] Zum Wechselbalg vgl. Speirs, 1951/1952, 117 sowie weiter unten.

[42] Vgl. Marshall, 1972, 731. Zur Typologie Eva/Maria in der *Secunda pastorum* vgl. Stearns, 1989.

[43] Auf die implizite Rolle Maks als Vater des Christuskindes verweist Mack, 1978, 81.

[44] Dies gegen die herrschende Forschungsmeinung; vgl. oben Anm. 6.

[45] Marshall, 1972, 721 ff.

[46] Apoc. 13, 11: *Et vidi aliam bestiam ascendentem de terra, et habebat cornua duo similia Agni, et loquebatur sicut draco.* (Und ich sah ein zweites Tier aufsteigen von der Erde, das hatte zwei Hörner und redete wie ein Drache).

[47] In der Legende ist der Antichrist das Kind sündhafter menschlicher Eltern, die Vaterschaft des Teufels wird als sekundärer Akt eingeführt, da Satan erst nach der Empfängnis des Kindes diesem seinen Geist verleiht. Vgl. Marshall, 1972, 723; unten Anm. 54.

[48] Vgl. LCI 3, 7ff.

[49] Ross, 1972, 204.

[50] Vgl. Ross, 1972, 200f.

[51] Vgl. Ross, 1973, 183ff.; ausführlich: Cutts, 1970, Blanch, 1972.

[52] Vgl. Stearns, 1989.

[53] Zur Antichristvorstellung vgl. Preuss, 1906; Salaquanda, 1978. Den Bezug zum Antichristen sieht auch Diller, 1970, 34f.

[54] Zum Symbolbegriff vgl. oben Anm. 26, 27. Tatsächlich weist das Spiel alle Elemente einer rituellen Symbolik auf, wie sie Turner, 1989, 55f., anhand ethnologischer Befunde beschreibt: "Die Symbole weisen Merkmale der Verdichtung, der Vereinigung unvereinbarer Referenten und der Bedeutungspolarisierung auf. Tatsächlich verweist ein einziges Symbol auf viele Dinge gleichzeitig: es ist nicht ein-, sondern vieldeutig. Seine Referenten gehören nicht alle der gleichen logischen Ordnung an, sondern entstammen vielen Bereichen der sozialen Erfahrung und ethischen Bewertung. Und schließlich häufen sich die Referenten an den entgegengesetzten Bedeutungspolen. An dem einen Pol verweisen die Symbole auf soziale und moralische, an dem anderen auf physiologische Tatsachen."

[55] Dieses Konzept von Ritualität entwickelt Turner, 1989a.

[56] Vgl. Ross, 1972, 188ff. (mit weiterer Literatur).

[57] Die Terminologie in Anlehnung an Kuhn, 1980, 85-89, der zwischen Inszenierungstyp als Formkategorie und "Faszinationstyp" als spezifischem Rezeptionsmodus mittelalterlicher Literatur unterscheidet.

[58] Zur Trennung von Zuschauern und Darstellern vgl. Gumbrecht, 1992 sowie Turner, 1989a, 178ff. Zum Konzept der Fiktionalität als 'Situationsspaltung' in eine textinterne und eine textexterne Situation vgl. Warning, 1983.

[59] Individualisierung kann nach Gumbrecht, 1992, 834f. ein Merkmal von Theatralität sein.

[60] Dabei fordert interessanterweise gerade die in unserem Sinne fiktionale Szene der Hirtenbegegnung im ersten Teil die Partizipation der Zuschauer, während die Nativität als bloß szenische Umsetzung des Weihnachtsgeschehens erscheint. Da letzteres dem Selbstverständnis des Spiels nach ein Faktum darstellt, ist die Nativitätsszene freilich eher Präsentation denn Theater.

[61] Vgl. oben, Anm. 55.

[62] Turner, 1989a, 42.

[63] Vgl ebd., 44.

[64] Zur 'Realistik' des Wakefield-Masters vgl. Weimann, 1967.

[65] Termini in Anlehnung an Schütz/Luckmann, 1994/1, bes. 63-69 (zur Welt in aktueller und potentieller Reichweite) sowie 372ff. (zum Rezeptwissen). Es ist wichtig zu betonen, daß das von den Hirten aufgerufene Wissen in ihren Zuständigkeits- und Verfügbarkeitsbereich fällt und nicht wie das kirchliche Wissen einer 'symbolischen Sinnwelt' angehört, die auf einer abstrakten und institutionell kontrollierten Ebene anzusiedeln ist. Zu diesem Modell der Sphären von Handlung und Wissen vgl. auch die konzise Darstellung bei Soeffner, 1991, 69-73.

[66] Vgl. hierzu Jungman, 1982.

[67] Vgl. hierzu oben Anm. 17 sowie Anfang dieses Abschnitts.

[68] Vgl. Kuhn, 1980, 87, der das geistliche Spiel ebenfalls als Vermittlung zweier Sphären auffaßt, indem er vorschlägt, "das volkssprachige geistliche Spiel, neben der ständigen Fortdauer der liturgienahen 'Feier', strukturell auch als eine 'Ermöglichung des Unmöglichen' zu begreifen (...), nämlich als Durchsetzung einer spielerisch-'öffentlichen' Realpräsenz der christlich-transzendent-kultischen Real-Präsenz, was auch die religiös inkonstistente Zunahme additiver 'Spiel'-Realismen erklären könnte".

[69] Es darf nicht aus dem Auge verloren werden, daß die *Secunda pastorum* keineswegs ein repräsentatives Beispiel ihrer Gattung ist, auch wenn die Aufnahme in Anthologien und Literaturgeschichten dies nahelegen könnte (vgl. hierzu Meredith, 1994).

Munich / Potsdam

Der Malleus Maleficarum *als Grundlage eines Hexenprozesses im Herzogtum Braunschweig (1610)*

Stefanie Hölscher, Ina Lommatzsch

I.

> Meine Mutter wollt und mußt aber vor Dunckelwerden Wolfenbüttel noch erreichen, tröstete mich, so gut es anging, und bald hatten wir auch das Lechelnholz und die Spitze des Schloßturms der fürstlichen Residenz und Festung vor uns. Letztere ward uns jedoch von Zeit zu Zeit durch eine schwarze Rauchwolke verdeckt, die gern zum Himmel aufgestiegen wäre, wenn sie nicht der Sturmwind Gottes immer wieder zur Erde und uns grade entgegen gepeitscht hätte. [...] 'Sie brennen wacker heut wieder!' sagte ein Bauer, der uns begegnete. 'Hülfe Gottes, wo kommen die Unhulden und Hexen all zutage!'[1]

Wilhelm Raabe beschreibt hier die Flucht seines Helden Lorenz Scheibenhart in Begleitung der Mutter von Braunschweig nach Wolfenbüttel im Jahre 1604, vorbei an einem Hexenverbrennungsplatz Braunschweigs im Lechelner Holz. Hier starb vermutlich auch die Schöninger Bürgerin Catharina Winckelmann sechs Jahre später, da die Stadt Schöningen dem Herzogtum Braunschweig zugeordnet wurde. Auf die bisher unveröffentlichte Akte, die sich mit diesem Prozeß beschäftigt, stieß Dr. Herbert Blume (TU Braunschweig) im Rahmen einer Forschung über die Geschichte der Stadt Schöningen im von Herrn Jürgen Könnecke geleiteten dortigen Archiv.

Die erhalten gebliebene Aktenlage des Prozesses umfaßt:

1. drei Niederschriften der Geständnisse Catharina Winckelmanns;
2. zwei Gutachten der Juristenfakultät Helmstedt;
3. zwei Briefe des Fürstlich-Braunschweigischen Richters des Peinlichen Gerichts, Arndt von Kunstedt an unbekannte Empfänger;
4. zwei Briefe desselben, a) an den Amtmann zu Schöningen, Christoph Gutzmann, b) an den Amtmann zu Lichtenberg;
5. ein Deckblatt;
6. drei Briefumschläge.

Am Prozeß beteiligt waren: die Angeklagte Catharina Winckelmann; nicht namentlich genannter Dekan, Senior und Lektoren der Fürst-Julius-Universität zu Helmstedt; der Fürstlich-Braunschweigische Richter des Peinlichen Gerichts Arndt von Kunstedt; der Amtmann von Schöningen Christoph Gutzmann; der Amtmann von Lichtenberg; ein Pastor Jacob. Die Schriftstücke dokumentieren den Zeitraum vom 4. Oktober bis zum 21. Dezember 1610 und sind offensichtlich unvollständig, da z.B. Anklageschriften und Zeugenaussagen gegen die Beschuldigte fehlen.

Aus der vorliegenden Akte ist nun folgender Prozeßverlauf rekonstruierbar: Am 4. Oktober 1610 werden vom Fürstlich-Braunschweigischen Richter und Beisitzer des Peinlichen Gerichts, Arndt von Kunstedt, an den Amtmann von Schöningen und an den von Lichtenberg Aufforderungen verschickt. Der Schöninger Amtmann Christoph Gutzmann soll bisher vorliegende Informationen über Catharina Winckelmann überprüfen, um die Anklageschrift innerhalb kürzester Zeit formulieren zu können.

Unterstützung soll er vom Lichtenberger Amtmann erfahren: Dieser wird aufgefordert, Berichte des Verwalters von Sulder anzuhören, schriftlich zu fixieren und Gutzmann zuzuschicken.

Etwa einen Monat später, am 5. November 1610, erstellen der Dekan, der Senior und andere Doktoren oder Lektoren der Juristenfakultät der Fürst Julius-Universität zu Helmstedt ein Gutachten, daß Catharina Winckelmann mit "scharpfer peinlicher Verhör unnd frage, jedoch menschlicher weise"[2] zu inquirieren sei. Damit ist der Prozeß gegen sie rechtlich legitimiert.

Am 24. November 1610 versendet in Wolfenbüttel Arndt von Kunstedt die Akten gegen die Angeklagte sowie das von ihm vorerst gefällte Urteil. Da noch Unklarheiten bestehen, wird ein intensives Verhör der Angeklagten angeraten. Absicht ist, dieses Protokoll dann für eine erneute Rechtsbelehrung nach Helmstedt zu schicken, was dem Usus der Urteilsfindung entsprach.

Das erste vorliegende Verhörprotokoll entsteht in der Zeit vom 30. November bis zum 1. Dezember 1610. Es umfaßt 66 Antworten Catharina Winckelmanns, wobei die erste peinlich, der Rest gütlich erreicht wurden. Bei der 47. Antwort findet sich der Zusatz "aufugit", was den Widerstand der Frau zu dokumentieren scheint. Nähere Angaben fehlen jedoch. In dieser ersten Befragung denunziert die Beschuldigte mehrere Frauen, worauf sich das zweite Gutachten der Juristenfakultät Helmstedt am 5. Dezember 1610 bezieht: Deren weiteres Schicksal erfordert umfangreiche Nachforschungen. Aufgrund des Verhörs wird eine erneute Befragung angeraten, diesmal vor einem Peinlichen Halsgericht. Wiederholten sich dann ihre Aussagen, so sei sie zur "woluerdienten straff, und anderenn zum abschrecklichenn Exempell mit dem fevr vom lebenn zum todte zu straffenn von rechts wegen".[3] Es liegt nahe, anzunehmen, daß dieses Schreiben als Empfänger den Fürstlich-Braunschweigischen Richter Arndt von Kunstedt hat — er gibt das Gutachten und die Entscheidung aus Helmstedt weiter.

Catharina Winckelmann wird tatsächlich wieder befragt, wie die Juristen aus Helmstedt angeraten hatten. Insgesamt trägt diese erneute Befragung nichts zu ihrer Rettung bei: Läßt man sie zunächst von einigen Aussagen Abstand nehmen, so treibt man sie durch geschicktes Fragen doch wieder zu den gewünschten Geständnissen.

Am 21. Dezember 1610 wird in Schöningen das endgültige Protokoll über die Beklagte angefertigt. Aufgelistet werden ihre mehrfach wiederholten Bekenntnisse — sowohl unter Tortur als auch gütlich. 51 Punkte zu ihrer Belastung werden aufgeführt: Es handelt sich dabei um eine Zusammenfassung der in den vorher abgehaltenen Verhören gewonnenen Antworten. Catharina Winckelmann gesteht alle Aussagen ein letztes Mal und wird folglich vom Peinlichen Halsgericht verurteilt: "Ist auch darauff laudt der vrtel mit dem fewer vom leben zum Tode gebracht"[4].

II

Soweit die rekonstruierbaren Fakten. Dieser durchaus üblichen Prozeßpraxis lagen juristische und theologische Schriften zugrunde. Den wohl stärksten Einfluß übte dabei der *Hexenhammer* aus, der "[...] neben den jesuitischen Moraltheorien das größte Kompendium unzüchtiger Vorstellungen, der größte Kehrichthaufen, den die Welt je gesehen, das scheußlichste Erotikum [ist], dem gegenüber Sades Werke als Marlitt-Romane anzusehen sind [...]."[5]

Das Handbuch der Hexenjäger war dennoch zum Zeitpunkt seiner Erstauflage 1487 eines der erfolgreichsten Bücher. Herausgegeben von den dominikanischen Inquisitoren Jakob Sprenger und Heinrich Institoris stellt es eine Kompilation von Wissen über das Hexenwesen dar. Ihm vorangestellt ist die Bulle 'Summis desiderantes affectibus' des Papstes Innozenz VIII., die gleichzeitig mit der 'Apologia' Jacob Sprengers als Manifestation des Hexenhammers richtungsweisend war. Eine in der Forschung überwiegend als gefälscht angesehene[6] 'Approbatio' der Kölner theologischen Fakultät folgt der päpstlichen Bulle und fundiert den Hexenhammer.

Der *Malleus maleficarum* erhebt den Anspruch, lediglich vorhandenes Gedankengut zusammengetragen zu haben, was der Handbuchcharakter des Werkes zusätzlich unterstützt. Betont wird durch die Herausgeber immer wieder die Traditionsgebundenheit der Darstellung, als Eigenleistung wird allein das Umfassende und Systematische dieses Werkes definiert.

Der *Hexenhammer* ist in drei Teile gegliedert: Der erste Teil subsumiert 18 Fragen, die sich mit der gegenseitigen Verbindung der drei konstituierenden Elemente Dämon, Hexer und göttlicher Zulassung befassen und dem Benutzer Aufschluß geben sollen über den Umgang mit diesen. Unter Berufung auf eine Unzahl kirchlicher Autoritäten wollen Institoris und Sprenger die Mitwirkung des Teufels bei allen Hexereien beweisen.

Der zweite Teil erörtert in 28 Thesen die Auswirkungen von Hexerei auf Mensch, Tier und Pflanze und die Aufhebung dieser sowie die genaue Spezifizierung der Hexentaten.

Der dritte Abschnitt des *Hexenhammers* reglementiert den Hexenprozeß. Bezogen auf das Hexereiverfahren ist der dritte Abschnitt des *Malleus maleficarum* als das Fundament für formale Kriterien einer Verurteilung von Hexen zu betrachten.

Obwohl der *Hexenhammer* zwar äußerlich durchaus strukturiert erscheint, zeigt sich bei näherer Betrachtung, daß das innere Konzept jeder Logik entbehrt. So wird nach einem einfachen Frage-Antwort-Schema vorgegangen, dem entweder jegliche Belege fehlen, oder aber dem aus dem Zusammenhang gerissenen Bibelzitate als Beweis genügen.

Trotzdem erlangte der *Hexenhammer* eine erstaunliche Verbreitung — eine maßgebliche Rolle spielten die 1487 zusammengetragenen Richtlinien bis in die Spätzeit der Hexenprozesse. Wie stark dieser Einfluß noch in dem Schöninger Prozeß, der immerhin rund 125 Jahre später stattfand, war, soll eine Analyse der Befragungspraxis zeigen.

III

Lediglich in einem Protokoll sind die den Antworten zugrundeliegenden Fragen mit aufgeführt. Jedoch ermöglichen in den anderen Protokollen die Antworten indirekt Rückschlüsse auf die Ausforschung — Grund dafür ist die Suggestivbefragung, in der sich die vorgefaßte Meinung der Inquisitoren widerspiegelt. Der *Hexenhammer* geht nicht auf diese Art des Verhörs ein, formuliert lediglich, daß die Angeklagte während der Folter über gewisse Artikel ausgefragt werden soll, wegen derer sie gefoltert wird. Die Peinliche Gerichtsordnung Kaiser Karls V. von 1532 (Carolina) hingegen verbietet mit Artikel 56[7] Suggestivfragen rigoros. Der Angeklagten ist diese Methode durchaus bekannt, so widerruft sie eine Aussage, die sie auf Einflüsterung des Scharfrichters gemacht hatte.[8]

In diesem Zusammenhang sollte der Aspekt der Folter während des Verhörs betrachtet werden. Wie bereits erwähnt, wird lediglich einmal der Zusatz 'peinlich' — bei der ersten Frage — angeführt, in der Folge weisen sämtliche weiteren Fragestellungen den Zusatz 'gütlich' auf. Ergänzend dazu gibt der *Hexenhammer* die Anweisung, die Folter mit leichter Frage beginnen zu lassen, weil es sich für die Angeklagte somit einfacher gestaltet, die Schuld einzugestehen. Die Befragte gibt denn auch zu, nur mit einem Mann zweimal Verkehr gehabt zu haben — erst im wesentlich späteren Verlauf des Verhörs gesteht sie, Menschen und Tieren geschadet zu haben.

Ein weiterer Aspekt — der sich allerdings nicht einwandfrei anhand des Prozeßprotokolls belegen läßt — ist die Wiederaufnahme der Folter. Da die Wahrscheinlichkeit nicht gering ist, daß eine Angeklagte die Folter ohne ein Geständnis abzulegen übersteht, ergibt sich im Denken der Inquisitoren die Notwendigkeit zur Wiederholung der Folter, um ein Geständnis zu erhalten. Der *Malleus maleficarum* erreicht dies, indem er zwar die Wiederholung oder Neuaufnahme der Folter ausdrücklich verbietet, nicht aber die *Fortsetzung* derselben,[9] weil die Angeklagte vielleicht "eingeschlafen" ist oder die Folterer übermüdet waren. Catharina Winckelmann ist nach Aktenlage mindestens dreimal befragt worden, doch findet sich nur einmal der Hinweis auf eine peinliche Befragung.

Zudem gibt der *Hexenhammer* an, daß ein Verhör nur an besonders heiligen Tagen oder während der Feier der Messe stattfinden soll.[10] Zwar läßt sich nicht genau sagen, zu welcher Tageszeit Catharina Winckelmann befragt wurde, doch fallen die zwei Befragungen sowie der vermutliche Todestag auf kirchliche Feiertage: 30. November 1610, der Zeitpunkt des ersten Verhörs, Andree apostoli (festa fiori); 21. Dezember 1610, der Zeitpunkt der dritten Befragung und der vermutliche Todestag, Thome apostoli (festa fiori).

Der *Hexenhammer* gibt außerdem detaillierte Hinweise auf den Einsatz von Vertrauenspersonen.[11] So wird bei der Befragung Catharina Winckelmanns ein Pastor Jacob als Vertrauensperson eingesetzt, indem er ihr die Beichte abnimmt. Ihm gegenüber bemerkt sie, durch die Tortur zu unwahren Angaben gezwungen worden zu sein.[12] Aufgrund dieser Aussage wird die Beklagte ein weiteres Mal befragt.

Der Einfluß des *Hexenhammers* auf die Prozeßführung erstreckt sich jedoch nicht nur auf die Befragungspraxis, sondern findet sich auch in dem der Befragung zugrundegelegten Hexenbild wieder, dem Catharina Winckelmann in vielen Bereichen entspricht. So gesteht sie sehr früh, am Tanz auf dem Brocken teilgenommen[13] und den Teufel als Buhlen, also als Sexualpartner, gehabt zu haben[14]. Sein Name sei Beelzebub gewesen und sie hatte ihn bei einem Besuch "beij ihrer weschen der Cruellschen"[15] kennengelernt. Diese hatte sie auf ihn aufmerksam gemacht und ihn als wackeren Knecht bezeichnet.[16] Falls Catharina Winckelmann Interesse an ihm hätte, würde sie ihn ihr verschaffen können: "Bekandt darauff die Cruellsche begehrt, sie solte bei ihm liggn, solches sie auch gethan vnd wehre solch werck kalt, vnd nicht menschlich sondn vnnaturlich geweßn"[17].

Schon in diesem kleinen Teil der Bekenntnisse finden sich Hinweise auf den *Hexenhammer*: Die Art, wie Catharina Winkelmann ihren Buhlen kennenlernt, wird dort mehrmals in eben dieser Weise dargestellt. Eine Frau wird zur Teufelsbündlerin, indem sie von einer anderen zum Geschlechtsverkehr mit dem Dämon verleitet wird: "[...] und die Tante sagte zu ihr: 'Wähle dir einen von diesen Jünglingen aus, und wen du willst, den will ich dir geben, und er wird dich zur Braut machen'! [...]"[18]. Die Teufelsbuhlschaft nimmt einen hohen Stellenwert im *Hexenhammer* ein: Die Autoren begründen die fast ausschließliche Rekrutierung weiblicher Personen als Helfer des Bösen mit deren Anfälligkeit aufgrund ihrer fleischlichen Lust. Also kann die Hölle sie durch diese Schwäche an sich binden, indem den Hexen jeweils ein dämonischer Liebhaber zugeteilt wird, der ihre sexuelle Begierde stillen kann. Daß Catharina Winckelmann bei den Befragern keinen gegenteiligen Eindruck erweckt hat, zeigt sich in ihrem Geständnis, zweimal mit einem Schäfer namens Lambert Ehebruch begangen zu haben.[19]

Des weiteren sollte Catharina Winckelmann Gott abschwören[20] — im *Hexenhammer* eine der Grundbedingungen für die Hexerei.[21] Damit hat sie den Teufelspakt geschlossen. Belastend kommt in diesem Zusammenhang hinzu, daß Catharina Winckelmann gesteht, Oblaten beim Abendmahl entwendet und in einer Schachtel aufbewahrt zu haben.[22]

Was gewinnt sie bei einem solchen Pakt? Nicht viel, wie es scheint. So empfängt sie zwar noch vor dem ersten Verkehr mit dem Beelzebub einen Taler von ihm[23], er bringt ihr später noch einmal drei Schafe mit[24] — aber alles verwandelt sich in "Dreck undt Schapschieße", und nicht einmal "sie wiße [...], ob ihr Buhle sie ernehret, od. sie ihne".[25] Der *Hexenhammer* kennt diese Art der Belohnung: Die Hexe soll nämlich nicht etwa durch plötzlichen Reichtum auffallen.[26]

Catharina gesteht, als Ergebnis des Beischlafes mit dem Beelzebub Hollen geboren zu haben, die von ihr sowohl Menschen als auch dem Vieh zugewiesen werden können. Im zweiten vorliegenden Protokoll beschreibt sie auf Nachfrage diese Wesen:

"Die jungen weren gewesen als Mucken, Sie weren aber nicht alle gleich, Es were an Viehe von den Abdekern im aufhengen befunden, das Sie den viehe beim herzen gelegen, in einer gelbn hautt und gewesen alß beren, oder Rogener, Waren auch von allerlei farben, [...]".[27]

Der *Hexenhammer* erwähnt, daß Hexen unvollkommene Tiere machen können.[28] Eben diese Beschreibung läßt sich wohl auf die von Catharina Winckelmann erwähnten Hollen übertragen. Die Winckelmannsche rechtfertigt die Zuweisung der Hollen mit dem Benehmen der Behexten ihr gegenüber: Eine hatte schlecht über sie gesprochen[29], eine andere ihr zustehendes Geld veruntreut[30].

Die Beklagte erwähnt auch den Milchzauber: Sie bekennt, daß die Schwiegermutter Heinrich Gärmers sie in der Kunst unterwiesen hat, so mehr Butter als eigentlich möglich herzustellen.[31] Für den *Hexenhammer* ist der Milchzauber oder die Erzeugung von Butter durch Hexenwerk eine der wichtigsten Tätigkeiten einer Zauberin.[32]

Zu ihrer Entlastung bringt Catharina immer wieder vor, nicht nur Schlechtes getan zu haben — mit ihren Fähigkeiten hat sie andere Zauber abgewendet, manchmal sogar ihre eigenen, wenn die Opfer ihr Mitleid erregten.[33] Im weiteren widerruft sie einen Besuch des Teufels in ihrer Zelle, auch die Zahl der gezeugten Hollen sei zu hoch veranschlagt worden — nur zwei seien es in Wahrheit gewesen.[34] Die Zuweisung derselben jedoch gibt sie zu. Die Teufelsbuhlschaft, den Ursprung der unnatürlichen Wesen, grenzt sie auf einen kurzen Zeitraum ein.

Zudem sind noch die zahlreichen Besagungen zu beachten, die die Gequälte macht. So weist sie darauf hin, daß eine weitere Frau ihr die "Segen", wie sie sie nennt, beigebracht hat.[35] Einer anderen Frau sagt sie nach, ihren Geliebten gezwungen zu haben, ihr zu Willen zu sein — auch wenn er dazu weite Wege zurücklegen mußte.[36] Der *Hexenhammer* kennt solchen Liebeszauber ebenfalls.[37]

Die Besagungen entsprechen dem Hexenbild der Inquisitoren: In ihren Augen ist es nicht möglich, daß eine Frau als Hexe solitär auftritt — sie gingen von einer Gruppenbildung aus. Dem *Hexenhammer* ist es schon Beweis genug, wenn die betroffene Frau früher einmal in einer Gegend gewohnt hat, in der schon weitere Frauen der Zauberei überführt worden sind.[38] Deshalb werden ständig Namen von Catharina Winckelmann genannt — die Befrager verlangen es.

IV

Da der *Hexenhammer* einerseits im Volk verankertes Gedankengut aufnimmt, andererseits das Hexenbild über Kanzeln und Fakultäten prägt, ist ein gewisser Einfluß auf die Prozesse, denen er quasi als theoretisches Rüstzeug dient, zu erwarten gewesen. Doch auch wenn der primäre Wirkungsbereich der Autoren Sprenger und Institoris der oberdeutsche Raum war, finden sich im Schöninger Prozeß deutlich Aspekte, die eine Prägung durch den *Hexenhammer* aufweisen. Es konnte gezeigt werden, daß zahlreiche Entsprechungen vorliegen — von der Befragungsstruktur bis hin zu einzelnen Details, wie dem Einsatz von Vertrauenspersonen, oder auch im zur Indizienbildung herangezogenen Hexenbild. Daß die Helmstedter, die bei Hexenprozessen als besonders scharf galten, sich auf den *Hexenhammer* stützen, ist insofern nicht verwunderlich, als dieser der Etablierung einer Maximalversion von Hexenprozeß als Vielzweckinstrument, etwa gegenüber der Carolina, dient.

In welchem Sinne der Hexenprozeß als Instrument im Fall Catharina Winckelmanns eingesetzt wurde, ist nicht zu erschließen, da die Anklageschrift nicht gefunden werden konnte. Diese könnte Aufschluß darüber geben, ob etwa eine verdachterweckende Tätigkeit oder Denunziation zu ihrer Verhaftung führten.

Letztendlich dürften jedoch die Gründe der Verhaftung Catharina Winckelmanns für das Urteil keine Rolle gespielt haben, denn wie so viele ähnliche Prozesse zeigen, führt der Weg aus dem Räderwerk der Hexenjustiz zwangsläufig auf den Scheiterhaufen.

Notes

[1] Hoppe, Karl (Hg.), Wilhelm Raabe. *Sämtliche Werke im Auftrage der Braunschweigischen Wissenschaftlichen Gesellschaft*. Bd. 2, bearbeitet von Karl Hoppe und Hans Oppermann (Göttingen: Lorenz Scheibenhart, 1970). S.310f.

[2] Schöninger Prozeßakte, VI.

[3] Schöninger Prozeßakte, XXII.

[4] Schöninger Prozeßakte, XXXVIII.

[5] Paul Englisch, *Geschichte der erotischen Literatur* (Stuttgart, 1927). 103.

[6] Hierzu: André Schnyder, Malleus Maleficarum Von Heinrich Institoris (alias Kramer) unter Mithilfe Jakob Sprengers aufgrund der dämonologischen Tradition zusammengestellt. Kommentar zur Wiedergabe des Erstdrucks von 1487 (Hain 9238; Göppingen: 1993), Litterae Nr.116.

[7] Gustav Radbruch, (Hg.), *Die Peinliche Gerichtsordnung Kaiser Karls V. von 1532* (Carolina). Stuttgart, 1975.

Artikel 56: Item in den vordern artikeln ist klärlich gesetzt, wie man eynen, der einer missethat die zweifellig ist, auß marter oder bedrohung der marter bekent, nach allen vmbstenden derselben missethat fragen, vnd darauff erkündigung thun, vnd also auff den grundt der warheyt kommen etc. solchs würdet aber etwa damit verderbet, wenn den gefangen jn annemen oder fragen, die selben vmbstende der missethat vorgesagt vnd darauff gefragt werden [...].

[8] Vgl. Schöninger Prozeßakte, XXVII.

[9] Vgl. Jacob Sprenger, Institoris, Heinrich: Der Hexenhammer (Malleus maleficarum). Aus dem Lateinischen übertragen und eingeleitet von J.W.R. Schmidt (München 1993). Teil III, 88; 135. Im folgenden zitiert als: Hexenhammer.

[10] Vgl. *Hexenhammer*, Teil III, 99.

[11] Vgl. *Hexenhammer*, Teil III, 101f.

[12] Vgl. Schöninger Prozeßakte, XXV.

[13] Vgl. *Schöninger Prozeßakte*, XV, Frage 39, 40.

[14] Vgl. *Schöninger Prozeßakte*, IX, Frage 3; X, Frage 7.

[15] Vgl. *Schöninger Prozeßakte*, IX, Frage 4.

[16] Vgl. *Schöninger Prozeßakte*, X, Frage 5.

[17] Schöninger Prozeßakte, X, Frage 7.

[18] *Hexenhammer*, Teil II, 30.

[19] Vgl. *Schöninger Prozeßakte*, IX, Frage 1.

[20] Vgl. *Schöninger Prozeßakte*, X, Frage 9.

[21] Vgl. *Hexenhammer*, Teil II, 29.

[22] Vgl. Schöninger Prozeßakte, XXIX.

[23] Vgl. *Schöninger Prozeßakte*, XVI, Frage 43.

[24] Vgl. *Schöninger Prozeßakte*, XVI, Frage 43.

[25] Schöninger Prozeßakte, XVI, Frage 43.

[26] Vgl. *Hexenhammer*, Teil I, 215.

[27] *Schöninger Prozeßakte*, XXVI. Vgl. Lohmeyer, Wolfgang: *Der Hexenanwalt*. München, 1979. 61. In der Gegend um Hildesheim kennt man die Hollen ebenfall Dort werden sie jedoch als winzige, durchscheinende Geisterchen definiert. Damit die sichtbar werden, bedient man sich einiger Eier, die in eine zinnerne Schüssel, die vorher auf einem Leichnam gestanden haben muß, aufgeschlagen werden. Erst dann lösen die so entstandenen Hollen angehexte Krankheiten au

[28] Vgl. *Hexenhammer*, Teil I, 13.

[29] Vgl. Schöninger Prozeßakte, XXVIII.

[30] Vgl. Schöninger Prozeßakte, XXVIII.

[31] Vgl. *Schöninger Prozeßakte*, XXXVI, Frage 36.

[32] Vgl. *Hexenhammer*, Teil II, 147f.

[33] Vgl. Schöninger Prozeßakte, XXVIII.

[34] Vgl. Schöninger Prozeßakte, XXV.

[35] Vgl. *Schöninger Prozeßakte*, IX, Frage 2.

[36] Vgl. *Schöninger Prozeßakte*, XIV, Frage 32.

[37] Vgl. *Hexenhammer*, Teil I, 118f.

[38] Vgl. *Hexenhammer*, Teil III, 51.

Technische Universität Carolo-Wilhelmina zu Braunschweig

Von Hexerei erzählen. Narrative Strategien im Malleus maleficarum[1]

André Schnyder

Das Thema dieses Artikels spiegelt die Interessen eines Literaturwissenschaftlers wider, nicht jene des Historikers; es zielt also auf eine Analyse des Textes als Text ab, erst in zweiter Linie geht es um die historischen Sachverhalte, von denen der Text[2] spricht. Die vorzulegende Textinterpretation muss in einem grösseren Zusammenhang, der hier nur angedeutet werden kann, gesehen werden. Es geht dabei um die Struktur des *Malleus*, um das klare Bewusstsein der Autoren über ihre Methoden und über die persuasiven Wirkungen der Formen, derer sie sich bedienten. Eine wichtige Form darunter ist das Exemplum. Da es nicht sinnvoll ist, hier eine eigene Definition dieses vielumstrittenen Begriffes zu entwickeln und zu begründen,[3] so stelle ich bloss eine kurze Beschreibung an den Anfang, skizziere dann global die Bedeutung des Exemplums für den *Malleus* insgesamt, schreite schliesslich zur Hauptsache, zur Detailanalyse eines herausragenden Exemplums aus dem Werk, fort.

Als "Exemplum" soll uns hier der im Hinblick auf einen allgemeinen Sachverhalt erstattete Bericht über ein einmaliges, also datierbares, lokalisierbares und allenfalls durch weitere Namen (etwa Personennamen) individuiertes Ereignis gelten. Der rapportierte Einzelfall kann die im Kontext formulierte generelle Aussage verdeutlichen, illustrieren oder belegen; Ziel ist es immer, durch diese Verfahren überzeugend auf den Leser zu wirken. Es lässt sich somit im "Exemplum" ein historischer, berichtender Teil und eine systematisierende, generalisierende Aussage unterscheiden. Dabei kann in Exempla des *Malleus* der narrative Teil bei wohlbekannten (da z.B. aus der Bibel stammenden) Ereignissen auf wenige Worte schrumpfen: dies ist das eine Extrem; die Vorgangsschilderung im gleich zu besprechenden Exemplum füllt anderseits mehr als eine Seite der Druckausgabe; dies das gegenteilige Extrem.

Das von mir erstellte Repertorium der Exempla im *Malleus* listet für das ganze Werk 279 Stück auf; dabei entfallen 90 auf den ersten, 174 auf den zweiten, bloss 15 auf den dritten Teil.[4] Diese Streuung und Ballung erscheint keineswegs zufällig, ist doch Teil 2 der detailliert beschreibenden, auf empirischem Material beruhenden Darstellung der Hexerei und der Möglichkeiten ihrer Bekämpfung vorbehalten; entsprechend finden wir hier die meisten Exempla. Demgegenüber kommt der weitgehend logisch deduzierende, zudem auf hoher Abstraktionsebene argumentierende erste Teil ebenso wie der dritte, der die praktischen Anweisungen für die Prozessführung enthält, mit weniger Exempla aus. Die wichtigste Quelle für

Exempla ist die Bibel; sie liefert 120 Geschichten. Weitaus vorherrschend sind bei den nicht-biblischen Berichten Fälle, wo Institoris und Sprenger sicher oder sehr wahrscheinlich aus ihrer eigenen Erfahrung als Inquisitoren oder vom Hörensagen, vermutlich aus Berichten von Amtskollegen, schöpfen. Für die folgenden Untersuchungen bleiben die Exempla auf biblischer Basis ausser Betracht. Da es sich bei ihnen ja um allgemein bekannte Geschichten handelte, konnten Institoris und Sprenger den Erzählteil auf knappe Andeutungen beschränken; das bildet natürlich keine günstige Voraussetzung für die Analyse des Erzählstils. Unter den verbleibenden Exempla gilt dann das Interesse jenen, die sicher oder höchst wahrscheinlich von den Autoren selber in Erfahrung gebracht worden sind und die sie — dies die zweite Abgrenzung — auf analytische Weise erzählen.

Damit ist ein weiteres für unsere Textuntersuchung wichtiges Konzept eingeführt; seine Bedeutung ist hier knapp in Erinnerung zu rufen. Analytisches Erzählen stellt das epische Gegenstück zum analytischen Drama dar. Das Erzählen beginnt nicht am Anfang des Geschehens sondern irgendwo im Verlauf desselben.[5] Die Voraussetzungen der Ereignisse sind damit dem Hörer (oft auch den meisten Figuren der Erzählung) verborgen, und sie werden erst während des Berichts aufgedeckt. Meist handelt es sich dabei nicht um harmlose Vorfälle sondern um ein düsteres Geheimnis, eine Schuld, ein Verbrechen, das aufgedeckt werden muss. Hinweise auf weitere Merkmale des analytischen Erzählens werden an gegebener Stelle noch folgen.

In unserem so abgegrenzten Corpus lässt sich etwa ein Dutzend analytischer Exempla finden (Nummern nach dem Repertorium im Kommentarband [Anm. 1]): 1.71, 2.28, 2.39, 2.68, 2.90, 2.101, 2.102, 2.111, 2.121.[6] In den meisten dieser Geschichten (Ausnahmen: 2.28, 2.39) wird das Hexereiverbrechen im Rahmen eines Prozessberichts geschildert, damit potenziert sich der analytische Charakter, insofern der Prozess das Musterbeispiel für die nachträgliche Erklärung von bereits Geschehenem ist; das analytische Verfahren begegnet somit auf der Inhalts — wie auf der Darstellungsebene.

Im Hinblick auf unser Ziel einer genauen Textanalyse konzentriere ich mich nun auf das Paradebeispiel unter unseren Exempla, den Bericht über den Ravensburger Prozess gegen Agnes Balneatrix und Anna von Mindelheim. Am Schluss werde ich dann die Verhältnisse bei einigen andern einschlägigen Exempla streifen.

Das Exemplum über das Ravensburger Hagelwetter (2.121) verspricht durch seinen Umfang und durch die dank aussertextlicher Quelle gesicherte Teilnahme des Berichterstatters Institoris am Geschehen besonders aufschlussreiche Beobachtungen. Von dieser Teilnahme des Institoris am Prozess (und zwar als Inquisitor) im Herbst 1484 wissen wir durch den

Brief des Ravensburger Rates an den Erzherzog von Österreich, Sigismund von Tirol (vgl. unten, Anm. 1).

Zur Bequemlichkeit des Lesers folgt hier der Abdruck des Exemplums; die beigefügte englische Übersetzung ist jene von M. Summers.[7]

Textgliederung und Numerierung fehlen in der Vorlage

1. Ad ea tamen que per nos reperta sunt expedit conuertere.

It is better to add an instance which came within our own experience.

2. In diocesi namque Constantiensi ab oppido Rauenspurg ab viginti octo miliaria teuthonicalia versus Saltzburgam grando seuissimus excitatus cunctas fruges, segetes et vinetas adeo in latitudine vnius miliaris contriuerat, quod tertius annus vix iudicabatur frugiferus in vinetis.

For in the diocese of Constance, twenty-eight German miles from the town of Ratisbon in the direction of Salzburg, a violent hailstorm destroyed all the fruit, crops and vineyards in a belt one mile wide, so that the vines hardly bore fruit for three years.

3. Unde res gesta, cum per notarium inquisitionis innotuisset et, quod propter clamorem populi inquisitionis opus esset, dum certi per maleficia imo omnes pene oppidani talia contigisse iudicarent, quare consulibus ad[8] id consentientibus, per quindenam iuxta iuris formam super heresim dumtaxat maleficarum a nobis inquiritur et ad duas dumtaxat personas pre alijs, que tamen in paruo numero non erant, diffamatas peruenitur, nomen vnius Agnetis Balneatricis alterius Anna de Mindelheim.

This was brought to the notice of the Inquisition, since the people clamoured for an inquiry to be held, many beside all the townsmen being of the opinion that it was caused by witchcraft. Accordingly it was agreed after fifteen days' formal deliberation that it was a case of witchcraft for us to consider; and among a large number of suspects, we particularly examined two women, one named Agnes, a bath woman,[9] and the other Anna of Mindelheim.

4. Quibus captis et seorsum ad distinctos carceres positis ignorante penitus vna de altera sequenti mane Balneatrix questionibus leuissimis a rectore seu ciuium magistro magno fidei zelatore, Gelre cognominato et ab alijs ex consulibus sibi adiunctis

These two were taken and shut up separately in different prisons, neither of them knowing in the least what had happened to the other. On the following day the bath-woman was very gently questioned in the presence of a notary by the

in presentia notarij exponitur. Et licet maleficium taciturnitatis indubie penes se habuisset, de quo et semper iudicibus timendum est, eo quod in primo aggressu non iam muliebri sed virili animo se innoxius[10] affirmabat, diuina tamen fauente clementia, ne tantum facinus impune transiret, subito libere et a vinculis absoluta licet in loco torture et cuncta flagitia ab ea perpetrata detexit.

chief magistrate, a justice named Gelre very zealous for the Faith, and by the other magistrates with him; and although she was undoubtedly well provided with that evil gift of silence which is the constant bane of judges, and at the first trial affirmed that she was innocent of any crime against man or woman; yet, in the Divine mercy that so great a crime should not pass unpunished, suddenly, when she had been freed from her chains, although it was in the torture chamber, she fully laid bare all the crimes which she had committed.

5. Nam a notario inquisitionis interrogata super articulos ex depositione testium circa nocumenta hominibus et iumentis illata, ex quibus iam violenter reddebatur tanquam malefica suspecta; cum nemo testis de fidei abnegatione ac carnali spurcitie cum demone incubo aduersus eam deposuisset, eo quod illa secretissima sint illius secte cerimonialia, attamen, vbi post nocumenta animalibus et hominibus illata vti rea respondisset, cetera omnia de fidei abnegatione et spurcitijs diabolicis cum incubo demone peractis interrogata publice fatebatur, asserens se vltra decem et octo annis illi incubo cum omnimoda fidei abnegatione succubuisse.

For when she was questioned by the Notary of the Inquisition upon the accusations which had been brought against her of harm done to men and cattle, by reason of which she had been gravely suspected of being a witch, although there had been no witness to prove that she had abjured the Faith or performed coitus with an Incubus devil (for she had been most secret); nevertheless, after she had confessed to the harm which she had caused to animals and men, she acknowledged also all that she was asked concerning the abjuration of the Faith, and copulation committed with an Incubus devil; saying that for more than eighteen years she had given her body to an Incubus devil, with a complete abnegation of the Faith.

6. Quibus expletis, vbi super grandinem prefatam, an ne aliquid de illis sciret, inquireretur, respondit, quod sic. Et interrogata, quomodo et qualiter, respondit: "In

After this she was asked whether she knew anything about the hailstorm which we have mentioned, and answered that she did. And, being asked how and in what way,

domo eram et hora meridiei demon me accersiuit et vt super campum seu planiciem Kuppel (sic enim nominatur) paululum aque mecum deferendo me transferrem inunxit. Et dum interrogassem, quidnam operis in aqua explere vellet, pluuiam se velle causare respondit. Portam ergo ciuitatis exiens ipsum demonem sub arbore stantem reperi." Interrogata autem a iudice, sub qua arbore, respondet: "Sub illa ex oppositio illius turris" ipsum denotando. Et interrogata quid sub arbore egisset, respondit: "Demon, vt foueam paruam foderem et illi aquam infuderem, iniunxit." Et interrogata, an ne pariter consedissent, respondit: "Me sedente ipse demon stabat." Interrogata demum, quibus ne verbis aut modis aquam mouisset, respondit: "Digito quidem moui, sed in nomine illius diaboli et omnium aliorum demoniorum." Et rursus iudex: "Quid actum fuit de aqua?" Respondit: "Disparuit et sursum in aerem diabolus duxit." Et demum, an ne aliquam sociam habuisset, interrogata respondit: "Ex opposito sub tali arbore" (aliam captam maleficam Annam vicem Mindelheim denominando) "consodalem habui. Quid autem egerit, ignoro." Et finaliter interrogata Balneatrix de interuallo temporis ab aque assumptione vsque ad grandinem respondit: "Tanta dilatio fuit, quousque ad domum peruenissem[11]."

7. Sed et hoc mirabile: Cum sequenti die altera questionibus etiam leuissimis exposita primo fuisset vt-

she answered: "I was in my house, and at midday a familiar came to me and told me to go with a little water on to the field or plain of Kuppel (for so is it named). And when I asked what he wanted to do with the water, he said that he wanted to make it rain. So I went out at the town gate, and found the devil standing under a tree." The judge asked her, under which tree; and she said, "Under that one opposite that tower," pointing it out. Asked what she did under the tree, she said, "The devil told me to dig a little hole and pour the water into it." Asked whether they sat down together, she said, "I sat down, but the devil stood up." Then she was asked, with what words and in what manner she had stirred the water; and she answered, "I stirred it with my finger, and called on the name of the devil himself and all the other devils." Again the judge asked what was done with the water, and she answered: "It disappeared, and the devil took it up into the air." Then she was asked if she had any associate, and answered: "Under another tree opposite I had a companion (naming the other captured witch, Anna von Mindelheim), but I do not know what she did." Finally, the bath-woman was asked how long it was between the taking up of the water and the hailstorm; and she answered: "There was just sufficient interval of time to allow me to get back to my house."

But (and this is remarkable) when on the next day the other witch had at first been exposed to

pote digito vix a terra eleuata post libere soluta prefata omnia non discrepando in minimo nec quo ad locum prout altera fassa fuerat, quia vicem sub tali arbore et alteram sub alia, nec quo ad tempus, quia hora meridiei, nec quo ad modum, quia per motionem aque in foueam immisse in nomine diaboli et omnium demoniorum, nec quo ad interuallum temporis, quia dum eius diabolus aquam accepisset in sublime eleuando, regressa ad domum superuenisse grandinem affirmabat singula detexit.

the very gentlest questions, being suspended hardly clear of the ground by her thumbs, after she had been set quite free, she disclosed the whole matter without the slightest discrepancy from what the other had told; agreeing as to the place, that it was under such a tree and the other had been under another; as to the time, that it was at midday; as to the method, namely, of stirring water poured into a hole in the name of the devil and all the devils; and as to the interval of time, that the hailstorm had come after the devil had taken the water up into the air and she had returned home.

8. Sicque tertia die incinerantur et Balneatrix contrita et confessa plurimum se deo commendauit asserens se libenti animo mori, vt demonis iniurias posset euadere, crucem in manibus tenendo et amplexando, quam tamen altera spernebat, que etiam vltra viginti annos incubum demonem cum omnimodo fidei abnegatione habuerat, primam in multis maleficijs hominibus, iumentis et terre frugibus illatis excedens, vti processus ad consolatum repositus demonstrat. (145D-147A)

Accordingly, on the third day they were burned. And the bathwoman was contrite and confessed, and commended herself to God, saying that she would die with a willing heart if she could escape the tortures of the devil, and held in her hand a cross which she kissed. But the other witch scorned her for doing so. And this one had consorted with an Incubus devil for more than twenty years with a complete abjuration of the Faith, and had done far more harm than the former witch to men, cattle and the fruits of the earth, as is shown in the preserved record of their trial.

Den Kontext der Geschichte im Werk bilden Erörterungen über das Wettermachen der Hexen, *super modum quo grandines et tempestates ... concitare solent* (144C). Anders als sonst entspricht unserem Kapitel im empirisch orientierten zweiten Werkteil keine theoretische *Quästio* im ersten.[12] Institoris und Sprenger sahen wohl bei der Frage des Wettermachens keinen Bedarf nach gründlicher theologischer und physikalischer Klärung, und sie orteten wohl auch keine Notwendigkeit für einen stringenten, spekulativ geführten Beweis für die Richtigkeit ihrer Theorie. So behandelt das Kapitel in lockerer Fügung einfach einzelne Aspekte des Wettermachens, formuliert anhand ausgewählter Einzelfälle allgemeine Regeln und illustriert sie damit gleichzeitig; so geht es um die physikalisch-ontologische Möglichkeit der Teufel, ins Wettergeschehen einzugreifen, die nötige Zulassung durch Gott, den Sinn dieser Zulassung (die Dämonen sind die in göttlichem Auftrag an den Menschen tätigen Schergen *tortores* 145A). Nacheinander greifen die Autoren auf das Buch Hiob, auf Niders *Formicarius* und zuletzt auf Vorgänge, *que per nos reperta sunt* (145D), zurück. Am Ende wird dann das Induktionsverfahren in rascher Verkürzung als abgeschlossen postuliert werden: *sufficiant ista cum reuera quasi innumera circa huiusmodi maleficia illata recitari possent* (147A). Es lässt sich also bei der Organisation der Exempla innerhalb des Kapitels ein Fortschreiten von altem zu neuem Material, von schriftlich durch Dritte Verbürgtem zu selbst Eruiertem, vom *apriori* — da biblisch belegbar — Glaubwürdigen zu Material, das die Feuerprobe kritischer Prüfung erst noch bestehen muss, vom knapp Angedeuteten zum breit Entwickelten[13] beobachten.

Nach einem kurzen Satz, der vom theoretischen Kontext zum "Tatsachenbericht" überleitet, folgt die Nennung der Lokalitäten. Zweierlei fällt dabei auf: die Überdeterminiertheit und die Erwähnung des weit entfernten Salzburg. Letztere fände eine Begründung, wenn damit auf die Kirchenprovinz, also auf die nach der ebenfalls erwähnten Diözese Konstanz nächsthöhere kirchliche Verwaltungseinheit gewiesen würde. Indessen gehört Konstanz zur Provinz Mainz. Sucht man nach einer anderen Deutung für diesen auffälligen Befund, so bietet sich als plausibelste Möglichkeit die von Müller geäusserte Annahme, Institoris habe diesen Passus in Salzburg geschrieben, sich also vielleicht überhaupt in der Zeit seines spurlosen Verschwindens von Mitte Februar 1486 bis Mai 1487, von seiner erzwungenen Abreise aus Innsbruck bis zu seinem Auftauchen in Köln anlässlich der Begutachtung des *Malleus* durch die dortigen Theologen, an der Salzach aufgehalten.[14] Die Erwähnung der Diözese Konstanz verrät im Übrigen die klerikale Perspektive des Autors, ist aber wohl namentlich dadurch motiviert, dass diese Diözese zum Inquisitionsgebiet des Institoris — und auch Sprengers — gehörte; damit wird seine Aktivität rechtlich legitimiert.[15]

Der zweite Satz stellt in seiner Gesamtheit die Folgen des Unwetters unter gebührender Betonung ihrer Schwere[16] in den Mittelpunkt. Erwartet man — gelenkt vom Kontext — sofort einen Hinweis darauf, dass Hexen das Unwetter erzeugt hätten, so vermisst man einen solchen freilich. Man steht damit vor einer offenen Frage, einem Rätsel. Bedingt ist diese "Verrätselung" durch das analytische Erzählen, die Tatsache, dass der Bericht nicht *ab ovo* beginnt, also nicht mit den Worten der Hexe *In domo eram et hora meridiei demon* aus Abschnitt Nr. 6.[17]

Drei Phasen sind — in idealtypischer Formulierung — für die analytische Erzählung konstitutiv: das Wahrnehmungs und Unbestimmtheitsmoment, d.h. der Bericht über ein vorerst rätselhaftes Faktum, das analytische Moment dann, also die Darstellung, wie eine Betrachterfigur, möglicherweise gegen verschiedene Widerstände und Hindernisse, es unternimmt, das Rätsel zu lösen, schliesslich das Klärungsmoment, das den Abschluss der Analyse bildet und die Lösung des eingangs in Erscheinung getretenen Rätsels bringt. Fragt man nach dem Figureninventar der analytischen Erzählung, so lassen sich zwei Grössen unterscheiden: die Betrachterfigur und die Gegenfigur. Diese ist Trägerin des Rätsels, jene versucht es aufzuhellen. Beide Positionen können auch durch mehrere Personen besetzt sein.[18]

Der zweite Satz unseres Exemplums konstituiert somit das Wahrnehmungs und Unbestimmtheitsmoment, wobei auffällt, dass sich anhand von *iudicatur* nur ein sehr diffuses Subjekt der Wahrnehmung ausmachen lässt.[19] Der nächste Satz (*Unde res gesta-Mindelheim* 146A,[20] Absatz Nr. 3) leitet bereits die analytische Sequenz, somit die zweite Phase, ein; er stellt sehr verknappt zunächst alle handelnden Personen — ausgenommen den Dämon[21] — vor, nämlich: *populus, notarius inquisitionis,*[22] *consules*, den Berichterstatter in seiner Rolle als Inquisitor (*nos*) und schliesslich — mit spannungserzeugender Hintanstellung — die zwei namentlich genannten Hauptverdächtigen; sie bilden die Gegenfiguren, alle andern haben die Funktion der Betrachterfigur. Der Satz leistet ein zweites, indem er das Wechselspiel zwischen den weltlichen und kirchlichen Instanzen, zwischen dem Inquisitor und dem gläubigen Kirchenvolk, sichtbar macht. Alle erfüllen vorbildlich die ihnen zukommenden Rollen: das Volk schreit nach Hilfe[23] und wirkt durch Anzeige des Gerüchts bei der Aufdeckung des Verbrechens mit (*clamor, diffamatas*), die weltliche Behörde ist kooperativ (*consentientibus*), die Inquisition nimmt dank ihrer Aufmerksamkeit wahr, was sich abspielt (*innotuisset*), hält sich bei ihrem Handeln streng an das Recht (*iuxta iuris formam*), spart nicht Zeit noch Mühe (*per quindenam*). Trotz des grossen Erzähltempos[24] überhastet sich die Geschichte auf ihrer Wahrheitssuche nicht, denn sie beteuert uns — zwar zwischen den Zeilen, jedoch klar genug, — dass über die zwei Frauen der Stab noch nicht gebrochen sei; sie sind erst *diffamate*, nicht schon *conuicte*. Dabei hat freilich die Suche nach der Wahrheit des Inquisitors seit Beginn des Satzes deutliche Fortschritte gemacht: von der völligen Ahnungslosigkeit der Menschen — an sich konnte das Unwetter ja auch natürliche Ursachen haben — geht es Schlag auf Schlag über den diffusen aber vielfach erhobenen[25] *clamor* (der indessen noch deutlich als subjektives Dafürhalten — *iudicarent* — charakterisiert ist) zum sich verdichtenden Verdacht gegen zwei Frauen, die jedoch nicht die einzigen Tatverdächtigen sind (*pre alijs*).

Zwei weitere Sätze führen uns nun zu dem Augenblick, wo ein umfassendes Geständnis vorliegt, wo das analytische Moment in das Klärungsmoment übergehen wird (*Quibus captis-cuncta flagitia ... detexit* 146B, Absatz Nr. 4).[26] Es zeigen sich verschiedene Gefährdungen für die Suche nach der Wahrheit, teils sind sie auch nur *e negativo* angedeutet. Das gilt etwa für das Verhalten der weltlichen Behörden; hier sind sie zwar kooperationswillig, teilweise sogar in ungewöhnlich hohem Masse; doch weiss der Leser des *Malleus* aufgrund anderer Fälle, dass dies nicht die Regel zu sein braucht.[27] Schwerer wiegt der Widerstand der Beschuldigten. Er kann sich durch Kollusion äussern, durch hartnäckiges Schweigen oder aggressives Leugnen. Die Kollusion wird hier nur indirekt durch die Erwähnung der getroffenen Gegenmassnahmen — die Verlegung der beiden Beschuldigten in getrennte Kerker zur Verhinderung von Absprachen — sichtbar gemacht, vom Bestreiten der Schuld ist dagegen direkt die Rede. Verantwortlich wird dafür das Vorhandensein eines Schweigezaubers gemacht. Damit nun erscheint im analytischen Moment eine neue Dimension, die religiöse. Es geht hier nicht einfach um die rechtsrelevante Feststellung eines Faktums durch die Justizbehörde, sondern um den Kampf mit dem Dämon.[28] Dieser steckt, verhüllt, dort im Text, wo vom Schweigezauber die Rede ist (*licet maleficium taciturnitatis indubie penes se habuisset* 146A), die Gegenmacht wird hingegen sprachlich für alle sichtbar gemacht, wenn gesagt wird, dies sei möglich geworden *diuina ... fauente clementia* (Gottes Eingreifen ist auch 146D impliziert: *sed et hoc mirabile*).

Nachdem so die einander widerstrebenden Mächte bezeichnet sind, kann erzählerisch breit entfaltet werden, was das *detexit*[29] als Resultat bereits pauschal vorweg genommen hat (*Nam a notario-peruenissem*, Abschnitte Nr. 5 und 6). Vom Inhalt des Geständnisses her, sind im ersten Abschnitt zwei Bereiche erkennbar: *circa nocumenta* und *cetera omnia de fidei abnegatione et spurcitijs*; diese entsprechen zugleich einem zeitlichen Ablauf,[30] indem die Angeklagte zuerst wegen des Schadenzaubers, über den Zeugenaussagen vorliegen, dann über den Pakt, wozu es keinen Zeugenbericht gibt, befragt wird. Damit sind zwei aus der Sicht des Institoris sehr wesentliche Momente berührt. Einmal ist klargelegt, dass Schadenzauber ohne den Teufelspakt nicht möglich ist. Dies verstand sich keineswegs von selber, vertraten doch gewisse Zeitgenossen die Ansicht, beide Sachverhalte existierten auch unabhängig voneinander. Dies wiederum hatte natürlich Rückwirkungen auf die Diskussion über die Schuld von Wetterzauberinnen. Mit dem hier erzählerisch geleisteten "Nachweis" des Zusammenhangs befinden wir uns auf der Ebene der dämonologischen Theorie; das zweite Moment in unserem Problemkomplex betrifft eher den pastoralen Aspekt der Hexereifrage. Wie kann der besorgte Seelenhirt seine Gläubigen von der Gefährlichkeit und der Strafwürdigkeit der Hexen überzeugen? Nach der — vielleicht auf einschlägiger Erfahrung beruhenden — Ansicht des Institoris waren viele Laien dieser These nicht ohne weiteres günstig gesonnen. Es mussten deshalb geeignete Mittel zur Beeinflussung angewendet werden. Institoris ist sich nun aber gewiss, dass die Laien "eher von der Liebe zum Irdischen als von jener zum Spirituellen bestimmt sind" (142Cf., vgl. Anm. 1). Genau dies wird vom Beginn unseres Berichts demonstriert; die Ravensburger denken vorerst an ihre zerstörten Äcker und Gärten. Der Inquisitor nimmt diese Sorge ernst und greift ein, doch er führt den Geschädigten im Verlauf des Verfahrens die tieferen Ursachen des Schadenzaubers vor Augen und zeigt, welche höheren Werte durch die Hexerei gefährdet sind. Und den gleichen Erkenntnisweg sollen auch die Leser des *Malleus* zurücklegen.

Der sprachlich hier abgebildete Vorgang der Wahrheitssuche wird also auf diese Weise komplexer. Er führt nicht nur von einem Vorkommnis, dessen Ursache zunächst unklar ist (bzw. trivial scheint), dessen materielle Verheerungen aber offenkundig sind, über mehr oder minder klare Beschuldigungen der Öffentlichkeit zu einem rechtmässig und sachgerecht-klug[31] abgewickelten Verfahren, an dessen Ende die ausführliche Erklärung des Anfangsereignisses steht. Es werden vielmehr dabei auch dem Wettermachen zeitlich[32] und kausal vorausliegende, keinerlei *corpora delicti* zeitigende Verbrechen aufgedeckt.

Diese tieferen Ursachen kommen bald nach dem Beginn des Klärungsmoments zur Sprache (*...cum nemo testis-succubuisse*, Absatz Nr. 5). Von der bisher alles dominierenden Frage nach den Hintergründen der Unwetterkatastrophe her ergibt sich damit ein retardierender, die Geduld des Lesers auf die Probe stellender Einschub. Er hat zunächst Aussagen über sonstigen Schadenzauber der Angeklagten und namentlich — hier findet der Hexereivorwurf sein Zentrum — über den Pakt und den Sexualverkehr mit dem Dämon zur Kenntnis zu nehmen. Mit Blick auf die Exempelfunktion lässt sich sagen, dass im vorliegenden Fall keineswegs nur eine Demonstration von Fragen, die der unmittelbare Kontext stellt, durchgeführt wird, sondern dass sich eine Art Gesamtperspektive auf das Hexereiproblem ergibt. Der eine Kasus wird damit paradigmatisch für die ganze Sache.

Erst nach dieser Retardation wird nun der vordergründig wichtigste Punkt, das Wettermachen,[33] wieder aufgenommen und jetzt in allen wesentlichen Aspekten, dem Wann, Wo, Wie, Mit-Wem, dargestellt. Institoris wählt hier die Form des Verhörprotokolls. Dessen stereotype, wiederkehrenden Signale — *interrogata* und *respondit* — gliedern den Ablauf, ein zweimaliges *demum* markiert das zielstrebige Insistieren des Inquisitors auf seinem Befragen, das *finaliter* führt die letzte Frage herbei.[34] Auf inhaltlicher Ebene öffnet die vorletzte Frage nach einer Komplizin den Ausblick auf den Fortgang von Untersuchung und Bericht. Die Verwendung der direkten Rede[35] in den Antworten der Angeklagten wirkt rhetorisch ebenso überzeugend wie jene der Protokollform; beide Mittel suggerieren dokumentarische Treue[36] und Unmittelbarkeit des Berichteten.

Die Darstellung des nächsten Verhörs wird durch eine knappe Wertung, welche die Rezeption durch den Leser in die gewünschte Richtung lenkt, eingeleitet: *sed et hoc mirabile* (Absatz Nr. 7). Es geht hier nicht um die Aufdeckung neuer Befunde, sondern — was bereits der frühere Hinweis auf die Abschirmung der beiden Verdächtigen voneinander vorbereitet hat — um die Bestätigung des Entdeckten durch ein zweites, gleichlautendes, dabei angeblich "unabhängiges" Geständnis. Entsprechend kann sich die Schilderung nun erheblich kürzer fassen, auf das komplexe Nebeneinander von Bericht, direkter und indirekter Rede verzichten. Ein relativ langer Satz genügt; er ist im inhaltlich entscheidenden Passus durch die Anapher *nec quo ad* durchschaubar gegliedert. Die wesentlichen Momente erscheinen als Stichworte — *locus, tempus, modus, interuallum* — und fungieren als Rubriken. Sie erinnern an die Fragen im ersten Verhör, ohne dass aber in der Anzahl und Abfolge eine genaue Entsprechung gesucht würde.

Den ebenso zügig gegebenen Abschluss bildet der Bericht über die Hinrichtung der Hexen am dritten Tag[37] (Absatz Nr. 8). Obwohl im Kontext nicht erforderlich, verzichtet der Autor nicht darauf, das unterschiedliche Sterben der zwei Frauen zu einem moralisch erbaulichen Tableau zu stilisieren.[38] So stehen die zwei Angeklagten, die Gegenfiguren, summarisch aber klar als Individuen profiliert vor uns. Als einzige erscheinen sie mit vollem Namen, als einzige spricht Agnes ausgiebig in direkter Rede,[39] als einzige sagt sie mehrfach "Ich",[40] einzig bei Agnes und Anna erfahren wir etwas aus ihrem Vorleben. Diesen Merkmalen der Darstellung entsprechen wesentliche, wenn auch hintergründige Inhaltsaspekte. Die zwei Frauen stehen hier als schuldige, damit in Vereinzelung geratene Mitglieder der Gesellschaft vor Gericht, sie haben sich nicht allein durch ein Delikt gemäss weltlichem Recht sondern, was viel schwerer wiegt, durch die Abschwörung des Glaubens aus der Gemeinschaft ausgeschlossen.[41]

Unser Exemplum hat die Form eines Prozessberichts. Welche Wirkungen auf den Leser können sich dadurch ergeben? Zunächst entsteht so der Eindruck eines Erlebnisberichtes, denn jener, der erzählt, ist der Inquisitor selber; was er erlebte, ist der Ablauf des Prozesses. Traditionellerweise vermittelt ein Erlebnisbericht den Eindruck der Authentizität; dieser Effekt dürfte auch hier vom Autor gesucht sein. Zweitens ist mit dem Prozessbericht eine bestimmte Art des Erzählens, die analytische, gegeben. Der Autor erhält die Möglichkeit, den Leser optimal in seinem Sinne zu beeinflussen, indem er ihm die Lösung eines Rätsels präsentiert. Das besagt etwas Doppeltes. Einmal wird dadurch von vorneherein das Interesse geweckt und in Beschlag genommen; sodann wird dem Leser kein Glauben im Vorneherein abverlangt. Er sieht sich vielmehr mit einem unbestreitbaren, aber in seinen Ursachen vorerst dunklen Faktum konfrontiert. Dann kann er geleitet vom Erzähler Schritt für Schritt die "einleuchtende" Lösung des Rätsels nachvollziehen, nachentdecken. So hört, sieht, erfährt er, benötigt dabei keinen Glauben.[42]

Der Blick auf die Diskussion über das Wettermachen beim Zeitgenossen Ulrich Molitoris zeigt uns noch einen weiteren möglichen Grund dafür, wieso das analytische Erzählen des Prozessberichts den Intentionen der *Malleus*-Autoren entgegenkam.[43] Die These, mit der Molitoris seine Darstellung des Problems beschliesst, lautet, die Hexen g l a u b t e n aufgrund der Vorspiegelungen des Dämons bloss, Unwetter erzeugen zu können, seien aber realiter nicht dazu in der Lage.[44] Dabei hat am Beginn des Dreiergesprächs über die Hexerei Sigismund, einer der Gesprächspartner im Trialog des Molitoris, folgende Wahrheitsbedingung formuliert. Als einleuchtend und zwingend gelten demnach weder durch Tortur erzielte Geständnisse noch zwar allgemein verbreitete aber ungeprüfte Vorstellungen, vielmehr gilt nur das, was autoritativ abgesichert oder durch Vernunftargumente nachgewiesen ist.[45]

Unser Exemplum zielt nun genau auf den umstrittenen Punkt, ob nämlich die Hexe in entscheidendem Masse am Wettermachen beteiligt sei. Es will einen Beleg dafür liefern; dabei gibt es die entscheidenden Aussagen in Ich-Form als Erfahrungsbericht der einzigen denkbaren Augenzeuginnen, der Hexen selber; sie fungieren mithin als Autorität für die These der zwei Inquisitoren; zudem ist ihre Aussage, wie ja am Schluss bemerkt wird, schriftlich festgehalten. Die Erwähnung der Folter, die bei Molitoris als Hindernis der Wahrheitsfindung erscheint, widerspricht der eben vorgeschlagenen Deutung nur auf den ersten Blick. Institoris befand sich hier wohl in einem Zielkonflikt. Einerseits war für ihn die Folter Teil des elementaren Kampfs, den er als Inquisitor mit dem Dämon und dessen Vertreterin in Menschengestalt, der Hexe, zu liefern hatte (vgl. oben, Anm. 1);[46] es verbot sich von daher also, ihre Anwendung zu verschweigen, denn darin lag in seinen Augen (und denen mancher Zeitgenossen) gerade der Wahrheitsbeweis. Dagegen galt die Folter bei aufgeklärten Beobachtern als Zeichen für die Unwahrheit der damit erzielten "Geständnisse". In diesem Dilemma hat der Erzähler hier eine Art Gratwanderung versucht, indem er die Folterung nicht verschweigt, ihre Schärfe aber minimalisiert,[47] zudem durch das parallele Geständnis der andern Beschuldigten die "Freiwilligkeit" beider Aussagen zu betonen sucht.[48]

Der Ich-Bericht scheint übrigens nur innerhalb der Textsorte "Verhör" denkbar; einzig dort ist es nämlich zulässig, dieser gefährlichen Feindin der Menschheit, der Hexe, das Wort zu erteilen, denn der institutionelle Rahmen gewährleistet die Kontrolle über ihre Aussagen. So sind diese präformiert durch die Fragen des Inquisitors, und sie durchlaufen dann bei der Aufzeichnung erneut eine Kontrolle durch den Protokollanten. Der Bericht in Form eines Verhörs kombiniert also die überzeugende Unmittelbarkeit der Ich-Aussage mit der beruhigenden doppelten Überwachung dessen, was die angeklagte Hexe sagt, durch Fragesteller und Schriftführer.

Der *Malleus* will nicht zuletzt ein "Aufklärungsbuch" im Hinblick auf die weite Verbreitung, die Erscheinungsweisen und die Gefahren der Hexerei sein. Die Autoren rechneten also mit Lesern, die zwar das gleiche wie sie selber sahen, diese Wirklichkeit jedoch anders deuteten als sie, die Inquisitoren, es für richtig hielten; sie betrachteten also etwa die Hexenwerke oder die Mitwirkung der Hexen bei den Übeltaten der Dämonen als imaginär. Aufklärung implizierte somit hier, bereits Geschehenes einer Analyse, die zur richtigen Einsicht führte, zu unterziehen. Von diesem Ansatz her ergibt sich eine Verbindung zum Problembereich der Erzählformen im *Malleus*. Das "analytische Erzählen", das Erzählen von hinten her, rückwärts in die Vergangenheit hinein zwecks Erhellung eines vorerst unverständlichen Ereignisses entspricht genau dem eben umrissenen "aufklärerischen" Anliegen des Werks.

Über die damaligen Vorgänge in Ravensburg liegt im Brief des Stadtrates an den Tiroler Erzherzog Sigmund den Münzreichen ein zweiter Bericht der Ereignisse vor.[49] Auch wenn die zwei Quellen das Geschehen aus unterschiedlicher Perspektive und auf unterschiedliche Weise darstellen, bietet sich uns doch die Chance, mindestens ansatzweise die Erzählung des Institoris kritisch auf ihren Wirklichkeitsgehalt hin zu prüfen. Im Brief des Rates findet sich keine Andeutung von einer Dramatik der Situation, einer Notlage des Volkes, die das Eingreifen der weltlichen und geistlichen Obrigkeit erfordert hätte.[50] Vielmehr scheint alles mit einem routinemässigen, bürokratischen Vorgang begonnen zu haben. Der Inquisitor erscheint im Ort, predigt mehrmals von den Gefahren der Hexerei, fordert zur Anzeige auf, die Leute kommen zahlreich und denunzieren Verdächtige, einige werden verhaftet... Welche Version verdient stärker unseren Glauben? Dass der Bericht des Rates genau zu dem, was uns einerseits im Falle Innsbruck aktenmässig verbürgt ist,[51] anderseits im 3. Teil des *Malleus* als Prozesseinleitung empfohlen wird, passt, dies stimmt skeptisch gegenüber der Version im *Malleus*.[52] Der Verdacht, dass im Exemplum — durch bewusste Manipulation des Autors oder nach unwillkürlicher Arbeit in seinem Unbewusstsein — die Vorgänge zugespitzt und der zu vermittelnden Botschaft dienlich gemacht wurden, ist deshalb gross.

Blicken wir von dieser einen Geschichte nun noch kurz auf die andern vergleichbaren in unserem Buch (vgl. oben, S.)! Die analytische Form ist meist dadurch gekennzeichnet, dass der Gewinn einer Erfahrung, der Erwerb einer Erkenntnis, deren Subjekt die Betrachterfigur ist, dargestellt wird; erzählt wird somit die "Geschichte der Erfahrung einer Geschichte".[53] Von diesem Ansatz her lassen sich noch einige zusätzliche Erkenntnisse über die Funktion unserer einschlägigen Exempel gewinnen. Wir mustern zunächst die Betrachterfiguren, die darin auftreten, jene Figuren also, die mit einem Rätsel konfrontiert sind und es zu lösen suchen. Es sind dies (unter Beschränkung auf die hier ergiebigen Fälle, wo es um einen Prozess geht):

1.71 Dorfschulze
2.68 Richter — Angeklagter
2.90 *honestus laborator* — dessen Freunde — Richter
2.101 Leute am Tor
2.102 Ehemann — von diesem hergeholte Zeugen
2.111 Ehemann / Vater
2.122 Volk — Stadtrat — Notar der Inquisition — Inquisitor.

Es fällt auf, dass oft Autoritätspersonen als Betrachterfiguren fungieren, seien dies nun ein *pater familias*,[54] oder Mitglieder der weltlichen Behörden. Daneben sind auch Angehörige der jeweils von Hexerei bedrohten Gemeinschaft überhaupt zu registrieren (2.101, 2.122). Vorerst unerwartet ist das relativ seltene Auftreten des Inquisitors. Wie ist dieser Befund zu erklären? Es ist vorerst die Grundabsicht des *Malleus* zu berücksichtigen, alle Christen nämlich — wenn auch nicht als Leser und damit unmittelbare Adressaten des Buchs, so doch als Hörer seiner Doktrin — über die Gefahren der Hexerei zu informieren und gegen die Hexen zu mobilisieren. Eine besonders wichtige Aufgabe als Vermittler und Vorbild fiel dabei aber natürlich den Personen zu, die auf verschiedenen Ebenen und in verschiedenen gesellschaftlichen Formationen Autorität ausübten. Diesem Profil nun entsprechen die in den Exempeln auftretenden Betrachterfiguren recht oft. Eine Bestätigung für die Gewolltheit dieser Entsprechung erscheint mir auch *per negationem* darin gegeben, dass Frauen keine wesentliche Rolle spielen.

Förderlich ist weiter der Blick auf das, was die Betrachterfiguren tun. Sie tragen Entscheidendes zur Lösung jedes Falles bei.[55] Meist kann der Inquisitor erst in Aktion treten, weil die Laien die Bedingungen dafür geschaffen haben, indem sie durch ihr Reden in der Öffentlichkeit dubiose Sachverhalte ruchbar gemacht haben. Dabei gewinnen die Betrachter ihre Einsichten nicht durch theologisch geleitete Spekulation sondern durch angemessenes und kluges Handeln in Situationen, die manchmal — wenigstens zu Beginn — ganz alltäglich scheinen,[56] manchmal aber von vorneherein aussergewöhnlich sind. Freilich ist es in der Mehrzahl der Fälle der Inquisitor, der mit seinen Mitteln den Kampf der Gemeinschaft gegen ihre inneren Feinde zu Ende führt, doch steht dies selten im Vordergrund der

Erzählungen oder mindestens nicht von Anfang an. Das Exemplum erscheint so als Medium für die Belehrung über die Hexerei und für die Einübung in ihre Bekämpfung — ein Kampf, an dem alle Christen mit ihren je spezifischen Mitteln an ihrem jeweiligen Platz in der *societas christiana* teilzunehmen hatten; über die jeweils zentrale Figur in diesen Geschichten, die Betrachterfiguren, ergeht dabei an die Gläubigen ein starkes Angebot zur Identifikation mit diesem Kampf.

Zum Schluss sei eine Reihe unserer Beobachtungen unter den Gattungsaspekt integriert. Man hat in der neueren Forschung vorgeschlagen, das Exemplum nicht als Form sondern als Funktion zu definieren.[57] Anderseits hat man betont, wenn das Exemplum nicht als Form oder gar "Urform" hypostasiert werden solle, dass dann die einzelnen Exempla in ihren jeweiligen Kommunikationszusammenhängen zu analysieren seien; dabei dürfte sich eine Verbindung zwischen der primären F u n k t i o n und der ihr dienenden, mithin sekundären F o r m ergeben.[58] Die Fruchtbarkeit dieses Ansatzes erweist sich auch hier. Unser analysiertes Exemplum ist formal gesehen ein vielschichtiges und anspruchsvolles Gebilde; es fallen dabei namentlich die Vielfigurigkeit, die Verwendung der Protokollform und von Elementen des Erlebnisberichtes, der Verweis auf Prozessakten und die analytische Struktur auf. Diese Komplexität lässt sich am plausibelsten erklären, wenn man darin eine Mitgift sieht, mit welcher die Autoren ihre Geschichte, der sie sehr unterschiedliche Aufgaben und Leser zudachten, ausstatteten. Durch die Buchform des *Malleus*, durch seine Sprache und durch die Gattungsform der "Summe" war sein primärer Verwendungszweck festgelegt: Kommunikation unter Fachleuten und Amtskollegen, unter Theologen, Kirchenrechtlern, Inquisitoren. Sie waren über den Wetterzauber der Hexen, über die erfolgversprechende Strategie bei einem Prozess zu informieren. An sie erging durch den Text zudem der Appell, dem aus seiner Praxis erzählenden Amtskollegen aufmerksam zu folgen und sich seine Handlungsweisen zu eigen zu machen. Als weitere direkte Leser kamen danach wohl auch lateinkundige Laien, Juristen, hochgestellte Fachleute in Verwaltung und Rechtspflege und Politiker in Frage.[59] Sie waren vornehmlich zum strafrechtlichen Eingreifen im Bereich der weltlichen Justiz zu motivieren; entsprechend wurden ihnen in Gestalt der rühmend erwähnten Ravensburger Behörden Identifikationsfiguren geboten. Dann kam schliesslich die Mehrheit der Bevölkerung, die nicht Lesefähigen, dazu. Auch sie mussten für den Kampf gegen die Hexerei gewonnen werden. In ihrem Fall war der *Malleus* auf Vermittlung angewiesen, erreichte er doch mit unserer Geschichte dieses Zielpublikum nicht direkt, sondern erst auf dem Umweg der Übersetzung, allenfalls der Umformung, danach der Weitergabe, etwa von der Kanzel herab. Das Werk hat aber jedenfalls bereits in seiner originalen Form beste Voraussetzungen für eine solche Vermittlung, indem es auf das Fassungsvermögen und die Mentalität auch der Laien eingeht. Unser Exemplum erscheint so als Gebilde mit einer Vielzahl an Bezügen, die nicht alle gleichzeitig aktualisiert werden mussten, wohl aber in unterschiedlicher Auswahl und Akzentuierung in einer Vielzahl von Gebrauchskontexten aktualisierbar waren.

Notes

[1] Der Beitrag wurde am Internationalen Kongress der *Fifteenth-Century Studies* in Kaprun (3.-7. Juli, 1995) vorgelegt; für die Drucklegung wurde der Vortragstext leicht überarbeitet und durch den Fussnotenapparat ergänzt.

[2] Der Malleus-Text wird im Folgenden zitiert nach: Malleus Maleficarum von Heinrich Institoris (alias Kramer) unter Mithilfe Jakob Sprengers aufgrund der dämonologischen Tradition zusammengestellt. Wiedergabe des Erstdrucks von 1487 (Hain 9238), hg. von A. Schnyder, Litterae Bd. 113 (Göppingen: Kümmerle, 1991). Dazu gehört der Kommentarband: André Schnyder, Malleus Maleficarum von Heinrich Institoris (alias Kramer) unter Mithilfe Jakob Sprengers aufgrund der dämonologischen Tradition zusammengestellt. Kommentar zur Wiedergabe des Erstdrucks von 1487 (Hain 9238), Litterae Bd. 116 (Göppingen: Kümmerle, 1993).

[3] Grundlegende Informationen vermittelt der Artikel "Exemplum" von Christoph Daxelmüller in: *Enzyklopädie des Märchens. Handwörterbuch zur historischen und vergleichenden Erzählforschung*, ed. Kurt Ranke. (Berlin: de Gruyter, 1984), 4 Sp. 627-649.

[4] Setzt man die Textmenge in Relation zur Anzahl der Exempla, so ergeben sich folgende Werte (eine volle Druckseite gilt immer als 4 Sektoren gemäss dem Nachdruck von 1991), im 1. Teil kommt 1 Exempel auf 3,5 Sektoren, im 2. Teil eines auf 2,2, im letzten dann bloss noch eines auf 19 Abschnitte.

[5] Der Begriff ist hier im Sinn der meist im Zusammenhang mit der Dramenanalyse angewendeten Definition zu verstehen: die wesentlichen Verwicklungen eines Geschehens liegen dem Beginn des Erzählens voraus und werden erst nachträglich eingebracht (vgl. dazu Dietrich Weber, *Theorie der analytischen Erzählung* (München: Beck, 1975).

[6] Nr. 2.77, der Bericht über die Begegnung des Institoris mit einem Besessenen, wird hier nicht in Betracht gezogen, denn die Geschichte ist zum einen bereits früher ausführlich interpretiert worden (vgl. André Schnyder, "Der Inquisitor als Geschichtenerzähler. Beobachtungen zur Ausgestaltung des Exemplums im *Malleus maleficarum* (1487) von Institoris und Sprenger," *Fabula* 36 (1995), 1-24), zum andern trifft der Begriff des analytischen Erzählens hier den Sachverhalt nicht ganz. Analytisches Erzählen liegt zwar insofern vor, als die Ursachen für die Verhexung des Priesters im Rückblick dargestellt werden; liest man die Geschichte jedoch als Beispiel für eine bestimmte Form von Besessenheit — und

unter diesem Gesichtspunkt wird sie im *Malleus* eingeführt — dann spielt das analytische Moment keine wesentliche Rolle.

[7] Montague Summers, trans., Malleus maleficarum with an Introduction, Bibliography and Notes (London: Pushkin, 1948), 148-149.

[8] Der Erstdruck hat hier *an*.

[9] Hier liegt ein Missverständnis der engl. Übersetzung vor; es handelt sich bei *Balneatrix* um den Geschlechtsnamen.

[10] Sic! — Die fehlerhafte Form des Adjektivs scheint, dieser Behauptung grammatischen Nachdruck verleihen zu wollen. Die letzte Ausgabe von 1669 liest dann *innoxiam* (161b).

[11] Korrigiert aus dem *peruenissent* des Erstdrucks (die letzte Ausgabe des *Malleus* von 1669 hat ebenfalls die Form in der 1. Person).

[12] Vgl. die Gegenbeispiele (theoretische Quaestio und empirisches Capitulum), 1.8 (52B) bzw. 2.1.6 (114A), 1.9 (55D) bzw. 2.1.7 (115A), 1.10 (59B) bzw. 2.1.8 (118D) u.a.

[13] Die Länge der drei Geschichten in unserem 15. Kapitel (Nr. 2.119 und 120 bleiben wegen ihres Exkurs-Charakters hier ausser Betracht) beträgt: 14 Zeilen für das Hiob-Exemplum, 21 für den Bericht aus Nider (2.118) und deren 106 schliesslich bei unserer Geschichte. Dabei überrascht der Umfang des ersten Exemplums, werden doch aus der Bibel bezogene Geschichten wegen ihrer Bekanntheit meist nur sehr knapp anzitiert. Die hier vorliegende Ausnahme liesse sich damit erklären, dass es den Autoren auf die lange, damit vor allem auf das Laienpublikum emotional wirkende Liste der vom Dämon verursachten materiellen Schäden ankam (vgl. Anm.); bei diesem stattlichen Inventar mit seinen Zahlen war wohl auch dem Gedächtnis des sonst bibelfesten Lesers nachzuhelfen.

[14] Vgl. Karl Otto Müller, "Heinrich Institoris, der Verfasser des Hexenhammers, und seine Tätigkeit als Hexeninquisitor in Ravensburg im Herbst 1484 in Ravensburg," *Württembergische Vierteljahreshefte für Landesgeschichte* Neue Folge 19 (1910), 397-417, 409 Anm. 3) Müller rechnet mit einer Distanzangabe zwischen Ravensburg und Salzburg (es wäre also etwa zu lesen: *in oppido Rauenspurg vigintiocto miliaria teuthonicalia ad Saltzburgam verso*). Möglich wäre aber auch ein Fehler bei der Entfernungsangabe oder bei der Masseinheit, dann wäre an die Ausdehnung des Unwettergebietes von Ravensburg in Richtung auf Salzburg hin gedacht (*ab oppido Rauenspurg ... versus Saltzburgam*). Der Fehler kann ebenso gut auf das Konto des Druckers, der z.B. eine Abkürzung verlesen hat, wie auf die mangelhaften Lateinkenntnisse des Autors (wie Müller meint) gehen.

[15] Institoris war am 13. 3. 1479 von Sixtus IV. zum Inquisitor für die Alemania superior ernannt worden (vgl. Heinrich Wibel, "Neues zu Heinrich Institoris," *Mitteilungen des Instituts für Österreichische Geschichtsforschung* 34 (1913), 121-125, 122), Sprenger dagegen am 19. 6. 1481 für die Kirchenprovinzen Mainz, Trier und Köln (vgl. Kommentarband [Anm.], 82 Nr. 119). Diese Gebiete — erweitert durch Bremen und Salzburg — erscheinen in der Bulle vom 5. 12. 1484,

welche ja beide Dominikaner gemeinsam speziell mit der Hexereiinquisition beauftragte (ebd., 45-47 Nr. 27).

16 Es ist daran zu erinnern, dass für die Autoren des *Malleus* die Laien am besten über den Hinweis auf materielle Schäden der Hexerei zu ihrer Verfolgung zu motivieren waren, denn *magis terrenis implicantur affectionibus quam spiritualibus* (142D).

17 Dass dies ohne Weiteres möglich gewesen wäre, zeigt sich, wenn man ein anderes, motivisch sehr ähnliches Exemplum über Wetterzauber vergleicht (2.43., 104A-104C). Dieser Bericht stellt die Verschwörung zwischen Hexe und Dämon an den Anfang, fährt dann genau chronologisch weiter. Wird im Ravensburger Fall also analytisch erzählt, so dort synthetisch.

18 Vgl. Weber [Anm.], 17-27.

19 Ebenso enthält das *excitatus* einen vorerst nur vagen Hinweis auf menschliche Urheberschaft des Unwetters.

20 Allenfalls könnte man die Namennennung (*nomen-Mindelheim*) zum Folgenden rechnen. Insgesamt ist der Satz grammatisch nicht gut durchschaubar, auch wenn über seinen Sinn kein Zweifel herrscht; die verfügbaren Übersetzungen zerhauen eher den gordischen Knoten, als dass sie sich bemühten, die logischen Verkettungen sorgfältig wiederzugeben. Als Hauptsatz fasse ich: *Unde res gesta ... per quindenam ... a nobis inquiritur et ad duas dumtaxat personas ... diffamatas peruenitur.*

21 Dass der Teufel im Exemplum überhaupt nur flüchtig erwähnt wird, mag auf den ersten Blick verwunderlich erscheinen, ist er doch der Anstifter der bösen Tat und der materielle Verursacher des Unwetters. Aber das Verfahren des Erzählers findet darin seinen guten Grund, dass er, obwohl der Kampf der Inquisition eigentlich ihm gilt, allerdings nicht vor ein hiesiges Gericht zitiert werden kann. In anderen Exempla kommt er freilich zu Wort; vgl. etwa 133D (Dialog Hexe-Dämon), 128Cf. (Schreie des Teufels aus einem Besessenen heraus).

22 Dieser *notarius* wird auch später noch erwähnt; um wen es sich handelt, bleibt unklar. Betrachtet man den Ablauf des Berichts, dann erscheinen der *notarius* und der *iudex* (bzw. *nos*) deutlich unterscheidbar. Jener nimmt die *fama* über den diabolischen Ursprung des Gewitters auf, setzt die Inquisitionsmaschinerie in Gang, führt später einen Teil des Verhörs (dies offenbar in der Phase, wo es um die summarisch berichtete Verifikation der von den Zeugen vorgebrachten Anschuldigungen geht [Abschnitt Nr. 5, *a notario inquisitionis interrogata super articulos ex depositione testium*]). Der Inquisitor selber wird als *iudex* zweimal im Verlauf des ausführlich wiedergegebenen Verhörs über die Umstände des Wetterzaubers fassbar (Abschnitt Nr. 6), er ist auch die zuletzt eingeführte (Abschnitt Nr. 3, *a nobis inquiritur*) und am längsten vorhandene Betrachterfigur.

23 Die Situation wirkt archetypisch, erinnert an die Bibel, selbst wenn mir dort keine genaue Parallele nachweisbar ist (vgl. immerhin II Esr 5,1, Is 15,8, Ps 9,13).

24 Über den Bericht hin sind Zeitangaben verteilt, welche das Erzähltempo erfassen lassen (146A *sequenti mane*, 146D *sequenti die*, 146D *tertia die*). Dem an

einem Tag ablaufenden Verhör der Agnes werden 61 Zeilen, jenem der Anna noch deren 15 gewidmet, gleich viel wie der "Voruntersuchung" von 2 Wochen. Das Berichtstempo ist also zunächst sehr rasch, wird dann gemächlicher, gewinnt wieder an Schnelligkeit: Beschleunigungen und Verlangsamungen, die zugleich mit der Bedeutung des jeweiligen Abschnittes konform gehen. Im Zentrum des Interesses stehen Verhör und Geständnis der Agnes über ihren Wetterzauber; jenes der Anna hat bloss noch die Funktion einer zusätzlichen Beglaubigung der hier zentralen Frage, obwohl ihr Fall an sich gesehen schwerer wiegt.

25 Wirkungsvoll arbeitet der Berichterstatter hier mit einer Steigerungsfigur: *dum certi per maleficia imo omnes pene oppidani talia contigisse iudicarent* (146A).

26 Es entsteht der Eindruck, dass umstandslos sofort gefoltert wurde; das stünde im Widerspruch zu dem im 3. Werkteil vertretenen Ratschlag für die Prozessführung (vgl. 210A-216A, v.a. 210C: *ad maleficam questionandam non sit pronus* [*iudex*]). Doch könnte dieser Eindruck einfach durch die raffende, sich auf das im Kontext Wesentliche beschränkende Erzählweise des Exemplums bedingt sein und nicht den Tatsachen entsprechen. Dass ein sehr kurzes, aber rechtskonformes Verfahren in der Realität durchaus vorkam, zeigt etwa der Hexereiprozess gegen Catherine Quicquat in Vevey. Die jüngst publizierten Akten belegen folgenden Ablauf: Verhaftung und erstes gütliches Verhör am 15. 3. 1448, weiteres gütliches Verhör und — nach der rechtsüblichen dreimaligen *monitio*, die Wahrheit freiwillig zu gestehen — Folterung am 16. 3., abschliessendes Verhör am 17. 3. (Palmsonntag), Todesurteil am 18. 3. (vgl. Martine Ostorero, "Folâtrer avec les démons." *Sabbat et chasse aux sorciers à Vevey (1448), Cahiers lausannois d'histoire médiévale 15* (Lausanne: Université, 1995), 242, 246, 254. Die Hinweise auf das bei Agnes "sicher" vorhandene *maleficium taciturnitatis* und auf ihre heftigen Unschuldsbeteuerungen lassen im Übrigen auf ein vorangegangenes "gütliches" Verhör schliessen.

27 Vgl. 75Df., 115A, 156Af., 219Cf.; anderseits werden Behörden gelegentlich auch für ihre Mitarbeit gelobt: 136D.

28 Vgl. v.a. III 16; dazu bringt Hans Fehr reiche Belege für diese religiöse Auffassung des Prozessverfahrens, z.T. schon aus dem Frühmittelalter ("Gottesurteil und Folter. Eine Studie zur Dämonologie des Mittelalters und der neueren Zeit," in: Edgar Tatarin-Tarnheyden, Hg., *Festgabe für R. Stammler zum 70. Geburtstage am 19. Februar 1926* (Berlin: de Gruyter, 1926), 231-254.

29 Das Wort tritt zweimal in ähnlichem Zusammenhang und an analoger Stelle auf (beim Bericht über das Geständnis der Agnes und der Anna am Schluss von Absatz Nr. 4 und 7, je am Satzende), bildet somit eine Art Epiphora.

30 Vgl. den entsprechenden Hinweis im Text: *vbi post*.

31 Man beachte in diesem Zusammenhang den Hinweis auf die Vermeidung einer Kollusion durch Abschirmung der zwei Verhafteten voneinander.

32 Dieser Gesichtspunkt wird noch durch die Angabe, dass der Verkehr mit dem Dämon in einem Fall über 20 Jahre gedauert habe (Absatz Nr. 8), unterstrichen.

[33] Einzig die vierte (von insgesamt acht) Fragen zielt in andere Richtung, offenbar nämlich auf den sexuellen Verkehr mit dem Dämon: *an ne pariter consedissent* (Absatz Nr. 6).

[34] Gefragt wird darin nach der Zeitspanne bis zum Ausbruch des Gewitters. Der Bericht lässt die Angeklagte nicht mit der Nennung einer abstrakten Grösse antworten (was wohl als epochentypisch gelten kann). Ihr Hinweis, die Zeit habe ihr gerade zur Rückkehr nach Hause gereicht, ist geeignet, ein weiteres Mal Widerwillen und Hass gegen die *malefica* zu bestärken; der Bericht versteht es also, auch anscheinend sachbezogene Informationen in den Dienst der Affekterregung, des *movere*, zu stellen.

[35] In der vorletzten Antwort erscheint kurzfristig ein Einschub des Berichterstatters (*captam ... nominando*).

[36] Am Ende (Absatz Nr. 8) wird in beglaubigender Absicht noch auf das tatsächliche Protokoll im Ravensburger Archiv verwiesen.

[37] Es fällt schwer zu glauben, dass sich für Institoris in der Tatsache der Hinrichtung beider Hexen *tertia die* (Absatz Nr. 8) nicht eine spirituelle "Pointe" verbarg (vgl. auch oben, Anm.); zur Bedeutung der Dreizahl im *Malleus* vgl. Kommentarband [Anm.], 438. Anderseits liegt eine so kurze Prozessdauer durchaus im Bereich des Möglichen (vgl. Anm.), Tatsachentreue des Berichts und überhöhende Symbolik brauchen einander nicht auszuschliessen.

[38] Vgl. dazu die Bemerkungen bei Assion über den "dualistischen Erzählgestus" (Peter Assion, "Das Exempel als agitatorische Gattung. Zu Form und Funktion der kurzen Beispielgeschichte," *Fabula 19* (1978), 225-240, 234f.).

[39] Nur in Absatz Nr. 6 findet sich eine eindeutig direkte Frage des Inquisitors: *Quid actum fuit de aqua* (daneben gibt es dort einige Zweifelsfälle, wo elliptisch nur mit dem Fragepronomen formuliert wird).

[40] Vgl. 146B eram ... me, 146C mecum ... me ... transferrem ... interrogassem ... reperi ... foderem ... infunderem ... me sedente ... moui ... habui ... ignoro ... peruenissem (zur letzten Form vgl. Anm.).

[41] Vgl. die eine neuerliche Bekräftigung darstellende Wiederholung der Kernbegriffe *fidei abnegatione maleficijs hominibus, iumentis et terre frugibus illatis* am Ende von Absatz Nr. 8.

[42] Über das analytische Erzählen als Insinuationstechnik (allerdings anhand fiktionaler Texte) vgl. Weber [Anm.], 154-157.

[43] Da die Arbeit des Molitoris, *De lanijs et phitonicis mulieribus*, kurz nach dem *Malleus* erschien, ist dieser nicht als direkte Replik auf jene zu fassen; man darf aber davon ausgehen, dass Molitoris Gedankengänge formulierte, die bei den Zeitgenossen generell bekannt waren, die also Institoris und Sprenger in ihre Argumentation einbeziehen konnten.

[44] Vgl. Jürgen Mauz, "Ulrich Molitoris aus Konstanz (ca. 1442-1507). Leben und Schriften" (Diss. Universität Konstanz, 1983), danach zitiert (gekürzte Druckausgabe: *Ulrich Molitoris. Ein süddeutscher Humanist und Rechtsgelehrter*

[Wien: Schendl, 1992]), *Nam quis ebes mentis est. qui credere posset quod ex huiusmodi fatuitate et mulierum stulta operatione. vna tam immensa spera* <sic> *aeris. et alia elementa deberent commouere in tantum vt grandines et fulmina prouocarentur* (319). Das Schlusswort unseres *Malleus*-Kapitels nimmt derartige Einwände auf, indem Institoris konzediert, oft seien Hexen bei Verheerungen durch Unwetter nicht beteiligt (147A).

[45] Vgl. Mauz [Anm.], 286: Ac ego nude fame non intendo facile enim dictum sequitur vulgus ne confessione torturali satiabor cum metu tormentorum quis inducitur quandoque ad confitendum id quod in rerum natura non est Verum ea que oculis non conspeximus. auctoritate tum vel concludenti ratione percipere desideramus. nam recta disputatio auctoritate et ratione concluditur.

[46] Zu beachten ist ferner, dass für ein Todesurteil — und ein solches dürfte man in Ravensburg angesichts der möglicherweise pogromhaft aufgeregten Stimmung erstrebt haben — ein Geständnis erforderlich war (210A).

[47] Je einmal bei Agnes und Anna, wird herausgestrichen: *questionibus leuissimis* (146A und D), ferner bemerkt: *subito libere et a vinculis absoluta* (146B).

[48] Freiwilligkeit bei den einschlägigen Geständnissen wird auch am Kapitelschluss (147A) geltend gemacht.

[49] Vgl. den Abdruck des Dokumentes im Kommentarband [Anm.], 47f. Nr. 28.

[50] Beide Texte stimmen anderseits in wichtigen Fakten überein: Substanz der Geständnisse (Wetterzauber, Pakt und Buhlschaft, Viehschädigung), Mehrzahl der Verdächtigen, Hinrichtung von 2 Personen.

[51] Vgl. Hartmann Ammann, "Der Innsbrucker Hexenprozess von 1485," *Zeitschrift des Ferdinandeums für Tirol und Vorarlberg* 34 (1890), 3-87, 4-5.

[52] Das gilt selbst dann, wenn man sich vergegenwärtigt, dass auch im Brief von 1484 ein Interesse, das die Fakten deformieren konnte, mitspielen mochte, etwa der Wille des Rats, seine Willfährigkeit gegenüber dem Inquisitor zu betonen.

[53] Vgl. Weber [Anm.], 27.

[54] Bei 2.102 und 2.111, wo ein Ehemann gegen die Frau um sein Kind kämpft, erinnere man sich des Grundkonsensus der patriarchalischen Gesellschaft, dass die Kinder in gewissem Sinne dem Vater gehören, wie das auch im *Malleus* formuliert wird (vgl. 140D unter Zitierung der *Summa theologiae* 2-2,108,4,ad 1).

[55] Ausnahmsweise spielt nun die Betrachterfigur eine eher negative Rolle (so der Richter in 2.68).

[56] Vgl. z.B. 2.101 (Szene am Tor), 2.102 (Verhalten der Gebärenden: das von der Alltagsnorm Abweichende [und damit indirekt das Normale selber!] ausdrücklich angesprochen), 2.122 (Gewitter).

[57] Vgl. Daxelmüller [Anm.], 627.

[58] Zur hier besonders bedeutsamen agitatorischen Funktion des Exemplums vgl. Assion [Anm.]. Im 16. Jh. wird dann das Exemplum durch die Möglichkeiten des Flugblattes ergänzt; einen inhaltlich einschlägigen Fall führt vor: Frank Baron, "Ein Einblattdruck Lucas Cranachs d.J. als Quelle der Hexenverfolgung in

Luthers Wittenberg," in *Poesis et Pictura. Studien zum Verhältnis von Text und Bild in Handschriften und alten Drucken. Festschrift für Dieter Wuttke zum 60. Geburtstag*, hg. von Stephan Füssel (Baden-Baden: Koerner, 1989), 277-294, bes. 288.

[50] Ein solcher Laie ist etwa der bayrische Jurist und hohe Verwaltungsmann Ulrich Tenngler, der in seinem wichtigen Rechtsbuch *Layenspiegel* die Thesen des *Malleus* rezipiert und weiterverbreitet (vgl. *Der Teufelsprozess vor dem Weltgericht nach Ulrich Tennglers Neuer Layenspiegel von 1511 (Ausgabe von 1512)* hg. und eingeleitet von Wolfgang Schmitz (Köln: Wienand, 1980), 43-45.

Universität Bern

Zur Bedeutung von Gewalt in der Reynaert-*Epik des 15. Jahrhunderts*

Rita Schlusemann

Das mittelniederdeutsche Versepos *Reynke de vos*, das 1498 von der Mohnkopfdruckerei in Lübeck gedruckt wurde, bildet das Ende einer stattlichen Anzahl mittelalterlicher Übersetzungen und Bearbeitungen des berühmten niederländischen Versepos *Van den vos Reynaerde* aus dem 13. Jahrhundert.[1] Der *Reynke* ist die Übersetzung und Bearbeitung einer mittelniederländischen Vorlage, die als solche nicht erhalten ist. Diese Vorlage ist ihrerseits in ein Geflecht von Überlieferungen einzuordnen. Obwohl die Literatur über den mittelalterlichen *Reynaert*-Stoff sehr umfangreich ist, fehlt es bislang an einer Studie zur Gewalt in der *Reynaert*-Epik.

Zahlreiche Abschriften, Übersetzungen und Bearbeitungen des *Van den vos Reynaerde* entstanden bis in die heutige Zeit. Einen regelrechten Boom erlebte die *Reynaert*-Epik jedoch im 15. Jahrhundert, vor allem im letzten Viertel des Jahrhunderts. Fragmente einer Handschrift des *Van den vos Reynaerde*, die erst 1971 wiederentdeckt wurden, werden auf das Ende des 15. Jahrhunderts datiert. Die lateinische Übersetzung des Epos, *Reynardus vulpes*, die zwar bereits vor 1279 entstand, ist in einer Inkunabel aus dem Jahre 1474 erhalten.[2] Mit *Reynaerts historie* (RII) entsteht spätestens zu Anfang des 15. Jahrhunderts[3] eine bearbeitete Fassung, die erhaltenen Textzeugen stammen wiederum aus späterer Zeit. Eine vollständige, aber sehr fehlerhafte Handschrift von etwa 1470 (B) und ein Fragment aus dem Jahre 1475 (C) sind von diesem Text erhalten.[4] Bei *Reynaerts historie* wurde der erste Teil des *Van den vos Reynaerde* leicht verändert und eine zweite Prozeßhandlung hinzugefügt.[5]

Die Bearbeitungen aus dem letzten Viertel des 15. Jahrhunderts kann man in Prosa und Versbearbeitungen einteilen. In Prosa erschien eine niederländische Inkunabel, gedruckt 1479 bei Gheraert Leeu in Gouda, und die englische Übersetzung von William Caxton, die 1481 erschien und 1489 nachgedruckt wurde.[6] Wichtig für die folgenden Überlegungen ist eine gedruckte Versfassung (RIII), versehen mit Titeln, Prosakommentaren und Holzschnittillustrationen, von der nur Bruchstücke erhalten sind, die sogenannten "Culemannschen Bruchstücke".[7] Diese Fassung erschien zwischen 1487 und 1490 bei Gheraert Leeu in Antwerpen.[8] Erhalten sind sieben zum Teil beschädigte Blätter mit 223 Versen sowie vier Holzschnitte, von denen einer doppelt erscheint.

Die niederdeutsche Inkunabel *Reynke de vos* geht über Zwischenstufen zurück auf diese nur fragmentarisch erhaltenen Versinkunabel.[9] Der niederdeutsche Text ist eingeteilt in vier Bücher, versehen mit neuen Prologen und Prosakommentaren, und illustriert mit 89 Abbildungen, von denen 36 Wiederholungen sind. Man hat es also mit 53 verschiedenen Illustrationen zu tun. Von den "Cambridge Fragments" sind nur drei verschiedene Holzschnitte und wenige Verse erhalten, doch ist es aufgrund der Parallelausgabe von Jan Goossens, der die Vorlage des *Reynke de vos* rekonstruiert hat,[10] möglich, einen eingehenden Vergleich der Entwicklung von der niederländischen zur deutschen Tradition vorzunehmen, auch in Bezug auf die Darstellung von Gewalt. Im folgenden soll die Darstellung von Gewalt im *Reynke de vos* in Text und Bild im Vergleich zu der Vorlage, die nur etwa 10 Jahre vorher in Antwerpen entstanden ist, analysiert werden.

Der Term "Gewalt" hat sich aus dem althochdeutschen "waltan" entwickelt. Man kann nach verschiedenen Lexika grob zwei Arten von Gewalt unterscheiden: zum einen ist damit gemeint Anwendung von Zwang oder ein unrechtmäßiges Vorgehen, wodurch man jemanden zu etwas zwingt oder auch die physische Kraft, mit der man etwas unrechtmäßig erreicht. Es kommt auch vor in Ausdrücken wie "der Wahrheit Gewalt antun", "einer Sache Gewalt antun". Zweitens versteht man darunter Macht, Befugnis, Recht und Mittel, über jemanden zu bestimmen; damit ist gemeint staatliche, richterliche, priesterliche und göttliche Gewalt.[11] Erstgenannte Bedeutung hat sich entwickelt von lat. *violentia* und beinhaltet u.a. im Strafrecht rohe, verbrecherische Gewaltsamkeit und Verbrechen wie Notzucht, Raub und Nötigung, die zweite stammt von lat. *potestas* mit den Assoziationen Macht, Kraft und Herrschaftsbefugnis.[12] In meinem Beitrag möchte ich diese beiden Aspekte von Gewalt und ihre Darstellung in den Epen berücksichtigen.

Um den Text und die Illustrationen des *Reynke de vos* mit der Vorlage vergleichen zu können, kann man auf die Rekonstruktion der Quelle des niederdeutschen Textes von Jan Goossens zurückgreifen.[13] Für die Rekonstruktion der Bilder in der Antwerpener Inkunabel (RIII) ist vor allem der sogenannte Wynkyn-de-Worde-Zyklus ergiebig gewesen. Goossens hat unter Hinzuziehung verschiedener illustrierter Textfassungen 39 Illustrationen für *Reynaert III* nachgewiesen.[14] Betrachtet man die Illustrationen im *Reynaert III* und im *Reynke* unter dem Aspekt der Gewaltdarstellung kann man nach den genannten zwei Arten unterscheiden. Die erste, die physische Gewalt abbildet, ist zu unterscheiden in die Gruppe des Aufzeigens von direkter Gewalt und die Gruppe der drohenden Gewalt, siehe hierzu Abbildungen 1 und 3.[15] Diese zeigen zwei der erhaltenen Illustrationen aus *Reynaert III*, Abbildung 2 und 4 jeweils dazu die spiegelbildliche — "eindeutig eine recht genaue — seitenverkehrte" Illustration aus dem englischen Zyklus von Wynkyn de Worde.[16]

Zur ersten Gruppe von Gewalt kann man im *Reynaert III* 18 der 39 Illustrationen zählen, davon 15, die direkt physische Gewalt zeigen und drei, bei denen drohende Gewalt angedeutet wird.[17] Formen von Amtsgewalt, sei es königlicher oder geistlicher Gewalt zeigen 15 Bilder, siehe als Beispiele Abbildung 5 und 6 (WdW 1 und WdW 12).[18] Abbildung 5 zeigt den Hoftag zu Pfingsten mit dem König als Vorsitzendem, in Abbildung 6 erteilt der Dachs auf dem Weg von Reynaerts Höhle zum Königshof die Absolution. Insgesamt wird Gewalt in 33 der 39 Illustrationen des *Reynaert III* gezeigt (etwa 87%). Nur sechs der 39 rekonstruierten Holzschnitte zeigen keine Form von Gewalt.[19]

Im *Reynke* haben 33 der 89 Illustrationen mit physischer Gewalt zu tun — 25 mit direkter Gewalt, acht mit drohender Gewalt[20] — und 33 mit Amtsgewalt (zusammen etwa 74%).[21] 23 gehören zu keiner der beiden Gruppen. Damit hat die Anzahl der Gewaltdarstellungen im Bildteil vom *Reynaert III* zum *Reynke de vos* abgenommen. Geht damit eine grundsätzliche Verringerung der Gewalt auch im Textteil des niederdeutschen Epos einher?

Gewalt ist in den Verstexten der *Reynaert*-Tradition zunächst nicht in der Erzählwirklichkeit präsent. In vielen Fällen werden Episoden, in denen Gewalt eine wichtige Rolle spielt, als etwas bereits Geschehenes von einer Figur nachträglich erzählt, wie zum Beispiel die Tötung der Kinder des Hahns Cantecleer. Der Hahn berichtet beim Hoftag von Reynaerts Hinterlist. Abbildung 7 zeigt, wie der Fuchs, als Einsiedler verkleidet, dem Hahn zu verstehen gegeben habe, er brauche sich um die Sicherheit seiner Kinder keine Sorgen zu machen. Im Hintergrund der Abbildung sieht man, wie der Fuchs gerade im Begriff ist, ein Huhn zu töten. Hier zeigt die Abbildung sehr illustrativ den Gegensatz zwischen Wort und Tat bei dem Fuchs.[22]

Das erste Beispiel von sich direkt in der Erzählwirklichkeit abspielender physischer Gewalt ist die Falle, in die der Bär Bruun gerät bei seinem Auftrag, Reynke an den Hof zu holen. Zu diesem Botengang gibt es im *Reynke* wie im *Reynaert III* vier Illustrationen, ausgewählt habe ich die Darstellungen im *Reynke*. Die erste Illustration (Abbildung 8, R 13) zu diesem Thema zeigt den Bären mit der schriftlichen Nachricht vor der Höhle des Fuchses, die folgende (Abbildung 9, R 16) beide auf dem Weg zum Hof des Bauern Rystevyl. In der dritten Illustration (Abbildung 10, R 17) hierzu werden zwei Szenen abgebildet. Im Hintergrund sieht man die zeitlich vorangestellte Szene, in der der Fuchs dem Bären den Baumstamm zeigt, im Vordergrund ist der Bär bereits eingeklemmt. Anhand der Illustrationen wird nicht deutlich, daß der Fuchs die Keile aus dem Baumstamm reißt und somit indirekt verantwortlich für diese Gewaltanwendung und indirekt für die spätere durch den Bauern und die anderen Bewohner ist. In der folgenden Abbildung (11, R 18) wird das Schlagen und Stoßen des Bären durch den Bauern und andere Bewohner des Hauses und des Dorfes direkt gezeigt.

Man kann also entsprechend der Darstellung im Text von einer Steigerung der Gewalttätigkeit in der illustrierten Darstellung in der Reihenfolge der Holzschnitte sprechen. Im Hintergrund sieht man bei der letztgenannten Abbildung zu dieser Episode den Fuchs auf einer Anhöhe liegen, der sichtlich Vergnügen am Leid Bruuns hat:

> Dat meende ok reynke. vnde sach rustevyle
> Van verne komen, myt deme byle
> He reep tho brune. wo steyt yd nu
> Eteht nicht tho vele. dat rade ik yw
> Des honniges. segget my. ysset ock gud
> Jk see dat rustevyle kumpt hir yth
> Vyllichte wyl he yw bedencken
> Vnde wyl yw yp de maltyd schencken.
> (R 655-62)

Indem er ihm zuspricht, er solle nicht so viel Honig essen, kommt seine sadistische Haltung zum Vorschein.

Im Vergleich zu *Reynaert III* gibt es hinsichtlich der Illustrationen keine Unterschiede in der Darstellung der Gewalt in den Bruun-Szenen, im Text wird an manchen Stellen im *Reynke de vos* etwas hinzugefügt, z.B. tritt ein Schmied auf, der Hammer und Feilen mitbringt, und andere, die mit Schaufeln und Spaten schlagen (R 715-8). Dagegen wird die Tätigkeit des Pastors harmloser. Im *Reynaert III* kommt er zusammen mit den "prochiane" (R III 738)[23], die so gut sie können auf den Bären einschlagen (R III 765). Im *Reynke* wird als Schlagwerkzeug des Pastors ein langer Stock genannt (R 711). In der niederländischen Fassung agiert der Pastor mit seinem Kreuzstab (R III 762 und 768) und wird dabei von seiner Frau Julocke unterstützt (R III 763). Im niederdeutschen Epos wird an dieser Stelle der Pastor nicht mit seiner Frau aktiv, denn Frau Yutte war vorher als seine "papemeyersche", also als seine Haushaltsgehilfin, eingeführt worden (R 681). Bei einem Befreiungsversuch des Bären stürzen kurz darauf fünf Frauen in den Bach, unter ihnen im *Reynaert III* die Frau des Pastors (R III 791), der dann auch demjenigen direkt für ein Jahr Vergebung der Sünden und Ablaßbefreiung verspricht, der seine Frau aus den Fluten rettet:

> Hy riep edel prochiaen
> Ghinder vliet vrou iudelocke
> Beide myt pelse ende myt rocke
> Nv toe dien hair helpen mach
> Jc geef hem jaer ende dach
> Vol pardoen ende recht oflaet
> Van alle sondeliker daet.

(R III 796-802)

Im *Reynke* jammert der Pastor in diesem 9. Kapitel des ersten Buches "nur" um "vruw yutte. myn maget" (R 756).[24]

In seiner Studie zu Tabus und dem Umgang damit in der *Reynaert*-Tradition mit dem Titel *De gecastreerde neus* hatte J. Goossens bereits anhand der Kater-Szene beim niederdeutschen Bearbeiter "een grote eerbied voor de priesterlijke waardigheid" konstatiert,[25] die den Niederdeutschen u.a. die Attribute, mit denen der Pastor den Kater Hintze schlägt, verändern ließ. Statt dem "spinrok" seiner Frau (R III 1187) nimmt er im *Reynke* den Stiel einer Harke (R 1194). Auch die Bären-Szene zeigt in dieser Hinsicht bereits einige Veränderungen: der Geistliche schlägt hier nicht mehr mit dem "cruus staff" (R III 762, 768), sondern mit einem neutralen langen Stock (R 711).

Der Niederdeutsche hat die Illustration der Kastrationsszene — die Szene, in der der Pastor durch den Kater Hintze eines seiner Geschlechtsteile beraubt wird, gestrichen, entweder aus ökonomischen Gründen und/oder aus Gründen der "Selbstzensur".[26] In der englischen Serie wird das Geschehen eindeutig gezeigt (Abbildung 12), im *Reynke* findet sich nur eine äußerst harmlose Illustration für die Kater-Szene (Abbildung 13), die aber noch zweimal wiederholt wird. Damit scheiden ökonomische Gründe wie Platzersparnis aus. Für Zensur spricht auch, daß der niederdeutsche Bearbeiter, wenn er aus rein wirtschaftlichen Gründen gehandelt hätte, sonst auch andere Illustrationen hätte streichen können. Er hat aber gerade diese Illustration, die Gewalt und Sexualität kombiniert, aussortiert und durch eine wesentlich weniger prekäre ersetzt.

Gewalt im *Reynke* wird hier reduziert, aber es wird offensichtlich sorgfältig ausgewählt, wer gewalttätig ist bzw. wem Gewalt zugefügt wird. Die Bereitwilligkeit der Geistlichkeit zu physischer Gewalt soll abgeschwächt werden, wie auch die häusliche Situation des Pastors verharmlost wird. Dem Autor des *Reynke* ist daran gelegen, die Geistlichkeit in ein weniger kritisches Licht zu stellen. Die allgemein vertretene Auffassung zum Bearbeiter des *Reynke*, dieser habe eine stark religiös geprägte Haltung, wird durch diese Analyse bestätigt.[27] In diesem Zusammenhang ist bereits von einem seelsorgerischen Anliegen des *Reynke*-Autors gesprochen worden, das zu den religiös geprägten Erbauungsschriften im Lübeck des ausgehenden 15. Jahrhunderts passe.[28] Der Niederlandist J. Reynaert hat in seinen Forschungen zu ethischer Literatur zum Ende des 15. Jahrhunderts im Vergleich zum Anfang des 14. Jahrhunderts eine Verstärkung der christlichen Moralisierung festgestellt. Ältere ethische Texte würden um 1500 so rezipiert, daß christliche Kommentare hinzugefügt würden, mit anderen Worten eine 'Spiritualisierung' der weltlichen Ethik finde statt.[29] Die Entwicklung des *Reynaert*-Stoffes zum Ende des 15. Jahrhunderts in Lübeck paßt sehr gut in dieses Bild: sie repräsentiert eine Spiritualisierung der weltlichen Epik,[30] allerdings nicht in der Zeit, sondern von einem Ort zum anderen. Die moralisierenden Kommentare der niederländischen Quelle, die in der Antwerpener Ausgabe, die Gheraert Leeu zwischen 1487 und 1490 gedruckt hat, erhalten ist, werden im niederdeutschen Text der Mohnkopfdruckerei christlich volksmissionierend umgeschrieben.[31] Damit schließt der epische Text gut an bei den 30 bisher bekannten produzierten Texten der Mohnkopfdruckerei, die einen stark religiös-erbaulichen Charakter haben.[32]

Im Gegensatz zu der oben genannten Tendenz zur Reduktion physischer Gewalt fügt der niederdeutsche Bearbeiter eine gewalttätige Szene ein, die nicht in der niederländischen Vorlage vorkam: es handelt sich um die Vergewaltigung der Wölfin, nachdem Reynke Kater Hintze bei der Scheune des Pastors verlassen hat.[33] Die Einfügung zeigt, daß im niederdeutschen Epos sogar Gewalt hinzugefügt wird, wenn es gilt, den Fuchs deutlich als Prototyp des Bösen darzustellen.[34] Ein grundsätzlicher Unterschied zwischen der niederländischen und der deutschen Tradition besteht demnach darin, daß dort der Fuchs nicht direkt gewalttätig wird, hier aber der Fuchs von Anfang an durch die Vergewaltigung zum Straftäter wird. Ausführlich geht der Bearbeiter im 4. Punkt der Glosse bereits vorher ein auf die Vergewaltigung, die er als Sünde bezeichnet und die die Kette des Teufels nach dem Verrat und dem Diebstahl noch weiter verlängert hätte.[35] Während in der niederländischen Tradition sowohl in Text und Bild hauptsächlich die List des Fuchses betont wird, zeigt sich im *Reynke* deutlicher eine Kombination von Gewalt und List, die in der Glosse zum 14. Kapitel im 6. Punkt formuliert wird: "wo wol yd ere menynge nicht en was. dat se [die Wölfin, R.S.] myt ghe walt vnde myt lyst des vosses meer wart gheschendet."

Ein folgendes Beispiel ist die Ermordung des als Boten mitgeschickten Hasen. Sein Tod sowie die näheren Umstände werden in Text und Bild ausführlich dokumentiert. Nachdem Reynke durch das Versprechen, als Pilger nach Rom reisen zu wollen, unter Begleitung des Hasen Lampe und des Widder Bellyn den Hof König Nobels verlassen durfte, führt er seine Begleiter zu sich nach Hause, um den Hasen seiner Familie als Mahlzeit anbieten zu können. Die sich in der Höhle abspielende Ermordung wird in der Illustration vor der Höhle abgebildet (Abbildung 14).[36] Es folgt ein Holzschnitt, wie Reynke dem Widder die Tasche mit dem Hasenkopf umhängt und wie der Widder sich auf den Weg begibt (Abbildung 15), und ein Holzschnitt, der die gewaltsame Handlung des Fuchses durch den Kopf des Hasen beweist (Abbildung 16). Hier gibt es weder im Text noch in den Illustrationen nennenswerte Unterschiede zur niederländischen Tradition.

Dagegen sind im Zweikampf, dem letzten Beispiel zur physischen Gewalt, im niederdeutschen Epos einerseits Kürzungen gegenüber der niederländischen Tradition, andererseits Erweiterungen vorhanden. Die Kürzungen können auf Grund der Auslassung größerer, mehrerer Textabschnitte[37] weitestgehend als Ermüdungserscheinungen zum Ende des Epos hin gedeutet werden,[38] auch nimmt die Anzahl der Illustrationen ab bzw. der Abstand zwischen Illustrationen beträchtlich zu.[39] Erweiterungen betreffen in diesem Textabschnitt im *Reynke* hauptsächlich eine Hervorhebung der sexuell-sadistischen und fäkalischen Aspekte (R 6495-524, 6714-34).[40] Auch betont Reynke in einer hinzugefügten Rede gegenüber seiner Frau nicht nur, daß er zum Kanzler ernannt worden ist, sondern auch, daß der Wolf durch ihn seine Potenz verloren habe:

> Jk hebbe en ok halff gheblendet
> Dat to syn hele slechte gheschendet
> Jc hebbe en ghelubbet. ya alzo seer
> Der werlde wert he neen nutte meer
> Wy slogen kamp. ik helt en vnder
> Wert he ghesunt dat deyt my wunder
> (R 6813-8).

Das Duell, das zusammen mit der Vorbereitung dazu im *Reynke* doch immerhin etwa 450 Verse (R 6163-602) einnimmt, wird in nur einem Holzschnitt gezeigt, der auch nicht wiederholt wird (Abbildung 17).[41] Vielleicht hat man es hier mit Gründen der Platzersparnis und/oder Ermüdung zu tun.

Bei der Darstellung physischer Gewalt wird im *Reynke* ein Unterschied gemacht, wer die Gewalt ausführt. Während der Priester im *Reynke* wesentlich braver wird, findet eine Vereindeutigung der Fuchsgestalt zum unberechenbaren Gewalttäter statt, der seine List gewissenlos gebraucht.

Auch die zweite Art von Gewalt, die ich hier behandeln möchte, spielt meines Erachtens in der *Reynaert*-Epik eine sehr wichtige Rolle, die hier nur angeschnitten werden kann. Im öffentlichen Recht und in der älteren deutschen Rechtssprache bedeutet Gewalt auch Herrschaft, Regierung oder Herrschaftsgebiet. Der direkte Zusammenhang zwischen Gewalt und Recht drückt sich auch in dem Sprichwort "Gewalt geht vor Recht" aus, das auf Habakuk 1,3 zurückgeht und sich auch bei Luther findet. Die besprochenen *Reynaert*-Epen sind Darstellungen von Gerichtsverhandlungen, bei denen der Löwe mit dem Zepter in der Hand als König und Richter Recht sprechen soll. Viele der Abbildungen, in denen er vorkommt, zeigen ihn in dieser Haltung (Abbildung 18). Dieser Holzschnitt zeigt den Richter bei der Ausführung seines Amtes. Nachdem er sich die Beschuldigungen angehört hat, spricht er nach der Hinzuziehung des Rates das Urteil:

> Reynke de vos is schuldich des dodes
> Men schal en bynden vnde vangen
> Dar to by syneme halze vp hangen
> ...
> De konnynck dat ordel suluen aff sprack
> (R 1818-23).

Reynke ist als Verräter gefesselt. In der folgenden Illustration steht das Urteil der richterlichen Macht kurz vor der Ausführung (Abbildung 19). Reynke steht bereits auf der Leiter beim Galgen. Die folgende Darstellung zeigt dann meines Erachtens symptomatisch die Wende in der Erzählung. Reynke ist vom Galgen herabgestiegen und sitzt zwischen dem König und der Königin (Abbildung 20). Er ist nicht mehr gefesselt, der König hat kein Zepter in der Hand. Demonstriert wird ein geselliges Beisammensein und Gespräch der drei — der Fuchs hat dem Löwen seinen Kopf zugewendet — unter Ausschluß der anderen Tiere, die im Hintergrund zu sehen sind. Das Königspaar hat seine Macht als Herrscher und Richter endgültig in der folgenden Illustration abgegeben (Abbildung 21) und teilt diese jetzt mit Reynke, der sich, in der Mitte postiert, mit ihnen zusammen erhaben auf einem Podest niedergelassen hat. Die anderen Tiere befinden sich unterhalb. Symbolisch dargestellt wird der Abstieg vom Galgen und der Aufstieg zu einer Machtposition, auch wenn es sich in diesem Teil des Epos noch nicht um die Berufung zum Kanzler handelt.[42]

Dem Fuchs gelingt diese Statusveränderung auch durch den Einsatz von Sprache. Durch eine Kombination von List, die er im besonderen mit seiner Sprache anwendet, und Gewalt ist Reynke in der Lage, sich aus verschiedenen mißlichen Situationen zu befreien. Gerade diese Kombination betont der Niederdeutsche deutlicher als die niederländischen Texte. Im Zusammenhang mit der Vergewaltigungsszene spricht der Bearbeiter sie direkt aus, sie spielt natürlich eine entscheidende Rolle im Zweikampf, als der Fuchs zunächst durch kluges Reden den Wolf so weit bringt, daß dieser abgelenkt wird und der Fuchs dann in der Lage ist, sich zu befreien:

> De wyle de wulff teghen reynken sus sprack
> Reynke syne anderen hant vnder stack
> Deme wulue twysschen syne benen
> Vnde grep ene vaste. alze was syn menen
> By synen. ya. ik en segge nicht meer
> Reynke duwede ene vaste vnde seer
> De wulff reep vnde beghunde to hulen
> ...

Reynke knep. vnde toch. en. dat he schryede
So seer. dat ysegrym blod spyede
Van pynen brack eme vth syn sweet
Dar to he achter ok glyden leet
Reynke de den wulff seer hatet
Hadde en by synen bröderen ghevatet
Myt synen henden vnde tenen so vast
...
He knep en. he sloch. he kleyede. he beet
Jsegrym hulede. he reep. he scheet
He dreff also grod myszghebeer (R 6495-6523).

Auch hier erweitert der Niederdeutsche die Taten und Folgen der Gewalt (Hervorhebung). Durch diese Kombination von Sprache und physischer Gewalt besiegt Reynke den Wolf und erhält auch noch, wie eigentlich schon viel früher bildlich symbolisiert wird, die eigentliche Machtposition in der Gesellschaft.

Im Duden wird "Sprachgewalt" definiert als eine souveräne und wirkungsvolle Beherrschung der sprachlichen Ausdrucksmittel,"[43] im Van Dale als "meesterschap" über die Sprache.[44] Die *Reynaert*-Epen thematisieren meines Erachtens das Spannungsfeld von physischer Gewalt, Gewalt im Sinne von Kraft der Sprache und der Herrschafts- bzw. richterlichen Gewalt. Durch ihre körperliche Gewalt sind der Wolf und der Bär dem Fuchs überlegen, so daß dieser nur über seine Sprache und List in der Lage ist, physische Gewalt auszuüben, wie sich in der Vergewaltigungszene und im Zweikampf zeigt. Über den Einsatz dieser Mittel gelingt es ihm aber zugleich, in den Bereich der herrschaftlichen Gewalt vorzudringen. Der König ernennt ihn zum Reichsverweser. Der Fuchs hat damit am Ende auch den König und Richter in seiner Gewalt. Der Rechtsstaat hat aufgehört zu funktionieren oder, um es anders zu formulieren: die Gewalt der Sprache und damit Gewalt durch Sprache, ergänzt durch körperliche Gewalt, hat richterliche Gewalt ersetzt. Die einzige Hoffnung, die dem niederdeutschen Bearbeiter bleibt, drückt er selbst in der Glosse zum 11. Kapitel aus. Dort heißt es:

> wente Dauid heth ok de boezen gheyste vosse... De boezen ghan dorch ere boezheyt in de grunt der erden der vordomenisse vnde alle bedregers werden ghegeuen in de gewalt des swerdes. alze des scharpen ordels des lesten gherichtes. vnde entfangen deel vor ere valscheyt in den pynen. myt den vossen. den boezen geysten. (R 11/4).

Der Bearbeiter hofft also unter Verweis auf den Psalm Davids (63,10) auf die Gewalt des Schwertes beim letzten Urteil.

Notes

[1] Für einen Überblick über die Reynaert-Epik siehe Reynaerts historie — Reynke de vos. Gegenüberstellung aus den niederländischen Fassungen und des niederdeutschen Textes. Mit Kommentar hrsg. von Jan Goossens (Darmstadt: Wissenschaftliche Buchgesellschaft, 1983). Siehe auch Naar de letter 5. Tentoonstelling (29 september 1972 — 8 februari 1973). Hg. Instituut de Vooys (Utrecht: Instituut de Vooys, 1972).

[2] S. zur Übersicht der Textzeugen des *Van den vos Reynaerde* und des *Reynardus vulpes* jetzt Louk Engels, "*Reynardus vulpes* als bewerking van de *Reinaert*," in *Verraders en bruggenbouwers*, Hg. Paul Wackers (Amsterdam: Prometheus, 1996), 63-84, 282-291, hier 282.

[3] Amand Berteloot, "Zur Datierung von *Reynaerts historie*," in *Sprache in Vergangenheit und Gegenwart*, Hg. W. Brandt (Marburg: Hitzeroth, 1988), 26-31.

[4] Siehe hierzu Goossens, *Reynaerts historie — Reynke de vos*, wie Anmerkung 1, XII. Handschrift B enthält 20 Stellen (und nicht 22), die für Illustrationen vorgesehen waren, von denen jedoch keine erhalten ist. Nähere Informationen hierzu bei Jan Goossens, *Die Reynaert-Ikonographie* (Darmstadt: Wissenschaftliche Buchgesellschaft, 1983), 6-9.

[5] Für eine Interpretation von *Reynaerts historie* siehe die Dissertation von Paul Wackers, *De waarheid als leugen. Een interpretatie van Reynaerts historie* (Utrecht: HES, 1986).

[6] Eine diplomatische Ausgabe des niederländischen Prosadrucks in *Van den vos reynaerde. I. Teksten. Diplomatisch uitgegeven naar de bronnen vóór het jaar 1500 door W.Gs. Hellinga* (Zwolle: W.E. Tjeenk Willink, 1952); die englische Ausgabe von 1481 in *The History of Reynard the Fox.* Translated from the Dutch Original by William Caxton, Hg. Norman F. Blake (London: Oxford University Press, 1970); die englische Ausgabe von 1489 *The Historye of Reynard the Foxe (1489).* Facsimile-Ausgabe des in der Pepysian Library des Magdalene College erhaltenen Exemplars aus dem Jahre 1489, Hg. J.A.W. Bennett (London, 1976).

Beide Texte sind nicht illustriert und sollen im folgenden nicht berücksichtigt werden. Für einen genauen Vergleich der Prosainkunabeln mit *Reynaert II* siehe Rita Schlusemann, *Die hystorie van reynaert die vos und The history of reynard the fox. Die spätmittelalterlichen Prosabearbeitungen des Reynaert-Stoffes.* (Frankfurt, Bern, New York: Peter Lang, 1991).

[7] Sie wird auch bezeichnet als "Cambridge Fragments" (D, *Reynaert III, R III*).

[8] Zu den Rekonstruktionsversuchen siehe u.a. *Naar de letter*, wie Anmerkung 1, und Niclas Witton, "Die Vorlage des Reinke de Vos," in *Reynaert — Reynard — Reynke. Studien zu einem mittelalterlichen Tierepos*, Hg. Jan Goossens und

Timothy Sodmann (Köln/Wien: Böhlau, 1980), 1-159. Siehe auch Goossens, *Reynaert-Ikonographie*, wie Anmerkung 4, 9-10.

[9] Eine Facsimileausgabe des Textes in: *Reinke de vos, Lübeck 1498*. Nachdruck des einzig vollständig erhaltenen Exemplars in der Herzog August Bibliothek, Wolfenbüttel (32.14 Poet.). Mit einem Nachwort von Timothy Sodmann (Hamburg: Kötz, 1976). Eine Gegenüberstellung der niederländischen Tradition und des niederdeutschen Textes bietet Goossens, *Reynaerts historie — Reynke de vos*, wie Anmerkung 1, die auch Überlegungen zu den Zwischenstufen enthält.

[10] Siehe Goossens, *Reynaerts historie — Reynke de vos*, wie Anmerkung 1.

[11] Siehe u.a. *Duden. Das große Wörterbuch der deutschen Sprache in 6 Bden*. Hrsg. und bearbeitet vom wissenschaftlichen Rat und den Mitarbeitern der Dudenredaktion unter Leitung von Günther Drosdowski. Bd. 3 (Mannheim, Wien, Zürich: Bibliographisches Institut, 1977), 1027; *Brockhaus Enzyklopädie* in 20 Bden. Bd. 7 (Wiesbaden: Brockhaus, 1969), 265; *Langenscheidts Enzyklopädisches Wörterbuch Deutsch — Englisch* (Berlin: Langenscheidt, 1990), 687. Eine dritte Bedeutung, elementare Kraft von zwingender Wirkung wie Naturgewalt ist im Zusammenhang dieses Beitrags zu vernachlässigen.

[12] Siehe *Brockhaus*, wie Anmerkung 11, 265.

[13] Goossens, *Reynaert-Ikonographie*, wie Anmerkung 4.

[14] Goossens, *Reynaert-Ikonographie*, wie Anmerkung 4, bezeichnet nur 38 Illustrationen als sicher rekonstruiert, doch sollte man auch die spätere Studie Jan Goossens, *De gecastreerde neus. Taboes en hun verwerking in de geschiedenis van de Reinaert* (Leuven: Acco, 1988), hinzuziehen.

[15] Die Abbildungen sind folgenden Quellen entnommen: die Abbildungen aus *Reynaert III* und dem Wynkyn-de-Worde-Zyklus nach dem Anhang bei Kenneth Varty, "The Earliest Illustrated English Editions of *Reynard the Fox*," in Goossens/Sodmann, *Reynaert — Reynard- Reynke*, wie Anmerkung 7, 160-195; die Abbildungen aus dem *Reynke de vos* nach der Ausgabe von Sodmann, *Reinke de vos, Lübeck 1498*, wie Anmerkung 9.

[16] Die älteste überlieferte illustrierte englische Fassung ist zwar von Richard Pynson (1501-5), aber zwei Drucke von Wynkyn de Worde haben je eine Illustration, die aus einem noch älteren Reynaert-Illustrationszyklus des Wynkyn de Worde stammen muß, der aber nicht erhalten ist. Bei den Texten handelt es sich um *The Horse, The Shepe and the Ghoos* (1499 oder 1500) und *Bowge of Courte* (spätestens 1500). Mit anderen Worten, ein zeitlich vor Pynsons Druck entstandener *Reynard*-Druck Wynkyn de Wordes war mit einer Illustrationsserie ausgestattet, die nach den Illustrationen im niederländischen *Reynaert III* angefertigt worden war. Für eine ausführliche Darstellung der Problematik siehe Varty, "Earliest English Editions", wie Anmerkung 15, und Goossens, *Reynaert-Ikonographie*, wie Anmerkung 4, 11-14.

[17] Die Illustrationen, die direkt Gewalt zeigen, sind die Abbildungen nach dem Zyklus des Wynkyn de Worde mit folgenden Nummern bei Goossens, *Reynaert-*

Ikonographie: Abb. 10, 18, 22, 26, 36, 39, 53, 52, 80, 88, 95, 101, 107, 124, 131. Drohende Gewalt zeigen die Abbildungen Nr. 56, 115, 127. Es kommen also auch einige Illustrationen vor, die mehrere Arten von Gewalt zeigen, wie zum Beispiel auch Abbildung 5 (WdW 1), bei der im Vordergrund der Löwe seines Amtes waltet, während im Hintergrund der Fuchs einen Hasen oder ein Kaninchen bedroht (s.a. Abb. 22 und 36 bei Goossens, *Reynaert-Ikonographie*, wie Anmerkung 7). Diese habe ich dann nicht doppelt gezählt, sondern nach der Art der Gewalt im Bildvordergrund eingeteilt.

[18] In Abbildung 6 erteilt im unteren Teil der Dachs auf dem Weg zum Hof dem Fuchs die Absolution. Bei Goossens, *Reynaert-Ikonographie*, die Abbildungen mit den folgenden Nummern: 2, 6, 14, 48, 61, 65, 68, 72, 76, 84, 89, 99, 103, 111, 122, 133.

[19] Die Nummern 30, 34, 44, 92, 118, 120. Es kann sich hierbei natürlich nur um Annäherungswerte handeln, da der Zyklus nicht vollständig rekonstruiert werden konnte und es mindestens vier Fälle von Illustration bei Wynkyn de Worde gibt, die nicht eindeutig zu der Gruppe der dem *Reynaert III* zuzuordnenden Abbildungen gezählt werden können. S. Goossens, *Reynaert-Ikonographie*, wie Anmerkung 7, 20. Außerdem muß man nach dem Befund der Abbildungen in den Culemannschen Bruchstücken davon ausgehen — eine Illustration kommt doppelt vor (siehe Abbildung 3), — daß auch im *Reynaert III* verschiedene Abbildungen mehrfach abgedruckt wurden, so daß sich dann das Verhältnis der Abbildungen mit oder ohne Gewalt wiederum ändern würde. Die genannten Zahlen sollen vielmehr als grobe Indikation der Gewaltdarstellung verstanden werden.

[20] Direkte Gewalt in den *Reynke*-Illustrationen 7, 9, 10, 11, 17, 18, 19, 24, 48, 49, 52, 53, 54, 57, 58, 70, 71, 77, 78, 81, 82, 85, 87, 88; drohende Gewalt: 23, 25, 26, 31, 74, 79, 80, 86.

[21] Amtsgewalt die *Reynke*-Illustrationen 4, 5, 6, 8, 12, 21, 22, 27, 28, 29, 30, 32, 33, 37, 38, 39, 40, 41, 42, 43, 44, 45, 46, 47, 50, 51, 66, 67, 68, 72, 73, 83, 84.

[22] Zur Diskrepanz zwischen Wort und Tat in der mittelniederländischen *Reynaert*-Tradition siehe Paul Wackers, "Words and Deeds in the Middle Dutch Reynaert Stories," in *Medieval Dutch Literature in its European Context*, Hg. Erik Kooper (Cambridge: CUP, 1994), 131-147.

[23] Alle Verweise und Zitate aus *Reynaert III* und *Reynke de vos* nach der Ausgabe Goossens, *Reynaerts historie — Reynke de vos*, wie Anmerkung 1, Angabe der Verse; bei den Prosaglossen: zitiert nach dem Kapitel, nach welchem die Glosse erscheint, und dem Teil der Glosse, z.B. 14/3.

[24] Erst in der Glosse zum 14. Kapitel, die die beiden vorherigen Kapitel kommentiert, spricht der Autor im 7. Punkt davon, daß der Pastor eine Haushälterin und Kinder habe, was der christlichen Ehre unziemlich sei:

Dat seuende dat de poete hir menet andrepende den gheystlyken de buten der rechten gheystlyken regulen leuen. wente he secht hyr van deme papen dede hadde eyne meyerschen vnde kyndere dat vntemelyk is in der kristene ee. (R 14/7)

[25] Goossens, *Gecastreerde neus*, wie Anmerkung 14, 18.

[26] *Reinke de vos, Lübeck 1498*, wie Anmerkung 9, XI. Goossens, *Reynaert-Ikonographie*, wie Anmerkung 4, 21, hat offensichtlich nach längeren Erwägungen diese Illustration nicht in seine Rekonstruktion des Illustrationszyklus des *Reynaert III* aufgenommen. In einer späteren Publikation (Goossens, *Gecastreerde neus*, wie Anmerkung 14, 76-77) gibt er vier Gründe an für das Vorhandensein dieser Illustration in der *Reynaert III*-Tradition: 1. die englische Illustration hat mit einem Holzschnitt des niederdeutschen Zyklus von 1498 einen gemeinsamen Ursprung; 2. im Antwerpener Druck aus dem Jahre 1566 wird eine Szene abgebildet, die der dargestellten unmittelbar vorangeht. Martinet und Julocke schlagen bereits auf den Kater ein, als der "Mann des Hauses" erst angelaufen kommt; 3. der niederdeutsche Holzschnitt ist dreimal abgedruckt; 4. die englische Reihe zeigt zwei verschiedene Phasen aus Tibaerts Abenteuer mit dem gleichen Hintergrund. Das könne am besten erklärt werden, wenn auch die Quelle vergleichbar wäre.

[27] Siehe Jan Goossens, *De gecastreerde neus*, wie Anmerkung 14.

[28] W. Kämpfer, Studien zu den gedruckten mittelniederdeutschen Plenarien. Ein Beitrag zur Entstehungsgeschichte spätmittelalterlicher Erbauungsliteratur (Münster, Köln: Böhlau 1954).

[29] Jo Reynaert, "Profaan-ethische literatuur in het Middelnederlands: enkele grote lijnen," in *Grote lijnen. Syntheses over Middelnederlandse letterkunde*, Hg. Wim van Anrooij, Frits P. van Oostrom (Amsterdam: Prometheus, 1995), 99-116, 200-205, im besonderen 110-111. Siehe auch: *Wat is wijsheid? Lekenethiek in den Middelnederlandse letterkunde*, Hg. Jo Reynaert (Amsterdam: Prometheus, 1994).

[30] Siehe jetzt auch Paul Wackers, "*Reynke de vos*: lekenethiek tussen verhaal en intellectuele reflectie," in: *Die spätmittelalterliche Rezeption niederländischer Literatur im deutschen Sprachgebiet*, Hg. Rita Schlusemann und Paul Wackers (Amsterdam: Rodopi, 1997), 197-211, der anhand einer Analyse der Glossen zu vergleichbaren Ergebnissen kommt.

[31] Man vergleiche die einzig verwertbare Glosse in den Fragmenten aus Cambridge zu Kapitel 18 mit der entsprechenden deutlich erweiterten Glosse in R zu Kapitel 17, s. Goossens, *Reynaerts historie — Reynke de vos*, siehe Anmerkung 1, 118 und 133-135.

[32] Siehe Tim Sodmann, "Die Druckerei mit den drei Mohnköpfen," in *Franco-Saxonica. Münstersche Studien zur niederländischen und niederdeutschen Philologie. Jan Goossens zum 60. Geburtstag*, Hg. Robert Damme, Loek Geeraedts, Gunter Müller, Robert Peters (Neumünster: Karl Wacholtz Verlag, 1990), 343-360.

[33] Diese Szene wird nicht illustriert, denn auch die Vorlage besaß keine Abbildung dazu.

[34] Goossens, *Gecastreerde neus*, wie Anmerkung 14, 19.

[35] Dat veerde dat hir de lerer menet is. beroem. wente nicht allene was reynke to freden in velen sunden men he makede de keden syner boszheyt lenger vnde vaster dar myt. dat he syk syner sunde begunde to beromen. sunderlyken der ebrekerye myt der wulfynnen (R 14/4).

Es sei sogar noch schlimmer, daß er sich dieser Sünde rühme, indem er die Kinder der Wölfin als seine Stiefkinder bezeichne. Auf diese Weise würde er die Kette seiner Bosheit noch länger und fester machen. Durch Todsünden würde die Kette länger, mit der ihn zuletzt der Teufel mit dem ewigen Leid festbinden würde (Goossens, *Reynaerts historie — Reynke de vos*, wie Anmerkung 1, 14/3).

[36] Hier ist im *Reynaert III*-Zyklus deutlich zu erkennen, daß Reynaert vor seiner Höhle steht, während man im *Reynke* auch annehmen könnte, es handele sich um einen Berg.

[37] So werden zum Beispiel der erste und der dritte Teil von Rukenaus Rede weggelassen (B 4746-4805, 5067-5210) und auch ein Teil des Zweikampfes zwischen Reynaert und Isegrim (C 7036-7067). Zur Übersicht der ausgelassenen Stellen siehe Goossens, *Reynaerts historie — Reynke de vos*, wie Anmerkung 1, 536-546.

[38] Goossens, *Gecastreerde neus*, wie Anmerkung 14, 55.

[39] *Reynke* hat insgesamt 242 Folios. Zwischen dem Ende des 2. und dem Beginn des 3. Buches gibt es 40 Seiten ohne Abbildung (zwischen f. 143v und 163v), im 3. Buch u.a. 19 (zwischen 164r und 173v), 16 (173v und 181v), 18 (194r und 203r, 212v und 221v). Vor Folio 143v dagegen beträgt der Abstand bis auf zwei Ausnahmen (zwischen f. 87v und 92v sowie 94v und 102r) höchstens acht Seiten.

[40] Goossens, *Gecastreerde neus*, wie Anmerkung 14, 56.

[41] Im niederländischen *Reynaert* sind es sogar beinahe 700 Verse (B 6442-7445). Auch im *Reynaert III* zeigte offensichtlich nur ein Holzschnitt den Zweikampf (Abb. 131 bei Goossens, *Reynaert-Ikonographie*, wie Anmerkung 4).

[42] Diese ist übrigens in keiner der Illustrationen abgebildet, wie überhaupt der zweite Prozeßteil deutlich weniger Aufmerksamkeit und Würdigung in den Illustrationen erhält.

[43] *Duden*, wie Anmerkung 11, Bd. 6, 2455.

[44] *Van Dale Groot Woordenboek Duits — Nederlands* (Utrecht/Antwerpen: Van Dale Lexicografie, 1985), 1201.

Rijksuniversiteit Groningen

Inventing the Middle Ages as Recreation: the Testimony of the Chapbook

Albrecht Classen

One of the best arguments in favor of literary studies today might be that the texts under investigation tell us as much about people and their imaginations, feelings, fears, aspirations, and desires as any specific sociological, psychological, economic, or historical document might do. A literary narrative represents a projection of an individual's concept of him/herself and of past and future developments of society, it mirrors social conditions and religious experiences, and examines types of behavior and individual decisions.[1] Literary history, on the other hand, charts the progressive evolution of those projections and attempts to establish large-scale categories of cultural periods or epochs.[2] These projections are not necessarily "realities" in the narrow sense of the word, but rather imaginations. Nevertheless, the literary expressions are the stuff people think and dream about and are thus "real" as well. Literature can either look forward (utopia) or backward (nostalgia), but either way a poet explores the paradigmatic conditions of human life, not necessarily the concrete physical aspects of life. Of course, some writers try to do just that by presenting a critical analysis of contemporary existence. But even such endeavors reflect on the mental horizon and inform us about the individual's or society's norms, ideals, value system, aspirations, and projections.[3]

These general observations apply to classical as well as medieval literature, or, for that matter, to all periods in literary history. To illuminate this fascinating point, the subsequent investigations are focused on late-medieval prose romances, which were mostly printed and found a wide distribution. In German these romances are known as "Volksbücher," or chapbooks, although both terms erroneously imply certain low-class cultural attributes and make the representatives of this genre smack like 'trivial literature.'[4]

Several sociological and technological criteria need to be considered to understand the historical emergence of the "Volksbuch" and to correct the false impression that early-modern prose novels do not belong to the literature of the intellectual elite. First, since the middle of the fifteenth- century German prose novels, similarly as in France and England, began, as a general trend, to replace verse romances, which can be explained by changing attitudes among the audience and a transformation of the social composition of this audience (increasingly the readers and listeners lived in cities and received a solid education). When Johann Gutenberg invented the printing press in ca. 1455/56, he provided the technical means for a massive book production which quickly affected all areas of literature, and so also the "Volksbuch." All these factors joined hands to support the development of this genre which soon turned into the tremendous success story of the fifteenth- and sixteenth-centuries book markets.[5] The term "influential" is correct only insofar as the "Volksbücher" seem to have exerted the largest popularity among all literary genres and found the widest distribution among readers of all social classes.[6] Whether these chapbooks also constitute the most sophisticated and the most brilliant literary documents of their time is an entirely different and very subjective question and does not really concern us here.[7] We know that initially many of these so-called "Volksbücher" were written for and by members of the upper aristocracy, but soon, once the printers got hold of them, these texts also found many enthusiasts among the lower classes. In this sense the use of the term "Volksbuch" (people's book) would be fully justified not before the middle of the sixteenth century. Nevertheless, for historical reasons and because of a lack of convincing alternatives, Germanists have more or less accepted the label for a wide variety of these texts.[8]

The sheer number of German chapbooks is staggering, and many still await their critical examination. Others have been reedited and studied by modern scholarship and do no longer require detailed introductions. It is the purpose of the subsequent paper to investigate the extent to which some of these texts reflect early-modern mentality and what they might tell us about fifteenth- and sixteenth-century readers' attitude about their own past.[9] It does not matter what criteria we utilize to determine the closure of the Middle Ages and the coming of the Renaissance, whether we refer to the discovery of the printing press (ca. 1455), to the fall of Constantinople (1453), to the discovery of America (1492), or maybe even to the use of gunpowder in warfare.[10] In any event, by about 1500 or so medieval Europe was no longer the same as it was hundred years before. Modernity, in its multiple and global facets, had become a fact of life, even if the political structures had not yet changed that much, even if medieval economy had given way to early forms of capitalism, and even if the Church continued to dominate society as the most powerful religious institution (the Reformation was not going to change this structure all that much!).[11]

People continued to live at the same locations and hardly moved, they believed in the central, though by now only nominal, role of the German Emperor, and did not basically change their attitudes towards foreigners and non-believers because of the discovery of America, for instance. To be sure, a new form of social mobility in favor of the burgher class was discernible, and so was the steady decline of chivalry and the aristocratic life style. And finally, anticlericalism reached an unforeseen pitch, certainly closely coupled with a new form of individualism and eventually leading to the Reformation.[12] As much as these various aspects have been studied by scholars from many different disciplines, as little have we examined how people reacted to those changes and what impact these changes had on their ideas, their value system, and their overall framework of mind in terms of self-perception and orientation towards the past.[13] A close reading of two of the perhaps best-known Geman chapbooks will provide us with crucial data to gain some understanding of late-medieval mentality, particularly of a pervasive form of nostalgia for the past because these texts were widely disseminated and appealed to large sections of fifteenth- and sixteenth-century audiences.[14]

The first example is Thüring von Ringoltingen's *Melusine* from 1456, the second is the anonymous *Fortunatus* from 1509.[15] Whereas *Melusine* is a literary translation of a French source and also finds many parallels in medieval tales in Latin,[16] *Fortunatus* appears to be more or less an original contribution, although the narrative motif can be found in earlier sources as well, such as in the *Gesta Romanorum* (Ch. 120).[17] Both chapbooks, as different as they are in their outlook and overall value system, share important aspects pertaining to the perception of traditional medieval society. Both contain, in comparison with the courtly romance composed in verse, disturbing and new narrative elements such as magic, fairies as half-humans, money as a new means of social interaction, social mobility of the main characters, and their tragic destiny as a consequence of this upward move on the social ladder.[18] Moreover, both prose novels offer perspectives of an idyllic past and also project utopian visions of a new society, but in both cases neither the backward trend nor the aspiring for new forms of human society are realized, instead fail in face of social realities which clash with the protagonists' dreams.[19] Finally, both authors obviously endeavor to cope with profound tensions impacting their societies, and thus reflect the birth pangs of a new world emerging from the slowly collapsing ruins of the Middle Ages.[20]

In a nutshell, Thüring's *Melusine* describes the history of Reymund's and Melusine's marriage, the latter being half a fairy or snake, half human. She meets him in a very difficult situation and rescues him with the help of an intelligent strategy with which a deadly accident and his responsibility can be covered up. Soon after they marry, and she builds many castles and churches and thus lays the foundation for a powerful noble family. All her children are marked, however, by signs of their mother's magical origin. The tragedy begins when Reymund, instigated first by his brother, later by crimes committed by one of his own sons, searches after his wife's true nature and then reveals it to the public, although she had forbidden him to inquire about her whereabouts on Saturdays. Because of his transgression she has, to Reymund's chagrin, to leave both him and her children, and even human society at large. Melusine's sons make several attempts later to win new glory, but they quickly reveal their shortcomings of character and also fail.

The anonymous *Fortunatus* also deals with the sudden rise of the protagonist from a low social status to that of a very wealthy and politically influential person. Fortunatus meets the goddess Fortuna and receives from her a money pouch which never becomes empty. With these new means he travels all over the known world of medieval Europe, but repeatedly encounters grave dangers for his life. Once having returned home, he can marry an impoverished count's daughter and thus rise into the ranks of nobility. Twelve years later Fortunatus goes on another trip, this time concentrating on the eastern parts of the Mediterranean and Asia. At his life's end he writes a book about his experiences and hands it over to his two sons. These two young men quickly prove to be failures and are not able to utilize the magic objects to their advantage. Whereas the older one, Ampedo, simply wants to stay home and does not develop as a character, the other one, Andolosia, uses the money pouch to travel and see the world as his father did. In his case, however, he does not gain knowledge of the world, but instead strives to win public esteem and recognition as a nouveau-riche aristocrat. In the end the money does not help him avoid being kidnapped and murdered, whereas Ampedo dies out of grief over his brother's disappearance.

Little wonder that both novels attracted a wide readership and thus stimulated many new prints far into the sixteenth and seventeenth centuries. In cheap paper editions these "Volksbücher" even entered the book markets of the nineteenth century, as Goethe and many of the Romanticists testify.[21] The authors provide exciting literary material, such as travel adventures, social conflict, murder, exchanges with beings of a demonic race, rape, incest, magical objects such as Fortunatus's purse and travel cap. They also portray the courtly life style, discuss the problems of social mobility, and explore various aspects of courtly love. What concerns me here is, however, not how and why Thüring von Ringoltingen, for example, introduces the notion of mystical beings, half human and half snake, as meaningful as it might be. Likewise, my interest does not focus on Fortunatus's and Andolosia's travels, a significant aspect of the early modern exploration of the world. Instead the particular question here raised is what both authors, representative for their audience and many contemporary writers, have to say about the Middle Ages, that is, how they viewed the social structure of their own past and how they evaluated life at large within a late-medieval context. It is obvious, though, that part of the "Volksbuch's" success rested in its deliberately conservative orientation and strategic ignorance of social, economic, cultural, and religious realities.

Thüring's prologue provides many clues as to the author's mental horizon, to his literary taste and his conviction regarding his audience's expectations. The first sentence offers several significant markers which set the tone for the entire romance to follow. Thüring calls his work an "abenteürlich buch" (11) in which he will tell us about this mystical figure Melusine who was both a "merfaÿm" (mermaid) and human being, that is, "ein geborne künigin" (born as a queen). Since he needs to explain how this combination is possible, he points out that Melusine came from "Awalon," which is the classical reference to the medieval utopia, the distant island of all of Arthurian romances where only the few chosen may go, a sort of a secular paradise of mythical dimensions.[22]

Although Melusine is portrayed as only half human, her descendents nevertheless gained great repute within medieval society: "Es seind auch von ir kommen gar grosse mæchtige geschlecht" (a large and powerful family derived from her), that is, they gained the ranks of kings, dukes, counts, and knights. Since Melusine's descendants are still living, Thüring claims the veracity of his tale, which probably had served, in its Latin and French sources, as a legitimizing document for the historical family of Lusignan.[23] Moreover, the author discusses the "monstrous" appearance of the female character again, stressing that despite her origin all her children were normal human beings and entered the ranks of medieval aristocracy. In other words, for Thüring there is nothing more noteworthy to report but those events relating to the upper social classes of the feudal world. Consequently the account of Melusine and Reymund is set within aristocratic society.

The initial tragedy that will bring together Reymund and Melusine is brought about by a boar attacking Reymund's lord, Count Emmerich. Trying to defend him, Reymund inadvertently kills the Count and is near desperation, when Melusine intervenes and offers him her help, then her hand, and finally access to all her powers. As decisive strategy to establish his own family with sufficient lands, she recommends him to request a fiefdom from his new lord, Count Bertram, of such a size as a hind can cover — an old fairy tale motif. The narrator does not express any concern about salary, payment, or any other form of monetary exchange for service, instead Reymund relies on the traditional concept of vassalage which is rewarded with land according to the principles of feudal society (30). As the motif implies, the hind is cut into long strips which, knotted together, make up such a long rope that Reymund indeed gains a large piece of land with the help of this device.

The subsequent wedding with its religious ceremonies and public celebrations in a tournament are closely modelled after traditional courtly romances (39-42). The same applies to the formal interactions between the freshly married couple and the other members of the court, be it the various types of courtly entertainment such as dancing, singing, and reciting (42), be it the handing out of gifts by the host Melusine to demonstrate the extent of her wealth (43f.). The literary framework for these events is directly borrowed from the medieval world, as the courtiers sing "hofflieder [ ] oder ander [ ] gesanng" (42; courtly songs and other songs). Melusine's major effort to establish her family consists in a major building program, which entails, primarily the erection of a strong castle along with the necessary defense components such as trenches and towers.[24] After the completion of this castle, named after Melusine, that is, Lusinia, the narrator points out that she had a series of smaller castles built, and also a monastery; but there is no word about urban dwellings, about burghers, about the craftsmen's lodging or any other reference to characteristic features of life in the fifteenth century.

Thüring himself lived in Bern the life of a city aristocrat, but did little in economic and political terms to improve the newly acquired social standing of his father. His only major contribution was the "translation" of *Melusine* from the French into German, and with this work provided his audience with a literary platform for their nostalgic projections of an aristocratic past.[25]

Melusine's sons participate in crusades against the heathens (51 ff.), they help the daughters of kings to escape from oppression by unwelcome suitors, and marry them in turn (59ff.), and they participate in wars between Christian kings and thus win the hands of their daughters (65ff.). Whereas all these events belong to the medieval past, the narrator includes, at least for once, a reference to the attack by the Turks against the European heartlands (77ff.), although the battle is fought, again, with nothing but the traditional weapons characteristic of chivalry: "Vnd besunder Reinhart von Lusinÿen / der ein starcker ritter vnd vnuerzagt was / der schlug der heÿden gar vil ze tod / vnd verwundet ir on zal / vnd zerspielt gar manchem seinen helme mit seiner manlichen ritterlichen hand" (81; especially Reinhart of Lusinien, a strong and courageous knight who killed many heathens and wounded scores, and split many helmets with his manly and chivalric hand).

The killing of a giant is another borrowed element from courtly romances and plays a significant role in the life of Geoffroÿ. Both the giant's appearance and equipment in the vein of Hercules with his club (101),[26] and Geoffroÿ's exclusive resort to his sword could have been directly lifted from any Arthurian tale and demonstrate the extent to which the literary tradition continued to play a major role even at a time when technology and social conditions had entirely transformed reality and thus had made this fictional account a pure product of the narrator's fantasy. Actually, Geoffroÿ deliberately searches for a giant because he needs this fairy tale figure as a means to confirm his chivalric virtues and his personal accomplishments, making him worthy of leading his country: "dann er wolt in mit streit besteen" (101; because he wanted to face him in a fight). After the giant has been overcome, the hero blows in his horn to inform the population about his accomplishment, reminiscent of Roland's blowing a horn to call Charlemagne (*Song of Roland*) and Erec's blowing in a horn to signal his victory over Mabonagrin (Hartmann von Aue, *Erec*). Immediately following this achievement he is called upon to free another land from the threat by an equally dangerous giant, and he agrees to accept this challenge as well because his calling as a knight is to win honor ("hehen preiß," 106), to protect widows and orphans ("wittiben vnd weysen zu beschirmen," 106), and to fight heathens ("alle vngelaubigen zuertreiben," 106).

Chaucer's "Knight's Tale," composed shortly before 1400, also presents this traditional picture of knighthood, yet the Middle English author explicitly takes his audience into antiquity where the narrative motif of Fortune's fickleness can easily be developed since the historical framework allows for the discussion of the timeless motif.[27] Chaucer, like many other of his contemporary writers, consciously turned to the past for his literary material to examine human nature, and thus followed a standard practice of his time. But his "Knight's Tale" does not represent a nostalgic view of the past, instead it utilizes the past as a fictional stage for the discussion of human characteristics and the effects of fortune.

Thüring von Ringoltingen, on the other hand, is primarily enraptured by the fantastic elements to be found in medieval romances and incorporates them as entertaining pieces in his prose novel without achieving a specific learning effect. The adventure in itself, and the excitement derived from chivalric experiences, dominate this tale, as the fantastic element gains overriding control. Geoffroÿ finds, for example, his long deceased grandfather who is enshrined in a glass coffin in the mountain "Awelon," another reference to the utopian idea of the grail romance tradition (139). He also has to fight against more giants and takes one of them, whom he had killed, with him on a cart and displays him in public, thus functionalizing him as a museum piece taken from the medieval world (145). In other words, as much as Thüring's audience is given access to a past long gone through his literary projection, the same process is also taking place within the narrative. Geoffroÿ does not only kill the giant, he also puts an end to medieval mythology and, although not aware to himself, to his own existence as a knight. The narrator still follows his destiny for several chapters in which he kills his uncle in revenge for his instigating Reymund to spy on his wife on a Saturday, and then rebuilds the monastery which he had burnt down earlier out of anger over his younger brother's decision to join the order. As soon as this narrative thread is completed, Thüring simply breaks off and turns to the life of two of Melusine's other sons, first Ditterich (157), and then Gÿs (158ff.). They also fail to accomplish their goals as knights and become victims of greed and lust.

Thüring frankly admits in his epilogue that his novel was conceived in the tradition of courtly romances, yet he believes that he outdid those models: "Vnd mich beduncket aller der hÿstorien keine fromder noch abenteẅ rlicher zesein dann dise" (176; it seems that no other account was stranger or more adventurous than this one). Thüring knows of and lists some of the classical romances such as *Iwein*, *Tristan*, and *Parzival*, but he claims that his text is superior to all of them because the protagonists belong to a family still living, which allegedly attributes *Melusine*, as a late-medieval version of the twelfth and thirteenth-century courtly romances, the character of a true account: "für ein warheit" (176).

As far as the social-historical context is concerned, the Bernese author successfully projects a fantasy product that is hardly connected with reality. The more Thüring attempts to increase the dramatic and adventurous elements in his tale, the more he reveals his true interest in a poetic dream which offers literary entertainment, psychological excitement through the elements of magic and horror, and a highly effective framework for public recreation.[28] This recreation is possible not only because the audience is confronted with images of a past long gone, but also because enigmatic features dominate the tale and invite the reader to pursue his or her own fantasy with the given literary material. Finally, although Melusine and her sons are the descendents of a mythical world and do not fully belong to the human race, the difference between these protagonists and the readers/ listeners is progressively reduced, that is, the "monsters" turn into benevolent and sympathetic figures. This process of familiarization begins with Melusine and her two sisters, who make valiant attempts to return into human society through marriage, after her mother Persina had placed a curse on them for the abduction of their father, King Helmas, into the mountain "Awalon." Melusine is the most successful of all three sisters and almost would have been redeemed if Reymund would not have been tempted by his brother to transgress the taboo. Meliora and Palantine have to wait for one of Melusine's sons to rescue them from their remote places of banishment, but are never graced with this fortune. The reason is the same as with Melusine: their nephews prove to be foolish and irresponsible and thus lose both their prizes and destroy the women's hope for a rescue.

All of Melusine's sons are marked by birth defects, be it a huge tooth, or be it a lion's claw growing in the face of one of them. Some of their features are very fearsome and grotesque, yet the narrator emphasizes that they all would later gain a great reputation as knights and thus would be well liked by their people (48f.). Geoffroÿ initially behaves very rashly, displays brutality, and monstrous strength, and this both against enemies of humanity (giants, 101ff., e.g.) and against his own brother Fraÿmund (107-109). Later, however, he learns self-discipline and begins to understand his family history, which convinces him to reform and to do penance for his crimes (155ff.). Once Geoffroÿ has died, his brother Ditterich steps into his place, then the latter also dies and bequeathes his lands to his children (173). Their history, in turn, is also briefly mentioned, until the next generations have arrived who are contemporaries of the Bernese author. Within only one final chapter the mythical past is quickly overcome and fixated in the narrative account.

Instead of being living testimonies to the dangerous world of chivalry, Thüring's audience is allowed to relax and to enjoy the fantasy world of the Middle Ages as a distant past which has survived only in the ornamental decoration of coats of arms (176) and in this prose narrative. The monsters have disappeared, and with them the heroes who could and actually did eliminate them.[29] At a time when modern technological inventions, the now dominant role of money, the centralization of government, and the global exploration made great strides, Thüring's tale exerted a surprising appeal and offered a unique form of literary recreation; the Middle Ages just had passed, and yet in *Melusine* a dramatized and highly fictionalized image of that age emerged to the great delight of a large cross-section of early modern audiences.

In how far do these observations also apply to the anonymous *Fortunatus*?[30] The frontispiece illustration in the Munich print from 1509 (München Bayrische Staatsbibliothek, Rar. 480) shows the ponderous Fortunatus sitting on a throne-like furniture, holding the pouch in his lap and taking some money out of it, looking meditatively into the distance, while his two sons play at his feet. Is it indeed, as John Van Cleve has claimed, "Fortunatus's conscious decision to secure wealth for himself because it is the most significant determinant of the quality of human existence"?[31] Does this text really represent the modern age with its early forms of capitalistic interaction? Has the author indeed composed a vehement literary manifesto against the evil influence which money exerts on the individual, or can we see this text, similarly as Thüring von Ringoltingen's *Melusine*, as a typical reflection of the recreative fictionalization process of the Middle Ages? The vast popularity of *Fortunatus* both in Germany and all over Europe far into the seventeenth and even eighteenth centuries demonstrates its great significance for the early modern book markets and the audiences.[32] The question is whether this popularity was due to the modern thematics of the narrative (money), or whether this "Volksbuch" was in conformity with traditional reader expectations and combined them with innovative elements.

Without any doubt the intriguing experience by the protagonist is indeed the fortunate acquisition of endless amounts of money. With the help of the magical purse Fortunatus can purchase anything he desires, and thus can win all pleasures of this world. The situation turns out to be highly problematic, though, because from the very moment when he utilizes the money he also faces dangerous, even life-threatening forms of jealousy and envy (434-436). In fact, Fortunatus had learned, even before he received the gift of the miraculous purse, that money and wealth are easily subject to being stolen and thus put the owner in a highly hazardous position. The young man had worked for a Florentine merchant in London, but neither the money nor the political safeguards given by the king protected the merchant and his entire family from being hanged simply because of suspicion that they might have stolen royal jewels (419ff.). Fortunatus escapes the same destiny by sheer luck, and not because of personal skill or particular support from a powerful member of the royal court. In many respects this "Volksbuch" portrays the impact of fortune and illustrates the consequences of the proverbial "wheel of fortune," as Boethius had discussed it in his *De consolatione philosophiae*.

After Fortuna's wheel finally has turned for the protagonist and has given him the magical purse, he is immediately tossed from his elevated position and must fear for his life because his newly acquired rank and reputation seem unjustified according to feudal class structures. Consequently he learns to hide his wealth and to act according to his traditional station in life (437). In particular, Fortunatus utilizes the money moderately and secretly to equip himself for a long journey that will take him over almost the entire European continent (440ff.).

Before he embarks on this trip, the narrator includes a brief comment which highlights the peculiar function of the "Volksbücher" as recreational reading material. The protagonist has arrived in Nantes and observes a big public celebration in preparation of the king's arrival. The narrator interjects the statement that in the present time members of the lower classes tend to spend outrageous amounts of money for their festivities and falsely pretend to belong to the higher class: "so wissen sy nit wie sy gnug kostlichait treiben sollen" (437; they do not know how to use their wealth appropriately). By contrast, the Duke of Nantes receives praise by the narrator because he stages his festivities in line with his station (437), which illustrates the author's subtle intentions with his narrative, which is to project a conservative, but idealized image of the world of the aristocracy and thus to entertain his audience with a nostalgic view of what the past was like.

This is not to ignore the new role which money and rational discourse play in this "Volksbuch," because even the extensive travels across Europe require, as Fortunatus's future companion Lüpoldus informs him, large amounts of cash ("fast vil bar gelt," 441).[33] But the protagonist has not acquired his wealth by typical means of early-modern capitalistic business, which certainly was one of the major economic factors triggering the transformation of the Middle Ages. Instead, the money has come to him in a miraculous fashion and simply provides him with the necessary means to follow similar travel routes as most late-medieval travellers had taken.[34] These travels are a combination of pilgrimage and modern touring of exciting places. They include an exploration of the alleged access to the Purgatory (443ff.) in Ireland, and a visit of Rome, then even of Jerusalem. Fortunatus does not go beyond the traditional range of medieval travellers, though, in fact, he is the medieval traveller per se who reiterates and reconfirms the medieval expectation of informative and religious travels.[35] Accordingly, Fortunatus keeps his promise to the goddess Fortuna and every month endows a poor bride with sufficient money to ensure a successful marriage (454f). But he also experiences great dangers again that teach him how little money can effect to defend a just cause because he has to flee Constantinople after his companion Lüpoldus has killed their host while he was trying to steal from him (458ff.).

By the early sixteenth century, if not already much earlier, money had become the most important factor in the life of most people, which certainly undermined traditional feudal society on a large scale.[36] Fortunatus, on the other hand, demonstrates the evil effects of money and operates with his new-found means only in a very conservative, and especially morally and ethically positive manner as long as he is travelling. As soon as he settles back home in Cyprus, however, he becomes a victim of his magical purse and builds, similarly as Melusine did for Reymund and herself, a splendid castle and then marries into an impoverished noble family. Here we find in him the social aspirant who climbs into a higher social class, although his origin had been rather humble ("purger," 388, 'burgher'), whereas now his goals are to enter the aristocratic circles himself. The future in-laws oppose his wooing their daughter because they do not trust money as the sole basis for a family: "er hat weder land noch leüt / hatt er dann vil bar gelt gehebt oder noch / so secht ir wol er hat vil gelts verpauen das kainen nutz tregt / so mag er daz ander auch onwerden vnd zu armot kommen" (467, he has neither land nor people, and although he has had much money or still owns much, you see that he used it all for his building which does not bring profit. He can lose all the rest as well and become poor again).

The negative evaluation of money seems, at first, not well grounded, as Fortunatus does win the princess's hand and can establish a family with her. He even gains possession of the estate of another impoverished count and can thus satisfy the mother-in-law's worry about his lack of "land noch leüt" (476, neither land nor people). With his bride and the new estate Fortunatus turns into a traditional land-holding nobleman without the official title.

The wedding takes place in the same traditional fashion as in Thüring von Ringoltingen's novel *Melusine*, that is with chivalric festivities and celebrations which even the king of Cyprus attends and who thus legitimizes Fortunatus's rise into the highest ranks of society (479). As much as the purse represents a magical gift from Fortuna, as much does Fortunatus's fortune rest on the circumstances of his life. As the wheel had turned, so he had risen to the heights of society. His life is that of a fairy tale figure, and as such he does not represent a threat to feudal society. In particular, he does not, because of his rise on the social ladder, undermine the traditional class structure, even though the narrative incorporates, considerably more than other prose novels or chapbooks from that time, references to the class of burghers (merchants) and the purchasing power of money.[37] Significantly, Fortunatus operates primarily as a wealthy and independent person, not as a merchant, and in this sense can indeed dare to align himself with nobility.

Already his father had displayed a behavior typical of an aristocrat, enjoying his life with "stechen turnieren / vil knecht / costliche roß / rait dem künig zu hoff" (389; jousting, hiring servants, buying expensive horses, going to the king's court), although this lead to his financial ruin: "vnd kam also zu armut" (389, he became poor). In a way Fortunatus and his own sons will experience the same destiny, though on a different level and over a longer time span. Certainly, he is able to secure the economic situation of his family, but only by means of the magic purse. He never acquires, however, a noble title, and does not establish a family business. Instead Fortunatus spends his time with aristocratic entertainent for the first twelve years of his married life, when boredom sets in and he prepares his next travels (482). Both his successful return and a peaceful conclusion of his life are the result of his reasonable manners and wise handling of money, and the narrator idealizes, indeed, the nobility of his character and his understanding of wisdom as the highest virtue in this life (504-507).

The narrative does not maintain this idyllic character, however, and reveals, in the second part, how condemnable social mobility can be. After his son Andolosia's many attempts to gain, even more than his father, recognition at the international courts, both brothers die without heirs, and thus the family disappears from the annals because both sons are defeated in their efforts and demonstrate that money alone cannot sustain nobility (579).

Fortunatus had recognized from very early on what a dramatic role fortune might play in the life of an individuum (e.g. destiny of the Florentine merchant in London, 419ff.). Obviously he tried to learn from this early realization, but still has to confront many other situations which endanger his life because of his inexplicable wealth and high public esteem. Fear for his life and the lure of money give him gradually sufficient maturity to handle the magic purse wisely and to the benefit of all people involved. He even copies his experiences down in a book which he bequeathes to his sons (463, 507), but neither his teachings (506f.) nor the written instructions will eventually prevent disaster falling upon the sons. Contrary to his advice, they split the two magical objects (purse and hat) among them, and whereas Ampedo stays at home, Andolosia joins the various royal courts and aspires for the highest social rank. With his endless wealth he outshines even counts and barons, creating hatred among them, and thus bringing doom upon himself (568). Consequently, all the hopes which Fortunatus's inheritance had instilled in them fail because they lack the wisdom their father had acquired and face even worse enemies than he.

In the epilogue we hear the narrator's voice again, warning against the temptations of money and worldly riches:

> hette der iung Fortunatus im walde betrachtlichen Weißhait / für den seckel der reichtumb / von der junckfrawen des gelücks erwølt vnnd begert / sy wære ym auch mitt hauffen gegeben worden / den selben schatz ym nyemandt hett mügen enpfieren. (579)
>
> [If the young Fortunatus had chosen wisdom instead of the money purse from the virgin of fortune, he would have gained it in large measure. This treasure nobody would have been able to take away from him.]

The narrative's message is loud and clear. Wisdom is to be preferred over money, since it provides endless happiness and richness in the spiritual sense of the word (580).[38] But how does this popular narrative inform us in terms of audience expectations and attitude towards the past? Does this "Volksbuch" also provide reading enjoyment derived from medieval nostalgia? Would the contemporary audience have rejected its own world in consequence of this text's teaching, or was it a mirror of their social reality?

Significantly, neither Fortunatus nor Andolosia advocate the life of merchants or of any other kind of urban profession. On the contrary, they utilize the magical power handed over to them by the goddess Fortuna, to secure their social move upwards toward the highest position in life, equal to kings and dukes, for instance. In other words, this "Volksbuch" aims at a projection of past lifestyles by idealizing the world of aristocracy that did not have to worry about money and only strove toward the realization of its ethical and moral ideals. Fortunatus, as different as he seems to be compared with such figures as Wolfram's Parzival, Gottfried's Tristan, Konrad von Würzburg's Engelhard, or Chaucer's protagonists in his *Canterbury Tales*, moves in the same direction and idealizes the life style of late-medieval aristocracy and belittles that of the burghers and merchants.

Social and economic historians would quickly point out that these literary projections have little in common with the realities of other, non-literary documents created during the late Middle Ages. In other words, neither Thüring's *Melusine* nor the anonymous *Fortunatus* instruct us about the actual economic and social conditions during that period. On the contrary, they tell us, in more or less precise terms, what was going on in people's mind when they were reading either of these two "Volksbücher," what they hoped to find in these popular texts, and what they were supposed to make of them once they found them in printed form.

Fortunatus always lives the life of a nobleman and interacts primarily with members of the aristocracy, except for the one-time service for the Florentine merchant Jeronimus Roberti in London (408ff.). After his travels he settles in Cyprus and marries into a count's family, and enjoys the king's friendship. Andolosia spends his time with members of the British court and aspires to rise even above his father in social terms, which, of course, leads to his downfall as well. At the end the King of Cyprus takes over the palace that Fortunatus had built because there are no heirs (579). In other words, this "Volksbuch" also presents a very traditional image of society in which the urban class has certainly gained a strong foothold, but leads, in narrative terms, only a shadowy existence. In particular, those who miraculously acquire huge amounts of money are eventually defeated and disappear from the narrative horizon, thereby reconfirming nobility's social preponderance at least in literary terms.

The anonymous author presents the tale as a moral exhortation to pay heed to wisdom and to prize it much higher than money: "erkyeß Weißhait für reichtumb" (580; choose wisdom over wealth).[39] But this lesson finds its confirmation primarily for those who believe in the tradition of feudal society and search for a literary projection of the medieval past. It also served as a fantasy for those who desired fictional recreation in a world where money rules, but where the memory of a different social system was still alive.[40]

Both literary functions were significant enough to overrule the potential need among sixteenth- and seventeenth-century audiences for a critical analysis of their own reality. Although *Fortunatus* certainly views the role of money in a negative light, the dominant narrative thrust aimed for the idealization of the courtly world. The large number of prints far into the 1590s indicates that, like in the case of Thüring's *Melusine*, the fascination with the Middle Ages had not abated and was actually on the rise, the further away the readers/listeners of this "Volksbuch" were removed from

away the readers/listeners of this "Volksbuch" were removed from that past.[41] In a way, *Fortunatus* and *Melusine*, among other German prose novels, provided a literary forum for the development of an early-modern form of "Romanticism" a long time before the actual Romanticists discovered the Middle Ages in the 1790s.[42] Gradually, more realistic reflections of contemporary reality came into sixteenth-century literature, such as *Till Eulenspiegel*, *Claus Narr*, *Der Pfaffe vom Kalenberg*, and *Wendunmuth*, but in many representative examples of this kind of popular literature the authors continued to idealize aristocracy, feudalism, and the concept of chivalry, such as in *Hug Schapler*, *Pontus und Sidonia*, *Kaiser Octavian*, and *Euriolus und Lucretia*.

The outcome for literary history was that the Middle Ages turned into a fantasy product which could be utilized both for recreation and didacticism. This is not to doubt that many of the "Volksbücher" easily can be approached as reflections of late-medieval or early-modern mentality and literary echoes of the "Alltag" (everyday life),[43] but a major objective of these texts certainly was to idealize the past and project an idyllic image of the world of nobility. Emperor Maximilian I of Hapsburg was, as many members of the upper ranks of the aristocracy were, one of the leading proponents of this nostalgic movement at the turn of the fifteenth to the sixteenth century, and he gained for himself the endearing title "the last knight." In his own verse romances *Theuerdank* and *Weisskunig* he still relied on verse for his composition, but his thematic orientation was the same as in the prose novels discussed above.[44]

Notes

[1] This question is thoroughly discussed by Terry Eagleton, *Literary Theory. An Introduction* (Oxford: Basil Blackwell, 1983).

[2] Good examples for the various approaches and understanding of literature can be found in Wilfred L.Guerin et al., *A Handbook of Critical Approaches to Literature*. Third Edition (New York-Oxford: Oxford University Press, 1992).

[3] The underlying theoretical paradigm for this understanding of literature is best expressed by "Mentalitätsgeschichte" or "histoire de la mentalité;" see, for a summary of the current trends in this scholarly approach, Peter Dinzelbacher, ed., *Europäische Mentalitätsgeschichte. Hauptthemen in Einzeldarstellungen*. Kröners Taschenausgabe 469 (Stuttgart: Kröner, 1993), xv-xxxvii; from a historian's point of view, see the now classical study by Carlo Ginzburg, *The Cheese and the Worms. The Cosmos of a Sixteenth-Century Miller*. Trans. by John and Anne Tedeschi (Baltimore: The Johns Hopkins University Press, 1980/1992).

[4] Francis Brévart, "Spätmittelalterliche Trivialliteratur. Methodologische Überlegungen zu ihrer Bestimmung und Erforschung," *Archiv für das Studium der*

neueren Sprachen und Literaturen 224/139, 1 (1987):14-33; Peter Nusser, *Trivialliteratur*. Sammlung Metzler 262 (Stuttgart: Metzler, 1991); Bradford K. Mudge, "The Man with Two Brains: Gothic Novels, Popular Culture, Literary History," *Publications of the Modern Language Association* 107, 1 (1992), 92-104.

[5] For the historical and sociological background of the "Volksbuch," see my monograph *The German Volksbuch. A Critical History of a Late-Medieval Genre*. Studies in German Language and Literature 15 (Lewiston-Queenston-Lampeter: Edwin Mellen Press, 1995).

[6] Bodo Gotzkowsky, "Volksbücher". Prosaromane, Renaissancenovellen, Versdichtungen und Schwankbücher. Bibliographie der deutschen Drucke. Part 1: Drucke des 15. und 16. Jahrhunderts (Baden-Baden: Koerner, 1991).

[7] See Xenja von Ertzdorff, *Romane und Novellen des 15. und 16. Jahrhunderts in Deutschland* (Darmstadt: Wissenschaftliche Buchgesellschaft, 1989); see also my article "Late Middle High German, Renaissance, and Reformation," *A Concise History of German Literature to 1900*. Ed. Kim Vivian. Studies in German Literature, Linguistics, and Culture (Columbia, S.C.: Camden House, 1992), 58-90.

[8] Jan-Dirk Müller, "Volksbuch/Prosaroman im 15./16. Jahrhundert - Perspektiven der Forschung," *Internationales Archiv für Sozialgeschichte der Literatur*. 1. Sonderheft: *Forschungsreferate* (Tübingen: Niemeyer, 1985), 1-128.

[9] For a similar approach, but with the focus on different text examples, see Werner Röcke, "Mentalitätsgeschichte und Literarisierung historischer Erfahrung im antiken und mittelalterlichen Apollonius-Roman," *Geschichte als Literatur. Formen und Grenzen der Repräsentation von Vergangenheit*. Eds. Hartmut Eggert, Ulrich Profitlich, Klaus R. Scherpe (Stuttgart: Metzler, 1990), 91-103.

[10] Among the many studies on this topic, I refer to: Erich Meuthen, *Das 15. Jahrhundert*. Oldenbourg Grundriß der Geschichte 9 (Munich-Vienna: Oldenbourg, 1980); Stephan Skalweit, *Der Beginn der Neuzeit, Epochengrenze und Epochenbegriff*. Erträge der Forschung 178 (Darmstadt: Wissenschaftliche Buchgesellschaft, 1982); Barbara A. Hanawalt, "Centuries of Transition: England in the Later Middle Ages," *Recent Views on British History. Essays on Historical Writing since 1966*, ed. Richard Schlatter (New Brunswick: Rutgers University Press, 1984), 35-69; Ferdinand Seibt and W. Eberhard, eds., *Europa, 1400. Die Krise des Spätmittelalters* (Stuttgart: Klett-Cotta, 1984); Peter Moraw, *Von offener Verfassung zu gestalteter Verdichtung. Das Reich im späten Mittelalter 1250-1490*. Propyläen Geschichte Deutschlands 3 (Berlin: Propyläen, 1985); Ernst Schubert, *Einführung in die Grundprobleme der deutschen Geschichte im Spätmittelalter*. Grundprobleme der deutschen Geschichte (Darmstadt: Wissenschaftliche Buchgesellschaft, 1992).

[11] In many respects Johan Huizinga's seminal study The Waning of the Middle Ages. A Study of the Forms of Life, Thought and Art in France and the Netherlands in the XIVth and XVth Centuries (Garden City, N.Y.: Doubleday

Anchor Books, 1954) still represents the best summary of the cultural transition leading away from the Middle Ages into the modern age; with respect to the concept of "modernity," see the individual contributions in the volume Innovation und Originalität. Eds. Walter Haug and Burghart Wachinger. Fortuna Vitrea 9 (Tübingen: Niemeyer, 1993). For a discussion of the modernity of the Middle Ages, see Modernes Mittelalter. Neue Bilder einer populären Epoche. Ed. Joachim Heinzle (Frankfurt a.M.: Insel, 1994).

[12] See, for instance, William Keffigan and Gordon Braden, *The Idea of the Renaissance* (Baltimore-London: The Johns Hopkins University Press, 1989); Edelgard E. DuBruck, *Aspects of Fifteenth Century Society in the German Carnival Comedies. Speculum Hominis*. Studies in German Language and Literature 13 (Lewiston-Queenston-Lampeter: The Edwin Mellen Press, 1993); *Anticlericalism in Late Medieval and Early Modern Europe*. Eds. Peter A. Dykema and Heiko A. Oberman. Studies in Medieval and Reformation Thought LI (Leiden-New York-Cologne: Brill, 1993).

[13] Preliminary attempts were made by Klaus Thieme, "Petrarcas Masken (Der Einzelne vor der Tradition)," Horst Wenzel, ed., *Typus und Individualität im Mittelalter*. Forschungen zur Geschichte der älteren deutschen Literatur, 4 (Munich: Fink, 1983), 141-163; Douglas Gray, ed., *The Oxford Book of Late Medieval Verse and Prose*. With a Note on Grammar and Spelling in the Fifteenth Century by Norman Davis (Oxford: Clarendon Press, 1985); see also A.C. Spearing, *Medieval to Renaissance in English Poetry* (Cambridge: Cambridge University Press, 1985); Thomas Cramer, ed., *Wege in die Neuzeit*. Forschungen zur Geschichte der älteren deutschen Literatur, 8 (Munich: Fink, 1988); James F. Poag/Thomas C. Fox, eds., *Entzauberung der Welt. Deutsche Literatur 1200-1500* (Tübingen: Francke, 1989); Albrecht Classen, *Die autobiographische Lyrik des europäischen Spätmittelalters, Studien zu....* Amsterdamer Publikationen zur Sprache und Literatur 91 (Amsterdam-Atlanta: Rodopi, 1991).

[14] Concerning questions of literacy and book markets, see Rudolf Hirsch, Printing, Selling and Reading 1450-1550 (Wiesbaden: Harrassowitz, 1967); Rolf Engelsing, Analphabetentum und Lektüre. Zur Sozialgeschichte des Lesers in Deutschland zwischen feudaler und industrieller Gesellschaft (Stuttgart: Metzler, 1973); ibid., Der Bürger als Leser: Lesergeschichte in Deutschland 1500-1800 (Stuttgart: Metzler, 1974); Michael Giesecke, *Der Buchdruck in der frühen Neuzeit. Eine historische Fallstudie über die Durchsetzung neuer Informations- und Kommunikationstechnologien* (Frankfurt a.M.: Suhrkamp, 1990).

[15] For bibliographical and historical information about both texts, see my *The German Volksbuch*, 1995, 141 ff., and 163ff.

[16] Bea Lundt, "Schwestern der Melusine im 12. Jahrhundert: Aufbruchs-Phantasie und Beziehungsvielfalt bei Marie de France, Walter Map und Gervasius von Tilbury," B.L., ed., *Auf der Suche nach der Frau im Mittelalter. Fragen, Quellen, Antworten* (Munich: Fink, 1991), 233-253.

[17] See Hans-Jörg Uther, "Fortunatus," *Enzyklopädie des Märchens*. Ed. Rolf Wilhelm Brednich et al. Vol. 5 (Berlin-New York: de Gruyter, 1987), 7-14, especially 9ff.

[18] Regarding of the new weight which money enjoyed in the post-medieval world, see, although problematic in many respects, John Van Cleve, *The Problem of Wealth in the Literature of Luther's Germany* (Columbia, S.C.: Camden House, 1991).

[19] Walter Haug, "Weisheit, Reichtum und Glück. Über mittelalterliche und neuzeitliche Ästhetik," *Philologie als Kulturwissenschaft. Festschrift Karl Stackmann*, ed. Ludger Grenzmann et al. (Göttingen: Vandenhoeck & Ruprecht, 1987), 21-37.

[20] Anna Mühlherr, *'Melusine' und 'Fortunatus'. Verrätselter und verweigerter Sinn*. Fortuna vitrea 10 (Tübingen: Niemeyer, 1993), propounds that both novels do not make any sense, are expressions of insurmountable ambivalences of the narrative thrust, and thus stand in for the enigmatic nature of the magical world. Such a theory sounds very intriguing, but quickly reveals its complete lack of tenability. Mühlherr argues that these novels cannot be interpreted and thus indicates her own failure to comprehend the significance of the textual messages. Neither of these "Volksbücher" represents a simple folksy tale; instead they are highly complex narratives reflecting their society, as I will argue in the subsequent part of my investigation.

[21] Both for the critical text edition and for extensive commentaries on both chapbooks, see *Romane des 15. und 16. Jahrhunderts. Nach den Erstdrucken mit sämtlichen Holzschnitten*. Ed. Jan-Dirk Müller. Bibliothek der frühen Neuzeit I (Frankfurt a.M.: Deutscher Klassiker Verlag, 1990). All quotes are taken from this edition.

[22] Geoffrey Ashe, "Avalon," *The Arthurian Encyclopedia*. Norris J. Lacy, Ed. (New York-London: Garland, 1986), 32-35.

[23] Xenja von Ertzdorff, "Die Fee als Ahnfrau. Zur 'Melusine' des Thüring von Ringoltingen," *Festschrift für Hans Eggers zum 65. Geburtstag*. Ed. Herbert Backes. Beiträge 94. Sonderheft (Tübingen: Niemeyer, 1972), 428-457.

[24] The illustrator makes a clear attempt to copy medieval fortification architecture; and the guard in front of the main gate holds a lance as his only weapon, 46.

[25] Hans-Gert Roloff, Stilstudien zur Prosa des 15. Jahrhunderts. Die Melusine des Thüring von Ringoltingen (Cologne: Böhlau, 1970), 94, 194, et passim.

[26] William C. McDonald, "The Fool-Stick: Concerning Tristan's Club in the German Eilhart Tradition," *Euphorion* 82, 2 (1988), 127-49, especially 142ff.

[27] See: *The Works of Geoffrey Chaucer*. Ed. F.N. Robinson. Second Edition (Oxford-London-Melboume: Oxford University Press, 1957) 25ff.

[28] See Glending Olson, Literature as Recreation in the Later Middle Ages (Ithaca: New Cornell University Press, 1982); in my study on Oswald von Wolkenstein, (Zur Rezeption norditalienischer Kultur des Trecento im Werk Oswalds von

Wolkenstein (1376/77-1455). Göppinger Arbeiten zur Germanistik 471 [Göppingen: Kümmerle, 1987],) I reached a very similar conclusion about these erotic love songs.

[29] Albrecht Classen, "Monsters, Devils, Giants, and other Creatures: 'The Other' in Medieval Narratives and Epics, with Special Emphasis on Middle High German Literature," *Canon and Canon Transgression in Medieval German Literature*, ed. A. Classen. Göppinger Arbeiten zur Germanistik 573 (Göppingen: Kümmerle, 1993), 83-121; see also Mary B. Campbell, *The Witness and the Other World. Exotic European Travel Writing, 400-1600* (Ithaca-London: Cornell University Press, 1988), 165ff.; Jeffrey Jerome Cohen, "The Limits of Knowing: Monsters and the Regulation of Medieval Popular Culture," *Medieval Folklore* III (1994):1-37, especially 35-37.

[30] See: *Romane des 15. und 16. Jahrhunderts*, ed. J.-D. Müller, 1990. See his extensive introductory remarks and bibliographical material on this novel.

[31] John Van Cleve, *The Problem of Wealth*, 1991, 97; see also Dieter Kartschoke, "Weisheit oder Reichtum? Zum Volksbuch von Fortunatus und seinen Söhnen," *Literatur im Feudalismus*. Literaturwissenschaft und Sozialwissenschaften 5 (Stuttgart: Metzler, 1975), 213-259; Walter Raitz, *"Fortunatus". Text und Geschichte*. Modellanalysen zur deutschen Literatur 14 (Munich: Fink, 1984).

[32] Albrecht Classen, "Die Weltwirkung des *Fortunatus*. Eine komparatistische Studie," *Fabula* 35, 3/4 (1994):209-225; id., "Die Rezeption des deutschen *Fortunatus* in England - Thomas Dekker und seine Dramatisierung des 'Volksbuchs'," *Neohelicon* XXI/1 (1995), 289-311.

[33] Wolfgang Haubrichs, "Glück und Ratio im 'Fortunatus'. Der Begriff des Glücks zwischen Magie und städtischer Ökonomie an der Schwelle der Neuzeit," *Zeitschrift für Literaturwissenschaft und Linguistik* 50 (1983), 28-47.

[34] Marjatta Wis, "Zum deutschen Fortunatus. Die mittelalterlichen Pilger als Erweiterer des Weltbildes," *Neuphilologische Mitteilungen* 63 (1962):5-55; F. Hassauer, "Volkssprachliche Reiseliteratur — Faszination des Reisens und räumlicher Ordo," *La littérature historiographique des origines à 1500*. GRMLA 11, 1 (Heidelberg: Winter, 1986), 259-283; Peter Moraw, "Reisen im europäischen Spätmittelalter im Licht der neueren historischen Forschung," *Reisen und Reiseliteratur im Mittelalter und in der Frühen Neuzeit*, ed. Xenja von Ertzdorff and Dieter Neukirch. Chloe 13 (Amsterdam-Atlanta: Rodopi, 1992), 113-139.

[35] Anne Simon, "The Fortunatus Volksbuch in the Light of Later Medieval Travel Literature," *Fifteenth-Century Studies* 12 (1987),175-186; her analysis does not provide new insights and only summarizes the basic facts of Fortunatus's travels.

[36] Bernd Sprenger, *Das Geld der Deutschen. Geldgeschichte Deutschlands von den Anfängen bis zur Gegenwart* (Paderborn-Munich-et al.: Schöningh, 1991), 102ff.; for a more global view of the rise of the early modern world, based on a market system and the cities, see George Huppert, *After the Black Death. A Social*

History of Early Modern Europe. Interdisciplinary Studies in History (Bloomington: Indiana University Press, 1986), especially 41ff.

[37] In a previous study, "Mentalitäts- und Alltagsgeschichte der deutschen Frühzeit: *Fortunatus*," *Monatshefte* 86, 1 (1994): 22-44, I argued that the anonymous author indicated "daß zu seiner Zeit Vertreter des gehobenen Bürgertums die Dominanz auf dem Finanzmarkt und in der Geschäftswelt übernommen haben, Fortunatus also keinesfalls als ein Einzelfall anzusehen wäre," 31. In light of the conclusions of the present investigation I would like to rewrite part of my previous statement. Both *Melusine* and *Fortunatus* seem to serve more as correctives to current social conditions than as reflections of their time and society. Insofar as *Fortunatus* indicates the audience's general desire to return to the medieval past, this narrative expresses a nostalgic perception of earlier times and a sharp criticism of the modern world in which money plays, after all, a major role.

[38] For a further investigation of this topic, particularly in comparative terms, see Hannes Kästner, *Fortunatus, Peregrinator Mundi. Welterfahrung und Selbsterkenntnis im ersten deutschen Prosaroman der Neuzeit*. Rombach Wissenschaft - Reihe Litterae (Freiburg i. Br.: Rombach, 1990).

[39] D. Kartschoke, "Weisheit oder Reichtum?," 1975; Hannes Kästner, *Fortunatus*, 1990; Hans-Jürgen Bachorski, *Geld und soziale Identität im "Fortunatus". Studien zur literarischen Bewältigung frühbürgerlicher Widersprüche*. Göppinger Arbeiten zur Germanistik 376 (Göppingen: Kümmerle, 1983).

[40] P. Rohrmann, "The Central Role of Money in the Chapbook *Fortunatus*," *Neophilologus* 59 (1975):262-272.

[41] B. Gotzkowsky, *"Volksbücher"*, 1991, 420-436.

[42] Ulrich Müller, "Das Nachleben der mittelalterlichen Stoffe," *Epische Stoffe des Mittelalters*. Eds. Volker Mertens and U. Müller. Kröners Taschenausgabe 483 (Stuttgart: Kröner, 1984), 424-448.

[43] Stephanie Beate Pafenberg, *"Torechte Gemueter": Character and Culture in the Chapbook "Fortunatus" (1509) (Cyprus)*. Ph.D. Diss. St. Louis, MO, Washington University, 1992; A. Classen, "Mentalitäts- und Alltagsgeschichte," 1994.

[44] See, for instance, Kaiser Maximilian I., *Theuerdank*, 1517. With an epilogue by Horst Appuhn (Dortmund: Harenberg, 1979).

University of Arizona

The Current State of Research on Late-Medieval Drama: 1996-97. Survey, Bibliography, and Reviews

Edelgard E. DuBruck

This article is a regular feature of Fifteenth-Century Studies. *Our intent was to catalogue, survey, and assess scholarship on the staging and textual configuration of dramatic presentations in the late Middle Ages. Like all such dated material this assessment remains incomplete. We shall therefore include 1997 again in the next listing [vol. 26]. Our readers are encouraged to bring new items to our attention, including their own work.*

Again, a number of studies were devoted to general considerations of the European medieval stage. Michel Bitot edited an essay collection in honor of André Lascombes on *Medieval and Renaissance Culture* with several studies on the theater, while Meg Twycross brought out the papers from the Sixth Triennial Colloquium of the International Society for the Study of Medieval Theatre, with one third devoted to English, and the remainder to continental plays (French, German, Spanish, Dutch, Danish, and Bohemian), mostly Shrovetide drama. In his turn, Francesc Massip published the papers of the Seventh Colloquium of the SITM (Société Internationale pour l'Étude du Théâtre Médiéval). Stephen K. Wright pondered "The Betrayer's Art," translation of medieval drama for modern readers, and Clifford Davidson contributed an excellent collection of articles on *Fools and Folly* (reviewed subsequently). Dunbar H. Ogden continued to investigate set pieces and special effects in European liturgical drama, such as lights, thunder, an earthquake, appearances and disappearances, special effigies, a furnace, flying machines—and writing on a wall. Much of this technology may also be discussed in Davidson's *Technology, Guilds, & Early English Drama* (to be reviewed in 1998).

The French and German religious theater was the topic of Edelgard E. DuBruck's article on the "Late-Medieval Theater of Salvation in Continental Europe," a plenary presentation at the Third International Congress on Fifteenth-Century Studies in Kaprun, 1995. Some of her conclusions were that the passion stage was exemplary, that attendance at the plays procured indulgences, that this drama justified Christ's sacrifice and urged imitation of his life. Salvation theater was a European phenomenon, but direct influences of French texts on those of other countries are difficult to prove (while possible).

General studies on English drama were composed by Douglas, Greenfield, Stokes (and Alexander), and Tiner. Krystan V. Douglas published a *Guide to British Drama Explication, I (Beginnings to 1640)*, while

Peter Greenfield wrote on dramatic records (Southampton) and contributed a census of medieval drama. James Stokes and Robert J. Alexander investigated the drama records of Somerset and Bath.

Eleven titles concerned English religious drama. Diana Wyatt considered the Pater Noster Plays in Beverley, Lincoln, and York, comparing them to Corpus Christi drama. Precise information was hard to come by, since the texts are lacking. Allegorical moralities in pageants of thirteen stations, these plays were influenced by similar drama in the Low Countries in the fifteenth century; here, the Seven Deadly Sins were related, one by one, to the petitions of the Pater Noster. A collection of articles on *English Parish Drama* by Alexandra Johnston and Wim Hüsken is reviewed below, as well as Elizabeth A. Witt's *Contrary Marys in Medieval English and French Drama*.We list here also Gary D. Schmidt's work, *The Iconography of the Mouth of Hell*because of the constant use of this major accessory on the mystery stage. While Schmidt did not explore the cultural background of this image of damnation, his book offered an interesting collection of appearances.

Pamela King and Meg Twycross pondered the York *Doomsday* project, while Peter Happé investigated the "Devil's Languages in Some Corpus Christi Plays." From Davidson's pen came "Saints in Play: English Theater and Saints' Lives," and Colin Counsell studied the *Castle of Perseverance* for spatiality and gaze. While the ultimate vantage point for gazing would be the bird's eye view, Counsell explained, a human's perspective remains incomplete. Anne L. Brannen undertook an interpretation of the Bassingbourn St. George Play, whereas Sarah Beckwith treated the aspect of memory in the York Corpus Christi cycle. The staging of the *Castle* was compared to that of *l'Omme Pecheur* by Peter Happé, reminding us that much information on the staging of morality plays can be inferred from that of mysteries. The two plays involved scaffolds on different levels which could be redesignated, i.e., serve on different days, for hell, paradise or the towers of a city. Unfortunately, in this article, Rey-Flaud's famous *Cercle magique* was consistently misspelt.

Eight entries concerned English secular theater. Happé published *John Bale* and "Spectacle in Bale and Heywood." "Two Fools from Sussex" were presented by Louis Cameron, and Sarah Carpenter wrote on "Women and Carnival Masking." "Household Business" was the subject of Viviana Comensoli, the York Mercers' *Lewent Brede* had Twycross's interest, and Christ Humphrey studied seasonal drama and local politics in Norwich. For A. Leslie Harris, the parody of chivalric romance in the *Tournament of Tottenham* was unquestionable at a time when the kings exercized increasing control over tournaments. This mock-epic (staged in modern times) has been compared successfully to Wittenwiler's *Ring*. Also,

Glenn Wright investigated parody, satire, and genre of the *Tournament.* The Cornish *Ordinalia* were studied for place names and political patronage (Gloria Betcher), and Evelyn Newlyn pondered the Middle Cornish interlude for genre and tradition. These interludes lacked structural symmetry. There were three characters: a female matchmaker offered a bride to a man and gave her practical advice. Traces of these plays were found on borough accounts and a charter fragment. From all the above it is clear that again in this year contributions on English drama were plentiful, and that most of them had excellent quality.

Studies on the French comic stage have been enriched by the tenth volume of André Tissier's *Recueil de farces* reviewed below. Nina Glaser investigated "Jenin, fils de rien," from Tissier's volume three (see my article in Jean-Claude Aubailly et al., eds. *Et c'est la fin*) and came to conclusions similar to mine, i.e., that this is a "serious" farce,—but she went one step further. In an emblem of all writing, the seemingly fatherless charlatan (the anonymous author?) revealed his radical alienation from the world in a gesture which abolished what it created. Jelle Koopmans's *Théâtre des exclus* will be reviewed in 1998. Alan E. Knight wrote on "Theatre and the Socialisation of Youth in Lille."

As for French religious theater, Paula Giuliani translated Arnoul Gréban's *Mystery of the Passion. The Third Day* (reviewed subsequently). Records of early French drama were studied by Graham A. Runnalls, who also attempted a classification of passion mysteries, establishing nine families of which the most complicated was that of Arras-Gréban-Michel-Valenciennes. Especially interesting were the manuscripts of texts meant for presentation.

Unfortunately, entries on German medieval theater were missing, except for a Swiss Last Judgement Play (Chur) investigated by Hansjürgen Linke, who corrected several editor misreadings of the manuscript in the "Teufeleien" (devils' scenes). We shall discuss as yet Robert Aylett's *Translations of the Carnival Comedies of Hans Sachs* (1994) in 1998. On Dutch theater we have Femke Kramer's "Rederijkers on Stage: A Closer Look at 'Metatheatrical' Sources," and Elsa Strietman's discussion of *The Temptation of Christ in the Desert*. Terry Gunnell's *Origins of Drama in Scandinavia* was reviewed by Martin W. Walsh, who discovered unprovable assumptions (e.g., that the Eddic poems were dramatized) and much circumstantial evidence. The title of the monograph is misleading, and there are leaps in time and logic, but in spite of the scantness of information Gunnell's was an intriguing attempt, perhaps just an introduction to the subject.

James Wyatt Cook and Barbara Collier Cook brought out an edition and translation of *Antonia Pulci. Florentine Drama for Convent and Festi-*

val which will be reviewed in 1998. Female interpretation was studied by Dympna Callaghan, and Nerida Newbigin examined art and drama in fifteenth-c. Florence. While a number of Florentine plays did not reach print, a vast corpus of manuscripts contained *feste*, *edifici*, *rappresentazioni*, and *storie*. Moralities and saints' plays were performed by boys' fraternities, and N. depicted the influence of art on the stage. Were Predella panels the equivalent of pulp fiction? she asks. The question of theater iconography remains truly intriguing.

*Witchcraft in Celestina*was published by Dorothy S. Severin in 1995, and, simultaneously, Richard Castells issued *Calisto's Dream and the Celestinesque Tradition*, proving that once Calisto wakes up, he sinks from the spiritual level of desire to the physical plane, a correct observation according to Severin (and us), Castells's reviewer. On Catalonia, Max Harris has contributed "A Catalan Corpus Christi Play: The Martyrdom of St. Sebastian with the Hobby Horses and the Turks," an interesting reminder of the battles between Catalans and Moors ("Turks"). The play originated in Lleida in 1150, then was staged in Zaragoza in c. 1300. The fifteenth-c. representations in the Barcelona Corpus Christi pageant resembled a passion play, with the Christian riders carrying a frame of wood and paper, with neck and head of a horse. St. Sebastian, martyred in Rome in c. 288, was said to have been born near Barcelona. Finally, Massip penned an article on the political stage in the service of Catalan kings.

BIBLIOGRAPHY

Beckwith, Sarah. "The Present of Past Things: The *York Corpus Christi Cycle* as a Contemporary Theater of Memory,"*Journal of Medieval and Early Modern Studies*, 26 (1996), 355-79.

Betcher, Gloria. "Place Names and Political Patronage and the Cornish *Ordinalia*," *Research Opportunities in Renaissance Drama*, 35 (1996), 111-31.

Bitot, Michel, ed. "*Diverse toyes mengled*": *Essays on Medieval and Renaissance Culture in Honour of André Lascombes*. Tours: Université François Rabelais, 1996.

Brannen, Anne L. "Parish Accounts in Context: Interpreting the Bassingbourn St. George Play," *Research Opportunities in Renaissance Drama*, 35 (1996), 55-72.

Callaghan, Dympna. "The Castrato's Song. Female Interpretation on the Early Modern Stage," *Journal of Medieval and Early Modern Studies*, 26 (1996), 321-53.

Cameron, Louis. "Two Fools from Sussex," *REED Newsletter*, 21 (1996), 16-18.

Carpenter, Sarah. "Women and Carnival Masking," *REED Newsletter*, 21 (1996), 9-16.

Castells, Richard. *Calisto's Dream and the Celestinesque Tradition: A Re-reading of Celestina*. Chapel Hill: University of North Carolina Press, 1995.

Comensoli, Viviana. *"Household Business": Domestic Plays and Early Modern England*. Toronto: University of Toronto Press, 1996.

Cook, James Wyatt, and Barbara Collier Cook, eds. and tr. *Antonia Pulci. Florentine Drama for Convent and Festival*. Chicago: University of Chicago Press, 1996.

Counsell, Colin. "Traversing the Known: Spatiality and the Gaze in Pre- and Post-Renaissance Theatre," *Journal of Dramatic Theory and Criticism*, 11 (1996), 19-33.

Davidson, Clifford, ed. *Fools and Folly*. Kalamazoo: Medieval Institute Publications, 1996.

—. "Saints in Play: English Theater and Saints' Lives," in*Saints: Studies in Hagiography*, ed. Sandro Sticca. Binghamton: MRTS, 1996. 145-60.

—. *Technology, Guilds, & Early English Drama*. Kalamazoo: Medieval Institute Publications, 1996.

Douglas, Krystan V. *Guide to British Drama Explication, I: Beginnings to 1640*. New York: G.K. Hall, 1996.

DuBruck, Edelgard E. "The Current State of Research on Late-Medieval Drama 1994-95: Survey, Bibliography, and Reviews," *Fifteenth-Century Studies*, 23 (1997), 236-57.

—. "Le Fond sérieux de la farce médiévale. Une dimension insoupçonnée," in *Et c'est la fin*, eds. Jean-Claude Aubailly et al., 3 vols. Paris: Champion, 1993. I: 469-78.

—. "The Late-Medieval Theater of Salvation in Continental Europe," *Fifteenth-Century Studies*, 23 (1997), 171-83.

Giuliano, Paula, tr. *Arnoul Gréban. The Mystery of the Passion. The Third Day*. Asheville: Pegasus, 1996.

Glaser, Nina. "'Fils de rien'," *Modern Language Notes*, 111 (1996), 709-21.

Greenfield, Peter. "Census of Medieval Drama Productions," *Research Opportunities in Renaissance Drama*, 35 (1996), 133-52.

—. "Using Dramatic Records: History, Theory, Southampton's Musicians," *Medieval English Theatre*, 17 (1995), 75-95.

Gunnell, Terry. *The Origins of Drama in Scandinavia*. Cambridge: D.S. Brewer, 1995.

Happé, Peter. "The Devil in the Morality Plays: The Case of Wisdom," in Bitot, *Diverse toyes*, 113-24.

—. "Devil's Languages in Some Corpus Christi Plays," in *Tudor Theatre*, ed. André Lascombes. 3 vols. New York: Peter Lang, 1996. 3: 43-60.

—. *John Bale*. New York: Twayne, 1996.

—. "Spectacle in Bale and Heywood," *Medieval English Theatre*, 116 (1994), 51-65.

—. "Staging *l'Omme Pecheur* and *The Castle of Perseverance*," *Comparative Drama*, 30 (1996),377-92.

Harris, A. Leslie. "Tournaments and the *Tournam33ent of Tottenham*," *Fifteenth-Century Studies*, 23 (1997), 81-92.

Harris, Max. "A Catalan Corpus Christi Play: The Martyrdom of St. Sebastian with the Hobby Horses and the Turks," *Comparative Drama*, 31 (1997), 224-47.

Humphrey, Christ. "'To Make a New King': Seasonal Drama and Local Politics in Norwich, 1443,"*Medieval English Theatre*, 17 (1995), 29-41.

Johnston, Alexandra, and Wim Hüsken, eds. *English Parish Drama*. Amsterdam: Rodopi, 1996.

King, Pamela, and Meg Twycross. "Beyond REED? The York *Doomsday* Project," *Medieval English Theatre*, 17 (1995), 132-48.

Knight, Alan E. "Theatre and the Socialisation of Youth in Lille," *Research Opportunities in Renaissance Drama*, 35 (1996), 73-84.

Koopmans, Jelle. *Le Théâtre des exclus au Moyen ¢ge*. Paris: Imago, 1997.

Kramer, Femke. "Rederijkers on Stage: A Closer Look at 'Metatheatrical' Sources," *Research Opportunities in Renaissance Drama*, 35 (1996), 97-109.

Linke, Hansjürgen. "Bündner Teufeleien," *Zeitschrift für deutsches Altertum und deutsche Literatur*, 124 (1995), 265-71.

Massip, Francesc. "La Fête du roi: les débats du théâtre politique," in Bitot, *Diverse toyes*, 179-87.

—, ed. *Formes Teatrals de la Tradicio Médiéval: Actes del VII Colloqui de la Société pour l'Ⓔtude du Théâtre Médiéval.* Barcelona: Institut del Teatre, 1996.

Newbigin, Nerida. "Art and Drama in Fifteenth-Century Florence," *EDAMR*, 19 (1996), 1-22.

—. *Feste d'Oltrarno: Plays in Churches in Fifteenth-Century Florence*. Rome: Olschki, 1996.

Newlyn, Evelyn. "The Middle Cornish Interlude: Genre and Tradition," *Comparative Drama*, 30 (1996), 266-81.

Ogden, Dunbar H. "Set Pieces and Special Effects in the Liturgical Drama, II," *EDAMR*, 19 (1996), 22-40.

Rey-Flaud, Henri. *Le Cercle magique*. Paris: Gallimard, 1973.

Runnalls, Graham A. "Les Mystères de la Passion en langue française: Tentative de classement," *Romania*, 114 (1996), 468-516.

—. "Records of Early French Drama: Archival Research on Medieval French Theatre," *Medieval English Theatre*, 17 (1995), 5-19.

Schmidt, Gary D. *The Iconography of the Mouth of Hell*. Selinsgrove: Susquehanna University Press, 1995.

Severin, Dorothy S. *Witchcraft in Celestina*. London: Dept. of Hispanic Studies, Queen Mary and Westfield College, 1995.

Stokes, James, and Robert J. Alexander. *Records of Early English Drama: Somerset [and] Bath*. Toronto: University of Toronto Press, 1996. Two vols.

Strietman, Elsa. "Representations of *The Temptation of Christ in the Desert* in Medieval Dutch and English Drama," in Bitot, *Diverse toyes*, 147-75.

Tiner, Elza C. "Patrons and Travelling Companies in Coventry," *REED Newsletter*, 21 (1996), 1-37.

Tissier, André, ed. *Recueil de farces (1450-1550)*, 12 vols. Genève: Droz, 1996. Vol. 10.

Twycross, Meg, ed. *Festive Drama*. Papers from the Sixth Triennial Colloquium of the International Society for the Study of Medieval Theatre (SITM). Cambridge: D.S. Brewer, 1996.

—. "The York Mercers' *Lewent Brede* and the Hanseatic Trade," *Medieval English Theatre*, 17 (1995), 96-119.

Witt, Elizabeth A. *Contrary Marys in Medieval English and French Drama*. New York: Peter Lang, 1995.

Wright, Glenn. "Parody, Satire, and Genre in *The Tournament of Tottenham (1400-1440)*," *Fifteenth-Century Studies*, 23 (1997), 152-70.

Wright, Stephen K. "The Betrayer's Art: Translating Medieval Drama for Modern Readers," *Research Opportunities in Renaissance Drama*, 35 (1996), 85-96.

Wyatt, Diana. "The English Pater Noster Play: Evidence and Extrapolations," *Comparative Drama*, 30 (1996-97), 452-70.

REVIEWS

Davidson, Clifford, ed. *Fools and Folly* (Kalamazoo: Medieval Institute Publications, 1996). Pp. 176.

The all-pervasive fool represents folly, of course, but in many nuances, as demonstrated in Brant's *Ship of Fools* (1494). In the introduction to his collection of articles Davidson explains that the fool can be frivolous, vicious, or just plain stupid, and that, furthermore, we distinguish the natural from the artificial fool who may satirize and ultimately be wise. Foolishness chosen by Christ or by the disciple of *docta ignorantia* (Nicholas of Cues) is a sign of humility but can also be a flare of liberation, witness Erasmus of Rotterdam at a time of haughty intellectualism.

We are especially interested in the stage fool, as might be expected, and there is plenty of evidence for this figure in D.'s collection. Sandra Billington ("The *Cheval fol* of Lyon and Other Asses," 9-33) shows the symbolic use of horses and donkeys in medieval French and English drama. A crazy horse was paraded in a burlesque procession in fifteenth-c. Lyon in revolt against the political power structure. Billington fails to mention here the undoubtable influence of the fourteenth-c. *Roman de Fauvel* by Gervais du Bus (a notary of the royal chancellery), where the horse, known as chivalric animal, has become a metaphor of deceit and satanic folly. In contrast, the ass was associated with harmless fool-behavior. In mystery plays, of course, the donkey was a symbol of humility, present at Christ's birth and mounted by him to enter Jerusalem. The ass has its own feast, the *asinaria festa*, where the verse from the *Magnificat*, "Deposuit potentes," is acted out to form a glorification of foolery, informing the allegory of Fortune's Wheel as well. Progression from negative to positive takes place in the Digby *Conversion of St. Paul*, while the Chester *Balaam and His Ass* contrasts King Balack (on horseback) with the humble Balaam on his ass.

Martin W. Walsh contributed an excellent article on "The King His Own Fool: *Robert of Cicyle*," 34-46. The metrical romance, *Kyng Robert of Cicyle*, an anonymous fourteenth-c. English poem, tells the fate of Robert who learned total humility the hard way. Forced into the role of a grotesque court fool, he undergoes violence, and his 'madness' is thought to be incurable, since he insists on his kingship. While the poem accurately describes the living conditions of a court fool, it also teaches damnation for *superbia*, the deadliest of the Seven Sins, which finally leads to an identity crisis, and this in Passion week; but Robert is restored by an Angel on Ascension Day, running the gamut (according to Walsh) from a beastly wild-man to the Pauline fool-in-Christ. If the romance were staged, it might be a morality play; it was indeed presented in England on three occasions in the next 150 years (1481-82, 1531, and 1623). Later, a fool figured in *Richard II, Hamlet,* and *Lear.* There seem to exist no continental versions of this (essentially Franciscan) tale, *Robert of Cicyle.*

D.'s collection would not be complete without a treatment of the famous *Ship of Fools* in Alexander Barclay's 'translation' (Robert C. Evans, 47-72). Evans's purposes were to survey past scholarship on Brant and Barclay; to see in how far Brant studies can be applied to the English author, and finally to plead for a new edition of Barclay's work. While the latter's fools have influenced English drama, the impact on predication is bound to be greater (in turn, medieval sermons and their *exempla* were a source for Brant's work—note of the reviewer). It is quite incorrect to derive Barclay's text from the Latin version by Locher alone (1497; 5,672 vv. versus 7,034 vv. in Brant's original), as E. has done on page 35; I have proved long ago that the English 'translator,' unable to read Brant's Middle Alsacian German, used the French translations, especially Pierre Rivière's text (1497, adding 11,461 vv. to Locher's text!). Barclay had studied in Paris between 1490 and 1500: see E. DuBruck, "Barclay's Veritable Source: A *Ship of Fools* by Pierre Rivière," *Michigan Academician*, 4 (1971), 67-75, and *Pierre Rivière. La Nef des folz du monde*, ed. E. DuBruck, 2 vols. (Ann Arbor: UMI, 1977).—It would perhaps have been profitable for the readers of this collection to have been given a short summary of the various kinds of fools mentioned by Barclay (Brant).

Peter Happé ("Staging Folly in the Early Sixteenth Century: Heywood, Lindsay, and Others," 73-111) shows that the development of the fool's stage character in England was decisively influenced by Erasmus's *Praise of Folly* (1509), Sebastian Brant's *Ship* (this author is called "Stephen" on page 74!), and the inherent theatricality of the figure. The stage fool could entertain, embody the foolishness of another character allegorically, or satirize, like the French *sot*. Happé discusses Heywood's *Witty and Witless, A Play of Love, The Pardoner and the Friar*, and *The Four PP* (Palmer, Pardoner, Poticary, and Peddler), Skelton's *Magnyfycence*, Lindsay's *Ane Satire of the Thrie Estaitis*, and others. Of all sixteenth-c. playwrights Heywood seems to be the most emphatic, criticizing the whole of society. In Bale, the vices are essentially evil, while Lindsay makes folly and its ambiguity a means of protection in a dangerous political climate.

"The Fool as Social Critic: The Case of the Dutch Rhetoricians' Drama" (112-45) by Wim N. Hüsken highlights the relationship of fools and Dutch literary guilds. Influenced by the French *puys* of the fifteenth century, these guilds featured fools in their processions and participated in royal entries. After Brant had equated fools with sinners, they became scapegoats as well as satirists of society in their most favored stage role: that of the peasant (as especially in the German carnival plays—note of the reviewer). Hüsken subsequently investigates the drama of rhetoricians, such as in the *Handschrift Van Hulthem* (beginning fifteenth century), the fool in the *Spel van den Somer ende van den Winter* (c. 1436), and a Neidhart play (1395 and 1419) at Arnhem. He also reviews prose narratives with dialogue (first half of the sixteenth century), as, for example, *Nyeuvont, Loosheit ende Practike*, with its interaction of the fool (a ventriloquist?) and his bauble. Dutch dinner plays have only few actors, since space is limited; the plots often resemble those of French farces, but sometimes convey moral lessons. Pieces critical of the clergy aroused the complaints of authorities (e.g., the *Dinner Play of Two Fools*, Brussels, 1559). While the Middle Ages and Brant related folly to vice, the Dutch plays generally teach how to avoid evil behavior, and their fools do not seem to be foolish at all, Hüsken concludes.

Finally, Robert W. Leslie offers here "Sienese Fools, Comic Captains, and Every Fop in His Humor" (146-69), following the literary line from the Sienese fool to Ben Jonson's 'humors' plays. The Siena figure shows neither wit nor wisdom, at least in the eyes of the Florentine neighbors who consider him a dumb brute, a natural fool. Treated harshly in Pietro Aretino's *La Cortigiana* (c. 1535), he is predisposed to become the foolish and boastful captain of the Italian stage, the *miles gloriosus* of the *commedia dell'arte*, usually accompanied by a gluttonous servant. In Antonfrancesco Grazzini's *La Strega* (c. 1547), Taddeo Saliscendi is the Sienese fool, hoping for military fame. Captain Martebellonio (note the name!) of Giambattista Della Porta's *Gli duoi fratelli rivali* (c. 1595) boasts about divine ancestry or capability. (We find the retelling of the plots a bit lengthy here.) Meant for the English society of his day, Jonson's 'humors plays' have been influenced by Italian drama (e.g., *Every Man out of His Humor*, 1610; Sir Politic Would-Be in *Volpone*), but in the later pieces the fop's role is diminished. Generally, though, the Italian stock figure has indeed enriched the English stage. In conclusion, let me quote Leslie's list of characteristics for this fool:

Middling social status, upward social aspirations, gullibility, boastfulness, amorous intent, mediocre and/or plagiarizing poet-musician, ostentation in dress—usually wearing an assortment of foreign garments, affectation of characteristics seen as soldierly, swearing, swordplay, whoring, bullying social inferiors (157-58), in one word, a fop. D.'s collection, rich enough to be a valuable addition to university, as well as individual libraries and drama departments, is provided with an index of six pages (double columns).

Giuliano, Paula, tr. *Arnoul Gréban. The Mystery of the Passion. The Third Day* (Asheville: Pegasus, 1996). Pp. xxiii, 205.

Giuliano's translation fits well into "The Early European Drama Translation Series" by Martin Stevens and Stephen K. Wright and is welcomed by specialists in drama as well as General Education students and teachers. A good introduction describes Gréban's *Passion* (played on the third out of four days of mystery performance), surviving in nine whole and partial manuscripts from the fifteenth and sixteenth centuries. Then, G. embeds it in its larger context (the *Mystère*), its sources and performance history. Generally, French fifteenth-c. passion plays are based on *La Passion du Palatinus* (fourteenth century), derived from the *Passion des Jongleurs* (early thirteenth century). Gréban's immediate sources for his *Mystère de la Passion* (1452; 35,000 lines), however, are—besides the four gospels—Eugène Marcadé's *La Passion d'Arras* (first quarter of the fifteenth century), the *Legenda Aurea*, the *Postillae* of Nicolas of Lyra, the *Meditationes Vitae Christi*, all from the thirteenth century, and the *Passion Isabeau* (1398).[1] The playwright improves upon these sources by carefully interweaving scenes, providing their causal linkage, and motivating the action of characters even by their psychology. He combines epic description with lyrical interludes in various verse forms, monologs and dialogs—making the *Mystère* a true *Gesamtkunstwerk*.

Arnoul Gréban (c. 1420-?), organist and choirmaster at Notre Dame in Paris, had studied theology at the Sorbonne. His *Mystère* was enormously successful, performed three times in Paris alone before 1473. The *Passion de Troyes* borrowed from it, and Jean Michel directly copied sixty-five percent of Gréban's Second and Third Days for his 1486 *Mystère de la Passion*. Gréban still pleases modern audiences. What is especially valuable here, G. has a chapter on the *Mons Passion* of 1501, a Gréban/Michel performance known to us by Gustave Cohen's edition of the *Livre de conduite du régisseur et le compte des dépenses* (Paris: Champion, 1925). Since sixty-seven stations were necessary (possibly ninety-eight) on the simultaneous stage, any one location must have served for different scenes, indicated by signs, as G. explains, facilitating typological associations (known already through preaching and such compendia as the *Biblia Pauperum*). Thus, the devil can sit temporarily on God's throne, and the space for Adam and Eve will become that of Christ and Mary. After listing props, costumes, and stations, G. summarizes the other days of the *Mystère* and explains the work principles of her translation. Trying to retain Gréban's syntax wherever possible, she even attempts to find English equivalents for slang and proverbs (forever problematic for translators); proverbs were accessible in James Woodrow Hassell's *Middle French Proverbs, Sentences, and Proverbial Phrases* (Toronto: Pontifical Institute of Mediaeval Studies, 1982). The translator gives some notes at the bottom of the pages, but we might have expected more annotations, especially for readers not yet familiar with interesting facets of drama research. Thus, for example, during the nailing of Christ and the descent from the cross, the actors' repeated lines indicated *rondeau*-like verse structures (pp. 130-33, 141, 183-84), as well as the simple verbal equivalent of repeated actions to accomplish the task.[2] Also, G. could have devoted a few lines to the wide spread of passion plays in the rest of Europe, especially in Germany. Many used the same episodes as the French mysteries, although direct influence would be difficult to prove.[3] G.'s translation is a wonderful achievement: she has succeeded in tracing all the fine nuances of the original and in finding their faithful equivalent in the lively English idiom of 1996. Let me give an example from the Prologue, the original of which she provides in the appendix, pp. 198-201:

> Ce devost salu accomply
> Seigneurs, humblement je vous supply
> Que ung peu de scilence prestez
> Et l` entendement aprestez
> A incorporer la doulceur
> Charité et parfaicte amourcharity,
> Ou ceste passion admainne
> Et joinct toute nature humaine.
> (vv.19,918-24).

> (This devout salutation being finished
> Lords, I humbly beg you to
> lend a little silence
> and ready your understanding
> to take in the compassion
> and perfect love
> to which this passion leads
> and joins all human nature.)

Johnston, Alexandra, and Wim Hüsken, eds. *English Parish Drama* (Amsterdam: Rodopi, 1996). Pp. 157.

In her introduction to this collection of essays Johnston explains that paradramatic activities in the parishes have never been the object of a critical or even just descriptive study, while salvation history, of course, is well represented on the stages of York, Coventry, and Chester. David George writes on "Rushbearing: A Forgotten British Custom" (17-29), which originated in the need to cover the packed-earth floors of medieval houses. Not every dwelling was covered every day, and especially after the winter the old rushes were quite filthy. Gradually, a small procession would first take the rushes to church in spring, and this activity soon developed into a secular fair with morris dancing in front of the rushcarts and with occasional disturbances. Rushbearing was still reported recently (1991) in Westmorland.

"Rushbearings and Maygames in the Diocese of Chester before 1642" was Elizabeth Baldwin's topic (31-40). Rushbearing was customary in Cheshire as well as Lancashire: there are records of payments to the rushbearers, for allied activities, and for food and drink provided. In Lancashire, the associated violence was condemned, and wakes were known for the same disruptive behavior, bear-baiting, etc. Garlands and dancing were the rule in Maygames, where a fool presented himself with his bauble.

In " 'Owre Thanssynge Day': Parish Dance and Procession in Salisbury (41-63)," Audrey Douglas investigated the combination of parish processions with dance. Perhaps a secular custom, it generated supplementary income for the churches from the fourteenth to the seventeenth century. Salisbury had a separate dancing day in Whitsun week, sometimes simply called procession day. Its three parishes engaged in it, and dances were also held in Rogation week and on Corpus Christi. While payments were made to banner bearers or bell ringers, and to dancers (*trepidantes*) on "Frick" Friday (frick=move briskly) just before Whitsunday, the income still remained sizable. With economic depression in the late sixteenth century, Salisbury experienced problems with policing the activity, thus ushering in the demise of the dance.

James Stokes reviewed "Bull and Bear Baiting in Somerset: The Gentles' Sport" (65-80) and explained that this activity was part of an attempt to suppress church ales. In this brutal show, a bear or a bull was chained then baited with dogs and tormented by them. These events were finally outlawed in the nineteenth century. Their symbolic meaning (the same as for mere masquerades of this show on the continent) was subdoing an evil force, like a disobedient wife (!), lastly any excess or loss of control. Headless bear figures signified the devil.

Barbara D. Palmer contributed "Parish Entertainment in West Yorkshire" (81-93), referring mostly to paradramatic activities from the sixteenth century to modern times. The West Riding parishes had dances and processions, rushbearings, summer games, Maypoles, and Lords of Misrule (Boy Bishop, Kitchen King). All involved disguises and some mimetic or parodic activity frequently aimed at authorities, attesting to social or religious tensions.

"'What Revels are in Hand?' Dramatic Activities Sponsored by the Parishes of the Thames Valley" (95-104) by Alexandra Johnston was an attempt of gathering evidence from eighty parishes: churchwardens' accounts and records of prosecutions. Four specific types were documented:

1) Folk Plays (king games or summer lords and ladies, as early as the fifteenth century, where a Robin Hood acted as an outlaw, gather-

ing money for a parish—and where summer lords represented law and order);

2) Biblical Plays (non-cycle plays as, e.g., *Jacob and His Twelve Sons* in 1481 Thame, and Easter Plays);
3) Plays on other themes, and
4) Itinerant Parish Plays. Most were money-making ventures. Unfortunately, this essay is not free of typos.

Peter H. Greenfield reported on "Parish Drama in Four Counties Bordering the Thames Watershed" (107-18), adjacent to those discussed by Johnston. Some of these activities dated from the fifteenth century, and records for rented playing paraphernalia were found in Tewkesbury and Bishop's Stortford. Smaller towns had king's ales and Maygames—the variations were complex.

Parish churchwardens' accounts are the principal source of knowledge for "Parish Drama in Worcester," as investigated by David N. Klausner (119-35). Also, the weekly accountbook kept by William More (1517-35) yielded valuable information. Church ales were often connected with a play in this wealthy parish. More's donations to such entertainments were relatively few and infrequent; perhaps, professional groups were hired instead.

James M. Gibson contributed a fine article on " '*Interludum Passionis Domini*': Parish Drama in Medieval New Romney" (137-48), a passion play at Whitsuntide as early as 1428 and 1456. No copy of the playbook survived, but records revealed a cast list (with minstrels, bann criers, and fool, while Lucifer and Christ were missing). There were four separate plays: the Ministry of Christ, the Betrayal and Buffeting, Christ's Death and Descent to Hell, and the Resurrection. Administration and finance in a city without guild structure were handled by entrance fees and the cooperation of the citizens. The all-male cast was chosen early in the year, and all had to learn their parts by Pentecost.

Finally, John M. Wasson mentioned "A Parish Play in the West Riding of Yorkshire" (149-57) entitled "Canimore and Lionley." We have neither a manuscript nor even a clue as to the contents of the 1614 play staged in Methley, but the title reminds us of dramatized versions of Cervantes's "Cardenio and Lucinda" staged shortly after Thomas Shelton's translation of *Don Quixote* (1612). In any case, the choice made for the Methley performance seemed unique.

All the contributors are editors in the *REED* project. Johnston's and Hüsken's slim volume represents a valuable addition to drama studies, medievalism, and research on English paraliterary activities.

Tissier, André, ed. *Recueil de farces. (1450-1550)*, 12 vols. (Genève: Droz, 1996), vol. 10. Pp. 436.

After several attempts by other scholars, Tissier is publishing a complete series of farce editions (1986-98). Volume 10 contains seven plays edited with the same care as the previously published pieces.

The first two plays are exceedingly scatological. While the first, "Le Pet" (The Fart), is at least witty, the second, "Tarabin, Tarabas et Triboulle-Ménage," shows very little in the way of plot development and makes us wonder what type of audience did in fact appreciate it. "Le Pet" (XLVIII) has had two previous editions, that of the *Recueil of the British Museum* (c. 1532-47), and another in Montaiglon's *Ancien Théâtre Français* (1854). A burlesque parody of forensic judgements, a time-honored genre since Aristophanes, this comedy is created by treating a trivial subject seriously, namely, a fart caused in the effort of putting a heavy package up on a table: what is it and who, husband or wife, is responsible for it? An eager lawyer is consulted, and a judge decides that in a marriage all things are in common, also such little accidents as a fart. One must remember that in the Middle Ages the natural functions of the body were not taboo, especially in popular theater. The unknown author lived in the Northeast of France, and the piece, in traditional octosyllabic lines, is datable 1476.

"Tarabin, Tarabas et Triboulle-Ménage" (XLIX) presents three figures: a debating old husband/young wife team and their valet *badin*,[4] arbiter and scapegoat. The basic text comes from the *Recueil Cohen*, i.e., Gustave Cohen's copy from a sixteenth-c. collection (c. 1540). It had been edited in haste and has faulty readings and contestable punctuations or spellings. The text must have been well known, for T. has found allusions to its title in seven fifteenth- and sixteenth-c. works, including that of Rabelais.

Tarabas and his wife consider themselves *mal-mariés*, he because his whole life seems to depend upon her *cul*, i.e., her (carnivalesque) *bas-ventre* (Bachtin), dirty and smelly because of urine, feces, and sex; she because of his quarrelsome and lunatic *tête*, the seat of his ill-used intelligence which she describes in an emphatic *annominatio* (vv. 8-15). Triboulle attempts to make a volatile peace, whereupon the two burden him with many heteroclite household objects, which he has to wash and clean, surely the result of the woman's uncleanliness. He finally gives up and leaves their service. The entire piece swarms with scatological references which must have amused the audience. Not mentioned by T. was the fact that the first half of the play is a parody of medieval debates, just like between Lent and Easter, Summer and Winter, Body and Soul, Brain and Brawn, Water and Wine, etc. The conclusion not made by Triboulle is, of course, that *tête* belongs to a ménage just as much as *cul*.

The farce "Mahuet Badin, natif de Bagnolet, qui va à Paris au marché pour vendre ses oeufs et sa crème" (L) states its subject in the title. A mother sends her son to Paris, to sell eggs and cream to (at) the Market Price.[5] Mahuet (the syllables hu-et mean 'fool' in Middle French) does not succeed, for he lets a potential buyer, Gaultier, have the eggs for free just because the latter affirms that he is in fact Market Price (personified—having been forewarned of the young man's stupid illusion). As Mahuet is hungry, he dunks his bread into the cream—but cannot retrieve his hand from the narrow pot. In addition, Gaultier, feigning to clean Mahuet's face, blackens it with soot and advises him to break the pot on the first person he sees—which is Gaultier, as Mahuet takes the advice literally. Thus, the cheater is cheated, once again. Mahuet returns home only to find that his mother does not recognize him with a black face: he has lost his identity, just like "Jenin, fils de rien" (Tissier, vol. 3, XVIII).[6]

Since there are two texts, that of the British Museum and a more elaborate version in the *Recueil Cohen*, both of the early sixteenth century, T. prints both on pages facing one another, allowing comparison. There is no doubt that the Cohen text has the better dramaturgy. In view of the numerous Norman and Picard expressions, the farce could have originated in Western France, but in any case close to Paris. Perhaps both versions came from a lost original. The *badin* Mahuet is no *ingénu*, by the way, but simply stupid, easy prey for spongers. The comic element here is based on the false comprehension of language and on gestures.

"Le Gentilhomme et son page" (LI) appeared originally in a sixteenth-c. manuscript in a collection called *Farces, moralités* of the Bibliothèque Nationale, also known as *Recueil La Vallière*. The copyist is of Norman origin, and the play dates from the end of 1525, since there are several allusions to recent historical events. It was probably staged in Paris to celebrate the peace that ended the Italian War. The piece is a dialog between master and servant, and while dramatic monologs and dialogs are known to be constitutive elements of theater, it would be wrong to postulate an evolution of these genres to full-fledged drama, as T. warns on page 191. The gentleman, *miles gloriosus*, evokes first his warrior exploits, then his noble acquaintances and a life of hunting, card- and dice-games, again his feats in battle. As he notices that his valet is about to leave him for good, he tries to retain him by promises as well as threats, alluding also to his lands and success with women. But to no avail: the servant has made his decision, all the more so since the master is impoverished and does not pay him. In a last aside to the audience, the pageboy suggests that they leave with him. While T. points to the complexity of the valet who is the 'motor' of the man's constant bragging, he fails to notice that we confront here a serious societal problem: the degeneration of a nobility which has lost its function, is impoverished, and lives of its fanfaronades. The best example of this type will be Don Quixote.

The fifteenth-c. *farce-sottie*, "Le Pauvre Jouhan" (LII), is based on a first edition in the *Recueil Trepperel* (beginning of the sixteenth century). As indicated by his name, Jouhan (=Jehan, Jean) is cuckolded by the young wife he loves. He is simple-minded, middle-aged, but has been married recently and enjoys the conjugal bed. The woman, called Affriquée (=decked out, vain), is more interested in clothes than in people and withholds herself even from her lover, Glorieux, who by the way is just as vain as she, but tries extortion to make her comply. She provides the movement in the play, as she ambulates between him and her husband.

The piece is a *sottie* at the same time, since the fourth personage is a wise fool, a *sot*, who gives asides to the audience and is a kind of observer and commentator. He even sings several times and invites the public to join in. Against marriage altogether, he opposes "his ridiculous wisdom to the folly of people who claim to be sensible" (Pauphilet—my translation). T. correctly points out that the play is not antifeminist, because the men, Jouhan and Glorieux, are silly in their own way (237).

The short farce, "Les Femmes qui aiment mieux suivre Folconduit et vivre à leur plaisir que d'apprendre aucune bonne science" (LIII), appeared first in an edition by Nicolas Rousset (1612), consisting of 168 lines. The personages are four: Master of good conduct, Folconduit, Lady Promptitude (to do evil), and Lady Tardy (to do good). The two women ask the Master for advice but then return to Folconduit (Crazy Conduct), hoping to learn life's wisdom from him, rather than from books. The latter refuses at first,—a few slaps in the face make him comply, however. Dated 1530-35, the play has sometimes been categorized as a morality on account of the allegorical names, but T. considers it a farce, for the women are certainly of flesh and blood, cognizant of the necessities of life: they bring a food basket to the Master. Also, they are lively, gossipy, capricious; they apparently have their own mind when they make their decision to avoid book knowledge. Finally, as a rule, moralities are not as short as this piece.

"La Cornette" (LIV) is featured for the first time in the *Histoire du théâtre français, depuis son origine jusqu'à présent* of the brothers Parfaict, III (1745), where this copy of a lost manuscript was appended to a *Mystère*. Both texts ended in the words "Fin sans fin" typical for writings by Jean d'Abondance, a lawyer (or just a clerc) of the basoche and royal notary of Pont Saint Esprit (Avignon). Dated 1535 the farce appeared in various later copies, of which T. selected the Méjanes version (1785) for his edition.

The crux of the play is a misunderstanding celebrating feminine ruse. A young wife deceives her elderly husband right and left with the help of her valet Finet, and her spouse's two nephews complain to one another about her disorderly conduct. She in turn tells her man about these complaints, using the pronoun *elle* but referring it to his headdress (*la cornette*), which is not up to snuff, turning right and left. Her husband throws the nephews out of the house. What T. has not brought out here is the symbolism between *cornette* (visibly cuckolding the man) and the name of Jean d'Abondance (a pseudonym reminding us of cornucopia—which is even affirmed by his devise "Fin sans fin"). Tissier's tenth volume thus presents seven farces of various dramatic potentials, with abundant textual notes and glossary; the introductions are valuable in themselves—if sometimes redundant.

Witt, Elizabeth A. *Contrary Marys in Medieval English and French Drama* (New York: Peter Lang, 1995). Pp. 196.

The grounds for comparison of the Mary figures, as specified by Witt, are that the English cycle dramas and the French passion plays flourished at thesame time (fourteenth and fifteenth centuries), that they were performed on feast days of the liturgical year and treated religious world history. They shared a civic nature, and their purpose was to educate the audience in Christian doctrine. But while the English plays saw Mary as a figure more divine than human, the French Marys were "pathetically human" (4), a "spiritual threat to mankind" (ibid.). Conforming to the misogynist stereotypes of the era, the French Marys presented a potential danger to God's plan for the redemption of sinners by their attitude to Christ's death.

In the first chapter, W. discussed the theological, social, and historical foundations for the ideas about Mary. She quoted outstanding feminist scholars of our time to support her view that the Mother of God, as seen in the Middle Ages, conformed to misogynist ideas about women based above all on the Bible, which placed the female under the authority of men, with women's sole function to propagate the race. In turn, women were considered lacking spirituality and chastity, even nuns were thought to be inferior to monks. The Biblical stance was reinforced by the Church Fathers, above all Thomas Aquinas who "proved" that women were inferior by nature and in need of control. Mary was for them an unattainable model, but, at the same time, an instrument of this control.[7]

The second chapter was devoted to the English cycle drama: *Chester, N-Town, Wakefield*, and *York*. Of Christocentric status, Mary had a semi-divine role. She was an object of veneration because of the unusual source of her motherhood and the identity of her child, while she was unable to understand these circumstances. She faced Christ's death with grief, but realized that it was necessary for the salvation of humankind. She was even empowered to intercede for man, but mostly in a passive way, and her motherhood fulfilled the proper function of the female sex. Because she was separated from other women—by her miraculous birth and high lineage, by her exemplary childhood, Christ's birth, her death and assumption—she was not an effective role model. Iconic rather than real and human, she received power in spite of her femininity.

The Mary of the French passion plays was the subject of chapter three. The titles include: *Passion du Palatinus, Passion d'Autun, de Semur, d'Arras, Le Mystère de la Passion* by Arnoul Gréban and that by Jean Michel (who added on to Gréban). No goddess figure, Mary was "pathetically human" (92), as was Christ, and showed typical female behavior. Concerned about her son's safety—and her own—she tried repeatedly to prevent his death above all in the four questions to Christ (which Gréban, incidentally, took from the *Passion Isabeau*, 1398, but indirectly, from the *Meditationes Vitae Christi* [thirteenth century], where they were much less elaborate—note of the reviewer[8]) during a supper at Martha's house. This Mary was not able to control her grief at the cross, and her maternal concern prevented her from seeing the larger picture. She also felt that her maternity placed an obligation on Christ, and she was like a real woman in that she was often "obstinate, bossy, and unreasonable" (97). No intercessor for humankind in the French passions (but rather in miracle plays), she required male control, even though she was the most perfect of women.

Witt's conclusion voiced her reasons for the divergent views of medieval playwrights on both sides of the Channel. Although all authors used the same sources, 1) there occurred a change in artistic emphasis: while earlier art and literature tended to stress the divine, the Franciscans brought about natural images of humanity, first in Italy (e.g., in the *Meditationes*), and later in the North; 2) England was characterized by religious conservativism and a relative lack of heresies (but what about Wyclif?); 3) all medieval authors and artists elaborated existing trends rather than pursuing innovation. Finally, W. stated that both types of Mary answered the need for "male dominance over the female sex" (132). Whether unattainable goddesses or pathetic females, these Marys were beyond emulation.

In a valuable appendix, the author describes the French and the English dramas briefly and characterizes both Marys' roles. Her bibliography is limited to "Works Cited" and lacks important scholarly studies, such as Maurice Accarie's bookon Jean Michel's *Mystère de la Passion*,[9] while it is perhaps overloaded with feminist items. A good index concludes the monograph.

Our criticism concerns style and scope as much as some points in contents. The work is very repetitious: the entire elaboration of pp. 7-138 could have been condensed to a single article, thereby gaining concision. Mistakes in spelling or typos are relatively few in number (but "Palatine" is consistently misspelt as "Pala*n*tine"). Some readers may find the feminist stance throughout hard to take; while it opens new perspectives on late-medieval drama, it is very doubtful that the audiences would have perceived Mary from this viewpoint, i.e., as a "non-empowered" female. The playwrights on both sides of the Channel gave the public (i.e., men *and* women) what it wanted to see.

The Marys' "anti-semitism" (75, 110) is the same anti-Jewish sentiment as can be found in the Bible and in medieval Latin treatises *Adversus Judaeos*. Associated with the devil in French and German plays (and not only by Mary), the Jews are Christ's enemies who seek his death. The realm of the devils is parallel, but in opposition, to the action of heavenly agents. In any case, this anti-Jewish sentiment is not identical with modern anti-semitism (of which it remains one component).[10]

The reason why the French Mary argues point by point (in the four requests) is scholastic influence on one of Gréban's sources (the *Passion Isabeau*) and the debate tradition. Medieval French drama has many 'forensic' passages, and this is one of them. To accuse Mary of "obstinacy" in this case is quite incorrect (98-99).

Notes

[1] E. DuBruck, ed. La Passion Isabeau. Une édition du manuscrit fr. 966 de la Bibliothèque Nationale de Paris (New York: Peter Lang, 1990).

[2] L. Müller, Das Rondel in den französischen Mirakelspielen des 15. und 16. Jahrhunderts (Marburg: 1884).

[3] See E. DuBruck, "The Late-Medieval Theater of Salvation in Continental Europe," Fifteenth-Century Studies, 23 (1997), 171-83.

[4] A figure of malicious naïveté, often an ingénu rather than a sot—see our characterization in *Fifteenth-Century Studies*, 16 (1990), 320.

[5] French *à* is used with prices, but sometimes means "to," if an indirect object follows.

[6] See E. DuBruck, "Le Fonds sérieux de la farce médiévale," in *Et c'est la fin*, eds. Jean-Claude Aubailly et al., 3 vols. (Paris: Champion, 1993), 1: 469-78 (470-71), and Nina Glaser, "Fils de rien," *Modern Language Notes*, 111 (1996), 709-21.

[7] Also: E. DuBruck, "Thomas Aquinas and Medieval Demonology," *Michigan Academician*, 7 (1974), 167-83.

[8] DuBruck, above n. 1, 13-29.

[9] M. Accarie, Le Théâtre sacré de la fin du moyen âge. Étude sur le sens moral de la Passion de Jean Michel (Genève: Droz, 1979).

[10]See: "Do worden die Judden alle geschant." Rolle und Funktion der Juden in spätmittelalterlichen Spielen (München: Fink, 1992). Manya Lifschitz-Golden, Les Juifs dans la littérature française du moyen âge (mystères, miracles, chroniques) (New York: Columbia University Press, 1935).

Marygrove College

Reviews

William F. Pollard and Robert Boenig, eds., *Mysticism and Spirituality in Medieval England*. Cambridge: D. S. Brewer, 1997. Pp. xi, 260; black-and-white illustrations.

This volume of essays explores the profound influence of earlier mystical and spiritual treatises upon key late fourteenth- and early fifteenth-century mystical texts and figures. While offering valuable discussions of the thematic continuities among these works the volume also provides new contributions to our understanding of such important late medieval mystics as Julian of Norwich, Margery Kempe, Richard Rolle, and *The Cloud* author. The collection should, therefore, be useful both to those seeking an introduction to the variety and richness of late medieval mystical and spiritual writings and to those more learned in these traditions. Limitations of space require that I provide only the most general summary of the central argument of each of the volume's eleven essays.

The collection begins with Thomas H. Bestul's, "Antecedents: The Anselmian and Cistercian Contributions." In this essay Bestul argues that eleventh- and twelfth-century Latin devotional literature, specifically the writings of Anselm of Canterbury, Bernard of Clairvaux, and Aelred of Rievaulx, amplifies the thinking of such earlier figures as Augustine of Hippo and Gregory the Great in its emphasis on affective spirituality and intimacy of contemplation. These early works lay the foundations for an exploration of the inner life by later mystics.

In "Pseudo-Dionysius and the *Via* towards England" Robert Boenig examines the ways in which Pseudo-Dionysian thought, particularly its considerations of the ineffability of language and resolution into silence as a way of approaching the divine, permeates the writings of late Middle English mystics. He argues that although tracing a direct path of transmission is virtually impossible, Pseudo-Dionysian ideas probably came to England in three ways: through the writings of the Victorines, through Thomas Becket and the archepiscopal court at Canterbury, and through the writings of the Dominicans.

René Tixier's, "Þis louely blinde werk': Contemplation in *The Cloud of Unknowing* and Related Treatises" offers a detailed analysis of the Dionysian nature of contemplation in those works commonly ascribed to *The Cloud* author. The "spiritual work of self-abandonment," Tixier suggests, ultimately "causes the materiality of the text to disappear progressively behind the experience which it seeks not only to describe but also — and primarily — to induce."

Two articles in this collection study the works of Richard Rolle. In "Richard Rolle and the 'Eye of the Heart'," William F. Pollard defends Rolle against those critics (particularly David Knowles) who would deny Rolle's mystical authenticity. The essay traces the mystic's development of the image of the *oculus cordis* which, Pollard argues, "resolves for Richard the conflicting functions of the affective and rational approaches to God and is influenced by both Dionysian and Dominican thought." Michael P. Kuczynski discusses Lollard revisions of Rolle's *Psalter* in "Rolle among the Reformers: Orthodoxy and Heterodoxy in Wycliffite Copies of Richard Rolle's *Psalter*." He argues in the essay that Lollard interpolations of the *Psalter* are not clear examples of heterodoxy; rather, they reveal what is in fact an orthodox understanding that the Psalms "speak beyond their limited historical circumstances directly to present concerns."

Another pair of essays examine the connections between the affective piety of anchoritic literature and both earlier and later mystical thought. In his "Enclosed Desires: A Study of the Wooing Group," Denis Renevey explores the ways in which Augustinian and Anselmian conceptions of meditative practice coalesce in the texts of the Wooing Group. He discusses specifically the Augustinian notion that union with God is achieved through introspective contemplation of the created world and the contradictory Anselmian claim that complete rejection of the self brings the contemplative to a deeper understanding of her sinful nature.

Anne Savage, in "The Solitary Heroine: Aspects of Meditation and Mysticism in *Ancrene Wisse*, the Katherine Group, and the Wooing Group," recognizes that while the affective piety expressed in these texts developed into a "widespread popular piety" by the late fourteenth century, they in fact respond in very specific ways to the contemplative demands of female anchoritic life. In particular, these works provide models of heroic feminine spirituality which inspire the anchoress aggressively to defend her virtues while they at the same time articulate for these women both formal and informal meditative practices that focus upon the goal of union with Christ in a "specifically *incarnational* embrace."

Two more essays on female spirituality and mystical experience in this volume are Ritamary Bradley's, "Julian of Norwich: Everyone's Mystic," and Susan Dickman's, "A Showing of God's Grace: *The Book of Margery Kempe*." By examining the uses of the word *asseth* and its associated vocabulary, Bradley elucidates Julian's claim that even in our wretched state we are lovingly redeemed through a "transforming salvation in Christ in solidarity with him." Dickman offers a corrective reconsideration of Margery's spirituality by examining her work within the context of contemporary Continental visionaries and holy women.

In "Further Thoughts on the Spirituality of Syon Abbey" Roger Ellis analyzes the central themes illustrated in the Brigittine "logo," a manuscript illumination found on texts read within and produced by Syon Abbey. He suggests that while the spirituality of Syon Abbey is an "amalgam" of elements drawn from diverse religious traditions, it is at its core a "Trinitarian vision which emphasizes the incarnate and crucified Christ and the compassion and love of the Virgin Mary."

Finally, Douglas Gray argues in "Medieval English Mystical Lyrics" that although this tradition can claim no singular great mystical figure or work, it nonetheless is broadly connected — through its emphasis on visual and affective imagery — with late medieval contemplative writing and thought.

This volume is diverse in its approach as well as in its conclusions. Perhaps its most important contribution to the study of contemplative practice and thought is its insistence on both the continuities and varieties among late medieval mysticisms.

Kathleen M. Hewett-Smith
University of Richmond

James S. Grubb, *Provincial Families of the Renaissance: Private and Public Life in the Veneto.* Baltimore and London: The Johns Hopkins University Press, 1996. Pp. xvii, 343.

James Grubb, Professor of History at the University of Maryland, Baltimore County, has produced a solid, thoughtful and useful study of upper-class society in Verona and Vincenza during the fifteenth century. He focusses on thirteen families that left *ricordanze*, or memorial books, whose authors recorded all manner of family affairs. Though common in contemporary Tuscany (and in Tuscan historiography), these sources are rare outside, and thus offer uncommon glimpses into the structure and dynamics of several generations of "long forgotten families from two semi-important cities". Grubb sees his contribution as filling a gap created by extravagant scholarly attention paid to the major Italian urban centers on the one hand, and on the other works on provincial cities that ignore "the domestic and the ordinary" (p. xi) in favor of administrative and economic considerations. He wisely rejects any claims to either city's representativeness of Italian life, but offers his study as a balance to the dominant trends, one that helps contextualize Venetian and Florentine work by providing a comparative perspective. Methodologically he does precisely this: establishing the pictures formed by the memorial books and other archival sources from the Veneto, and explaining them by, or testing them against, similar materials, generally from Florence. Thus, the comparisons flow both ways, tempering conclusions drawn from Florentine historiography, and establishing both the commonalities and uniqueness of provincial life. While this approach is of obvious value to the specialist, it also serves as a fine introduction to the issues and literature for the novice or generalist.

His first four chapters cover marriage, children, death, and household and the family. In each case he draws out the data or reflections from the Veneto *ricordanze* (and wills and tax *estimi*) and holds them up against the picture we have of Tuscany or Venice, or from prescriptive works of the period. From names assigned to children to euphemisms for death, Grubb revels in the minutiae that coalesce to provide a clearer picture of the *mentalitè* of the provincial families, and of the processes of their daily lives. In Chapter Five he explores the provincial economic picture from the contract and the shop up, rather than from aggregate data or guild regulations and prescribed practices. His sixth chapter covers "land" and the Veneto variation on leasing and cropping and the role of the villa. Hampered by his small sample, he can but present the prevailing view (Renaissance landowners enjoyed their rustic sojourns) alongside the dissenting (for at least one the villa was a purely economic proposition). In completing his picture he sets his patricians in two matrices: of local nobility, in the process presenting a lucid discussion of the issues surrounding urban nobility as concept and reality; and of religious belief and practice, from superstition to support for parishes and resistance against imposed bishops.

Although his sample is small, Grubb treats it in a sweeping and often sensitive way, avoiding any temptation to generalization. Yet, due to his thematic approach, I never came to know any of his families in the way I am certain he did: entangled in the anecdotal, statistical and contextual, the families — let alone the individuals — are washed out and run together. The human cost of doing social history, I suppose.

Joseph P. Byrne
Belmont University

Colin Imber. *Ebu's-su'ud. The Islamic Legal Tradition*. Stanford: Stanford University Press, 1997. 288 pp.

This volume is the first in the series *Jurists: Profiles in Legal Theory*, edited by William Twining and Neil MacCormick, to address legal theory and practice in the non-Western world. Its clear prose style, glossary, and avoidance of foreign terms make it a useful introduction to early modern law both for students of Ottoman history and for non-specialists of the period interested in comparative studies. Its topic makes it an especially valuable contribution to legal scholarship on the Ottoman Empire. Sultan Suleyman I (1520-1566), known as The Magnificent to Europeans, was known to Ottomans as The Lawgiver. Ebu's-su'ud (1490-1574) was the jurist responsible for Suleyman's reputation. Ebu's-su'ud virtually established foundations of the Ottoman legal system that would last through the 19th century. He not only produced Suleyman's famous law code (*kanunname*), but rationalized the Ottoman judiciary under the authority of a single supreme legal official, the *Sheikhu'l Islam*, a post that Ebu's-su'ud held for 29 years.

Perhaps of most general interest to scholars of the early modern period is Colin Imber's discussion of how Ebu's-su'ud redefined the relationship between the authority of the law and the power of the sultan. Contrary to stereotypes of Ottoman sultans as unrestrained despots, they were in fact limited in the scope of their authority by Islamic law. In effect, by the late fifteenth century, the Ottomans had two bodies of law. Sultans could issue secular decrees, forming a body of customary imperial law called *kanun*, which addressed primarily administrative, fiscal, and criminal matters. But, in theory, *kanun* law could neither conflict with, nor be imposed in areas already covered by, Islamic law. Moreover, temporal rulers had no power to either interpret or change Islamic law, which was based on long- established interpretations of scripture. However, Imber shows, in practice the *kanun* often conflicted with the dictates of the Ottomans' official school of Islamic law, the *Hanafi* school, particularly in taxation. Ebu's-su'ud reconciled these conflicts and broadened Ottoman rulers' power by elaborating a theory of rule by divine right, and of the Sultan's authority as a necessary precondition to the rule of Islamic law. Ebu's-su'ud's legal reasoning supported Sultan Suleyman's claim to be Caliph, a successor to the Prophet and God's representative on Earth. This claim made the sultan the executor of Islamic law, in violation of previous, mainstream *Hanafi* tradition, and enabled Sultan Suleyman to broaden his legal jurisdiction through the codification of laws and standardization of legal practice.

In the second half of the book, Imber questions Ebu's-su'ud's longlasting reputation as the scholar who reconciled Islamic and *kanun* law. Imber focuses his discussion on four legal areas: land tenure and taxation, trusts in mortmain, marriage and its dissolution, and crimes and torts. Imber recognizes that Ebu's-su'ud's motivation was pious: he, like most other legal scholars, revered Islamic law as an ideal law for an ideal world. However, Imber also argues that Ebu's-su'ud was a practical man, whose scholarship served very worldly needs. His codification of *kanun* laws on land tenure in terms of *Hanafi* law also served to increase the power of the Sultan over his subjects. And his justification of trusts that lend at interest, against critics who argued that the charging of interest violated Islamic law, met the critical need of Ottoman subjects for a source of credit. By presenting translations of key texts, Imber leaves it to the reader to make a final judgement of the degree to which Ebu's-su'ud truly reconciled *kanun* and Islamic law.

This volume is a unique and valuable contribution not only to Ottoman legal history, but to legal scholarship on the Islamic Middle East in general. Its focus on a single scholar in a particular period contrasts with the continuing preponderance of ahistorical studies of Islamic law. It also complements studies on theories of kingship and the caliphate, which have previously focused on the Islamic Middle Period, before the rise of the Ottoman Empire. Finally, Imber's contention that Ebu's-su'ud did not practice innovation enjoins a current and important debate about whether the gate of *ijtihad*, or permissibility of new legal interpretation in Islamic law, had closed after the Middle Period.

Elizabeth Thompson
University of Virginia

Seth Lerer, *Courtly Letters in the Age of Henry VIII. Literary Culture and the Arts of Deceit*. Cambridge: CUP, 1997. xiv + 252 pp.

This new monograph in the Cambridge Studies in Renaissance Literature and Culture brings together literary and historical analysis and theories of readership to interpret the court of Henry VIII. In an imaginative study, Lerer links Chaucer's *Troilus and Criseyde*, the king's love letters, manuscript anthologies, and the verse epistles of Wyatt and Tottel to define a political culture that he calls "Pandaric." Just as scholars become voyeurs who pry into archival secrets for intellectual satisfaction, Lerer argues, the early Renaissance courtier mimicked Pandarus's mixture of observation and deceit, public spectacle and private masking. In this "sixteenth-century encounter with a fourteenth-century text" the author locates "the moment when the early modern reader may emerge."

As the subtitle and cover illustration of Thomas Cromwell suggest, the courtiers who attended Henry VIII lived in a world of secrecy and manipulation. The "surreptition and surveillance that defined the actions of the courtier and diplomat" turned the court into a voyeur's arena. Henry's courtiers, "minions" such as William Compton and Francis Bryan, acted as royal panders in procuring "women, information, and advantage" for a king who thrived on control and dissimulation.

Through his letters and actions, Henry VIII created the Pandaric culture of his court. The second chapter begins on Twelfth Night 1516, with the king watching a children's show of "Troilus and Pandar." With John Skelton's *Magnyfycence* and Edward Hall's *Chronicle* that both address the king's preference for the company of his male courtiers, these texts suggest that the court was "a world of masks." The third chapter focuses on the collection of Henry's letters to Anne Boleyn, written between 1527 and 1529. In these letters, the author argues, Henry draws Anne into his male world, hunts her as prey, constructs and clothes his own body, and gives it to her in a Christ-like offering evocative of the Eucharist. The one-sided correspondence was Henry's "literary fashioning" of himself.

The literary world of commonplace books, manuscript marginalia, verse epistles, and courtly lyrics allows the author in the last two chapters to explore the shift from a handwritten to print culture. One effect was a fragmentation of texts and a subsequent reforming of separate bits into a different whole by the reader in private. The anthology of Humphrey Wellys, the Devonshire Manuscript, Wyatt's verse, and Tottel's *Miscellany* reveal a literary culture of unstable texts and diverging public and private reading responses.

Lerer makes a better textual argument for the Pandaric culture than he can support in the historical sources. While indebted to G. R. Elton's study of Henrician religious policy, as enforced by Cromwell, and David Starkey's work on the English court, this Henrician court seems devoid of real queens and ladies in waiting, royal spectacle, and the king's own prodigious vanity. When the Spanish Ambassador and Ferdinand of Spain corresponded about Catherine of Aragon's fertility, and thus supposedly became panders and voyeurs, they also reflected the historical realities of their era. Royal heirs, conception, childbirth, bodily functions, and marital problems were not private matters; producing a son would become the litmus test for Catherine's tenure as queen. Such a written discussion of her body under those circumstances seems neither intrusive nor erotic. Nor should we be surprised to learn that in his love letters to Anne Boleyn, which created "something of a surrogate physicality," Henry mentioned nothing of his "marriage, his purported affairs, his appetites or appreciation of the female form." Given his desires and Anne's agenda, Henry would have had no reason to expound upon these topics.

These distinctions aside, however, Lerer has written an elegant book. His chapters are grounded in close readings of literary texts, and he has presented a nuanced, challenging argument in well-turned phrases free of theoretical jargon. It is also, unfortunately, free of any bibliography. But this fine study should serve as a model for those of us drawn to the borders of history and literature.

Mary Hill Cole
Mary Baldwin College